THE INSPECTORS GENERAL
OF THE UNITED STATES ARMY
1777–1903

by

David A. Clary

and

Joseph W. A. Whitehorne

OFFICE OF THE INSPECTOR GENERAL
AND
CENTER OF MILITARY HISTORY

UNITED STATES ARMY
WASHINGTON, D.C., 1987

Library of Congress Cataloging in Publication Data

Clary, David A.
The Inspectors General of the United States Army,
1777–1903.

Bibliography: p.
Includes index.
1. Military inspectors general—United States—History.
2. United States. Army. Office of the Inspector General
—History. I. Whitehorne, Joseph W. A., 1943–
II. Title.
UB243.C56 1987   355.6'3'0973   86–25931

CMH Pub 70–16

First Printing—CMH Pub 70–16

For sale by the Superintendent of Documents, U.S. Government Printing Office
Washington, D.C. 20402

Foreword

The Office of The Inspector General, with its attendant inspection and investigating functions, has been a part of the Army for nearly two hundred and ten years. It has served throughout that period as the eyes and ears of the Army's leaders and often as the Army's conscience as well. As such, it has come into contact with nearly every issue, problem or triumph in which the Army has been involved. As a consequence, the inspectorate has achieved a unique insight into the Army's development and history. Despite this involvement, few soldiers and even fewer citizens know of inspector general activities or their value and influence in making the Army more effective, efficient, and humane.

Inspectors general, past and present, have every right to be proud of the record of their organization. Until now, access to that record and the perspective it can give to military events has not been available. This volume begins to change that by telling the story of one of the oldest elements of the Army staff. It also tells the story of the United States Army as inspectors have seen it. With this book, it is hoped that inspectors, soldiers, and interested readers all will better understand what the inspectorate has done and, in so doing, will develop ideas as to what it can do now and in the future. This is a story that has long merited telling. It is hoped that its appearance will enhance the inspectorate's capability to assist, train, and generally contribute to continued improvements in the modern Army.

Washington, D.C.
16 May 1986

NATHANIEL R. THOMPSON, JR.
Lieutenant General, USA
The Inspector General

Preface

An army's history encompasses far more than a description of the battles fought or a listing of the wars won and lost. Like any complex organization, a larger part of its story rests with a description of the development and relationship of those elements that combine to give it character and to support it in its endless preparations to carry out its missions. In fact, most of an army's history necessarily should deal with its daily record over long years of peace, interspersed rarely with conflict. The record of the United States Army shows that it, too, has spent most of its time at peace. And even in war, some of its greatest accomplishments have been outside the realm of combat. The record of these more prosaic achievements is often lost because of their undramatic nature, despite their importance to the full organization. Futhermore, the long periods of peace seldom have been given exclusively to the preparation for war. Civil missions, equipment testing and procurement, and the countless small tasks given to keeping a large group of men assembled and available compose the bulk of an army's experience. Therefore, it follows that the story of an army is not simply an account of military events, but the chronicle of an organization. Great captains and blunderers, heroes and cowards—all have their day when battle comes. But in the longer periods between battles, the military organization must remain intact and ready. It must eat, sleep, house and clothe itself, train itself, stay healthy, and remain on good behavior. Many people—soldiers, all skilled professionals, but few of them listed among the great captains—must spend their time ensuring the well-being and effectiveness of the Army.

This is an account of one group of those soldiers, the inspectors general of the United States Army, from the eighteenth century until the early years of the twentieth. Their responsibility was to ensure that the highest authorities knew always the state of the Army—how well it fed and clothed itself, trained itself, and the rest. In the words of one senior inspector, "to touch most firmly those things the generals most need to know." They were an essential part of those unsung elements that kept the Army intact in peacetime, and organized and ready for conflict when wartime came. When war did come, they were expected to oversee the expansion of the force, to teach and enforce its standards, and to assist in its management and improvement when necessary—and, again, to keep the highest authorities advised on the condition of the Army. The inspectors general were instrumental in making the Army what it was. It was their vision as reported to the War Department that formed the basis for many far-reaching decisions. Accordingly, the history offered here is not only an account of the activities of the inspectors general, but also it is the story of the Army from a unique perspective.

Several themes run through the story: One is the natural tension existing between the Army and the government it serves. The inspectors general often found themselves affected by this division. They were really the only officials in a position to know firsthand what was going on throughout the Army. That made them important to the highest military commander, who needed such information in order to exercise command effectively. But, the information of inspectors general was equally valuable to civilian members of government who had valid reasons for needing to know the state of the Army. This tension was a major factor in the life of the inspectorate until the divided authority over the military was resolved by reforms in 1903; however, to a lesser extent it persists to the present day. Another theme of the inspectors general history is organizational. Although it remained strictly military in perspective and objective, the inspectorate became increasingly structured over the years. Much of its history gravitated around the formalization of an inspection bureaucracy, especially after the Civil War. Symbolic of this were the growing efforts to create an Inspector General's Department. Such a department was never established by law; however, the effort to create one was nevertheless successful. The need for the function performed by the inspectorate was such that over time it became an institutional part of the Army without anyone realizing that no direct official act had caused it to exist. Thus, by the end of the nineteenth century, the Inspector General's Department was an enduring part of the Army, established on the assumption that it had been authorized since the days of von Steuben and Hamilton. Underlying the theme of organizational development, there is yet another thread. This has to do with the practical issues of doing business. Topics such as the confidentiality of investigations, proximity to the commander, and scope of activity have been matters of concern from the beginning of the American inspection effort. The precedents set by their resolution have determined the way inspectors conduct their business to the present day.

In a way, the inspectorate has been a kind of bureaucratic laboratory. For over two hundred years, inspectors have been performing essentially the same missions for the same larger organization. The technology and other outward appearances may change, but the problems and issues have been constant. The inspectors inspect, investigate, assist, and teach; and have done so since 1778. All the various issues of organization, such as integrity and confidentiality have been discussed since Valley Forge. A modern inspector need only search the history of his predecessors to discover that there is rarely such a thing as a "new" issue. Invariably, he will find that five or ten or twenty or more years earlier the same issue had appeared, had been discussed, and had been resolved.

This cycle of issues has been a regular feature of the inspector general experience, of which every inspector need be aware. The old saying that we study history to avoid the sense of panic when confronting something new to us never has been proved more true than when viewing the record of the inspectors general.

This project grew out of the personal interest of Lt. Gen. Richard G. Trefry, The Inspector General, 1977–1983, who appreciates the value of history to current public administration. He was interested in a document of his organization's existence as well as a record of the roots of contemporary practices and relationships. The universal growth of interest in inspection activities throughout the government made it imperative in his view to gather the scattered information about the United States Army's inspectors general into a coherent whole. Otherwise, the Army's extensive experience and established procedures and relationships could neither be shared nor defended. The decision was made to present the history in chronological parts, the first ending in 1903. This volume covers that early period. It was prepared in first draft by David A. Clary, who developed the basic structure of the book. Joseph Whitehorne assisted in the research and continued it while rewriting the draft to add new information and to develop various points. He also guided the work through the stages of editing and production. General Trefry's successor, Lt. Gen. Nathaniel R. Thompson, Jr., continued to underscore the importance of the historical effort and gave it his welcome support. This work is written with the serving inspectors general in mind. We recognize that there will be few historians in this group, but we are equally certain that all soldiers recognize the value of the experience of their predecessors. It is our hope that this history will serve the practical purpose of explaining how inspection in the Army evolved and why things are done the way they are. Above all, we hope the reasons for the existence of a separate inspectorate, its traditions, and its place in history become apparent. They provide a guide and an inspiration to meet the challenges of the present.

No one who undertakes a project on this scale can work without the assistance of a great many others. It is impossible personally to thank all the librarians and archivists who aided in the research. Among those who deserve special mention are Michael Musick, Charles Shaughnessy, Old Army and Navy Branch, and Sara Jackson, National Historical Records Publications Commission, all at the National Archives, Washington, D.C.; John Slonaker, Richard Sommers, David Keough, Valerie Metzler, Norma Umbrell, and Dennis Vetock of the United States Army Military History Institute, Carlisle Barracks, Pennsylvania; Alice Wickizer and her staff of the Government Documents and Publications Department, Indiana University Library, Bloomington, Indiana; and Marilyn Irwin, Lily Library and Rare Books and Manuscripts Repository, Bloomington, Indiana. Ronald B. Hartzer ran down some elusive publications, and Jesse B. Clary handled the mechanical production of the first draft. Thanks also are due to Lt. Gen. Richard G. Trefry, TIG, USA (retired); David Trask, Center of Military History, Department of the Army; and Jay Luvaas, Army War College, who read the draft. Special thanks go to the members of the Inspector General word processing center for typing the untold number of drafts leading to the final form: Lynne M. Reid, Denise P. Lindsey, Mary A. Lorber, Crystal L. Smith, Tracy D. Cotton, Theresa K. Middleton, and Denise R. Jones. Last, but not least, our deepest appreciation to Rae T. Panella, Anna B. Wittig, Cheryl A. Morai, and Arthur S. Hardyman of the Center of Military History for their superb, conscientious efforts in editing the manuscript into publishable form. All the foregoing deserve a measure of credit for any merits in the final product. Blame for any shortcomings should not be laid at the door of those good people, however, but at our own.

Washington, D.C.   DAVID A. CLARY
16 May 1986   JOSEPH W. A. WHITEHORNE

Contents

	Page
INTRODUCTION: ORIGINS OF MILITARY INSPECTION	3
Military Self-examination	3
European Examples	4
American Situation—British Example	5
American Traditions	7

Part One: A Tradition of Inspection, 1775–1821

Chapter

	Page
1. THE FIRST AMERICAN ARMY, 1775–1778	11
A Militia Army	11
Organizational Problems	12
Inadequate Staff Support	14
Disorganization in the Line	14
Congress Takes a Hand	16
Congress Becomes More Active	17
Recruitments in France	17
The First Inspector General	18
The Second Inspector General	20
The Campaign of 1777	21
Inspector General Conway	22
Valley Forge	31
2. STEUBEN AT VALLEY FORGE, 1777–1778	33
A Volunteer for the American Cause	33
Steuben's Challenge	36
Steuben Trains the Troops	38
The First Regulation	40
Proving the Worth of Training	42
Inspector General Steuben	43

3. DEFINING THE INSPECTOR'S ROLE, 1778–1779   45

   Limiting the Inspector's Authority   45
   Steuben Tries To Assert Himself   46
   Steuben's Blue Book   48
   Charter for the Inspector General   50

4. INSPECTION AND THE AMERICAN VICTORY,
   1780–1784   52

   The Inspector's Authority Widens   52
   Reducing the Army and the Inspectorate   56
   Demobilization and Border Defense   58
   Steuben's Legacy   59

5. DECLINE, REVIVAL, AND VICISSITUDES OF
   INSPECTION, 1784–1798   61

   Very Little Army To Inspect   61
   Birth of the United States Army   62
   Anthony Wayne and Inspection   64
   James Wilkinson and the Army   69

6. HAMILTON AND THE PROVISIONAL
   ARMY, 1798–1800   73

   Establishing an Army for War   73
   The Inspector General as Second in Command   75
   Inspector General Hamilton   77
   Hamilton and the Paper Army   79
   Hamilton and the Real Army   80
   Hamilton and the Army of the Future   81

7. DISGRACE OF AN INSPECTOR GENERAL, 1801–1813 . . .   84

   The Jeffersonian Army   84
   The Adjutant and the Inspector   87
   The Madisonian Army   89
   Facing Another War   90
   Reestablishment   91
   Smyth Goes to War   94
   The Office Is Abolished   96

8. ORIGINS OF THE OFFICE OF THE ADJUTANT
   AND INSPECTOR, 1813–1815 98

   Army Reformation, Inspectorate Restoration 98
   Adjutant and Inspector General Pike 103
   The Inspectorate and the Army After Pike 105
   The Adjutant and Inspector General's Office 107
   Adjutant and Inspector General Parker 111

9. END OF THE ADJUTANT AND INSPECTOR
   GENERAL, 1816–1821 115

   A General Staff and New Inspectors 115
   The State of the Army 118
   Calhoun and Army Reform 121
   Inspectors and Army Reduction 123

Part Two: The Inspectors General of the Army, 1821–1881

10. ESTABLISHING THE INSPECTOR GENERAL, 1821–1825 .. 131

   Choosing and Regulating the Inspector 131
   Inspecting the Army 136
   Gaines: The Commander as Inspector 140
   The Inspector and Property Management 142
   More Changes in the Inspectorate 143
   A New Inspector General 145

11. INSPECTION AND THE FORTUNES OF THE
    COMMANDER, 1826–1849 149

   The Nation's Military Forces 149
   The Inspectorate and the Commanding General 151
   Reporting the State of the Army 153
   The Productive Inspector Wool 154
   Gaines, Congress, and Disciplinary Reform 156
   Powers and Agents of the Commanding General 157
   More Attempts at Army Reform 159
   The Inspectors and Army Control 160
   The Inspectorate and the Seminole Wars 164

Decline of the Commanding General 167
New Commander and Divided Inspectorate 172
Another War—No Central Inspectorate 177
The Place of the Inspector General 181

12. INSPECTION BETWEEN THE WARS, 1849–1861 183

The Army's Continued Mission 183
A Leaderless Army 185
An Energetic Inspector 190
The Secretary's Inspector 192
Living Conditions 193
A Busy Decade for Churchill 194
Regulations and the Inspector General 200
Another War—The Inspectors Depart 201

13. THE INSPECTORATE DURING THE CIVIL
WAR, 1861–1865 204

Inspectors Without Portfolio 204
Class of 1861: Inspectors General 206
Class of 1861: Assistant Inspectors 209
Inspectors Without an Inspectorate 213
A Presence in Washington 217
Scattering the Inspectors' Attention 218
Bringing the Inspectors Into Line 220
The Washington Office 224
An Undefined Inspectorate 227
The Inspectorate at War's End 228

14. SECURING A PERMANENT PLACE, 1865–1866 232

New Orders for the Inspectors 234
Reduction of the Regular Establishment 238
Serving the Secretary of War 239
The Subsistence Sales List 240
A Symbol of Permanence 241

15. FOUNDATIONS OF A BUREAUCRACY, 1867–1869 242

Founding a Bureau 242
Making the Organization Useful 244
Taking Charge of the Inspectorate 246

A Formal Bureau is Acknowledged 249
The Inspectorate and Army Reorganization 252
Continuing the Routine 256
The Senior Inspector Takes Over 257

Part Three: A Tradition of an Inspection Department, 1881–1898

16. MARCY AND THE ADVENT OF THE
    DEPARTMENT, 1870–1881 265

    The Commanding General's Ordeal 265
    Marcy Tries To Assert His Authority 266
    The Inspectorate Declines 269
    An Independent Inspectorate 271
    Reducing the Army and the Inspectorate 273
    Marcy Loses Control 274
    The Inspector General's Department Emerges 277
    Another Reorganization Scare 279
    Marcy's Last Year 281
    Special Investigations and Services 283
    Property Inspection 285
    Disbursing Accounts 287
    Other Occupations of the Inspectors 289
    The Old Soldier Retires 292

17. PASSING OF THE OLD GUARD, 1881–1889 294

    Portents of Reform 294
    Breckinridge Joins the Department 295
    The Department Enlarged and Ratified 299
    Davis Has a Brief Reign 300
    Baird Succeeds Davis 302
    Breckinridge Takes Charge 305
    Special Investigations in the 1880s 306
    Soldiers' Home, Military Prison, Cemeteries 309
    Military Colleges 311
    Disbursing Accounts 312
    Property Inspections 314
    The Sales List 315
    Signs of Change 315

18. BRECKINRIDGE'S WIDENING SCOPE, 1889–1898   318

New Department Under New Leadership   318
Ending Sunday Inspections   320
Building a Definite Sphere   322
A Setback and Renewed Advance   326
An Uncertain New Patron   329
Independence Gained   330
Independence Lost   332

19. THE DEPARTMENT IN SERVICE TO THE
SECRETARY, 1889–1898   335

Paragraph 955   335
West Point   337
The Military Prison   337
The Soldiers' Home   338
Home for Disabled Volunteer Soldiers   339
Disbursing Accounts   341
Property Inspections   342
Military Colleges   343
The National Guard   345
Balancing Two Interests   348

20. REFORM DURING THE BRECKINRIDGE ERA,
1889–1898   350

Soldier Life and Discipline   350
Educating the Enlisted Men   351
Military Training   352
Supply Services   355
The Army, the Inspectors—Ready for War?   357

Part Four: The Inspector General's Department of the New Army, 1898–1903

21. INSPECTION DURING THE WAR WITH SPAIN, 1898   361

The Situation in 1898   361
Where Were the Inspectors?   363
The Whereabouts of General Breckinridge   369
The Aftermath   372

Chapter	Page

22. INSPECTING THE NEW ARMY 376

    Breckinridge and the Dodge Commission 376
    Increasing the Army Temporarily 378
    Serving the Secretary's Interest in Economy 379
    Military Colleges and the National Guard 380
    Old Business and New 383
    The State of the New Army 384
    Inspecting a Worldwide Army 385
    Supply Services 386
    The Inspector General's Wide View 387

23. INSPECTION AND REORGANIZATION OF THE
    WAR DEPARTMENT, 1898–1903 389

    Secretary Root Takes Charge 389
    The General-Staff Idea and Inspection 393
    The General Staff Bill 396
    Breckinridge Saves His Department 400
    A Charter for the Future 402
    The Veterans Depart 406

Appendixes

A. INSPECTORS GENERAL 411

B. BIOGRAPHICAL NOTES 415

SELECTED BIBLIOGRAPHY 431

LIST OF ABBREVIATIONS 451

INDEX 453

Maps

No.

1. Military Departments, October 1850 189

No.   *Page*

2. Military Divisions, April 1870 268
3. Military Divisions, December 1880 307

Illustrations

Maj. Gen. Thomas Conway 23
Maj. Gen. Friedrich von Steuben 36
Maj. William North 51
Capt. Edward Butler 67
Maj. Thomas H. Cushing 70
Maj. Gen. Alexander Hamilton 78
Brig. Gen. Alexander Smyth 93
Brig. Gen. Zebulon M. Pike 105
Brig. Gen. William H. Winder 107
Battle of New Orleans, 1815 112
Brig. Gen. Daniel Parker 116
Col. John E. Wool 117
Col. James Gadsden 126
Col. George Croghan 146
Battle of Moncaco Lake, 1837 165
Defense of Quartermaster's Train on the Chihuahua Column,
   1847 178
Col. Ethan A. Hitchcock 180
Ringgold's Battery at Palo Alto, 1846 185
The Assault on Chapultapec, 1847 187
Col. George A. McCall 190
Ascending the Tablelands of Texas 196
Col. Joseph K. F. Mansfield 202
Commissary Department Baggage Train, 1861 205
Brig. Gen. Randolph B. Marcy 207
Col. Henry Van Rensselaer 209
Col. Edmund Schriver 221
Going Into Battery Before Petersburg, 1865 223
Col. James A. Hardie 225
Ohio Infantry at the Bloody Angle, 1864 230
Charge of the Fifth Regulars at Gaines Mills, Va., 1862 235
Brig. Gen. Delos B. Sacket 282
Brig. Gen. Nelson H. Davis 301
Brig. Gen. Absalom Baird 303
Brig. Gen. Roger Jones 316

Infantry Tactical Drill, 1892 322
Inspection at Proving Ground, 1892 328
Eighteenth Pennsylvania Infantry Regiment at the
    Allegheny Co. Centennial, 1888 345
Inspection of Engineer Troops, 1892 347
Maj. Gen. Joseph C. Breckinridge 353
Inspector General Insignia, 1895–1961 355
Bloody Ford, Cuba, 1898 370
Second Kansas National Guard, 1898 381
Brig. Gen. Peter D. Vroom 407

Illustrations courtesy of the following sources: The cover *Steuben at Valley Forge* (Edwin Austin Abbey) (cover for the softbound version of this book) is from the Pennsylvania Museum and Historical Commission; portrait of Baron von Steuben (Ralph Earl) is from the New York State Historical Association, Cooperstown; portrait of William North (Charles Willson Peale, gift of Dexter M. Ferry, Jr., copyright, Founders Society) is from the Detroit Institute of Arts; portraits of Alexander Hamilton (artist unknown) and Thomas H. Cushing (Ezra Ames) is courtesy of The Society of the Cincinnati, Washington, D.C.; portrait of William Winder is from B. J. Lossing's *Field Book of the War of 1812*; portrait of Zebulon Pike is from the Independence National Historical Park Collection, Philadelphia; portraits of Croghan, Conway, Butler, Gadsden, Sacket, Davis, and Baird are from the U.S. Army Signal Corps; portrait of Alexander Smyth is from the U.S. Army, DAIG, Washington, D.C.; portraits of John E. Wool and Ethan A. Hitchcock are from the Special Collections, University of Texas at Arlington Library; portraits of Hardie, Van Rensselaer, Mansfield, McCall, Jones, Marcy, and Vroom are from the National Archives; portrait of Joseph C. Breckinridge is from the Military History Institute, Carlisle Barracks, Pennsylvania; the following illustrations are from William Walton's *The Army and Navy of the United States from the Period of the Revolution to the Present Day*, Inspection of Engineer Troops: 1892 (W. T. Trego), The Battle of Moncaco Lake: 1837 (Gilbert Gaul), Ringgold's Battery at Palo Alto: 8 May 1846 (W. T. Trego), The Assault on Chapultepec: 12 September 1847 (Andre Castaigne), Defense of Quartermaster's Train on the Chihuahua Column: 1847 (artist unknown), Commissary Department Baggage Train: 21 July 1861 (W. T. Trego), Charge of the 5th Regulars at Gaines Mills, Virginia: 27 June 1862 (W. T. Trego), Ohio Infantry at the Bloody Angle: 12 May 1864 (Andre Castaigne), Going into Battery Before Petersburg: 1865 (W. T. Trego), Inspection at Proving Ground: 1892 (V. Perard), Infantry Tactical Drill: Summer 1892 (N. G. Ferris); portrait of Edmund Schriver is from Collection of the Newark Museum; Eighteenth Pennsylvania Infantry Regiment at the

Allegheny Co.: 1888 Centennial is from DAIG, Washington, D.C.; Second Kansas National Guard field inspection photograph: 1898, courtesy of John Hyson; *Bloody Ford, Cuba* (Charles Johnson Post), *Battle of New Orleans* (artist unknown), and *Ascending the Tablelands of Texas* (artist unknown) photographs are from the Army Art Collection; Inspector General Insignia: 1895–1961 (Ronald M. Shuler); portrait of Daniel Parker is from Hazen Memorial Library, Shirley, Massachusetts.

THE INSPECTORS GENERAL
OF THE UNITED STATES ARMY
1777–1903

Origins of Military Inspection

In 1777, George Washington determined that the Continental Army required the services of an inspector general. At about the same time, the Continental Congress decided that it also needed an inspector general, to keep the government informed about military affairs. In that instance, both commander and government perceived a fundamental need for military information. Their respective desires, however, were as much conflicting as mutual, reflecting a tension between army and government that, when it came to military inspection, had arisen many times before in other countries. The relationship of the inspectors to the military chain of command and to representatives of the government was a delicate one. The need for commanders to have full authority and flexibility within their units had to be balanced with the government's need for information about its forces. The resolution of this balance would determine to a large extent the degree of control exercised by either element. The inspectors' proximity to their commanders and the amount of information passed between them and to those outside the chain has been an issue to the present time.

Military Self-Examination

To ensure success, a commander must know intimately the strengths and limitations of his military force and its readiness to express his will. In peace or war, the competent commander knows how many men he has, how they are organized, and how well they are trained and ready for movement or combat. He keeps track of the quantities and qualities of arms and ammunition, and the equally essential food, shelter, and transportation of his force. Warfare is a personal art, no matter on how grand a scale. Successful armies evidence high morale, which might be equated with devotion to the job of soldiering. Because little things can seriously erode morale, the commander must know how well his men are housed, clothed, and fed; whether discipline is fair and appropriate; and whether officers are fit for their assignments. Military duty, in peace and war, may be directed by commanders, but it depends upon private soldiers; the commander must know whether his soldiers are content to do their duty.

In Western armies during the past three centuries, the gathering of information about a commander's own force has become formalized in the term *inspection*. That formalization, often by the assignment of inspection duties to a particular agency, does not contradict the fact that inspection has long been viewed as integral to command. Thus, as Charles James defined *inspection* in

1802, it is "a strict examination, a close survey. It likewise signifies superintendence," he continued. "In a military sense it admits of both interpretations, and may be considered under two specific heads, each of which branches out into a variety of general, regimental, and company duties."[1] The term *inspector-general*, defined as "an officer at the head of a system of inspection, having under him a body of inspectors; a superintendent of a system of inspection," was in the English language by 1702, and until the late nineteenth century usually meant a military official, after which it transferred to police and other civil organizations. British Army regulations used the term *inspecting general* for the same official in the 1790s, but *inspector-general* seems to have been more common. Inspectors general were assigned particularly to categories of regiments (infantry or cavalry) in British service, and the general definition of their duties was to monitor or to direct training and efficiency, and to report formally upon their observations.[2] *Inspector* enjoyed usage in America as early as 1685, when "inspectors of brick" were appointed in Boston to monitor the quality of brick offered for sale. The inspector as an internal authority of civil agencies dates in America from as early as 1711, when Boston appointed inspectors of schools. Not a nation with a permanent military force, the United States did not hear native use of the term *inspector-general* until 1777. The next usage, *inspector of police* (1778), followed the adoption of the term in the American military.[3]

European Examples

In the West, the first modern military inspectors were two French *inspecteurs* appointed in 1668—an inspector general of infantry and an inspector general of cavalry. Louis XIV expanded the system during his reign, appointing additional inspectors general, assigned to geographical departments. Their duties were to review the troops once a month and to report to the king. They examined everything, including books and records, and were told especially to remove from the ranks soldiers unfit for duty. Observing France's military prowess during Louis' reign, the rest of Europe adopted the idea. Despite this prominence, the French inspectors general did not have regular military commissions, but were answerable directly to the sovereign. In wartime, however, the king's inspectors general ranked equivalent to generals, brigadiers, or colonels. They were strictly the sovereign's agents in the army; they did not inspect the king's personal troops or the artillery. By the late eighteenth century,

---

1. Charles James, *A New and Enlarged Military Dictionary, or, Alphabetical Explanation of Technical Terms* (London: Military Library, 1802). Dictionary references in this volume are to entries for the words discussed, unless otherwise stated.

2. Ibid. The hyphenated form "inspector-general" persisted in the United States Army into the 20th century.

3. *A Dictionary of American English on Historical Principles*, 4 vols. (Chicago: University of Chicago Press, 1938–44) (hereafter cited as *DAE*); *A Dictionary of Americanisms on Historical Principles*, 2 vols. (Chicago: University of Chicago Press, 1951) (hereafter cited as *DAHP*). The *DAHP* mostly follows the *DAE* on "inspector," with some American jargon and slang variations.

they numbered eleven inspectors general of cavalry and eleven of infantry. France's army also had a regularly commissioned *inspecteur de construction*, who was predominantly a supervisory engineer, approving plans for fortifications and the like.[4]

Perhaps no other person in the modern period came so close to embodying Machiavelli's vision of the prince as commander and head of state as did Frederick the Great of Prussia. Instead of appointing a general to command the whole army, he filled the role himself. At the same time, he remained sovereign of his state. By the 1770s he had perceived that if he was to meet both responsibilities he must appoint others to serve as his eyes and ears in the army:

> Inasmuch as one individual cannot supervise all of these details of regimental service I have appointed an inspector to look after each unit. These officers are responsible for the execution of instructions issued to the troops. They also are the instrument whereby equality of discipline is attained, so that one man is treated as another without undue mildness or severity. The inspectors report to me regarding the conduct of the officers, bring those to my attention who through bad behavior, negligence, and stupidity are courting dismissal, and recommend those who have earned distinction through their industry or talent. They inspect the regiments frequently, have them drill, improve their shortcomings, and hold the reviews if governmental duties prevent my traveling in the province myself. And finally, they preside over muster days and see to it that the cantons will not be deceived by the captains, which in former days happened only too often.[5]

Of the inspection duties listed by Frederick II, only the last was of purely civil concern—of greater moment to the state than to the army. The others covered the very things that every good commander needed to know about his troops. Although this information was also of interest to the government that paid for the army, it was that about which commanders could be particularly sensitive, especially when they felt their own authority challenged. Frederick avoided civil-military conflict over inspection because he was the supreme military as well as civil authority. Had that not been the case, and had eighteenth-century France not been so authoritarian, both the French and Prussian systems would have generated disputes between soldiers and their governments.

The American Situation and the British Example

By the mid-eighteenth century, military inspection had become essential to modern armies. The tactics of the day, founded on volley fire and massed bayonet charges, required stern discipline and extensive drill and training. But careful training meant a high public investment in each soldier.[6] Inspection as a monitor of public investment in the army became increasingly concerned with troop drill and tactical proficiency. Thus, when the rebellious Americans formed their own armies in the 1770s, they soon perceived a need for training, and with

---

4. James, *Military Dictionary*.
5. Frederick II ("the Great") of Prussia, *Frederick the Great on the Art of War*, ed. and trans. Jay Luvaas (New York: Free Press, 1966), 79.
6. Russell F. Weigley, *History of the United States Army* (New York: Macmillan, 1967), 19–20.

this need the importance of inspection. Before the uprising was two years old, the military command had come to appreciate the importance of inspection as a function of command, and particularly as a monitor of martial readiness. At about the same time, the civil power, embodied in the Continental Congress, seized upon inspection as a way to oversee the military establishment. As might have been predicted, government and commander soon came into conflict over the person and role of the inspector. The United States imported a number of French, Prussian, and other European officers in the early years of the Revolution. But the country resisted the importation of French or Prussian inspection systems, because the confederation of more or less independent states lacked a supreme autocrat. Besides, the country was essentially English in tradition and outlook, no matter the rebellion. British armies had greatly impressed Americans with their effectiveness in the French and Indian War, and British training manuals were in the native tongue. Deliberately following tradition, the United States modeled its army on that of Britain.[7]

At least as far as military leaders were concerned, one aspect of the British military establishment compatible with American sentiments was its inspection system. The British government was not as unstructured as that of the United States, but neither was it as authoritarian as that of France or Prussia. The civil power in Britain supervised the military by the appointment of high officials and by the control of the purse. Commanders were held accountable for the public interests in economy and propriety; that accountability made propriety a command responsibility. Inspection, therefore, was integrated with command and at the same time supported the public interest in an efficient and properly behaved army. Through it, the interests of commanders and politicians were expected to be served equally.

By the late eighteenth century, the British Army had *inspecting field officers of districts*, officers detailed from the line to monitor distribution of monies and supervise recruiting officers in their districts. With press-gangs an important source of recruits, recruitment had to be supervised to avoid excesses that would bring forth violent public reaction. Inspecting field officers could also order detachment courts-martial, and would supervise medical examinations of recruits. The recruiting service as a whole came under its own inspector general, whose regulations and procedures were binding even on regiments that did their own recruiting.[8] In other cases, the British Army also detailed officers as *inspectors of clothing*, who compared delivered uniforms with standard patterns, and there was a permanent *inspector of hospitals*, who was the surgeon general's principal subordinate. One other person in the army who bore the title *inspector-general* was the inspector general of cavalry. He was a general officer who inspected all cavalry regiments, reported the condition of the horses, and received regular accountings from all corps. He answered to the commander in chief, and was the sole inspector of any cavalry regiment about to be disbanded.[9] The

7. Ibid., 22–23.
8. James, *Military Dictionary*.
9. Ibid.

variety of functions meant that inspection in the British Army of the late eighteenth century was not a formal bureaucracy, but an activity to which officers were assigned when necessary and when the activity was outside the normal course of military service. Otherwise, inspection was a function of command. The British establishment called for a great deal of responsibility to be delegated downward—sergeants actually trained the troops, for instance—with accountability upward ensured by rigorous, periodic inspections. At each stage of the command pyramid, an officer used inspection to ensure that those below him were on the job.

In the British routine, a general inspection was made annually by generals commanding districts, and included a complete examination of all regiments in each district. Each regimental commander was to make a regimental inspection monthly, while every Monday morning company commanders or subalterns were to hold a "private inspection of companies." Other regular examinations included "inspection of necessaries," or all property supposed to be in the hands of soldiers, and "private inspection of arms" before every general parade. Regardless of level, every inspection was all encompassing. Each soldier was individually examined, along with his clothing, arms, and property; each unit's books were reviewed; and evidences of training and discipline were put on review. Housing, food, medical care, transportation, and general administration were also objects of inspection.[10] The British system of inspection was only partly useful as a model for the Continental Army of America. It depended upon a corps of officers and noncommissioned officers of long experience, supervising sufficiently cowed, lifelong soldiers. It was also practical only for an organization long trained and essentially uniform in procedure. By itself, the British system would not accomplish much in the wildly diverse gatherings of short-term militia and volunteers who composed the first rebellious forces. Nor could it do much even for a Continental Army without much collective experience, facing immediate challenges from a determined and competent enemy.

American Traditions

Most of all, the British system of inspection would be ineffective as a means of control without the hard discipline and penalties for desertion that held the British ranks together. The thirteen colonies entered the Revolution with faith in the militia, every citizen providing his share of the common defense. Instead of press-gangs and iron discipline, the army of the Revolution began with exhortations. For example, the militia regulations of Massachusetts stated that it was the pride and duty of every citizen to defend his country. An army created out of such sentiments could not be modeled on any European system, although it might borrow and adapt such European ways as suited American realities. The early American army was a product of its own colonial

---

10. Ibid.

traditions, and had to be molded in a manner that accorded with its heritage. The British system of inspections as a means of command accountability and control was suitable enough, but it did not answer for the inexperience of officers and men in the American service. The Prussian system of inspection appeared to offer a possible monitor of training, but it did not answer the problems created by the variety of colonial units and practices. The French idea of the *inspector general* suggested a mechanism for uniformity, but it was coupled with the threat of interference in the chain of command.[11]

None of the European examples, working as they did in experienced professional armies, was wholly useful to the army of the American Revolution. All other considerations aside, when it came time to form a permanent army for the American cause, it had to be an integrated force with a common organization and tactics. Above all, it had to be trained so far as it could be in the circumstances. When the Continental Army's leaders considered the problems of organization, tactics, and training of a regular force in 1777, they looked naturally to European inspection systems for ideas, but they also looked to American experience. This in its own way was as extensive as that in the mother country. The Massachusetts Bay colony had been the first to form its militia into regiments (one per county), in 1636. Three years later, Virginia imposed uniform regulations on its militia. Those were the first American efforts to form military organizations on something larger than merely local defense. In each case, the two colonies perceived that uniform tactics and training were essential if the militia units were ever to be proficient alone, or able to join into larger formations. Massachusetts placed each regiment under a sergeant major, who was assisted by a *muster master*. Virginia appointed a *muster master-general* to enforce its regulations, although captains were responsible for training their men (with no time set aside by law for drilling).[12] As it happened, the militia organizations of the colonies left much to be desired as military forces. But they were familiar and comfortable, and they offered American precedents to modify European examples. When the Continental Army obtained its first real inspector general, he turned out to be a Prussian recruited in France who labored to adapt British ways to American conditions. But it is a fitting comment on the strength of colonial traditions that this man made his greatest contribution to the cause, and is best remembered today, as the man who trained the Continental Army—the job of a *muster master-general*.

---

11. *The Exercise for the Militia of the Province of the Massachusetts-Bay* (1758), as quoted in Douglas Edward Leach, *Arms for Empire: A Military History of the British Colonies in North America, 1607–1763* (New York: Macmillan, 1973), 89.

12. Louis Morton, "The Origins of American Military Policy," *Military Affairs* 22 (summer 1958): 78.

Part One

A Tradition of Inspection, 1775–1821

CHAPTER 1

The First American Army
(1775–1778)

The first wholly American army came into existence almost inadvertently, as a product of circumstances and cautious reaction. It was, accordingly, characterized by organizational and administrative shortcomings that often bordered on the chaotic. The American army came about as a result of the rush of events beginning with the fighting at Lexington and Concord, Massachusetts, in April 1775. Royal governments collapsed one after the other in each colony while military confrontation with crown forces became a certainty.[1] The Congress attempted to establish a military force and appointed George Washington to its command. He was widely respected as a military authority, in a country where there were comparatively few trained soldiers.[2] He was in fact a scholar of military arts, and had been acquiring and reading military treatises for over a quarter of a century. He took his studies seriously, urging others to do the same. Equally important, he had had experience with British regular forces during the French and Indian War. Also interesting was the beginning of his military career: His first commission, November 1752, was as one of four district adjutants in Virginia—his duties those of an instructor and an inspector.[3]

A Militia Army

Washington accepted command of "all the Continental forces" on 16 June 1775. But he did not assume charge of an army, even in name. Even the Continental forces (as opposed to those of the various colonies) were anything but a regular military force. In authorizing the muster of troops under its

1. Don Higginbotham, *The War of American Independence: Military Attitudes, Policies, and Practice, 1763–1789* (New York: Macmillan, 1971), 68. See also John Shy, "American Society and Its War for Independence," in Don Higginbotham, ed., *Reconsideration of the Revolutionary War: Selected Essays* (Westport, Conn.: Greenwood, 1978), 72–82.
2. Merrill Jensen, *The Founding of a Nation: A History of the American Revolution 1763–1776* (New York: Oxford University Press, 1968), 605–13; Shy, "American Society," 72–82.
3. Oliver L. Spaulding, Jr., "The Military Studies of George Washington," *American Historical Review*, 29 (July 1924): 675–80. For Washington's early military career, see James Thomas Flexner, *George Washington: The Forge of Experience, 1732–1775* (Boston: Little, Brown, 1965); for his career in the Revolution, see James Thomas Flexner, *George Washington in the American Revolution (1775–1783)* (Boston: Little, Brown, 1968).

sponsorship to aid the forces around Boston, Congress merely asked for 10 companies of riflemen (6 from Pennsylvania and 2 each from Maryland and Virginia), of specified complement. "Continental" they might be, but they were merely the old colonial militia in broader trappings.[4] As it developed, militia in any form proved less than a complete answer to the colonies' collective need for armed forces. The reason was an imperfect understanding of the militia tradition, owing to the lapse of decades since the militia had been both necessary and appropriately employed. When conflict with Indians was frequent throughout the colonies in the late seventeenth century, the militia organizations had been maintained at a fairly high degree of readiness.[5] But when the Indian danger receded from the seaboard during the eighteenth century, the necessity for armed readiness abated and the quality of most militia declined. Worsening relations with the mother country in the 1760s forced a retransformation of militia toward the original military purpose. The return to old values, however, was not quite complete by April 1775, and even in the first clashes with British troops several militia units distinguished themselves for their failures.[6] Whatever its shortcomings as a fighting force, the less than complete subordination of militia to the high command offered a degree of political security to the Continental Congress that its members could not feel with a professional army. Congress was from the outset fearful of the specter of Cromwell's new model army, which had supported Cromwell against Parliament in establishing a British military dictatorship in the seventeenth century. The congressional delegates took great pains to assert their authority over the army, controlling the principal officers and binding Washington to hold councils of war with them over every major decision.

Organizational Problems

When it assigned Washington to the head of the Continental forces, Congress appointed a committee to prepare his instructions. The members also established the organization of the line command and staff departments, authorizing two major generals and eight brigadiers under Washington, with an Adjutant General's Department and offices of Commissary General, Quartermaster General, and Paymaster General. Although that Continental organization was at first superimposed upon the collection of militia and volunteers around Boston, by 30 June Congress had decided to authorize the first increment of what would be the Continental Army, for which it adopted a modified version of the British Articles of War. When Washington reached Boston on 4 July 1775, he issued a general order announcing that the "Troops of the United

---

4. Weigley, *History of the United States Army*, 29. When the Continental Army was formed, the ten companies became the 1st Continental Regiment.

5. Morton, "Origins of Military Policy," 80.

6. Ronald L. Boucher, "The Colonial Militia as a Social Institution: Salem Massachusetts, 1764–1775," *Military Affairs* 37 (December 1973): 125–30. See also Don Higginbotham, "The American Militia: A Traditional Institution with Revolutionary Responsibilities," in Higginbotham, *Reconsideration of the Revolutionary War*, 83–103.

Provinces of North America'' were thereafter under the authority of the Continental Congress.[7]

It soon became apparent, however, that the ''Troops of the United Provinces'' were scarcely under anyone's authority, and barely worthy of the title of troops. Washington had been led to expect that he would find 24,500 New England soldiers when he arrived at Boston. When he asked for an exact figure, he was told that about 18,000 to 20,000 men were around Boston. After he insisted upon an accurate count, he finally learned that he had under him 16,600 privates and noncommissioned officers, with only 13,743 infantry and 585 artillery men present and fit for duty. Worse, it had taken over a week to produce those numbers. Bungled staff work that made counting heads so difficult was but a symptom of the chaos that characterized the early revolutionary army. Because the forces were largely militia units from the colonies, along with less than adequately prepared collections of volunteers and adventurers, there was no uniformity in the sizes of organizations, procedures, drills (for those units that tried to drill at all), appearance, or equipment. Especially debilitating was a generally poor selection of officers.[8]

The development of a strong officer corps was a problem only partially solved during the Revolution, and then mainly in the regular formations of the Continental Army. The reasons were many, foremost among them probably the general absence of military tradition and experience in the colonies. In militia organizations, company officers who could be voted in and out of their positions at the whim of their men could not be expected to be an outstanding lot. Regardless of organization, officership tended to be a reward for social position in civilian life, and some ''gentlemen'' were wont to pursue military duty only so far as it suited them. Whatever the reasons, the chief defect of the Continental Army was the generally low quality of its combat leaders. Only a handful of general officers were truly proficient, and even some of the better ones had flawed characters. Nor were there enough good junior officers and noncommissioned officers to institute an effective level of training. Although the situation improved somewhat after the first years of the war, the undependable officer corps was one reason why Washington adopted fabian tactics against the British.

Even in 1775, the Army's leaders regarded experience as an essential qualification for high military position. To some extent, it was possible to fill certain high positions with men who had solid military backgrounds, despite the penchant of Congress to use other considerations in making appointments. Of 13 general officers commissioned in 1775, all had had war experience, 8 as lieutenant colonels or higher. Like Washington, many of those had seen service in the French and Indian War. Of 73 general officers in the Revolution, 16 had held commissions in European armies, while only 21 had had no military experience before 1775. But there were limits to how much talent could be drawn from Europe. American officers had strong nativist feelings, and the

---

7. Weigley, *History of the United States Army*, 29–30; Jensen, *Founding of a Nation*, 605–13.

8. For an excellent overview of the early army disorganization, see William A. Ganoe, *History of the United States Army*, rev. ed. (New York: Appleton-Century, 1942), 2–9.

larger share of Europeans who offered their services proved to be unemployed (often unemployable) adventurers.[9]

Inadequate Staff Support

Capable officers were in such short supply that many of the best potential staff officers simply had to be employed in line commands. That left staff services woefully wanting. Maj. Gen. Horatio Gates served as Washington's Adjutant General from June 1775 to June 1776, but thereafter was too valuable for such a role. His successors were little more than military secretaries, so Washington usually served as his own staff.[10] For technical services, Congress managed to provide enough engineers and other specialists, mostly by enlistment of Europeans. But Congress could also be meddlesome, appointing supervisory boards and investigating committees to assert its supremacy over the army. The delegates had a propensity for second-guessing the commander's judgment on the appointment of high officers, especially when the war was quiescent. When disaster threatened, however, the Congress was inclined to look to Washington for advice.[11]

Of essential staff services, supply was the most chaotic operation of the Continental Army during the Revolution. Except for small arms, artillery, and ammunition—which were usually ample—the troops often wanted for nearly everything throughout the war, suffering from shortages of food, forage, fuel, straw, clothing and blankets, shoes, and vehicles for transport. That the Army's needs could not be met can be attributed to unsound currencies, limited domestic materials and manufactures, absence of popular support, congressional interference or inaction, and ineptitude. The inexperienced Americans seemed unable to develop a smoothly working administrative system for army supply. The Quartermaster Department, repeatedly reorganized, had several changes in leadership, and came into frequent conflict with departments for purchasing, for clothing, and for subsistence—which themselves were in a constant state of flux. Nonetheless, it developed during the war a sounder organization and working procedure than it would have for many decades thereafter.[12]

Disorganization in the Line

The line organization of the early Continental Army was nearly as chaotic as its logistical arrangements. In 1775 it comprised 38 regiments of widely

---

9. Weigley, *History of the United States Army*, 64–65; Sidney Forman, "Why the United States Military Academy Was Established in 1802," *Military Affairs* 29 (spring 1965): 17–18; Robert Kenneth Wright, Jr., "Organization and Doctrine in the Continental Army, 1774 to 1784" (Ph.D. dissertation, College of William and Mary, 1980), 203–05; Richard Kohn, "American Generals of the Revolution: Subordination and Restraint," in Higginbotham, *Reconsideration of the Revolutionary War*, 104–23.

10. Weigley, *History of the United States Army*, 49–50.

11. Ibid., 44–45.

12. Ibid., 51–61; Erna Risch, *Quartermaster Support of the Army: A History of the Corps, 1775–1939* (Washington: Department of the Army, 1962), 1–73.

ranging sizes (600 to 1,000 men), according to the practices of the various colonies. Washington reorganized the force into 6 brigades (usually of 6 regiments each), and into 2 divisions of 2 brigades each. Brigades, divisions, and regiments were essentially administrative units. The tactical designation of the regiment was the battalion, the main unit of maneuver in an army that would fight as a tactical whole. In outlining his organization, Washington followed contemporary European practices, in which tactical formations between the battalion and the whole army (that is, brigades and divisions) remained uncommon until the 1790s.[13]

To keep his soldiers in line, Washington favored the sort of harsh discipline common in the British Army, with an emphasis on corporal punishment. The death penalty was limited to treason, mutiny, and desertion, but the lash was freely used. Washington also approved unauthorized punishments, such as running the gauntlet, but he generally evinced a distaste for punishment as a necessary evil. He showed restraint in approving death sentences, hoping that their rarity would increase the deterrent effect.[14] Traditionally, harsh punishments were used as a form of cohesion in the military forces of the day. The Continental Army required more than stern punishments to hold it together, however. Above all, if militia, state, and continental units were to function as an army, they required a common system of tactics and training. But that was nowhere in sight in the uprising's first year. There was no central tactical drill standard and the various published British books were in scarce supply. Few officers were experienced enough to conduct drills and training from memory. Colonel Timothy Pickering produced the first American tactical manual, for the militia of Essex County, Massachusetts, in 1775. Not just a compilation of European texts, Pickering's volume offered several original ideas, with simplified maneuvers. It was adopted by the state of Massachusetts in 1776, and was much copied by other American units. Nonetheless, a general system for the whole American army was still lacking.[15]

The Army was divided by more than disorganization and absence of central tactical guidance. As Washington sought to assemble Continental units answerable to the Continental Congress, he found himself in competition with the colonies. New England, especially, offered lavish inducements to meet its quota of men. Massachusetts established an exceedingly generous daily food ration, and further determined that each militia private should receive $36.00 per month in pay. The Continental Army could not compete with that; it could muster only about 9,000 troops along with 14,000 militia to meet the invasion of New York by British and Hessian forces during the summer of 1776.[16] The

---

13. Weigley, *History of the United States Army,* 62; Ganoe, *History of the United States Army,* 7–12.

14. Weigley, *History of the United States Army,* 63; Maurer, "Military Justice Under General Washington," *Military Affairs* 28 (spring 1964): 8–16.

15. Henry Knox to John Adams, 13 May 76, quoted in Forman, "Why the United States Military Academy Was Established," 18; Joseph R. Riling, *Baron Von Steuben and His Regulations* (Philadelphia: Ray Riling Arms Books, 1966), 1–2.

16. Ganoe, *History of the United States Army,* 13–14.

results were dismaying, regulars and militia alike falling back before the British and Hessians. Some did well enough, but generally the sorry New York campaign seemed to prove that American troops were no match for European professionals. The militia evaporated, and what was left of the Continental Army was scheduled to expire with most of the enlistments at the end of the year.[17]

Congress Takes a Hand

Congress, meanwhile, had been at work. Early in the year, bowing to Washington's wishes, it had re-formed the Continental Army, giving it a compact form of 28 regiments, theoretically of 728 officers and men each. All units were to have Continental (not state) designations. But the elimination of surplus, undersized regiments excluded some officers and discouraged reenlistments, while the Continental designations cooled ardor in state governments. More positively, Congress had appointed a committee of seven to look into creating a war office. That came to nothing until strong appeals from Washington led to the establishment of the Board of War and Ordnance on 12 June. The board was responsible for recruitment and levies upon the states (which proved to be an impossible job), as well as all congressional correspondence related to the war. In practice, it concerned itself with preparing estimates of supplies, accounting for material on hand, and establishing manufacturing of arms—"continual employment, not to say drudgery," in the words of John Adams.[18]

Washington ended the discouraging chain of events with unexpected successes at Trenton and Princeton, New Jersey, driving the British and Hessians from most of the state. These gave hope to the Army's supporters and encouraged new enlistments to the rapidly dwindling force.[19] There were definite signs of improvement when after recovering New Jersey, the Continental Army settled into winter quarters at Morristown to await the coming maneuver season. The manpower question was momentarily solved, but the matter of training and tactics had not yet been addressed. The British were now fully committed to a military solution to the Revolution, and the stunning rebuff following upon their triumph around New York put their pride at stake. The warm afterglow of Trenton notwithstanding, 1777 promised to be another year of trial for Washington and his army. The Commander in Chief knew he must develop some means of effective training, discipline, and organization, lest the Army's fortunes plummet once again. Washington labored through the winter and spring of 1777 to assemble a respectable army, but the flush of spirit following upon Trenton and Princeton faded quickly and recruitment proceeded slowly. Many

---

17. Weigley, *History of the United States Army*, 35–37; Higginbotham, *War of American Independence*, 148–65.

18. Weigley, *History of the United States Army*, 46, 62–63.

19. Weigley, *History of the United States Army*, 39–40; Higginbotham, *War of American Independence*, 165–71; Douglas Southall Freeman, *George Washington*, 7 vols. (New York: Scribner, 1948), 4: 332–35, 404–05.

men enlisted in state programs for service in militia as home guards which contributed almost nothing to the national cause but obstruction.[20]

By 1777, from a military point of view, the Continental Army's general officers preferred a larger regular army with less reliance than formerly on militia, though there were others in Congress and elsewhere who held the opposite opinion. Compromises dictated by events fixed the Revolutionary army as a mixed force by the end of 1777, which continued to the end of the war. It became so ingrained in national consciousness that the mixed force formed the basis for Washington's proposed peacetime establishment in 1783.[21]

Congress Becomes More Active

The Revolution was at a crisis in 1777, however, and Congress became more active in its attempts to develop and support an effective military force to confront the British challenge. Some of its actions took the form of tinkering with things best left to the Commander in Chief, but delegates noticed "the absence of a regular inspector." On 18 April 1777, Congress "requested" one general to "inspect the magazines of provisions under the care of Commissary Wharton."[22] Inventory control is always important to military logistics; however, of more pressing moment to Congress was the ineffectiveness of the Board of War and Ordnance, a source of unrewarding drudgery for its members. After considering replacing it with a number of boards of people not members of Congress, the legislators at last produced a re-formed Board of War on 18 July 1777, a group of three delegates. But those appointed to the duty mostly did not want it, and it was not until early 1778 that the board met for the first time. It effectively ceased to exist within a year, although Congress added two members to the cipher in October 1778.[23] The unproductive panel could do no good, but it did offer a platform for persons inclined to interfere in the Continental Army.

Recruitments in France

Congress had a more profound effect upon the Continental Army in 1777 through the actions of its agents in Paris, Silas Deane and Benjamin Franklin. Europe happened to be in a lull between wars, and the continent was replete with unemployed, often merely self-styled soldiers looking for adventure and

20. Weigley, *History of the United States Army*, 40.

21. Paul David Nelson, "Citizen Soldiers or Regulars: The Views of American General Officers on the Military Establishment, 1775–1781," *Military Affairs* 43 (October 1972): 126–32.

22. Worthington C. Ford et al., eds., *Journal of the Continental Congress, 1774–1789*, 34 vols. (Washington: Government Printing Office, 1934–37), 18 Apr 77 (hereafter cited as *JCC*). See also Raphael P. Thian, *Legislative History of the General Staff of the Army of the United States (Its Organization, Duties, Pay, and Allowances), from 1775 to 1901*, S. Doc. 229, 56th Cong., 2d sess., 1901, 87. This appears to be the first use of the term "inspector" by the Continental Congress.

23. Weigley, *History of the United States Army*, 46–47.

glory—and if they could get them, high military rank and peacetime nobility. The American Revolution was across the sea, but it offered the only possibility for such ambitions. Especially after the Declaration of Independence in July 1776, Deane and Franklin were constantly besieged by Europeans looking for commissions in the American service. Most were without merit, or merely looking for adventure. Many were exceedingly persistent. Wrote Franklin to one, "If, therefore, you have the least remaining kindness for me, if you would not help to drive me out of France, for God's sake, my dear friend, let this your twenty-third application be your last."[24]

The American commissioners for a time had the authority—or assumed that they did—to commit the Congress to granting commissions to Europeans whose services might be valuable. A number of officers crossed the Atlantic firmly believing that their commissions were in hand. The only defense against them, until Congress cut back on foreign recruiting later in 1777, was the judgment of the American agents. Franklin proved himself discreet and a fair judge of talent. Deane, however, was more easily fooled into accepting highly imaginative credentials and offering some fantastic commitments to questionable volunteers. The parade of foreigners was sufficiently large, and enough of them were incompetent or offensive, that Washington cast a cold eye on the whole business. In fact, he had a real dread of too many foreign officers in his army. Besides the expense and nuisance involved, he was most worried about the foreigners driving out good American officers, and about possible spying.[25]

The First Inspector General

One of Franklin's more impressive finds was Augustin Mottin de la Balme, who arrived in America in the spring of 1777. He bore a letter from Franklin to John Hancock introducing him as a man of high character and an experienced cavalryman who might be useful in forming a mounted branch for the Continental Army. Mottin de la Balme was in fact an able cavalry officer, with experience in the French gendarmerie as an instructor of cavalry during the Seven Years' War, then ten years of service in the French Army as an inspector of academies. He retired as a major, with pension, in 1773, and was the author of several books, including two accepted as authoritative on cavalry training and tactics. In 1777, at the age of forty-one, he presented himself to Franklin and sought his military fortune in America.[26]

---

24. Ganoe, *History of the United States Army*, 41. For Franklin's various missions to Paris in the period of the Revolution, See David Schoenbrun, *Triumph in Paris: The Exploits of Benjamin Franklin* (New York: Harper & Row, 1976).

25. For a succinct analysis of Washington's reaction to the foreigners that descended upon him in 1777, see Forman, "Why the United States Military Academy Was Established," 18.

26. Mark M. Boatner III, *Encyclopedia of the American Revolution* (New York: David McKay, 1974), 748–49; Gilbert Bodinier, *Dictionnaire des Officiers de l'armee royale qui ont combattu aux Etats-Unis pendant la guerre d'Independence 1776–1783* (Vincennes: Bureau d'histoire, 1982), 355–56. See Appendix B.

Congress respected Franklin's judgment, and was dutifully impressed with Mottin de la Balme's credentials, handsome bearing, and zeal for the American cause. The legislators appointed the French cavalry expert a *lieutenant-colonel of horse* on 26 May 1777. But the minuscule mounted force of the American army was equivalent only to four small regiments, dispersed mainly as messengers and escorts. That was a small stage for a performer of de la Balme's energy, and in all likelihood it probably had no place for an additional lieutenant colonel. Possibly at the Frenchman's urging (he was not shy about forcing himself on Congress' attention), the delegates gave him what appeared to be a grander role in the cause, and introduced a new term into the lexicon of American public letters. On 8 July 1777, Congress "*Resolved*, That Lieutenant-Colonel Mottin de la Balme be appointed inspector-general of the cavalry of the United States of America, with the rank and pay of colonel."[27] Exactly what Congress meant by the term *inspector-general* was not apparent in the record of the appointment. There is, however, reason to believe that the delegates had begun to fish for titles that would suit the pretensions of some of the more promising (or demanding) European volunteers, without committing the American authorities to too many general officerships for foreigners at the expense of natives. The title *inspector-general of the cavalry* acknowledged de la Balme's expertise, and implied a high advisory capacity without power of command over Americans. The rank of colonel accorded with the probable size of any Continental cavalry force, which was bound to be modest.

Mottin de la Balme clearly perceived himself as the organizer and trainer of the American mounted force, although it is not apparent that he made much progress toward that end. He revealed his conception of his assignment when he left it. On 3 October, upon learning that the Polish volunteer Casimir Pulaski had been appointed chief of cavalry, the Frenchman fired off to Congress a letter of resignation. He had not crossed the ocean, he said, to train cavalry that would be led into battle by someone with less experience, zeal, courage, and knowledge of cavalry service than he. Congress noted his resignation on 11 October 1777, but did not proceed with accepting it until 13 February 1778. De la Balme was left with his rank of colonel, and was otherwise informed that his services were no longer required; however, such was his interest in the rebellion that he continued to volunteer his services until he was killed in action in 1780.[28]

---

27. Boatner, *Encyclopedia of the American Revolution*, 748–49; *JCC*, 26 May and 8 Jul 77; Francis B. Heitman, *Historical Register and Dictionary of the United States Army, From Its Organization, September 29, 1789 to March 2, 1903*, 2 vols. (1903; reprint, Urbana: University of Illinois Press, 1965), 1:84.

28. Boatner, *Encyclopedia of the American Revolution*, 749; *JCC*, 11 Oct 77, 13 Feb 78. It should be observed that the end of de la Balme's service has been reported as 11 October 1777, with no record of further tenure. Heitman, *Historical Register*, 1:38, 84. See also J.P. Sanger, "The Inspector-General's Department," in Theo. F. Rodenbaugh and William L. Haskin, eds., *The Army of the United States . . .* (New York: Maynard, Merrill, 1896), 12–32, and the *Annual Report of the Inspector General 1900* (hereafter cited as *ARIG*), app. L, H. Doc. 2, 56th Cong., 2d sess. 1, pt. 3: 228. See Appendix B.

The Second Inspector General

Less fortunate than Mottin de la Balme's American career, at least for the American cause, was that of Philippe Charles Jean Baptiste Tronson du Coudray, also a veteran of the French Army. Tronson du Coudray was an artillerist, and like Mottin de la Balme was an author of standard references in his specialty. Born in 1738, educated first as a mining engineer, he rose steadily in the ranks, and after the Corsican campaign of 1768–1769 became an adjutant of artillery. He had at least once commanded a brigade of artillery before offering his services to Silas Deane late in 1776. Deane offered him a commission as major general and chief of artillery and engineers in the American forces, blithely ignoring the fact that Brig. Gen. Henry Knox was the chief of artillery under Washington.

That mistake could have been resolved amicably enough, but for Tronson du Coudray's own personality. He was well connected in French court circles, and was accustomed to having his own way. Worse, he was exceedingly pompous, supercilious, and a general troublemaker, a veteran of thirty duels. He arrived in America in June 1777 with a retinue of eighteen officers and ten sergeants, bearing written information from Deane that he was to be in charge of all artillery. Upon hearing that news, Brig. Gen. Henry Knox, Maj. Gen. Nathanael Greene, and Maj. Gen. John Sullivan threatened to resign. Washington exercised his persuasive powers to the fullest to keep his three generals. Meanwhile, he protested to Congress the imposition upon him of an officer of whose qualifications he knew nothing. Washington's displeasure was aggravated by information from trusted French officers that Tronson du Coudray might not be the engineer he claimed.[29] Nevertheless, du Coudray pressed his claim, while Washington struggled to keep his principal commanders from walking off in a huff. Congress, meanwhile, was in the middle, inclined to uphold the commitments of its agent in Paris, but not altogether willing to dismiss the protests of the American officers as without justification. The legislators dispatched du Coudray to make a study of the defenses of Philadelphia along the Delaware River, which resulted in excellent reports but no real action. On 16 July 1777, the delegates appointed a committee of three members to negotiate some sort of acceptable arrangement with the Frenchman.[30]

---

29. *Webster's American Military Biographies* (Springfield, Mass.: G. C. Merriam, 1978), 106 (hereafter cited as *AMB*); Ganoe, *History of the United States Army*, 41; Flexner, *Washington in the Revolution*, 195; James Ripley Jacobs, *The Beginning of the U.S. Army, 1783–1812* (Princeton: Princeton University Press, 1947), 11; Wright, "*Organization and Doctrine*," 205; Howard C. Rice, Jr., and Anne S. K. Brown, trans. and eds., *The American Campaigns of Rochambeau's Army, 1780, 1781, 1782, 1783*, 2 vols. (Princeton: Princeton University Press; Providence: Brown University Press, 1972), 1:50; Bodinier, *Dictionnaire des Officiers*, 403–04. See also Paul K. Walker, *Engineers of Independence: A Documentary History of the Army Engineers in the American Revolution, 1775–1783* (Washington: Corps of Engineers, 1981), 8–17, and Schoenbrun, *Triumph in Paris*, 90–93, 110, 158.

30. *JCC*, 16 Jul 77. See also Thian, *Legislative History*, 87. For Tronson du Coudray's reports, with commentary, see Walker, *Engineers of Independence*, 148–55; "Coudray's Observations on Forts for Defense of the Delaware, July 1777," *Pennsylvania Magazine of History and Biography*, 24 (1900): 343–47; and Worthington C. Ford, ed., "Defenses of Philadelphia," *Pennsylvania Magazine of History and Biography*, 18 (1894): 334–37.

On 11 August, Congress reached a compromise, appointing Tronson du Coudray "inspector-general of ordnance and military manufactories, with the rank of major-general." Just exactly what he was to do was to be determined by a committee of four members of Congress. Meanwhile, inserting the temperamental Frenchman into the Continental Army, and at that making him a major general over the heads of so many Americans, was a prescription for trouble in Washington's command. But the troublesome "volunteer" solved the entire problem with a characteristic demonstration of his martial dash on 16 September 1777. He is said to have galloped his horse onto a ferry on the Schuylkill River with so much vigor that he landed in the water on the other side and drowned.[31]

Congress never had a chance to define the duties of its inspector general of ordnance and military manufactories. Presumably he would offer technical oversight in the manufacture of artillery hardware, and du Coudray did have some abilities in that area. But the energetic Frenchman was more inclined to haunt the field of action with the main army. He was in practice, then, a highly ranked supernumerary. In fact, his title and rank were most likely a congressional compromise, giving him the show of agreement with Deane's commitment to him, without any substance that would have discomfited Washington or his American officers. The title *inspector-general* was mere flattery that meant nothing in military terms.

The Campaign of 1777

Meaningless titles adorning temperamental foreigners did Washington's cause little good during the campaign of 1777. He had more important things on his mind, and was understandably impatient with the nuisances that Silas Deane's beneficiaries could cause. He remained concerned principally with being ready for the campaign about to open. The Continental Army, albeit loosely organized and mostly amateur, had nonetheless benefited from the experience of the previous year. The initiative in 1777 rested with the British. Washington was not sufficiently confident in his force's martial ability to make the first move. The British, for their part, had determined to put down the Revolution by force, and must therefore take the offensive. Washington was content to let them do that, reacting according to his army's abilities but careful always to keep the Continental Army alive as the main embodiment of the struggle.

The British, amazingly, accommodated him. Instead of pursuing the Continental Army as the core of the uprising, the British sought territorial gains. Worse, they cast off their advantages of size, experience, and logistical support

---

31. *JCC*, 11 Aug 77; Thian, *Legislative History*, 87; Flexner, *Washington in the Revolution*, 195; Rice and Brown, *American Campaigns*, 1: 50; Sanger, "Inspector-General's Department," 228. Various sources give the date of du Coudray's death as 8, 11, 13, 15, 16, or 17 September. Heitman accepts 15 September. Heitman, *Historical Register*, 1: 38, 329. Most French sources, however, record it as the 16th.

by dividing their forces and immobilizing them so that separate parts could not support each other. A complicated, two-pronged invasion of upper New York under Maj. Gen. John Burgoyne, intended vaguely to isolate New England, was so obviously dangerous to them that Washington felt no concern about it. He sent a force under Horatio Gates to assist the terrain in bringing Burgoyne to grief. The main army followed Washington out to meet Maj. Gen. Sir William Howe's campaign against Philadelphia. Howe's force sailed from New York and up Chesapeake Bay, and in late August began its march through hostile territory stripped of provisions. Washington moved to confront the challenge, suffering defeats at Brandywine and Germantown in September and early October. Congress decamped from Philadelphia to establish a temporary capital at York, Pennsylvania, and the British occupied Philadelphia for the winter. Meanwhile, Burgoyne came to grief at Saratoga, New York, where he surrendered his forces on 17 October.[32]

Superficially, the results of the campaigns of 1777 appeared mixed, with the balance in favor of the British. That balance actually lay the other way. The capture of Burgoyne's force was a serious military loss, and a worse political one, for the British. Nor had the royal forces had things all their own way farther south. Howe's hostile reception in Pennsylvania had revealed clearly that there was no widespread loyalist support in the colonies, no matter how lukewarm was public support for the American effort. Washington had met tactical defeat, but he had proved himself skillful enough as a battlefield commander, and his soldiers had fought stoutly enough to give their opponents a resounding shock. The Continental Army was still together, and with more experience and training it could become a redoubtable force on the battlefield. There were members of Congress, however, who were not so convinced, driven as they were from their homes in the city. The positive aspects of the main army's defeats were not apparent to those not soldiers. Moreover, it was patently simple to draw a contrast between Washington's losses and Gates' victory. The cause of the Revolution was fraught with discontent in high places, a situation made for grumbling, encouraging change for the sake of change—and fertile ground for the seeds of personal ambitions. It was in that climate that the Office of the Inspector General of the Continental Army came into being.

Inspector General Conway

One of Washington's officers was Brig. Gen. Thomas Conway, who was present at the battles of Brandywine and Germantown.[33] Conway was another of Silas Deane's contributions to the American cause. Born in Ireland in 1735, he was reared and educated in France, whose army he entered in 1749. A

---

32. The campaigns of 1777 are covered in Higginbotham, *War of American Independence*, 175–203.

33. Ganoe, *History of the United States Army*, 44. This story may be apocryphal, although not inconsistent with Conway's character.

colonel by 1772, he had seen service in campaigns in Germany in 1760 and 1761. Supposedly a talented disciplinarian, especially with infantry, in April 1777 he made his way to America on Deane's recommendation, and was appointed brigadier general in the Continental Army on 13 May. Conway was a large man with a chinless, rather popeyed face, much given to posturing and to intrigue. He had an ability to impress people at first meeting, giving rise to a general belief among civilians that he possessed great military talents. But he soon wore out his welcome with his pomposity and ceaseless bragging about his own merits. In time, his skills as a disciplinarian proved to be more those of a bully. He quickly established himself as a thorn in Washington's

MAJ. GEN. THOMAS CONWAY. *Inspector General of the Continental Army, 13 December 1777–28 April 1778.*

side, one of the few people towards whom the Commander in Chief ever expressed personal animosity.[34] Conway's talent, said Washington, "exists more in his own imagination, than in reality." He was also the junior brigadier general, and Washington predicted that to promote him over the heads of all others would cause most of them to resign, with good reason. In conclusion, Washington said he saw such a move imposing so many morale problems that his job would be impossible, hinting that he would resign.[35] The Commander in Chief would brook no repetition of the Tronson du Coudray business.

Washington probably believed that he had scuttled Conway's personal efforts at advancement, and turned his attention to the organization of his military force. The Continental Army was vastly better than it had been a year earlier, but it was still woefully untrained and loosely organized for the challenges it faced. Washington had been serving for too long as his own staff, and could not give his undivided attention to everything. Apparently he had decided by October 1777 that he needed an additional staff officer with oversight in all training and maneuvers, and attendant regulations. It is likely that he had learned

---

34. *Dictionary of American Biography*, 20 vols. (New York: Scribner, 1928–36), 4:365–66 (hereafter cited as *DAB*); Flexner, *Washington in the Revolution*, 262–268; Weigley, *History of the United States Army*, 50–51; *Bodinier, Dictionnaire des Officiers*, 105–06. See Appendix B.

35. Washington to Richard Henry Lee, 17 Oct 77, in John C. Fitzpatrick, ed., *The Writings of George Washington, From the Original Manuscript Sources*, 39 vols. (Washington: Government Printing Office, 1931–44), 9: 387–89. See also Henry Steele Commager and Richard B. Morris, eds., *The Spirit of Seventy-six . . .*, 2 vols. (Indianapolis: Bobbs-Merrill, 1958), 1: 652–53.

enough from European officers in his camp to become generally familiar with the services of inspectors general in foreign establishments.

Washington called a council of fourteen general officers on 29 October, and asked them among other things, "Will the office of Inspector-General to our Army, for the purpose principally of establishing one uniform set of maneuvers and manual, be advisable as the time of the adjutant-general seems to be totally engaged with other business?" General John Sullivan replied that an accomplished drillmaster familiar with large units would be a great asset, any one less qualified would be more trouble then he was worth.[36] The other officers were of like sentiments, and all signed a statement that such an officer was desirable, the manual of regulations to be first agreed upon by the Commander in Chief, or a board of officers appointed for the purpose. Washington passed the record of the council to Congress, with a recommendation that the position of Inspector General be established.[37]

Washington revealed very clearly his conception of what an inspector general should be. The officer was to superintend the training of the whole army, ensuring troop proficiency in a common set of tactics—really a sort of "drillmaster general." He had formerly entrusted responsibility for training to the Commander in Chief's first agent, the Adjutant General. That was probably an understandable influence of his own first military experience, as an adjutant in Virginia, his duties being those of an instructor and inspector of training. But Washington's own council had had to remind him of the need to subordinate the Inspector General to the Commander in Chief—the latter, not the inspector, should effect regulations. As proposed to Congress, the Inspector General would be the commander's agency for the promotion of tactical efficiency in the Army. The inspector's duties consequently would be quite specific: Washington's first conception of the Inspector General was limited in scope, but it focused on the Army's greatest immediate needs. It was bound to evolve in practice as part of the Commander in Chief's evolutionary development of army organization. But it turned out that there were others in Congress who seized upon the inspector-general proposal as a means to accomplish more—to reform things besides training and to tighten congressional control over the Army.

Washington's proposal lent itself more immediately to the ambitions of Thomas Conway. Present at the council of officers, he was the first to let Congress know that he would like the new job.[38] Even before he had done so, he had begun to make himself known to people in power. Conway apparently believed that Gates' star was on the rise after the victory at Saratoga, while Washington's was about to fall. He decided to ingratiate himself with Gates, and wrote him a flattering letter that disparaged Washington. Already there were mutterings in the Congress that the cause might be served better with

---

36. Sanger, "Inspector-General's Department," 228.
37. Ibid.
38. Ibid., 228–29.

Gates in command than with Washington. They remained nothing more than idle mutterings, and not even Gates put much stock in them. Gates' aide, Maj. James Wilkinson, had ambitions of his own. When the general heard from Conway, Wilkinson was greatly amused. Wilkinson stopped at the headquarters of Brig. Gen. William Alexander (Lord Stirling) at the end of October, and feeling the effects of alcohol, he grew voluble. After Stirling learned what Conway had been about, he relayed the information to Washington.[39] Conway had transcended the bounds of contemporary decency, and on 9 November Washington confronted him in a blunt letter with what he had heard.[40]

As November passed, members of Washington's staff began to believe that there was a plot afoot in Congress to replace him with Gates. There was in fact no organized conspiracy, but there were those who saw fit to advance Gates' cause, and for various reasons, Conway's name seemed to be frequently mentioned. Washington's staff, in particular Alexander Hamilton, persuaded him to deter any plotters with a series of strong letters. They were probably more alarmed when Gates was appointed to the Board of War on 27 November, and in any case Washington had made it well known by the end of the month that he wanted to hear the last of Conway.[41]

Meanwhile, Conway had developed the habit of threatening to resign if he did not receive what he believed he deserved. That alarmed some members of Congress who still thought that Conway was a man of rare talent, an asset to the cause, and they actively sought a suitable assignment for him.[42] Their opportunity came on 13 December 1777, when the Continental Congress authorized the appointment of inspectors general, "essential to the promoton of discipline in the American Army, and to the reformation of the various abuses which prevail in the different departments . . . agreeable to the practice of the best disciplined European armies." There were to be two inspectors general, who were to be "experienced and vigilant general officers, who are acquainted with whatever relates to the general economy, manoeuvers, and discipline of a well-regulated army."

The duties of the inspectors general were "to review, from time to time, the troops, and to see that every officer and soldier be instructed in the exercise and manoeuvers which may be established by the board of war, that the rules of discipline be strictly observed, and that the officers command their soldiers properly and do them justice." The inspectors general were required to notify regimental commanders of the time for their reviews, and the commanders were to prepare a number of returns according to models furnished by the inspectors. The returns were to inventory clothing; arms and accouterments;

39. Samuel White Patterson, *Horatio Gates: Defender of American Liberties* (New York: Columbia University Press, 1941), 216–19; Commager and Morris, *Spirit of Seventy-Six*, 651–52.

40. Washington to Conway, 9 Nov 77, in Fitzpatrick, *Writings of Washington*, 10: 29; Commager and Morris, *Spirit of Seventy-Six*, 653.

41. Commager and Morris, *Spirit of Seventy-Six*, 651–52.

42. Henry Laurens to Lafayette, 6 Dec 77, in Paul H. Smith, ed., *Letters of Delegates to Congress, 1774–1789*, 8 vols. (Washington: Library of Congress, 1976–81), 8:383.

recruits, with an account of recruiting money expended; the number and names of wounded men, identifying those fit for the invalid corps and those unfit for any service; losses by "death, desertion, or otherwise"; pay and rations; and all officers, "with observations upon the behavior, capacity, and assiduity of every individual." Regimental field officers were all to sign the returns before presenting them to the inspectors general, who were likewise to sign them and transmit them to Congress.

The congressional resolution also required that the inspectors general make their reviews at the beginning and end of every campaign, and at other times as the Commander in Chief might direct. But they would also make their inspections "as they themselves shall severally judge proper, or shall receive orders for that purpose from the board of war, first giving notice thereof to the Commander in Chief, and obtaining his leave for reviewing the said troops." More explicitly, Congress resolved that the inspectors general personally interview and observe unit members and their equipment down to the smallest detail necessary to give a clear understanding of the unit's condition. And Congress did not stop there. Inspection reports were to be prepared in triplicate, one copy for the inspector general concerned, one for the major of the regiment inspected, the third to Congress. Almost as an afterthought, the resolution directed the inspectors general to examine pay books, reporting to Congress any signs of "malversation or mismanagement," and announced that the "commissioners of the war office" would prepare any additional regulations for the Office of the Inspector General. Lastly, Congress resolved that two inspectors general be appointed for the moment, and elected Conway to be one of them. No one was ever advanced for the other position. The delegates closed their long resolution authorizing the addition of another major general in the Army, appointing Conway to the new vacancy.[43]

There were a number of questionable aspects of the position of the Inspector General as established on 13 December 1777. Foremost among them was the fact that the Continental Army was no longer big enough to hold both Thomas Conway and George Washington, and some of the framers of the resolution knew it. But the actual substance of the Inspector General's position was very defective from a military perspective. That may have reflected Conway's own contributions, as it is likely that he proposed the Inspector General as a potential field agent of the Board of War. By such means he could garner the position for himself and with it—what he wanted all along—his promotion to major general. Whether in Conway's hands or not, the Inspector General's office as defined 13 December represented a serious threat to Washington's control of the Army.[44]

The establishment of the Inspector General's position probably had been influenced by a number of factors. One was the recommendation of Washington and his generals that it be established, to reform the training and discipline

43. *JCC*, 13 Dec 77. See also Thian, *Legislative History*, 87–88.
44. Wright, "Organization and Doctrine," 195–96; Sanger, "Inspector-General's Department," 229.

of the army; Washington's recommendation had mentioned in passing the preparation of regulations. Another probable influence on the resolution was dissatisfaction on the part of some delegates over the way the war had gone; some of them may have preferred Gates in Washington's position, and may have believed that elevating Conway would encourage Washington to resign. Thus, the inspectorship became in some minds secondary to a change in army leadership. Allied with that was the feeling on the part of congressmen that Conway actually deserved an elevated position. For many members of Congress the inspectorship probably was of primary importance as a possible way to reform the military establishment. The solution they adopted—making the Inspector General a congressional agent within the army—also happened to suit both Conway's selfish purposes and those of Gates' proponents. That perhaps was secondary to the greater number of delegates. So recently driven out of Philadelphia, they believed that the army should be made to work better. Momentarily losing confidence in Washington, Congress thought it could do the job itself.

In asking for an inspector general, Washington implicitly acknowledged that the Army needed improvement. As commander, he wanted to undertake that improvement, and sought an inspector general to use as his tool. As commander, he expected to be held responsible for every aspect of military service to the country. The resolution establishing the Inspector General, however, did not hold the Commander in Chief responsible for the regulation or training of the army. It may be assumed that Congress would continue to hold Washington accountable for the army's performance, but the resolution would have undermined seriously his ability to control those under him. It did not give Washington control over the means of improvement. To begin with, the inspectors general were under the control of the Board of War, and not at all answerable to the army commander. The results of their inspections, for instance, were to be communicated directly to the Congress; the Commander in Chief would not receive a copy. Inspectors determined their own schedules, or were under orders of the Board of War, although the Commander in Chief would direct them to make reviews. Moreover, the manner in which inspections were to be conducted meant that regimental commanders would be accountable for administration and discipline to the inspector, not to their superior commanders. Altogether, those procedures nearly erased the normal chain of command, except as subordinate commanders were willing to follow purely military orders.

As a matter of civil supervision of the military, the resolution establishing the inspectors general went impossibly beyond the line of discretion in another very important regard. It reserved to the Board of War the authority to establish the "exercise and manoeuvers" to be practiced in the army. The Commander in Chief was not allowed to regulate his own force or determine such matters as small-unit tactics or even the standard march cadence. He could not even supervise instruction in the tactics imposed by the Board of War. That was the duty of the board's agents, the inspectors general. The latter was probably the most serious defect of the whole arrangement. Establishing the inspectors general as political inquisitors attached to the army was troublesome enough, although Washington probably could have found a way to live with it in practice (by managing to have communications routed through his hands, for instance). But granting to the Board of War the power to regulate the army without reference to the Commander in Chief was simply unacceptable. Taken to its logical conclusions, the resolution of 13 December would have effectively eliminated the command authority of the Commander in Chief. It would have transformed the Continental Army into a disunited collection of regiments politically monitored. As Alexander Hamilton observed later, at the least the system would produce confusion, inaction, and delays.[45]

An inspector general answerable to the Board of War but not to the Commander in Chief was a classic formula for conflict between the civil power and the military. But for the moment, that was almost an academic question. The immediate issue was that Congress had imposed upon Washington an officer it knew was utterly unacceptable to him and to most American officers. That Conway was a political appointee and not a line officer was irrelevant. Conway was in, and that was all that seemed to matter: "Conway is made a Majr. Genl. & Inspector of the Army," Francis Lightfoot Lee told his brother as soon as it happened.[46] His message was much discussed in the first few days after the resolution passed.

Telling Gen. William Whipple the news of Conway's appointment as the Inspector General, Delegate William Ellery said, "I am in hopes that the measures adopted and adopting will enable our army to take the field early in the Spring under great advantages."[47] That was a fairly common sentiment. A few people who would have liked to see Gates in Washington's position may have sponsored Conway in the hopes that his appointment would force Washington to resign. But it is likely that they were indeed very few. The majority apparently believed Conway's reputation as a disciplinary expert, and probably accepted his general concept of the Inspector General as the recommendation of an authority. They were awakened soon enough, but it remained to be seen how Washington would react when Conway presented himself at headquarters.

Conway arrived at Washington's camp at Valley Forge at the end of December, prepared to assume his duties as Inspector General. The Commander in Chief received him unenthusiastically. Looking over Conway's credentials, Washington observed that the Board of War's instructions said that the board was to furnish a set of regulations for maneuvering the troops. When he asked Conway if he had those instructions with him, the Inspector General replied that he did not. Washington avowed that Conway could not possibly serve as Inspector General until the instructions arrived; he then had an aide show Conway to the door.[48] Effectively locked out of the Continental Army,

45. Friedrich Kapp, *The Life of Frederick William Von Steuben, Major General in the Revolutionary Army*, 2d ed. (New York: Mason Brothers, 1859), 121–22.
46. Francis Lightfoot Lee to Richard Henry Lee, 15 Dec 77, in Smith, *Letters*, 8:417.
47. William Ellery to William Whipple, 21 Dec 77, in Smith, *Letters*, 8:453.
48. Flexner, *Washington in the Revolution*, 258–59, 262–63.

Conway left for York on 31 December to complain to his supporters in Congress. Two days later, Washington wrote to Congress opposing Conway's appointment and Conway's version of the inspectorship. He enclosed a record of the council of generals on 29 October, which he said showed "the office of Inspector-General was a matter not of such modern date as General Conway maintains it to be, and that it was one of the regulations in view to reform the Army." He thus suggested that the report of the October meeting should have been acted on first, without considering Conway. The officers he had intended to recommend for the position were those "foreign officers who had commissions and no commands, and who were of ability . . . particularly the Baron d'Arendt, with whom the idea originated, and whose capacity seemed to be well admitted."[49]

The next day, 3 January 1778, Washington had again to write to Congress to present his version of his meeting with Conway, in answer to Conway's official complaints. The letter was unusually blunt, but carefully crafted to place Washington on the higher and his antagonist on the lower plane of public conduct:

If General Conway means, by cool receptions . . . that I did not receive him in the language of a warm and cordial friend, I readily confess the charge. I did not, nor shall I ever, till I am capable of the arts of dissimulation. These I despise, and my feelings will not permit me to make professions of friendship to the man I deem my enemy and whose system of conduct forbids it. At the same time truth authorizes me to say, that he was received and treated with the proper respect to his official character, and that he has had no cause to justify the assertion, that he could not expect any support for fulfilling the duties of his appointment.[50]

Washington's partisans had by that time firmly established in their own minds, and in those of others, the notion that there was a conspiracy afoot to get rid of Washington—with full awareness of the unseemly connotations of that term. Gates and Washington exchanged a protracted correspondence, with the former denying any complicity in plots of whose existence he claimed no knowledge. The propounders of the conspiracy story then portrayed Gates as almost a fool, his manipulators that much worse for using him. Another part of the counterattack against Conway was a concerted effort to discredit him among his former proponents. Regarding his supposed military talents, Conway proved to be his own worst enemy, his manner soon trying the patience of everyone in York. When Congress proposed in January 1778 to mount an expedition against Canada under Lafayette, Conway was advanced as second in command, possibly to get him out of town. But Lafayette refused to accept him in that capacity, and he finally was reduced to accompanying him as third in command. Conway's continued scheming for a separate command, coupled with his disfavor among most of the high officers of the Army, prevented him from achieving his ambitions.[51] He was thoroughly discredited by this time. The President

---

49. Sanger says that Baron d'Arendt was a Prussian officer and colonel of the German regiment and an aide-de-camp to Washington. Sanger, "Inspector-General's Department," 229.

50. Washington to Pres of Cong, 3 Jan 78, quoted in John McAuley Palmer, *General Von Steuben* (New Haven: Yale University Press, 1937), 133.

51. *DAB*, 4: 366.

of Congress, Henry Laurens, had once looked upon Conway with favor. He finally put an end to all talk of a "cabal" against Washington, in a letter to his son John Laurens, one of Washington's aides, who showed it to the Commander in Chief. It became apparent that the whole affray was mostly idle talk from a handful of malcontents, of whom only Thomas Mifflin and Conway showed any real malice toward Washington. That ended the assertions from Washington's officers regarding cabals and plots. They did, however, claim victory. "The poor and shallow politicians," crowed Nathanael Greene, "unmasked their batteries before they were ready to attempt any execution."[52]

The business was nearly completed, except for the dispatch of Conway, still technically the Army's Inspector General. He had become almost a pariah, in his own words "ordered from place to place." The unfortunate expatriate Irishman blundered one last time, again offering his resignation. To his chagrin, on 28 April 1778, Congress voted to accept it. Conway exploded to Gates, "I had no thoughts of resigning," then spent the next several weeks in rather deranged attempts to persuade Congress to reconsider. In a duel with Brig. Gen. John Cadwalader near Philadelphia on 4 July 1778, Conway took a bullet in the mouth. Thinking he was dying, he wrote to Washington to apologize "for having done, written, or said anything disagreeable" to his excellency. He did not perish, however, and within a year resumed his career in the French Army.[53] With his departure, the incident of the "Conway cabal" was over, but not forgotten. It appears that there never was a real conspiracy to unseat Washington, merely some varied dissatisfactions with his performance as Commander in Chief. It is clear, however, that Washington and his partisans really believed that there was a plot to get rid of him. At least, they claimed that there was in order to strengthen their own case. But aside from giving historians something to speculate about over the next two centuries, the whole turmoil surrounding Washington and Conway in 1777 and 1778 had some fortunate effects for the American cause. Among others, it left Washington virtually immune to criticism for the remainder of the war.[54]

Equally important, and another aspect of the turmoil surrounding Conway that should not be forgotten, was the concept of the Inspector General itself. Washington and his supporters probably would not have raised such a controversy if the only issue at stake had been Conway's personal ambition for high rank. As Washington demonstrated at the end of December, Conway's guns were easy to spike. The Commander in Chief probably realized that it was but a matter of time before Conway's record and personality removed him from the

---

52. Jonathan Gregory Rossie, *The Politics of Command in the American Revolution* (Syracuse: Syracuse University Press, 1975), 201–02; Greene as quoted in Hugh F. Rankin, *The American Revolution* (New York: Putnam), 174. For an excellent discussion of the "Conway Cabal," see Rossie, *The Politics of Command*, 188–202.

53. Patterson, *Horatio Gates*, 265–69; Rankin, *American Revolution*, 174. See Appendix B.

54. The prevailing wisdom for some time has been that there in fact was no "cabal" as such. For typical accounts, see Flexner, *Washington in the Revolution*, 241–77, and Higginbotham, *War of American Independence*, 216–22.

scene. The question remains: Why then the outcry in Washington's camp against Conway, the insinuations that he was part of a vicious plot to overthrow the Commander in Chief? The reason has less to do with Conway than with the concept of Inspector General that the Congress, with Conway's assistance, had propounded. In defining the office the way it did on 13 December, Congress had inadvertently posed the real threat to Washington's command of the Army. Washington and his officers may have sought to discredit Conway as a way of discrediting the office of Inspector General as then presented. They succeeded.

The aftermath of the Conway episode both strengthened and clarified the position of the Commander in Chief. To begin with, it ensured that Washington would be allowed to select his own Inspector General in the future. Never again would Congress try to impose on him in such a high position someone he either did not know or did not want. More fundamentally, the whole myth of the "cabal" tainted any proposals to insert into the Army agents not subject to the orders of the Commander in Chief. Congress' conception made the Inspector General one of its own agents reporting independently about what went on—and worse, imposing regulations on the regiments without the knowledge of the army commander. After the Conway affair, the very idea suggested intrigue and an undermining of the Revolutionary cause. In fact, Congress became so sensitive about interference in Washington's command that early in 1778 its pertinent committees hesitated to visit Valley Forge, even on the most urgent business.[55]

Washington emerged from the Conway controversy solidly in control, and politically almost above reproach. He had also established the Commander in Chief as the sole military authority accountable to the civil power, in so doing founding a strong American tradition of separation between the military and political spheres. And Washington had not forgotten his original purpose. He had destroyed the office of Inspector General as a political intrusion into his chain of command; if Congress wanted to know the state of the Army, it would have to ask the Commander in Chief. There remained the need to establish an inspectorate commensurate with the authority of the army commander. Washington, not Conway or anyone else, would now define the role of the Inspector General—first, as the drillmaster-general he had originally proposed; later, in every way the eyes and ears of the Commander in Chief. But in the meantime, he had to find someone who could fill the job.

Valley Forge

While the Conway controversy continued, the Continental Army had more pressing needs. Washington decided to go into winter quarters in December 1777, despite complaints from York that he should do something about the British occupation of Philadelphia. But the troops had gone as far as they were

---

55. Higginbotham, *War of American Independence*, 220.

able without relief. Col. John Laurens wrote his father Henry Laurens describing the exhaustion and privations of the soldiers and the need to give them minimum comforts so they could be properly trained and rested.[56] The hardships of the Continental Army at Valley Forge which he described have become part of the American legend, but they were real enough. Food, clothing, shoes, blankets—nearly everything was in short supply or nonexistent. Conditions were aggravated by an unusually early and severe winter. Men greatly fatigued and underfed labored for two weeks to erect huts of fence rails and poles chinked with clay, moss, or straw. But even in that they were defeated, as straw was in such short supply that many thatched roofs went unfinished, and men had to sleep on brush or bare ground. When combined with the other deprivations—largely owing to a breakdown in transportation—such conditions help to explain why fully a third of the 9,000-man army was declared unfit for duty at the end of December 1777.[57]

As cries of "No meat! No meat!" echoed through the camp, Washington sat down on 23 December and literally begged Congress for help. "What then is to become of the Army this Winter?" He asked, "and if we are as often without Provisions now, as with it, what is to become of us in the Spring, when our force will be collected, with the aid perhaps of the Militia, to take advantage of an early campaign before the Enemy can be reinforced?"[58] Washington and the soldiers received their answer, piece by precious piece, as the transportation jam began to break early in 1778. The army never had enough to eat or wear that winter, but it gradually got more, enough to survive. As provisions arrived and the troops became fit for duty, the Commander in Chief turned his attention again to the need for regulation and training. That raised anew the question of the Inspector General. The answer to that question appeared disguised most improbably in the form of yet another "volunteer" from Europe, a man professing not only high military attainment but nobility as well.

---

56. John Laurens to Henry Laurens, 3 Dec 77, in Commager and Morris, *Spirit of Seventy-Six*, 1:639.
57. Risch, *Quartermaster Support*, 29–35; Ganoe, *History of the United States Army*, 50–53; Charles Knowles Bolton, *The Private Soldier Under Washington* (New York: Scribner, 1902), 75; John B. Trussell, Jr., *Birthplace of an Army: A Study of the Valley Forge Encampments* (Harrisburg: Pennsylvania Historical and Museum Commission, 1976). See also the selection of original reports in Trussell, *Birthplace of an Army*, 641–44.
58. Washington to Pres of Cong, 23 Dec 77, in Commager and Morris, *Spirit of Seventy-Six*, 1: 644.

CHAPTER 2

Steuben at Valley Forge

(1777–1778)

Born in Magdeburg, Prussia, on 17 September 1730, Friedrich W. A. von Steuben would grow up to become one of the better known figures of the American Revolution, a legend in his own time and after. Long familiar to schoolchildren as the Prussian who drilled the Continental Army at Valley Forge, his memory has served as the principal inspiration for the Inspector General's Department of the United States Army, its successor, and other organizations patterned after it. His genuine concern for individuals, personal integrity, and willingness to devote his time to the training of those less experi- enced epitomized the standards expected of those who followed him. The relationship he eventually developed with the commander in chief remains the pattern for modern military inspectors. It will be seen that the system and attitudes he developed set a permanent precedent still largely followed.

A Volunteer for the American Cause

Steuben entered the Prussian Army at the age of seventeen, eventually serving with credit in the Seven Years' War as an infantry officer, then as a staff officer. He was assigned to the general staff in 1761, and soon attained the rank of captain—his highest position in Prussian service. In January and February 1762 he received two personal letters from Frederick the Great, thanking him for certain minor services. That most unusual compliment to a junior officer was followed by a confidential assignment connected to Prussian negotiations with the Russians; then in May 1762, to assignment to the royal headquarters as a general staff officer and one of the king's aides-de-camp. Despite this modest prominence, Steuben became neither a lieutenant general nor one of the king's favorites, as he later claimed. But he did bring credit upon himself for his skills and energy. Most important, he acquired experience in the duties of a general staff, something almost unknown outside Prussia. After the Seven Years' War, he became chamberlain at the court of Hohenzollern-Hechingen, where he received a knighthood and the honorific title *Freiherr* (baron). But his prince's fortunes declined toward bankruptcy, and by 1775 Steuben was once again out of work and seriously in debt. After unsuccessful attempts to enter the service of France, Austria, and the Margrave of Baden, Steuben encountered an acquaintance of Benjamin Franklin who suggested the American cause as a possible outlet for the Prussian's military ambitions—not to mention a remedy for his penury.

Steuben arrived in Paris during the early summer of 1777, armed with letters to Franklin and others. It so happened that his reputation as a trained Prussian staff officer preceded him, and had been noticed by the French minister of war, the Comte de St. Germain, then engaged in introducing Prussian methods into France's army. St. Germain recommended Steuben to Franklin as just the sort of man the American cause needed, a practical expert on training, organization, and military administration. Franklin and Silas Deane were easily persuaded of Steuben's abilities, and given his financial straits, they may have believed that the Prussian would serve the United States more eagerly and faithfully than some of the aristocratic Europeans who had preceded him. The administrative and organizational skills which he would bring to America were such that he could be of value without threatening the positions of established commanders. He certainly needed the work.

Deane, Franklin, St. Germain, and the French author and merchant, Caron de Beaumarchais, it appears, were all involved in negotiations with Steuben. Since Steuben needed the employment for his pocketbook's sake, while his ego required a certain minimum status for its own well-being, restrictions on the American agents caused difficulty. Congress had limited the commissioners' authority, no longer allowing them to enter into contracts on Congress' behalf, nor even to guarantee rank or pay—two previous licenses that had brought some decidedly sorry "volunteers" to the American cause. Steuben, of course, was not likely to venture across the ocean without some assurances, and in any case could not afford to make the trip on his own. Beaumarchais removed the fundamental obstacle by arranging for his corporation, Hortalez and Company, to advance Steuben's traveling expenses. Reimbursement was no concern. The French and American recruiters believed that Steuben's own abilities would cause Congress to recognize and reward his value to the Revolutionary cause. They may also have believed that presenting him as a distinguished volunteer not demanding position and pelf would contrast strikingly with the likes of Tronson du Coudray. That the arrangement was unavoidable in the circumstances, along with the fact that Steuben was desperate for employment, could be glossed over. Steuben would appear as a man of rare talent and high position, who acted at great personal sacrifice solely out of dedication to the American cause—a royalist nobleman turned democrat.

It was probably Franklin who supervised the refinement of Steuben's resume. Fearing that Steuben's actual highest rank of captain would be unimpressive in Congress (and as likely, believing that it did not fairly represent his considerable talents) Franklin and the others elevated Steuben to the status of "a Lieutenant General in the King of Prussia's service," as Franklin wrote to Washington in September 1777. When Steuben left Marseilles on 26 September, he carried with him letters from Franklin, Deane, and Beaumarchais to Henry Laurens, Robert Morris, and others of influence, who were told that the "lieutenant general" had been as much as the right-hand man of Frederick the Great.[1] Steuben's introduction to the fledgling United States of America was disingenuous, but not really to his discredit. It is clear that the American and French parties in Paris perceived his potential value to the Revolutionary cause, so much so that they were willing to go to extraordinary lengths to win him a good reception in the New World. That would not be possible if Congress saw him as the unemployed fugitive from debt collectors that he was, especially since he followed a number of Europeans with grand reputations but poor records of performance. Franklin at least perceived that, given a chance, Steuben would prove his value. As events demonstrated, he did.[2]

Following his arrival at Portsmouth, New Hampshire, on 6 December Steuben wrote to Congress to volunteer his services. He asked only payment for his expenses, and if the outcome of the war was successful, reimbursement for the loss of his own European income (neglecting to mention that he had none). He wanted merely, he promised, to serve Washington as he had the King of Prussia in seven campaigns. Writing to Washington the same day, Steuben asked only to be granted citizenship in return for his services. After having served the King of Prussia, Steuben avowed, Washington was the sole person under whom he would wish to follow his profession of arms.[3] His letter to Congress created an immediate favorable reaction. In York, Henry Laurens, President of the Continental Congress, was decidedly impressed with Steuben's credentials. On 14 January he wrote him to acknowledge his letter to Congress and report that the delegates had that day "Resolved an Act . . . requesting you to join General Washington as soon as you can make it convenient to your Self." Congress had in fact presented Steuben with a brevet rank of captain, to protect him should he be taken by the British. But Laurens warned the arriving nobleman not to expect too much because of the Continental Army's hard conditions at Valley Forge. He said even Washington was living in a rude hut.[4] Laurens apparently believed that Steuben was so lofty of station, and the fortunes of the Continental Army so low, that the foreigner might quail at the thought of sharing the miseries of Valley Forge. He wanted to do what was possible to keep Steuben for the cause. In contrast, Washington's caution appeared a more realistic attitude in the circumstances. The Commander in Chief evidently knew by early January that Steuben was not all that he had been claimed to be, and word soon reached the Prussian that a part, at least, of his disguise had slipped.[5]

---

1. For the best account of Steuben's early years, see Palmer, *General Steuben*, 9–102, which is summarized in Palmer's entry on Steuben in the *DAB*, 17: 601–04, and for the most recent scholarly account of Steuben's career, see Philander D. Chase, "Baron Von Steuben in the War of Independence" (Ph.D. dissertation, Duke University, 1973), which focuses on his time in America.

2. Horst Dippel, *Germany and the American Revolution, 1770–1800: A Sociohistorical Investigation of Late Eighteenth-Century Political Thinking*, trans. Bernhard A. Uhlendorf (Chapel Hill: University of North Carolina Press, 1977), 110–11.

3. Kapp, *Life of Steuben*, 95–97; Ganoe, *History of the United States Army*, 54.

4. Laurens to Steuben, 14 Jan 78, in Smith, *Letters*, 8:594.

5. Steuben to Hamilton, 27 Jan 90, quoted in Kapp, *Life of Steuben*, 74.

MAJ. GEN. FRIEDRICH W. A. VON
STEUBEN. *Inspector General of
the main army, 28 March 1778–15
April 1784.*

Washington proposed to reserve judgment on Steuben, but he knew that action was required immediately to reform his army. The Conway controversy was drawing to an end, so he arranged for a congressional committee to visit Valley Forge in late January to help develop a plan for army administration. The need for an inspector general was still uppermost in his mind. In a letter to the committee on 28 January, he revealed that his original conception of that position, more or less a drillmaster-general with assistants down to brigade level, was still firm.[6] Despite his need, Washington did not rush into filling the position before careful scrutiny of the latest foreign volunteer after his arrival in camp. Steuben left York 19 February, and arrived at Valley Forge on the 23d. His reception there was merely polite, in contrast to events in York.[7] Steuben was an immediate success in the camp, and his military competence was apparent in his first encounters with Washington and his generals. Steuben's questionable credentials seemed unimportant after he had demonstrated his proficiency. In short, Steuben's combination of skill with agreeability made credible the office of the Inspector General so recently abused in the Conway controversy. Steuben soon won over the skeptical Washington and his officers. He became the obvious candidate for Inspector General, although after the Conway episode Washington and Nathanael Greene agreed that it would not be wise to make Steuben a major general, he still had to prove himself.[8]

Steuben's Challenge

It would require a combination of competence and good humor to grapple with the problems facing the Continental Army, which was at a low ebb in February 1778. "The situation of the camp is such that in all human probability the army must soon dissolve," Brig. Gen. James Mitchell Varnum predicted to

---

6. Sanger, "Inspector-General's Department," 229–30.

7. Palmer, *General Steuben*, 129–30; Flexner, *Washington in the Revolution*, 286–87. Palmer effectively demolishes the legend that Steuben was received grandly at Valley Forge, while Flexner believes the older tradition. Steuben was honored with a number of receptions in towns between York and Valley Forge. Kapp, *Life of Steuben*, 104–05.

8. Theodore Thayer, *Nathanael Greene: Strategist of the American Revolution* (New York: Twayne, 1960), 225.

Greene before Steuben's arrival. There was no meat, the horses were dying, and the bare country surrounding was a poor location for a camp. Varnum averred that either the army must be moved to where it could be supplied, or disband.[9] Steuben, beginning work as an adviser to Washington, proclaimed the money department "a mere farce," and said that paying quartermaster agents a commission according to what they spent was a prescription for waste. He proposed a staff overhaul to reform army supply, but nothing came of his suggestion.[10] There were many problems of discipline, supply, and training which he observed on his arrival at Valley Forge. He soon became involved in some aspect of their resolution regardless of who had the theoretical responsibility.[11]

Things were even worse than they looked. To begin with, there was no uniform organization of the army. "I have seen a regiment consisting of *thirty men*, and a company of *one corporal!*" said Steuben. "Nothing was so difficult, and often so impossible as to get a correct list of the state or return of any company, regiment, or corps." As serious was the loss of firearms, carried away not only by deserters but by men whose terms of service had expired. Henry Knox told Steuben that the magazines supplied 5,000 to 8,000 muskets in every campaign, just to replace those that had been carted home. Nor were the troops well managed. Many of the troops were scattered on various fatigue details while several thousand more were being used as officers' servants.[12] This manpower had to be restored to the tactical units to gain the full benefit of training. The situation was such that Steuben took it upon himself to prescribe an overhaul of army discipline, and to define the role of the Inspector General. He perceived more clearly than Washington that European methods of discipline could not simply be imposed upon the American army, because of differences in fundamental organization and an absence of national regulations and authorities. Steuben dismissed, for instance, the individual manual of arms as a waste of ammunition (he emphasized platoon firing), and observed, "In our European armies a man who has been drilled for three months is called a recruit; here, in two months I must have a soldier." Steuben proposed to simplify the drill manuals, and developed a new system that leavened British rigidity with French and Prussian practicality. Regarding the Inspector General, he maintained that, unlike in Europe, that officer must depart from purely military inspection and must also examine financial accounts. At least, someone must do so for the American army.[13]

---

9. Varnum to Greene, 12 Feb 78, in Commager and Morris, *Spirit of Seventy-Six*, 1: 650–51.

10. Kapp, *Life of Steuben*, 114–15, 123.

11. John McAuley Palmer, *Washington, Lincoln, Wilson: Three War Statesmen* (Garden City, N.Y., Doubleday, Doran, 1930), 47.

12. Kapp, *Life of Steuben*, 115–17.

13. Ibid., 123; Robert K. Wright, Jr., *The Continental Army* (Washington: Department of the Army, 1982), 140–42. National authorities in Europe had other means of ensuring financial accountability, leaving inspectors to observe purely military questions of efficiency and performance. No strong central authority existed in the United States or even, as regarded staff services, in the Army. Steuben wanted the Inspector General's purview in the Continental Army to be comprehensive.

It became steadily more apparent that Steuben would be placed in charge of the Army's reformation. He focused on first things first: "I found it useless to trouble myself about the many things which I could not remedy. I directed my attention to the organization and discipline of the army . . . . I found here neither rules, nor regulations, nor system, nor minister at war, nor pardon, nor reward . . . . All this required an immediate remedy. But how to commence, was the question."[14] The most pressing issue was training in the basics of soldiering. Thus, Steuben for the moment confined the role of the Inspector General to that of a drillmaster-general. That was a wise decision, for at the time the Continental Army knew neither how to drill nor how to march, limiting its performance on campaign and in battle. Henry Knox had recently established in New Jersey a gunnery school. That could eventually pay dividends for the artillery, but it did nothing for the infantry, which must rely on antiquated British manuals dating from as early as 1727.[15]

Steuben Trains the Troops

By the middle of March, Washington had determined to let Steuben show what he could do, reserving the Inspector General's position as a reward for success. Washington let him determine his approach for himself, and then followed his advice. Steuben decided to start small. On 17 March 1778, Washington ordered an additional 100 men to be attached to the Commander in Chief's guard; since the latter were all from Virginia, the others were to come from all other states. The men selected were to be of "robust constitution," and "well limbed, formed for activity, and men of established character for sobriety and fidelity. They must be Americans born."[16] What those men were to experience was new in the Continental Army, and their reactions were naturally varied. The guard participated in the Continental Army's grand entertainment for the spring of 1778—Steuben training the troops—which from the first day attracted sizable crowds. Training of the Commander in Chief's guard commenced on 19 March, with Steuben in charge. Steuben himself trained one squad first, then set his subinspectors, whom Washington had been appointing for several days, to drill other squads, while he supervised. Once the squads were trained, Steuben drilled them as a company, starting each day with squad drills, and ending with company exercises.[17]

From the outset Steuben devised an American body of tactics. He taught a greatly simplified manual of arms, because there was no time to follow elaborate European practices. He also disapproved of the British-inspired distance between the soldiers and American officers, who had been wont to leave

---

14. As quoted in Kapp, *Life of Steuben*, 123.

15. Forman, "Why the United States Military Academy Was Established," 19; Riling, *Steuben and Regulations*, 1; Wright, *Continental Army*, 140–42.

16. Orders, GHQ, Valley Forge, 17 Mar 78, in Ganoe, *History of the United States Army*, 55–56.

17. Palmer, *General Steuben*, 144–45.

instruction to sergeants. Steuben not only offered a good example, but specifically instructed officers in how to train their own men. After the model guard
company was ready, he extended his system to battalions, then brigades, and in
three weeks was able to maneuver an entire division for Washington. His
inspectors were his agents.[18] The results of the training were impressive and it
did not take long to persuade Washington that Steuben knew what he was
doing. Three days after the new drilling began, on 22 March, Washington
issued orders to the Army paving the way for Steuben's advent as Inspector
General by directing unit commanders to stop all drills under systems then in
use and to begin preparations to use Steuben's methods. A few days later, he
directed them to begin practicing under Steuben's supervision.[19] At that time,
Washington also appointed four lieutenant colonels to act as subinspectors,
while the next day he appointed brigade inspectors for all brigades.[20] On 28
March he appointed Steuben Inspector-General.

Washington told Congress on 30 April that, given his longstanding desire to
institute an inspectorship, he had "set on foot a temporary institution, which
from the success that has hitherto attended it, gives me the most flattering
expectations, and will I hope obtain [Congress'] approbation." The "Baron de
Steuben," he said, had at Washington's request agreed "with the greatest
chearfulness [sic]" to "take the office of Inspector General." He recounted
Steuben's training of the demonstration company, and reported the appointment of the pyramid of subinspectors and brigade inspectors following Steuben's
instructions. He asked for approval of the organization, and extra pay for all
inspecting officers. Lastly, Washington implied that Steuben had persuaded
him to adopt a somewhat broader conception of the role of inspector general
than that of a mere "drillmaster-general" making the office more comprehensive.[21] When it came to appointing foreign officers to high places, the late
request was characteristic of Washington's caution; he waited until the end of
April to ask Congress for a permanent berth for Steuben. But the Prussian had
long since proved himself, so ably in fact that Washington could consider a
major generalcy for him without expectation of the kind of outrage among
American generals that had accompanied Tronson du Coudray's similar promotion in the line or Conway's as a staff officer. Steuben had accomplished much
during the month of April, extending his operations on a large scale, with
increasingly complex maneuvers.[22]

---

18. Palmer, *Washington, Lincoln, Wilson*, 48.
19. Orders, GHQ, Valley Forge, 22 Mar 78, in Thian, *Legislative History*, 89; ibid., 24 Mar
78, in Palmer, *General Steuben*, 150.
20. Orders, GHQ, Valley Forge, 28, 29 Mar 78, in Thian, *Legislative History*, 89. From the
outset, the variously designated assistant inspectors general and brigade inspectors met with Steuben's
approval: "Among the many obligations which I owe to General Washington, I shall always
esteem it among the greatest, the selection which he made among the officers to aid me in this
work." Kapp, *Life of Steuben*, 125.
21. Washington to Pres of Cong, 30 Apr 78, in Fitzpatrick, *Writings of Washington*, 11:
328–31.
22. Kapp, *Life of Steuben*, 128.

It was not, of course, quite so simple. Steuben's lack of English caused him difficulty from the beginning. He developed his American drill regulations from his European background and his observation of American circumstances, then wrote the instructions in French. Pierre Duponceau, his secretary, translated them into literary English, but he was no military man. Washington's aides John Laurens and Alexander Hamilton then edited the instructions into military parlance, and Steuben memorized the text as well as his broken English allowed. He had a gift for languages, but he could not pick up a new one instantly.[23] Steuben's language difficulty was resolved quickly. According to Col. Alexander Scammell, "At the first parade, the troops neither understanding the command, nor how to follow in a movement, to which they had not been accustomed even with their instructor at their head, were getting fast into confusion." At this moment Capt. Benjamin Walker, then of the 2d New York Regiment, advanced from his platoon, and offered his assistance to translate the order to the troops. Captain Walker very soon became Steuben's aide in charge of correspondence and other documents.[24]

The training extended from the Commander in Chief's guard to the entire army, and the work came under the immediate direction of the lower inspectors and troop commanders. As the regiments were training, Steuben galloped about the camp, supervising. Steuben shocked American officers by personally teaching men the manual of arms and drill, but his success helped to convince them. Previously, as he recalled, " [T]he captains and colonels did not consider their companies and regiments as corps confided to them by the United States for the care of the men as well as the preservation of order and discipline. The idea they had of their duty was that officers had only to mount guard and put themselves at the head of their regiment or company when they were going into action." With Washington's support, Steuben set out to involve officers in training, making the subordinate inspectors—a body of officers drilled by Steuben—his agents.

The First Regulation

Supervising drill was but an immediate part of the Inspector General's duties. Much more important was the formulation of a body of regulations upon which drill and other military necessities were to be based. The contents of Steuben's regulations were an improvisation, melding foreign and domestic principles and Steuben's creativity into a system fit for American conditions. No less an improvisation was the way the regulations were first distributed. A unique solution was reached to assure rapid production: There were no printing presses at Valley Forge, while circumstances demanded the fastest possible dissemination of the regulations. The team of Steuben, Duponceau, Laurens,

---

23. Palmer, *General Steuben*, 140.
24. Scammell to Gen John Sullivan, 8 Apr 78, quoted in Riling, *Steuben and Regulations*, 8; Joseph B. Doyle, *Frederick William von Steuben and the American Revolution* (Steubenville, Ohio: H.C. Cook, 1913), 360. See Appendix B.

and Hamilton—joined in time by Lafayette, Greene, Walker, and others of Steuben's and Washington's entourages—prepared the instructions a chapter at a time. To distribute the drill regulations, brigade inspectors wrote out copies for themselves, then entered copies in the orderly books of the brigades and each regiment. From regimental orderly books copies were made for each company, from which each officer and drillmaster made his own copy. It required two to three days for each chapter to be distributed. Meanwhile, Steuben taught, supervised, and wrote. The first rudimentary regulations as transcribed were a combination of exact instructions for various maneuvers and timely advice for inspectors and other officers. Surviving examples demonstrate that Steuben's penchant for detail was all-encompassing, while his literary committee produced texts of great exactitude and clarity. Captain Nathaniel Webb's orderly book, for example, recorded the basic drill, and included such elementary things as when to start drill, how to stand, and how to form in ranks, as well as more complex maneuvers.[25]

One of the fortunate aspects of Steuben's regimen in April 1778 was a thorough overhaul of the Continental Army's organization. His first objective was training, but few regiments were ever full enough to serve as training units. The fluctuating personnel situation of the force also made continuous training advisable. Steuben divided the brigades into provisional training battalions of 112 to 224 privates, subdivided into companies and platoons, with officers and noncommissioned officers assigned appropriately. The regiments no longer matched the battalions, but when Steuben was finished with them, the latter had become uniformly known quantities able to maneuver in battle with calculable results. Thereafter, Steuben's organization made it possible to muster effective battalions for battle no matter how depleted the Army was.[26]

Steuben also perceived that the American units had difficulty in going from column of march into line of battle. The source of the problem was the customary marching formation of a column of files ("Indian file"), stringing the force out impossibly. That was one reason why many units had arrived late at the recent battles of Brandywine and Germantown. Steuben moved quickly to correct that bad habit, training battalions to occupy no more road space than they would require room in battle. At his instigation, on 10 April Washington outlawed the column of files. Thereafter, in all situations all sizes of units were to march exactly as they were taught on the drill field. The result was an army that marched faster and deployed faster for battle.[27] Steuben also wanted the Army to fight as well as to march, and that required weapons instruction. He prepared and taught a simplified manual of arms, with many fewer movements than those of European armies, and emphasized the use of the bayonet, the essential infantry assault weapon of the day. Previously lacking the discipline essential to bayonet charges, American soldiers had shied away from the

25. Palmer, *General Steuben*, 180–81.
26. Ibid., 152–54; Weigley, *History of the United States Army*, 64.
27. Palmer, *General Steuben*, 156–57; Weigley, *History of the United States Army*, 64.

weapons. Steuben himself observed that their chief utility in the Continental Army was as spits for roasting meat. He turned the Americans into confident bayonet fighters, something they demonstrated within a few weeks at Monmouth and the next year at Stony Point.[28]

Steuben's 1778 regulations represented a thorough reform of army administration as well as tactics, and were the first truly comprehensive set of rules the American army had. Informally distributed as they were, they taught the soldiers how to stand at attention, march, and behave in unison; and units how to form, and disengage from, larger units. More broadly, they set forth rules for camp sanitation, company administration, and daily routine. In property management alone, Steuben's regulations paid their way. To stop the massive losses of arms to deserters and to men mustered out, Steuben required that weapons remain with unit colors. Before he arrived the Army lost thousands of muskets every year; in 1779, it lost twenty.[29] Rules were also applied to military inspection, which was made a subject of the regulations. But it was not presented as an activity of designated inspectors, rather as a function of command. The regulations made inspection a routine duty of company commanders. At "troop beating," company officers were to "inspect into the dress of their men," to "see that the clothes are whole and put on properly, their hair combed, their acouterments properly fixed and every article about them in the greatest order." Steuben founded the army's long tradition of the Saturday morning inspection, when captains were to "examine into the state of the men's necessaries."[30]

Proving the Worth of Training

It was in refining the technical skills of the Continental Army that Steuben made his major contribution to the American cause in the spring of 1778. That had its own secondary, but very important, effect in raising morale. The intense training had been the great amusement of the Valley Forge encampment, beginning with Steuben's entertaining mannerisms. But as his labors, and those of his assistants and the troop commanders, began to produce results, when the Army mastered what had previously been difficult, the force felt a confidence it had never before known. The training routine also offered opportunities for healthy rivalries and prideful displays. By the end of April, the Continental Army was eager to demonstrate its achievements.[31]

The first positive result of Steuben's efforts appeared on 19 May, when Lafayette with 2,200 continentals and 800 militia were almost cut off by British forces at Barren Hill, across the Schuylkill River. To get out of the trap required a quick retreat, something the old straggling columns could never have

---

28. Palmer, *General Steuben*, 151–52.
29. Ganoe, *History of the United States Army*, 56–58, 61.
30. Ibid., 58.
31. Flexner, *Washington in the Revolution*, 289.

done. The British moved in for a predictable kill. But Lafayette merely gave an order, and the troops moved as Steuben had taught them, denying the British easy victory.[32] This small incident did not demonstrate that the Continental Army was a match for the British, merely that it could move as an army should. Steuben had worked wonders, but Washington still had on his hands a force that must avoid open challenges to an enemy superior in efficiency. Nor could Steuben, Washington, or anyone else change the hard fact that the best units had the best officers, while the others were content with lower standards of performance.[33] The officers with the drive and sense of professionalism necessary to recognize the value of Steuben's instructions, were the ones who applied them most effectively to their units.

Inspector General Steuben

In any event, Steuben had long since proved his value to the cause, and was firmly emplaced as the Inspector General. Washington had followed his letter to Congress of 30 April with a plan for the inspectorship; in it he showed his wish that it develop a system of manual and maneuvers, prepare all necessary regulations, and see that they were observed. Inspectors were to be "the instructors and censors of the Army in everything connected with its discipline and management," he said, in a reflection of Steuben's broader conception. The Inspector General, Washington proposed, was to serve under the Commander in Chief. His chief deputies were to inspect wings or divisions under the orders of major generals, while brigade inspectors would serve brigade commanders.[34]

Washington desired inspection to be a function of command, inspectors to be subordinate to commanders, and he wanted no revival of the Conway version of the inspector as political overseer. Nevertheless he maintained a strong functional relationship within the inspectorate. Inspectors might inspect at the orders of commanders, but they were to do so exactly as the senior inspector ordained. His orders of 4 May 1778 explicitly directed subordinate inspectors to look to Steuben for all technical direction to assure standardization in all procedures in the Army.[35] With these orders, Washington at least ended the menace of interference in his command associated with the earlier version of the Inspector General's duties. On 5 May 1778, Congress approved his plan for "a well-organized inspectorship" in general terms, without the pointed details that had made Conway such a menace. The resolution otherwise appointed Steuben to be Inspector General, with rank and pay of a major general, including back pay for his services since February; established two ranks of inspectors under the Inspector General, one for two or more brigades, the other for brigades; authorized additional pay for inspectors because of the demands of their duties;

32. Palmer, *General Steuben*, 169–70.
33. Weigley, *History of the United States Army*, 64.
34. Sanger, "Inspector-General's Department," 231.
35. Orders, GHQ, Valley Forge, 4 May 78, in Kapp, *Life of Steuben*, 134.

and authorized Washington to appoint all inspectors below the Inspector General.[36]

Washington announced Steuben's appointment at a reception following a grand review for the French, and later in orders to the Army on 9 May. Steuben had hitherto served as a gentleman volunteer. The immediate necessity for his unfettered services—not to mention his likable nature—had permitted him to get along well with Washington's generals. But, appointing him a major general, albeit in a carefully stated staff position, raised some of the resentments that had characterized the appointments of Tronson du Coudray and Conway. Additional unhappiness had been building since early April over the interruption of command associated with Steuben's training methods. Although Washington had managed to soothe feelings while supporting his Inspector General, he realized that sooner or later the commanders, not the inspectors, would have to command their own troops.[37] Despite these unsolved matters, Steuben himself was not finished. And despite his own broader conception of the position, the Inspector General had so far been little more than a "drillmaster-general." That had been so because it had been necessary, but a permanent training system was now in place that did not require Steuben's full-time involvement. The regulations existed only in the orderly books. Furthermore, a real system of inspections, except as a function of unit command, had not yet been developed. Nor had the Inspector General's "department"—in the sense of a sphere of activity, as the word usually meant at the time—been defined. The issue remained of great interest because Washington at last had an inspector general acceptable— and subordinate—to himself. He now perceived that that officer must be more than a chief drillmaster, but exactly how much more remained to be determined. Steuben had accomplished much as a volunteer. But now that he was officially on the payroll, his efforts to determine his place in the Army were bound to bruise some egos, including his own.

---

36. *JCC*, 5 May 78. See also Thian, *Legislative History*, 89–90, and Sanger, "Inspector-General's Department," 231.

37. Orders, GHQ, Valley Forge, 9 May 78, in Thian, *Legislative History*, 90; Palmer, *General Steuben*, 167–69.

CHAPTER 3

Defining the Inspector's Role
(1778–1779)

Steuben's promotion may have encouraged the Prussian to think about a possible command in the line. Without a doubt, his transformation from volunteer to major general caused some American officers to fear that he harbored such ambitions. An explanation of relationships was definitely in order. The role of the Inspector General and the extent of his authority was unclear to the officers of the line. It was further evident that the functions of Steuben's position had not been developed thoroughly by the Congress either. The way in which solutions would be reached would determine the continued usefulness of the Inspector General to the Army.

Limiting the Inspector's Authority

Determining the exact status of the new Inspector General and his relationship to commanders and other inspectors required further work. Congress continued to appoint senior officers as inspectors of forces other than Washington's, without reference to Steuben although the recent law implied that Steuben should have technical supervision over them.[1] Washington, also, continued to define the roles of his inspectors. On 4 June, he assigned the four subinspectors to various line divisions for field operations, saying that since they had no specific commands, they would act as adjutants general while on the march. That established a principle, eventually to become permanent in the Continental Army, that inspectors were to handle paper work and act as adjutants along with their inspection duties.[2] But it further reduced Steuben's control over junior inspectors, who were in fact considerably less subordinate to him than they had been in April.

Steuben was at the same time advancing his own designs for his position. By early June 1778, he had proposed a plan of legal authority for the Inspector

---

1. *JCC*, 14 May, 14 Oct, 4 Dec 78; Thian, *Legislative History*, 90, 90n. The resolution of authority is discussed briefly below.

2. Orders, GHQ, Valley Forge, in Thian, *Legislative History*, 90; Wright, "Organization and Doctrine," 233–35; Wright, *Continental Army*, 144–45. On 16 May 1778, Congress directed the Quartermaster General to furnish Steuben "with two good horses for his use." *JCC*, 26 May 78.

General that would in effect have made the position equal to that of the Commander in Chief, answering separately to Congress. That was too much for some officers, who already believed the Inspector General had too wide a reach. Hamilton said that the novelty of the office excited questions about its boundaries, the extent of its operations alarmed the officers of every rank for their rights, and that their jealousies and discontents were rising to a height that threatened to overturn the whole plan.[3] These senior officers' concerns caused Washington to publish a general order on 15 June 1778 to regulate Steuben's operations, curbing the independence that had accelerated training but interrupted command.[4] The new regulations were to stand until "the duties of the office of Inspector-General shall be defined and fixed by Congress."[5] They began with a synopsis of the Inspector General's functions. Inspectors were to prescribe rules and standards for drill and maneuvers, and set policies for garrison and camp routine. They also monitored all guards and camp security and determined all necessary rules and procedures.

That was a sweeping purview, but the powers of the Inspector General were tightly confined. The order further specified that the commander approve and authorize any rules generated by an inspector. All orders were to be communicated through the Adjutant General to subordinate inspectors, who were to relay them to division and brigade commanders. In addition, divisional and brigade inspectors were to "assist in their execution" (of maneuvers and exercises) "under the immediate orders of the major-generals, brigadiers, and colonels commanding."[6] This order of 15 June established a principle that would govern in the United States Army over the next two centuries. It was, in short, that inspection is a function of command, and that the inspector is an agent of the commander. Although the subordination of the Inspector General to the army commander would be challenged many times, it was not until the late nineteenth century that the fundamental principle was seriously threatened with compromise. Even then an attempt to grant independence to the Inspector General, as an agent of the civil power, failed to overcome the strength of the deeply rooted tradition.

Steuben Tries To Assert Himself

Steuben challenged the check on his authority, first by seeking a line command, then by attempting to free the Inspector General from the army commander. He made his move after his contributions during the spring of 1778 had proved their value in the Monmouth Campaign and while he briefly commanded three brigades after the Battle of Monmouth. But the resentment against having any foreigner high in the line persisted, and frustrated him.

---

3. Palmer, *General Steuben*, 172–74; Hamilton as quoted in Sanger, "Inspector-General's Department," 232.
4. Palmer, *General Steuben*, 172–74.
5. Orders, GHQ, Valley Forge, 15 Jun 78, in Thian, *Legislative History*, 90–91.
6. Ibid.

When he court-martialed an officer for disrespectful conduct, the man was acquitted. Washington ordered Steuben to relinquish his command as soon as the normally assigned commander returned from temporary duty. But the Prussian protested, asking to be given a permanent position in the line.[7] He was not pleased with the restrictions inherent in the 15 June order and he asked Washington for permission to go to Philadelphia on personal business, hoping to lobby with Congress to improve his situation.[8] Washington agreed but asked Steuben to take with him a copy of his 15 June order along with a letter to Laurens. Steuben's original objective changed when, upon his arrival in Philadelphia, several powerful friends informed him that they agreed with Washington on denying a line command for him. But they supported the Prussian's desire to be chief of all inspectors, which Congress soon granted. Mollified, Steuben meanwhile set about lobbying for a charter for his inspector general's department. He suggested that his office should answer to the Board of War, reporting to both the board and to the Commander in Chief, with differences between the Inspector General and the commander to be resolved by the board.

In August a committee of Congress proposed a plan for the Inspector General's activity much as Steuben had outlined, and asked Washington to comment. While the Commander in Chief praised the adoption of many fundamental principles of inspection, he condemned the direct communication between the inspectorate and the Board of War on the grounds that inspectors would thereby be independent of commanders. When the committee finally produced a plan for the Inspector General (in February 1779), it was a compromise, but one acceptable to Washington and Steuben both.[9] This compromise meant that by the end of the summer of 1778, Steuben and Washington were agreed. The Inspector General had come to see that his office should not have powers of command. Thus began his most useful period. Over the following years, Steuben would become much more than a drillmaster-general. He would be a staff officer in the fullest sense, Washington's most important source of support. Because of his training in the Prussian Army, he was able to offer the best staff advice available in the world. Given his experience, ability, and views on an administrative hierarchy, no British or French officer could have equaled him.[10]

So Steuben resumed the training program. More fundamentally, he laid the groundwork for the full scope of the Inspector General's activity, beginning with the institution of a system of inspection. Without awaiting the action from Congress, Steuben established an inspection service for the whole army, in service to the Commander in Chief. He and his subordinate inspectors visited

7. Palmer, *General Steuben*, 91–92; Washington to Pres of Cong, 26 Jul 78, in Fitzpatrick, *Writings of Washington*, 12: 235; Thian, *Legislative History, 90.*

8. *Palmer, General Steuben*, 174–76, 192–93.

9. Steuben's Philadelphia adventure is discussed in Palmer, *General Steuben*, 195–96; see also Sanger, "Inspector-General's Department," 232–33, and *JCC*, 20 Aug 78. For Washington's commentary on Steuben's design, see Washington to Pres of Cong, 12 Sep 78, and "Observations on Congress's Plan for the Inspector General's Department," both in Fitzpatrick, *Writings of Washington*, 12: 436–44.

10. Palmer, *General Steuben*, 195–99; Palmer, *Washington, Lincoln, Wilson*, 44.

all organizations, reporting all defects in discipline, administration, supplies, and equipment. His criticism was constructive, and because he was not a threat to the line, it was accepted well enough. His results he transcribed for Washington, while his prestige gave him authority without the necessity of powers of command.[11] It was in instituting his inspection service that Steuben laid the foundation for the fundamental function of the future inspectors general of the United States Army. He went at it in customary fashion, participating personally, applying great energy with patient exactitude. His aide William North described Steuben the inspector as being fair and extremely thorough. He set high standards and insisted on their being met to the point that doing so became instinctive throughout the force. North knew of officers spending their own pay to keep their men looking as they should so as not to embarass their units' reputations.[12]

Steuben's Blue Book

The Army settled into winter quarters late in 1778, with training and the inspection service running under their own power. Steuben turned his attention to the publication of drill regulations in final form. The preparation of regulations for the manual of arms and maneuver had been among the Inspector General's first duties, one which preceded even training. But late in 1778 the regulations comprised only the scattered entries in orderly books produced during the Valley Forge training period in the spring. If uniformity of movement was to become permanent in the Army, its guiding rules had to appear in more durable and accessible form. It was decided therefore to codify them in a publication. To do this, Steuben and his literary committee, in particular Duponceau and Walker, began work late in 1778 in Philadelphia, where they took up residence for the duration of the job. The first half of the text went to Washington on 26 February 1779, the remainder on 11 March. Washington approved this immediately, followed on 29 March by Congress, which authorized printing and distribution. Those concerned were so delighted with Steuben's product that on 5 April Congress passed a resolution honoring him for the improvements his efforts promised.[13] Steuben next turned to the task of getting his regulations printed and distributed. To supplement his text, he appended explicit drawings of the manual of arms and basic troop movements, prepared by Pierre Charles L'Enfant, a military engineer and architect, who later gained fame as the city planner of Washington, D.C.[14]

Steuben and his staff met with a great deal of frustration in printing and binding the *Regulations for the Order and Discipline of the Troops of the United States*, which they had hoped to have available by spring. The printing industry suffered from shortages of paper, ink, and other materials, but bind-

11. Palmer, *General Steuben*, 198–99.
12. Thian, *Legislative History*, 89n.
13. Palmer, *General Steuben*, 202–04; Thian, *Legislative History*, 93–94; *JCC*, 5 Apr 79.
14. Riling, *Steuben and Regulations*, 9.

ing proved to be the major obstacle as production dragged through the summer
and into the fall of 1779. High-quality materials were scarce, and at last the
binders adopted substitutes in order to get the job done. Among the substitu-
tions was blue paper for half-covers, instead of full leather. That accident gave
Steuben's regulations the name they would bear thereafter—Steuben's "blue
book." Recalled William North in 1814, "except the Bible, it was held in the
highest estimation."[15] In final form, the blue book presented complete infantry
drill regulations, and more. It also offered regulations for field service, the
basics of organization, essential commands and movements, marching, camp
layout, and sanitation—all stated simply and directly. It was all the manual the
Continental Army needed, with instructions for everyone from colonel to private,
in concise but explicit form. It was also an immediate and enduring success,
with at least seventy-five editions published through 1809, as well as uncounted
militia manuals largely based upon it.[16]

The *Regulations for the Order and Discipline of the Troops of the United
States* were a literary refinement of the first drafts reproduced in so many
orderly books during 1778. They were ideally formed for an army in which
training of recruits was a constant burden. The heart of Steuben's regulations
was his simplified and carefully described and illustrated *Manual Exercise*,
what is today called the manual of arms. It was eminently workable, and like
the rest of the text, well suited to the American army.[17] But the blue book also
guided the officers. Chapter 20, "Of the Inspection of the Men, their Dress,
Necessaries, Arms, Accoutrements and Ammunition," established a tradition
of inspection and observance on the part of company officers that endured
through the following centuries. The blue book placed great emphasis on inspection as a function of command. Officers were to examine arms and ammunition
every day, while noncommissioned officers were to supervise the personal
hygiene of the men. Captains were required to make general inspections of their
companies every Saturday morning. As a reflection of Steuben's philosophy,
inspection was indeed integral to command because it was the best means
whereby an officer could learn about his men and the state of their equipment.[18]
It was the chief tool of the commander.

However, the blue book was almost silent about the formal inspectorate
represented by the Inspector General. It offered nothing about authorities or
questions of line and staff. Rather, the regulations told how an inspection
should be conducted, with the inspector passing along the front of a battalion
from right to left, accompanied by the commander and his staff, proceeding
down to the inspection of companies. That completed, the colonel was to form

15. North, as quoted in Riling, *Steuben and Regulations*, 15–18.
16. Riling, *Steuben and Regulations*, 19–21, 27–31; Palmer, *General Steuben*, 202–04;
Regulations for the Order and Discipline of the Troops of the United States (Philadelphia: Styner &
Cist, 1779). The bulk of Riling is a facsimile reproduction of this first Styner & Cist printing.
17. *Regulations for Order and Discipline*. 16–30.
18. Ibid., 88–90. Some of the language appeared almost unchanged in the Army's first comprehensive set of general regulations after the Revolution, produced by Winfield Scott in 1821.

his battalion and cause it to perform any exercise or maneuvers the inspector thought proper to order. That may have been a practical working manual for inspectors, but it gave them no advice when a commander challenged their presence or requests.[19]

A Charter for the Inspector General

While Steuben was working to produce the blue book, Congress at last produced a charter for the Inspector General, on 18 February 1779. It passed a resolution which authorized the position with rank of major general and specified that forming a system of regulations for maneuvers and discipline was the inspectors' principal task. The Inspector General and subordinate inspectors were also to inspect troops for efficiency and appearance when directed to do so by their commanders. General Washington was authorized to appoint as many subinspectors as he desired. Each brigade major was to double as brigade inspector for his own brigade, thus perpetuating the combination of adjutant and inspector begun at various levels the year before. The resolution put an end to more than a year of dispute over the role and authority of the Inspector General and his assistants. The Inspector General reported to the Commander in Chief, who gave him his orders. His reports were directed to the commander, with a copy to the Board of War. The commander was firmly in control of all officers of his command, appointment of the Inspector General being no more subject to the Congress than the nominal veto power that governed all general officers. The inspector, simply put, was clearly the unfettered agent of the commander.[20]

The Inspector General's charter of February 1779 was a very workable compromise of competing interests and ambitions. It removed the occasion for civil interference in command that had been inherent in earlier definitions of the Inspector General. Within the Army, it neatly resolved the tensions between line and staff that would have been aggravated if the Inspector General had headed a separate organization comparable to that of the Quartermaster General. At each step of the command pyramid, commanders had inspectors serving as their eyes and ears, monitoring those under them, and each command level was subject to similar inspection from the level above. That was acceptable because the inspector from above was seen as the agent of the superior commander, not a power to himself, and because inspection standards, set by the Inspector General, were uniform throughout the Army.

Meanwhile, Steuben completed his part in the blue book production and rejoined the Continental Army at Middlebrook, New Jersey, on 27 April 1779. Shortly thereafter, he made, at Washington's behest, a special inspection of the whole Army, looking particularly for understrength regiments. That led to a consolidation in order to keep at full strength the training and maneuver battal-

---

19. Ibid., 126–27.
20. *JCC*, 18 Feb 79. See also Thian, *Legislative History*, 92–93.

ions that Steuben had developed the year before. It seemed that the Inspector General was beginning to demonstrate his usefulness for all sorts of special assignments. For instance, he also formed a special light infantry force (later commanded by Anthony Wayne). This unit was trained for special assault and skirmishing duties derived from Steuben's knowledge of equivalent French and German forces such as Chasseurs and Jaegers. Steuben added Capt. William North to his staff in May, completing an exceedingly close trio that included also Ben Walker.[21] North would continue the inspectorate after the breakup of the Continental Army in 1783. This completion of his staff meant that Steu-

MAJ. WILLIAM NORTH. *Inspector of Troops, 15 April 1784–25 June 1788.*

ben's inspection service came into full flower during 1779, allowing detailed inspections of everything and everyone in the army. Through the mechanism of inspection, Steuben and his assistants were able to enforce accountability for supplies, using the individual soldiers' books and company books, which he and his aides compared against each other. Special attention went to the care of the sick. In short order, the monthly general inspection was an essential part of the army routine.[22] Steuben's inspection system promoted economy sufficiently that in June and July Congress awarded inspectors extra pay and allowances. And, as a mark of Steuben's rising influence, the Congress was to expand Steuben's sphere further.

---

21. Palmer, *General Steuben*, 207–10. See Appendix B
22. Palmer, *General Steuben*, 210–11.

CHAPTER 4

Inspection and the American Victory

(1780–1784)

The Continental Army endured a ghastly winter at Morristown, New Jersey, in 1779 and 1780, its officers and men experiencing great hardships because of problems in the staff departments and in the response of Congress to them. The need for action led to changes in the Army structure to meet the crisis. Critical breakdowns in supply, transport, and administration revealed the lack of depth and experience in the staff departments. It was only natural that a growing number of these duties would fall on one of the few officers available with the knowledge and background to attend to them properly. The recognition that these functions had to be performed to avert greater crisis muted any protests as to the expansion of the Inspector General's sphere.

The Inspector's Authority Widens

By early 1780, Steuben had made the Inspector General the chief administrator and virtual chief of staff of the Army; his counterparts at the lower levels were the lesser inspectors. As de facto chief of staff, he became the Commander in Chief's principal agent for bargaining with Congress, often representing Washington at meetings in Philadelphia. Thus, while the fortunes of the Continental Army waned, those of the Inspector General continued to rise. Since Steuben's appearance at Valley Forge, the Inspector General had served largely as a "muster master-general," mustering, organizing, and training troops. The inspectorate had since received a number of administrative redirections, but the mustering of troops—to a great extent, verifying the presence of men for pay, rations, and other disbursements—was integral to their inspection. The Continental Army's Mustering Department, therefore, had become superfluous. So, on 12 January 1780, Congress resolved that the mustering of the troops be performed by the inspectors of the Army.[1] This absorption of the Mustering Department was but a part of Steuben's expansion of his sphere of interest. He had been gaining strength at the expense of other depart-

---

1. *JCC*, 12 Jan 80. See also Thian, *Legislative History*, 95.

ments for several months, and in particular had preempted the pursuits of the Adjutant General in January 1778, who had succumbed to Steuben's charm when the latter arrived at Valley Forge. The two worked together to standardize army paper work, inevitably mixing the interests of their two departments. In May 1779 Congress reduced the members of the Adjutant General's Department to the Adjutant General, two assistants, and a clerk, and in June it directed the Adjutant General to serve as assistant inspector general. Six months after absorbing the Mustering Department, Steuben moved to gather in the last of the Adjutant General's province. On 7 May 1780 the Inspector General proposed a plan for the new Inspecting and Mustering Department, which subordinated the Adjutant General to the Inspector General. Washington endorsed the proposal, and on 14 July recommended it to Congress as essential.[2]

Congress adopted Steuben's "Plan of the Inspecting and Mustering Department" on 25 September 1780, with only minor changes.[3] In the future, the Inspector General would be appointed by Congress, and allowed two secretaries in addition to the aides he was permitted from the line of the Army. Also with the main army, there was to be one assistant inspector general, "who shall be adjutant-general for the time being."[4] Each separate army of two or more divisions would also have an assistant inspector general, who would further serve as deputy adjutant general. The resolution further prescribed one inspector to each division, one to the corps of cavalry, and one to the corps of artillery. Inspectors were to come, when possible, from the line of colonels and lieutenant colonels, and were to be given additional compensation while serving as inspectors. In addition, a subinspector was to be assigned to every brigade, and one each to the corps of cavalry and the corps of artillery, if the commander so desired. Subinspectors were to be taken from the line of majors in their brigades. The Commander in Chief or army commander was also permitted to appoint inspectors and subinspectors for active service militia on the same basis as the appointments that were allowed to the continentals.

Congress vested greater authority in the Inspector General in 1780 than it had in February 1779, making him the source of the Army's regulations and policies. The Inspector General and his assistants were required to review and muster the troops once a month, examining the number and condition of the men, their discipline, clothes, arms, accouterments, and camp equipage; verifying the number of rations drawn; and singling out soldiers or recruits unfit for service, finally reporting all to the commanding officer. No soldier could be discharged or transferred, however, unless the paper work was signed by the major general, brigadier, or commandant, and a surgeon's certificate attached. Commanders were also to prepare three muster rolls at the time of inspection, signing and swearing to them. Each roll was to be certified by the mustering

---

2. Wright, *Continental Army*, 145; Sanger, "Inspector-General's Department," 234–35. An important part of the plan was increased compensation for inspectors, which Washington defended vigorously.

3. The resolution appears in *JCC*, 25 Sep 80.

4. Ibid.

(inspecting) officer, with a copy each to the commander, the mustering officer, and the regimental paymaster. Procedures for accountability to Congress were also clarified in that the monthly muster abstracts were to be forwarded to the Commander in Chief, with a copy to the Board of War.

Congress built a number of financial safeguards into the inspection and mustering system. No commander could muster his own regiment; that had to be done by another inspector assigned by the Inspector General. Assistant inspectors general in separate armies were to heed the instructions of the Inspector General. The commissary of issues was directed to deliver to the Inspector General or the latter's agent an account of rations actually issued. All muster rolls were to be sworn to before a general officer, and the resolution specified the wording of the oath. Inspectors could demand from commanders all papers and vouchers relating to the enlistments and musters of the troops. Inspectors also were to keep accounts with the commanding officers of all arms and accouterments delivered and returned. Officers of the inspectorship retained their rights of command and promotion in the line. But they were to suspend exercise of their commands while serving as inspectors, or were authorized to command by the Commander in Chief. They were also exempt from routine duties so they could devote themselves fully to inspection.

The Inspector General was expected to visit every element of the army to assure uniformity. He was also to keep books registering documents passing through his office and to maintain copies of all resolutions of Congress and regulations of the Board of War. All regulations relating to the Inspecting and Mustering Department were to be approved by Congress. But, if circumstances required, the Inspector General could, with the "approbation" of the Commander in Chief, proclaim temporary regulations, subject to later congressional approval. Finally, the resolution continued Steuben in office, and empowered him to appoint all officers for the inspection service, subject to the approval of the Commander in Chief.[5]

The plan for the Inspecting and Mustering Department was comprehensive. In one act, Steuben supervised a system which had a chance to deal with the almost chaotic circumstances of the Continental Army. The whole purpose was to ensure economy and efficiency by controlling such abuses as the fraudulent issues of rations. The plan also showed congressional disinterest in interfering with Washington's powers of command. The subordination of the Inspector General to the Commander in Chief was complete. For instance, inspection abstracts no longer went equally to the Commander in Chief and the Board of War. Instead, they were transmitted explicitly to the former, with a copy to the latter. On the other hand, Congress retained its final power of approval or rejection, while leaving the initiation of orders and regulations up to the commander. Despite these changes, the plan also ratified a more powerful Inspector General. He answered to the Commander in Chief, but within the Army establishment he enjoyed a great deal of independence and influence—

5. Ibid.

not least because, controlling the Adjutant General, he controlled the Army's communications and paper work. Unlike the earlier definition of his authorities, the new plan allowed the Inspector General to assign inspectors as he thought fit, subject to his technical direction. This relationship was structured in such a way that it safeguarded the integrity of command. In military matters, commanders still ruled their troops and were, nonetheless, subject to a full and independent inquiry on matters of concern to the Commander in Chief.

Steuben had been rebuffed when he tried to establish an independent inspectorate in 1778. But by September 1780, he had achieved a position of influence that would have been inconceivable two years before. His tactics may have been fabian, but more likely he was able to gain his expanded position because his plan seemed to be the best solution to the Army's administrative problems. At the same time, his record and his clear subordination to Washington made him a man who could be trusted not to abuse his wide powers. Steuben had started in the Continental Army as a "drillmaster-general" before becoming a "muster master-general." Then, as his title implied, he was the Commander in Chief's principal inspector. But by September 1780 he had become much more, in fact the second most important man in the Army. The merger of the departments was but a symbol of the fact that everything related to the management of the army, excepting only the initiation of military orders, was within his purview. His abilities had continued to attract new responsibilities until he was now Washington's chief source of information and advice. It was in the nature of things that even military orders would reflect his influence. His plan put him at the head of a large staff organization, so Steuben's effects on operations became more than the product of one man. The Inspecting and Mustering Department established in September 1780 may actually be viewed as the American army's first form of a general staff.

Shortly after the enlarged department was established, Steuben was assigned to an independent command in Virginia. He was expected to provide support to Maj. Gen. Nathanael Greene's forces operating against Lord Cornwallis in the Southern Department. Steuben did not do well in this position. He was unable to inspire the local militia to rally, nor was he able to enlist the sympathy or support of state officials, many of whom he antagonized. Then, in June 1781, while in command of a scratch force of militia and a few continentals, he was defeated by a British force at Point of Fork, Virginia.[6] Thus, in the only independent command of his career, Steuben was a failure on the field of combat. Worse, however, was the larger fiasco of his entire service in Virginia. It was not the Old Dominion alone that could bear responsibility for Steuben's inability to raise men, arms, and supplies. He may have been one of the best staff officers in the world during his day, but Steuben lacked the diplomatic and political skills necessary to succeed in Virginia in 1781. He had alienated nearly everyone who should have supported him.

---

6. Hugh F. Rankin, *The War of the Revolution in Virginia* (Williamsburg: Virginia Independence Bicentennial Commission, 1979), 16–17, 21, 36–39, 41–43, 66, 73–74.

Fortunately, the indecisive operations in central Virginia did not hinder the entrapment of Cornwallis at Yorktown and his subsequent surrender on 19 October. With the exception of a few minor scattered engagements thereafter, the war in real terms was over. It took another two years, however, to complete the negotiations to end the conflict officially. Consequently, the United States had to keep an army in the field. Washington returned the main army to positions in the Hudson Highlands in order to contain the strongest British forces based in New York City. Greene's Army of the South remained mostly in the Carolinas where its elements operated against Tory forces and guarded British enclaves in the coastal cities. The last of these, Charleston, was evacuated in December 1782, and the remnants of Greene's force garrisoned it until disbandment the next August. The primary concern of the army everywhere starting in 1781 was an orderly dissolution.

Reducing the Army and the Inspectorate

Before victory had even seemed possible, on 7 February 1781 Congress established a consolidated War Department under a "Secretary at War" (a British title dating from the reign of Charles II), answerable to Congress.[7] The new department assumed the record-keeping and liaison activities of the Board of War. It was required to investigate the "present state" of the army, and to transmit and execute the military orders of Congress. But civilian fears of the military retarded the selection of a secretary until 30 October. Then, Congress selected a general, Benjamin Lincoln, who had a reasonably good record and had demonstrated ability as an administrator. The division of authority between Washington and Lincoln was not clear, but the two usually worked well together. They conflicted over only one issue: the inspectorate.[8]

Lincoln believed that the greatest deficiencies in the army lay in the Inspector General's Department, whose officers were encumbered by not only line command but also inspections, leaving them little time to forward their returns. As a corrective measure, he asked inspectors to report directly to him. When Washington learned of that, he ordered them to report only to the Commander in Chief. Lincoln's demand, he said, would in effect make the inspectors and those they reported on independent of the army commander.[9] Despite Washington's intervention, staff services in the Continental Army came increasingly under civilian control during the war's last two years. Superintendent of Finance Robert Morris gradually took over the purchasing responsibilities of all supply departments. He turned increasingly to contracting for rations, and abolished the army commissariat. Difficulties with contractors, however, continued, and even as the Army and its programs were reduced, many things remained in

---

7. The title of Secretary at War was changed to Secretary of War in 1789.
8. Weigley, *History of the United States Army*, 48.
9. Ibid.; Harry M. Ward, *The Department of War, 1781–1795* (Pittsburgh: University of Pittsburgh Press, 1962), 16.

short supply, especially clothing. On 7 May 1782, to correct abuses in the supply system, Congress provided for the appointment of inspectors of contracts and supplies for the two armies. They were to report fraud, neglect of duty, or other misconduct threatening public property to the Inspector General. The acting inspectors of the two armies, Col. Ezekial Cornell in the main army and Col. Francis Mentges in the Southern Army, became inspectors of contracts and supplies.[10]

Washington began to reduce the size of the Army after Yorktown, placing Steuben in charge of the program. The Inspector General began with a general effort to re-form units into compact sizes, eliminating officers when their number exceeded that required by the number of men under their command. The reduction of the Army entailed a reduction also in the Inspecting and Mustering Department. On 10 January 1782, Congress repealed its resolution of 25 September 1780 and set forth a revised "Plan for Conducting the Inspector's Department." Somewhat briefer than the earlier charter, the new plan followed much the same spirit. The Inspector General was to be appointed by Congress from among the general officers, and was allowed only one secretary, taken from the line and given the pay and emoluments of an aide-de-camp. Each separate army was to have one inspector, taken from the field officers of the line. The plan did not include assistants, subinspectors, or the like.[11]

The Inspector General or inspector of a separate army was, as directed by the Commander in Chief or army commander, to review and muster the troops "of every denomination in service," in accustomed fashion, examining men, horses, and property and reporting "deficiencies, neglects, and abuses, and, if possible, the manner in which they happened; and at the same time pointing out the alterations and amendments they may think necessary in any branch of the military system." After every review, the commander was to exercise his troops in the manual and evolutions for the inspector, and the latter would report on their discipline. If the inspector wished to see a certain maneuver, he had to furnish a plan in advance to the commander, who might or might not comply "as he may think proper."[12]

At every review, company commanders had to submit enlistment papers and three copies of the muster rolls (signed but no longer sworn to) to the inspector, who would transmit them upward as before. The inspector was to transmit immediately an abstract of the musters to the commander, who was to send a duplicate to the Secretary at War. The inspector was also to report men unfit for service, the previous procedures for discharge remaining in force except that now the army commander or Commander in Chief's signature was required. The inspectors were authorized to receive returns of supplies from the Quartermaster General and the Clothier General. In addition, inspectors were also expected to visit military hospitals to determine their condition and advise the

10. Risch, *Quartermaster Support*, 70–73; Sanger, "Inspector-General's Department," 236.
11. *JCC*, 10 Jan 82.
12. Ibid.

commander. The Inspector General himself, again, was expected to visit every part of the Army to see that uniformity prevailed. Congress intended also to ensure subordination of the inspectorate to the army commander, and diligence in inspection by specifically saying inspectors were subject only to the orders of Congress, The Secretary at War, the Commander in Chief, or the commanding officer of a separate army. The Inspector General was to specify the form of all returns. Each inspector of a separate army was further permitted to take an officer from the line of captains or subalterns to assist him. Finally, Congress continued Steuben as Inspector General.[13] As a result, during most of 1782, the strength of the department included the Inspector General, two assistant inspectors general, two assistant inspectors, and twelve brigade inspectors.[14]

The new organization was greatly consolidated and simplified, essentially in accord with precedent. Its primary emphasis, however, had shifted from the proclamation of regulations to inspection, in particular, to monitoring training and economy. That inspectors dealt equally with commanders, the Secretary at War, and Congress, however, represented a blurring of the distinction between civil oversight of the military and military command principles. In practice, Washington's continued personal requirement that inspectors report only to him avoided any dangers of interference in his command. His interest in daily events sustained his policy on the inspectorate. This was shown when the Army encamped in New York and monthly musters and inspections became the established routine. Washington issued frequent orders commenting on the inspection reports, usually expressing his pleasure at good reports and his hope that, in a typical instance, "any little irregularities which have crept into the service may be immediately remedied."[15] Such orders made up a substantial share of those issued during the Army's last encampment.

Demobilization and Border Defense

Congress took no action regarding a permanent military establishment in 1783. On the contrary, most of the delegates were eager to dispose of what army the United States had left. It was motivated not only on the grounds of economy, or because many believed that the conclusion of peace with Britain made a military force unnecessary, but also, persistent fears about the threats an army posed to public liberies prevented Congress from even approaching agreement on the nation's permanent military needs. Those fears were aggravated in March when a group of army officers issued the "Newburgh Addresses," demanding their financial and political rights in an ominously threatening manner. Washington calmed the tempers of his officers, and the

---

13. Ibid.

14. Sanger, "Inspector-General's Department," 235–36; Ward, *Department of War*, 235.

15. Edward C. Boynton, comp. and ed., *General Orders of George Washington, Commander in Chief of the Army of the Revolution, Issued at Newburgh on the Hudson, 1782–1783* (1909; reprint, Harrison, N.Y.: Harbor Hill, 1973). The typical order cited was issued 5 June 1782. Ibid, 27.

crisis passed. But two months later a group of officers gathered in Steuben's quarters to form the Society of the Cincinnati, once again arousing groundless but nevertheless real fears of a military or aristocratic counterrevolution. Meanwhile, Washington reported that the enlisted men were rioting and insulting their officers; they wanted their pay and discharges. By the middle of June, all but about seven hundred of them had been released, but without having been paid.[16]

The Continental Army melted away after the peace with Britain, but not all of its business was concluded. Steuben carried important burdens during the transition to peacetime. Washington sent him to Canada in July 1783 to arrange for the transfer of military posts in the United States from British to American control.[17] Steuben next turned his attention to the details of demobilization. Henry Knox commanded the troops remaining in service, but he lacked an inspector. On Steuben's recommendation, his aide William North became inspector for Knox's troops in October 1783. Freed of inspection duties, the Inspector General himself spent the months of October and November supervising the dissolution of posts, issuing orders for the transport and care of the sick and invalids, and emptying the remaining hospitals. In short, Steuben disbanded the Continental Army.[18] When Commander in Chief George Washington prepared to return to civilian life, his last official letter, that of 23 December 1783, was to Steuben: "I wish to make use of this last moment of my public life to signify in the strongest terms my entire approbation of your conduct, and to express my sense of the obligation the public is under to you, for your faithful and meritorious service."[19] Steuben entered civilian life the following April.

Steuben's Legacy

Steuben had made a remarkable contribution to the first army of the United States, and he left to its successors a rich legacy. The most famous of his achievements were the training program at Valley Forge and the manual of tactical and administrative regulations that evolved from it. They entitled him to a share of credit for the American victory equal to that of any other major general. Nor did the impact of his achievements stop with the Revolution, for Steuben's blue book enjoyed currency for decades, and profoundly influenced

---

16. Weigley, *History of the United States Army*, 77–78. A good, concise summary appears in Higginbotham, *War of American Independence*, 409–12, whereas a recent, popular account is James W. Wensyel, "The Newburgh Conspiracy," *American Heritage*, 32 (April–May 1980): 40–47. A recent, full history of the Society of the Cincinnati is Minor Myers, Jr., *Liberty Without Anarchy: A History of the Society of the Cincinnati* (Charlottesville: University of Virginia Press, 1982). The organization began as a social group of Continental Army officers, with some political overtones. Following the Newburgh addresses, its very existence caused the more fearful parts of the public to suspect a plot with antidemocratic intentions.

17. Steuben to Washington, 23 Aug 83 (from Saratoga), and Frederic Haldimand to Washington, 11 Aug 83, both in Jared Sparks, ed., *Correspondence of the American Revolution . . .* , 4 vols. (Boston: Little, Brown, 1853), 4: 39–40, 41–43.

18. Kapp, *Life of Steuben*, 524.

19. Washington to Steuben, 23 Dec 83, quoted in Thian, *Legislative History*, 85.

later army regulations. . . . Steuben also left his stamp on the office of Inspector General. Some of his influences lasted only a generation; for example, the custom that the Inspector General was effectively the chief of staff or alter ego of the Commander in Chief. For three decades after the Revolution, when the United States addressed the establishment of an army, it referred to the Continental Army as its prototype. In 1798, and again in 1812–1813, the general second in command to the nominal army commander received the title "Inspector General," mostly because that was what Washington had called his most visible assistant. That Steuben had actually been a staff officer most of the time, rather than a commander of troops, was irrelevant. There was magic in the evocation of things as they were in the Continental Army.

Thanks to Washington and Steuben (and the legacy of the Conway affair), military inspection in the United States Army would remain a function of command; it never became an external political agency intruding itself into the Army. The army commander lost control of the staff departments during the nineteenth century, but the Inspector General remained his servant, his eyes and ears in the military line organization. The inspector answered to the commander, while the commander remained solely accountable for the efficiency of his command. In addition, Steuben also established the principle that inspection should concern itself with more than purely military efficiency and should extend throughout the Army's staff departments and services. As long as that principle was observed, there was in fact one command authority over the entire U.S. Army, one person answerable to the public for all the Army did. When the principle eroded, the commander's control of staff departments slipped away and the War Department fragmented into a collection of bureaus. As oversight for the entire organization passed increasingly to the Secretary of War late in the nineteenth century, the force of Steuben's principle of comprehensive examination drew the Inspector General into service to the Secretary of War. Thanks to Steuben, a system of inspection was regarded as essential to the management of the army, regardless of the focus of authority. Those developments lay in the distant future in 1784, when the American army practically disappeared. When the army again grew and became a permanent function of the government of the United States, the example of Steuben and the Continental Army ensured that a system of inspection would develop with it.

CHAPTER 5

Decline, Revival, and Vicissitudes of Inspection

(1784–1798)

In 1784, the little army that remained in regular service had only the eighty privates and their officers guarding stores that the War Department wanted to sell off. The twenty-five men at Fort Pitt were commanded by a lieutenant who believed that his duty was to guard, not preserve, the stores. The hoard of powder at the fort deteriorated while the soldiers occupied themselves with nonmilitary pursuits. The fifty-five men at West Point were more efficient. They were the remnants of Alexander Hamilton's battery of the Continental Army, under the command of Capt. John Doughty, highest ranking officer continued in service. The stores they guarded were for the most part useless surplus left over from the war.

Very Little Army To Inspect

Whether William North accomplished much as inspector during the first years after the Revolution is not now apparent, although the fragmentary evidence suggests that he did very little. He lived for a time, after the war, with Steuben in New York, then the seat of government, and busied himself improving his social position. Serving in such a minuscule army, his paper work at the War Department would have taken little time. Although North had been brevetted a major on 11 September 1783, Congress did not increase his pay in recognition of his position as inspector until 22 March 1785. That measure may have been intended to encourage him to travel on duty, but North was known to take only one official journey—he was sent to inspect troops camped on the Mingo River, in Ohio, in 1786. At the conclusion of that journey, Congress probably granted North a permanent promotion to major. North married the daughter of the mayor of New York City on 14 October 1787, and ceased to serve as inspector as of 28 October. He spent the next few years developing a rich estate near Schenectady and pursuing his political career. But, as later events demonstrated, he never lost touch with the army, nor gave up his hopes for military advancement.[1]

---

1. *JCC*, 22 Mar 85; Thian, *Legislative History*, 103; Heitman, *Historical Register*, 1: 38, 751; Doyle, *Steuben*, 356–60; *DAB*, 7: 563–64.

The office of inspector thus remained vacant for five years with Congress discontinuing the office of inspector of troops on 25 June 1788, telling the Secretary at War to develop some other means of inspection. Secretary Knox told Congress a month later that the recruits then being raised in Connecticut, New Jersey, and Pennsylvania would be mustered and inspected by Mr. John Stagg, chief clerk of the War Department, who was a Continental Army veteran, formerly a brigade major. Paralleling his activities were those of Francis Mentges, who continued to serve as inspector of contracts as he had since 1782. Except for their labors, inspections of troops in service were incumbent upon majors of regiments—in other words, the American army was militia, conducted as militia always had been. There was no real general inspectorate, nor even a semblance of one until at least 1792.[2]

Birth of the United States Army

A revitalized American army, however, appeared a real possibility early in 1789. William North, among others, hoped to be a part of it. But he was soon discouraged, believing that the future would follow the course of politics and favoritism. He complained to Steuben that the army as proposed was too small and was dominated by Henry Knox.[3] The army did not start out as something that a man of North's ambition would want to make a career in. Congress established the War Department on 7 August 1789; Knox continued in office, thereafter answering to the President instead of directly to Congress. He gained an extra clerk in 1790, and by 1792 had a staff of ten people—still inadequate to supervise a widely scattered force. On 29 September 1789, Congress legalized the army of 700 three-year men it earlier had called for, together with the artillery companies already in existence. An authorized 886 officers and men were to be arrayed in an infantry regiment of eight companies and an artillery battalion of four. But only 672 men were actually in service. To supplement them, the President was authorized to call out militia when needed to fight Indians. Thus the United States Army had its uneasy birth. Congress clearly regarded it as, at best, a distasteful necessity, and at worst a threat to the republic.[4]

Congress was hostile to an increase in national military programs because, among other reasons, the national budget was always under a strain. Equally pertinent, most congressmen's districts were east of the Appalachian Mountains, where Indians posed no threat to their constituents. The frontier could not be ignored indefinitely, however. Encouraged by the British still occupying posts

---

2. *JCC*, 25 Jun 88; Thian, *Legislative History*, 103; Sanger, "Inspector-General's Department," 237; Knox to Pres of Cong, 3 Jul 88, quoted in both Thian, *Legislative History*, 103, and Sanger, "Inspector General's Department," 237; Heitman, *Historical Register*, 1: 38. Thian erroneously attributes Knox's letter to Washington.

3. North to Steuben, 8 Jan 89, in Doyle, *Steuben*, 359.

4. Ward, *Department of War*, 101–04; Jacobs, *Beginning of the U.S. Army*, 41–42; Weigley, *History of the United States Army*, 88–89; Heitman, *Historical Register*, 2: 560.

in American territory in the Northwest, the large and powerful tribes there by 1790 demanded a curtailment of white settlement. In fact, they wanted it driven back to the line of the Ohio River. Harassing settlers, soldiers, and peace delegations, they began to do just that. It occurred to Congress that the campaigns of the Indians might be an opening wedge for British advances against the United States.[5] Consequently, it was as stimulated to action as it could be to act expeditiously. On 8 December 1790, Washington asked for an expanded U.S. Army, and Congress gave it to him just four months later, on 3 March 1791. A second infantry regiment was authorized, along with two regiments of six-month volunteers and such militia as the President cared to call out. In the Army organization, Congress permitted a major general, a brigadier general, a quartermaster, and a chaplain. Most staff services were provided by brigade majors, adjutants, regimental paymasters, and quartermasters detailed from the line. There was no formal provision for an inspectorate. A provision of the previous year authorizing two inspectors remained in force, but the vacancies were not filled.[6]

Arthur St. Clair became major general commanding the Army—that is, leader of the planned expedition into the Northwest—in March 1791. Mr. Francis Mentges, still serving as inspector of contracts, was the closest thing the War Department had to an inspector general. Mentges' management of supply contracting proved to be as poor as the management of troops and militia in the hands of St. Clair. The expedition did not start until September, and it ran into an ambush on 4 November that left 672 men dead—about half the force. The remainder, including the supply contractors, ran for their lives, scattering most of the Army's inventory to the winds. In the aftermath, the six-month levies went home without pay, while a committee of Congress railed at "the gross and various mismanagements and neglects in the Quartermaster's and contractors' departments."[7] In amongst this chaos, many of the duties associated with inspectors continued to be carried out. Besides the mustering and inspecting duties that probably were fulfilled by brigade majors, the St. Clair expedition had, by accident, a general inspector. He was Lt. Col. Winthrop Sargent, territorial secretary in the Northwest and perforce a political ally of Governor St. Clair. Sargent was St. Clair's Adjutant General, but because of his disagreeable nature, officers hesitated to report to the commander through him. To remove him as an irritation, St. Clair used him a great deal to inspect militia outposts

5. Jacobs, *Beginning of the U.S. Army*, 42–43; Weigley, *History of the United States Army*, 90. The Secretary of War was responsible for Indian as well as military affairs.

6. Weigley, *History of the United States Army*, 91; Heitman, *Historical Register*, 2: 561. This legislation has erroneously been cited as the authorization for the position of Adjutant and Inspector General. Weigley, *History of the United States Army*, 123n. The position actually dates from 5 March 1792, but was not filled while that legislation was in force.

7. Sanger, "Inspector-General's Department," 237; Francis Paul Prucha, *The Sword of the Republic: The United States Army on the Frontier 1783–1846* (Toronto: Macmillan, 1969), 22–27; Risch, *Quartermaster Support*, 99–100.

and detachments. He was wounded, but survived the debacle of November 1791.[8]

The St. Clair disaster induced yet another army reorganization. On 5 March 1792, Congress authorized recruitment of the two infantry regiments and the artillery battalion to full strength, and an additional three infantry regiments to serve for three years, along with four troops of dragoons. To promote recruitment, the law ended deductions for clothing and medical services, and offered an enlistment bounty of $8.00. On the advice of Treasury Secretary Alexander Hamilton, Congress sought to end corruption and inefficiency in contracting by transferring to the Treasury Department responsibility for purchase of army supplies. That ended the function of the War Department's inspectors of contracts, and set the stage for bureaucratic squabbles that would bedevil army supply for several years.[9]

Anthony Wayne and Inspection

Secretary Knox, in 1790, had proposed the creation of a "legion" to guard the frontier, and now urged Washington to form the Legion of the United States. By 4 September, Maj. Gen. Anthony Wayne—who took command 12 April, to date from 5 March—had organized his force sufficiently in western Pennsylvania to proclaim the formation of the Legion. Congress was notified on 27 December, although the Legion was not completed until the spring of 1793.[10] . . . Wayne, as always, was a competent and energetic man. The Legion organization—arranged in four sublegions—was a compact, manageable force for what lay ahead. This was once again no permanent military establishment, but like the Continental Army was a field force with an immediate mission: to meet the enemy in the Northwest. The distinct command structure permitted a systematic recruitment of the Legion, which Wayne simultaneously set about training. By late 1792 he had assembled his force for training at a place he called Legionville, west of Pittsburgh. Wayne ignored those who wanted action before his force was prepared. Instead, he concentrated on everything from basic drill, march and battlefield movements to camp sanitation and property accountability—consciously modeling his program on that of Steuben in the Continental Army. In fact, he asked for a supply of Steuben's regulations. In September, Knox told him that "Baron Steubens [sic] blue book is out of print—but we will have an edition printed with all expedition."[11] His stress on

---

8. Jacobs, *Beginning of the U.S. Army*, 104–05; Prucha, *Sword of the Republic*, 24. For Sargent's own record of the expedition, see "Winthrop Sargent's Diary While With General Arthur St. Clair's Expedition Against the Indians," *Ohio Archaeological and Historical Quarterly*, 33 (July 1924): 237–73.

9. *An Act making further and more effectual provision for the protection of the frontiers of the United States*, Statutes at Large 1, sec. 7, 241 (1792); Jacobs, *Beginning of the U.S. Army*, 125; Ward, *Department of War*, 143–44; Risch, Quartermaster Support, 100.

10. 1 Stat. 241; Heitman, *Historical Register*, 1: 139. See also the excellent background summary in Prucha, *Sword of the Republic*, 28–29.

11. Spaulding, *United States Army*, 120; Jacobs, *Beginning of the U.S. Army*, 130–37; Knox to Wayne, 21 Sep 92, in Richard C. Knopf, ed., *Anthony Wayne, a Name in Arms; Soldier, Diplomat,*

basics and his insistence on standards meant that Wayne brought a strong system of inspection back into the Army, along with Steuben's regulations. Section 7 of the act of 5 March 1792 provided that the Adjutant General would also undertake the duties of inspector. Until a permanent tenant of the office could be found, on 10 March 1792 Lt. Henry DeButts was designated to act as adjutant and inspector; he was listed in that capacity until 23 February 1793, although his functions in the office overlapped those of others.[12]

The Adjutant General, who was also to carry the duties of inspector, was known as the "Adjutant and Inspector General" by the time the Legion was formed. The origins of the combined office probably lay in congressmen's memories that, under Steuben, Washington had been served by such a consolidated functionary during the Revolution. In an age when military paper work, burdensome as it could be, remained relatively limited, the combination of the functions of records management, mustering, and inspection probably worked well enough. It certainly ensured that, at each level, inspection would remain an agency of the commander, not a power to itself. Knox apparently offered the position of Adjutant General to Winthrop Sargent in April 1792, but without enough attached rank to induce him to give up his political position. The office therefore went empty, and in fact never was filled as originally constituted. Knox nonetheless believed it an important one, for he told Wayne on 20 July that he would do all he could to find another qualified officer.[13]

Wayne, more clearly even than Washington, made inspection an extension of his own will as commander. Lacking a permanent Adjutant and Inspector General, he employed his aides Capt. Henry DeButts, Maj. Michael Rudolph, Capt. Edward Butler, and Maj. John Mills as his inspectors, sometimes one or another, sometimes all of them. They oversaw and actually conducted training, as had Steuben and his agents in 1778; they inspected detachments, recruits, and supplies; they interceded where transportation bogged down; and they, in fact, served in his absence wherever, whenever, and however Wayne thought fit. Each of Wayne's inspectors was a veteran of the Continental Army. In fact, each had spent the formative part of his adulthood in the military. That they all returned to the Army at the earliest opportunity suggests that they may never have quite adjusted to civilian life. Eagerness to return to the uniform and a cause fitted them for Wayne's purposes. Their attraction toward the military, moreover, permitted an unnoticed transfer of the rather loose inspectorate from

---

Defender of Expansion Westward of a Nation: The Wayne-Knox-Pickering Correspondence (Pittsburgh: University of Pittsburgh Press, 1960), 105. For a good summary of the challenge Wayne faced as he tried to assemble the Legion from unpromising materials, see Prucha, *Sword of the Republic*, 30–32.

12. *An Act making further and more effectual provision for the protection of the frontiers of the United States, Statutes at Large* 1, sec. 7, 241 (1792); Heitman, *Historical Register*, 1:38. Heitman's source for DeButts' appointment is not apparent, and in fact the office is not shown in the entry on DeButts' career, Heitman, *Historical Register*, 1:363.

13. Thian, *Legislative History*, 85; Ward, *Department of War*, 145; Knox to Wayne, 20 Jul 92, in Knopf, *Anthony Wayne*, 43.

the War Department to the staff of the Commanding General. This was because of Wayne's methods in preparing for the forthcoming campaign. As commander, Wayne instituted a training regime for the Legion modeled on that developed by Steuben for the Continental Army. His aides, as inspectors, were also his training officers, Rudulph first among them. The major general held his authority or that of his aides unassailable in the training program: "I am informed," he told Knox, "that Capt Stake has taken some umbrage at Major Rudulph's interference with the discipline of his *Troop*—if upon reflection, he shou'd persist in his intention to resign, I will most certainly indulge him, Altho' I know him to be a most Gallant Officer."[14]

The inspector, in other words, was the agent of the commander, and the commander would not tolerate even the suggestion of intercession in his organization by the Secretary of War or anyone else on behalf of a disgruntled officer. Wayne did not have to tell Knox not to interfere in his command. Rather, he let his officers know that Rudulph's orders were Wayne's orders, not those of a mere major—and not liable to cancellation by anyone other than Wayne. With this kind of command support, Wayne's training and inspection program started well, but it was improvised. By 28 September the major general felt the lack of a formal first assistant. With DeButts holding the seat of acting adjutant and inspector, but serving elsewhere, Wayne appointed Capt. Edward Butler "Deputy Adjutant & Inspector General *protem* [sic] . . . ." Soon after, answering the commander's pleas for a permanent tenant in the post, Knox told Wayne that "The Adjutant General will not be appointed until the arrival of the President which will be on the fourteenth [of October]."[15] Wayne, therefore, continued to improvise. Butler served him as adjutant (that is, as secretary and office manager) while Rudulph served as his training officer and chief troubleshooter.

Of all Wayne's aides, Butler was the least fortunate choice. Officers generally complained about his arrogance and purported incompetence, but Wayne retained him anyway.[16] Early in 1793, when Wayne established a pattern of sharing or rotating the duties of adjutant and inspector among his aides, Butler was included. His work was mostly that of an adjutant, the most important being the delivery of orders for training drills. Butler and Rudulph had been joined by Capt. John Mills, who impressed Wayne as he had Knox. The shortage of good officers complained about by Wayne in his letters to the Secretary perhaps explains Butler's continued service as adjutant, despite his defects.

Knox, meanwhile, was still trying to locate a permanent Adjutant and Inspector General. On 19 January 1793, he asked Wayne, "Would Colonel Sproat make a good Adjutant General and be acceptable to the Army?" Wayne responded on 31 January that he hardly knew the man, and doubted that the rest

---

14. Wayne to Knox, 28 Sep 92, in Knopf, *Anthony Wayne*, 109.
15. Wayne to Knox, 18 Sep 92, and Knox to Wayne, 5 Oct 92, both in Knopf, *Anthony Wayne*, 108–09, 114.
16. Jacobs, *Beginning of the U.S. Army*, 156.

of the Army did either. But he earnestly desired that the position be filled.[17] Although he continued to be hampered by the absence of competent senior officers, Wayne had his training program in high gear throughout 1793 and on into the following year. As soon as a supply of Steuben's blue book was available, he had handed every officer a copy and saw they used it. The British, meanwhile, continued to supply and to encourage the Indians north of the Ohio River to disregard American overtures and to insist on the withdrawal of all whites from their lands. While this increase in hostile activity alarmed many in the government, "Mad Anthony" Wayne refused to launch an impetuous campaign until his Legion was ready. On 11 September he learned

CAPT. EDWARD BUTLER. *Inspector of the Army, 18 July 1793–13 May 1794; 1 August 1796–27 February 1797.*

that the "procrastinated and fruitless, but absolutely necessary negociations [*sic*] with the Indians" that had taken all summer, had broken down. By the summer of 1794, he planned, he would have an efficient military force at hand. Meanwhile, perhaps thankful for the extra training period because the season was too late for a campaign, Wayne spent the fall and winter moving the Legion into advanced positions in Indian country.[18]

As Wayne prepared for the approaching war, he made a last effort to fill in his principal staff position. He nominated John Mills for the job in March 1794. "It is hoped," Knox assured him, "that Major Mills's nomination to the office of Adjutant & Inspector will be productive of all the advantages incident to so important an office." But the nomination brought no results, except for Mills' appointment as Acting Adjutant and Inspector on 13 May.[19] Thus did Mills replace the contentious Butler, but the latter remained on Wayne's staff as an aide and inspector. Wayne was so short of competent staff officers that he had to use those available in unusual ways. A principal duty of an inspector was to muster troops to verify their presence for payment of wages. As the Legion, national volunteers, and militia began to mobilize for campaign early in the

---

17. Knox to Wayne, 19 Jan 93, and Wayne to Knox, 31 Jan 93, both in Knopf, *Anthony Wayne*, 175, 179–80.

18. Prucha, *Sword of the Republic*, 34–36; Weigley, *History of the United States Army*, 93; Reginald Horsman, "The British Indian Department and the Resistance to General Anthony Wayne, 1793–1795," *Mississippi Valley Historical Review*, 49 (September 1962): 269–90.

19. Knox to Wayne, 31 Mar 94, in Knopf, *Anthony Wayne*, 316; Heitman, *Historical Register*, 1: 38.

summer of 1794, and the army gathered its supplies, Wayne was hampered by shortages of competent paymasters as well as other staff assistants. That, combined with regional economic peculiarities, caused him to find some odd employment for his aide Butler. Wayne informed Knox on 10 June that he was using Butler as a courier taking the muster-in pay to volunteers in Kentucky.[20]

Wayne was determined to get the job done, no matter what it required. His flexibility and determination paid off in August 1794. On 20 August, in a perfectly executed bayonet charge against a strong, but unknown to Wayne, weakly manned, position at Fallen Timbers, Ohio, the Legion of the United States won a swift, stunning victory over the Miami Indians. The shock of the Legion's advance was so great that, when the losers sought the protection of Fort Miami, the British garrison locked them out.[21] The distinguished performance at Fallen Timbers of the officers of Wayne's improvised inspectorate—that is, his personal staff including aides-de-camp Henry DeButts, Capt. T. Lewis, and Lt. William Henry Harrison, along with Acting Adjutant and Inspector John Mills—was the incentive for Wayne's writing to Knox on 28 August of their "most essential services by communicating my orders in every direction & by their Conduct & bravery exciting the troops to press for Victory."[22] At this moment of triumph, however, the Legion of the United States threatened to dissolve, especially as enlistments expired. The volunteers left first, and Butler was ordered to muster and discharge the Kentucky troops. Wayne railed at Knox to help keep the Legion at full strength, and to garrison the several posts in the Northwest, but Knox refused to test congressional willingness to do so in poor economy.[23]

Wayne's success in Ohio, the waning fortunes of the Legion notwithstanding, probably ensured the permanence of the United States Army. The Legion and its predecessors had traditionally been established as a short-term measure—like the Continental Army, they had existed to take the field against a particular enemy. The failure of the earlier armies to achieve success, compared with the outcome of Wayne's regimen, demonstrated that a trained force of regulars must always be at hand, lest it take another two years to prepare for the next emergency. Furthermore, it appeared likely that the British would soon abandon their posts in the Northwest. The American frontier territories must therefore be garrisoned; militia had not done that effectively in the past. But as Wayne's Legion deteriorated, so did the system of training and inspection with which he had managed it. Once again, a uniformed functionary occupied himself with paper work. It was too small a job for Mills, who was succeeded by Maj. Jonathan Haskell of the 4th Sublegion on 27 February 1796. He in turn was replaced on 1 August by Edward Butler.[24]

---

20. Wayne (at Greeneville) to Knox, 10 Jun 94, in Knopf, *Anthony Wayne*, 340.
21. Jacobs, *Beginning of the U.S. Army*, 173–76; Prucha, *Sword of the Republic*, 36–38.
22. Wayne to Knox, 28 Aug 94, in Knopf, *Anthony Wayne*, 353.
23. Wayne to Knox, 17 Oct 94, in Knopf, *Anthony Wayne*, 360; Prucha, *Sword of the Republic*, 37–38.
24. Heitman, *Historical Register*, 1: 38; *The National Cyclopaedia of American Biography* (New York: James T. White, 1909), 12: 336 (hereafter cited as *NCAB*).

James Wilkinson and the Army

The Army had been redesignated a "Legion" in 1792 because the terminology was current, and possibly in a romantic evocation of the ancient Roman Republic. As Wayne organized and trained it, the Legion was a compact, flexible tactical force, four self-contained little armies under one command. But with the war over, the Legion was poorly organized to garrison the many posts of the Northwest, including those abandoned by the British in 1796. Accordingly, the Legion of the United States became the United States Army on 30 May 1796. As reorganized 1 November, the authorized force of 3,359 officers and men was arrayed in four regiments of infantry, a small body of light dragoons, and a Corps of Artillerists and Engineers. The reduction of strength from the U.S. Legion's authorized 5,414 was no small matter in the reorganization.

The legislation re-forming the United States Army also established a general staff, which included one major general, one brigadier general, two aides-de-camp, and a brigade major, Quartermaster General, Paymaster General and "one inspector, who shall do the duty of Adjutant General." The inspector, quartermaster, and paymaster might be taken from the line, or from civilian life. However, Congress decreed "That the general staff as authorized by this act shall continue in service until the 4th day of next March, and no longer."[25] Wayne's emphasis on an inspector as adjutant and aide-de-camp to the commander was in principle realized in the organization, but there was nothing permanent about it. The position of "inspector, who shall do the duty of Adjutant General," remained as ill-defined as it had ever been. Without a Commanding General with Wayne's ability to make good use of staff officers, the position was ineffective, almost unnoticed. Inevitably, the clerical duties of an Adjutant General, for which the inspector was a misnamed, lower-paid substitute, took precedence over all other responsibilities. Even Butler may have become bored as he returned to his regiment in February 1797. He was replaced 27 February as Acting Adjutant and Inspector by another veteran of the Revolution, Maj. Thomas H. Cushing of the 1st Infantry.[26]

Cushing was hardly in his new assignment before Congress revised it. On 3 March 1797, the act of the year before was repealed, so far as it related to the major general and his staff. The United States Army was now to be headed by a brigadier general, who was supported by a staff of officers whose purposes were exceedingly vague, even obscure. They included a brigade major, a brigade inspector, a Quartermaster General, a Paymaster General, and a Judge Advocate. The basic functions of the latter three had been defined by custom, but the responsibilities of the brigade major and brigade inspector were not specified. Furthermore, the legislation said that the brigadier general could

---

25. *An Act to ascertain and fix the military establishment of the United States, Statutes at Large* 1, sec. 3, sec. 12–14, 483 (1796); Thian, *Legislative History*, 104; Heitman, *Historical Register,* 1: 139, 2: 563.

26. Heitman, *Historical Register*, 1: 348; *NCAB*, 12: 560. See Appendix B.

MAJ. THOMAS H. CUSHING. *Inspector of the Army, 27 February 1797–22 May 1798, and Acting Adjutant and Inspector General, 15 June 1800–26 March 1802.*

choose his "inspector from the captains and subalterns in the line," entitling them to extra pay and emoluments. Since Cushing had retained his position in the line, Wilkinson ignored his rank and permitted the major to remain as inspector.[27]

James Wilkinson was the Army's brigadier general who discovered that his inspector was occupied with military paper work—if, indeed, he was occupied with anything. In the absence of any equivalent of a modern Inspector General, the brigade inspector notwithstanding, Wilkinson had to tour the army to discover conditions for himself. What he found displeased him. The smart fighting force that had triumphed at Fallen Timbers had by 1797 become little more than a collection of small ineffectual bands scattered throughout the wilderness. The absence of enforced standards was very clear and Wilkinson's experience as his own inspector general left him fuming with indignation as he returned east later in 1797. He was appalled at the condition of the army—and, most likely, equally upset that the state of things had been unknown to him before his personal inspection. If anyone in the army possessed the strength of will for realignment, it was Wilkinson. But he needed to know at all times what was deficient before he could order its correction. Given the widely scattered army and the absence of any real inspectorate, that was impossible.

The U.S. Army organized in 1796 had, without anyone quite realizing it at the time, a mission without precedent in its own history. The Continental Army, the improvised forces that succeeded it, the Legion of the United States— all had been formed to take the field against an enemy. They were fighting forces motivated, not always well, to maintain efficiency. Most important, they were fairly cohesive bodies, relatively speaking, under the eyes of their commanders. The Continental Army was sufficiently large that the commander needed an extra set of eyes. He gave himself, with the approval of Congress, an Inspector General and organization to keep the Army in view. The temporary

---

27. An Act to Amend and Repeal in Part the Act Entitled "An Act to Ascertain and Fix the Miliary Establishment of the United States," approved 3 Mar 97, *Statutes at Large* 1, sec. 2 (1797); Thian, *Legislative History*, 86; Heitman, *Historical Register*, 1: 38, 2: 564. This legislation was continued by further legislation 27 Apr 98, but the Army's organization was immediately thereafter overtaken by other events.

armies that followed the Revolution had little in the way of a formal inspectorate, but they were compact enough that their commanders could observe most parts of them; these forces' failures were due to circumstances, including incompetent leadership, and not to lack of inspection.

Anthony Wayne had revitalized the principles of inspection for the Legion of the United States. But perhaps because the position of the chief inspector was never formally occupied, his inspectorate was personal and improvised. A small, coordinated group of staff officers acted as his personal agents, his eyes and ears, and messengers. He needed nothing more elaborate, because the Legion was mostly within his view. Wayne established very firmly a principle that inspection was the agency of the commander, the tool by which he made his army do his will. But it would appear that Congress and the War Department did not perceive the important role that Wayne's improvised inspectorate played in forging the Legion. Rather, they noticed how well he got along without a formally constituted organization for inspection. They therefore neglected to provide for effective inspection in the new army organization.

If the United States Army had remained a compact body, as the Legion of the United States had been, Wilkinson might have managed to keep his finger on all parts. Congress did not afford him any aides he might use as inspectors, and Wilkinson was not the sort of person who attracted a devoted staff. Nevertheless, with an army in the field, he could keep himself informed of its condition, and assert his control. But his army in 1797 was an army in name only. It was no longer a recognizable marching force supervised directly by its leader. Rather, it was on its way to becoming a continental constabulary, dispersed across the wilderness in small units, most of them unable to communicate with one another. Wilkinson might be the nominal commander of that scattering of armed bands, but it was impossible for him to keep them all in view at any one time. Since the commander could not be everywhere at once, he would require assistance if he was to know what was going on in the Army.

The mission that would occupy the Army for most of the nineteenth century— policing the West—had begun to take shape by 1797, not deliberately, but circumstantially. The organization established by Congress would have sufficed for a consolidated marching force. It was inadequate for a frontier constabulary in which local commanders were prone to regulate their own forces as they saw fit. Its greatest administrative shortcoming was the absence of any systematic way of keeping the commanding general informed, so that he could oversee the efficiency of his army. So, as an unhappy Wilkinson ended his tour of inspection as in 1797, it is likely that he gave some thought to the Army's administrative defects. At the least, he must have concluded that he needed some means of knowing what those unrestrained satraps, the post commanders, were up to—and some way of ensuring that they served the public interest before their own.

Before anything could come of Wilkinson's frustrated complaints, war threatened once again. Congress addressed the reconsolidation of the army into a fighting force. To oversee national mobilization, the lawmakers revived

Washington's former rank of lieutenant general. Congress also remembered the
Commanding General's principal assistant during the Revolution, and decided
that the lieutenant general's second in command should be called the ''Inspector
General.''

CHAPTER 6

Hamilton and the Provisional Army
(1798–1800)

Wilkinson retained Thomas Cushing as his brigade inspector under the act of 3 March 1797, ignoring the law's restriction of his right of appointment to junior officers. That apparently left his inspector without the compensation to which he would have been entitled since he was a major rather than a captain or subaltern. It took a special law on 22 May 1798, amending the 1797 legislation, to pay Cushing and thus allow Wilkinson to retain the inspector he wanted.[1] Thereafter, Wilkinson's chosen inspector vanished amid a flurry of real and apparent changes in army organization.

Establishing an Army for War

From March to July 1798, Congress passed at least twenty pieces of legislation aimed at strengthening the national defense. The object of military attention at that time was France, with which relations had been deteriorating for some time. Among the new developments was an expanded fortification construction program, real and potential increases in the Regular Army, and a so-called provisional army that grew and grew over the next year, but only on paper. This was a reaction to the conflict in Europe beginning with the revolution in France. These wars with revolutionary France had, since the early 1790s, their own unhappy effects on relations between the United States and various foreign powers. Britain indulged in customary highhandedness on the seas, capturing American sailors on their own ships and impressing them into British naval service. As the United States and Britain edged toward war over that issue, danger was averted by Wayne's victory in the Northwest and the Jay Treaty of 1794. In the treaty, the British agreed to evacuate the posts they occupied on American soil and to arbitrate debts left over from the Revolution.

The French overreacted to the Jay Treaty, assuming it meant more than it really did in terms of Anglo-American relations, because of the decided Anglophilia of leading Federalists in the United States. An American delega-

---

1. *An Act to amend the Act intituled [sic] "An Act to amend and repeal in part the act intituled 'An act to ascertain and fix the military establishment of the United States.'"* Statutes at Large 1, sec. 1–2, 531 (1798); Thian, *Legislative History,* 105. See Appendix B.

tion that went to Paris late in 1796 was at first rebuffed, then in 1797 met with an insulting demand for loans and a hefty bribe for the three French agents identified by the Americans as "X, Y, and Z." The aftermath of the "XYZ Affair" was an increase in tensions that led Federalists to demand that the United States prepare for war.[2] One of the most prominent Federalists, Alexander Hamilton, was the strongest advocate of an expanded army. In February 1798 he prepared a proposal, which Secretary of War James McHenry sent to Congress on the 15th, to increase the Regular Army to 20,000 enlisted men, and to provide for a provisional army of 30,000. That brought only piecemeal legislation over the next month.[3]

The authorized strength of the army stood at 3,870 enlisted men and 289 officers on 27 April 1798, although the actual complement was considerably less. On 28 May, Congress authorized the President to raise a "Provisional Army," by expanding the Regular Army to a maximum of 10,000 enlisted men. The general staff of the army would comprise a lieutenant general with four aides-de-camp and two secretaries, an unspecified number of major generals with four aides among them, and an Inspector General, an Adjutant General, a Quartermaster General, a Paymaster General, and a Physician General. The Inspector General was to have the rank of major general, and was entitled to appoint two aides with the rank of major. The President could also appoint assistant inspectors and subinspectors wherever needed. The consent of the Senate was required for appointment of the Inspector General, although if the President believed it advisable to fill the position while the Senate was not in session, he was empowered to do so temporarily. In addition, the Inspector General and other new officers could "continue in commission during such term only as the President shall judge requisite for the public service." Finally, no officer appointed under the legislation was entitled to pay until actually called into service.[4] . . . The position of the Inspector General of the provisional army was clearly modeled on what developed during the Revolution— the Adjutant General, for instance, was ranked brigadier general, and would probably have been subordinated to the Inspector General. Like Steuben, the new Inspector General would effectively be chief of staff to the lieutenant general, and at the same time head of an inspectorate reaching down to the brigade level. But as events soon demonstrated, the intention was to have a new Inspector General who was more than a chief of staff.

---

2. Ganoe, *History of the United States Army*, 108; Weigley, *History of the United States Army*, 98–104; Freeman, *George Washington*, 7: 521–34; Stephen G. Kurtz, *The Presidency of John Adams: The Collapse of Federalism, 1795–1800* (Philadelphia: University of Pennsylvania Press, 1957), 308–33; Page Smith, *John Adams*, 2 vols. (Garden City, N. Y.: Doubleday, 1962), 2:973–83; Bernhard Knollenberg, "John Adams, Knox, and Washington," *Proceedings of the American Antiquarian Society*, 56 (October 1946): pt. 2, 207–38.

3. Jacobs, *Beginning of the U.S. Army*, 222–23. Fort McHenry at Baltimore, Maryland, was named for President Adams' Secretary of War, James McHenry.

4. *An Act authorizing the President of the United States to raise a provisional Army, Statutes at Large* 1, sec. 6, 7, 9, 10, 558 (1798); Heitman, *Historical Register*, 2:564–65; Thian, *Legislative History*, 105–06.

A number of Federalists promoting an expanded army had ambitions of their own—Hamilton being first among them. The principal check upon their designs lay not in the opposition of the Republicans, but rather in their own camp. President John Adams was suspicious of the intentions of Hamilton and others, and not at all enthusiastic about the creation of a larger army. His influence ensured that the provisional army was not so large as its promoters desired, nor that he would be forced to call it into existence. As leading Federalists fell into sordid squabbling over who would or would not be among the major generals—with Hamilton and Charles Cotesworth Pinckey always near the top of the list—Adams' limited interest in calling up the provisional army declined toward nullity. In the end, he never felt it necessary to raise the force to its authorized strength.[5]

The nation could think of only one man to command the new army—George Washington. Hamilton—whose most recent military association with the old general (except for endless correspondence on martial subjects) was as his adjutant during the Whiskey Rebellion—put up the appearance of favoring the former president's appointment. Washington, however, was averse to the whole idea, and not at all enamored of Hamilton's strong views. He replied firmly to all inquiries that he was reluctant to assume the office of commander in chief, but was willing if need be—provided he could pick his own subordinate commanders, free of the political brawling among Federalists with military ambitions. Washington pointedly did not mention Hamilton for any position in the army.[6]

The Inspector General as Second in Command

Hamilton lost no time in gathering support for his own attempt to take effective control of the provisional army. It was obvious to him, and to everyone else concerned, that Washington, if he accepted command, would at most be a figurehead, his second in command would be the real controller of the army. The former President's influence was great, however, and Hamilton sought it in his own behalf.[7] Hamilton's desire to play a major role was obvious, and so strong that he managed to change the conception of the Inspector General's position in the Army: "Inspector General, with a command in the line," he had defined it to Washington. Before long, everyone who competed with Hamilton for the position of second in command sought the job of inspector general. In that interpretation, the Inspector General would in fact be the commander of the army, in the expected absence of Washington. That was not the role played by Steuben in the Continental Army, and this probably was not the role envisioned by Congress when it reestablished the title. But by June

5. Jacobs, *Beginning of the U.S. Army*, 224–25.

6. James Thomas Flexner, *George Washington: Anguish and Farewell (1793–1799)* (Boston: Little, Brown, 1972), 393–96.

7. Hamilton to Washington, 2 Jun 98, in Richard B. Morris, ed., *Alexander Hamilton and the Founding of the Nation* (New York: Dial Press, 1957), 438–39.

1798, "Inspector General" was a title of convenience for the second in command, and not at all the title of a staff officer in charge of a system of inspection. Adams soon became alarmed by what he perceived as too many plots to give control of the provisional army to Hamilton, whom he had his own reasons to distrust. In addition, he believed that the navy was more important than a larger army. So the President dragged his feet throughout June, showing no inclination to call out the provisional army. Finally, to confound the Hamiltonians, Adams nominated Washington, without the latter's knowledge, to the lieutenant general's position on 2 July. Congress approved unanimously five days later, while Adams and McHenry exerted great efforts to persuade Washington to accept. The old soldier finally agreed, on the condition that he have no duty or pay until he actually took to the field. He never did.[8]

Washington nevertheless was drawn into the political maelstrom brewing over the appointment of his principal staff and subordinate commanders. His inspector, quartermaster, adjutant, and chief of artillerists and engineers, he told McHenry on 5 July, "ought to be men of the most respectable character and of first rate abilities," as the Commander in Chief must rely on their knowledge to form his own decisions. Washington went on to say that all must be men of unquestionable integrity and prudence with his fullest confidence. The Inspector General, Washington made clear, should be an upstanding character— implicitly, not the sort inclined to the kind of political maneuvers then occupying Hamilton and others interested in the job. Furthermore, Washington wanted the Inspector General's role to be like Steuben's, not a line officer as Hamilton had suggested.[9] Washington wanted the Inspector General to do Steuben's job. One of the major generals of the line should serve as his second in command. But he did not reckon with the redefinition of the Inspector General worked by the influence of Hamilton. Besides Hamilton's focus on that position, it is likely that those hungering after position realized that the next—and perhaps last, if the troops were not raised—general officer's post to be filled would be that of the Inspector General. That officer would control the organization of the army—including the selection of officers.

There were other obvious candidates for second in command, in Washington's opinion. But Hamilton had powerful political forces arrayed in his support. Accordingly, under McHenry's prodding, Washington agreed to accept three major generals: in descending order, Hamilton, Charles C. Pinckney, and Henry Knox. He immediately wrote Hamilton a letter describing the patriotic reasons for giving way to Pinckney. Hamilton knew he had won, however, and stood firm. President Adams was forced by political circumstances to go along, and on 18 July 1798 Hamilton became Inspector General, therefore the senior major general and second in command to Washington.[10]

---

8. Flexner, *Washington: Anguish and Farewell*, 390–400; Jacobs, *Beginning of the U.S. Army*, 223.

9. Washington to James McHenry, 5 Jul 98, quoted in Thian, *Legislative History*, 4.

10. These negotiations are discussed in Flexner, *Washington: Anguish and Farewell*, 400–02.

As the result of additional legislation in July, the Inspector General appeared as in the legislation of 28 May, but with a somewhat altered organization. He was entitled to 2 aides and 2 assistant inspectors taken from the line, while the Adjutant General also received 2 assistants. Lastly, the legislation empowered the President to appoint 4 teachers of the arts and sciences for the instruction of the artillerists and engineers.[11] The power of the new Inspector General was for the moment secure, but not because of the legislation of 16 July. Hamilton was the senior officer on the job, for Pinckney's commission as major general dated from one day after his own, 19 July. So long as Washington showed no inclination to exercise his own powers, Hamilton was preeminent.[12]

Inspector General Hamilton

At least potentially, Hamilton carried more authority over the army than anyone who ever bore the title Inspector General before or after him. But his authority meant nothing unless the expanded army came into being. "At present there is no more prospect of seeing a French army here than there is in Heaven," snorted President Adams, refusing to mobilize. Hamilton apparently did not disagree, but he did everything he could to override Adams' decision not to raise the army. He worked hard over the next months to recruit the new regiments. Stymied at that, he sought to commission enough officers to command 30,000 soldiers. Besides incurring the fearful wrath of the Republicans, the differences between Adams and Hamilton over the Army issue produced a split in the Federalist Party that led to its electoral defeat in 1800.[13]

Hamilton was the dominant figure in the United States Army for two years. But what were his intentions? The Republicans, remembering Hamilton's previous utterances, his role in the Whiskey Rebellion, and the recent passage of the Alien and Sedition Acts, believed that he planned to establish an authoritarian government by military means. When he hinted at such a notion in 1799, even his friends, including Gouverneur Morris, believed the same. At the least, Hamilton appeared bent on using his position to the disadvantage of the Republicans, whom he rigorously excluded from commissions, with the apparent acquiescence of Washington and McHenry. Adams predicted that that would backfire, and he proved correct.[14]

---

11. *An Act to augment the Army of the United States, Statutes at Large* 1, sec. 3–4, 604 (1798); Thian, *Legislative History,* 106; Heitman, *Historical Register,* 2: 566. For his aides, Hamilton eventually appointed Capt. George Izard and Lt. Ethan Allen Brown; Jacob Brown later served as his military secretary. Sanger, "Inspector General's Department," 238–39.

12. Heitman, *Historical Register,* 1: 793.

13. Kurtz, *Presidency of John Adams,* 308; Adams as quoted in Smith, *John Adams,* 2: 983; William H. Gaines, Jr., "The Forgotten Army: Recruiting for a National Emergency (1799–1800)," *Virginia Magazine of History and Biography,* 56 (July 1948): 267–79.

14. Leonard D. White, *The Federalists: A Study in Administrative History* (New York: Macmillan, 1954), 275; Kurtz, *Presidency of John Adams,* 330; Smith, *John Adams,* 2: 983, 1004–07, 1033–34. Weigley believes that Hamilton intended all along to use the military as a political instrument to impose the kind of strong central government he believed the country needed. Weigley, *History of the United States Army,* 102–03.

MAJ. GEN. ALEXANDER HAMILTON.
Inspector General, 25 July 1798–15 June 1800.

On the other hand, aside from his excessive partisanship and unrestrained tongue, Hamilton made no positive movements to dominate the country. Just exactly what his intentions were for the new army remain unclear. He conceived of his position as one in which he could form and discipline the new regiments, molding them to his desires—absolute control of the army, if not the country. Being head of a large standing army likely suited Hamilton's romantic dreams, and there was always the possibility that military triumph might give him a permanent position of influence in national politics.[15] Whatever his ultimate objectives, Hamilton was immediately the dominant power in the army. He tried early to take over the War Department. McHenry wrote Hamilton on 25 July to tell him of his appointment as Inspector General. He wrote Washington at the same time to tell him that the President had gone home for the summer, and that it was planned to have Hamilton revise the army regulations.[16] As soon as Hamilton received the news in New York of his appointment on the 28th, he went to Philadelphia at once, presuming from his old friendship with McHenry that he would have complete control of matters. On the 30th, he offered to relieve the Secretary of War of the "vast mass of details" he must look after. But McHenry kept the department's reins in his own hands. Hamilton therefore returned home, writing Washington a letter criticizing McHenry rather harshly.[17]

Hamilton reached an uneasy truce with McHenry, whom he soon began to bombard with suggestions: As a major general, he outranked Brigadier General Wilkinson, although he had urged the latter's promotion. Washington refused to support that, and nothing came of the suggestion. In any event, Wilkinson proved subordinate enough, and the two got along well after Wilkinson reached New York in early August. Hamilton's actual relationship to the Regular Army was unclear because of a blurred chain of command, but the relations between

---

15. Richard H. Kohn, *Eagle and Sword: The Federalists and the Creation of the Military Establishment in America, 1798–1802* (New York: Free Press, 1957), 252–54. Kohn finds no basis for believing that Hamilton wanted to take over the country.
16. Bernard C. Steiner, *The Life and Correspondence of James McHenry, Secretary of War under Washington and Adams* (Cleveland: Burrows Brothers, 1907), 316, 319.
17. Ibid., 319–20; Hamilton to McHenry, 28, 30 Jul 98, in Henry Cabot Lodge, ed., *The Works of Alexander Hamilton*, 9 vols. (New York: Putnam, 1885–86), 6: 90, 91.

the two officers were tranquil. Wilkinson occupied himself with his regular duties, while Hamilton looked to the future. He became a one-man general staff, planning, organizing, and looking forward to the day he would command the provisional army—and so occupying most of 1798. But the longer Adams declined to call out the new army, the more Hamilton's frustration grew.[18]

Hamilton and the Paper Army

Legislation of 3 March 1799 contained a number of features apparently intended to curb Hamilton's ambition. The new position of General of the Armies of the United States, for instance, was a redesignation of the top post created as a suggested protection from the designs of the Inspector General. But the aging Washington was still the logical candidate, so Hamilton enjoyed his seniority and a dominant position that would have allowed him to overcome that vague obstacle. It is also apparent that a provision limiting his extra pay to $50.00, "in full compensation for extra services and expenses in the execution of his office," was a suggestion that Congress would hear from Hamilton no Steubenesque postwar plea for extra reward. Despite these minor limitations, the Inspector General emerged in a commanding position, controlling not only his own apparatus but also that of the Adjutant General, at least so far as the latter was his deputy. That control was realized at lower levels, where deputy inspectors general were ex officio deputy adjutants general in the armies to which they were attached. Hamilton, in other words, appointed and owned the Adjutant General's staff. That did not seem to bother William North, one-time inspector, who became Adjutant General 19 July 1798; he remained until discharged 15 June 1800.

The organization of 3 March 1799 was Hamilton's high point, integrating the Regular Army and any provisional force into one gigantic establishment with the Inspector General at its center. But once again, it was an exercise of paper work and a distinctly hollow victory in the political push and pull of the times. Washington never became General of the Armies of the United States, continuing in the inactive commission of lieutenant general until his death in December 1799. Not even the Quartermaster General was promoted as authorized to major general.[19] President Adams refused to raise additional troops, and Congress showed little inclination to pay for them. Moreover, the idea of a 51,000-man army with no war to fight was absurd in 1799. Not even at the height of its crises or triumphs had the Continental Army been able to attract anywhere near such a complement. Hamilton, with McHenry's considerable assistance, had created a potentially magnificent army, but in reality it lacked substance.

Hamilton never saw his expanded army, but it was not for want of trying on his part. He had come to an accommodation with McHenry, and bombarded the

---

18. Jacobs, *Beginning of the U.S. Army,* 227–29.
19. Heitman, *Historical Register,* 2: 567.

Secretary with an endless series of proposals and suggestions, many of them reflected in McHenry's message to Congress in December. Hamilton maintained his predictions of an impending war with France. One of his principal concerns was the nation's failure to shore up coastal defenses, and he urged major efforts to finance and build them.[20] The strength of an enlarged army also remained of great concern to him. By then, the nation's failure to meet what he believed to be an obvious threat from France caused Hamilton to abandon what little faith he had in the country's people. He avowed that national conscription by lot among all persons 18 to 45 years old would be required "in case of invasion," the number necessary to complete the entire army of 50,000. He believed a draft essential, even in the event of a direct assault by a foreign power dismissing the militia as not worth consideration.[21]

Hamilton and the Real Army

No enemy invaded the United States, and Hamilton's "entire army of fifty thousand" never rose, however coerced, to meet it. The growing futility of planning for an army of paper soldiers ultimately caused Hamilton to turn his attention to the real army. The first sign of his new interest was mixed—the publishing of regulations for a uniform that would clothe the grand army if it was raised but for the moment would clothe the present force. On 9 January 1799, the clothing of soldiers from the Commander in Chief to the lowest private was specified by the War Department. The Inspector General, particularly, stood out. He, his aides, and inspectors general, especially, were "to be distinguished by a blue plume."[22] His interest in the uniform showed that Hamilton's attention had passed increasingly to the small army already in existence. On 4 February 1799, he received command of all troops in the Northwest and the Great Lakes.[23] But Hamilton had already begun to sound like a commander, one with the eye of an inspector. He had, for instance, drafted a blistering circular letter to the commander at West Point on the subject of discipline, accusing him of tolerating laxity and low standards among his troops.[24]

Despite Hamilton's best efforts, the morale of the army remained low through 1799, and the quality and efficiency of the troops probably declined as well. The majority of troops in the Southwest were sick during the summer, and work on fortifications stalled. Things were somewhat better on the East Coast and north of the Ohio River, but the old problems persisted not only of indiscipline and self-interested officers but also of generally inadequate supplies that

---

20. Washington to McHenry, 13 Dec 98, in Morris, *Hamilton and the Founding*, 439. This letter was drafted by Hamilton.

21. Hamilton to James Gunn, 22 Dec 98, in Morris, *Hamilton and the Founding*, 439.

22. Orders, War Office, 9 Jan 99, in U.S. War Department, *Uniform of the Army of the United States;* Hamilton to McHenry, 18 May 99, in Morris, *Hamilton and the Founding*, 443.

23. Sanger, "Inspector General's Department," 238–39.

24. Hamilton to Commanding Officer at West Point and Dependencies (Circular), 30 Jan 99, in Morris, *Hamilton and the Founding*, 441–42.

were of poor quality as well. Hamilton protested vigorously, demanding reforms in supply procedures, but McHenry was not to be budged.[25]

Hamilton and the Army of the Future

Hamilton spent most of his time in the office instead of inspecting, still harboring hopes of a grand army. Consequently, he found time to ponder larger questions of the nation's military establishment. Cavalry, he told McHenry in July, was never well understood in the United States, whereas there were various theories of the "system" of cavalry in Europe. He believed it very important to experiment, and to devise a system of cavalry "adapted to the geographical circumstances of the country. For this purpose alone a small body of cavalry is indispensable." But he got none. In September, Hamilton urged the establishment of a "corps of invalids" for retired or disabled soldiers, suggesting that the United States was "perhaps the only country in which an institution of this nature is not to be found—a circumstance, which, if continued, will be discreditable." He also proposed a school for children of men in the Army and Navy, but still met only deafness.[26] McHenry was probably weary of Hamilton's grand vision of a great army, and no longer inclined to support even the smallest gestures toward achieving it. But the Secretary of War was receptive to another of Hamilton's projects—the establishment of a national military academy.

Hamilton had long promoted a system of military instruction, belaboring the idea with Washington in 1796. On 23 November 1799, he gave McHenry an elaborate plan for a complete military school system. A "fundamental" school with a two-year course would provide basic education to officer candidates for all branches of the Army and the Navy. Branch schools would continue the instruction for the artillerists and engineers, the cavalry, the infantry, and the Navy. There were to be professors of mathematics, geography, natural philosophy (physical sciences), and chemistry (including mineralogy). The school faculties would also include architects and drawing masters, riding masters, and fencing masters. To preside over the educational system, Hamilton called for a "director-general." The proposal was an immediate success among Hamilton's superiors. Washington endorsed it, as did President Adams in a strong, almost contentious statement to Congress in January 1800. When Congress asked McHenry what the educational structure would cost, he was able to demonstrate that its promotion of efficiency would save money. Submitting construction cost estimates for school facilities, McHenry persuaded Congress in the strongest terms. Hamilton's plans met approval in the Senate, but the House of Representatives left for recess and delayed its consideration of the measure until the following December. There the academy idea rested.[27]

---

25. Jacobs, *Beginning of the U.S. Army*, 228–32, 233–34.
26. Hamilton to McHenry, 2 Jul, 17 Sep 99, in Morris, *Hamilton and the Founding*, 443, 445.
27. Hamilton to Washington, 1 Dec 96, and Hamilton to McHenry, 23 Nov 99, in Morris, *Hamilton and the Founding*, 438, 445–46; Forman, "Why the United States Military Academy Was Established," 23–25.

The campaign to raise a large army had opened a wide division in the ranks of the Federalists since 1798. By early 1800, Adams' efforts to end tensions with France—the justification for the great army—served to worsen conflicts in the party ranks. The President was persuaded by early spring that McHenry and others in his cabinet were conspiring against him, even working against his reelection. So Adams cleaned house, among other things demanding McHenry's resignation on 5 May. But the President had difficulties locating a qualified successor. At last, after several knowledgeable individuals declined the honor, Samuel Dexter agreed to become Secretary of War as of 13 May, the effective date of McHenry's resignation. But he was reluctant to move into the office, and the War Department remained leaderless. Brigadier General Wilkinson, never slow to detect the way the winds blew, began to curry favor among the Jeffersonian Republicans, and ran the War Department.[28]

Hamilton's last hopes for military glory had by that time been dashed, and the Inspector General was out of office. On 14 May 1800, Congress repealed most of its military measures of the previous two years, discharged most of the men recruited, and reduced the Army to an authorized 4,436 officers and men—and thereafter budgeted for only about 3,400. Among other casualties of that legislation was the office of the Inspector General, which was disbanded. Except for the existence of an Inspector of Fortifications and an Inspector of Artillery and a few other staff officers, the general staff resembled its former self. A brigadier general headed the organization, and under him again were the ill-defined brigade major and brigade inspector. Even the Adjutant General disappeared from the organizational listing.[29] As a result of these changes, Hamilton requested permission on 13 May to resign his commission as of 1 June. He was turned down, because it was believed advisable for him to muster out personally the larger bodies of troops then to be discharged. That was his only real service as an inspector in the traditional sense, and it was probably thrust on him because of his political relations with the theoretical forces he had created. The discharges having been completed, Hamilton's resignation was accepted on 15 June. Thomas H. Cushing returned the same day to his role as "Acting Adjutant and Inspector." He took up residence in the new capital of Washington in the District of Columbia, and resumed his former routine.[30]

Hamilton left his mark on the U.S. Army, because he was a man of instinctive military sense and of wide interests and unbounded energy. His hopes for a military academy would soon be realized, although not exactly as he had proposed. His exhortations on discipline were welcome, and came at a time when the Army most needed them. Hamilton's abandonment of brutality in favor of incarceration for deserters had long-reaching effects, starting the

    28. Jacobs, *Beginning of the U.S. Army*, 239–40.
    29. Heitman, *Historical Register*, 1: 38, 2: 568; Thian, *Legislative History*, 86. The Inspectors of Artillery and Fortifications were to be detailed from the line.
    30. Heitman, *Historical Register*, 1: 38; Thian, *Legislative History*, 86; Sanger, "Inspector-General's Department," 239. Hamilton became president general of the Society of the Cincinnati and resumed pursuit of his ambitions through conventional methods.

Army on the road away from corporal punishment, eventually making "guardhouse" synonymous with "jail" in the minds of many, both military and civilian. But as his frustrated efforts to expand the Army reflected, the Inspector General left no lasting imprint on army organization. Hamilton was Inspector General in name only, at least if the term is to connote the head of a system of inspection. He was in effect the dominant officer of the organization, and behaved as a commander so far as the Secretary of War permitted him to. But the army he hoped to raise never came forth, and his role as commander went unrealized. Although Hamilton the Inspector General contributed little to the evolution of the U.S. Army's inspectorate, his possession of that title did have its own curious effects. Because of Hamilton, the title of Inspector General was divorced from inspection, and unalterably attached to the chain of command. When next the term Inspector General appeared, it would denote the Secretary of War's principal commander. The Army was to lack a commanding general for many years, and the Inspector General became its totem head. The precedent for this leadership requirement in 1812, as in 1798, reached back to the Continental Army, as misconceived by the nation's leaders. But Hamilton's title really ratified that use of the term.

Meanwhile, the Army tried to recover from its brush with partisan politics. Wilkinson moved to set right what he had believed wrong in army administration. The country was divided into twelve military districts for purposes of administration on 30 November 1800. There was also an attempt to ensure the honesty of inspection and mustering. The order prescribing the districts said that "the muster and inspection of a garrison should not be made by any officer belonging to it."[31] The clear implication was that someone else must be assigned to inspection and mustering. The recognition that it was desirable for the army to have within it a disinterested group of officers in order to avoid conflicts of interest and to gauge efficiency was clearly recognized in this provision. It was an unintentional endorsement of Washington's concept of inspection which, eventually, would require a formal system.

---

31. John R. Parsons, Jr., *History of Inspection in the Armed Forces* (Washington: Department of Defense, 1981), 15.

CHAPTER 7

Disgrace of an Inspector General

(1801–1813)

The accession of Thomas Jefferson to the presidency in March 1801 signified one of the major political transitions in American history. Liberal republicanism was supplanting centrist, conservative federalism. It was no accident that the new order of things had its effects on the army, for the military establishment had been a point of contention between political parties for some time. The Federalists founded the military system during the early national period, and they remained its defenders. They argued strongly for a large navy, coast and border defenses, and an adequate Regular Army. They were somewhat divided over what *adequate* might mean, but at the least they wanted the country to field enough soldiers to garrison the Indian country and to ensure preparedness for the next war.[1]

The Jeffersonian Army

The Republicans, under Jefferson's leadership, were of quite a different mind. Jefferson was hostile to the idea of a standing army, seeing it as an inherent menace to public safety. Had he been able, he would have eliminated the army altogether in favor of a universal system of militia. But the Militia Act of 1792 proved unenforceable, so the Regular Army endured as a necessary evil. Jefferson remained ambivalent—he reduced the Army as soon as he could after taking office, although he later proved willing enough to expand it when foreign affairs appeared dangerous. His chosen successor, President James Madison, and a thoroughly Jeffersonian Congress raised the Regular Army to the highest authorized strength it would achieve before 1898.[2] Both presidents showed an interest in the functions of the army. Thus, if Jefferson had any

---

1. Donald R. Hickey, "Federalist Defense Policy in the Age of Jefferson, 1801–1812," *Military Affairs*, 45 (April 1981): 63–70.

2. Ganoe, *History of the United States Army*, 108; Jacobs, *Beginning of the U.S. Army*, 236; Ward, *Department of War*, 132–33; Leonard D. White, *The Jeffersonians: A Study in Administrative History, 1801–1829* (New York: Macmillan, 1959), 212–13; Weigley, *History of the United States Army*, 104–05. See also Samuel P. Huntington, *The Soldier and the State: The Theory and Politics of Civil-Military Relations* (New York: Vintage, 1964), 196–98, and Dumas Malone, *Jefferson and the Ordeal of Liberty* (New York: Little, Brown, 1962).

ambitions for the Army, he desired that it be useful to the nation. To that end, he and Hamilton, cooperating for the moment, arranged for the establishment of a national military academy. They sowed the seeds of a future professionalism with that deed, but for some years the Army's chief distinction was its dedication to the laborious and nonstrategic activities of road building, river clearing, and exploration—habits firmly established during the Jeffersonian years. Otherwise, the Army declined drastically while Jefferson was in office—a victim not so much of Republican malice as of presidential neglect. Jefferson had other things to think about, and remained indifferent to army administration, which he left up to the Secretary of War.

The position of Secretary of War would have challenged the most energetic of men. From 1798—when procurement authority, except for the actual execution of contracts, returned to the War Department from the Treasury—to 1812, it was generally believed that the small size of the Army made it unnecessary to maintain in peacetime the staff departments required in wartime. So the Secretary of War served personally as Quartermaster General, Commissary General, Master of Ordnance, Indian Commissioner, Commissioner of Pensions, and Commissioner of Public Lands. He bought all supplies, but only after funds had been appropriated by Congress, which required that all procurement be conducted on a yearly basis. For subsistence, Anthony Wayne had urged in the late 1790s "the absolute necessity of some [more] effectual and certain mode of supplying the Army than that of private Contract," but the contract system continued. The system did not, perhaps could not, work, with the Army scattered all over a nearly roadless country, lacking any real supply organization worthy of the name. Some officers protested the constant shortage of food, clothing, and shelter, and described the living conditions of the men as "inhuman."[3]

Merely to administer the disorder of the War Department was nearly impossible. But the Secretary of War's situation was made even worse by the fact that he was also effectively the army commander. In keeping with Jeffersonian sentiments, no officer was allowed to command the whole army until 1821. That may have been intended to prevent an ambitious general from marching on Washington and seizing control of the country. More immediately, in Jefferson's administration the absence of a single commander prevented Brig. Gen. James Wilkinson from taking over the Army. Although Wilkinson was the senior officer in the United States Army, no one in the administration trusted him, despite his attempts to curry their favor.[4]

Jefferson appointed Henry Dearborn to superintend the War Department and its many and conflicting interests. Once a physician, Dearborn had been a Massachusetts Minuteman in 1775, then a gallant and energetic soldier who

3. Jacobs, *Beginning of the U.S. Army*, 225–29, 236, 252–53; Risch, *Quartermaster Support*, 116–19; White, *The Jeffersonians*, 215–28.

4. William B. Skelton, "The Commanding General and the Problem of Command in the United States Army, 1821–1841," *Military Affairs*, 34 (December 1970): 117.

had finished the Revolution as a lieutenant colonel. But by 1801, he was a superannuated drudge even more thrifty than Jefferson.[5] He remained, however, an advocate of a small, well trained, national army to oppose outside aggression. The militia in his and Jefferson's view was sufficient only for the maintenance of internal order. This philosophy, in part, explains his interest in the active army despite his constricting views on economy.

Before Dearborn could curtail him, Wilkinson attempted early in the Jefferson Administration to assert his authority over the Army. He did so by attacking one of its symbols: the queues sported by one and all in defiance of changing tonsorial customs. Wilkinson ordered hair to be cut short, on the grounds of cleanliness and neatness, on 30 April 1801. Officers and men alike protested strongly losing their pigtails, but despite some cases of resistance, eventually they complied.[6] Thereafter, the Jeffersonians progressively exerted their control over the Army, and tried to displace Wilkinson. They began by trying to professionalize the Army, then by reducing it. Adams had appointed a mathematics teacher for the artillerists and engineers, under the legislation of 1798, in January 1801. The Jefferson Administration continued the policy of employing a few teachers, mostly well-qualified Europeans. On 12 May 1801, Dearborn told Wilkinson that the President had decided to establish a military school at West Point with Maj. Jonathan Williams as the inspector of fortifications.[7] The position of Inspector of Fortifications, although first conceived to do what the title implied on behalf of the Secretary of War, became a misnomer. The incumbent was more a school principal than a superintendent of fortifications.[8]

The United States Military Academy at West Point was one of Jefferson's long-term objectives for the improvement of the Army. But it was of a piece with one of his immediate goals—reduction of the military force so far as circumstances would permit. On 19 December 1801, the Army numbered 248 officers, 9 cadets, and 3,794 enlisted men, in 4 regiments of infantry, 2 of artillery and engineers, and 2 companies of light dragoons. Still relying on the militia for peacetime security, Jefferson believed the active army was excessive for its mission of policing the frontier and guarding arsenals.[9] As a consequence, Jefferson proposed a "Military Peace Establishment," and Congress debated the subject during the first three months of 1802. Some members of the House of Representatives believed that Jefferson's cuts in the Army were too modest. They focused particularly on the provision of an aide-de-camp to the brigadier general, an office one of them described as a "perfect sinecure." But the

5. Jacobs, *Beginning of the U.S. Army*, 245–46; Heitman, *Historical Register*, 1: 363.

6. Jacobs, *Beginning of the U.S. Army*, 261–62.

7. Dearborn to Wilkinson, 12 May 01, quoted in Forman, "Why the United States Military Academy Was Established."

8. See Appendix B.

9. Ganoe, *History of the United States Army*, 108; Jacobs, *Beginning of the U.S. Army*, 236. See also A.D. Schenck, "The United States Army in the Year 1810," *Journal of the Military Service Institution of the United States*, 32 (1911): 443–44.

opponents decided not to fight the bill on that issue alone. It was nevertheless plain that Congress wanted no elaborate staff system for the Army.[10]

The act of 16 March 1802 reduced the number of infantry regiments from 4 to 2, cut the artillery to 1 regiment, eliminated the small mounted force, and established the Corps of Engineers. Infantry regiments had but 1 battalion, arrayed in 10 companies composed of 4 officers and 76 enlisted men. The artillery had 4 battalions, each with 5 companies of 3 officers and 76 enlisted men. The general staff was headed by the brigadier general, who was entitled to an aide and whose only immediate assistants were an "Adjutant and Inspector of the Army" and a "Paymaster of the Army," each detailed from the line. Beneath them stood the Army's roster of paymasters, assistant paymasters, military agents, surgeons, and surgeons' mates.[11] Wilkinson, too, suffered from the new arrangement. The law allowed him a salary of $225.00 per month, with rations, expenses, or other compensation. That was not enough to permit him to pursue his most important duty, which was to inspect the Army. Always resourceful, however, the brigadier general managed to supplement his income; a War Department accountant reported in 1811 that he had embezzled $7,891.03 from various official accounts.[12]

The Adjutant and the Inspector

Wilkinson had always placed great stock in inspection as a tool of command, serving as his own Inspector General since the 1790s. He now lacked the wherewithal to inspect and even a semblance of power to command. As the small Army passively existed during the first decade of the nineteenth century, Wilkinson turned his attention progressively toward more rewarding interests. He had always been a man of questionable character, but he soon became positively sinister. He got himself placed on a pension from the Spanish government in exchange for occasional information and possible future services. Later, he became involved in Vice-President Aaron Burr's vague plot to create an independent western empire, turning informer when the plot was revealed. His shadowy conduct was indicative of the small demands made on his official time.

The brigadier general was a functional nonentity whose position might as well not have been filled. Dearborn ran the Army, bypassing Wilkinson as much as possible. Although he was wont to handle much of his own correspondence, the Secretary used the Adjutant and Inspector of the Army as his office assistant and delegate. Thomas Cushing remained in that position until April 1807. He served Dearborn, not Wilkinson, and the Army soon learned

---

10. Debates, 21 Jan 02, in Thomas Hart Benton, *Abridgement of the Debates of Congress, From 1789–1856*, 16 vols. (New York: Appleton, 1857–1861), 2: 535–86.

11. *An Act fixing the military peace establishment of the United States*, Statutes at Large 2, sec. 3–4, 132 (1802); Thian, *Legislative History*, 107; Heitman, *Historical Register*, 2: 569.

12. Jacobs, *Beginning of the U.S. Army*, 254.

that the Adjutant and Inspector spoke for the Secretary, not for himself and not for Wilkinson. It was perhaps fitting, therefore, that Fort Dearborn, at Chicago, was established and so-named in response to instructions in Cushing's hand.[13] This arrangement with the Adjutant and Inspector spending his time as the Secretary's adjutant, and with the frustrated Wilkinson ineffective meant that the Army had no real inspectorate. That was not because its force was too small, which it was, but because there was no reason in Dearborn's mind to institute a formal inspection. But in the absence of critical review, the Army's situation encouraged inefficiency. The force was down to 2,732 men in 1805, scattered among forty-three posts. The largest group was the 375-man garrison at New Orleans, the next largest the 220 men at Detroit. The smallest post numbered 3 men at Fredericktown, Maryland. Thus the Army existed in name only.[14]

The War Department staff produced one piece of worthwhile paper work in 1806, when the Articles of War were revised. The original code had been adopted in 1776 and revised slightly in 1786. The new version, mostly an inventory of crimes and misdemeanors, reflected the more liberal spirit of the times by curbing the arbitrary brutality that had characterized Army justice. This more enlightened approach to military punishment can be seen as having its origins in some of Alexander Hamilton's recommendations while he was inspector. The continuity of ideas in the Army may be seen in that the text survived with only the most minor alterations into the 1890s. In fact, although there were various amendments, no wholly new code was adopted until 1916.[15]

Cushing returned to his line command and was succeeded as Adjutant and Inspector by Maj. Abimael Youngs Nicoll, an artillerist, on 2 April 1807. Nicoll had the distinction of being the first of the Army's hierarchy young enough not to have been a veteran of the Revolution—although he was the son of one. He was a graduate of Princeton and also a medical doctor, but he had been an artillerist since 1791 and a major since 1804. His relative youth brought him limited influence among the older men inhabiting the War Department. As had Cushing, he served mostly as the Secretary's adjutant.[16] Nicoll arrived in 'Washington during a time of increasing tensions between the United States and Britain. Jefferson had to admit by 1808 that the militia system was a failure, for the states were unable to raise the units requested of them. So the President asked Congress to triple the size of the Regular Army to nearly 10,000 men.

13. Cushing to Commander at Detroit, 9 Mar 03, Jacobs, *Beginning of the U.S. Army*, 255.
14. Walter Millis, *Arms and Men: A Study in American Military History* (New York: Putnam, 1956; reprint, New York: New American Library, n.d.), 59.
15. Jacobs, *Beginning of the U.S. Army*, 272–73; Jack D. Foner, *The United States Soldier Between Two Wars: Army Life and Reforms, 1865–1898* (New York: Humanities Press, 1970), 3–5. The Army also adopted its increasingly confused system of brevet commissions in 1806. Ganoe, *History of the United States Army*, 121; Weigley, *History of the United States Army*, 110–11.
16. Heitman, *Historical Register*, 1: 748; A. Elwood Corning, "Little Known Facts and Well Known Folks of Newburgh and Vicinity," Newburgh, New York, *News*, 8 June 1940, clipping in IG biographical files, Office of the Inspector General.

Congress complied on 12 March 1808, setting the Army's strength at a maximum 9,921 officers and men. The force included 5 new infantry regiments, 1 regiment of riflemen, and 1 each of light dragoons, artillerists, and light artillery, along with the small Corps of Engineers. There was also new money for coastal fortifications, and $200,000 for state militias. Despite this surge of activity, the office of Adjutant and Inspector was unaffected by the legislation. Inspection, however, was, at least in principle. When a "suitable proportion of the troops authorized by this act shall be raised," the President was authorized to appoint two brigade inspectors, taken from the line. They, presumably, were to be shared by the three brigadier generals. The brigade inspectors and all other staff officers were to be United States citizens. But except for them, the Army had a no more real staff than it had before.[17]

The Madisonian Army

Despite the legislation, the government was not committed wholeheartedly to an increase in the army, nor even to making it more efficient. Recruiting lagged, as a new administration—that of James Madison—took office in 1809. Madison was even more equivocal toward the army than Jefferson had been. Only 6,744 officers and men were in service by 1812, not the authorized 10,000. This neglect could not be justified with the growing tensions between the United States and Great Britain. While Madison pursued a wavering foreign policy and a vacillating policy on the military for three years, relations with the British deteriorated fitfully, compelling the President in 1810 to recommend filling out the Regular Army and assembling equipment for 20,000 volunteers and 100,000 militia. But he offered a budget that made that impossible, so nothing happened. Madison's Secretary of War, meanwhile, tried to take control of the War Department. Like Dearborn, William Eustis was a former physician, and a parsimonious individual. But he lacked even Dearborn's capabilities as an administrator. The growing but still small Army continued to vegetate.[18]

While the army as a whole went from bad to worse, the Adjutant and Inspector enjoyed a somewhat stronger position. By 1809, orders of the War Department were routinely issued from the "Inspector's Office." They ranged from the important to the routine. On 27 April 1809, all officers on furlough or absent from their corps were to report without delay to the Adjutant and Inspector, Nicoll, to explain the authority for their absence. Thereafter they were to report monthly. On 17 July, Nicoll was granted furlough, and Lt. Col. John Whiting

17. An Act to raise for a limited time an additional military force, Statutes at Large 2, sec. 3–4, 8–9, 481 (1808); approved 12 March 1808, 2 Stat. 481; Thian, Legislative History, 107–08; Heitman, Historical Register, 2: 570–71; White, The Jeffersonians, 213, 531–35; Weigley, History of the United States Army, 109.

18. Jacobs, Beginning of the U.S. Army, 342–43; Irving Brant, James Madison, 6 vols. (Indianapolis: Bobbs Merrill, 1941–1961), 5: 123–29, 437; Weigley, History of the United States Army, 112.

of the 4th Infantry was appointed to assume the duties of the Adjutant and Inspector of the United States Army.[19] The importance of the inspectorate was clear when Congress decreed on 30 April 1810 that the Inspector of the Army was among the officers of the United States whose letters and packets "shall be received and conveyed by post free of postage." That reflected the volume of the Adjutant and Inspector's correspondence, for he served more as adjutant than as inspector. Nicoll was not about to make more of the office than that, because he was absent during most of 1811. When Nicoll took another furlough on 25 June 1811, Eustis told Col. William Beall to act as Adjutant and Inspector. Five days later, the duty again went to Col. John Whiting. Nicoll was again absent from his command on 30 August, with Capt. James Gibson acting in his place. Eustis wearied of ordering changes of addresses in Nicoll's office and demanded, "Until further orders all letters and returns for that office will be simply addressed 'to the Adjutant and Inspector of the Army.' "[20]

Facing Another War

Meanwhile, war with Britain appeared ever more likely. But Madison and Congress vacillated once again. When the President brought himself to ask for 10,000 additional regulars, 50,000 federal volunteers, and $3 million to pay for it all in 1811, Congress authorized a Regular Army of 25,000, a volunteer army of 30,000, and a budget of $1 million. But the government was reluctant to implement the legislation, so nothing important came of that flurry of lawmaking.[21] This lack of firm activity was to be regretted when war finally erupted in June 1812. It burst upon an American nation that was decidedly belligerent but, except for a sufficiently empowered central government, no more prepared for military adventure than it had been in 1775. The tiny Regular Army of less than 7,000 men was scattered among small outposts. The troops were mostly untrained and commanded by men of little talent or energy, a mixture of aging veterans of the Revolution and well-connected men drawn from civilian life. There were only seventy-one graduates of West Point available. The administrative apparatus for army supply was insufficient for peacetime, and hopelessly inadequate for a continental war. Furthermore, there was little

---

19. General Order (GO), Inspector's Office, 27 Apr 09, and Orders, W. Eustis, 17 Jul 09, both in U.S. War Department, General Orders Relating to Inspection, and the Inspector General's Department, collected by A.C. Quisenberry (n.p., 1893) (hereafter cited as GORI&IG). This remarkable compendium was assembled by the Inspector General's chief clerk in 1893 and was updated at irregular intervals over the next decade and a half. Athough one of the records of the Inspector General's Office, it was for some unknown reason not incorporated into the body of that office's records in the National Archives. The original reposes in the staff offices of the Navy and Old Army Branch Office of the National Archives, Washington, D.C., and comprises every general order affecting inspection, beginning with the two cited above. A copy is in DAIG.

20. *An Act regulating the post-office establishment, Statutes at Large* 2, sec. 24, 592 (1810); Thian, *Legislative History*, 108; Orders, W. Eustis, 25 Jun, 30 Jun, and 30 Aug 11, all in GORI&IG.

21. Brant, *James Madison*, 5: 396–401; Weigley, *History of the United States Army*, 114–115.

vigorous direction given by the Congress. It knew instinctively that it must prepare for war. To do so it drew upon fading recollections of the Revolution, and acted with an incredible combination of meddling and bungling. The lawmakers' intense preoccupation with minor details knew no limits; on 11 January 1812, for example, they fixed the exact amount of soap and candles to be provided to enlisted men with their rations.[22]

The Army appeared adequate in June 1812, but only on paper. When war was declared on the 18th, its authorized force included 17 regiments of infantry, 4 of artillery, 2 of dragoons, 1 of riflemen, and the Corps of Engineers. But except for 7 infantry and 2 artillery regiments, and part of the dragoons and engineers, most of the army was recently authorized and as yet unraised. The organization of regiments varied from 10 to 18 companies each until Congress standardized them on the 23d—25 infantry regiments then were all to have 10 companies of 90 privates each. The states were also asked to place their militia on call.[23] Nor was the army organized or staffed to wage a big war. The average age of its generals was about sixty years. And as had been the case since Wilkinson was shunted aside, there was no commander of the whole U.S. Army. Secretary Eustis supervised nine military districts, each under a general officer.[24]

A serious problem of the organization was Congress' persistent tampering with the military supply system, which in 1812 was in a state of collapse. Legislation fixing the peacetime military establishment on 16 March 1812 abolished the positions of quartermasters and turned their duties over to yet another system of "military agents," intended to be directed by the Secretary of War. The lawmakers reversed themselves twelve days later—at least for the war emergency—and established a Quartermaster Department headed by a Quartermaster General. But the department was divided into eight districts, only four of which (all north of the Potomac) were accountable to the Quartermaster General; the others answered to the Secretary of War via military commanders. The first Quartermaster General, an old soldier of the Revolution, lasted less than a year.[25]

Reestablishment

It was in this distressing context that the title of Inspector General reappeared in the United States Army. Congress began to prepare for war on 11

22. Weigley, *History of the United States Army*, 115; David A. Clary, *These Relics of Barbarism: A History of Furniture . . .* ", 31; Clifford L. Egan, "The Origins of the War of 1812: Three Decades of Historical Writing," *Military Affairs*, 38 (April 1974): 72–75; U.S. War Department, Adjutant and Inspector General's Office, *Military Laws and Rules and Regulations for the Armies of the United States* (Washington: n.p., 1813), 75 (hereafter cited as *1813 Regulations*).

23. Marvin A Kriedberg and Merton G. Henry, *History of Military Mobilization in the United States Army, 1775–1945* (Washington: Department of the Army, 1955), 44–47; Weigley, *History of the United States Army*, 118–19.

24. Weigley, *History of the United States Army*, 119; Kriedberg and Henry, *History of Military Mobilization*, 46.

25. L.D. Ingersoll, *A History of the War Department of the United States . . .* (Washington: Francis B. Mohun, 1879), 181; Risch, *Quartermaster Support*, 136–39.

January 1812, much as it had in 1798. Legislation authorized the appointment of "one Inspector General," with the rank and pay of a brigadier general. He was permitted two assistant inspectors, taken from the line, with the compensation of lieutenant colonels. An officer detached to serve as an assistant to the Inspector General was not to lose his rank as a result. Finally, the law required that no staff officer appointed under its provisions could receive pay until actually called into service. The whole law was lifted almost bodily from that which had enabled Hamilton to become Inspector General despite the misgivings of others.[26] Even though Congress did not specify the functions of the Inspector General, the War Department did, revealing that the office bore not only Steuben's indelible stamp but also a small touch of Hamilton's. The "Regulation of the Duties of the General Staff," 4 May 1812 specified that the inspector would note discipline, facilities, and equipment and would also conduct musters and examine financial accounts.[27]

The statement of duties was explicit enough, but it actually served to complicate further the chain of command. An inspector, as Washington and the reluctant Steuben had defined the job, was supposed to monitor discipline; but the new regulations said he was "to superintend and enforce discipline," which was the job of a commander acting on the reports of an inspector. That provision in the War Department regulation probably reflected the memory of Hamilton's tenure in the office. So did, it is likely, the first duty—to organize the Army—although Steuben's role at Valley Forge may have helped to legitimize that provision. Nevertheless, with no commander other than the Secretary of War, the Inspector General's real place in the scheme of things remained to be seen.

On 16 May 1812, Congress authorized the President to appoint, from among the captains and subalterns of the line, "so many subinspectors as the service may require, not exceeding one to each brigade." On 26 June, Congress authorized two brigade inspectors taken from the line, one permanent inspector general, two assistant inspectors general taken from the line, and an Adjutant and Inspector of the Army also taken from the line. The distinction between the new brigade inspectors and the subinspectors previously authorized for brigades was not immediately apparent. By that point, not even the lawmakers, it appears, knew just whom they were talking about.[28] Nevertheless, Congress and the War Department had to come to grips with the office of Inspector General, for the nation had already declared war on Britain, as of 18 June. The preoccupation with details persisted anyway. On 6 July, Congress allowed the President to appoint a Deputy Inspector General in any army other

26. An Act to raise an additional military force, Statutes at Large 2, sec. 4–6, 25, 671 (1812); Thian, Legislative History, 108.

27. Regulation of the Duties of the General Staff, Adjutant General's Office (hereafter cited as AGO), 4 May 1812, in GORI&IG.

28. An Act making further provision for the Army of the United States, Statutes at Large 2, sec. 3, 735 (1812); An Act respecting the pay of the Army of the United States, Statutes at Large 2, sec. 1, 782 (1812); Heitman, Historical Register, 2: 572–73; Thian, Legislative History, 108.

than that in which the Inspector General served. The Inspector General's mail remained free from postage.[29]

Eustis selected an Inspector General that same day. A week later, on 14 July, he announced he had appointed Col. Alexander Smyth of the Rifle Regiment to be Inspector General of the Army with the rank of brigadier general. Eustis' instruction suggested that Smyth would have power to command. As for the Adjutant and Inspector of the Army, Eustis put him out of business in the same order, placing Major Nicoll under the Adjutant General, Thomas Cushing, as one of his assistants.[30] Smyth was the third Inspector General, so-called, of the United States Army. He was the first to disgrace himself in the position—so thoroughly that the job

BRIG. GEN. ALEXANDER SMYTH. *Inspector General, 6 July 1812–3 March 1813.*

was abolished in order to get rid of him. But in July 1812, he appeared a not illogical candidate for the office.

Alexander Smyth was born in Ireland in 1765, migrating with his minister father to Virginia at about the start of the American Revolution. Educated at home, then in the law, he became a deputy county clerk when he was 20 years old, and was admitted to the bar four years later. He practiced law throughout his life, and was active in Virginia politics as well. From 1792 to 1809, he was a member of the Virginia legislature, in the upper house during the last year. Probably because of Smyth's political connections, the Virginian President Jefferson (exponent of the citizen-soldier) commissioned him colonel of the Rifle Regiment, 8 July 1808. He was ordered to Washington in 1811 "to prepare a system of discipline for the army." His work was published the next year as *Regulations for the Field Exercise, Manoeuvres, and Conduct of the Infantry of the United States*, approved by the War Department. His reputation as the author of a drill manual apparently impressed Eustis, or someone. It should actually have served as a warning. Smyth's regulations were merely an abridged translation of the French Army's infantry regulations of 1791, not wholly applicable to American practice. The colonel's contribution to the cause

---

29. An Act making further provisions for the Army of the United States, and other purposes, Statutes at Large 2, sec. 2–3, 784 (1812); Thian, *Legislative History*, 109.

30. Orders, W. Eustis, 14 Jul 12, in GORI&IG. Thomas Cushing, former Adjutant and Inspector, was now Adjutant General; William North had been offered the post but had declined it. On 16 July, Eustis appointed Capt. William King, of the 15th Infantry assistant to the Inspector General. Orders, W. Eustis, 16 Jul 12, GORI&IG.

of discipline, accordingly, was not much. Steuben's regulations remained such as the Army had, republished in 1808 and again in 1812, accompanied by some of Dearborn's penny-wise economy regulations. Several private imprints were also published. However, among the old veterans designating themselves military men in 1812, Eustis did not have many candidates to undertake the Inspector General's first duty. That was to organize the Army—which was then totally unorganized. Smyth had produced a volume of regulations—however useless, they were credentials.[31]

The new Inspector General was a handsome man, whose rather boyish good looks reflected a similar character. He was addicted to comically pompous bombast that most people treated with ridicule, although Eustis may have been favorably impressed with so many brave words. Winfield Scott, who was among those unfortunate enough to serve under Smyth, later characterized him with a great deal of charity, but clearly enough to demonstrate what kind of man had become the Inspector General. Scott felt that Smyth had no talent for command, and, although able in some fields, his tendency to brag and his pomposity made him ridiculous in the eyes of his soldiers.[32]

Smyth Goes to War

Smyth was less an inspector general than Hamilton had been, his title notwithstanding. His rank was just brigadier general, so he was not the senior officer of the Army; at the time, no one was, although the various Revolutionary veterans commissioned as brigadiers claimed seniority by tenure. Eustis tried to run the war himself, handing out inadequate orders to the various theater commanders and department heads. If Smyth had had the ability or the inclination to fulfill his mandate under the legislation establishing his office, he might have been of real service—despite Eustis' ineptitude and the general atmosphere of chaos. But Smyth wanted glory, and Eustis permitted him to pursue it. The Inspector General left for the battlefield in early September, leaving no one behind to organize the army or to fulfill any of the other duties expected of an inspector general. The small staff remaining in Washington processed returns and did other paper work.

The proponents of war against Britain had had one great aim in view from the outset—the annexation of Canada. To that end, they had fanned hastily organized forces of regulars and militia across the northern border. In the east,

---

31. *DAB*, 9: 373–74; Heitman, *Historical Register*, 1: 905; *1808 Regulations*; U.S. War Department, *An Act for Establishing Rules and Articles for the Government of the Armies of the United States* (Washington: R.C. Weightman, 1812); Virgil Ney, *Evolution of the United States Army Field Manual: Valley Forge to Vietnam*, Appendix B, Report of the Field Manual Review Board (Ft. Belvoir, Virginia: U.S. Combat Development Command, 1966), 7–8. The *1812 Regulations* apparently do not differ from the *1808 Regulations*. Smyth has been dismissed as "just a commonplace braggart without redeeming qualities," Jacobs, *Beginning of the U.S. Army*, 384–85.

32. Winfield Scott, *Memoirs of Lieut.-General Scott, LL.D.*, 2 vols. (New York: Sheldon, 1864), 1: 54n.

troops under Gen. Henry Dearborn—the ailing former Secretary of War had donned uniform, along with many other vintage warriors of the Revolution—were to attack Montreal along the Lake Champlain route. In the center, Stephen Van Rensselaer, a major general of New York militia, was to invade Canada across the Niagara River frontier. To the west, Brig. Gen. William Hull—another veteran of the Revolution—was to take an expedition out of Detroit into Upper Canada.

Inadequate preparation and incompetent leadership had begun to corrode the entire enterprise by late summer. Hull allowed himself to be outfoxed by much smaller British and Canadian forces, and on 16 August surrendered Detroit and all troops under his nominal command without firing a shot. The British and their Indian allies followed that with a brutal campaign that left them in control of Lake Erie and the Michigan country. Hull's performance was disgraceful, and earned him a court-martial and a death sentence for cowardice—remitted only because of his record during the Revolution. After their triumph, the victorious British under General Isaac Brock rebounded to the Niagara River, which he and about a thousand men reached on 23 August. They dug into strong defensive positions anchored by Fort George. The goal of taking Canada, if not the safety of the United States, seemed imperiled. It was to the Niagara that Alexander Smyth went to the rescue.[33] At this point, Hull's sorry showing, when combined with problems in the forces along the eastern frontiers, unruly and disorganized combinations of regulars and volunteers, and growing chaos in supplies and financing, should have impelled the government to halt, take stock, plan a course for the future, and organize the Army to follow its plan. But the nation's leaders did nothing of the kind, and accordingly gave the Inspector General little to do as inspector general. With another impetuous dash at the border in the making, Smyth determined to be a part of it.

Dearborn established himself in Albany to organize supplies and reinforcements. Van Rensselaer faced Brock over the Niagara, torn between his own reluctance and fears of a British attack on the one hand, and Dearborn's demands for action on the other. His force grew throughout September, and when Smyth arrived with 1,700 regulars at the end of the month, the American position was secure. Van Rensselaer had about 8,000 troops altogether, half of them regulars, facing about a thousand regulars and 1,200 militia and Indians strung along the river opposite. Smyth refused to cooperate with Van Rensselaer because the latter was not a regular. Van Rensselaer was not the sort of man inclined to court-martial the insubordinate Smyth, as he should have. Thus the results of his generalship were not surprising—he launched a cross-river assault against Queenston Heights on 13 October.[34]

---

33. For the general course of the war, see the recent account of Pierre Berton, *The Invasion of Canada, 1812–1813* (Boston: Little, Brown, 1980) as well as Henry Adams, *History of the United States During the Administrations of Jefferson and Madison*, 9 vols. (New York: Scribner, 1889–1891), pertinent parts of which are contained in Harvey A. DeWeerd, ed., *The War of 1812* (Washington: Infantry Journal, 1944).

34. Berton, *Invasion of Canada*, 219–49. British General Brock died in the action.

The better American troops, in particular regulars led by Winfield Scott, fought gallantly, but the battle of Queenston Heights was a debacle. Van Rensselaer left the Army, and Smyth became the senior officer on the Niagara frontier. "I must not be defeated," he declared when he took command, and ordered construction of enough boats to take 4,000 men to the Canadian shore. That was ridiculous, for half of his army was unfit to fight and most of his regulars were untrained recruits; furthermore, his hospitals and cemeteries were full and militia desertions exceeded a hundred men per night. Nevertheless, Smyth tried to launch a new invasion, predicting martial glory. He was ridiculed by his disenchanted soldiers. After weeks of indecision, he made two remarkably inept efforts, fully anticipated by the British, to launch attacks across the Niagara River. The lack of leadership, poor preparation, and demonstrated indecision infuriated the exasperated American soldiers. On 27 November, following the second invasion try, the troops were demoralized.[35] What happened next was described by, among others, Maj. John L. Thompson who said that all military discipline collapsed.[36] That was an understatement. Smyth's army exploded in rage. Officers broke their swords, and privates their muskets. The militia ran wild, shouting and firing their weapons. Before long they focused on the cause of their discontent, and began shooting at Smyth's tent, riddling it. One of his aides was almost killed, having his belt and cap shot away. Smyth increased his personal guard, then moved his headquarters repeatedly to protect his life. His continued service in the Army was impossible, and politically unacceptable.

The Office Is Abolished

Smyth asked for leave to return home to Virginia, and Dearborn, with the hearty support of Eustis, granted it to him. The office of Inspector General, thoroughly debased by his performance, disappeared with him. On 3 March 1813 Congress abolished it, replacing it with an Inspector General's Department headed by an adjutant and inspector general. Smyth held no commission in the line, so he was "disbanded," no longer an officer. The erstwhile Inspector General asked to be returned to the Army, to "die, if Heaven wills it, in the defence of his country." His petition was denied, but Smyth did not disappear entirely from the Army's future. Beginning in 1817, he served in the House of Representatives for all but one term until his death in 1830. His committee assignments included military affairs.[37] Alexander Smyth, one of the strangest people ever to don a general's uniform in the American army, was not totally to blame for his failure. Because he was incompetent, he was least able to judge

---

35. Ibid., 257–62.

36. As quoted in Ganoe, *History of the United States Army*, 126. Other officers, including Peter B. Porter, offered strikingly similar descriptions.

37. *An Act for the better organization of the general staff of the Army of the United States*, *Statutes at Large* 2, sec. 1–4, 11, 819 (1813); Sanger, "Inspector General's Department," 241. *DAB*, 9: 374. Smyth's role in later army legislation is discussed below.

his own limitations. Responsibility for his assignment as Inspector General, and for allowing him to neglect the proper duties of that office, rested with the Madison Administration, and, in particular with Secretary of War Eustis.

The American army's education did not have to be so difficult. Not only were the wherewithall and the talent available to create a respectable military organization, the tools were also at hand. One would have been a consolidated system of command, under a single Commanding General. Granted, that posed political difficulties, and Eustis was at least wise enough to realize that none of the most prominent candidates for such a position was competent enough to make it effective. But although Eustis was a poor substitute, he continued to function as a commander in a rather loose way. The Army never was consolidated during the war. A unifying factor still available to Eustis—or to a commander if he had located one—was the office of the Inspector General. As constituted in the legislation, that official enjoyed wide powers, and in the absence of a Commanding General could have organized the Army and made it efficient. He would at least have made it possible to know how many men were in service, where they were, and how efficient they were, in order more effectively to dispose of them. Given that only 12 percent of the Army during the war were regulars or long-term volunteers, the rest being militia, a coordinated system of training and inspection, such as Steuben had developed during the Revolution, should have seemed essential.[38] Thanks to Smyth, however, the office of Inspector General disappeared in early 1813, and with it its potential utility in training and organizing the Army. And thanks to Eustis, who had treated the position as merely another commission without reference to its stated purpose, its value to the Army had never been tested.

---

38. H.A. DeWeerd, "The Federalization of Our Army," *Military Affairs*, 6 (1942): 143–52.

CHAPTER 8

Origins of the Office of the Adjutant and Inspector

(1813–1815)

The American cause was enhanced in December 1812, when William Eustis stepped down as Secretary of War. He was succeeded on 13 January 1813 by John Armstrong. The new Secretary accomplished some good. Unfortunately, his efforts could not overcome the problems imposed by his own personality. He did not have the support of the Congress or most of the cabinet because of his reputation as a plotter and critic against politicians with whom he disagreed. His irascible, unsympathetic nature quickly alienated most of the senior army commanders and those few in the government willing to give him a chance. Without support, his indecisiveness and his penchant to overmanage left the Army no firm direction when it was most needed.

Army Reformation, Inspectorate Restoration

Armstrong was energetic, with results both good and ill for the Army and for the cause. He had been a major critic of the administration's handling of the war. When Eustis departed under fire from Congress, Madison appointed Armstrong, a veteran of the Revolution, hoping the New Yorker would bring Northern support and do a better job. Although Armstrong spent much of his secretarial energy in plots to displace the leadership of the Republican Party, more serious, for the war effort, was his sometimes unfounded faith in his own military ability. Eustis had never permitted anyone else to command the Army, and had tried to manage the war from the War Department on his own. But at least he had not tried to play general himself. Armstrong, however, neglected his true office, and at least twice took to the field during campaigns, thoroughly scrambling command relationships with his presence and his orders. Needless to say, army command was never unified during his tenure.

Even the Secretary's martial pretensions had their beneficial effects, however. He perceived early that, as de facto commander, he required competent staff support. He encouraged Congress in March 1813 to follow through on a Eustis proposal to provide the Secretary with a general staff to furnish all administrative services. Unlike their predecessors, the new staff officers were to be based in Washington; they were the permanent management staff of the War Department. The result of that, and some of Armstrong's other reforms, was a considerable improvement in supply and logistics—although they remained inadequate throughout the war. More immediately beneficial to the Army was Armstrong's effort to eliminate superannuated, incompetent generals from the roster, which the enemy had serendipitously begun during the way of 1812. The generals newly appointed were, with some exceptions, energetic, efficient, and competent. They were also younger than their predecessors; under Armstrong their average age declined to thirty-six years by 1814.[1] Armstrong's most visible contribution to army organization was the act of 3 March 1813, which increased the force to 57,351 officers and men and authorized a simple form of a general staff. Among its members were 1 adjutant general and inspector general along with 8 inspectors general and 16 assistant inspectors general. There were also a separate medical staff, Quartermaster Department, and Ordnance Department.[2]

The legislation used the word *department* in its two current senses. As a separate bureaucratic organization or subdivision of a larger organization, the word identified the establishments of Quartermaster and Ordnance, both termed *departments*. That usage was relatively recent, and apparently an Americanism. More common at the time was the definition of department as a sphere of activity. It was in that sense that the legislation referred to staff activities such as those of the inspectors and adjutants.[3] The Inspector General's Department, as an organization, therefore was not established in the 1813 legislation. Although it may not have been a formal organization, the Inspector General's activity was a welcome restoration within the Army. The legislation said that the departments of the Adjutant General and the Inspector General would include an ''Adjutant and Inspector-General, with the rank, pay, and emolument of a

---

1. *Concise Dictionary of American Biography*, 2d ed. (New York: Scribner, 1977), 29 (hereafter cited as *CDAB*); Weigley, *History of the United States Army*, 121–23; White, *The Jeffersonians*, 237–38; Brant, *James Madison*, 6:68, 167, 261; E. Edward Skeen, *John Armstrong Jr., A Biography* (Syracuse, N.Y.: Syracuse University Press, 1981), 53. The legislation of Armstrong's period is discussed below. For Armstrong's presentation of his wartime record, see John Armstrong, *Notices of the War of 1812*, 2 vols. (New York: Wiley and Putnam, 1840).

2. 2 Stat. 819; Heitman, *Historical Register*, 2: 574–75. Regarding training, riding masters and sword masters continued in the Dragoons.

3. *The Oxford English Dictionary* (hereafter cited as *OED*) lists the first use of the term to identify the major divisions of government in a statement by George Washington in 1791. Its application to a lesser bureaucratic organization, as opposed to a sphere of activity or interest, apparently originated with the establishment of the Ordnance and Quartermaster's Departments on 3 March 1813. It should be noted that standard references, including Heitman's *Historical Register* and such texts as the National Archives inventory of the Records of the Office of the Inspector General, state that the Inspector General's Department was created in the 1813 legislation. Not only is that an error in etymology, but a close examination of the law and of resulting army organization demonstrates that no such organization came into existence at that time. It may also be observed that the formation of separate departments was still tentative in 1813: Only the Ordnance Department had an apparent chief, the Commissary General of Ordnance. There were eight ''Quartermaster-Generals [*sic*].'' Purchasing came under one Commissary General of Purchases, with deputies and assistants, but was not distinguished from the general staff. The medical staff had preeminent a Physician and Surgeon-General and an Apothecary-General.

brigadier general,'' along with the inspectors general, adjutants general, and assistants of each title. Inspectors general were to have the ''brevet rank and pay and emoluments of a colonel of infantry,'' while assistant inspectors general were treated as brevet majors of cavalry. The latter were to be taken from the line, while inspectors general ''may be taken from the line or not, as the President may deem expedient.'' Finally, the appointment of the highest officer, the Adjutant and Inspector General, was to be accomplished rather indirectly, Congress formally decreeing ''That the President of the United States be, and is hereby, authorized, if he shall deem it expedient, to assign one of the brigadiers-general to the principal Army of the United States, who shall, in such case, act as Adjutant and Inspector-General, and as chief of staff of such Army.''[4] The legislation continued the two brigade inspectors, taken from the line and previously in existence, but did not regard them as part of the Inspector General's ''department.'' Since there were only thirteen brigade majors authorized, it may be assumed that brigade inspectors functioned as brigade majors—that is, as adjutants and aides or secretaries to the brigadier generals. The role of the Adjutant and Inspector General, however, was clearly specified in the law. He was not the head of a War Department organization, but specifically the chief of staff for the main army—effectively Steuben's role, although without such specific authorization. After Smyth's poor performance, it is likely that Congress wanted no more inspectors general in position of command.

The distribution of inspectors general and assistant inspectors general, when compared with the number of general officers, suggested that the former were to serve as inspectors, possibly chiefs of staff, to major generals—ordinarily, district commanders. The assistants performed like services for brigadier generals, who were mostly field commanders. The inspectors had no separate existence as a group, and no central coordinating authority. Inspection, accordingly, was restored as a function of command, as it had been under Washington and Wayne. The Adjutant and Inspector General was a linguistic anomaly, probably adopted as a way of vacating Smyth's hold on office. The officer functioned as did other inspectors general and adjutants general. His title signified only his place in the most important field army, although there could have been an inspector general and an adjutant general immediately under him in that army. To clarify the duties of inspectors general and others, Congress also adopted ''Rules and Regulations of the Army for 1813.'' The regulations were essentially Steubenesque, but they elaborated on various staff services. The duties of inspectors general were summarized as follows: ''These will be divided under the following heads, viz: Mustering and inspecting troops of the line, and militia detachments serving with them; Selecting places of encampment, and posting guards; Superintending the police of the camp and of the march; Inspecting parades; and Making half yearly confidential reports to

4. *An Act for the better organization of the general staff of the Army of the United States,* *Statutes at Large* 2, sec. 1–4, 11, 819 (1813).

the War Department, of the state of the Army, division, or detachment, to which they belong."[5]

Steuben would for the most part have recognized the duties of inspectors general in 1813, and been comfortable with them. He might have been startled, however, by the inspectors' power to issue orders in some circumstances, and Washington would have blanched at independent communications between inspectors and the War Department. In the absence of a single army commander, however, the War Department merely stepped into the place Washington would have filled. The integrity of command was not in principle compromised, except as an army commander might regard his inspector as a War Department spy. That was because each commander was required to review and comment upon the reports before they were forwarded to the War Department.

Mustering and inspection were the first of the duties of inspectors general, imposed in order to correct the chaotic lack of information on manpower that had characterized the Army in 1812. Inspectors general were to muster troops once every two months before they were paid. Pay was to be issued according to muster rolls signed by an inspector general or his assistant, or in their absence by a designated officer. Three copies of muster rolls were to be prepared: one for the district paymaster and two for the War Department (one for the department's accountant, the other for the Paymaster General). Semiannual musters of the whole Army, "whether regular or militia," were to be made on or before 1 January and 1 July, "and rolls thereof, in alphabetical order, forwarded to the War Department as promptly therafter as possible." Mustering clearly was an accounting device for the War Department, independent of army commanders. Inspection, however, was a tool of command. Inspections were to be of two types, "stated and occasional." The former were to take place at the end of every month, the latter "as often as the General commanding the district, the Chief of the Staff, or the Inspector General, may think proper." Both focused on arms, equipment, clothing, and all other objects of economic concern. Army horses were to be inspected quarterly. Unfit animals were to be branded in the presence of an inspector and given to the Quartermaster Department for sale. A return of every inspection was to be filed in the appropriate Inspector General's office, "for the information of the general commanding the district, and half yearly returns of inspection shall be made to the War

---

5. *Rules and Regulations of the Army for 1813*, Doc. 125, 13th Cong., 1st sess., *American State Papers, Military Affairs*, vol. 1 (1813) (hereafter cited as *ASP-MA*) 1. The War Department, through the Adjutant and Inspector General's Office, published these as *Military Laws and Rules and Regulations for the Armies of the United States* (*1813 Regulations*, previously cited), with additional material. It appears that they first became public in *Niles' Weekly Register*, which published the regulations serially in early 1813. Those governing Adjutants General, Inspectors General, the Topographical Engineers, the Purchasing Department, and the army uniform appeared on 22 May. *Niles' Weekly Register*, 4 (22 May 1813): 187–89. Regarding uniforms, the regulations of 1813 made only one distinction for inspectors. Along with adjutants and other staff officers, they were "permitted to embroider the button holes of the collar only." United States War Department, *Uniform of the Army of the United States, Illustrated, from 1774–1889* (Washington: Quartermaster General's Office, 1889).

Department.'' The inspectors were also expected to be responsible for camp selection and security, control of prisoners, supervision of sutlers, and enforcement of march discipline.[6]

These latter duties were some of the more curious parts of the regulations. To begin with, inspectors served their commanders as provosts and legal officers as well as inspectors. That answered the absence of law enforcement and judicial officers in the army establishment, but it was a considerable extension of the inspector's authority. Steuben had drawn upon himself and his subordinates whatever staff services were either unprovided or which he could absorb, in effect becoming both staff and chief of staff. The 1813 regulations made mandatory such a broadened roll of the inspector. Even more interesting was the granting to inspectors of the power to punish disorderliness or deviation from the order of march. That was clearly and traditionally a command power. So long as inspectors remained loyal agents of commanders, as Wayne's inspectors had, it would work well enough. But the power held the potential for a division of authority within a command that could have serious, disruptive effects on the organization. Officers and men must not only answer to their supervisors, but to inspectors as well. The duty of inspecting parades, as described by the regulations, made the inspector the eyes of the commander in the daily review.

In selecting places for encampment and posting guards, the regulations very briefly made inspectors agents of their commanders: "This duty shall be performed under the directions of the commanding general; and the Inspector, in performing it, shall call to his aid an officer from each corps of engineers." The latter provision meant that both construction and topographical engineers were to be involved in the layout of camps. The confidential half-yearly reports to the War Department were clearly a device by which the department hoped to acquire factual information on the efficiency and honesty of its military units.[7] The 1813 regulations, the most extensive guidance inspectors had yet received, owed a great deal to Steuben's legacy. While they stressed thoroughness and unbiased frankness, more interesting is what they did not say. They did not mention the preparation of regulations or training. As recently as 1812, the preparation of regulations and the organization and training of the army were among the first duties of the Inspector General. But without a single inspector general for the whole U.S. Army—the Adjutant General was a grandly titled inspector, adjutant, and chief of staff for one of the field armies—such a duty could not be fulfilled by the inspectorate. And an inspectorate, thanks to the 1813 regulations, is what the Inspector General's department had finally become, free of responsibilities more properly placed elsewhere. Preparation of regula-

---

6. *Rules and Regulations of the Army for 1813*, Doc. 125, 13th Cong., 1st sess., 1813, *ASP-MA*, 16:384.

7. The 1813 regulations of the War Department had a further provision governing inspectors. When the militia drafts of 100 men gathered and were organized as a company, each unit was to be mustered and inspected by an inspector general, assistant inspector general, or designated Regular Army officer, the muster report to serve as the basis for pay. *1813 Regulations*, 239–40.

tions for congressional approval rested with the War Department staff, while training was the responsibility of line commanders. Inspectors were to monitor adherence to the former and the efficiency of the latter, free of vested interest in either.

Another break with the past occurred in 1813. The administrative function of the adjutant had long dominated inspection. When the staff was small, it generally had little time for inspection. But when the Inspector General had been revived in 1798 and again in 1812, he dominated the Adjutant General, as Steuben had in the Continental Army. In 1813, however, the function of Adjutant General finally achieved its status as the first and most important of staff services, a logical reflection of its control of official communications. While adjutants general in 1813 were entitled to $90.00 per month in pay, $30.00 worth of forage, and six rations, inspectors general received just $75.00 in pay, $12.00 in forage, and six rations.[8]

The new inspectorate should have been of immeasurable value in organizing the large army Congress called for in March. But that proved difficult to demonstrate, because the recruiting effort was a dismal failure. Congress had increased the Army to an authorized forty-four infantry regiments and over 57,000 officers and men, and in addition had invited members of volunteer and militia formations to enlist in the Regular Army for one year. But by the end of 1813, no more than 20,000 regulars were on hand.[9]

Adjutant and Inspector General Pike

The War Department, meanwhile, used the new position of Adjutant and Inspector General where it appeared that help was needed most—in the northern theater of the war. Henry Dearborn continued in nominal command in New York, but he was impotent to command the forces under him. He claimed illness as his excuse for inaction, and wanted to retire. He was no source of inspiration for his troops, who called him "Granny."[10] Despite his evident infirmities, Congress and the War Department wanted action in Dearborn's theater, and the old general could not offer it personally. Rather than replace him, Armstrong gave him a chief of staff. Zebulon Montgomery Pike was promoted to brigadier general on 12 March 1813, assigned to Dearborn's army, and named Adjutant and Inspector General. The appointment may have come as a surprise to many observers. On the surface, Pike appeared almost as odd a person for such an assignment as Smyth before him. He had greater military experience than Smyth, but his only combat had come in a confused action on

8. *Niles' Weekly Register*, 4 (8 May 13): 158.

9. Kreidberg and Henry, *History of Military Mobilization*, 48–51; Weigley, *History of the United States Army*, 120.

10. Pierre Berton, *Flames Across the Border: The Canadian-American Tragedy, 1813–1814* (Boston, Little, Brown, 1981), 41.

the Canadian border in November 1812, when his troops got lost in darkness and shot at one another.[11]

Pike was born in 1770, the some of an army officer. He became a cadet in his father's regiment while a boy and then a lieutenant in 1799. His rise in the small army was steady, making captain in 1806, major in 1808, and lieutenant colonel in 1809, all in the Infantry. After serving briefly as a quartermaster officer, Pike became a colonel on 6 July 1812.[12] He was fairly well known to the public before 1812, because of his adventures as an explorer. Wilkinson sent him from Saint Louis to discover the source of the Mississippi River in 1805. He returned a few months later with erroneous findings. Wilkinson next sent him into Spanish territory at the head of an exploring party in 1806. That was, of course, an illegal invasion of a foreign domain, and it came to grief when Pike and his men were captured and interned for several months.

Pike, however, was what Smyth merely professed to be: an effective commander. He was bold, even impetuous. He had eloped with his cousin, infuriating her rich father, and declared, "Whilst I have breath I will never be the slave to any." Like Smyth, Pike lusted for fame and glory and was devoted to the grand turn of phrase, but fortunately not to purple proclamations. When he became adjutant general and inspector general, he wrote to his father that he hoped to be "the happy mortal destined to turn the scale of war." Failing that, "may my fall be like Wolfe's—to sleep in the arms of victory." To his patron Wilkinson he wrote, "If we go into Canada, you will hear of my fame or of my death. For I am determined to seek the 'Bubble' even in the cannon's mouth."[13]

When Pike arrived at Sackets Harbor, Dearborn handed him command of an attack on York, capital of Upper Canada on the north shore of Lake Ontario. It was a complicated land and naval assault, but Pike had everything well in hand from the embarkation to the landings on 27 April 1813. Supported by fire from ships, his troops advanced smartly through thick woods, destroying a force of British grenadiers, then pushing into the town's outer works. They seized a battery in a sharp fight, then advanced against a blockhouse from which the British withdrew, even though it held a large ammunition magazine that the commander did not want to fall into American hands. Therefore he had a fuse train lit, without taking care to warn either his own men or the Americans. As Pike sat down with his maps to plan his next move and interrogate a

---

11. W. Eugene Hollon, *The Lost Pathfinder: Zebulon Montgomery Pike* (Norman: University of Oklahoma Press, 1949), 205–06.

12. Heitman, *Historical Register*, 1: 792; *DAB*, 7:599–600; ibid., 40. On Pike's career, see Hollon, *The Lost Pathfinder*, and on Pike's New York period in particular, W. Eugene Hollon, "Zebulon M. Pike and the New York Campaign, 1813," *New York History*, 60 (July 1949): 275–95. Important sources on his earlier period are Donald Jackson, ed., *The Journals of Zebulon Montgomery Pike, With Letters and Related Documents*, 2 vols. (Norman: University of Oklahoma Press, 1966); Elliott Coues, ed., *The Expeditions of Zebulon Montgomery Pike*, 3 vols. (New York: Harper, 1895); and Prucha, *Sword of the Republic*, 88–94. See also Donald Jackson, "How Lost Was Zebulon Pike?" *American Heritage*, 16 (February 1965): 10–15, 75–80.

13. Both quotes in Hollon, "Zebulon M. Pike and the New York Campaign," 27 and 202. The allusion was to British General James Wolfe, who died during his victory at Quebec in 1759.

BRIG. GEN. ZEBULON M. PIKE. *Adjutant and Inspector General, 12 March 1813–27 April 1813.*

prisoner, the magazine erupted in a gigantic, deadly fountain of timbers and stone. Over 100 Americans and 40 British troops, mostly local militia, were killed outright.

Pike was among the casualties, crushed by a huge boulder. When others rushed to his aid, it is reported on good authority that he said, "Push on, my brave fellows, and avenge your general!" As he was carried from the field to the ship where he died, the soldiers gave him a resounding cheer. His last official act was to receive the news that the Stars and Stripes had risen over the blockhouse, even as the enemy fled.[14] This display of gallantry and leadership in Pike's last hours as Adjutant and Inspector General could not have been more different from Smyth's. That he received the cheers of his men, rather than their gunfire, demonstrated that he was a good appointment. But like Smyth, he had never done anything remotely suggested by his title: He was a troop commander. Ultimately, he was not even remembered for that, but for Pike's Peak, a mountain named for him that he did not discover and had not climbed.

The Inspectorate and the Army After Pike

Pike's death left a vacancy in the War Department as well as in Dearborn's command. Armstrong apparently wanted an adjutant and inspector general at hand to be his own chief of staff. When he asked for one while Pike was in the North, he was turned down on the ground that there could be only one Adjutant and Inspector General, who must be either appointed and confirmed in that office or a brigadier general designated by the President. Neither came forth for a year after Pike's death. In the interim, the office was served by successive assistant adjutants general.[15] Despite the absence of formal, presidential and legislative action for the senior position, Armstrong did manage to appoint a

---

14. Berton, *Flames Across the Border*, 46–51; Hollon, "Zebulon M. Pike and the New York Campaign," 275–95. Pike's commission as brigadier general arrived after his death, so he actually was a locally brevetted brigadier during the campaign against York.

15. Heitman, *Historical Register*, 1: 39; Thian, *Legislative History*, 86. Those handling the affairs of the office were Maj. C. K. Gardner until 30 December 1813, and Col. J. DeB. Walbach from that date until 28 May 1814. Walbach was relieved by Maj. John R. Bell, assistant inspector general.

number of inspectors general (colonels) and assistant inspectors general (majors) during 1813, the twelfth and the last named in August. There were six of each rank, and except for one they were all assigned to the headquarters of the several districts. Abimael Y. Nicoll, who doubtless had never left the Washington office, was the senior inspector general, assigned to duty in the War Department.[16] Nicoll probably continued to serve as an adjutant to the Secretary of War.

The Army's inspectorate began to prove its value late in 1813 and into 1814. Here and there the troops became more efficient, better regulated. That made up for the failure of the recruiting program, so on 30 March 1814 Congress continued the general staff in the same form as the year before. The lawmakers ceased trying to inflate the paper army, being satisfied with the addition of a regiment of coast defense troops in July 1813 and three more regiments of riflemen in March 1814, raising the authorized force to 62,274 officers and men. But recruiting lagged until a British invasion threatened. The Regular Army included about 35,000 men by September 1814, while about the same number of militiamen were available for extended duty. They were supplemented by hundreds of thousands of militia theoretically available in their own districts to repel raids and invasions.[17] Manpower, however, had not been the Army's major problem. The improvement of the Army depended upon the character of the various commanders, who thanks to Armstrong's appointments and the passage of relics like Dearborn were an increasingly effective lot overall. It is clear that some of them regarded inspectors general and assistant inspectors general principally as training officers, although the regulations did not assign that duty to them. Nonetheless, training was required, and that role was ordained for inspectors by tradition reaching back to the Revolution.

For instance, Winfield Scott, commanding the left division of the 9th Military District in the North, established a celebrated camp of instruction in New York in March 1814. There he trained the forces that stood up against the British regulars at Chippewa and Lundy's Lane later in the year. Scott, an adjutant, had originally assigned the training program to the district inspector, Maj. Azor Orne. But he was compelled to assume responsibility for the program personally when his commander, Maj. Gen. Jacob Brown, ordered Orne to join him at Sackets Harbor. This reassignment had little practical effect. In fact, Orne could never have done better than Scott. Housing 3,000 regulars and volunteers in tents, Scott put them through a rigorous program of drill and instruction, and turned them into a formidable military force—a far cry from the chaotic mobs that had carried the burden of war thus far. The program was

---

16. *Army Register, 1813*; Doc. 125, 13th Cong., 1st sess. (1813), *ASP-MA*, 16:384; *Niles' Weekly Register* 4 (1 May 1813): 146–47. Sylvester Churchill, a future inspector general, became an assistant inspector 29 August 1813, and served on the staffs of Wilkinson, Izard, and Macomb during the war. He became acting adjutant general of the Champlain Department in 1815. Franklin Hunter Churchill, *Sketch of the Life of Bvt. Brig. Gen. Sylvester Churchill, Inspector General U.S. Army, . . .* (New York: Willis McDonald, 1888), 16–17.

17. Weigley, *History of the United States Army*, 121; Heitman, *Historical Register*, 2:567–77.

BRIG. GEN. WILLIAM H. WINDER.
*Adjutant and Inspector General, 9
May 1814–2 July 1814.*

complete, from battle maneuvers down to the smallest details. Remembering the earlier problems, Scott made camp and field police and sanitation, and personal hygiene, part of his course. Meanwhile, he also gathered supplies, obtained intelligence about the enemy, and did all the other preliminary work for the coming campaign.[18]

The Adjutant and Inspector General's Office

Thanks to Armstrong's interest in attaching the Adjutant and Inspector General to his own retinue, that vacant office became his chief administrative agency by early 1814, actually issuing orders to the Army. That was not what Congress had intended for the position, but it answered the Secretary's need for an adjutant general senior to all others. With inspecting officers otherwise occupied, the Adjutant and Inspector General's Office frequently assigned line officers to muster and inspect troops, usually retroactively—in other words, to afford the soldiers back pay.[19] The vacancy was filled finally on 9 May 1814, when the President appointed Brig. Gen. William H. Winder to the office of Adjutant and Inspector General. Winder was a prominent Maryland attorney who had been commissioned a lieutenant colonel of infantry 16 March 1812, colonel four months later, and brigadier general on 12 March 1813. The 39-year-old general may have appeared to be one of the Army's rising young stars. He had served creditably enough on the northern frontier, but his actual military experience was very limited. Winder had been captured in his only action and paroled in June 1813, and was unavailable for field service until June 1814. His appoint-

---

18. Jeffrey Kimball, "The Battle of Chippewa: Infantry Tactics in the War of 1812," *Military Affairs*, 31 (winter 1967–68): 169–86; Charles Winslow Elliott, *Winfield Scott: The Soldier and the Man* (New York: Macmillan, 1937), 146–53; Weigley, *History of the United States Army*, 129. See also Benson J. Lossing, *The Pictorial Field-Book of the War of 1812*, 2 vols. (New York: Harper & Bros., 1860), 802, for Maj. Thomas S. Jessup's account of the training of the 25th Infantry under Scott's direction.

19. Orders, Adjutant and Inspector General's Office, 19 Apr 14 and 27 Apr 14, in GORI&IG. The first-cited order appointed officers to muster and inspect troops at posts in the 5th Military District for March and April. The second-cited order appointed Lt. F. Baden of the Ordnance Department to muster and inspect troops at Greenleaf's Point, Washington, D.C., for the months of March and April.

ment as Adjutant and Inspector General, accordingly, may have served merely to find work for an officer otherwise unemployable. In any case, Winder had started high in the army, and risen fast. "It is a misfortune," Winfield Scott recalled of Winder's situation, "to begin a new career with too much rank, or rather, too late in life."[20] Winder's appointment evidently displaced Maj. John R. Bell, who had been the most recent interim tenant of the office. On 24 May, the War Department ordered, "Major J.R. Bell, Acting Inspector General, will perform the duties of Adjutant General in the room for Colonel Walback until further orders."[21]

At least potentially, the Adjutant and Inspector General in the War Department stood at the top of two pyramids—one of adjutants general, the other of inspectors general. Winder could therefore have been the chief of staff of the Secretary of War, who remained a poor substitute for a Commanding General. In actuality, however, the two did not get along, and both were swiftly overtaken by events. The staff of adjutants and inspectors continued to run the office in the War Department. By the summer of 1814, among their paper work were fruits of the inspectorate established the year before—in particular, half yearly confidential reports to the War Department. Two such documents survive for the period ending 30 June 1814.

Assistant Inspector General Nathaniel N. Hall reported on Sackets Harbor, under the command of Brig. Gen. Edmund P. Gaines, following almost point by point the format required in the regulations. The 1st Regiment of Light Dragoons, he said, showed good discipline, and had their papers in order. In the 2d Regiment, however, the papers were in a "confused state," with even records of terms of enlistment lost; that caused the men to complain. Hall did believe that a new commander, recently appointed, was working to improve things in that regiment. Artillerists at Sackets Harbor impressed Hall very favorably. He praised their commander, saying that the discipline of his troops and their drill was as good as any in the service. Generally, however, Hall complained that troops at Sackets Harbor followed drill manuals selected personally by the various company officers, with a general absence of uniformity. Turning to the infantry, the men of the 13th Regiment, said Hall, were mostly green, but were developing well under the influence of a common drill manual for the regiment. The 29th Infantry was "destitute of discipline in general," by which Hall meant proficiency in drill more than deportment, although he said the men also lacked the "habit of obedience." The regimental major was "destitute of the qualifications for an officer," while "the rank and file almost to a man are lousy," there barracks in a "filthy state," and the sickness rate high.

Hall was more pleased with the 1st Rifle Regiment, which he said was well led and drilled. Provisions, however, were "very indifferent," mostly inferior

20. *DAB*, 10: 382–83; *AMB*, 485; Heitman, *Historical Register*, 1: 1049; Scott, *Memoirs*, 1: 92.
21. Orders, War Department, 24 May 1814, in GORI&IG.

at Sackets Harbor, although the forage supply was good. The general hospital was maintained in a "remarkably high state," while some of the regimental hospitals exhibited an "indifferent state," the artillery hospital a notable exception. Hall discovered "no errors" in courts-martial in the command, and said that the weapons on hand were sufficient but old. Finally, he reported that he had mustered the command for their pay.[22]

Major Daniel Hughes conducted a tour of military posts in the 7th Military District before returning to line command 1 June 1814. He found the barracks at New Orleans "large, airy and commodious," capable of holding 700 men. One building, he said, needed new floors, and there were some surface draining problems. The garrison had been there for six months, during which he had inspected it several times, and was improving steadily in its efficiency. The men's health was good, better than it had been in the past, while the general hospital was in fine order, "extremely well conducted" by a surgeon, mate, and two civilian physicians under contract. But the quartermaster, Hughes complained, was uncooperative, his refusal to provide straw, mosquito bars, and other necessities causing the sick to suffer needlessly. Hughes also made similar reports on conditions at Fort Saint Charles and Fort Claiborne. Hughes' itinerant inspectorate was a taste of things to come for the Army's inspectors. Once the war ended, the large forces would disband, and what was left of the U.S. Army would disperse in small posts across the continent. Inspection would be their chief contact with the higher military establishment. As prophetic as Hughes' routine were some of his comments. He closed his report with a complaint that would recur for decades: The troops of the 2d Infantry, he said, were overworked building posts that were soon abandoned. "This duty had considerably thinned the ranks of the Regiment."[23]

The adjutants and inspectors in the War Department processed the flow of inspection reports, musters, and other paper, but it appeared that there was nothing for the Adjutant and Inspector General to do. Under the law, Winder should have borne that title only as chief of staff of the main army. Armstrong, however, wanted a chief of staff of his own. But it soon became apparent that he did not want Winder. . . . If anyone filled the role of Adjutant and Inspector General as Congress had conceived it, it was Winfield Scott, who had become Dearborn's Adjutant General during 1813. General Brown had replaced the doddering Dearborn by the summer of 1814, while Scott in his camp of instruction had created the first thoroughly trained, professional body of American soldiers since Anthony Wayne's Legion of the United States. Brown and Scott took their troops into Canada in July, beating British regulars at Chippewa on the 3d in a brutal, stand-up confrontation. A greater battle occurred on the 25th

---

22. Nathaniel N. Hall, Confidential Report of the State of the Post of Sackets Harbour, now under the immediate command of Brig. Gen. Gaines, of the commanding officers of the Regiments, Corps & detachments & their Staff and the progress made by each corps or detachment, 30 June 1814, in Inspection Reports 1814–1842, RG–159.

23. Confidential Report of Maj. D. Hughes, the Asst Inspector Genl of the Posts and Troops in the 7th Military District, ending 30 June 1814, in Inspection Reports 1814–1842, RG–159.

at Lundy's Lane, where Scott took an important hill in a murderous series of charges, then beat off three great counterattacks. The Americans proved that they could stand up to the best professionals in the world, but they were as bruised as the enemy. Among the casualties were Brown and Scott, both wounded, and the Americans retired from the field during the night.[24]

Scott, therefore, was Pike's real successor. He was that in his official position, and in practice. He earned the title by virtue of his place and his activities in the main army. But there is no evidence that he was ever considered for the job. Winder had the title before Scott's labors had borne fruit. In any case, Scott was the last person who would have willingly played servant to Armstrong. For better or worse, Winder was Adjutant and Inspector General of the Army. Thanks to Secretary Armstrong, it proved to be for the worse. Armstrong was, as usual, engaged in a series of plots and conspiracies to undermine the Republican Virginia dynasty. He wished that New Yorkers and other friends might rise, to carry him into the White House on their shoulders. But for a year he had found himself frustrated at every turn by a Virginian, Secretary of State James Monroe. They feuded ceaselessly. In fact, they had but one point of agreement—that Washington was safe from British attack.

But the capital's safety began to erode in April, when Napoleon conceded defeat, leaving the British almost unlimited manpower with which to wage the American war. President Madison had peace commissioners at work in Europe, but they made little headway. Madison received news from them on 26 June that "there can be no doubt that if the war continues, as great a portion of that disposable force as will be competent to the objects of the British government will be employed in America."[25] When it became apparent that Washington, D.C., itself could be threatened by this enlarged British force, President Madison took it upon himself to plan for his capital's defense. In addition to issuing calls for militia, he created a new military district, the 10th, to which he named Winder as commander. Winder was picked both because he was available and because he was the nephew of the governor of Maryland whose state would have to provide the bulk of the militia if the British attacked. Winder assumed command on 2 July 1814, stepping down from the Adjutant and Inspector General position at the same time. He was disastrously defeated at Bladensburg in August, after which the British burned Washington's public buildings. Winder lingered in the Army after that until his honorable discharge in June 1815.[26]

---

24. These actions are admirably placed in the context of the Army's evolution in Weigley, *History of the United States Army*, 129–30. See also Louis L. Babcock, *The War of 1812 on the Niagara Frontier* (Buffalo, New York: Buffalo Historical Society, 1927); Ernest Cruikshank, *The Battle of Lundy's Lane* (Welland, Ontario: Lundy's Lane Historical Society, 1893); Berton, *Flames Across the Border*, 317–59; and chapter 3 in Fletcher Pratt, *Eleven Generals: A Study in American Command* (New York: Sloane, 1949).

25. Walter Lord, *The Dawn's Early Light* (New York: Norton, 1972), 17–18.

26. *AMB*, 485; *DAB*, 10: 382; Heitman, *Historical Register*, 1: 1049.

Adjutant and Inspector General Parker

Winder had not served long enough as Adjutant and Inspector General, nor had he enjoyed sufficient support from the Secretary of War, to define the office. The adjutants and inspectors composing the office staff continued their routine as if he had never been present. Armstrong, meanwhile, became the target of immediate public outrage over the occupation of Washington, which the British evacuated after vandalizing it. Monroe became interim Secretary of War on 17 August, and Armstrong resigned on 3 September. The interim Secretary of War also remained Secretary of State, and was spread thin by his attempts to manage the entire administration while also cultivating his presidential ambitions. He therefore needed staff support more than had Armstrong, and at last consolidated them in the office of the Adjutant and Inspector General, which by late September was the issuing address of the Army's orders.[27]

Daniel Parker was appointed Adjutant and Inspector General, with the rank of brigadier general, on 22 November 1814, as confirmed by the Senate. He was at the time chief clerk of the War Department, and apparently had been an aide to Secretary Armstrong during the battle of Bladensburg. A native of Massachusetts, Parker had spent the first decade of the century on his 1,200-acre estate near Paris, in France. There, despite his questionable relationship with Mrs. Henry Preble, he was regarded by Parisians as an informal American minister to France. William Crawford, Minister to France in 1813 and, later, Secretary of War, spent considerable time at Parker's estate.[28] Parker was not a military man, and evidently Monroe did not want one. He was an administrator with well-developed political connections, well suited to preside over office details. When he announced Parker's appointment as Adjutant and Inspector General, Monroe said clearly, "This office is considered as connected with this Department, and unconnected with the line of the Army."[29] That is what Armstrong had wanted all along.

An effective administrative organization was especially required, because the Army was about to demobilize, with all of the procedures and paper work that discharge of a large and varied force entailed. Peace commissioners set to work in earnest at Ghent, Belgium, in the fall of 1814, their demands shifting with each news of events on the several battle fronts. The war finally appeared a frustrating stalemate, and in December peace was concluded on the basis of

---

27. See, for instance, the order of the Adjutant and Inspector General's Office that appointed an infantry officer to "muster and inspect" two regiments "from the time they were last mustered up to September 30, 1814" and the one that transferred Assistant Inspector General Maj. George P. Peters to the Adjutant General's Department as an assistant adjutant general, to rank from 29 August 1813, which appear to be the only such orders from that period. Orders, Adjutant and Inspector General's Office, 26 Sep and 28 Sep 1814, in GORI&IG.

28. Heitman, *Historical Register*, 1: 796; Lord, *Dawn's Early Light*, 171; Francis S. Drake, *Dictionary of American Biography Including Men of the Time* (Boston: James R. Osgood, 1872), 687; Chase C. Mooney, *William H. Crawford, 1712–1834* (Lexington: University Press of Kentucky, 1974), 58–59. Parker's time in France overlapped Armstrong's.

29. Orders, Adjutant and Inspector General's Office, 23 Nov 14, in GORI&IG.

BATTLE OF NEW ORLEANS. *Andrew Jackson's inspector at this fight, Maj. Arthur P. Hayne, was cited for gallantry and credited with organizing the motley forces available for victory.*

the *status quo ante bellum,* the diplomats' way of saying there was no change. Two weeks later, as if to seal the treaty but in ignorance of it, Andrew Jackson won a stunning victory over the British near New Orleans. Nevertheless, dismissal of the Army began late in 1814, and accelerated after the Treaty of Ghent. There is some reason to believe that Parker may have assumed functional control over the disparate force of adjutants and inspectors, and in January he added at least one assistant inspector general, by transfer, to the staff at the War Department. The War Department ordered on 21 February that no soldier enlisted for the duration could leave his regiment before he was mustered, inspected, and paid by an inspector general "or officer doing that duty." The inspector was to send to the Adjutant and Inspector General's office all certificates of service-connected disability, for filing pending pension applications.[30]

With Madison increasingly distracted, Parker became the chief administrative official of the Army, at least so far as personnel was concerned. His responsibilities expanded after 3 March 1815, when Congress ordered drastic reductions in the Army, down to 12,383 officers and men. The act was a stopgap measure, reflecting disagreement on how small the Army should be, until a permanent decision could be made. The discharges contemplated were nevertheless wholesale, cutting the force to eight infantry regiments, one light artillery regiment, a corps of heavy artillery, a rifle regiment, and the Corps of

---

30. Orders, Adjutant and Inspector General's Office, 11 Jan and 21 Feb 15, in GORI&IG.

Engineers. The dragoons were gone, as were the staff services and departments necessary to implement the discharge, let alone manage the Army. Of the inspectorate, there remained only four brigade inspectors, taken from the line, with no apparent presence in Washington.[31] The reductions were too drastic, particularly the elimination of almost the entire staff. Monroe left the War Department in March, and his successor was not immediately in sight. President Madison therefore ordered the "provisional" retention of critical positions, including the Quartermaster General and the Adjutant and Inspector General. Daniel Parker was retained to preside over the dissolution of the Army, but only "until circumstances will permit of [his] discharge, without material injury to the service," as the War Department put it officially.[32]

The roster of adjutants and inspectors declined, despite the retentions in high places. Parker began to shift those remaining to where he believed them to be most needed. In April, for instance, Col. A. P. Hayne, a past and future Inspector General, was assigned as an adjutant general to replace another who had resigned.[33] The pressure of demobilization paper work had begun to make adjutants more useful than inspectors. Accurate records and accounts were very important because the great question facing the officer corps was who would and who would not be retained in service. In a reversal of tradition, the failures of the early part of the war had led to prejudice against officers of the prewar period, the implication being that seniority would count against a man's chances of continued service. A board of general officers assembled to select those to be retained expressed alarm at the difficulty of the task, and the extent of dismissals and reductions in rank that would occur.[34]

The peace establishment was finally announced on 2 December 1815. It showed an adjutant and inspector general on the general staff. The Army also included two adjutants general and four brigade inspectors, "officers of the line." Also during the year, *Scott's Exercise* codified by a board of officers under Winfield Scott, finally supplanted Steuben's blue book, replacing it with tactics reflecting French inspiration. The U.S. Army was theoretically prepared to fight the war just ended.[35] . . . But the Army was not ready for peace, at least in the eyes of Congress. Further reductions were in store, and the provisional arrangements for army administration were questionable. The new Secretary of War, William Crawford, recommended a permanent staff structure for the War Department in 1815, but no one heard him.[36] Short of the obvious, there were even more difficult choices ahead at the end of 1815. Some way had to be

---

31. *An Act fixing the military peace establishment of the United States, Statutes at Large* 3, sec. 3, 224 (1815); Thian, *Legislative History*, 110; Weigley, *History of the United States Army*, 139; Carlton B. Smith, "Congressional Attitudes Toward Military Preparedness During the Monroe Administration," *Military Affairs*, 40 (February 1976): 22–23.

32. Mooney, *William H. Crawford*, 80; Heitman, *Historical Register*, 2: 578–79; Orders, Adjutant and Inspector General's Office, 17 May 15, as quoted in Thian, *Legislative History*, 110.

33. Orders, Adjutant and Inspector General's Office, 5 Apr 15, in GORI&IG.

34. *Niles' Weekly Register*, 8 (29 Apr 1815): 146.

35. Ibid., 9 (30 Dec 15): 301; Ney, *Evolution of the Field Manual*, 8.

36. Risch, *Quartermaster Support*, 178–79.

found to ensure that no incompetents or drunkards remained in the officer corps. Moreover, there was reason to believe that there were far more able and efficient candidates than there would be places for in the coming years. How, then, to select the better from the merely good?

A possible answer would present itself before long. It was the Army's inspectorate, finally shaped into effectiveness during the war, but falling apart in the aftermath. Inspection reports offered an opportunity to see who the good officers really were, based on their character and performance, and on the efficiency of their subordinates. Parker had before him an opportunity to demonstrate the importance of inspection as a permanent activity in the Army. In the event, he did so, and when the military establishment hit its statistical bottom, inspection remained separately and permanently accounted for. But the Adjutant and Inspector General was not able to demonstrate his own necessity. His office passed from existence.

CHAPTER 9

End of the Adjutant and Inspector General (1816–1821)

William H. Crawford—like Armstrong, an old associate of Daniel Parker—became Secretary of War 15 August 1815. He held the job a little over a year, leaving 22 October 1816. He was hardly a full-time secretary, being considerably preoccupied with his ambitions of occupying the White House. Because he was too busy to run the War Department personally he needed an effective staff, but the staff he enjoyed was likely to disappear at any time—it rested only on the provisional arrangements made by the President in 1815. Experience during the war had shown that it was no longer possible for one man with a few clerks to run the Army with any effectiveness. Crawford therefore argued strongly for a permanent general staff, and on 24 April 1816 Congress gave him that staff.

A General Staff and New Inspectors

The new legislation substantially ratified Madison's provisional staff, retaining most important officers and services. Parker was secure, the law affirming the position of Adjutant and Inspector General. There was also to be one inspector general, and an "assistant . . . to every brigade, which shall supersede the brigade . . . inspectors now existing."[1] The legislation further set up

---

1. Mooney, *William H. Crawford*, 80–81; Weigley, *History of the United States Army*, 133; Risch, *Quartermaster Support*, 178–79; An Act for Organizing the General Staff and Making Further Provisions for the Army of the United States, approved 24 April 1816, 3 Stat. 297; Thian, *Legislative History*, 110. On 15 March 1816, incidentally, the Army uniform was completely respecified. Only passing attention was given to inspectors and other staff officers, who were to wear the same "cocked hats without feathers, yellow gilt bullets buttons, and buttonholes in the herring bone fashion" as general officers. In addition, "All General Officers will be permitted to embroider the buttonholes. The Adjutant Generals [*sic*], Inspectors General, Quartermaster General and their deputies and assistants, will be permitted to embroider the buttonholes of the collar and cuffs only." When the uniform was next respecified, 27 March 1821, inspectors remained similarly undistinguished in their dress. In the following decades, inspectors general wore the uniform of their rank, decorated as specified for general staff officers. Orders, Adjutant and Inspector General's Office, 15 Mar 16 and 27 Mar 21, and subsequent regulations, in *Uniform of the Army of the United States*. The first distinction for officers of the Inspector General's Department appeared with the uniform regulations of 1872, when they and officers of other departments were to have initials embroidered onto the shoulder knots of dress uniforms—"I.D." for inspectors, "A.D." for adjutants, "M.D." for medical officers, and so on, the "D" meaning "Department." That practice continued in subsequent uniform regulations.

BRIG. GEN. DANIEL PARKER. *Inspector General, 22 November 1814–1 June 1821.*

two large geographic divisions, North and South, each headed by a major general. Each of these divisions was divided into two subdistricts headed by brigadier generals. It would appear that the intention of the law was to give each major general his own inspector general and each brigadier an assistant inspector general. It could not be that simple, however, because although the law included two adjutants general who could be assigned each to a division, there was only one new inspector general cited in the law. He could not be paired so easily with the continued position of the Adjutant and Inspector General filled by Daniel Parker. Parker had become the Army's chief administrator by then, the equivalent of what the Adjutant General later became. There was no way he could be spared from his existing functions at the War Department; consequently, one of the division commanders could not have his own inspector officially. It will be seen that this limitation was not observed; each major general assured that the size and trappings of his staff mirrored that of his colleague.

Arthur P. Hayne, at twenty-six, became the first person to occupy the new position of Inspector General on 3 May 1816. A native of South Carolina, Hayne had entered the Army as a lieutenant of dragoons in 1808 and was promoted to captain the next year. He was assigned as Inspector General with the rank and compensation of colonel on 12 April 1814, although his line promotion to major did not occur until 1 August. Probably to raise his pay, Hayne was reassigned as an adjutant general 1 March 1815, to date from the beginning of his inspectorate. He reverted to the status of Inspector General with his new appointment, 3 May 1816, retaining the rank and pay of a colonel.

Hayne had been Andrew Jackson's Inspector General during the war and since its end. His conduct during the campaign against the Creeks had been commendable, while his actions during the battle of New Orleans earned him a brevet as lieutenant colonel (his permanent rank remained major, even while he was an inspector). Hayne was effective in upholding Jackson's standards, which demonstrated that, through training, leadership, and efficient staff supervision, good armies could be forged from militia, volunteers, and regulars alike. Since Hayne still served Jackson in 1816, and Jackson commanded the Division of the South, Hayne was assigned to that division. His appointment,

COL. JOHN E. WOOL *Inspector General, 29 April 1816–25 June 1841.*

therefore, was merely a formality ratifying Jackson's staff arrangements.[2] Then with Congress threatening to reduce the Army yet further, its higher officers were sensitive about their own survival, and exceedingly jealous of prerogative and appearance. Jacob Brown, commanding the Northern Division, was not about to let himself be outclassed by his counterpart in the South. In fact, Brown preempted Jackson with his acquisition of an inspector general on 29 April. Lt. Col. (Maj.) John Ellis Wool, a New Yorker, got the job. He had raised and led a company of volunteers from Troy, New York, when the War of 1812 opened. He became a captain of the 13th Infantry in April 1812, then major in the 29th Infantry a year later. Wool was seriously wounded in the attack on Queenston, and it was on 11 September 1814 that he gained his brevet as lieutenant colonel for gallant conduct at the Battle of Plattsburgh. After the war, on 17 May 1815, he was assigned to the 6th Infantry, where he became inspector general for the Northern Division.

There was no legitimate place for an inspector general other than the one Hayne occupied. Nevertheless, like Hayne, Wool was an inspector general with the rank of colonel. Exactly how Wool attained his inspectorate is not clear. Why, however, is readily apparent—one major general was not to be denied something enjoyed by the other. The bigger the staff, the greater the general, and Brown was senior to Jackson. In any case, Wool served as Brown's inspector general for five years before his status was confirmed. The illegality of his promotion apparently caught up with him in the meantime. He was reduced to the lineal rank of lieutenant colonel of the 6th Infantry on 20 May 1820, to date from 10 February 1818, the reason for that date not apparent in the records. Wool remained on the books of the 6th Infantry as a lieutenant colonel until 1 June 1821. He continued as inspector general, however, and in fact bore that title for a quarter century, until 1841.[3]

2. John Howard Brown, ed., *Lamb's Biographical Dictionary of the United States* (Boston: James H. Lamb, 1900), 3:611–12 (hereafter cited as *LBD*); *Who Was Who in American History: The Military* (Chicago: Marquis Who's Who, 1975), 246; Heitman, *Historical Register*, 1: 515.

3. *DAB*, 10: 513–14; Heitman, *Historical Register*, 1: 1059–60; William Barrett Skelton, "The United States Army, 1821–1837: An Institutional History" (Ph.D. dissertation, Northwestern University, 1968), 78–79. For Wool's career, in general, see Harwood P. Hinton, "The Military Career of John Ellis Wool, 1812–1863" (Ph.D. dissertation, University of Wisconsin, 1960), which emphasizes his wartime experiences.

The State of the Army

The army that the two inspectors general examined in the years after the War of 1812 was a loosely organized collection of armed bands distributed around the country. Soldiers occupied small posts built with their own hands, using materials drawn from the surrounding forests and tools provided by the quartermasters. Thanks to the war and advances in metallurgy, there was a better stock of tools, so saw wood became increasingly important in post construction. But the structures were primitive, mostly timber-frame, not too well built to begin with, and quick to deteriorate—the Army's general housing custom for the next half century and more. The appropriations to support military post construction were inadequate until 1817, and they were terminated completely for five years beginning in 1820. Barracks rooms were tiny, and very crowded. The continuing high rate of desertion was understandable— the men ran away from conditions that no self-respecting person would tolerate.[4]

Construction was not the only burden on the soldier. The Adjutant and Inspector General's Office issued a general order on 11 September 1818 directing all posts to establish vegetable gardens, and "more extensive cultivation" at certain designated posts, with careful records to be kept. The purpose of the order was to "promote the health of the troops" by providing cheap sources of fresh food. But it led to agricultural operations at some places that surpassed the abuses of the prewar period and finally had inspectors general utterly frustrated. There was accordingly little that was military about the Army's routine by 1818. Niles' Register reported in December that since April the 6th Infantry, at Plattsburgh, New York, had performed 25,716 days of manual labor—exclusive of military duty or agricultural pursuits.[5] Not only did the burden of labor make military life unrewarding, but a commentary in the press in 1816 reflected the kind of administrative inefficiency that did little to reduce the desertion rate: "It is positively stated in a western paper that the troops at Detroit, Michilimachinac, &c have not received one dollar of their pittance of pay for the last fifteen months. WE HOPE THIS IS NOT TRUE. But the mere suspicion of such a thing is degrading to the character of government, and ought to be repelled."[6]

Henry Clay had a rather different point of view. He told his colleagues in the House of Representatives in January 1817 that he still thought the government paid more money and got less military services than any other country in the world, and his object was to know if any proper expenditure of the military department might not be retrenched.[7] In fact, a "proper examination" was then under way, as reflected in the semiannual reports of inspectors general, assistant inspectors general, and acting assistant inspectors general who were hard at

---

4. Prucha, Sword of the Republic, 175; Risch, Quartermaster Support, 210; Clary, "These Relics," 31–40, 249–54.
5. GO, Adjutant and Inspector General's Office, 11 Sep 18, reprinted in Niles' Register, 15 (3 October 1818): 91; the labor report appeared in Niles' Register, 15 (19 December 1818): 294.
6. Niles' Register, 10 (17 August 1816): 415.
7. Benton, Abridgement of the Debates (10 January 1817), 5: 685.

work before Clay spoke, producing confidential and nonconfidential reports that described the condition of the Army's buildings, the efficiency of its troops, and—increasingly—the character of its officers. Capt. James Pratt, in the Northern Division, discovered little evidence of wasteful spending, but considerable efficiency in an underbudgeted organization. Fort Shelby, for instance, was "fast falling to decay, while the Company composing its garrison maintains its high standing." Another company, commanded by a second lieutenant, "has improved in Arms and dress to a considerable degree, tho more destitute of Clothing than any other Compy." Pratt's report was not confidential, so his characterizations of officers were mostly overly complimentary.[8]

Pratt was only acting as an inspector. Major John M. Davis, however, had been an assistant inspector general since October 1814, and knew how to be critical when his reports were protected by confidentiality. He forwarded to the Secretary of War, through the inspector general of the Division of the South, his semiannual confidential report on the units within his purview, on 30 April 1817. He covered all bases. Camp Montgomery, for instance, had "tolerably good barracks" built from materials from an abandoned post. Eliminating post stockades, he suggested, would "add much to the health and comfort of the troops." Another new post was a "square log work with Block Houses at diagonal angles," with barracks around the square. Provisions there were in short supply because of poor roads.

Davis reported the construction of new posts all over his district, which he thought proper because of possible attacks by Seminole Indians. Confronting that threat were units "under excellent discipline." In general, he said of the 1st Brigade (4th and 7th Infantry): "They are in habits of obedience, the prescribed uniform is strictly adhered to, and the [illegible] of interior economy appears to be their greatest care—notwithstanding all the economy that can possibly be used the expenditures may appear great, yet I cannot well see how the[y] could in any way be curtailed." The officers, he said, were able and willing, the food furnished by contractors good, and the forage not so good. In addition to the description part of his report, Davis appended, as required, a confidential report on the brigade officers, most of whom he described very favorably—"among the best Officers in the Army," and "both valuable officers and well acquainted with their duty" being typical comments. But of Lt. Col. William McRae of the Artillery, he said, "Is a good meaning innocent man, attentive to his personal appearance, of good Character—a good police officer—not very well calculated for active service [,] rather slow, and not very systematic." Davis noted charges placed against one officer for being absent without leave, while another had "disgraced himself" by setting an armed

---

8. *ARIG*, Semi-annual Report of Capt. James Pratt, 15 Jan 17, in Inspection Reports 1814–1842, RG 159. Pratt spelled the place's name "Shelty," which must be erroneous, for there is record of neither post nor officer by that name. At various times Fort Shelby existed at Detroit, Mich., Rock Island, Ill., and Prairie du Chien, Wisc. Pratt's inspection report is the only one to survive from the Northern Division during this period. Heitman, *Historical Register*, 2: 544.

party against a citizen. They beat the man up in the middle of the night, and the responsible officer earned himself a court-martial. Yet another officer was under arrest for ''charges that appear more of a personal nature than from the good of the service,'' so Davis expressed hopes for a verdict of acquittal.[9]

Hayne, as Divisional Inspector, processed and forwarded the reports of assistants, and also prepared his own. Further reductions in the Army apparently were pending, so character assessments of officers were first among his services to his commander, Jackson, and to the War Department, for whom he prepared confidential reports yearly. They listed every officer in the Southern Division, each assessed in a capsule report. Hayne's assessments varied in their usefulness, although some could be quite frank. Brigadier General Edmund P. Gaines, he said in November 1817, was ''An Officer of long experience, in whose Department the utmost harmony prevails, & whose correct conduct has long won the esteem of all under his command.'' Gaines was a powerful man, and Hayne trod lightly around him. He was more frank discussing Assistant Adjutant General Clinton Wright, ''An Officer of intelligence—heretofore his conduct has been marked by too much levity, but of late, I understand, very much altered for the better.'' Assistant Inspector General Davis was ''An officer of experience & distinction.''[10]

Most officers received favorable comments from Hayne, but the exceptions were notable. William McRae was ''An officer of correct deportment but not calculated for the Army.'' Major George M. Brooke was ''An Officer of much distinction & bravery, but of very dissipated habits.'' Major John Hicks was ''An Ordinary officer,'' while Maj. James Bankhead was ''An intelligent man, but not a good Officer,'' and Capt. William Bailey was ''An ordinary officer. Genl Gaines & Maj. Davis, both state he has disgraced himself.'' Eighth Department commander Eleazer W. McDonald was ''An Officer of dissipated habits.''[11] Hayne's confidential report accompanied voluminous nonconfidential descriptions of the men and posts of the Southern Division. Those comprised capsule descriptions of the physical condition and military usefulness of the several posts, and included discussion of ''progress made in military discipline'' and of the staff services. Hayne was especially energetic in 1817, recommending replacement of subsistence contracting by a Commissariat Department (which took place in 1818), raising the pay of subalterns, and proposing a new set of general regulations he had prepared himself.[12]

---

9. Jno. M. Davis to Hayne, 30 Apr 17, Inspection Reports 1814–1842, RG 159.

10. Hayne, Confidential Report of the Southern Division of the Army, 1817, approved 27 Nov 17 by Andrew Jackson, Inspection Reports 1814–1842, RG 159.

11. Ibid.

12. Hayne, State of the Posts in the 6th and 7th Military Department, and State of the Posts in the 8th Military Department, with a note on the 9th Department, approved 27 Nov 17 by Andrew Jackson, Inspection Reports 1814–1842, RG 159. Brown of the Northern Division evidently did not see fit to forward Wool's reports to Washington, as none survive in the records for this period. Assistant Inspector General G.H. Marigault of the Northern army resigned 17 June 1817, and was replaced by Capt. John Biddle of the Artillery, promoted to major. GO, Adjutant and Inspector General's Office, 19 Jun 17, in GORI&IG. In the Southern Division, meanwhile, Jackson was

Calhoun and Army Reform

The Army's inspectorate worked efficiently enough throughout 1817, but the War Department did not. President James Monroe experienced difficulty in finding a Secretary of War: Several people turned it down before John C. Calhoun entered the post on 8 October 1817. The job had been vacant for a year, and was occupied only part-time much longer. In fact, Calhoun was the first permanent head of the War Department since Armstrong had left in disgrace.[13] The Secretary's job had been hard to fill because it was a monumental challenge, one not likely to prove rewarding in the country's antimilitary political climate. The War Department faced a debt of $45 million in unsettled accounts, and overlooked a military force scattered everywhere and apparently beyond control. But Calhoun was undeterred, and reduced the outstanding accounts to $3 million and brought the Army into some semblance of order. During his tenure, the staff services were strengthened and given permanent form, the Military Academy made great advances as the heart of growing professionalism, and the Corps of Engineers spent $3 million on modern coastal fortifications. The Secretary's success was not unmixed, however. He was unable to have the Regular Army reorganized exactly as he wanted it, an "expansible" core of national defense. His fortification program diminished after the first rush, and soon after Congress authorized Calhoun's proposed line of posts up the Missouri River, it halved the program for reasons of economy. Nevertheless, the number of posts had grown to seventy-three by 1818—up from twenty-seven in 1801.[14]

Calhoun believed that the Army's peacetime pursuit should be preparing for war. The success of generals like Harrison, Jackson, and others in assembling efficient formations of volunteers and regulars during the War of 1812 had persuaded him that the Regular Army should be the potential heart of any mobilization. He therefore wanted to organize the peacetime Army so that it could be expansible in an emergency, gaining size and efficiency quickly while additional units took form. That, he believed, would prevent the chaos that had characterized the 1812 period, as well as the disasters that had befallen disorganized, untrained masses when they confronted a determined enemy.

---

engaged in a private war with the Spanish in Florida during 1817, eventually leading to annexation of that territory. For a recent account, see Virginia Bergman Peters, *The Florida Wars* (Hamden, Conn.: Archon Books, 1979). With military activity, Jackson needed an efficient inspectorate.

13. Smith, "Congressional Attitudes Toward Military," 23.

14. Charles M. Wiltse, *John C. Calhoun, Nationalist, 1782–1828* (Indianapolis: Bobbs Merrill, 1944), 138–39, 149, 167–85, 203–16, 248; White, *The Jeffersonians*, 256–59; Oliver Lyman Spaulding, *The United States Army in War and Peace* (New York: Putnam, 1937), 154; Leonard D. White, *The Jacksonians: A Study in Administrative History, 1829–1861* (New York: Macmillan, 1954), 203–12; Weigley, *History of the United States Army*, 133–34, 143, 144–53, 153–56, 158–59, 163–64. See also Vincent J. Fisher, "Mr. Calhoun's Army," *Military Review*, 37 (September 1957): 52–58.

An effective wartime Army required more than fighting units. At its head must be a competent organization to oversee supplies, logistics, ordnance, and other necessary staff services. Calhoun had little patience with the feeling prevalent in Congress that staff services were essential only in wartime. Rather, he said, they were equally essential during peace if they were to be available for war. He repeatedly stressed the need for an effective general staff, functioning in peacetime, ready for war.[15] In using the term "general staff," Calhoun did not mean the sort of planning and coordinating establishment associated with modern armies; that idea had only begun to take form in Europe. Rather, he referred collectively to the bodies of specialists responsible for the leadership of the Army, and in particular for the management of its material needs, such as quartermasters, surgeons, and ordnance specialists. They, he believed, required permanent organizations as efficient and as expansible as should be the fighting units.

John Williams, chairman of the Senate Committee on Military Affairs, asked Calhoun on 11 February 1818 to submit his suggestions for organizing the U.S. Army. When Calhoun replied, he not only gained his permanent general staff, but set off another ferocious debate over how big the Army should be. Despite the furor, the lawmakers did recognize the need to provide some form of permanent staff to manage the War Department. The legislation of 14 April 1818 established separate departments headed by the Quartermaster General, the Surgeon General, the Commissary General of Purchases, and others, including a new Commissary General of Subsistence—who thereafter superintended the supply of rations, ending the discredited contract system at last. What was left of the general staff, so-called, was the roster of general officers and others not assigned by department, including adjutants and inspectors. The latter received only one notice in the legislation in which the pay of inspectors general of divisions was equated to that of adjutants general at the same level.[16] Calhoun's new staff departments gave him the advice and information he wanted for a unified management of the Army but, in doing so, they introduced certain distinctions between staff and line that would grow into major difficulties in the future. In fact, trouble erupted immediately, as Calhoun and General Jackson fell into dispute over control of staff department officers assigned to the Southern Division.[17] Inspectors general remained as they were before; however, they did not constitute a separate department answering to the Secretary alone. No such disputes centered upon their accountability—at least not yet.

---

15. Weigley, *History of the United States Army*, 134.

16. Smith, "Congressional Attitudes Toward Military," 23; Ingersoll, *History of the War Department*, 182; An Act Regulating the Staff of the Army, approved 14 April 1818, 3 Stat. 426; Thian, *Legislative History*, 110.

17. White, *Jeffersonians*, 238–50; Risch, *Quartermaster Support*, 181–88; Weigley, *History of the United States Army*, 134–37. See also P.M. Ashburn, *History of the Medical Department of the United States* (Boston: Houghton-Mifflin, 1929), and Ingersoll, *History of the War Department*, on the early history of various staff departments.

Congress, meanwhile, told Calhoun to prepare a plan to reduce the Army to 6,000 officers and men—about half the then authorized force. He replied in December with his plan for an expandable army, but Congress would not hear of it. Congressional concern over the cost of the military increased during the depression of 1819. Although the War Department budget had fallen from $16 million in 1816 to less than $9 million since 1817, there remained a deficit of $45 million in unsettled accounts—nearly half the national debt. Many in Congress believed the country was not getting its money's worth from the War Department, and Calhoun admitted that little had been done previously to give exactness, economy, and dispatch to its monied transactions. But Congress generally believed that the military was inherently wasteful, and buried itself in proposals for army reorganization that all promised economy.[18]

Congress showed some attention to the welfare of enlisted men, even as it tried to reduce the army budget. The lawmakers probably observed the connection between the growing volume of manual labor and the climbing desertion rate, and decreed on 2 March 1819 that the soldiers be given extra pay if required to do such labor for more than ten consecutive days.[19] The law had little practical effect, despite its good intentions. Some officers quickly discovered clever ways to cheat the men of their extra-duty pay—successive nine-day assignments, for instance, were complained of for decades—but the extra pay contributed to the Army's growing costliness as it pursued its far-flung activities. General Henry Atkinson, for instance, embarked on an ambitious expedition up the Missouri River beginning in 1819, and indulged in a lot of expensive experiments with steamboats. The costs quickly got out of hand, greatly exceeding appropriations. Thereafter, the Quartermaster Department's principal expense was the provision of transportation, which usually caused it to ask Congress for supplemental funding.[20]

Inspectors and Army Reduction

Inspector General Hayne of the Southern Division suggested in 1819 that the Army was wasteful. Too many officers were inefficient: "An officer of amiable disposition, but wants industry," he said of a typical example. He believed that the posts were wastefully allowed to deteriorate and that troops were not necessarily placed where the real Indian danger was. The pattern of small posts scattered everywhere, Hayne believed, was an utter waste of money. In the Missouri country, he favored a few large posts, and the use of a disposable force of mounted men to patrol the distances between them. Cavalry, he maintained, was more efficient on the plains than dispersed infantry. But all

---

18. Weigley, *History of the United States Army*, 140–43; Smith, "Congressional Attitudes Toward Military," 23.
19. As quoted in Ganoe, *History of the United States Army*, 156.
20. Roger L. Nichols, "Army Contributions to River Transportation, 1818–1825," *Military Affairs*, 33 (April 1969): 242–49; Risch, *Quartermaster Support*, 188–93, 204–09.

Congress could see at the time was the cost of horses. Hayne's suggestions were totally unheeded.[21]

John M. Davis continued as an assistant inspector general in the Southern Division in 1820, but now he reported directly to Parker in Washington. Davis had become more critical of the Army and its situation. Fort Scott, Georgia, he had found in a miserable condition when he visited it—so bad that he left the place and returned after things had been cleaned up. But the division's posts were nearly all shabby and dilapidated, affecting morale. Discipline, Davis said, was as good as could be expected in the Army's sorry circumstances. Courts-martial were becoming more common, and he believed them wasteful. Trials were held for trivial offenses, and the difficulty of assembling officers to hold courts at tiny garrisons cost money and took time. He believed that commanding officers should examine charges brought before them carefully before calling for courts. In other matters, Davis believed supply to be generally well managed, although he complained that many cannon carriages were being allowed to deteriorate needlessly.

Davis found cause to speak favorably of most of the division's officers. But he delivered real tirades about several whom he thought should be cashiered for infractions, including a considerable amount of embezzlement. His report for 1820, in fact, was almost a long bill of indictment against a fair percentage of the officer corps. But dishonesty aside, he also found cause to revise Hayne's former high estimation of General Gaines.

This officer in many respects is remarkably circumspect in his conduct, and attentive to his duty and personal appearance, but I think he falls far short of that noble Independent disposition which ought to characterize a General in the American Army—I think he possesses a great deal of vanity, duplicity, and in many instances has suffered himself to be led astray from the common path of rectitude by those who ought to have but little influence over him.[22]

The reports of inspectors general confirmed what many in Congress suspected—the Army was not as efficient as it should be, and a substantial share of its officers might as well be dismissed in the public interest. At least in that respect, the inspectorate demonstrated its value. But the most influential inspector general, Hayne, resigned at the end of September 1820, to embark on a political career. He was replaced as inspector general of the Southern Division by James Gadsden, 1 October. Gadsden, who would later become famous for the Gadsden Purchase of land from Mexico in 1853, was appointed to satisfy Jackson, and to balance the appointment of Roger Jones, at the behest of

---

21. Hayne, Confidential Report of the Southern Division of the Army under the Command of Major General Andrew Jackson, for the year 1819, approved October 1819, in Inspection Reports 1814–1842, RG 159. Assessing the character of officers, Hayne noticed a future Inspector General, Capt. S.B. Archer of the Artillery: "In many respects, a first rate Officer."

22. Jno. M. Davis, AIG, to Daniel Parker, Adjutant and Inspector General's Office (hereafter cited as A&IGO), Confidential Report for the half year ending 30 June 1820, Inspection Reports 1814–1842, RG 159.

Brown, as adjutant general in the Northern Division. Both became colonels, although the permanent rank of each was only captain.[23]

Jackson and Brown, with other generals, competed for positions in an army that all knew would soon be much smaller. Calhoun was at work on a new proposal for army organization, and thanks to what he had already accomplished, the influence of staff officers in the War Department was growing. Brown and Jackson therefore wanted to put their proteges in line for influential positions, and may have begun to believe that a position of Commanding General was in the offing. Nonetheless, Jackson had more immediate reasons to think about his inspectors. When assistant inspectors general like Davis were able to communicate directly with the Adjutant and Inspector General, they were out of the control of the district commanders. Moreover, it was apparent that inspection reports would play a roll in determining which officers would remain in the Army after its reduction. The division commanders wanted to have a hand in those determinations—and they most definitely did not want Parker to have influence in their commands. As Jackson may have suspected, inspectors sang a different tune in their confidential reports when they went to Washington directly—as reflected in Davis' critical judgment of Gaines.

Jackson was struggling with Calhoun anyway over the control of staff officers in his division. He was not about to relinquish control of officers who were theoretically part of his own command staff, instead of in a separate department. The Adjutant and Inspector General in that instance quickly lost his private line of sight into the divisions. On 20 October 1820, by order of the Secretary, Parker told the Army that inspectors should report only through their division commanders to the War Department.[24] The order substantially changed command relationships. It gave division commanders Brown and Jackson power in two ways. First, they closed off an independent channel of communications, hence a potential source of outside interference, in their subordinates. Second, their power over their subordinates was increased by making the assistant inspectors general agents of the division commanders, removed from control by the brigadier generals—Davis might now speak as freely to Jackson as to Parker about Gaines, because the latter would no longer see his confidential reports. Inspection was reinforced as a tool of command, but it became a tool denied, in any formal sense, to generals lower than division commanders.

The struggle to reduce the Army, meanwhile, had become more intense. It resumed early in 1820 with an unsuccessful attempt to gut the appropriations bill for coastal defense. Members of Congress had also apparently become aware of inspectors' criticism of army officers, and reaffirmed their determination to decrease the size of the officer corps. The House of Representatives passed a resolution on 11 May directing the Secretary of War to submit a plan

---

23. Heitman, *Historical Register*, 1: 441, 582; J. Patrick Hughes, "The Adjutant General's Office, 1821–1861: A Study in Administrative History" (Ph.D. dissertation, Ohio State University, 1977), 27. Gadsden was an engineer, Jones an artillerist.

24. GO, A&IGO, 20 Oct 20, in GORI&IG.

for reducing the Army to 6,000 enlisted men. That measure was a compromise offered by Henry Clay as a
substitute for a very explicit bill that
would have slashed the Army and its
budget arbitrarily—eliminating all but
three generals and ending most staff
positions, leaving but one Inspector
General, one Adjutant General, and
the department heads.[25]

Calhoun answered the House resolution by proposing a 6,000-man army
and a revised organization of the general staff. His separate departments
remained, while the general staff
would also remain in large part unchanged. In other words, Calhoun
proposed to retain virtually the entire
army overhead. Of the various adjutants and inspectors, excluding the
Adjutant and Inspector General, he

COL. JAMES GADSDEN. *Inspector
General, 1 October 1820–13 August
1821.*

said, "All except three are officers of the line, and it is contemplated to have
them all of the line as vacancies occur."[26] The House received Calhoun's plan
on 12 December 1820, and immediately went to work on its own ideas. A bill
reported out of committee on 28 December offered a staff comprising one each
of the following: brigadier general (with an aide-de-camp), Adjutant General
(with an assistant adjutant general), assistant inspector general, Quartermaster
General, Judge Advocate, Paymaster General, Commissary General of Purchases (with an assistant commissary general of purchases), Commissary General of Subsistence, Surgeon General, and Apothecary General. There would
be two storekeepers, but no Adjutant and Inspector General, and no Inspector
General.[27]

The opposing positions were thus set, and the debate opened. It centered
almost entirely on the need for economy and general opposition to budgetary
deficits. Those lawmakers favoring a large army and navy could not deny the

---

25. Smith, "Congressional Attitudes Toward Military," 23; David Ted Childress, "The Army
in Transition: The United States Army, 1815–1846" (Ph.D. dissertation, Mississippi State University,
1974), 384–85; U.S. Congress, *Annals of Congress*, 16th Cong., 1st sess. (11 May 20), 2232–33.
The proposed legislation would eliminate the Adjutant and Inspector General and all assistant
adjutants and inspectors, among other positions.

26. *The Organization of the Army*, H. Doc. 31, 16th Cong., 2d sess. (Washington: Gales &
Seaton, 1820). The three exceptions were two adjutants general of divisions and Inspector General
Gadsden. Wool had already been relegated to a line position, effective two years earlier.

27. *Annals of Congress*, 16th Cong., 2d sess. (12 Dec 20), 607 (28 Dec 20), 687. Giving staff
officers titles as "assistants" would permit giving them lower rank and pay than the full title would
accord.

need for economy, and were reduced to suggesting lamely that there was no problem in the present arrangement. Just below the surface lay lingering fears of standing armies, which numerous speakers described as inherently dangerous to liberty. Their opponents stressed the likelihood of future wars, and the need to prepare for them. But no one wanted to abolish the United States Army altogether, or to make it utterly ineffective. The result was a compromise, developed by the Senate. That split the difference between Calhoun and the House, reducing the Army by 50 percent and cutting its appropriations.[28]

The act of 2 March 1821 reduced the Army by half, to an authorized 6,126 officers and men. Much of the hierarchy vanished from the organization, including the Adjutant and Inspector General. The line consisted of seven regiments of infantry and four of artillery. There was a Corps of Engineers and a Corps of Topographical Engineers, along with three separate departments—Medical, Pay, and Purchasing. The Quartermaster and Commissary were so reduced and interdependent that they were departments in common parlance only, although each eventually resumed its former status. Otherwise, the general staff comprised one major general and two brigadier generals (with four aides among them), an Adjutant General, and two inspectors general, the latter "with the rank, pay, and emoluments of colonels of cavalry."[29] Although a staff was substantially preserved, Calhoun was not pleased with the outcome, but he had not really lost the issue. True, his hopes for an expansible Army had been dashed, and the remaining staff was too meager to perform its prescribed duties, let alone to prepare for future wars. The U.S. Army and its budget had been reduced sharply, but in the circumstances they had to be. Nor could persistent fear of standing armies be erased entirely. But what emerged was a permanent army, effectively organized for its mission, and supported by Monroe's and Calhoun's arguments that it would always be necessary because wars would inevitably occur.[30]

The two inspectors general were expected to play important roles in the new army. They had, in fact, been established somewhat as substitutes for all the generals Calhoun wanted. Instead of two major generals, now there was one, and he would need to be well informed. The army might be smaller, but it remained so scattered that not even three generals could apprise themselves unaided . . . . The immediate question became who should the inspectors general be? Given the circumstances, this was the primary concern of the officers who feared for their employment. Jobs needed to be defined only after they were secure. Gadsden was already in one position, and logically could continue. Wool was conducting the same activity, but without a formal position. Parker

28. Smith, "Congressional Attitudes Toward Military," 23–25; Skelton, "Commanding General," 117–18.

29. *An Act to reduce and fix the military peace establishment of the United States, Statutes at Large* 3, sec. 6, 615 (1821); Heitman, *Historical Register*, 2: 580–81; Thian, *Legislative History*, 110. See also Risch, *Quartermaster Support*, 195–97. The organization had no cavalry. The provision governed compensation for forage, because inspectors were expected to travel.

30. Smith, "Congressional Attitudes Toward Army," 25.

was about to lose his office, but he had never been an inspector anyway, he had mostly been an adjutant. There were already two adjutants general, so Parker might not be the best candidate for the single Adjutant General's position that remained but the resourceful bureaucrat was never in peril. When the job of Paymaster General opened on 1 June 1821, Parker immediately moved into it.[31] Wool, then, might be equally secure. One inspector general's position was open, and with Parker accommodated, Wool was an obvious candidate. Calhoun moved quickly to establish the new organization. There was only one major general, so divisions were no longer appropriate. The President replaced them on 17 May with two departments, Eastern and Western—berths for the two brigadier generals. Effective 15 June 1821, Jacob Brown—senior major general before the reduction—moved to the War Department, establishing the office of Commanding General.[32] That opened another question affecting the two inspectors general: Would they move to the two departments, or would they answer to the Commanding General? The three generals all had strong opinions on that subject.

---

31. Heitman, *Historical Register*, 1: 38.
32. Skelton, "Commanding General," 117–18; Sanger, "Inspector-General's Department," 242.

Part Two

The Inspectors General of the Army

(1821–1881)

CHAPTER 10

Establishing the Inspectors General

(1821–1825)

The reduction of the Army as ordered by Congress happened swiftly, because by June 1821 appropriations were available for only a small force – not even as large as Congress had authorized the Army to be. The Army numbered 8,942 officers and men in December 1820; a year later the figure stood at 5,746. The number of active officers had fallen from 712 to 530. Reductions continued the following year, when the U.S. Army's residue was 5,211 people, including 512 officers. It was the second drastic reduction in six years, and it left the officer corps shaken and uncertain.[1] While it happened, officers scrambled furiously for position and influence, seeing one another as rivals. Every vacant commission was the object of attention that bordered on the paranoid.

Choosing and Regulating the Inspector

The posts of Adjutant General and Inspector General received particular scrutiny. They were bound to exert a great deal of influence in the small military hierarchy. The Secretary of War wanted them filled with capable officers, amenable to his wishes. The new Commanding General wanted the positions occupied by loyal officers, subject to his orders. The brigadier generals, Edmund P. Gaines and Winfield Scott, wanted the occupants of the offices to be friendly to them. Others, including the retiring Andrew Jackson, saw the positions as havens for their proteges. The politics of the officer corps, accordingly, caused Secretary Calhoun to move carefully, and to strike compromises.

John Wool apparently continued as a de facto inspector general, with his permanent base in the 6th Infantry, until 1 June 1821. As of that date, he occupied one of the two positions established for inspectors general. Calhoun had by that time decided to attach the inspectors general to the War Department, depriving the department commanders of those positions. Wool was a protege of Jacob Brown, new Commanding General and old rival of Andrew Jackson.

---

1. Strength figures used are those given in Heitman, *Historical Register*, 2: 626. See also Childress, ''Army in Transition,'' 282–84, for effects on the officer corps.

Wool's installation as a permanent inspector general was probably interpreted as a favor to Brown and his supporters in the officer corps. Jackson, however, was not without his own influence, despite his retirement. He also had a protege—James Gadsden, already a permanent inspector general. Gadsden balanced Wool in that position, but as Adjutant General he might offer a more effective counterweight to the Brown party in the army command. The position of Adjutant General, in any case, could not be filled casually. The logical candidate, on the grounds of ability, was Roger Jones. But he was another Brown protege, and for that reason his appointment, after Wool's, might divide the Army.

When Parker became Paymaster General 1 June 1821, after the abolition of the office of Adjutant and Inspector General, the Secretary ordered 1st Lt. Edmund Kirby to perform the duties of Adjutant General until the office was filled. Calhoun had by then probably selected Gadsden for the job, and had already ordered him to Washington. Gadsden was in Florida, but was actively campaigning for the assignment. He wrote to Calhoun on 18 July to report his rather leisurely progress to assume his post as Inspector General: "I have reported myself to you," he said, "as I am at a loss to know whether under the new organization of the Army the Inspectors are to obey the Instructions & report to the Major Genl commanding the Army, or the Brigadiers of Departments. A hint from you however on the subject, and I will report myself directly as the regulations prescribe." Gadsden knew very well what his reporting relations were to be, and by that letter merely certified his independence of the department commanders and his direct connection to the War Department. Calhoun replied on 25 July 1821, "The Inspectors, as well as the Adjutant General, are immediately attached to the Major General." The Secretary also granted Gadsden's request for leave for his health's sake, and told him that he had been appointed Adjutant General. In due course, orders announced Gadsden's appointment as Adjutant General, to date from 13 August 1821.[2] Jackson was satisfied, the large question of the Adjutant General was answered, and the smaller question of who would replace Gadsden was opened.

Jacob Brown and Andrew Jackson had proteges more important than Gadsden or Wool. They were the two brigadier generals, Brown's man Scott and Jackson's man Gaines. They had their own ulterior motives, and as department commanders were not pleased at the prospect that the Commanding General might have too much power over them. Scott focused first on the threat that the War Department's inspectors general might pose to his own independence when he wrote to Calhoun on 12 April 1821 to raise the question of the two inspectors general. He said that their continued existence was unnecessary in the new army organization. If they were attached to the War Department, he

2. Gadsden to Calhoun, 18 Jul 21, and Calhoun to Gadsden, 25 Jul 21, in Robert Meriwether and W. Edwin Hemphill, eds., *The Papers of John C. Calhoun*, 13 vols. (Columbia: University of South Carolina Press, 1959–1980), 6: 263–64, 280; GO No. 21, Adjutant General's Office (hereafter AGO), n.d., 1821, in GORI&IG. Erroneously it has been stated that the Adjutant General whose position was not abolished took over the job. Skelton, "United States Army," 76.

suggested that the Adjutant General handle everything that the Adjutant and Inspector General had overseen before reduction. If the inspectors general served the commander as roving inspectors of the department, "This would be in a great deal to supersede the Brigadiers; to place an inferior rank over a superior which would be absurd. It would show to the Congress & to the country, that either the Brigadiers or the Inspector General [sic] are useless." Brigadier generals, Scott said, were already required to make their own inspections, and should not themselves be inspected by colonels.[3]

With the establishment of the departments imminent, Scott raised the subject again on 9 May. He declared in a long letter to Calhoun reviewing his objections that to have inspectors general, ranking as colonels, inspecting brigadier generals would be insulting to the generals. Again he said he could see no reason for having inspectors at all, since the brigadier generals must inspect their own departments. But this time the practical Scott took a new tack. Since the brigadier generals' staffs were short, he said, putting the inspectors general on the department commanders' staff would be a good idea. At least, no officer would be inspected by an inferior.[4] . . . In one of the last orders he published as Adjutant and Inspector General, Parker announced on 17 May 1821 the establishment of the Western Department, commanded by Gaines, and the Eastern Department, under Scott. Major General Brown's headquarters was fixed at the District of Columbia. The headquarters of the Eastern Department would be at Governors Island, New York, while the Western would lodge at Louisville, Kentucky, "when the Generals are not on visits of inspection and tours of duty." Lest Scott think he had scored a triumph, on 19 May Calhoun wrote him that the President had decided that the inspectors general should "be attached to the Major General commanding the Army. You will therefore insert the enclosed among the regulations now in press."[5] The "enclosed" was a regulation, dated 18 May, authored by Calhoun himself. Scott was in charge of preparing the Army's first comprehensive new set of general regulations since Steuben's. He would, in fact, receive credit for authorship. But Calhoun's *Regulation Concerning Inspections in the Army* was an independent contribution. Scott might not have liked it, but he did as he was told. The regulation defined the Army's inspectorate:

The Inspectors General are under the direction of the Major General of the Army. Whenever they commence a tour of inspection, they will communicate information of its commencement to the General commanding the Department to be inspected; and on the termination of the tour, they will transmit a copy of the confidential report to the General Commanding the Department, who will transmit it to the Major General, after making remarks in writing upon such parts of it as he may think proper to notice. The reports of the Inspectors to be considered strictly confidential.[6]

---

3. Scott to Calhoun, 13 Apr 21, in Meriwether and Hemphill, *Papers of Calhoun*, 6: 48–49.
4. Scott to Calhoun, 9 May 21, in Meriwether and Hemphill, *Papers of Calhoun*, 6: 103–06.
5. GO, A&IGO, 17 May 21, in GORI&IG; Calhoun to Scott, 19 May 21, in Meriwether and Hemphill, *Papers of Calhoun*, 6:132.
6. John C. Calhoun, "Regulation Concerning Inspections in the Army," 18 May 21, in Meriwether and Hemphill, *Papers of Calhoun*, 6: 126. The identical text appeared in U.S. War
(Continued)

That provision ratified the communications of inspectors established previously in Calhoun's compromise with Jackson. It established the authority of the Commanding General to oversee the brigadiers, and at the same time reassured the department commanders that they would know what the inspectors said about them and their commands. Calhoun's regulation also supported Scott's contention that department commanders should serve as their own inspectors, and at the same time clarified their subordination to the Commanding General. Department commanders were to inspect all posts and forces under them every two years, and report to the major general "such facts connected with the connection of their Departments as they may judge necessary."[7] Colonels and field officers of artillery were also to inspect their regiments regularly under the orders of department commanders, at least once every six months. Calhoun's regulation reaffirmed very strongly that inspection was a function of command, and a responsibility of every commander. Inspection by an agent of higher authority would not be a substitute for, or an interference with, the authority of a lesser commander. Only the Commanding General enjoyed the services of his own, formally designated inspectors general; brigadier generals and lower commanders must provide such services for themselves. In either case, inspectors were but agents of commanders, not powers unto themselves.

Objects of inspection specified in the regulation included frontier defense, repairs needed at posts, new posts needed, the resources of the country, and communications difficulties. Inspectors were to look specifically at police, discipline, instruction, service, and general administration of the posts, the last of which was defined by the regulations. The "form and course of inspections" were outlined, beginning with general reviews, basic parade ground maneuvers, and examinations of troops front and back, along with their knapsacks and contents, weapons, ammunition, and so on. Commanders, not inspectors, issued the requisite orders. After troop examinations, the men could be paid. Then the inspectors were to move on to hospitals, magazines, quarters, sutlers' shops, and other facilities. Scott's text provided details on what an inspector should look for in barracks: how bunks, bedding, equipment, and other objects were to be arranged, including the case of culinary equipment. "Memoranda of censure" would report all deficiencies. Finally, when inspectors were not present, post commanders were to conduct the same complete examination monthly.[8] Scott's 1821 regulations also required that captains inspect their companies every Sunday, and lieutenants their sections every Thursday. Surgeons were to conduct their own inspections of their hospitals on Sunday. As if that were not enough, officers were also to make daily visits to the men's quarters, while the

(Continued)
Department, *General Regulations for the Army; or, Military Institutes* (Philadelphia: M. Carey & Sons, 1821), 325 (hereafter cited as *1821 Regulations*).
    7. Calhoun, "Regulation Concerning Inspections," in Meriwether and Hemphill, *Papers of Calhoun*, 6:126.
    8. *1821 Regulations*, 60–68.

visits of post commanders were to be frequent. Uniforms were to be kept clean, and underwear changed three times a week in midsummer and twice a week (Sundays and Thursdays) the rest of the year. The men were to wash their hands and faces daily after fatigue, "shave themselves (if necessary), and brush or comb their heads."[9] Scott clearly believed that inspection was the commander's most important management tool. From general to corporal, every leader was an inspector, satisfying himself that the men under him did what they were told, and that all was in order. Scott's formal integration of inspection into the process of command exceeded even the words and examples of Steuben and Wayne before him. His success in his camp of instruction during the war, and his acknowledged intellectual powers, made Scott an authority on troop management. Thanks to his regulations, in the United States Army inspection was management.

The importance Scott placed on inspection may have influenced his opposition to the inspectors general. Certainly his attempt to deny to the Commanding General something he regarded as essential to command was impertinent, and most probably it arose from a sense of his own authority as a prospective department commander. But more subtly, Scott may have been suspicious of the commander's first duty. A less than diligent commander, he may have feared, might neglect his proper attention to his command, believing that dispatch of an inspector general was sufficient oversight of the troops. A lazy commander, accordingly, might not even make sufficient use of an inspector's findings, leaving the command with a commander in title only. Conversely, an inspector not constantly responsive to the commander might develop ambitions of his own.

The Army's inspectorate was about to enter some of its finer hours. Inspection would be absolutely essential over the coming decades if the Army was to be kept well in hand. The force was thoroughly scattered in small outposts, and for want of roads or good mail service, practically out of communication with its titular head in Washington. Whether inspection succeeded in making a real contribution to army management ultimately depended upon the character and authority of the Commanding General, as well as the industry of the inspectors general. So long as the Commanding General was a person who took his duty seriously, and was allowed to do so, inspection was his handmaiden, the eye of the leader. But when the Commanding General was not inclined to exercise his powers of command, or was not allowed to, inspection provided information, but otherwise served little purpose. In those circumstances, the inspector defined his own job. An ambitious inspector general could establish his own niche in the bureaucracy, while an inattentive officer could let the function wither away. It is more than a little ironic that inspection's golden age ended while Scott himself was an almost powerless Commanding General.

In 1821, those developments lay far ahead. For the moment, Calhoun merely wanted to establish the inspectorate on a sound footing. He told the

9. Ibid., 47–48, 68.

President on 18 August 1821 that since Gadsden had become Adjutant General, the position of one inspector general was open. There were three applicants for the job, he said, and two others known to want it. The Secretary believed the position too important to fill casually because the quality of the army would depend largely on the quality of the individual selected to assure that standards were being met. Calhoun observed of the candidates that two were scheduled for promotion in the line, while another—Roger Jones, Brown's old Adjutant General and protege—had exerted too much political influence to suit the Secretary. He told the President that he favored Col. Abram Eustis and Bvt. Maj. Samuel B. Archer—especially the latter, who was the junior officer on the list.[10]

Calhouns's recommendations brought no response. He reminded President Monroe two months later that they still must give attention to the appointment of an inspector general as an early inspection of the Army in the South was advisable. In addition, Col. Robert Butler had been grumbling about his position in the army since reduction. Perhaps, Calhoun suggested, making him an inspector general might satisfy him and his influential friends.[11] Nevertheless, Bvt. Maj. Samuel B. Archer, of the Artillery, was appointed an inspector general, with the rank of colonel, on 10 November. He accepted 12 November. Archer was about thirty years old when he became an inspector general, a Virginian who had entered the U.S. Army as an artillery captain in 1812. His conduct during the war had earned him commendations, including a brevet for gallantry in action. He had drawn the favorable notice of Inspector General Hayne, among others, since the war. Like Gadsden before him, he came from Jackson and Gaines' part of the Army, balancing Wool, who came from Brown's.[12]

Inspecting the Army

When the staff of inspectors general was complete, Calhoun redefined their duties on 5 December 1821. Wool was given the responsibility to inspect all infantry posts and units. Archer was directed to inspect all artillery garrisons and the ordnance activities such as arsenals and foundries that supported them. Each officer was required to submit annual reports.[13] The reasons behind this division of responsibility are open to speculation. It may be that the specialization of the two inspectors general might have eased tensions between the Commanding General and the department commanders. On the one hand,

---

10. Calhoun to James Monroe, 18 Aug 21, in Meriwether and Hemphill, *Papers of Calhoun*, 6: 348–50.

11. Calhoun to Monroe, 14 Oct 21, in Meriwether and Hemphill, *Papers of Calhoun*, 6: 436.

12. GO No. 43, AGO, 21 Nov 21, in GORI&IG; Heitman, *Historical Register*, 1: 168; James Grant Wilson and John Fiske, eds., *Appleton's Cyclopaedia of American Biography* (New York: Appleton, 1888), 87. Calhoun wrote a letter to Archer on 10 November, but it has disappeared; Archer's reply of the 12th survives. Meriwether and Hemphill, *Papers of Calhoun*, 6: 504. See Appendix B.

13. GO No. 55, AGO, 5 Dec 21, in GORI&IG.

neither department commander needed to fear that an inspector general would be assigned full-time as his personal supervisor or spy. On the other hand, the arrangement prevented an inspector from coming too much under the influence of a brigadier general—inspection cut across department lines—thus denying any hint that Wool was Scott's or Brown's man, or Archer Gaines'. . . . The specialization of the inspectors may have served other ends as well. Calhoun and Brown alike may have decided to assign each man to the inspectorate where his particular skills would make him the best observer. Calhoun was greatly interested in the progress of coastal defense—the province of artillery and manufacturers—and not especially pleased with the general neglect of fortifications and heavy ordnance by an army preoccupied with the frontier. That may be why he preferred a capable artillerist like Archer for the inspector general's position.

Brown also had interests. He viewed himself as Commanding General in fact as well as in title, and set about trying to define his position at the head of the Army. He wanted to perfect the military establishment, and for that he needed information. Over the next few years, he wrote volumes of reports suggesting reforms, based on his own observations and on those of the inspectors general, as well as those of department commanders.[14] Brown, in other words, was the kind of Commanding General the department commander, Scott, feared because he used inspectors general as his eyes in the departments. He was also the sort of general that Scott the military theorist applauded, because he used inspectors general as his personal agents, taking inspection seriously and acting upon their findings. Archer went right to work with a vengeance, starting with Fort Stockton at Norfolk Harbor, Virginia, in December. He returned with his first annual report on 3 November 1822, having visited forts on the east and Gulf coasts and in Louisiana, at Springfield Armory and Watervliet Arsenal, at Plattsburgh, Niagara, Detroit, Pittsburgh Arsenal, and Baton Rouge, and points in between. His report took the form almost of a journal, describing each post in turn, with a staccato listing of inefficiencies and errors—mostly unelaborated adjectives. He established his pattern at Fort Stockton, whose entry was typical of the others:

Preparation of the Company Messes indifferent. Parade and Grounds appended to the Fort, indifferent as to cleanliness. Quarters the same. Arms in the hands of the company injured by injudicious cleaning, bright but not in good firing order. Appearance of the Company under arms respectable. Gun carriages on the platforms rotten past repair. The platforms in the same situation. Gun carriages, under the Sheds, and their implements very well preserved. The Black Hole [prison], small low and damp. The Arsenal and Storehouses good and sufficient, but very badly arranged. Books well kept and preserved. The Company books of the new Regulations not received. Magazine damp, powder very well piled. Hospital in good order the supplies abundant.[15]

The headings in Archer's report were police, discipline, instruction, service, and administration. Altogether, he usually filled a page for each post inspected.

---

14. Skelton, "Commanding General," 118.
15. Archer, Report for 1822, 3 Nov 22, in Inspection Reports 1814–1842, RG 159.

He found many substandard conditions, although some places received definite praise. The poor quality of the mess and general sloppiness of quarters and grounds drew the most notice from him, while the best he could say about instruction at the posts was "tolerable." Discipline he usually described simply as "good," while service—that is fatigue duty—was "fair" or "regular," meaning it was shared by all in just measure. Archer complained frequently, however, that the time devoted to construction and other fatigue duty prevented the troops from drilling. Nevertheless, his recommendations were only of the most incidental sort.[16]

Archer's first report opened up subjects that were to occupy inspectors for decades to come. The storage of ordnance property, for instance, he found inadequate even at Springfield Armory, while at the New Orleans Ordnance Depot in May 1822: "The Ordnance Stores &c. in charge of Lt. Ward are heaped together in such absolute confusion that it is impossible to form an accurate idea of the quantity, or of the quality of the greater part of them, to do either they should be removed and arranged, which with the force he has under his command would require some weeks to perform. Every thing that I have been able to examine is in very bad order."[17] . . . Unserviceable property was another problem. Archer found at every post quantities of property which should have been disposed of. But he opposed the current policy of selling it, which he said brought in only "a mere trifle," and was a practice that could be used to cover possession of stolen government goods. He also suggested that there was danger of "fraudulent substitution" of property going on sale, while the disposal itself made it easy to "conceal miss-management [sic] by disposing of that which should never have been received." . . . Archer found his particular specialty, the artillery, woefully inefficient. He recommended concentrating artillery units for training, even if that left many posts vacant. Saying that in wartime heavy artillery units were necessarily isolated, Archer suggested that they should spend peacetime in training. That was impossible because of the scattering and isolation of the companies. . . . Archer also had some ideas on officers' pay and "emoluments," or extra compensation for things like forage, rations, and quarters. "The emoluments of officers should always be increased with their rank" in order to provide incentive, he said. "The hope, of bettering ones [sic] situation, will make [an officer] submit to any discipline, and will lead him to engage cheerfully in any enterprise however laborious or hazardous, but when this hope is extinct or rendered too remote, the principal incentive to action is destroyed, how much worse then is it, when the consequence of promotion to rank, is the diminution of emolument, yet this is generally the case when a Lieutenant of Artillery is advanced to the grade of Captain," which usually meant assignment to a staff position without the compensation that came from service with troops.[18]

---

16. Ibid.
17. Ibid.
18. Ibid.

As required, Archer characterized the officers he encountered, listing by name those of bad habits who ought to be dropped or disciplined. Drinking was the most common shortcoming. But, said the Inspector General, "the vice, which has from all times been supposed common among Military Men, I mean excessive drinking, is scarcely known among the officers of the American Army." He then belied his own generalization. "Drunkenness, excessive, periodically," he said of one officer, and "Confirmed sot" and "Habitual indulgence in more liquor than his constitution can bear" he said of more than one.[19] Other officers were conducting inspections also because obviously Archer could not be everywhere. Asserting his own authority, General Scott detailed several officers to make inspections of arsenals and artillery units during 1822. They produced reports similar to those of post inspections, although the level of detail varied according to the inspector. Brevet Lieutenant Colonel Jacob Hindman made a thorough inspection of every artillery company in the northeast, discovering the usual variations in quality of mess and other aspects of administration. The most defective company was at West Point. Scott highly approved Hindman's report, and in sending it to Washington recommended moving the troops out of West Point. Hindman and Scott also echoed something that Archer complained of—that officers promoted to posts at arsenals had little to do, "are without occupation except as storekeepers or turn-keys."[20]

Archer's complaints about the mismanagement of public property brought a response from headquarters. Brown added to the duties of inspectors on 19 May 1823: "Hereafter the Inspecting Officers at the stated musters at the end of every second month, will examine, and note on the respective inspection returns, whether the officers commanding companies, and others charged with public property, furnish within the time prescribed the accounts, reports, returns, estimates and statements required by the Regulations."[21] That was the beginning of a role for inspectors in property management that would increase steadily in future years. Property and logistical issues often dominated inspectors' concerns as seen when Archer's peregrination resumed in December 1822. His annual tour began with an inspection of the armory at Harpers Ferry. "This Manufactory, considering it is a public institution, is certainly well managed," he said with an inadvertent touch of sarcasm. Archer was in fact fascinated by what he saw there, and devoted much of his report for 1823 to a long, gratuitous description of how muskets were manufactured. That completed, the Inspector General went to Norfolk Harbor in April, then to posts in the Carolinas, New York City, Boston Harbor, Portsmouth, Maine, and upstate New York. Visiting Springfield Armory, Archer inspected the artillery company at West Point,

---

19. Ibid. Archer listed quite a number of drunkards.

20. Reports of Lt. Col. William Lindsay, 3d Artillery Inspector, Dec 22, approved "and suggestions adhered to" by Scott, Feb 23, and Hindman to Scott, approved Feb 23, and endorsements, both in Inspection Reports 1814–1842, RG 159.

21. GO No. 38, AGO, 29 May 23, in GORI&IG. That was one of the earliest orders issued "By order of Major General Brown," instead of by order of the Secretary of War or without attribution.

then ended his tour at the Baltimore Arsenal. He did not inspect the Gulf Coast in 1823.[22]

The two major subjects of 1823 were the artillery and Fort Sullivan at Eastport, Maine. The former had not improved much since the previous year, and could only be "considered . . . as indifferent Infantry," in Archer's opinion. The men simply had not been trained to handle cannon, and only one company, thanks to its energetic commander, had held some form of training exercises. Archer said the reason for such negligence was that officers had not been trained in artillery duties, and in current circumstances had no call to learn them. On the positive side, most artillery units had improved the police of their stations. As for Fort Sullivan, where Archer arrived in July, "This Post should be abandoned, it is perfectly useless in time of war, or Peace. . . . It can afford no protection to the Town of Eastport during war, on the contrary it would then be absolutely necessary to remove the Garrison from the Island to save it from capture."[23] It was with similar comments that Archer had by 1823 established a comfortable routine as the Army's official tourist. His journeying around the Army occupied eight to nine months, after which he produced reports that were more commentary than description, bursts of quick characterizations without much elaboration. Wool, presumably, was doing much the same for infantry stations in the interior, although none of his reports from the early 1820s survives. Wool later would prove his value in other ways, and would become progressively less a roving inspector and more a chief assistant to the Commanding General.

Gaines: The Commander as Inspector

The army was so scattered, and the country so difficult to traverse, that two inspectors general could not cover everything in a year. The regulations required department commanders to make their own examinations, and that both Scott and Gaines did. Scott, however, never forwarded his own inspection reports to Washington, although he did pass on reports of inspections of artillery units conducted by his subordinates.[24] Gaines was more punctilious than Scott in submitting his annual reports. He soon made them semiannual, and long treatises that combined factual description of men and military posts with discourses on the state of the country and of the army. In his report for 1823, Gaines named the units in the Western Department, listed their locations, and described the positions of military posts. He also offered recommendations on establishing and expanding posts, especially to protect the Baton Rouge Arsenal, which he believed susceptible to isolation in the event of a slave rebellion—a danger he took seriously. Gaines also described the defenses of the Mississippi

---

22. Archer, Notes of a Tour of Inspection Commencing 10 Dec 22 (Report for 1823), in Inspection Reports 1814–1842, RG 159.

23. Ibid. Incidentally, the post was finally closed in 1873.

24. No inspection reports by Scott survive in the records, which are replete with those of Gaines.

River, and reported his findings during personal inspections of his posts; Baton Rouge received his most thorough scrutiny that year, its shabby hospital "but a mere shell." The department commander's reports filled in many details obscure to hurried inspectors general, with considerable attention to the condition of troops, rates of disease, and other important subjects, including the geography of the country west of the Mississippi.

Gaines was wide-ranging and verbose in his reports, never giving a subject a paragraph when a chapter could be written. His most elaborate essay in 1823 was on the lower Mississippi River. After detailed descriptions of supply depots and fortifications—he wanted more of the latter at the river's mouth—Gaines described the prevalence of diseases in the region. He gave the greatest attention to the hazards to navigation on the Mississippi, ending with an impassioned plea for a program to clear obstructions from the river. That, he said, would be justified on both commercial and military grounds, and in demonstration he described how it could be done and what he believed it would cost. Thanks to the opinions of Gaines and others, the following year Congress passed the first Rivers and Harbors Act, directing the Corps of Engineers to improve navigable rivers generally.[25] Gaines was equally full of suggestions on traditionally military topics. He advised General Brown on how to handle the Army's horrendous rate of desertion. The root cause, he said, was inattention by officers. Company commanders should know the character of their men, and keep watch over them off as well as on duty. Gaines believed that the abolition of stripes and lashes—whipping—as punishment for desertion had happened too quickly, producing an utter absence of restraint. He wanted to restore corporal punishment for "incorrigible drunkards and deserters," but opposed it for slight offenses. After closely reviewing the punishments used by European armies, Gaines said, "And I am convinced that shooting must occasionally be restored to in our service; as no punishment short of death, possesses a sufficient degree of terror to prevent the crime of desertion."[26]

Gaines was a hard man, of the old school, but he could not talk the government into restoring the death penalty for desertion in peacetime. More positively, however, he demonstrated as effectively as anyone since Anthony Wayne that inspection could be an effective tool of command, and that a properly conducted personal inspection could inspire a commander to think about larger issues affecting the army. He put so much store in inspection—not just as an implement of management, but as source of information on the scattered, almost invisible military units under him—that on 1 June 1824 he issued an order requiring all subordinate commanders to submit regular reports on the state and condition of their commands. Those reports gave him an

---

25. Gaines to Adjutant General (hereafter AG), Report for 1823, 28 Dec 23, in Inspection Reports 1814–1842, RG 159; Weigley, *History of the United States Army*, 166.
26. Gaines Report for 1823, RG 159.

immediate briefing on his units after he arrived in the Eastern Department in 1824, and some of them he transmitted to Washington for Brown's benefit.[27]

The Inspector and Property Management

The inspectors general, meanwhile, found their activities redefined slightly. Brown may have felt them slipping from his control, or wanted their assistance when they were not on tour. He ordered on 3 August 1824, "When not engaged in tours of inspection the Inspectors General will, in future, be stationed at General Headquarters." The same order required that, beginning 1 January 1825, all officers responsible for ordnance property were to submit quarterly inventories as instructed by the Ordnance Department, "which inventories, when verified by the inspector general of Artillery [Archer], will be by him transmitted to the War Department."[28] Archer's paper work expanded with that order. Another order six days later further tightened the War Department's control over "ordnance, ordnance stores, and munitions of war of all kinds." It directed inspectors general on their next tours to submit, along with their reports, schedules of ordnance property required for all posts, "both upon the peace and war establishments"—in other words, what was needed for the present, and what would be needed in an emergency. The inspectors were to consult with post commanders in preparing estimates, and to consider not only obvious military requirements but contributing factors such as local transportation difficulties. Wool was to prepare estimates for the infantry, and Archer, for artillery posts.[29]

The War Department, to prevent waste and theft, and under the pressure of tight budgets, continued to strengthen its control over public property in 1824 and 1825. After a jurisdictional dispute with the Commissary General of Purchases, Quartermaster General Thomas S. Jesup instituted a system of accountability for clothing and equipment issued throughout the Army in 1824; it became law in 1826, and remained essentially unchanged until World War II. The system standardized the distribution of regular issues, and required keeping a record on each soldier—an evocation of practices in Steuben's "little book" of the Revolution. The records, of course, were subject to examination by inspectors general.[30]

Congress lent a hand in property control on 3 March 1825 by authorizing the sale of unserviceable ordnance, arms, and military stores. To ensure that declarations of unserviceability were independent and honest, Congress ordered that "the inspection or survey of the unserviceable stores shall be made by an

---

27. An early example is from Lt. Col. W. Lawrence, commander of Madison Barracks, to Gaines. "Report of the State and Condition of My Command," 1 July 1824, in Inspection Reports 1814–1842, RG 159. Gaines and Scott alternated in command of the two departments for several years.
28. GO No. 55, AGO, 3 Aug 24, in GORI&IG.
29. GO No. 60, AGO, 9 Aug 24, in GORI&IG.
30. Risch, *Quartermaster Support*, 199.

inspector-general or such other officer or officers as the Secretary of War may appoint for that purpose.'' That was a significant, new, and long-lasting, responsibility for inspectors, as well as the first of a succession of services they were to perform for the Secretary of War rather than for the Commanding General.[31] The War Department implemented the legislation on 13 July 1825, telling post commanders to prepare returns of their unserviceable property, which they were to describe. ''As there may be a great difference in the 'stores' considered 'unserviceable,' '' said the order, ''in degree as well as in nature, the inspecting officer will describe the condition of every article examined, and in his remarks suggest in what manner it may best conduce to the public interest to dispose of them.'' Inspections were to be conducted by an inspector general ''when practicable,'' but for any post or arsenal not visited by an inspector general before 31 October, the commander or other officer designated by the War Department could perform the duty, transmitting his returns to the Adjutant General by 5 November.[32]

The new law and regulations were at the time a reasonable attempt to stem the waste and abuses that continued to deplete the War Department budget. But they led to a system of excessive accountability, with officers continually fearful of accusations of fraud or mismanagement, for which they were financially liable. Every tent or teacup that outlived its usefulness was subject to inspection, condemnation, consignment by boards, and sale or destruction—with elaborate records and statements at every stage of the process, all of which involved inspectors general or other designees. Worthless materials accumulated at every post, in the care of officers afraid to get rid of them lest they make a mistake. The burdens of inspectors general multiplied at the same time, their attention shifting from military efficiency to property forms and procedures. The change in emphasis, just beginning in 1825, was reflected in a general order which suspended the inspection returns that formerly had been the chief record of men present and absent. They were replaced by company muster rolls, forwarded directly to the Adjutant General without clearance by inspectors general.[33] The latter lost a role in mustering that they had carried since the Revolution.

More Changes in the Inspectorate

The day before Congress put inspectors into the property-condemnation business, the War Department revised its management of the inspectors general. The division of assignments between Archer, who examined the artillery, and Wool, touring the infantry, had not worked well, because it kept both inspectors away from their desks for too long. New orders on 2 March 1825 rescinded the earlier specialization and directed the two officers alternately to inspect

---

31. *An Act to authorize the sale of unserviceable ordnance, arms and military stores, Statutes at Large* 4, sec. 2, 127 (1825); Thian, *Legislative History*, 111.
32. GO No. 58, AGO, 13 Jul 25, in GORI&IG.
33. GO No. 53, AGO, 8 Jul 25, in GORI&IG.

posts throughout the entire army.[34] Even with this new arrangement, both officers remained firmly under the control of the Commanding General although the alternate inspection requirement may have been an effort to head off subordinate commanders' fears of domination.

In the case of property management, the War Department regarded formal inspection as a way of controlling expenses. But inspection itself was expensive, because of travel expenses. So the department kept inspectors general at home in alternate years, and generally reduced the amount of inspection in the Army. Scott revised the regulations slightly, the new volume appearing in 1825. The revisions had some changes affecting inspection: Department commanders were still required to make tours of inspection, but "as often as may be required by the War Department, or general-in-chief," with every post still to be visited at least once every two years. Artillery inspections remained as required in 1821, and in fact the "form and course of inspections," to the smallest detail, remained unchanged. Weekly company inspections were still to be made on Sundays. Regarding the "Inspectors' Department," the 1825 regulations repeated the text of 1821, with a signficant difference that increased the influence of the Commanding General and limited that of department commanders. The last sentence of the first paragraph now read: "The reports of the inspectors will be considered strictly confidential, so far as they relate to the character and habits of officers. In other respects, they will be subject, under the discretion of the general-in-chief, to be communicated to the commands affected by them, with a view to the correction of abuses."[35]

Inspection might as well have been cut back by 1825, for it had become almost perfunctory. Archer did not begin his tour until 21 March, at least three months behind his usual schedule, and he visited only a few posts along the Mississippi River and Red River. The thin substance of his report was another succession of unelaborated adjectives, the most signal comment a complaint that the "rapid destruction of Arms in the hands of the troops is an evil which requires a prompt and efficient remedy." His remedy was to end the frequent changes of hands to whom weapons were assigned. Artillery field officers, meanwhile, continued to tour their companies as required. They examined men and behavior, but for the most part ignored physical facilities. Typically, the colonels believed that their regiments looked good.[36] As far as some of the Army hierarchy was concerned, these official inspection reports were of little value. Archer, for instance, paid very little attention to the condition of the

---

34. GO No. 16, AGO, 2 Mar 25, in GORI&IG.

35. U.S. War Department *General Regulations for the Army; or, Military Institutes. Revised by Major-General Scott* (Washington: Davis and Force, 1825), 61–68, 367. As written in 1821, the sentence read: "The reports of the Inspectors to be considered strictly confidential." Copies of the general regulations were to be sent to all staff and field officers and all company commanders, "who will exhibit them at inspections." (p. 408 of *1825 Regulations*).

36. Archer, "Report of a Tour of Inspection of the Western Department of the Army of the United States, Commencing 21 March 1825" (Report for 1825), n.d., and a typical artillery report, Col. W. K. Armistead, 3d Artillery, "Report of Inspection, 13 January 1825," both in Inspection Reports 1814–1825, RG 159.

army's physical plant, which had been deteriorating for five years since 1820, when Congress imposed a moratorium on construction. Many posts were on the verge of collapse by 1825.

The Quartermaster Department was unable to obtain an accurate picture of physical conditions from the inspectors general, so it made its own survey in 1825, examining all military posts in order to support its request for a renewal of construction appropriations. The resulting descriptions were in very general terms, stressing the need for improvement. One point stood out, however. Apparently the way the army laid floors (or washed them) caused them to deteriorate quickly. The survey report repeatedly referred to the deplorable state of the floors at post after post, even in buildings otherwise described as in good condition. When the report did not condemn the flooring, it said that it had been "recently repaired."[37] The reports made it evident that governmental economizing had clearly gone too far, and the shabby state of troop housing was an important contributor to the high rate of desertion. If the inspectors general had pointed that out, corrective measures might have been instituted earlier. Things began to improve slightly only when the Quartermaster Department revealed the extent of the structural deterioration. The quartermasters were allowed to resume making repairs and building new barracks in 1825, although most of the work was done by the troops.

A New Inspector General

While Congress debated building appropriations, the Army's inspectorate underwent changes. Samuel B. Archer died on 11 December 1825. On the 17th, orders declared, "As a testimony of respect for the memory of Colonel Archer, late an Inspector General, in the Army, and an officer of distinguished merit, the officers of the General Staff will wear crepe and the hilts of their swords for the period of thirty days." The Army learned on the last day of the year that, on 21 December, it had acquired a new inspector general, George Croghan.[38] . . . George Croghan was a remarkable character. He was born near Louisville, Kentucky, 15 November 1791, the son of a veteran of the Revolution, Maj. William Croghan. George was no relation to the famous eighteenth-century Indian agent, George Croghan, but he was nephew, through his mother, to George Rogers Clark and William Clark. His uncles' famous exploits inspired the young Croghan with notions of a military career, upon which he embarked at the earliest opportunity. Volunteering in campaigns against the Indians beginning in 1810, Croghan served as aide to William Henry Harrison at the Battle of Tippecanoe in 1811. That earned him, at Harrison's instigation, a commission as captain in the 17th Infantry 12 March 1812. He became a major just over a

---

37. State of Barracks, Quarters &c. occupied by the troops, or in charge of the Quartermasters Department, April 1825, Records of the Office of the Quartermaster General (hereafter ROQMG), Miscellaneous Records Relating to Reservations and to Buildings 1819–1865, RG 92, National Archives.

38. GO No. 86, AGO, 17 Dec 25, and GO No. 89, AGO, 31 Dec 25, in GORI&IG.

COL. GEORGE CROGHAN. *Inspector General, 21 December 1825–25 September 1849.*

year later. Croghan served with such distinction in the defense of Fort Meigs in May 1813 that Harrison put him in command of Fort Stephenson, on the lower Sandusky River, with orders to burn and abandon the dilapidated old place if a strong enemy force approached. But the 21-year-old major defied those orders, barely talking his way out of a court-martial, and determined to hold Fort Stephenson with about 160 men and a cannon. He did just that when the British attacked in August, and became an instant and enduring national hero. The anniversary of the battle of Fort Stephenson was celebrated for over a century (Croghan was reinterred on the site in 1906), and in 1835 Congress struck a medal in Croghan's honor and gave each of his officers a sword as token of the nation's thanks. He was brevetted for his defense of Fort Stephenson, and became a lieutenant colonel before the end of the war. But he found no home in the peacetime army, and resigned his commission in 1817. He had married into the wealthy Livingston family of New York in 1816, and in 1817 moved to New Orleans, where his wife's relatives were well connected. Croghan drifted for the next few years, and fell into a number of bad habits, from which his own and his wife's family protected him thereafter. Their influence secured him the position of Postmaster of New Orleans in 1824.

Croghan was a well-educated man, graduate of the College of William and Mary in 1810, and extremely well-read. He was thoroughly versed in military subjects and much else, and in fact was one of the more literate inspectors general ever. His intelligence, drive, and critical eye and tongue fitted him well for his new position. His positive traits were truly strong, for they compensated for some serious defects. As the defender of Fort Stephenson in 1813, he was the very model of the dashing young officer of romantic fiction. He had a handsome, almost beautiful, face with soft eyes and a warm but determined expression. But the George Croghan of 1825 showed signs of dissipation, the eyes clouded and the face puffed. He became addicted to liquor and gambling while resident in New Orleans, and remained so for life.[39] He developed a habit of getting drunk, then allowing himself to be drawn into card games, signing

---

39. Francis Paul Prucha, ed., *Army Life on the Western Frontier: Selections From the Official Reports Made Between 1826 and 1845 by Colonel George Croghan* (Norman: University of Oklahoma Press, 1958), xiii–xxviii; *DAB*, 2: 557; Heitman, *Historical Register*, 1: 46–47, 339.

promissory notes he would not have acknowledged sober. He was a source of continual embarrassment to his family during his years as inspector general. He became the object of so many official complaints that his colleague, Inspector General Wool, several times was sent to investigate, returning with unfavorable reports. Each time, Croghan reformed for a while, and when sober he was a most effective inspector.[40]

Croghan served as Inspector General for more than twenty-three years, despite his defects. He kept his job because he usually performed it well, if not always on time, and because he enjoyed considerable protection. First among his guardians was his sister's husband, Quartermaster General Thomas S. Jesup. Croghan started borrowing money from Jesup the day before the latter's wedding in June 1822, when he received $1,250 to cover gambling debts. Jesup remained loyal for his wife's sake, however, and an easy touch for Croghan until the latter's death. The extent of his helpfulness was demonstrated in 1825, when it became necessary to clear Croghan's record so he could become Inspector General. Croghan's drinking and gambling had caused him to dip into the till while he was postmaster at New Orleans. In the easy climate of the times, that was not stealing, because he intended to pay it back, with the help of friends and family if necessary. Jesup went into debt in 1825 to cover $8,000 that Croghan owed the Post Office Department; it took five years for Croghan to pay him back, during which time he borrowed more.[41]

Croghan was recommended for the post of Inspector General by several important people when Archer died. His sponsors included William Henry Harrison and at least seven congressmen and senators, all of whom interceded with Secretary of War James Barbour. They had been trying for some time to get Croghan a government appointed in recognition of his war record, and at one time talked of a diplomatic assignment to Mexico. After his financial difficulties as postmaster, a return to the Army seemed to be a good idea. But Croghan himself expressed some uncertainty about the position of Inspector General.[42] He was nevertheless determined to succeed, and perhaps for the moment equally determined to reform. But at the same time, Croghan knew that his appointment from civilian life would bruise some feelings in the army. That was inevitable, given the politics of the officer corps, and the shortage of colonelcies. Croghan told Jesup early in February 1826 that he was grateful to all those who had gotten him the opportunity and he knew he would have to work hard to prove himself in the face of inevitable resentments from active officers.[43] His appointment ushered the Army's inspectorate into a long period of stability, free of the politics and tensions associated with commissions.

40. Prucha, *Army Life*, xx.

41. The remarkable relationship between Croghan and Jesup was brought to light by Chester L. Kieffer, *Maligned General: The Biography of Thomas Sidney Jesup* (San Rafael, California: Presidio Press, 1979), 98, 111. Jesup remained Croghan's ceaseless defender within the War Department.

42. Prucha, *Army Life*, xix.

43. Ibid., xixn.

Croghan served until 1849, while his colleague Wool remained until 1841. Only one other person, Sylvester Churchill, served as Inspector General before the Mexican War. The three men together carried the title of Inspector General for a total of sixty-eight years. It was during their tenure that inspection passed through a golden age, before undergoing vast alterations.

CHAPTER 11

Inspection and the Fortunes
of the Commander

(1826–1849)

American public attitudes toward the Army had begun to moderate by 1826. With the force reduced to insignificance, perceptions of any military threat to public liberty gradually vanished. The *North American Review* was typical of prevailing opinion in saying in 1826 that the Army was a reliable part of a greater community and nothing to be feared.[1] The relatively small size of the force and its deployment beyond the visibility of most of society unquestionably contributed to this reduction in public concern and interest. This was the position of the frontier army, with a few notable exceptions, for the remainder of the century.

The Nation's Military Forces

The *Review's* editorial may have been somewhat forward-looking at the time, but it did suggest the start of changing sentiments. At the same time, it passed over the fact that the army was not "mingled" with the nation, but was banished in small bands to the wilderness, where it was to watch the Indians. In any case, there had been a shift from outspoken fear and rejection of the military to an attitude of benign neglect. America could safely ignore its army. However, the military could not be ignored entirely because according to the chairman of the Senate Committee on Military Affairs in January 1826, about nine hundred soldiers deserted from the army every year, and this cost the public a fortune in wasted training and lost pay and equipment. Punishment by such means as the ball and chain and hard labor had not worked, the chairman reported, and something better must be attempted. He spoke in support of a bill to reduce desertion by increasing the pay of privates, and retaining part of it until the end of enlistment. There was only limited objection on the floor, mostly to increased pay for men who reenlisted, although some members objected to the withholding of pay as being unfair. The bill, a renewed War

---

1. *North American Review*, 23 (n.s., 14 October 1826): 245–74, reprinted in Russell F. Weigley, ed., *The American Military: Readings in History of the Military in American Society* (Reading, Massachusetts: Addison-Wesley, 1969), 71–77.

Department proposal, passed to its third reading, but no new law appeared in 1826.[2] The militia received equally fitful attention from Congress, which in 1826 told Secretary of War James Barbour to draw up a system of tactics and exercises for militia cavalry and artillery. Barbour established a board of regular and militia officers, chaired by Winfield Scott, to prepare the manuals. Meanwhile, he seized the opportunity to examine the condition of the militia officers, and others. He found that volunteers were widely regarded as more efficient troops than the militia, which in most states did not amount to much more than lists of names on outdated rosters. The scheduled militia musters, in fact, were generally disfavored as "schools of vice"; furthermore, there was no uniformity among the militia of the various states.

One of Barbour's respondents was former Inspector General Alexander Smyth, who was as usual out of step with the majority. His attitude had changed since 1813—now he wanted to improve the militia, in order to abolish the need for volunteer formations. Training the militia officers was sufficient, he said, to make militia effective. Another respondent was Alexander Macomb, hero of the battle of Plattsburgh, current Chief of Engineers, and future Commanding General. He offered an idea that decades later would become the pet cause of an inspector general—the recruitment of apprentice battalions. Macomb suggested that the army should accept boys fourteen to sixteen years old, apprenticed by their parents for fifteen years, during which time they would be trained to become noncommissioned officers. Not only would the army gain properly trained noncoms, Macomb averred, but it could return them to society at the end of their apprenticeship as potential leaders of militia. Although it was a novel idea, nothing came of it. The board of officers proposed several reforms, including reducing the number of men obliged to militia duty, making training more uniform, and so on, but the whole question came to naught in Congress, which took no action on any of the proposals.[3]

While Congress vacillated, the army went about its way. Croghan entered upon his duties as Inspector General early in 1826, and on 17 May was ordered to inspect posts on the upper Mississippi and Missouri rivers. He returned in October, ready to submit his report, and was somewhat at a loss on how to go about it. The regulations required certain topics to be addressed under separate headings, but there was some informality when it came to the format of the Inspector General's annual report. Adjutant General Roger Jones told Croghan that the reports were "constructed according to the dictate of the Inspector General himself." With that advice, Croghan submitted a long, and very engaging, first report.[4]

Congress renewed the privilege of free postage for inspectors general on 2 March 1827. That removed any obstacle to transmission of their reports, as

2. Benton, *Abridgement of Debates* (12 January 1826), 8: 371–74.
3. John K. Mahon, "A Board of Officers Considers the Condition of the Militia in 1826," *Military Affairs*, 15 (summer 1951): 85–94.
4. Prucha, *Army Life*, xx, xxiv (quoting Jones to Croghan, 3 Oct 26). Croghan's first report was Croghan, "Report of a Tour of Inspection during the Summer & Fall of 1826," n.d. (Report for 1826), in Inspection Reports 1814–1842, RG 159.

they were handed their instructions on 27 March. Also, it was recognition of their role as an important element of the staff. Wool was told to inspect all posts on the seaboard, from Maine to Virginia, while Croghan went to posts of the 7th Infantry in Arkansas, and stations along the Mississippi from New Orleans, Louisiana, to Fort Snelling, Minnesota, stopping by the Pittsburgh Arsenal on his way. Both were to depart "with as little delay as the season will permit," and to inspect all recruiting stations along their routes.[5]

Croghan was a replacement for Archer, who had concentrated on artillery and ordnance, but by 1827 Wool had made that area his principal object of attention. He considered it the most important part of the army. Wool had spent the winter of 1826 and 1827 developing a new classification of ordnance and ordnance stores, in order to raise their importance to equal other departments of the U.S. Army. That became his pet project for the year, and he was fairly outraged when the War Department failed to release the new classifications before he left on his inspection tour. They were issued at last, after his return, forcing him to repeat some inspections of arsenals. That delayed his report by three weeks, but he was happy to tell General Brown that he had observed overall, gradual improvements in the Ordnance Department—arsenal buildings were good, stores well cared for.[6]

The Inspectorate and the Commanding General

Wool's report was the last that Brown was to see, as the Commanding General died on 24 February 1828. He had been the one unifying force in an army that was really two armed camps. Edmund P. Gaines, in the Eastern Department, commanded 2,530 officers and men at twenty-seven posts, while Winfield Scott, in the Western Department, oversaw 2,203 officers and men at sixteen posts. Each department commander hated the other, perceiving correctly that he was a rival for the post of Commanding General. Gaines and Scott were strong-minded men, each surrounded by friends and regarded balefully by legions of enemies. As the Secretary of War considered which of the two to make Commanding General, it became apparent that either one, if disappointed, would stir up trouble that could wreck the organization.[7] In this atmosphere, the Senate Military Affairs Committee defined the role of Commanding General on 19 March 1828. He was a "medium of communication" between the government and the Army, keeping the former aware of military matters. He supervised discipline and ensured efficiency. He directed the recruiting service and the Artillery School. The commander also was to study American terrain in preparation for war, and to coordinate national mobilization. The statement

---

5. *An Act ammendatory of the act regulating the Post-Office Department, Statutes at Large* 4, sec. 4, 238 (1827).

6. Wool, "Confidential Report to General Brown," 16 Nov 27, in Inspection Reports 1814–1842, RG 159.

7. Watson, "Congressional Attitudes Toward Military," 615; Skelton, "Commanding General," 119.

said nothing about the Commanding General's relations with the Secretary of War or with the staff departments. It remained for the next tenant to determine what the office of the Commanding General really meant, and where the inspectors general stood in relation to the highest office.[8]

The next Commanding General surprised everyone. He appeared during a confusing change of leadership at the War Department. Secretary Barbour resigned as of 23 May 1828. The next day, the President promoted Alexander Macomb, Chief of Engineers, to the rank of major general—over the heads of Gaines and Scott. Peter B. Porter—who had once fought a duel with Alexander Smyth—became Secretary of War on 26 May. Macomb became Commanding General three days later. His appointment averted the dangers of the Gaines-Scott rivalry, but it angered both. Scott, characteristically, resigned in a huff. Porter managed to smooth his ruffled feathers enough to get a retraction, but Scott refused to have anything to do with Macomb except as strictly required by military duty. Scott, as feared, proved to be a source of dissension in the officer corps, but at least he did not lead a mutiny.[9] So Macomb entered office determined to make the Commanding General as much a reality as a title. He decided to make the inspectors general agents in his cause. But they were absent on their annual tours when he took office, sent off under orders issued 19 April. As Macomb sized up his inspectors from afar, Croghan picked that moment to succumb to his old weakness. He was to tour posts on the Great Lakes, in the Northeast (usually Wool's territory), at West Point, and down the East Coast. Croghan showed up at New London, Connecticut, too drunk to inspect the command. The commanding officer asked Quartermaster General Jesup to intercede. Evidently Jesup delivered a stern lecture, but within a year reports again circulated about Croghan's drinking and gambling. Moreover, he failed to turn in an annual report for 1828. Probably because of that series of events, Macomb placed his trust in Wool. Meanwhile, Gaines joined Scott in bypassing the new Commanding General, submitting to the Secretary of War a long, gratuitous report on the Indian menace and how to manage it.[10]

Amid that turmoil, the inspectors general acquired an additional power in April 1829, one that they had exercised occasionally since the Revolution. If a soldier was regarded as unfit for service on account of wounds, disease, or infirmity, the senior surgeon of his station was to provide the man's captain with a certificate of disability. When the captain presented that to an inspector

---

8. Skelton, "Commanding General," 119.

9. Ibid., 119; Heitman, *Historical Register*, 1: 16, 680, 800; Elliott, *Winfield Scott*, 241–49; Weigley, *History of the United States Army*, 170.

10. GO No. 14, AGO, 19 Apr 28, in GORI&IG; Chester L. Kieffer, *Maligned General: The Biography of Thomas Sidney Jesup* (San Rafael, California: Presidio Press, 1979), 111–12; Croghan's report dated 1828, an enclosure with Croghan to Macomb, 26 Aug 36 and postscript dated 1 Dec 36 (Report for 1836), in Inspection Reports, 1814–1842, RG 159; Edmund P. Gaines, "Indian Department," submitted to the Department of War 1 Jul 28, in Inspection Reports 1814–1842, RG 159. Why the latter was filed with inspection reports is not apparent, as it was really what would now be called a position paper.

general or post or regimental commander, either could grant a discharge.[11] However, discharges were a minor issue; the inspectors' first duty was to inspect. Croghan was dutifully dispatched to the West in the spring of 1829, while Wool passed a more interesting year. Macomb told them both on 16 May to inspect the conduct of officers, noncommissioned officers, and enlisted men, according to the regulations, and to make an assessment of the condition and efficiency of each individual and unit. He then gave them a list of specific points to consider. These included not only such traditional things as unit appearance and discipline but also requirements for inspectors to gauge the effectiveness of general orders and to recommend changes to the Articles of War.[12]

Croghan was delighted with Macomb's instructions. He took the opportunity to suggest to the Commanding General that he would not repeat his deplorable performance of 1828, promising strict adherence to the new requirements. He said he welcomed them as being much more helpful than previous guidelines for inspections.[13] Croghan's previous reports had in fact been long, detailed, and of high literary quality—that is, when he had himself well enough organized to get his reports in. But he adopted Macomb's listed points beginning in 1829 and his report that year was especially informative and engagingly presented.[14] They remain an exceptional documentary of the role, appearance and functions of the army as it began nearly a century of specialization in guarding the expanding frontier.

Reporting the State of the Army

Wool and Croghan were inspectors general during a unique period in the history of the U.S. Army. The force was widely scattered, and the authorities in Washington had substantially one source of knowing what went on at the isolated posts—the inspectors general. Furthermore, during Macomb's tenure as Commanding General, what the inspectors general had to say about the condition of the army was held in the highest regard, because it was the principal source of information that Macomb needed to assume control of his organization. Visits from the inspectors general, Macomb's personal representatives, were annual reminders that there was a Commanding General, and his desires were to be observed.

The Macomb years were a high point for the U.S. Army's inspectorate. The force was small—two men—but it was integrated, centrally directed, and a real

---

11. GO No. 7, AGO, 23 Apr 29, in GORI&IG; Sanger, "Inspector-General's Department," 243.

12. Macomb to Wool and Croghan, 16 May 29, as quoted in Prucha, *Army Life*, xxiv–xxvi. The original is in Letter Book, Volume I, Records of the Headquarters of the Army, RG 108, National Archives.

13. Croghan to Macomb, 13 Jun 29, quoted in Prucha, *Army Life*, xxvin.

14. Croghan, Report of Tour of Inspection during the Spring and Summer of 1829, n.d. (Report for 1829), in Inspection Reports 1814–1842, RG 159.

agency of the highest authority. It also had almost a monopoly on information about conditions in the scattered outposts that housed most of the troops. But neither circumstances outlasted Croghan and Wool. With the waning fortunes of the Commanding General, the place and purpose of the inspectors general became uncertain. After a while they were not Washington's only source of important information. Paper work and reporting systems multiplied throughout the nineteenth century, and the War Department had many ways of knowing where appropriations went, and how the public interest was or was not being served. Other staffs, including the Quartermaster Department and, especially, the Medical Department, developed their own inspection and reporting procedures, and eventually provided a wealth of detail on the personal and material state of the army. Therefore, the reports of the inspectors general during the quarter century preceding the Mexican War are unique in their importance, in the context of the time and in their informative value. They are often the only contemporary sources of information on conditions in the army, and they established patterns for generations of inspection reports that would follow them. They are also personal documents, expressions of the personalities of their authors. That makes them human, and therefore interesting.

Wool and Croghan followed a common set of rules, but they had different assignments and vastly different literary styles: Wool spent most of his time on the seacoasts and at Ordnance Department facilities, and concentrated on the improvement of ordnance and artillery. He contented himself with generalities about most other subjects, or ignored them altogether. He was also reluctant to point out deficiencies if he believed that they would be corrected without notice for the record. His reports, therefore, seldom make compelling reading. Croghan was quite another sort of man. He spent most of his time roaming the frontiers, where the majority of the army was scattered. He had to be more informative because the troops he surveyed were the farthest removed from headquarters. Croghan's educated style was characterized by a high sense of military propriety and a fine gift for controlled outrage. He presented the fullest picture of the army's social fabric and geographic setting and a very diverting one.

The Productive Inspector Wool

Wool lacked Croghan's easy literary style, but he was a far more productive inspector. Under "verbal instructions" from the Commanding General, he inspected the Artillery School of Practice at Fort Monroe, Virginia, in March 1829. He found there a new organization and a new commander, both improvements since his last visit. The officers, he said, were generally adept, although some were nervous during the inspection. Nevertheless, Wool was displeased that there was still more emphasis on infantry drill than on artillery practice, and he recommended some changes to make the place an effective service school.[15] Wool's scope was not limited to routine garrison visits. He also

---

15. Wool to Macomb, 13 Apr 29, in Inspection Reports 1814–1842, RG 159.

served the Secretary of War. From March through May 1829, he, a civilian official, and a lieutenant composed a board of inspectors to look into contracts at Harpers Ferry Arsenal, and to review the character of the superintendent. They discovered that diligent inspectors had been systematically fired from the arsenal, while lax ones remained. Furthermore, the superintendent owed money to a number of employees. He permitted a great deal of absence from work, while many defective muskets had been produced, with significant amounts of materials disappearing. The superintendent also was involved in some questionable real estate deals, and there was considerable conflict of interest among his employees. Among the abuses the board discovered were payments on warrants for work not done. At the least, said Wool and his colleagues, the superintendent was negligent. More directly, they found "a want of honesty and integrity on his part." Wool wrote the board's report.[16] The energetic inspector further devoted himself to another ordnance related task. Wool's major project for 1829 was the preparation of a detailed inventory of what ordnance property should be on hand at twenty-two garrisoned posts. From cannons to storage boxes, he prepared a catalog for every post, with explanatory remarks. It was a remarkable piece of work, winning the endorsement of the Ordnance Department the following year.[17]

While completing those assignments, Wool also managed to find time to make a regular tour of inspection. He visited the armories at Harpers Ferry and Springfield, and a host of arsenals and ordnance depots. Not surprisingly, given his orientation, he focused on the need to upgrade ordnance operations, which involved complicated financial and technical considerations. He recommended strengthening the Ordnance Department, and wanted to gather the scattered property supposed to be under its control, to "preserve it from waste and destruction." Wool also urged disposal of mountains of unserviceable ordnance property, although he said the job would be "difficult of execution." Nevertheless, he claimed that his personal exertions had served to improve things considerably.[18] In addition to his study on property, Wool submitted a separate report of his inspections in 1829 of military posts from Florida to New York and also New England. In it, he explained for Macomb's benefit his personal philosophy on the inspector's critical role in promoting efficiency:

I have uniformly made it my duty to notice all errors at the time of inspection, and not to mention them in my reports, unless they were of importance, provided the officers manifested a disposition to correct them. This mode I think preferable to confidential reports, which would scarcely be necessary if the inspecting Officers of Regiments would in their tours enforce a more rigid compliance with the regulations of the Army.[19]

---

16. Wool to Secretary of War, 26, 28 May 29, in Inspection Reports 1814–1842, RG 159.
17. Wool,"Estimate of Ordnance & Ordnance supplies for Military posts garrisoned in time of peace," 21 Oct 29, and Lt. Col. George Bomford, Ordnance, to Lt. Samuel Cooper, 4th Artillery, 14 May 30, in Inspection Reports 1814–1842, RG 159.
18. Wool to Macomb, 31 Oct 29, in Inspection Reports 1814–1842, RG 159.
19. Wool to Macomb, 10 Nov 29, in Inspection Reports 1814–1842, RG 159.

Wool's disinclination to recount deficiencies made his reports less entertaining than Croghan's, but they were instructive nevertheless. He was not reluctant to criticize when he thought criticism was merited, and he was especially displeased with the poor performance of the artillery colonels. They were to inspect their scattered companies regularly, and in the process keep them at a high state. As far as Wool was concerned, the artillery was in poor condition, and the colonels were to blame as they were not doing their job.[20] His reports were of great value because by then inspection was well established in the American army as a tool of command. It was the only tool of command in the artillery, since the companies were never assembled as regiments in one place where their colonels could supervise them directly. Wool believed that the colonels neglected their duty, and took it upon himself to reform the artillery and heavy ordnance. He wore himself out in the process, and by the fall of 1829 was incapacitated with a "severe headache" which threatened to delay his annual report, but the tireless inspector general overcame the pain and put his report into the mail on time.[21]

Gaines, Congress, and Disciplinary Reform

General Gaines, meanwhile, continued to produce his own voluminous inspection reports. His report on the Western Department and *Remarks Concerning the Militia of the United States* were published by Congress early in 1829, while later in the year, after another change of station, he sent in a 140-page report of inspection of the Eastern Department.[22] Gaines was faithful in his reporting, and as sweeping as ever. He focused his critical eye on the Ordnance Department and what it ought to be, subsistence and its organization, the Quartermaster Department, and other services. He also offered chapters on such topics as "sickly southern posts," books and records, the officer's oath of office, and anything else that came to his mind. His reports were mainly vehicles for recommendations, especially on the disposition of troops. In 1829 he gave a lot of attention to border and seacoast defenses, many of which he believed served no valid purpose. He recommended concentrating on harbor defense—an idea that finally became defense policy in the later 1800s. The wide-ranging general also believed that too much leeway was granted courts-martial, whose capricious punishments made miscreants "incorrigible." He recommended reform of punishments, forbidding cruelties like branding, as well as demeaning treatment of convicts. On the other hand, he asked for a return of lashing as a punishment.[23]

---

20. Ibid.

21. Wool to Macomb, 11 Nov 29 (two letters), in Inspection Reports 1814–1842, RG 159.

22. Edmund P. Gaines, "Report of a General Inspection of the Military Posts of the Western Department, and Remarks Concerning the Militia of the United States," Military Affairs (Mil. Aff.) Doc. 407, 20th Cong., 2d sess. (1829), ASP, 19; Gaines, "Report of an Inspection of the United States Forces and Military Posts in the Eastern Department . . . for the half Year Ending December 31st, 1829," received n.d. January 1830, in Inspection Reports 1814–1842, RG 159.

23. Gaines, "Report of an Inspection of . . . the Eastern Department for . . . 1829," cited in previous note. Gaines suggested that southern posts should be garrisoned by soldiers native to the South, who would be used to climate and resistant to its diseases.

Gaines was not alone in believing that the army should examine its disciplinary systems. The desertion rate was too high, and Congress again showed its concern. Congressman Nathaniel Macon of North Carolina and Senator Thomas Hart Benton of Missouri thought that the country and the U.S. Army would be better off without the United States Military Academy. They believed that that institution manufactured an isolated class of petty autocrats, who created conditions favoring desertion. Macon said he felt the academy created a gulf between officers and men and also denied the opportunity for qualified soldiers to rise to commissions.[24] Macon had a point, and Secretary of War John H. Eaton was inclined to agree with him. The country had long placed its faith in the militia, which presumed that every man could become a soldier. Every man by the same token could also become an officer in the militia. Why, therefore, should the officer corps of the Regular Army be restricted to a narrow class of people, frustrating the ambitions of potentially good officers in its own ranks? Those frustrations, some people believed, made a career as an enlisted man a dead end, and probably contributed to desertion.

As Congress debated improvements to the army's personnel situation, its official hope for national defense remained in the militia. But beginning about 1830, events occurred that undermined the last legislative props holding up the militia's increasingly hollow shell. Most states had long imposed fines for failure to appear properly equipped for militia day. Overdue militia fines were a principal reason that men were imprisoned for debt. But in the three decades before the Civil War, militia fines were repealed in state after state—first as part of a movement to end debt imprisonment, then as part of a general decline in militia. State militias were an avowed sham by 1860, existing only in the statute books and rarely performing musters.[25]

Powers and the Agents of the Commanding General

The quiet fading of the militia reinforced the importance of the Regular Army, which had problems of its own. Macomb had decided by 1830 to take firm control of the military establishment as part of a general reform. The War Department already showed tendencies of becoming a collection of independent bureaucracies, each reporting to the Secretary of War, with a Commanding General who commanded nothing. Of all the high army officials, only the inspectors general owed their principal loyalty to Macomb. So he determined to use them in his campaign to take charge of the army. Croghan proved undependable once again. Macomb dispatched him on a regular tour of inspection on 23 March 1830, to gather the information the Commanding General needed to oversee the field force. Having visited only Forts Preble and Sullivan and Hancock Barracks in the Northeast by early May, Croghan begged relief from

---

24. Macon to Benton, 1831, as quoted in Richard L. Watson, Jr., "Congressional Attitudes Toward Military Preparedness, 1829–1898", *Military Affairs*, 40 (December 1976): 617–18.
25. Lena London, "The Militia Fine 1830–1860," *Military Affairs*, 15 (fall 1951): 133–44.

his orders because of "family afflictions." Macomb let him go home, and received only a fragmentary annual report that year.[26] That probably confirmed Wool's status, apparent the next year, as Macomb's right-hand man, with Croghan relegated to the status of roving reporter.

In 1830 Macomb set about making the army's bureau heads subordinate to the Commanding General. His first target was the Adjutant General, who as controller of the Army's communications and general administration acted by that time as if the Commanding General did not exist—for instance by issuing orders in the latter's name, but without his knowledge. In the end, Macomb court-martialed Adjutant General Roger Jones for insubordination. To Jones' utter surprise, he was reprimanded by the court. After that, it was Macomb who defined the Adjutant General's duties, enforcing subordination to the Commanding General. Jones, good soldier and sagacious bureaucrat that he was, admitted defeat—probably content in the knowledge that Macomb would not always be Commanding General.[27] With Jones well in hand, beginning in 1831 Macomb used his clearly subordinate inspectors general and their inspections as a means of asserting his authority over the other staff department elements. He began with the most independent of all, his former province, the Corps of Engineers. His first blow was to order Wool to inspect the Military Academy, the corps' exclusive domain. The academy superintendent, Sylvanus Thayer, protested, as did the Chief of Engineers, but Macomb and Wool succeeded.[28]

Wool traveled all over the country that year, from New Orleans to Maine, and merely included West Point in his rounds—emphasizing that his visit there was a proper part of his ordinary routine. He generally found much to applaud in the United States Army that year, except for slovenly troops at Niagara, New York. West Point gave him an opportunity to aver the necessity for cavalry in the army, and to suggest that cavalry exercises be added to academy drills. He prefaced a long, critical discourse on the strengths and weaknesses of the West Point drill program, for which he offered improvements, with a statement of how his inspection of the academy was conducted so as not to offend the superintendent too much. He specified that he restricted his interest to military topics and facilities only and closed with praise for the appearance of the Corps of Cadets.[29] This visit to West Point and the roaming of most of the country on an inspection tour were only part of Wool's activities that year. The energetic inspector general also continued his crusade for the reform of the ordnance

26. Croghan to Sir, Oct 30 (Report for 1830), in Inspection Reports 1814–1842, RG 159. It should be noted that Prucha, in *Army Life*, xxiii, says that Croghan asked for and received several postponements of his departure until it was too late to inspect at all, and therefore made no tour in 1830. Actually, however, he reported on the three posts visited in April and May, after which he probably attended to his family problems. The report is apparently fragmentary; the last pages and signature block have not survived, and it is easy to miss as the work of Croghan.

27. Skelton, "Commanding General," 119.

28. Ibid., 119–20.

29. Wool to Macomb, 24 Oct 31 (Report for 1831), in Inspection Reports 1814–1842, RG 159. That his inspection was confined to purely military training meant that he did not presume to question the academic curriculum or its teaching.

establishment. Late in October he evidently believed that he had been criticized by Secretary of War Lewis Cass for some of his recommendations. In a letter to Macomb, he defended his good intentions by denying that any private concerns influenced his work. He emphasized the fact that the Ordnance Department took the majority of his time, and that he was "almost constantly engaged" in his work. He appended to his letter a report calling for more independent inspections as a way of improving the Army, and objecting to regimental inspections by colonels and lieutenant colonels, who he said got "in the way of the Inspectors General." He had also seen a British rifle battalion during the year, and thought it a good model for the United States Army to follow. He suggested further that American uniforms were inferior in cut to the British.[30]

Wool also put up a good front for the Secretary, writing directly to Cass the same day he wrote to Macomb. He recommended that the Secretary of War establish a permanent board of officers to act on improvements in weapons and other equipment, and reviewed his own work in helping the Ordnance Department gain control over its scattered property. He also presented Cass with a general review of the condition of forts and armories, and went on to call for more rules to govern sutlers.[31] This relatively uncontroversial tone characterized the next reporting year. While Wool was thus engaged, Croghan roamed over the West, around the Great Lakes, and across the New York frontier during the summer and fall, returning with a routine report. Gaines, meanwhile, took a break from his customary personal inspection, sending a subordinate to examine the 2d and 5th Infantry regiments, company by company. He transmitted the resulting report, which featured none of Gaines' usual exhortations, on to Macomb.[32] Macomb and the Corps of Engineers maintained a quiet truce through 1832, while his inspectors general were comparatively inactive. Because of illness in his family, Croghan delayed his departure several times, then did not inspect at all during the year. Nor does Wool appear to have done anything worth reporting.[33] Unprogrammed delays and the thoroughness of inspections in previous years ruled against any major new observations.

More Attempts at Army Reform

The U.S. Army continued in low repute in Congress that year. Ambrose H. Sevier, delegate from Arkansas Territory, told the House of Representatives that its ranks comprised the "refuse of society, collected in the cities and seaport towns; many of them broken down with years and infirmities." They were certainly a drunken lot, and in 1832 Secretary Cass moved to raise the Army's level of sobriety. After trying unsuccessfully to offer one cent a day in

---

30. Wool to Macomb, 31 Oct 31, in Inspection Reports 1814–1842, RG 159.
31. Wool to Cass, 31 Oct 31, in Inspection Reports 1814–1842, RG 159.
32. Croghan, "A tour of Inspection during the Summer and fall of 1831," Croghan to Macomb, 11 Nov 31 (Report for 1831), and Brig. Gen. H. Brady to Gaines, n.d., dated 1831 on endorsement, in Inspection Reports 1814–1842, RG 159.
33. Prucha, *Army Life*, xxiii. No reports by either Croghan or Wool survive for 1832.

lieu of the gill of whiskey, he added coffee and sugar to the rations as voluntary substitutes for liquor, and barred sutlers from selling "spirituous liquors" to the troops.[34] More substantial reforms were needed than voluntary temperance and Congress finally tried to set things right. It raised the authorized force to 7,129 officers and men in 1832, and added a battalion of mounted rangers to patrol the prairies. The following year, on 2 March 1833, the force rose to 7,194 officers and men, while the rangers became a regiment of dragoons. The same legislation at last answered the War Department's request for an attack on desertion. Congress abolished the enlistment bounty, reduced the term of enlistment from five years to three, and raised a private's monthly pay from $4.00 to $6.00 retaining the extra dollars for the first two years to discourage desertion. Reenlistment earned a man two months extra pay and the full $6.00 per month from the start of his second term. The law also provided that no man convicted of a crime could thereafter be recruited. Lastly, however, the lawmakers turned down Quartermaster General Jesup's request for something to improve the lot of officers in the frequently moving army. He wanted to provide furniture for their quarters, something Congress allowed in the navy but not the army, and he would be echoed in later years by inspectors general.[35]

Other minor attempts to improve the U.S. Army took place in 1833, some of them affecting the inspectors general. On 13 November, the War Department reiterated its orders of 1829, permitting inspectors general to discharge soldiers on a surgeon's certificate of disability. The same order ended the weekly Sunday inspections of companies and hospitals, moving the day to Saturday. Croghan recommended a year later a return of the weekly inspections to Sunday, because there was no longer "order and sobriety formerly observed on that day."[36] Whatever he thought, giving the soldiers a day off made enlisted life slightly less disagreeable. The change did not last long, however, and it ultimately took an inspector general with a different attitude to compel the army permanently to grant its soldiers a day of rest.

The Inspectors and Army Control

Croghan roamed the West that year, while Wool devoted his attention to inspections of artillery and ordnance operations. Once again, he inspected the

---

34. Watson, "Congressional Attitudes Toward Military," 616, 619. It is stated that "ardent spirits" were actually removed from the ration, effective 2 November 1832. Ganoe, *History of the United States Army*, 172.

35. Heitman, *Historical Register*, 2: 582–85; Watson, "Congressional Attitudes Toward Military," 623; Grace, *History of the United States Army*, 173; Otis E. Young, "The United States Mounted Ranger Battalion, 1832–1833," *Mississippi Valley Historical Review*, 41 (December 1954): 453–70; Weigley, *History of the United States Army*, 159–60; *Annual Report of the Quartermaster General* (hereafter cited as *ARQMG*) 1833, in Mil. Aff. Doc. 551, 23d Cong., 1st sess. (1833), ASP, 20. The formation of dragoons was encouraged by the Black Hawk War, fought more on the prairies than in the forests.

36. GO No. 107, AGO, 13 Nov 33, in GORI&IG; Croghan to Commanding General (CG), 15 Nov 34 (Report for 1834), in Inspection Reports 1814–1842, RG 159. The role of Inspector General Breckinridge in ending Sunday inspections is discussed below.

cadets at West Point. His repeated presence there increased the tensions between Macomb and the Corps of Engineers. West Point was long the corps' private preserve, offering an education that was not military, but was dominated by engineering and associated fields like mathematics and natural philosophy, added to a general education. The superiority of engineering was drummed into the heads of the cadets,[37] and any intrusion by Macomb or his agents threatened to undermine that philosophy. Macomb challenged the Corps of Engineers directly in 1834 and 1835, when he and Wool together inspected a number of the corps' fortification construction projects. That set off an uproar of complaints. According to Wool, there was "but one opinion among all the officers & that was extremely adverse to General Macomb's interference in any respect with the Corps of Engineers." But Macomb stood firm, going so far as to order the arrest of a captain at New York Harbor who refused to answer questions about his work.[38] The engineers maintained that theirs was a highly technical occupation not understandable by anyone else. Wool, who had immersed himself in the equally technical chemistry and physics of munitions manufacture, thought otherwise. He was not interested in questions of engineering, but in common sense and sound economy. What he discovered in his inspections embarrassed the corps.

Fort Delaware, Delaware, under construction in 1834, was a typical case. Wool visited the place in July 1834, and reported immediately to "My dear General," as he addressed Macomb. The place was in sad condition, badly deteriorated, although there was a large crew at work on a seawall and other structures. Wool looked carefully at construction expenses, and confessing that he was not an "Engineer by profession," he stated that there was a lot of wastage of sound materials in the demolition of old structures and construction of new ones. As for his right to raise such questions, he concluded, "although as I have before stated, not an 'Engineer by profession,' [I] shall hereafter give my opinion at length."[39]

While Wool affronted the Corps of Engineers, Croghan also was more active than he was formerly, in 1834 touring posts around the Great Lakes and in the upper Mississippi Valley. He offered a substantial annual report, prefaced with a set of recommendations "presumed upon ocular proof of the existence of certain evils and abuses that require immediate correction." He suggested requiring that servants of officers be mustered to support their pay; establishing post gardens at all posts, to be cultivated by men on detail; prohibiting company and private gardens at posts unless cultivated by civilians; repealing the law permitting extra-duty pay for men working for the staff departments; appointing sutlers to regiments instead of to posts; requiring that all sutlers be

---

37. Croghan to Macomb, 9 Dec 33 (Report for 1833), and Wool to Macomb, 23 Nov 33 (Report for 1833), in Inspection Reports 1814–1842, RG 159; James L. Morrison, Jr., "Educating the Civil War Generals: West Point, 1833–1861," *Military Affairs*, 38 (September 1974): 108–11. Morrison offers an excellent study of the West Point curriculum before the Civil War.

38. Skelton, "Commanding General," 120.

39. Wool to Macomb, 31 Jul 34, in Inspection Reports 1814–1842, RG 159.

army veterans; rescinding the order banning liquor from camp or garrison; and finally, repealing the order that prohibited Sunday inspections.[40]

When he received Croghan's report, Macomb was hard at work on a revision of the general regulations of the army. The revised regulations appeared in 1835, and demonstrated his triumph over the Corps of Engineers and the clear supremacy of the Commanding General. That was symbolized in the right of his inspectors general to inspect staff departments and installations under staff supervision. The long article on the "Inspector's Department" began:

1. It is through this department that the Secretary of War, and the Commanding General, are to be made acquainted with the actual state and condition of the army, and more especially the character and proficiency of the officers.

2. It is, therefore, made the duty of the Inspectors General, critically to inspect, as often as the Secretary of War or the Commanding General may direct, every branch connected with the military service, including the armories, arsenals, military posts, the departments of the staff, the department of the Commissary General of Purchases, the Military Academy at West Point, and the troops in general. At the end of every tour, or by the 15th of November in each year, they will transmit to the Commanding General, to be laid before the Secretary of War, reports of all that may have passed under their observation during their inspections.[41]

Specific headings were then given, accounting for virtually every bureau or function in the army. Each heading was followed by a paragraph giving a detailed list of things inspectors were to look for. The details were to a great extent derived both from the 1813 regulations and from Macomb's instructions of a few years previous, but with much more elaboration, and some changes. Regarding officers, for instance, the inspectors general were still in general terms to state whether they were honest, sober, and efficient, but the confidential reports characterizing them, which had been usual in years before, were not required. In fact, no such lists had been prepared since the conclusion of army reduction in the early 1820s. Inspectors general now were to make a special report on any officer deemed unfit for duty. The inspectors' approach was even more circumspect in other cases. In that of the staff departments, Macomb still felt it necessary to tread lightly around the Corps of Engineers. That department was not specifically mentioned in the article on the Inspector's Department. The Military Academy was the only Corps of Engineers program identified, although phrases like "other staff departments" and "other disbursing officers" clearly brought the corps within reach. Construction, however, was not a specific object of attention, although repairs to structures were. Except for actual fortifications, however, construction and repair was a Quartermaster Department responsibility.[42]

---

40. Croghan to Macomb, 15 Nov 34 (Report for 1834), in Inspection Reports 1814–1842, RG 159.

41. U.S. War Department, *General Regulations for the Army of the United States; Also, The Rules and Articles of War, and Extracts from Laws Relating to Them* (Washington: By Authority of the War Department, 1835), 131–37 (cited hereafter as *1835 Regulations*).

42. Ibid., 133.

The regulations for the Inspector's Department also set forth "Additional Duties of Inspectors General, when with an Army, including Militia and Volunteers, on active Service and in the Field." Those merely restated the broad staff duties given inspectors general in 1813, except that (probably to satisfy the Corps of Engineers) the inspectors general no longer supervised camp layout and location. The mustering and evaluation of militia and volunteer forces remained a prominent duty, as did inspection of condemned property.[43] As had been the case under the 1813 regulations, inspectors general were told to arrange their reports under the headings listed in the regulations, "and not blend the whole together, with one general remark. Each inspection report should be complete in itself, and contain a full and faithful representation, with such suggestions as they may consider necessary for the improvement of all the objects to which their attention may be directed."[44]

The regulations governing inspection procedures were substantially the same as those of 1825, although somewhat more generalized on what to look for in quarters, and giving more attention to inspection of post records. Post commanders were to inspect their posts monthly, while captains were to inspect their companies weekly (on Saturday) and lieutenants their sections every Wednesday. Hospitals also were to be inspected on Saturday, while the men were always to be inspected before being mustered for payment. There was also greater encouragement for personal cleanliness than there had been in previous regulations.[45] Inspectors general, under the 1835 regulations, were extensions of the will of the commander in chief. In peacetime, they were his eyes and his agents. In war or in the field, they served as chief of staff for the field army. Macomb evidently wanted his inspectors general respected as his emissaries. He would observe military custom regarding rank, but he would allow no failure to acknowledge the authority of the inspector to do his job.

Macomb had made his point in the new regulations, and apparently reneged in forcing his attentions on the Corps of Engineers. Wool spent the spring and summer touring a number of forts and arsenals, but he toured no construction projects and did not visit West Point. Of the troops in general, he reported "no material change since the inspections of 1834, either in appearance, discipline, police, or in the Company or Battalion drill." Wool was preoccupied with ordnance anyway, as evidenced by his special short report on arsenals in the Northeast.[46] Croghan made no regular tour of inspection in 1835, possibly because of a cholera epidemic. At the request of the Secretary of War, however, he made a special inspection of Fort Des Moines and other defenses in the region in October. He recommended that the "establishment at Rock Island" be "broken up," and tried to enlist Macomb's support for that in case the Secretary disagreed. Croghan also took the occasion to object to a proposed

---

43. Ibid., 136–37.
44. Ibid., 137.
45. Ibid., 67–70.
46. Wool to Macomb, 16 Oct 35 (Report for 1835), and Wool to Macomb, 4 Jun 35, in Inspection Reports 1814–1842, RG 159.

dragoon excursion beyond the Rockies under Col. Henry Dodge, as "it would end in the destruction and disbandment of the Corps. He might depart well mounted, but he would most assuredly return on foot."[47]

The War Department issued a manual of instructions and regulations for militia and volunteers early in 1836. It was prepared at Macomb's request by Assistant Adjutant General Samuel Cooper, regulations having long since ceased to be the responsibility of inspectors general. Regarding inspections, the pertinent sections were verbatim copies of the text of the Regular Army's 1835 regulations.[48] The manual was a last attempt to impose some order on manpower mobilization before the next emergency. It appeared none too soon, but was still largely disregarded at the state level. Virtually each militia, and even elements within each, carried on with their own particular drills and methods of operation.

The Inspectorate and the Seminole Wars

War with the Seminoles broke out in Florida in 1836, and the Army was woefully unprepared, its actual strength down to about 6,000—with only a little over 4,000 present and fit for duty. About a quarter of the force was rushed to the war zone, greatly straining the logistical system, while stretching the troops very thinly over other regions. Despite minor increases—another dragoon regiment and more ordnance officers—Congress did not expand the authorized strength of the army for two years. The war, it was assumed, could be conducted with volunteers. Congress and the Army alike underestimated the Seminoles.[49] The emergency, if it had been perceived as such as the time, could have been an opportunity to test out the new definitions of Commanding General and inspector general under the 1835 regulations. But the War Department looked elsewhere. In fact, its big project for 1836 was a great military road from Fort Jesup, Lousiana, to Fort Snelling, Minnesota, punctuated with posts from which troops would patrol the Indian frontier. Opposition rose against the idea within a year, and by 1841 the project was dead. Only the section of road from Fort Leavenworth to Fort Towson was constructed.[50]

The War Department's attention was also taken up with the Cherokee Indians. Instead of sending Wool to perform the Inspector General's duty in the war zone in Florida, the Secretary sent him to the Cherokee country to see

---

47. Croghan to Macomb, 25 Jan 36, in Inspection Reports 1814–1842, RG 159. It is suggested that cholera cut Croghan's tour short with the one post of Des Moines. Actually, there was no regular tour that year, perhaps because of the cholera. When Croghan went to Des Moines in October, the season was safe, after the first frost. Prucha, *Army Life*, 180.

48. U.S. War Department, *A Concise System of Instructions and Regulations for the Militia and Volunteers of the United States* . . . (Philadelphia: Robert P. DeSilver, 1836). See pp. 65–67 for inspection regulations.

49. Elliott, *Winfield Scott*, 288–310; Spaulding, *United States Army*, 162–63; Weigley, *History of the United States Army*, 161–62; Heitman, *Historical Register*, 2: 286–87, 626.

50. Harold L. Nelson, "Military Roads for War and Peace—1791–1836," *Military Affairs*, 19 (spring 1958): 11–14. Croghan, for one, pointed out the folly of running lines of communication parallel to a potential fighting front.

THE BATTLE OF MONCACO LAKE, 1837. *Inspectors John E. Wool and Sylvester Churchill were prominent in dealing with administrative aspects of the Seminole Wars.*

whether the Indians would observe the Treaty of New Echota, which required their removal to west of the Mississippi. Wool was empowered to command Tennessee volunteers, and could call out others if the Indians started any trouble. He requested regulars, but he did not get them. Wool sympathized with the Cherokees' being torn from their homes and forced away to a strange country. "The whole scene since I have been in this country," he wrote on 10 September 1836, "has been nothing but a heart-rending one, and such a one as I would be glad to get rid of as soon as circumstances will permit." When he tried to protect some Cherokees in Alabama, where their oppression by whites was the worst, the governor and state legislature charged him with usurping the power of civil authorities. The President had to refer the charges to an army court of inquiry, which cleared the Inspector General in September 1837.[51] It was not a good precedent that at the very moment the Inspector General's position was most clearly defined and placed under the Commanding General, the Secretary called Wool away for an assignment that another officer could have carried out. It was, of course, a testimonial to Wool's military and diplomatic abilities, and he was worthy of the assignment. But the diversion also suggested that the role of Inspector General was not regarded as very important when other tasks beckoned. Wool's assignment to the Cherokees in 1836 was not the last time that a Secretary of War would hand an inspector general a mission mainly because the officer appeared to be available.

---

51. Prucha, *Sword of the Republic*, 263–64.

As if the Cherokee problem were not enough, Wool was further distracted by his own financial interests. The military law of 1802 permitted extra rations for post commanders. The War Department had gradually extended the standard double rations to heads of staff departments, beginning in 1821. The department denied Wool's request for double rations in 1829, at the same time it approved that of the former clerk of the department, retroactively to 1822–1825. Wool was not a department head, but he was the senior inspector general. The Secretary of War decided in 1833 that he had been unfairly treated, and started giving him double rations. Wool then advanced a claim in Congress for retroactive payment, and Secretary of War Cass supported him. The House Committee on Military Affairs, impressed by Wool's record, also agreed and decreed that he receive rations retroactively for the same period as other staff officers. That conclusion was reached while Wool was engaged with the Cherokee problem.[52] While Wool was occupied away from the fighting in 1836, his colleague, Croghan, was equally diverted. He made a desultory tour of four posts on the Missouri and Mississippi rivers in the fall, then failed to get his report in on time. He attempted to make up for that by sending Macomb his annual inspection report for 1828, saying that the original had been in his trunk when it was stolen from a steamboat, and he had reconstructed the document from memory.[53]

With the Army's inspectors general otherwise occupied, commanders in the war zone improvised. They assigned the inspector's duty to at least two officers who would find themselves in similar positions later. Captain Ethan Allen Hitchcock, Gaines' assistant adjutant general, was assigned as acting inspector general of a force of 1,100 men under Col. Persifor F. Smith which was sent to Tampa in January 1836 as a reinforcement. In that capacity he wrote an account of a reconnaissance of the Dade massacre site on 22 February. Hitchcock would find himself a decade later an inspector general in Scott's force in Mexico.[54] Major Sylvester Churchill, of the 3d Artillery, gained similar inspection experience. He spent five years, 1836 to 1841, periodically serving as acting inspector general for the troops in Florida and working for Generals Thomas S. Jesup and Zachary Taylor, successive commanders there. His duties included inspecting troops and posts and mustering volunteers in and out of service. As inspector general for the Army of the South in 1836, he spent most of his time traveling to muster in volunteers. He discovered that even that had its hazards when he was hit by a tree, felled by a settler who gave no warning. Knocked from his horse and severely bruised, Churchill suffered from the injury the rest

---

52. *On Claim of an Inspector General of the Army for an Allowance of Double Rations*, Doc. 622, 24th Cong., 1st sess. (1836), ASP–MA, 6.

53. Croghan to Macomb, 16 Aug 36, postscript 1 Dec 36 (Report for 1836), and enclosure dated 1828, in Inspection Reports 1814–1842, RG 159.

54. Ethan Allen Hitchcock, *Fifty Years in Camp and Field: Diary of Ethan Allen Hitchcock*, W. A. Croffut, ed. (New York: Putnam, 1909), 86–89, 89–91. Hitchcock's service in Florida was cut short in March, when Gaines sent him to Natchitoches, Louisiana, to observe the rebellion in Texas. His private opinion of that situation, written before the Texan victory at San Jacinto, has been published as Marshall M. True, ed., "Ethan Allen Hitchcock and the Texas Rebellion: A Letter Home," *Vermont History*, 45 (spring 1977): 102–06.

of his life—much of which he spent as an inspector general of the Army. He, too, was involved in aspects of the Indian removal and then later was made a subdistrict commander near Saint Augustine.[55] . . . The principle of inspection worked well enough in the early mobilization of volunteers for the Second Seminole War, but a centrally directed inspectorate had nothing to do with it. In fact, as was to happen again in later wars, the Army's inspectorate fell apart. It failed to offer the Commanding General oversight on the whole army, and only incidentally contributed to the war effort.

Decline of the Commanding General

The war did not go well, and partly as a result, Macomb's control over the army began to slip. Secretary of War Joel R. Poinsett, late in 1837, proposed a reorganization of the U.S. Army, with all staff services under Macomb, whose role would have vaguely resembled that of the Chief of Staff created in 1903. Macomb was the chief influence on the proposal, which grew out of his struggle to define the role of the Commanding General. The actual direction of military operations would have rested with field commanders, reporting to the Secretary through the Commanding General.[56] Although nothing came of Poinsett's proposal, he had already implemented the idea so far as possible. In an order redistributing the troops on 19 May 1837, the War Department changed the boundaries of Gaines' and Scott's domains, which were at that time called military divisions, comprising seven geographical departments. The headquarters of the Eastern Division (headed by Winfield Scott) was fixed at Elizabethtown, New Jersey, while the Western Division (headed by Edmund P. Gaines) lodged at Jefferson Barracks, Missouri—neither very close to the scene of the Second Seminole War. The order further attached one of the inspectors general to each as "chief of the staff," to perform the duties of adjutant and inspector general. Accordingly, Inspector General Wool was assigned to the Eastern Division, and Inspector General Croghan to the Western Division. Each was subject to the orders of his division commander.[57]

Poinsett had at one stroke made the Commanding General a cipher. The commander's control over the staff departments vanished because he no longer had the inspectors general as his agents. His control over the line of the army had always been strained, given the attitudes of Scott and Gaines. With the inspectors general transferred to the division commanders, Macomb knew only what those commanders wanted him to know, except such reports as they were specifically required to send him. Macomb was never able to gain back what he had lost in his attempts to consolidate authority in the Commanding General,

---

55. Churchill, *Sketch of Life of Churchill*, 31–32, 36–37. As discussed previously, Churchill had been an assistant inspector general from 1813 to 1815. General Jesup was the Quartermaster General, commander in the battle zone because he wanted a field command, because the greatest difficulties were logistical, and because the war was not supposed to be worth the full-time presence of the Commanding General. About a quarter of the Army was involved.

56. Skelton, "Commanding General," 120.

57. GO No. 32, AGO, 19 May 37, in GORI&IG.

even after the inspectors general returned to his staff, and the central inspectorate that he had established was also demolished. The inspectors general ceased inspecting. Wool for a time was occupied with the Cherokees; he then joined Scott as a chief of staff who soon had another improvised assignment. Croghan made no inspections in 1837, spending his time mustering volunteers for the Second Seminole War.[58]

Croghan—reporting to Gaines, not Macomb—resumed his inspection tours in 1838, but Wool did not. During trouble on the Canadian border following the destruction of an American boat, the *Caroline*, Scott went to Buffalo in January as a mediator. He sent Wool to Vermont to preserve the peace in an area where local sentiment was strong for the "Patriots," groups of men, mostly Canadians, whose raids took them into Canada during a rebellion there that winter. Wool mustered volunteers and sent them to intercept arms and ammunition destined for Canada and also supported local authorities in thwarting Patriot activities in northern Vermont. But the absence of Regular Army troops in the area made it impossible for the United States to keep faith with Britain. A frustrated Wool was back in Washington by June, begging for troops for the border.[59]

Congress, meanwhile, had taken up the question of expanding the army, which was seemingly ineffectual with the Seminoles. The Senate debated a bill to expand the army in January. Its chief proponent was Thomas Hart Benton, who especially wanted to increase the Corps of Engineers, the Corps of Topographical Engineers, and the Ordnance Department. Opponents of the bill were equivocal, but were generally united in opposing increases in the officer corps; some favored expansion of the enlisted force only. But Benton had his way with expansions in the staff departments, and held forth through several attempts to table the item.[60] Herewith, the product of the debate was the act of 5 July 1838, which with supplemental legislation two days later raised the authorized force to 12,539 officers and men. One section governed the army's inspectorate: "The President is authorized to appoint two assistant adjutants-general, with the brevet rank of captain, who shall be taken from the line of the army, and in addition to their own shall perform the duties of assistant inspectors-general when the circumstances of the service may require."[61]

That combination of inspectors' and adjutants' positions was a reversion to the days of the War of 1812 and even the Revolution. It also followed the precedent established the year before by Poinsett, making each inspector general a divisional chief of staff and an adjutant and inspector general. It was inevitable, in the nature of things, that adjutants/inspectors would spend most of their time as adjutants. But the legislation did have a fortunate side-effect. It

58. Prucha, *Army Life*, 180.
59. Prucha, *Sword of the Republic*, 315–18.
60. *Congressional Globe*, 25th Cong., 2d sess. (24 January 1838), 133. Benton also wanted to end the practice of army engineers working for private concerns, and introduced an amendment to that end.
61. *An Act to increase the present military establishment of the United States and for other purposes, Statutes at Large* 5, sec. 7, 256 (1838).

permitted a return of the inspectors general to the War Department on the assumption that the increases caused by Benton's recent law would provide adequate division staffs.[62] Thus did Wool and Croghan return although never again would they be Macomb's instruments of control over the army. The reason was not just because of the interruption caused by their transfer to the divisions: Macomb was becoming powerless as the unintended consequence of some of Poinsett's reform efforts. Poinsett was not consciously bent on weakening the power of the Commanding General. Rather, he wanted to strengthen the office, that being as part of his general reform of the military establishment. But his actions had the opposite effect.

Poinsett was the most energetic and forceful Secretary of War in many years, a widely traveled man of great insight. He proposed a comprehensive overhaul of the militia system, and a more modern organization of the Regular Army. When Congress would not concur, he did what was in his power. He sent the Ordnance Board to study European systems in 1840, and made a tour of his own the same year. His findings strengthened the army's supply organizations, and also caused him to remark that the American army was "the best paid, the best fed, the best clothed, and the worst lodged army in Christendom."[63] That attitude caused him to formulate the Army's first policy on housing and construction in 1838, a year in which he also returned light artillery to the force. Poinsett was such a dynamic personality that power naturally gravitated to him, the staff departments looked to the Secretary, and the Army slipped away from Macomb. Then, too, Macomb's inspectors general were not much help to him after they returned from the divisions. Wool continued his preoccupation with ordnance, and naturally gravitated toward Poinsett, who shared his interest in improving that staff service. Croghan, meanwhile, again fell victim to his weakness in 1838 and 1839. Jesup remained in debt, bailing his brother-in-law out of his gambling losses. If he was ever inclined to wash his hands of the dissipated inspector general, he kept his feelings to himself, out of love for his wife, Croghan's sister.[64]

If either Croghan or Wool conducted a regular tour of inspection in 1839, no record survives. Apparently, as far as the War Department was concerned, the inspectors general were to roam from post to post, determining whether commanders adhered to department policy. However, that policy could change capriciously. The department ordered post commanders on 18 March 1839 to enforce the regulations requiring sutlers to procure the "Soldier's Book" and make it available to the troops. Inspectors general were to report to "General Head Quarters" those sutlers who did not stock the publication, and companies that were without them. But just a month later, the department determined that every recruit would receive a copy of the Soldier's Book (the personal record of

62. GO No. 58, AGO, 13 Dec 38, in GORI&IG.

63. J. Fred Rippy, *Joel R. Poinsett, Versatile American* (Durham: Duke University Press, 1935), 175–77; Spaulding, *United States Army*, 165–66; Weigley, *History of the United States Army*, 156, 171–72.

64. Kieffer, *Maligned General*, 112.

clothing and equipment, and other information) before joining his regiment, with its cost deducted from his first pay. What the inspectors general were to make of that was not explained.[65]

Mustering was a serious business to the cost-conscious War Department. It entailed substantially a counting of the men of a given unit, verifying their dates of enlistment and terms of qualifying active service during the calendar period for which the muster was conducted. The muster served as the basis for payment, ensuring that no one be paid for service not provided, as well as a headcount to verify unit strength. That was an especially important activity when volunteers individually and in units came and went constantly, as during a war. Mustering also served the political interest in ensuring that volunteers remained throughout their lawful terms, and equally that no one was forced to stay longer than his period of enlistment. This was not always done by commanders with the desired degree of accuracy. Macomb expressed his displeasure during 1839 that commanding officers were not performing their mustering duty as required and were often delegating it to others. So in October he issued new orders: Officers of the Inspector General's or Adjutant General's Department when practicable were to muster troops every two months for payment. Otherwise, "well qualified officers of the line" assigned by a general commanding an army, division, or department were to muster the men. The regulations also specified that inspections were to be made at every muster. Furthermore, reviews and field exercises and maneuvers were to precede the musters and monthly inspections. It was the responsibility of inspectors general, adjutants general, and commanding officers to ensure that all regulations governing inspections were observed, and that men and officers were properly equipped and in full dress uniform. Lastly, the Soldier's Book was to be accounted for at every muster and inspection, the inspector observing that all entries had been properly made, and that each man had his book.[66]

That order was an implication that the army's field commanders needed help from a knowledgeable source like the inspectorate. Hitherto, the inspectors had not even provided the most elementary advice ensuring that the payroll was properly disbursed. Shortcomings most likely had existed in the volunteer formations and new units of regulars formed since 1838, but in general the Army had had no systematic inspection to show them. Offsetting this, Poinsett relieved the inspectors general of the burden of examining unserviceable ordnance property in December. Now it was to be inspected by a designated Ordnance Department officer. Inspectors general were to continue as before to inspect armories, arsenals, and depots and to report their observations. But neither they nor the ordnance officers had the authority to dispose of con-

---

65. GO No. 11, AGO, 18 Mar 37, in GORI&IG; GO No. 26, AGO, 23 Apr 39, in Orders and Circulars 1797–1910, RG 94. Regarding inspections in 1839, Francis Paul Prucha conducted a thorough search of RG 159 and RG 94, and could find no record of what Croghan did that year. Prucha, *Army Life*, 180.

66. GO No. 54, AGO, 22 Oct 39, in GORI&IG.

demned stores. No condemned ordnance materials could be disposed of without a special order of the President—a recent instruction from Congress.[67]

The inspectors general resumed their routines in 1840, but their potential influence over the United States Army waned with that of Commanding General Macomb. The latter's loss of power was symbolized in the new general regulations issued in 1841, indicating that he had lost his fight to curb the independence of the Corps of Engineers. The regulations governing inspectors general were substantially the same as they had been in 1835, except in one respect: The United States Military Academy was conspicuously absent from the general statement of their purview—it was now under the regulations for the Corps of Engineers, the final regulation being "the superintendence and inspection of the Military Academy." Another significant alteration was the return of the weekly company and hospital inspection to Sunday, depriving the men of their day off.[68]

It was apparent that the tide was against Macomb, and that the Corps of Engineers was triumphantly independent of his oversight. He still retained his two inspectors general, however, and might have used them to restore some of his lost authority. But the Commanding General himself was in failing health by 1841, and his inspectors general were anything but helpful. Wool was distracted by his own ambitions, while Croghan's conduct became disgraceful. In fact, Croghan's drunkenness and financial difficulties aroused so many complaints that in 1841 Macomb ordered Wool to investigate his colleague. Wool returned a very unfavorable report. When the Secretary of War was on the verge of dismissing Croghan, however, it appeared that he reformed himself somewhat, and General Gaines interceded in his behalf. Croghan therefore escaped disciplinary action and remained an inspector general. But if he made a tour that year, he left no record of it.[69]

Wool was scheduled for promotion to brigadier general whenever Gaines or Scott replaced Macomb, whose death was expected at any time. Macomb became increasingly ineffective, so Secretary of War John Bell, who took office on 5 March, gradually assumed the managerial duties that his predecessors had shared with the Commanding General. The Secretary intended to pick Wool's successor personally. He summoned Maj. Ethan Allen Hitchcock to Washington to meet with him in May. Bell told Hitchcock that he had been "much talked of" for the position of an inspector general. Winfield Scott, however, had strongly opposed Hitchcock, distrusting him since the time some incidents had occurred between the two, and because of his long association with Scott's rival, Gaines. Hitchcock advised Bell not to overrule Scott, and when the Secretary offered him the leadership of the Indian Bureau, he also declined that.[70] Hitchcock was still at the War Department on 25 June. He

67. GO No. 63, AGO, 6 Dec 39, in GORI&IG.

68. U.S. War Department, *General Regulations for the Army of the United States, 1841* (Washington: by authority of the War Department, 1841), 148–54, 155 (hereafter cited as *1841 Regulations*).

69. Prucha, *Army Life*, xx, 180.

70. Hitchcock, *Fifty Years*, 139–31.

recorded in his diary that day, "Major-General Macomb died to-day at half past 2 p.m.—paralysis—third stroke." On the 29th, he wrote, "The General was buried yesterday in the Congressional graveyard about mid-day. Procession nearly a mile long, marshalled by General Jesup."[71]

New Commander and Divided Inspectorate

The Commanding General's position also died that day, although its title and rank lived on. Scott and Gaines both claimed the position by reason of seniority. The commission of each acutally dated from exactly the same time. Gaines, however, preceded Scott on the list, while Scott held a brevet commission older than Gaines'. Each was a capable man with serious personality defects; each also retained his partisans. Neither had earned any credit in the Seminole wars—both, in fact, had been reprimanded for personal feuding that bungled their two expeditions in 1836—although Gaines' association with the frustrating conflict was longer. Whatever the reason, Scott became major general as of the date of Macomb's death, and Commanding General 5 July 1841. Gaines, however, was not without influence in the new order, and to everyone's surprise refused to resign from the Army.[72]

Wool became a brigadier general with Scott's promotion, and vacated the position of inspector general. What probably ensued was an attempt to balance the egos of Scott and Gaines. The inspector general's position was the only opening in the War Department hierarchy, the other bureau chiefs secure until they chose to leave. Because of Wool's special interests, it was probably determined that the new inspector general should also be an artillerist, who was otherwise qualified for the position. It was probably also desired that the new man be acceptable to Gaines. On 15 September 1841, the War Department announced the appointment of Sylvester Churchill, effective 25 June.[73] Whether Churchill was actually Gaines' man is open to speculation. Gaines was probably as familiar with him as he was with Croghan, because Churchill had spent some of the previous five years as inspector general of the main army in Florida, which kept him active in Gaines' territory. At least, Gaines posed no strong objection to the appointment.

Churchill was born at Woodstock, Vermont, on 2 August 1783. He grew up on his father's farm and began a career as the publisher of a small local newspaper. However, in March 1812 he accepted a commission in the 3d Artillery, remaining in the Army for the rest of his life. He first served under Dearborn's command on the east side of Lake Champlain. In August 1813 he was promoted to captain and was transferred to the staff of General Wade

---

71. Ibid., 133.

72. Elliott, *Winfield Scott*, 241–49; James W. Silver, "Edmund Pendleton Gaines and Frontier Problems," *Journal of the Southern Historical Association* 1 (1935): 320–44; White, *Jacksonians*, 191–94; Weigley, *History of the United States Army*, 161, 170; Heitman, *Historical Register*, 2: 870.

73. GO No. 53, AGO, 15 Sep 41, in GORI&IG.

Hampton, first as ordnance officer, then as inspector general. For the remainder of the war he served as inspector on various senior staffs at Niagara and Plattsburgh, New York, rising to the rank of temporary major. He reverted to captain at war's end, rejoining the 3d Artillery at Plattsburgh. He then served from 1816 to 1824 as commander of the artillery defenses of New York City, based at Fort Columbus. While there, he was transferred to the 1st Artillery. From 1824 to 1828 he commanded the Allegheny Arsenal at Pittsburgh, Pennsylvania, then rejoined his regiment at Fort Johnson, Wilmington, North Carolina, to command Company D until 1835. He was promoted to major that year and reassigned to Fort Sullivan, Eastport, Maine. However, the outbreak of the Second Seminole War brought him to the South again. He first served on Jesup's staff as acting inspector general, spending most of his time mustering militia and volunteer forces. In June of 1836, as an additional duty, he commanded one of the columns evacuating the Cherokees from northern Alabama. He joined his regiment in 1838, commanding it as infantry in operations along the Saint Johns River. He ultimately became a subdistrict commander in the Saint Augustine area. He had shown himself to be an able and courageous field commander and administrator.[74]

Unlike Wool and Croghan, Churchill did not become an inspector general on the strength of a war record. Rather, his was a record of quiet competence and ability in a variety of responsible positions. He was respected and liked by all with whom he had served. That may have been his strongest qualification for the position, because it meant that he had earned no important enemies during three decades in the Army. Accordingly, and because of his seniority, nobody questioned Churchill's entitlement to a colonelcy and appointment as an inspector general. His career, particularly the last five years, had given him more pertinent experience than that possessed by any other candidate.

Churchill was 58 years old in 1841, eight years older than the deteriorating Croghan. The two together could not promise to provide as vigorous an inspectorate as before. The U.S. Army as a whole was becoming burdened with aging veterans of the last war, much as the Army of 1812 has been dominated by relics of the Revolution. Given the increasing independence of the staff departments, the strong sense of prerogative shown by the brigadier generals— Wool and, especially, Gaines—and the gravitation of power into the hands of the Secretary of War, it is not likely that Scott could have restored the power of the Commanding General even if either he or his inspectors had been younger. And then, circumstances were not promising for a strong inspectorate in any case. Scott had long maintained that inspectors general were unnecessary, that commanders should do their own inspecting. His attitude as a department commander had helped to weaken the position of Commanding General by the

74. Churchill, *Sketch of Life of Churchill*, passim; Brown, *LBD*, 2: 5; S. H. Churchill and N. W. Churchill, *The Churchill Family in America* (n.p.: Family of G. Churchill, n.d.), 98–99; Swan Dana Henry, *The History of Woodstock, Vermont, 1761–1886* (Woodstock: Woodstock Foundation, 1980), 45–46; Heitman, *Historical Register*, 1: 301.

time he inherited it. Like Macomb, Scott could have used the inspectors general to gain influence, but when he took office he showed no inclination to do so. He was a suspicious, cantankerous man, who saw enemies behind every tree and interpreted even compliments as personal attacks. Scott had not selected his inspectors general—they were in fact better known to Gaines than to himself—so he evidently placed little confidence in them. The Army's central inspectorate, already debilitated by the disruptions of the Second Seminole War, thus declined during Scott's tenure as Commanding General. As time went on, the inspectors all became more agents of the Secretary of War than they were of the Commanding General.

The trend began very soon: The Secretary of War apparently wanted regular inspections to go forth, and at the same time wanted Croghan to be more dutiful. Croghan accordingly was required to send his inspection reports directly to the Commanding General from each post as he inspected it in 1842. Instead of an inspection report that year, Croghan submitted at least nine separate letters from locations ranging from Detroit to Fort Leavenworth.[75] Also, the Secretary took a page from Macomb's book, and ordered the inspectors general to examine the business practices of the Corps of Engineers. The army was told in a general order on 1 June 1842 that the duties of the inspectors general, or officers acting as inspectors, included the examination and inspection of all supplies and materials procured for the construction of forts, or for harbor and river improvements, and all the related engineer property. They were also to examine all extracts and financial arrangements made by the Corps of Engineers and the Quartermaster's Department.[76] That order represented a significant expansion of the Inspector General's purview. Its purpose, however, was not to serve the interests of the Commanding General, but was to serve those of the Secretary, who was understandably interested in what the staff departments did with their appropriations. In tightening the accountability of those departments to the Secretary of War, the order further undermined the Commanding General's influence over the whole Army. He was left in nominal command of the line formations, superior in rank to all other officers, but that brought him nothing except courtesies.

There were now, in a sense, two commanders of the Army. The Commanding General theoretically commanded the troops, although in fact the division commanders exercised that power, and they had under them the department commanders. The Secretary of War commanded the War Department, which

---

75. Croghan's reports for 1842 are as follows: Detroit and Detroit Arsenal, n.d. June; Fort Gratiot, 21 June; Fort Brady, 25 June; Fort Mackinac, 28 and 29 June; Fort Crawford, 11 July; Fort Snelling, 16 July; Fort Atkinson, 27 July; Prairie du Chien, 29 July; and Fort Leavenworth, 16 August, in Inspection Reports 1814–1842, RG 159.

76. GO No. 32, AGO, 1 June 42, in GORI&IG; Sanger, "Inspector-General's Department," 243, dates the Secretary's original order to May. Paragraph 835 of the general regulations was the general statement of duty for inspectors general, including: "by the 15th of November of each year, the Inspectors-General will make and transmit to the Commanding-General, to be laid before the Secretary of War, reports of all that may have passed under their observation during their inspections." *1841 Regulations*, 148–49.

was a collection of bureaus whose officials happened to wear uniforms although they enjoyed considerable independence. The inspectors general were perforce divided. When they inspected troops, they served the Commanding General; when they inspected staff operations, they served the Secretary. That their reports all went to the Commanding General before going to the Secretary was a mere formality because the Secretary was not in fact a commander. He was, however, the voice of the government that the Army served. The divided inspectorate was therefore no longer an extension of the commander's will. It was a mechanism for civil oversight of a department of government—the bureaus of the War Department. Only to the extent that the inspectors general represented the Commanding General among the army line could they be regarded as functionaries of command, and because the Commanding General lacked any real command powers, the extension of his powers through the inspectors general was moot.

What began to develop in the 1840s, therefore, was a gradual transformation of the role of inspectors general. They would orient themselves increasingly in coming decades toward the administrative interests of the Secretary because that was where their services were needed and because that was the source of power and direction in the War Department. Inspectors general would endeavor to perform two jobs: as inspectors for the commanders and as agents of the political power. Their real place in the military establishment was therefore inadequately defined, and they could not be what Steuben had been or what Macomb had wanted them to be. Then, despite the pulling from two directions, inspectors general, unlike other staff officers, tended to think of themselves as military men rather than bureaucrats. Their orientation prevented their aligning themselves completely with the Secretary, as demonstrated by the record when Congress tried to abolish one of their positions.[77]

The end of the Second Seminole War permitted a reduction in the Army, and on 23 August 1842, Congress exercised its option. The authorized force was cut by a third, to 8,613 officers and men, and thereafter Congress held down appropriations so sternly that not even repairs of barracks, except for emergencies, could be ordered during fiscal year 1844. One provision of the legislation abolished the office of one of the inspectors general, this occurring within one month after passage of the act. However, since the Secretary of War had decided to use the inspectors general to monitor the disbursements of the staff departments, he would not lightly give up one of them. Secretary John C. Spencer, who had replaced Bell in the fall of 1841 and then expanded the purview of the inspectors general, observed that the legislation did not tell him how to discharge the extra inspector. So he kept Churchill, the junior of the two, in office. His successors (there were four secretaries in all between 1841 and 1845) followed suit—Secretary James M. Porter pointed out in his annual

---

77. *An Act respecting the organization of the Army, and for other purposes, Statutes at Large* 5, sec. 4, 512 (1842); Thian, *Legislative History*, 111; Weigley, *History of the United States Army*, 163; Risch, *Quartermaster Support*, 237–38.

report for 1843 that the act of 23 August 1842 had abolished a number of offices, and had directed the discharge of all but the one Inspector General. But, he said, the appropriations acts since that time had continued to support two inspectors general. He recommended that that part of the act be repealed, because he needed both his inspectors general.

The House Committee on Military Affairs looked into the services and history of inspectors general in the United States Army, observed that comparable officials served all European armies, and concluded that the information they provided was essential to the War Department. The members concluded that two independent inspectors general with at least the rank of colonel were essential, and recommended repealing the part of the law in question. The committee's reasoning reflected military, more than War Department, thinking about the status of inspectors general, stressing the need for impartiality: "Officers who are connected with a particular regiment or corps, might be tempted to favor their own, or to disparage others; and, whether they did or not, would be liable to such imputations. In either event, their efficiency would be impaired, and discontents and heartburnings excited in the army."[78]

As a deliberative body, Congress moved slowly. When President James K. Polk handed Churchill an honorable discharge in 1845, Secretary of War William L. Marcy went to Congress to try to get him back. A bill for that purpose passed the House of Representatives and reached the floor of the Senate on 8 January 1846. It attracted only one speaker, a member of the Committee on Military Affairs, who read letters from the Secretary of War and General Scott on the matter. He also observed that repeal of the 1842 measure had been urged by every Secretary of War since its passage, and said that his committee had found "abundant evidence that the officer discharged was not only a worthy officer, but that he was one whose conduct had met the approbation both of the Secretary of War and of the President of the United States." The committee would have preferred to see Churchill restored, but forebore making such a specific recommendation. On the strength of the panel's recommendation, the bill repealing the 1842 measure passed "without further delay," and became law 12 April 1846. Churchill was restored to his position, without loss of time, although Churchill's being restored as an inspector general did have its ironic aspects.[79] The number and rank of the inspectors general were all explained and justified in purely military terms. But the position was restored mostly because the Secretary, not the Commanding General, needed it.

Churchill's temporary absence was made worse by Croghan's recurrent difficulties. There might as well have been no inspector general in 1845, with

---

78. *Inspectors General of the Army*, House Report (H. Rpt.) 321, 18th Cong., 1st sess. (1844). The report also includes the various statements of the Secretaries of War asking for restoration of the position.

79. *Congressional Globe*, 29th Cong., 1st sess. (8 January 1846), 163; *An Act to repeal the act which abolished the office of one of the inspectors-general of the Army, and to revive and establish said office*, Statutes at Large 9, sec. 1,2 (1846); Thian, *Legislative History*, 111; Churchill and Churchill, *Churchill Family*, 98–99. The third source wrongly attributes Churchill's discharge to presidential malice; Polk more likely acted to bring the issue to a head.

Croghan in that position. His chronic indebtedness, mostly for gambling, kept most of his pay vouchers pledged to creditors. Serious mismanagement of Croghan's accounts became apparent in 1845, and he was charged with illegally receiving double payment. Charges and specifications were prepared and submitted to a court-martial, but Croghan sought to exonerate himself with a letter of explanation. After correspondence among the Secretary of War, the Adjutant General, the Paymaster General, and the President—but not, it is worth noting, any correspondence involving the Commanding General—the charges were dropped by President Polk, and the court-martial did not sit. Croghan was saved once again.[80]

Another War—No Central Inspectorate

The restoration of Churchill and the rescue of Croghan came none too soon, because on 13 May 1846 Congress declared war on Mexico. Subsequent legislation provided for a greatly expanded Regular Army, which grew from about 8,500 early in 1846 to 30,476 officers and men during the war. This force was supplemented by 73,532 volunteers. Unlike previous wars, the Mexican War was fought by long-term soldiers, regulars and long-term volunteers making up nine-tenths of the total force. In establishing that pattern for future wars, Congress adopted another—it relieved the wartime citizen-soldiers of some of the nuisances that afflicted regulars in peacetime. Sutlers were deprived of their liens on soldiers' pay, and were not allowed to sit at pay tables during the war. The sutlers' fists returned to the soldiers' pockets at the conclusion of the peace, however.[81] Another precedent for future wars developed in 1846, although it reflected what had happened in 1836. The Army's central inspectorate disappeared with the outbreak of hostilities. The expanded force still had but two inspectors general, and they made no tours of inspection. Croghan mustered volunteers in the South, then he joined Zachary Taylor's army on its way to Mexico. His self-destruction had finally caught up with him, and he was sick by the time he reached Monterrey, where he lost twenty pounds within two weeks. Bedeviled by family and financial problems, he spent more than a year looking for a way to leave Mexico.[82]

Churchill was also sent out to muster volunteers, which he did in several western states from late May to mid-July, accompanied by Lt. Richard P. Hammond, who in one way or another had been assistant to him for three years. After gathering the volunteers, Churchill joined Wool at San Antonio on 29 August, and spent the next month there. "I was most busily employed in camp and at Hd. Qrs.," he wrote in his journal, "inspecting men and horses for

---

80. Prucha, *Army Life*, xx–xxi.
81. Kreidberg and Henry, *History of Military Mobilization*, 70–77; Weigley, *History of the United States Army*, 182–83; H. A. DeWeerd, "The Federalization of Our Army," *Military Affairs*, 6 (1942): 147; Alfred J. Tapson, "The Sutler and the Soldier," *Military Affairs*, 21 (winter 1957): 175.
82. Prucha, *Army Life*, xxi, 180.

DEFENSE OF QUARTERMASTER'S TRAIN ON THE CHIHUAHUA COLUMN, *1847. This was the responsibility of Inspector General Churchill who served as the column's chief of staff.*

discharge, getting the muster rolls in and examining them, regulating camp duties and many important matters confided to me by Gen'l Wool.''[83] Churchill was, in other words, for the time being Wool's inspector general and chief of staff, as the regulations directed. When the army moved south, however, he became more a troop commander on the march, harking back to an inspector's functions under Steuben. For the remainder of the war, he acted much like Wool's second in command, ultimately earning a brevet commission as brigadier general for ''gallant and meritorious conduct'' at the battle of Buena Vista, in February 1847.

Croghan and Churchill performed valuable services, but those services were of value only to parts of the Army. There was not even the pretense of a central army inspectorate in their absence; nor was there any attempt to fill in behind them. Granted, most of the U.S. Army was in the war zone, but even there, no one suggested establishing a central system of inspection. Each army commander established his own. The Commanding General was not included in many central functions, languishing in Washington without authority to assume overall military direction of the war. When Scott did go to Mexico, it was as commander of a field army, not as Commanding General of the United States Army—inspectors general serving a meaningless Commanding General probably would have served no useful purpose in those circumstances. But,

83. Churchill, *Sketch of Life of Churchill*, 54, 106–07; K. Jack Bauer, *The Mexican War, 1846–1848* (New York: Macmillan, 1974), 146–47, 149; Heitman, *Historical Register*, 1: 301.

again, when an emergency occurred, the War Department had decided that the central inspectorate was unimportant. The inspectors general were available for assignment in the field, because there was no concept of anything better for them to do.

The absurdity of the Commanding General's position was affirmed in the next set of general regulations, issued in 1847, which offered an exceedingly vague and contradictory statement of his authority. Article X said that the Commanding General was in charge of the military establishment "in all that regards its discipline and military control. Its fiscal arrangements properly belong to the administrative departments of the staff, and to the Treasury Department under the direction of the Secretary of War." The Commanding General, however, watched over "every thing which enters into the expenses of the military establishment, whether personal or material," including the Military Academy. He also supervised preparation of budget estimates, "in carrying into effect these important duties, he will call to his counsel and assistance the staff, and those officers proper in his opinion to be employed in verifying and inspecting all the objects which may require attention," using the rules and regulations of the U.S. Army and the law as his guide. The power of the Commanding General, in other words, was whatever the Secretary and the bureau heads let him have, which was not likely to be much.[84]

As for the Inspector's Department, its regulations remained as before, while the Commanding General remained its theoretical point of contact with the Secretary. Field commanders were required to submit regular reports on the Indians, but inspectors general were not asked to observe the same subject. The forms of inspections remained as they had been for years, although their form was simplified, with explicit statements on how to give commands and the sequence for reviews. Troops were to be mustered and inspected every two months for payment, by an inspector general, an adjutant general, or someone specially designated. Every man was to be accounted for, and the inspection form was to include remarks on discipline, appearance, and so on.[85] These regulations had no overt effects on the inspectors general. The Army's inspectorate remained on paper much as it had been since 1835. But later as the influence of the Commanding General was eroding, so was the explicit role of the inspectors general. If there was to be an audience for their reports, it had to be the Secretary, who had the power to act on them, and not the Commanding General, who lacked such power. In any case, with a war in process their were evidently more important things than inspection, even for the Secretary's benefit. Inspectors general became mustering agents and field commanders, or assistants to other generals.

There may have been no formal inspectorate extending from the War Department down to the brigade level, but inspection nevertheless remained important

---

84. U.S. War Department, *General Regulations for the Army of the United States, 1847* (Washington: J. and G. S. Gideon, 1847), 8–9 (hereafter cited as *1847 Regulations*).
85. Ibid., 16–17, 81–85, 179–85.

COL. ETHAN A. HITCHCOCK. *Inspector General, Mexico expedition, 1847–1848.*

to commanders. Commanding General Scott, who commanded nothing, might get along without such assistance, but General Scott, commanding the army invading Mexico in 1847, needed an inspector general. Reconciling after years of feuds, Scott and Ethan Allen Hitchcock became friendly early in 1847. Hitchcock wrote in his diary on 5 February, "Was told to-day at Brazos by General Scott to consider myself his Inspector-General. Order to be issued and printed in Tampico. The General told me to do whatever I thought proper as Inspector-General and use his name as authority."[86]

Hitchock apparently let the regulations guide him on what was "proper," and Scott followed suit. Hitchcock in effect became chief of staff to the commander and the general factotum that, since 1813, regulations had conceived an inspector general to be when with an army in the field. Scott gave Hitchcock "charge of the provost guard and the examination of all suspected persons brought in," at Vera Cruz on 14 March. Scott sent Hitchcock out on the 26th to receive the bearer of a white flag proposing the city's surrender. The inspector general had yet other duties on the 29th, processing Mexican prisoners of war and receiving the paroles of their officers.[87] Despite such special activities, Hitchcock spent most of his time as an inspector and expediter, seeing that the whole command was always ready for battle; ensuring that sufficient arms, equipment, and animals were on hand; supervising camp sanitation to prevent disease; ordering brigades and divisions out for inspection; and so on.[88] Whenever a general officer was in the field at the head of troops, he had someone detailed to him as inspector general. Hitchcock's routine was repeated in almost every brigade, division, and army, ably or not according to the abilities of the officer assigned. But they were agents of the commanders they served, unconnected with a central inspectorate for the military establishment as a whole, because one did not exist. Their communications went to their commanders, and no further. In the field, at least, inspection was a function of command, as Washington and Steuben had wanted it to be. But the only central guidance came from the regulations, and not from any higher inspectorate.

86. Hitchcock, *Fifty Years*, 236.
87. Ibid., 240, 246, 247–48.
88. Ibid., 254; Bauer, *Mexican War*, 268.

The Place of the Inspector General

In 1848, as the war ended, Fayette Robinson produced a two-volume description of the United States Army for the benefit of citizens whose interest in things military had been roused by recent events. The Adjutant General, he said, was the "most important" staff officer under the Commanding General. "The next branch of the staff in dignity, and the only other one whose functions are purely military, is that of the Inspectors-General. This is the smallest of all the departments, being composed of but two officers, each of whom has the rank of colonel of cavalry."[89] Of course, the inspectors general did not constitute a department, for they were not formally so organized. Robinson said that they were to make frequent visits to posts and units, inspecting personnel and material. "They may report on anything—the character, moral and physical, of officers, nature of defences, health of posts, and the countless minutiae which make up the sum of the service. Their reports being the result of individual examination, are of course only valuable as such, in proportion to the estimate placed on the character and standing of the inspectors-general."[90] Although able to describe their functions, Robinson was somewhat at a loss to say where the inspectors general really fit into the larger scheme of things. Theoretically, he said, the senior inspector general might be the chief of staff of the Army under the Commanding General, albeit his potential authority had been usurped by the seniority of other heads. But, as happened in Mexico and was countenanced in the regulations, Robinson observed that when someone was detailed as inspector general of a particular field army, he was the chief of staff.

Not even the positive Robinson could fail to acknowledge that inspection was not regarded as sufficiently important to spread it thoroughly across the army. There had once been a system of inspections by brigade and division inspectors, he said, but not for many years. That was because the army was so scattered that such offices could not function. "In the interim," he concluded, "the duty of inspection has been confined to the inspectors-general of the whole army, and the generals and other officers commanding military departments and territorial divisions."[91] Robinson gauged the state of things at the end of the war accurately, although inadvertently. Without a central power at the head of the army, the value of a central inspectorate was questionable. The place of the inspectors general in the future would continue to be defined in conjunction with that of the Commanding General. But because they had already begun to serve the Secretary of War, their fortunes would not necessarily rise and fall along with those of the Commanding General. They would become less and less an extension of the commander, and more and more an agent of the War Department.

---

89. Fayette Robinson, *An Account of the Organization of the Army of the United States*, 2 vols. (Philadelphia: E. H. Butler, 1848), 1: 39–40.
90. Ibid.
91. Ibid.

The Army at the end of the Mexican War was transformed from its previous incarnation. It was organized on paper much as before. But in fact it was more widely scattered than it had ever been, broadcast across the entire continent. The more the force dispersed, the less likely it became that Scott or anyone else could take control of it. At the same time, its greater dispersal made inspection even more important, if there was to be any hope of anyone's knowing what was going on. And conditions had changed. The Army had always had a high rate of desertion, for instance, but in California, throngs of soldiers left after 1848, bound for the gold fields. "The struggle between *right* and six dollars a month and *wrong* and seventy-five dollars a day is rather a severe one," observed a newspaper.[92] The U.S. Army, and its inspectorate, must adapt to the new state of affairs. This transition began with the passing of George Croghan. The exhausted Croghan returned briefly to Kentucky at the end of the war, thence to New Orleans. There he died on 8 January 1849, victim of a cholera epidemic.[93] He had been the last of Macomb's inspectors general, and the last, no matter his personal defects, who remembered how important and effective inspection once had been to the Commanding General.

---

92. Pittsburgh, Pennsylvania, *Daily Dispatch*, 16 December 1848, quoted in Ralph P. Bieber, "California Gold Mania," *Mississippi Valley Historical Review*, 35 (June 1848): 12.
93. Prucha, *Army Life*, xxi.

CHAPTER 12

Inspection Between the Wars (1849–1861)

The U.S. Army had grown to nearly 100,000 men during the Mexican War. Observing previous experience, Congress could be expected to diminish the force and again to refuse to deal effectively with the Army's expensive needs. And it did, cutting strength to 10,763 by 1850. But this time, the Army could not be reduced so easily to near nonexistence, as had happened after previous wars. The Mexican War had transformed the United States into a truly continental nation with continental military obligations that had to be served. White Americans flooded into the newly conquered territories, and their demands for protection from increasingly belligerent native people could not be denied for long. By 1855 the authorized strength of the Army stood at 12,698, with the President permitted to enlist more by expanding the size of companies in the western territories. The theoretical authorized force was 18,318 officers and men.[1]

The Army's Continued Mission

The vastness of the territories gained from Mexico, and the urgency of their military needs, made the Army a continental police force, stationed mostly at small, scattered outposts. There were only 2,109 officers and men at 33 stations east of the Mississippi in 1850, as compared to 6,385 at 67 posts west of that river, not counting others at depots, West Point, and recruiting rendezvous and in transit. At least 32 new posts were established in territories acquired from Mexico before the middle of 1849, and construction and repair budgets exploded despite congressional opposition. In fiscal year 1851 the Quartermaster Department spent three times as much for barracks and quarters as it had in 1844. The burden was enormous, because shifting frontier needs required frequent changes in the locations of posts.[2]

The military budget was difficult to control during the years immediately after the war, especially in the Quartermaster's Department. During the middle

---

1. Kreidberg and Henry, *History of Military Mobilization*, 70–77; Risch, *Quartermaster Support*, 301; Heitman, *Historical Register*, 2: 594–97. The outstanding study of the Army's frontier military mission after the Mexican War is Robert M. Utley, *Frontiersmen in Blue: The United States Army and the Indian, 1848–1865* (New York: Macmillan, 1967).

2. Risch, *Quartermaster Support*, 301, 304; Spaulding, *The United States Army in War and Peace*, 229–30.

and late 1850s the Division of the Pacific, where costs were extremely high during the gold rush, annually spent twice what Congress had appropriated. Even as early as 1850 the transportation costs of the Army, grown in size 50 percent since 1844, had increased by 1,500 percent. Yet shortages of all essential requirements were everywhere the rule. This was because congressional appropriations never kept pace with realities, thus forcing the War Department regularly to seek supplemental appropriations to cover "arrearages." In 1850, Secretary of War Charles M. Conrad stoutly defended the requested Quartermaster Department budget of $4,295,000 (five times the 1844 appropriation) against the inevitable congressional reductions, and gave the legislators a lecture on the facts of life. He predicted that disbursements would reach $5 million by 1852, and pointed out that they routinely exceeded appropriations, something he regarded as administratively dangerous. Conrad urged in the strongest terms that for once the money be appropriated before it was spent.[3]

Congress did not entirely ignore the needs of the nation's soldiers, of course. But in what would become a tradition, the lawmakers tended to overlook the incumbents in favor of gestures toward the citizen veterans, dead and living, of the war just past. Congress appropriated funds for a United States military cemetery in Mexico City in 1850, creating a precedent for the future care of battlefield dead, and a future object of concern for inspectors general. It authorized the United States Soldiers' Home in 1851 to provide a refuge for destitute veterans of the Regular Army, supported by modest deductions from each soldier's monthly pay.[4] Eventually inspection of this home became also an item of interest for the inspectors general and one of the few duties performed by them by law for the Secretary.

The U.S. Army's new circumstances strained its budget enormously, with the single greatest cost being transportation. Everything conceivable was attempted to reduce shipping costs, including rigorous calculations of what must be transported—the total equipment and arms for a mounted soldier, for instance, weighed seventy-eight pounds, of which two blankets (one for the horse, the other for the man) weighed exactly nine pounds. The War Department issued orders on 8 January 1851 to institute large-scale farming at all posts—to reduce the need to ship food, and to turn a profit from sales of produce. The abandonment of Forts Kearney and Laramie on the northern Great Plains was proposed solely on the grounds that farming was not believed possible at either location. Unlike the military farming of the 1820s, long discredited, now operations were to be conducted on a commercial scale.

---

3. Risch, *Quartermaster Support*, 304, 306, 309–17; *Annual Report of the Secretary of War 1855* (hereafter cited as *ARSecWar*), Sen. Ex. Doc. 1, 31st Cong., 2d sess., pt. 2, pp. 8–9. Of the over $4 million requested, all but $530,247 for the seven old departments of the Army was destined for the four new departments of Oregon, California, New Mexico, and Texas. *ARSecWar 1850*, 109.

4. Edward Steer, "Genesis of American Graves Registration 1861–1870," *Military Affairs*, 12 (fall 1948): 149–61; Foner, *Soldier Between Wars*, 72. The cemetery at Mexico City still exists, representing the nation's first formal attention to its dead soldiers.

RINGGOLD'S BATTERY AT PALO ALTO, 8 MAY 1846. *The mustering and forwarding of volunteer regiments to Zachary Taylor's army was a major duty for inspectors early in the Mexican War.*

Produce would be sold at a profit, the soldiers having a share. The idea was to attract a civilian population that could eventually supply the army's needs locally, so that no longer would everything have to be shipped from the East. However, the program never really got started.[5]

A Leaderless Army

The Army was so widely scattered, with its expenses growing so greatly, that some means had to be developed to bring it all under control. The inspectors general potentially were a valuable source of information to that end, but their performance depended upon where the controlling authority would stand, especially since the office of Commanding General had lapsed while Winfield Scott commanded the invasion of Mexico. Afterwards, as Zachary Taylor approached the presidency, Scott forbore trying to give orders to his future Commander in Chief, and installed himself in New York City as commander of the Eastern Division while Taylor commanded the Western Division. After Taylor's inauguration, Scott was reinvested as Commanding General, but he refused to leave New York. He took his position seriously and literally, and tried to prevent civilian interference in his command. When Taylor died in July 1850, Scott returned to Washington, where he ran for President in 1852 against

---

5. *Annual Report of the Quartermaster General 1851* (hereafter cited as *ARQMG*), and *ARSecWar 1851*, both S. Ex. Doc. 1, 32d Cong., 1st sess., 108–13, 161, 164–65, 253.

another Mexican War general, Franklin Pierce, and lost. By the spring of 1851, the headquarters of the army was back in New York, where Scott remained until the Civil War. He spent the duration of the Pierce Administration in a vicious feud with Secretary of War Jefferson Davis—a vigorous, far-thinking reformer in the mold of Calhoun and Poinsett, although vastly more temperamental—over questions of authority and subordination. If the army had a master during the 1850s, it was the Secretary.[6] When Scott was reassigned to command the United States Army on 10 May 1849, the two senior brigadier generals were put in charge of the Eastern and Western divisions. "The Inspectors General of the Army," said the order announcing the assignments, "will report for duty [by letter] to the Major General Commanding-in-Chief."[7]

At the time, however, only one of the inspectors general, Sylvester Churchill, was active. He apparently remained based at the War Department in Washington, working in the vacuum that existed between the Secretary of War and the Commanding General. Croghan's position continued vacant for over a year. Finally, Maj. George A. McCall of the 3d Infantry was assigned as the other inspector general, with the rank of colonel, on 10 June 1850. McCall had graduated from West Point in 1822 and made captain in 1836. He served for a while as aide to Edmund P. Gaines. During the first year of the Mexican War he was twice brevetted for gallantry, then he served as an assistant adjutant general with a brevet rank of major. He ended the war as a major in the 3d Infantry. His appointment was partly a matter of convenience, because his regiment was in New Mexico and partly because he was a favorite of President Taylor; also, the Secretary of War desperately wanted information about that territory. Whatever the motivation, McCall went to New Mexico with instructions to examine political conditions, including the territory's statehood movement.[8]

McCall conducted the first general inspection of posts in the 9th Military Department, comprising the territory of New Mexico (the present states of New Mexico and Arizona, and some adjoining lands), during 1850. His regular inspections were rather perfunctory and were restricted to the most essential details of each post, never looking beyond their boundaries. But New Mexico was a volatile province, overrun by hostile Indians and inhabited by a mysterious and restless population chafing under American military rule. The Secretary of War, and the Congress, wanted to know more about what was going on there. So McCall spent most of the year under the Secretary's orders, preparing two special reports on New Mexico. One, submitted 15 July 1850, provided a

6. Elliott, *Winfield Scott*, 426–28, 648–58; White, *Jacksonians*, 190–96; Weigley, *History of the United States Army*, 189–94. On Jefferson Davis, see Hudson Strode, *Jefferson Davis, American Patriot, 1808–1861* (New York: Harcourt, Brace, 1955), especially 245–80.

7. GO No. 27, AGO, 10 May 49, in GORI&IG. The order was published in *Niles' National Register*, 75 (16 May 1849): 305.

8. Heitman, *Historical Register*, 1: 653. See also the introductory material in Robert W. Frazer, ed., *New Mexico in 1850: A Military View by Colonel George Archibald McCall* (Norman: University of Oklahoma Press, 1968).

general description of the territory, its Indians, and its non-Indian people— emphasizing population, customs, and institutions. The second, forwarded on 16 December, covered much the same ground, but focused on the territory's military needs. Early in 1851, McCall's reports went to Congress for its information.[9]

THE ASSAULT ON CHAPULTAPEC, 12 SEPTEMBER 1847. *Commanding General Winfield Scott deemed the use of inspectors essential to the success of his forces.*

Inspector General McCall was in 1850 the agent of the Secretary of War, not of the Commanding General. His reports were intended for the Secretary, and were addressed to the Adjutant General. The latter circumstance was symbolic of Scott's declining control over the Army, but it was not new. During the 1840s, after Macomb's death, the reports of inspectors general increasingly were addressed to the Adjutant General, the old tradition of confidential reports directly to the Commanding General fading away. And then, if the Adjutant General was subordinate to the Commanding General, that would have been nothing more than the custom that governed most other military paper work. But with Scott separating himself from the War Department, the Adjutant General became increasingly a channel of information for the Secretary, rather than for the Commanding General. The incumbent Adjutant General was Roger Jones. Earlier, Jones had lost a bid for bureaucratic autonomy when Macomb had been Commanding General. But, with the passing of Macomb and with Scott's self-exile from Washington, Jones' influence gradually increased to the point that he became one of the most important uniformed advisers to the Secretary. One of the results of this shift of power was that the inspectors became separated more and more from the Commanding General. Instructions for the inspectors general began to come through the Adjutant General, "by order of the Secretary of War," Scott was effectively excluded from much influence over inspectors' activities. After he returned to Washington in 1850, Scott made one last, feeble attempt to reclaim his inspectors general, at the same time that the Secretary wanted the inspectorate revitalized. On 16 October 1850, Churchill was assigned to inspect the

---

9. McCall's reports were published as *Report of the Secretary of War Communicating, in Compliance with a Resolution of the Senate, Colonel McCall's Reports in Relation to New Mexico,* S. Ex. Doc. 26, 31st Cong., 2d sess. (1851), and more recently in Frazer, *New Mexico in 1850.*

Eastern Division, McCall the new Pacific Division, and Bvt. Maj. Samuel Cooper the Western Division. That arrangement was revoked two months later, and new orders announced that "The Inspectors General of the Army are attached to General Headquarters, and will hereafter inspect, in regular rotation, the three Military Geographical Divisions." The three officers had the same divisional assignments, "after which they will report in person to the General-in-Chief for further instructions."[10]

Scott, like Macomb before him, may have feared that the inspectors general would become too attached to the division commanders, and planned to rotate them to prevent that. But if he hoped to use the officers to secure his control over the Army, or as a counterweight to the increasing power of the Secretary of War, he did not have the men with which to do it. Churchill was sixty-seven years old in 1851. Inspecting the Eastern Division along with carrying out the Secretary's special inquiries was as much as he could handle. Rotating him to one of the wilderness divisions was not a promising prospect. McCall was in declining health, in his fifties and a slow starter (he did not make his inspection of the Pacific Division until 1852).[11] And Samuel Cooper was yet another odd commodity—he had graduated from West Point in 1815, had become an artillerist, did not make captain until 1836, and remained in that rank until 1852. He became an assistant adjutant general by brevet in 1838, then lieutenant colonel and assistant adjutant general in 1847. He earned a brevet for "meritorious conduct particularly in the performance of his duties in the prosecution of the war with Mexico," a rather bland acknowledgment of bland performance when others earned so much more.[12] Cooper was in his late fifties, and was preoccupied with his own ambitions—succession to the aging Adjutant General Jones. In 1852, the War Department directed Churchill to inspect posts in the Western Division, McCall those on the Pacific—and Cooper to complete the inspections required of him in 1850. He apparently never got the job done, because he succeeded Roger Jones as Adjutant General on 15 July.[13] . . . Scott's inspectorate was of little value to him. Churchill and McCall moved at their own pace, largely doing the Secretary's bidding while Cooper was devoted to the interests of the Adjutant General. Scott himself was along in years, becoming increasingly indisposed physically, and was preoccupied with his prerogatives as Commanding General. If the western commands had not been in more energetic hands and if the Indians had not compelled a continued military vigilance, the Army would have reverted to the inadequate organization that marred it preceding the War of 1812.

Cooper's assignment to inspection signified the recognition that a two-officer force could not cover the greatly expanded army alone. But perhaps because Cooper's accomplishments were nil, the experiment of assigning an

---

10. GO No. 38, AGO, 16 Oct 50, and GO No. 55, AGO, 17 Dec 50, in GORI&IG.
11. Robert W. Frazer, ed., *Mansfield on the Condition of the Western Forts, 1853–54* (Norman: University of Oklahoma Press, 1963), xxvii, documenting McCall's rounds.
12. Heitman, *Historical Register*, 1: 326; GO No. 13, AGO, n.d. 1852, in GORI&IG.
13. Heitman, *Historical Register*, 1:326.

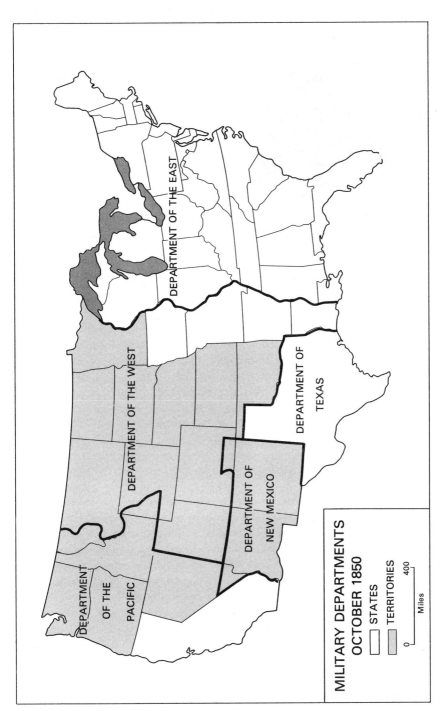

MILITARY DEPARTMENTS
OCTOBER 1850

STATES
TERRITORIES

0   400

Miles

DEPARTMENT OF THE EAST

DEPARTMENT OF THE WEST

DEPARTMENT OF TEXAS

DEPARTMENT OF NEW MEXICO

DEPARTMENT OF THE PACIFIC

MAP 1

COL. GEORGE A. MCCALL. *Inspector General, 10 June 1850–29 April 1853.*

acting inspector general was not tried again until late 1853, and then at the Secretary's instigation. Cooper himself helped to continue the undermining of Scott's authority by sustaining the independence of the Adjutant General's Office after he succeeded Roger Jones. The power of the position was derived from the Secretary of War rather than from the Commanding General. In the end, however, his loyalties lay elsewhere. He resigned from the United States Army in March 1861, during the secession crisis. He joined the Army of the Confederate States of America, to become its adjutant and inspector general. [14] . . . Even the more productive inspector general, McCall, failed when he was most needed. The Secretary of War determined in 1853 that a change of command was needed in the 9th Military Department (New Mexico), where there was widespread civilian dissatisfaction with the incumbent and a legacy of political and military misbehavior. McCall was ordered to inspect the department in anticipation of the change, but instead, he resigned on 22 April for reasons of health. He later served with the Union forces as a brigadier general of volunteers in the early days of the Civil War until poor health again forced his resignation. The appointment of a new inspector general was immediately necessary. [15]

An Energetic Inspector

Joseph K. F. Mansfield got the job, courtesy of Secretary of War Jefferson Davis, on 28 May 1853. Mansfield had been born in Connecticut in 1803, making him well along in years for the time although younger than Churchill. He had graduated in the West Point class of 1822 as McCall had, but he had a much better academic record. That auspicious beginning earned Mansfield a commission in the Corps of Engineers, which customarily took the academy's brightest and most energetic graduates. His rise in the small corps was slow, and he did not become a captain until 1838. He spent most of the decades before the Mexican War working on the construction of coastal fortifications. Mansfield served during the war as chief engineer for the army of General

---

14. Ibid.
15. Frazer, *Mansfield on Condition,* xxix.

Zachary Taylor, beginning as supervisor of the construction of Fort Brown, Texas. His "gallant and distinguished service in the defense of Fort Brown" earned him a brevet as a major, "gallant and meritorious conduct" in the battles around Monterrey made him a brevet lieutenant colonel, while similar conduct at the Battle of Buena Vista gained him a brevet colonelcy. Mansfield's performance during the war also drew the notice of Jefferson Davis, then serving in Taylor's army. When Secretary Davis needed an inspector general in 1853, he handed the post to Mansfield, who since 1848 had been in Washington as a member of the Army's Board of Engineers for Fortifications, then a very active and important body.[16]

Mansfield proved himself an exceedingly energetic and productive inspector general, but there was no possibility that Scott, in the style of Macomb, could use him to restore the power of the Commanding General. The new inspector general departed immediately on his first tour, and spent most of the next few years traveling throughout the West and preparing his reports. Besides, he was Secretary Davis' personal choice for the assignment, and the suspicious Scott probably regarded him as the Secretary's man. He proved in fact to be his own man, and a good one. But no one person could by himself constitute a unified inspectorate for a constabulary distributed over millions of square miles. The army was really a police force, with a chief in name only. The real decision-making power over daily operations rested with local post commanders, whose direction was from department and divisional commanders. It was to these officials that Mansfield proved himself most useful. When he was inspecting, they knew how many men they had, how efficient they were, how they were supplied and equipped, and how well they lived. And Mansfield was a peripatetic inspector: He toured New Mexico Territory in 1853, the Division of the Pacific in 1854, and the Department of Texas in 1856. In 1857 Mansfield served as Inspector General with the army sent to keep order in Utah during the "Mormon War"; another expression of the War Department's belief that in an emergency an inspector general was available because he was not occupied with anything important. Mansfield returned to his regular tour next year, inspecting the departments of California and Oregon in 1858 and 1859, then moving on to Texas, where he remained through 1860 and into 1861.[17]

Mansfield was a fitting successor to George Croghan. Although he lacked Croghan's literary gifts and sense of controlled outrage when something affronted his sensibilities, he compensated with his greater diligence and sobriety. His reports were readable enough, and highly informative. They combined travelogue, inspection, and commentary—a running narrative of his journey with comments on the countryside, punctuated with reports of the condition of posts and garrisons, followed by remarks on subjects of general interest to the army command.[18] Mansfield's typical inspection of a post included a head

---

16. Heitman, *Historical Register*, 1: 688; Frazer, *Mansfield on Condition*, xxviii–xxix.

17. Frazer, *Mansfield on Condition*, xxix.

18. Ibid., comprises Mansfield's reports for 1853 and 1854, along with some special reports to John E. Wool, commanding on the Pacific Coast. See also Martin L. Crimmins, ed., "Colonel
(Continued)

count (those present, absent, sick, those in the guardhouse, and so on) then characterized in general terms the discipline and instruction of the command, arms and equipment, condition of buildings, medical services, the funds remaining for subsistence and quartermaster operations, the fort's environment, and the abilities of the officers (whom he usually commended). Engineer that he was, Mansfield included detailed plats of the posts that he inspected, and—with apparently no objections from former fellow engineers—he gave careful attention to coastal fortification construction projects supervised by the Corps of Engineers. His emphasis was always on military readiness: whether the post was properly located, what the proximate dangers were, what the garrison should be—and so on.

Mansfield's "general remarks applicable to the whole command" sometimes echoed those of Croghan. He complained in 1853 that the clothing was "defective in cut," recommended a new knapsack and canteen, strongly recommended a new field tent he had observed (complete with diagrams), evaluated the Army's wagons and its "worthless" gum elastic whips, proposed additions to the rations, and otherwise ranged over every conceivable subject. Among the matters that caught his eye was the attempt to revive military agriculture. His feelings on that issue would have brought applause from George Croghan. He said it took the soldiers away from training and turned them into farmers, causing them to neglect all other duties in the effort to make a profit.[19] Whatever Mansfield's influence, the new farming program faded rather quickly. That was partly because he was not alone in his sentiments, but mostly because it was a failure. When he inspected in New Mexico, the farming program there was $14,000 in debt and declining rapidly. Despite their best efforts, Mansfield and Churchill could not inspect the whole army all the time. Scott, however, made the best of the situation. He traveled a lot on his own, and he managed to enforce the orders of 1849 and 1850 that the inspectors general addressed their annual reports to him, although Mansfield made some inspections on behalf of department commanders.[20]

The Secretary's Inspector

While Scott presumed to monopolize the time of his inspectors general, the Secretary of War sought to develop his own sources of information. He dispatched Bvt. Capt. Edward R. S. Canby, assistant adjutant general, on 30 November 1853 to make "minute" inspections of arsenals, depots, and mili-

(Continued)

J.K.F. Mansfield's Report of the Inspection of the Department of Texas in 1856," *Southwestern Historical Quarterly*, 42 (October 1938–April 1939): 122–48, 215–57, 351–87.

19. Ibid., 58–68, quotation on page 63.

20. See ibid., 81. In 1854, Mansfield began his report by saying that he "sailed from New York," possibly implying that his duty station was with Scott there. He reported to the department commander at the start of his inspection, however, and wrote numerous separate reports to department commander John Wool during 1854, copies of which he included with his report to Scott, but at Wool's request. Ibid., 186–97.

tary posts on the Arkansas and Red rivers. Canby began at Little Rock Arsenal, then gradually extended his tour along the Gulf Coast to Florida, visiting twenty-nine places by July 1854. The experience exhausted Canby, making him so ill that it took almost a year for him to submit a 150-page report. He was apparently regarded as an acting inspector general, but he reported to the Adjutant General for the benefit of the Secretary.[21]

Canby confessed to the Secretary that he started out with only the vaguest idea of what to do, possessing but a theoretical notion of what an inspector general was. He did well enough, however, addressing matters small and large. Among his major complaints was that he found no post where the records were complete. He recommended, as would a later inspector general, that when a post was abandoned its records should be transferred to a safe repository for permanent retention. Canby further identified weaknesses in the status of the units he inspected.

He believed that the troops were uniformly untrained, for three reasons: Post commanders changed too frequently, too much extra duty left the ranks too thin for training, and the scattering of troops in small bodies made training impossible. He was neither the first nor the last inspector to urge consolidation of military posts. "This is not only essential to the attainment of a proper degree of instruction and discipline," he said, "but is perfectly compatible with the objects—the protection of the frontier and the control of the Indians for which the troops are employed in the Indian country."[22]

Living Conditions

Canby, unlike Mansfield, did not pay much notice to the living conditions of the soldiers. But because of the overstressed army budget and the frequently shifting post locations, those conditions were often miserable. Quartermaster General Jesup begged Congress, in the strongest terms, in 1853 to give him a bigger budget to provide "better accommodations than have been provided for [officers and men] heretofore." Suitable housing standards had been set in navy and marine barracks and at arsenals, he said, but not at very many military posts.[23] Scott joined in commenting about the condition of the army's housing during the 1850s. It was the one issue that aroused utterances from the Commanding General that clearly were based on the comments of inspectors general. Mansfield encountered a few places where conditions were tolerable under the circumstances, but Fort Conrad, New Mexico, was more typical. He said in 1853 that the quarters of both officers and soldiers were falling to pieces, that the timbers had rotted away, that some of the troops were in tents, and that the public storehouses were worthless. Concerning the Presidio of San Francisco in

21. Max L. Heyman, Jr., *Prudent Soldier: A Biography of Major General E. R. Canby, 1817–1873* (Glendale, California: Clark, 1959), 87–94.

22. Ibid., quotation on pages 90–91.

23. *ARQMG 1853*, S. Ex. Doc. 1, 33d Cong., 1st sess., 2:132. For a detailed survey of army housing in the 1850s, see Clary, "These Relics," 48–66, 164–75, 264–71.

1854, he reported that the adobe buildings left by the Mexican government were miserable but that they were well kept. At San Diego he found the quarters of the soldiers to be worthless. And so it went, as the underbudgeted troops labored to throw together rude shelters and to tend to their other duties as well.[24]

Scott heard complaints from all sides about conditions in the West. On his own tours (and from Churchill) he learned that the few artillerists in the East were huddled in casemates, little more than man-made caves, at the coastal forts. In 1856, meanwhile, a commission of officers was dispatched to observe the war in the Crimea and to visit military establishments in Europe. The deplorable condition of sanitation in the war zone contrasted dramatically with the high quality of barracks and hospitals in the European military posts, and the whole tour only aggravated the American army's unhappiness about its own shabby physical plant. General Scott vented that frustration the following year when he asserted that the low quality of the quarters provided for the army was a principal cause "of desertion, disease, and mortality." The men, he said, lived in casemates in the coastal fortifications, and on the frontier "either in tents (winter as well as summer) or such miserable bush and mud huts as they have hastily constructed for the moment." But he acknowledged that the problem was only partly soluble, because the constant movement of the frontier of settlement made it inadvisable to establish permanent quarters for the army.[25]

A Busy Decade for Churchill

Although affected by the physical problems imposed by his increased age, Sylvester Churchill also continued to be relatively active during the 1850s.[26] In 1851 and again in 1859, he made extensive inspections of the area east of the Mississippi River, encompassing the Department of the East. In the intervening years, he was engaged in several special investigations and inspections desired by the secretaries of war. He inspected Springfield Armory in 1853 to evaluate the quality of the weapons being completely assembled for the first time on the principles of mass production. He gathered a group of active and retired artisans to examine the 1853 model rifle and to compare it to earlier, individually manufactured pieces. All of them pronounced the new weapon equal to or better than the older models. Churchill's report heartily endorsed the new system of interchangeable parts, recommending its continuance as more economical and efficient than the older system. In 1856 and 1858 he visited Florida and then Minnesota to investigate and report on the origins and prospects of Indian troubles that concerned the Secretary of War. During the latter visit, he assisted the governor of Minnesota to conduct a conference with the Sioux and

---

24. Frazer, *Mansfield on Condition*, passim, quotations on pages 51, 135, 143–44.

25. *ARSecWar 1856*, House (H.) Ex. Doc. 1, 34th Cong., 3d sess., 16; *Annual Report of the Commanding General 1857 (ARComGen)*, S. Ex. Doc. 1, 35th Cong., 1st sess., 49.

26. Material on Sylvester Churchill is drawn from an article by the author in *Civil War History*, vol. 32, June 1986, pp. 159–168, courtesy of Kent State University Press.

the Chippewa. His reports were thorough descriptions and analyses of the situations he observed, accompanied with supporting documents and clippings. He visited Fort Riley, Kansas, in 1855 with Bvt. Brig. Gen. Newman S. Clarke to investigate irregularities incident to the development of the military reservation around the fort.[27]

Churchill was even more involved in the conduct of special boards and projects for the Secretary. He began to pick up numerous complaints about the army uniform while mustering out the Mexican War volunteers. To these were added similar remarks gathered from officers with whom he talked on a tour inspecting Fort Columbus, New York, Fort Monroe, Virginia, and Jefferson Barracks, Missouri, in the fall of 1848. In March 1849, he wrote a lengthy description of their recommendations and complaints to the Commanding General suggesting favorable consideration. The officers felt that the uniforms looked old-fashioned, were too hot, and were impracticable for field duty. Simultaneously, he advised the Secretary of War, who requested that he serve as a board of one to review the various uniform changes proposed. Secretary George W. Crawford expressed the view that Churchill's long experience and reputation for good sense qualified him to make the necessary decisions. Churchill replied two days later saying he was familiar with the proposals, concurred in the changes as having come from those affected the most, and recommended their adoption. When the changes were approved in February 1850, the Secretary of War, through the Adjutant General, asked Churchill to have prepared the lithographic drawings to be distributed to manufacturers.[28]

Perhaps for Churchill the most time-consuming and frustrating project of the decade was the creation of a revised drill manual that he began on his own initiative. He was inspired in 1851 while observing Company A of the 3d Artillery at Fort Trumbull, Connecticut, conduct bayonet drill as described in a French work translated by the then Capt. George B. McClellan. He liked what he saw and considered it a great improvement over current U.S. practices.[29] Then, in January 1852, Adjutant General Roger Jones included Churchill among the bureau and department heads in a circular directing them all in the name of the General-in-Chief to submit recommended changes to the 1841 Army regulations that affected their respective departments.[30] Churchill replied on 11 February with a detailed review of the regulations as they affected the inspectors general. He also included some suggested changes in other areas, the need for which he had noted in the course of his inspections. Before submitting the papers, Churchill coordinated his response with fellow inspectors George A. McCall and Samuel Cooper, incorporating their views with his. Adjutant General Jones acknowledged his response with the offhand, informal note that

27. Franklin H. Churchill, ibid., 134–36.

28. Sylvester Churchill, Ltr to General-in-Chief, 29 Mar 49; Ltr to Secy of War, 27 Mar 49; Ltr from AGO, 27 Feb 50. Collection of Churchill Papers, Military History Institute, Carlisle, Pa. (hereafter referred to as Churchill Papers).

29. Franklin H. Churchill, ibid., 134.

30. Cir, Army HQ, AGO, 15 Jan 52, Churchill Papers.

ASCENDING THE TABLELANDS OF TEXAS. *The exploration of the trans-Mississippi area and the inspection of the units in the new territories were major concerns of the inspectors in the 1850s.*

perhaps Churchill should sometime correlate his views with comments addressing the 1841 regulations and their partially revised 1847 version.[31]

    Those experiences seem to have inspired Churchill to give increasing thought to the need for a really thorough review and overhaul of the Army regulations and the existing drill manuals. Whatever the case may be, he had written one complete draft and was in the process of rewriting that by the middle of 1856. His objective was to clearly and unequivocally state in one manual all the movements and procedures for all tactical and ceremonial drills, parades, and inspections, to include such things as salutes and honors. In order to come up with an acceptable consensus, he not only plumbed his own experience, but also queried regular and militia officers and the foreign attaches in Washington. Like Steuben with his famous blue book, he wanted a simple, accurate manual to train all American troops in a standardized drill. His work was sufficiently complete in January 1857 for a portion of it to be submitted to Secretary of War Jefferson Davis for his official sanction and agreement so the project could move forward to completion. Davis reviewed the draft, returning it to Churchill the next month. He directed Churchill to continue his work and formally submit it to the War Department.[32] . . . After further work and coordination, on 27

    31. Sylvester Churchill, Ltr to Bvt. Maj. Gen. R. Jones, 11 Feb 52; Ltr from R. Jones, AG, 12 Feb 52, Churchill Papers.

    32. Sylvester Churchill, Ltr to Jefferson Davis, 15 Jan 57; Ltr from Jefferson Davis to Secy of War, 27 Feb 57, Churchill Papers.

March 1858, Churchill sent out what must have been one of the earliest pre-printed questionnaires, consisting of a circular containing fourteen questions with multiple-choice answers and a place for remarks. The questions were tailored to address specific issues raised by criticisms of the earlier drafts. The circular was mailed to 105 regular and 20 militia officers along with an explanatory note and a request for prompt reply. The addressees included the adjutants general of Massachusetts, New York, and Virginia as well as such distinguished individuals as Bvt. Maj. Gen. Ethan A. Hitchcock, Prof. Denis Mahan, and former Capt. George B. McClellan.[33]

The warmth and high regard for Churchill held by men from many parts of the country was reflected in the responses that began to come in. For example, a reply from a fellow Vermonter and prominent scholar and politician, George P. Marsh, was lighthearted and humorous, deprecating his ability to match Churchill's military knowledge. He did say he thought a proposed revision was an excellent idea needed to "revive a martial spirit among the militia. The decay of which I think a dangerous evil." Churchill also got a reply from Illinois Governor William A. Bissell whom he had known since Mexican War days when Bissell commanded the 1st Illinois Volunteers in Wool's Column. Bissell said the manual looked good to him, but he did not feel his thirteen months military service qualified him to be critical of Churchill's greater experience. After warmly reminiscing about their days soldiering together, Bissell mentioned that many Illinois militiamen were eager to get in on the campaign against the Mormons. He estimated the state could raise about forty regiments to go to Utah. He concluded, "We are great soldiers, always ready to go," but he predicted an early end to the Utah campaign.[34]

Churchill's fellow inspector, Col. Joseph K. F. Mansfield, also wrote him an encouraging note after reviewing the 27 March circular. Mansfield deferred to Churchill's greater experience as an inspector, as well, and urged him not to let the opinions expressed in replies to the circulars to influence his sound judgment too much. Mansfield agreed with Churchill that such a total overhaul of the drill regulations was necessary and long overdue.[35] During all this, Churchill left his final draft with Winfield Scott at his headquarters in New York for review. Scott returned it after several weeks without comment, but he later told Churchill (in December 1858) that he would have a board of officers examine it once Churchill had it completed. As the author of a drill manual then very much in vogue, Scott was less than enthusiastic at the prospect of having it superseded. Churchill formally submitted the final draft for War Department approval on 21 February 1859. In his letter of transmittal, Churchill said he had amplified topics that were only alluded to in the Army regulations and he had

---

33. Sylvester Churchill, Ltr Bk entry 27 Mar 58, Churchill Papers.
34. Sylvester Churchill, Ltr from George P. Marsh, Burlington, Vt., 2 Apr 58; Ltr from Wm. A. Bissell, Springfield, Ill., 22 Apr 58, Churchill Papers.
35. Sylvester Churchill, Ltr from Joseph K. F. Mansfield, colonel and inspector general, USA, Middletown, Conn., 11 May 58, Churchill Papers.

simplified and standardized other drills and ceremonies. He cited his extensive consultations, surveys, and coordination while preparing the manual, concluding that his experiences as an inspector since 1812 had convinced him that a new standard manual was necessary. He included a synopsis of responses from his circular.[36]

Scott returned the draft requesting additions on the types of gun salutes to be used for various dignitaries. After further research and writing, Churchill resubmitted the final draft. The proposed manual was then reviewed by a board of officers whose deliberations lasted from 10 November to 5 December 1859. It approved the manual with a few minor changes. The manuscript was then further examined by Adjutant General Cooper and by Col. Joseph E. Johnston, acting inspector general, in what must have been one of the latter's few actions as an inspector before becoming Quartermaster General. They recommended approval as well. Accordingly, Secretary of War John B. Floyd wrote to the chairman of the Senate Military Committee in May 1860 requesting the necessary appropriation to cover publishing costs. As it turned out, Floyd got no answer, and in what must have been one of his last acts before resigning, he repeated his request in a similar letter on 28 December.[37]

The tensions generated by the secession crisis began to affect the smooth progress of Churchill's project. The first sign of this was the congressional reluctance to appropriate money for any military purposes followed by Secretary Floyd's resignation. Even though the manual had gone through the full approval procedure, Floyd's successor, Secretary Joseph Holt, declined to authorize its publication because he was an interim appointee and did not feel it his place to make a decision of such lasting consequence. Hearing this, the Lippincott Company of Philadelphia, which had won the printing bid, offered to print the manual at its cost if the War Department would guarantee the purchase of 1,500 copies at 75 cents each. Secretary Holt declined to go even this far, and there the matter had to rest until the departure of the Buchanan cabinet.[38] Thus the story belongs to the Civil War period, although it is best completed here.

Churchill brought up the matter of the manual in a talk with Simon Cameron, Lincoln's Secretary of War, shortly after he came into office. When Samuel Cooper resigned to join the Confederacy, Churchill also explained the situation to the new Adjutant General, Brig. Gen. Lorenzo Thomas. After the firing on Fort Sumter, Churchill formally wrote Secretary Cameron, saying that Lincoln's call for 75,000 militiamen made the publication of an updated drill manual even more urgent. He felt that all responsible army and militia officers agreed to the need because the existing regulations and manuals were contradictory, unclear,

---

36. Sylvester Churchill, Ltrs to Col. S. Cooper, AGO, Washington, 29 Jan 59 and 21 Feb 59, Churchill Papers.
37. Sylvester Churchill, Ltr from W. A. Nichols, Asst AG, Washington, 5 Dec 59; Ltrs from John B. Floyd, Secy of War to chairman, Military Committee, U.S. Senate, 23 May 60 and 28 Dec 60, Churchill Papers.
38. Sylvester Churchill, Memo, 1 Mar 61, Churchill Papers.

and in very short supply. Churchill said his long experience as an inspector, in seeing what was needed, combined with the rigid scrutiny by numerous senior officers to whom he had subjected his drafts, made his book a valuable means for assuring early and proper organization of the mustering forces. Churchill stressed that immediate printing was still possible if the Secretary approved and authorized the expenditure.[39] Despite this plea, again no money was forthcoming.

By this time, Churchill was beginning to feel the full ravages of his seventy-eight years and he was preparing to go on an extended leave before his scheduled September retirement. His physical afflictions and the disappointment of not being able to serve actively did not deter him from trying to see his manual published. He wrote his successor in the inspectorate, Maj. Gen. George B. McClellan's father-in-law, Col. Randolph B. Marcy, in September 1861, outlining the saga of the approved draft. He sent Marcy a full copy and urged him to push for its publication. Churchill again stressed that such a standard manual would be of great value in training the newly forming armies. He felt that Marcy's status as inspector general might help get the project renewed. Fully retired by now, Churchill was dividing his time between his Washington residence and that of his daughter and her husband in Carlisle, Pennsylvania.[40]

Marcy and McClellan appear to have given some brief attention to the manual among their other duties during the fall of 1861. Finally, in February 1862, General McClellan appointed another formal board consisting of Maj. Gens. Irvin McDowell and Fitz-John Porter, and Brig. Gen. William B. Franklin to meet with Churchill and then to review the manual for possible adoption. They convened for a day on 11 February at Churchill's Washington residence. The next day, the board members consulted with McClellan, saying that the demands on their time prevented a thorough review of the manual and they suggested deferring any action. McClellan agreed, adjourning the board to a later date which never came. General Franklin was tasked with informing Churchill and thanking him for his courtesy and interest.[41] . . . Churchill made his final attempt to get the manual published when he saw that his old friend and commander, former inspector Maj. Gen. John E. Wool, had been appointed in June 1862 to develop a large camp of instruction near Annapolis, Maryland. Churchill wrote Wool that month, regretting that ill health prevented his active role in the war. He reviewed the history of his manuscript, saying the one way he might help the cause would be to assist Wool in getting it published for use in training the great forces being raised. When Wool expressed polite interest, Churchill replied in July with a summary of the manual's contents, recounting his view that it would be a valuable asset for training new troops.

39. Sylvester Churchill, Ltr to Simon Cameron, Secy of War, Washington, 19 Apr 61, Churchill Papers.

40. Sylvester Churchill, Ltr to Col. R. B. Marcy, IG, USA, Washington, 24 Sep 61, Churchill Papers.

41. Sylvester Churchill, Headquarters, Army of the Potomac, Special Orders (SO) No. 40, 10 Feb 62; Ltr from W. B. Franklin, Brig. Gen. of Vols., Camp Williams, Va., 13 Feb 62. Churchill Papers.

Wool was unable to act on Churchill's hopes because of greater demands on his time that summer.[42]

Churchill died on 7 December 1862 and hope of getting his manual published died with him. The manuscript and supporting papers remained in the possession of his son-in-law, Spencer F. Baird of Carlisle, Pennsylvania, until 1872 when he donated them to the War Department. The final insult to the project came the next year when the War Department returned the papers to Mr. Baird as being of no use. One can only speculate on the effect the manual would have had on the quality of the untrained hordes thrown into battle by the Federals in the early years of the Civil War and to Churchill's reputation as perhaps a second Steuben. The absence of a standard drill manual in the Federal forces was one of the greatest problems in the first year of the war. It unquestionably impeded the efficiency of the units sent into combat and delayed the training both of officers and of men. The disregard for Churchill's project was one of the many tragedies in a tragic era.

Regulations and the Inspector General

While Churchill was working on his drill manual, the U.S. Army received a new set of general regulations in 1855, reissued essentially unchanged in 1857. It had little impact on the inspectors general. One interesting development was the increasing use of the term "department" in refer to the inspectorate. Properly speaking, this word still meant a sphere of activity more than an organization, but the context showed the growing tendency to regard the inspectors general as a formal department.[43] Even though no separate body of regulations existed for the Inspector General's Department, as was true for other departments, regulations for inspections did exist as did a brief statement of inspecting officers' duties, honors due the troops, forms for inspections, and other details that echoed previous regulations. The content of inspection reports was redescribed, much shortened from the 1840 regulations, at Churchill's recommendation.[44]

Once again, inspectors were required to comment on the efficiency and abilities of the officers they saw. In addition, when property or stores were reported as unserviceable, they were to be examined by an inspector general or other officer appointed by the Secretary of War. Separate inventories were to show the disposition and exact condition of each article inspected. Objects determined to be unserviceable after inspection could be sold at auction. No officer could drop property from his returns until it was condemned after inspection and ordered to be dropped. That was cumbersome, but it was the sort of reform that Croghan had demanded years earlier. The War Department

---

42. Sylvester Churchill, War Dept GO No. 59, 5 Jun 62; Ltrs. to Maj. Gen. John E. Wool, Cdg Distr and Camp of Instruction, Carlisle, Pa., 17 Jun and 7 Jul 62, Churchill Papers.

43. U.S. War Dept, *Regulations for the Army of United States and for Quartermaster's Department* (Washington: A.O.P. Nicholson, 1855), and *Regulations for the Army of the United States, 1857* (New York: Harper & Brothers, 1857), 2–3.

44. *1857 Regulations*, 63.

simplified matters further on 15 June 1857, probably because there were not enough inspectors general to go around. The required inspections of unserviceable property, said the department, "will, unless otherwise ordered, be made by the commanding officers of posts."[45]

The 1855 and 1857 regulations neglected to establish the place of the inspectors general in the U.S. Army, in peace and in war, as explicitly as had their predecessors. There was an apparent assumption that they served the Commanding General, but the same assumption governed all other staff officers. If the inspections and reports were to have any apparent purpose, it was to encourage efficiency in the methods of inspection, and only incidentally to inform higher authorities of what was discovered. Given the War Department's primacy over the line of command, its economic interests gained ascendancy over the military interests of the Commanding General. Inspectors general appeared destined to become, by degrees, the Secretary of War's auditors. Promoting this impression was the War Department's amendment to the regulations in 1858 which permitted inspectors general to take one servant on their tours, with the government compensating for the servant's transportation costs. Secretary of War John B. Floyd proposed the next year to increase the number of brigadier generals in the Army to ten. Congress asked, "What do you want with ten brigadier generals?" The Secretary answered that one was to command each of six departments, one was to serve as Adjutant General, one was to serve as Quartermaster General, and two were to serve as inspectors general. That is, the War Department proposed to promote the inspectors general, but not to increase their number. Neither, in any event, happened.[46]

The Army did not get its ten brigadier generals in 1859. Legislation proposed the next year would have allowed a total of eight, the inspectors general not among them. In fact, the purpose of the bill, prepared in the Senate, was to eliminate the administrative staff of the Army, making a total reduction in the staff departments of 60 officers, and of 73 in ordnance and the Corps of Engineers—matched by additions of 76 officers to the regiments. The inspectors general and the Pay Department would be abolished completely. The duties of the latter were to be filled by the Quartermaster Department. The inspectorate, apparently, would have ceased to exist. In any event, nothing came of that measure either, and the Army retained its organization and its inspectors general until the start of the Civil War.[47]

Another War—The Inspectors Depart

The army that the Senate proposed to reorganize in 1860 was hopelessly scattered. Its actual strength that year stood at 16,006 officers and men—929 of

45. *1857 Regulations*, 119; GO No. 8, AGO, 15 Jun 57, in GORI&IG.

46. GO No. 3, AGO, 24 Mar 58, in GORI&IG; *Reorganization of the Army*, H. Misc. Doc. 29, 53d Cong., 2d sess. (1859).

47. U.S. Congress, Senate, Committee on Military Affairs and the Militia, *Report* to accompany Bill S. 61, S. Rpt. 21, 36th Cong., 1st sess. (1860).

them in the Department of the East, 13,143 broadcast over the rest of the continent, and others at depots, West Point, recruit rendezvous, and in transit. Such a dispersed organization required more inspection, not less, if it was ever to be cohesive. Accordingly, on 6 March 1860 the War Department had appointed Bvt. Col. Joseph E. Johnston "to duty as Acting Inspector General of the Army, according to his brevet rank." But Quartermaster General Jesup died in early June, and on the 20th of June Johnston replaced him. He spent a distracted year in that position before going over to the Confederacy.[48]

The threat of civil war became a reality in 1861, and the Army prepared itself with a new issue of the general regulations although, for the

COL. JOSEPH K. F. MANSFIELD. *Inspector General, 29 May 1857–14 May 1861.*

inspectors general, they remained unchanged since 1855. The Inspector General's Department had no separate section but the duties of its officers were briefly described. Inspection, however, was thoroughly integrated into command. Regulations for troops on campaign made inspection down to the company level the duty of brigadier generals, who reported to their division commanders. The chief purpose was to track regimental strength and readiness. Recruits at depots and in parties were to be mustered, inspected, and paid as were all other troops. Commanding officers were to inspect all recruits, and form boards of inspection— consisting of commanding officer, medical officer, and three other senior officers—to review men unfit or disqualified for service. Elsewhere, public works were to be inspected annually by "such officers of the corps [of Engineers] as the Secretary of War shall designate," while the Ordnance Department managed its own technical inspections. That was the epitaph for Macomb's attempt to subordinate the Corps of Engineers.[49]

The role of the inspectors general in the coming war was yet to be determined. In the preceding conflict they had been detailed as mustering officers, assembling and forwarding volunteer formations. But in the Civil War, they were eliminated from that duty at the outset, as the responsibility for recruiting was

---

48. Risch, *Quartermaster Support*, 301, 332–33; GO No. 5, AGO, 6 Mar 60, in GORI&IG.
49. U.S. War Department, *Revised Regulations for the Army of the United States, 1861* (Philadelphia: J.G.L. Brown, 1861), 40–41, 46–49, 71, 72–73, 138–39, 370, 387. The regulations for the first time accounted (on p. 120) for inspection of waterborne troop transports, although the inspection was to be a technical one.

turned over to Secretary of the Treasury Salmon P. Chase. The program then ran afoul of political considerations. When a board of officers recommended to Chase that regiments be established on three battalions—keeping two in the line by rotation, while the third battalion was recruiting and training—he accepted the idea only for the regulars, but rejected it roundly for volunteers. In fact, the idea was not even applied to the regulars, which re-formed in three-battalion regiments, but with all battalions on line. The proposal would have limited the total number of regiments by keeping them all fully manned, and accordingly would have limited the number of commissions that state governors could grant. There was no role for the inspectors general in any of that.[50] . . . In any case, there were no inspectors general available for mustering when the war became serious in the spring of 1861. Sylvester Churchill, yielding to age, reluctantly had taken leave in April, retiring on 25 September 1861.[51] Joseph K. F. Mansfield relinquished his inspectorate soon after Churchill did, and died even sooner than his colleague. He was in the Department of Texas when the secession crisis broke there, when the department commander, Brig. Gen. David Twiggs, surrendered all his troops to the state's rebels without a struggle. Mansfield managed to return to Washington, where he received a brevet as brigadier general on 6 May, and a full commission in that rank on 14 May 1861. As energetic and gallant as ever, Mansfield died 17 September 1862, of wounds received at the Battle of Antietam.[52]

The Army and its inspectorate were about to be transformed by war once again, and by its aftermath. But this time the inspectorate would start with a clean slate. No inspectors general remained from the old regime, and in fact the old regime itself came to an end on 1 November, when Scott, returned from New York at last, retired. All that remained to guide their successors were the regulations, and those left the true role of the inspectors general begging for definition. In the last war the inspectorate had fallen apart, its two-man staff dispatched to other duties. With manpower short in 1861, as it always was in emergencies, it appeared likely that the new inspectors general, whoever they were, could easily scatter to the winds.

---

50. Armin Rappaport, "The Replacement System During the Civil War," *Military Affairs*, 15 (summer 1951): 95–106. Volunteer regiments remained in the old ten-company format, an unavoidable reality in face of strong sentiments among the states, which provided the regiments and commissioned their officers.

51. Churchill, *Sketch of Life of Churchill*, 58–59; Heitman, *Historical Register*, 1: 301.

52. Frazer, *Mansfield on Condition*, xxix; Heitman, *Historical Register*, 1: 688. Twiggs, incidentally, was dismissed from the Army, and went over to the Confederacy, which made him a major general. He died in July 1862. Heitman, *Historical Register*, 1: 976.

CHAPTER 13

The Inspectorate During the Civil War

(1861–1865)

As the government acted in haste to raise and organize a great United States Army during the summer of 1861, it gave passing attention to the military inspectorate. On 3 August, Congress empowered the President to appoint, with the consent of the Senate, five assistant inspectors general, "with the rank and pay of majors of cavalry . . . to have the pay, rank, and allowance and perform the duties of similar officers in the present military establishment." Another grab-bag of provisions masquerading as legislation—among other things—the abolishment of the lash as punishment in the Army—said three days later "That the President of the United States is hereby authorized to appoint two additional inspectors-general to have the same rank and receive the same pay and allowances as now provided by law for inspectors-general." But another law enacted the same day repealed that very provision.[1]

Inspectors Without Portfolio

If the distracted War Department hierarchy examined that legislation closely, all it could have discovered was confusion. The five assistant inspectors general, ranked as majors, were to have the compensation and were to perform the duties of "similar officers" already in the organization. But the only "similar" officers were two colonels, entitled inspectors general. There had been no assistant inspectors general for many years. There was further confusion over the number of inspectors general desired. In principle, two positions for inspectors general already existed: Churchill was soon to vacate his office by retirement and Mansfield had already left to command troops, although he apparently retained his permanent commission as an inspector general. The 6 August legislation offered two more inspectors general before evidently snatching them away. The number of inspectors who could be appointed at Churchill's retirement ranged, according to interpretation, from as few as one to as many as

---

1. *An Act providing for the better organization of the military establishment*, Statutes at Large 12, sec. 2, 287 (1861); *An Act to promote the efficiency of the Engineer and Topographical Engineer Corps and for other purposes*, Statutes at Large 12, sec. 4, 317 (1861); *An Act to promote the efficiency of the Engineer and Topographical Engineer Corps, and for other purposes*, Statutes at Large 12, sec. 3, 318 (1861); *Legislative History*, 111–12.

COMMISSARY DEPARTMENT BAGGAGE TRAIN, 21 JULY 1861. *Procurement and logistical support were a major concern for Civil War inspectors.*

four. The War Department appointed three, until Mansfield's death made his position available as well.

The appointment and early disposition of the inspectors general and assistant inspectors general demonstrated that the War Department had no interest in establishing a unified, central inspectorate serving a unified, central command. Much as in 1812, the department proposed to direct the war itself, via theater commanders, although there was a succession of nominal commanding generals from Scott to Ulysses S. Grant—the latter finally exerting some central military control over all theaters. The title of Commanding General was an honor to the lead player, but gave him no power to direct the whole military play. So that inspectors general in the Civil War could be something different from their predecessors in the earlier conflicts, a fully empowered Commanding General might have made them his means of enforcing control over the army. So too might the Secretary of War have done so, had he planned to retain military control in his own hands. But what actually happened was something less. Inspectors general were appointed because the appointees were deemed worthy of promotion to colonel, regardless of their intended functions. They, and especially assistant inspectors general, were also appointed because the Secretary needed capable aides to serve him in roles ranging from messenger boys to confidential agents. Only inadvertently was there planted the seed of a centralized inspectorate.

Class of 1861: Inspectors General

A review of the careers of the principal characters shows that the new inspectors general and assistant inspectors general were a varied group; they played equally varied parts in the wartime drama. The first officer promoted to inspector general was Randolph B. Marcy, assigned on 9 August 1861. Born in Massachusetts in 1812, Marcy graduated from West Point in 1832, and was among the twenty-nine cadets of that class who volunteered to go along with General Scott's "Northwestern Army" to put down the Sacs and Foxes in the Black Hawk War during the summer of 1832. That expedition was broken up because of cholera.

Marcy then went to the 5th Infantry, not making captain until 1846. He spent the intervening period, except for two short stints as a recruiting officer, in Michigan and Wisconsin. In 1846, he went to Texas, where he served during the military occupation and the opening skirmishes of the Mexican War. But he was soon assigned to duty as a recruiting officer, and although he returned to Texas in 1847, he remained out of the fighting and accordingly missed the promotions, brevets, and reputation-building that the war offered to others. He ended the conflict as he had begun it, a captain. After that, Marcy roamed the Southwest for the next twelve years, becoming one of the more famous of the Army's many explorers and adventurers in the interwar period. He escorted an immigrant train and opened a new trail from Arkansas to New Mexico in 1849, and two years later led an expedition to establish sites for new military posts in the Southwest. In 1852, assisted by a young second lieutenant, George B. McClellan, Marcy led an exploration of the headwaters of the Red and Canadian rivers. Two years later, he surveyed the Indian lands of Texas. His reports of his adventures were published by Congress, and enjoyed great popularity.

After brief service fighting the Seminoles in Florida, in 1857 Marcy accompanied the expedition into Utah to subdue the Mormons during the "Mormon War." That force had to winter at Fort Bridger under very distressing conditions, its supplies cut off by Mormon raiders. Marcy led about one hundred men on a heroic 1,300-mile round trip through unknown wilderness, during the worst winter in memory, to bring relief to the force. That exploit drew the extended attention and admiration of the Secretary of War, who devoted a substantial part of his annual report to an account of Marcy's dramatic adventure. It also earned Marcy an appointment as acting inspector general for the Department of Utah. Late in 1858, he was assigned to Scott's headquarters at New York to prepare a guidebook for the westward-moving emigrants, published by the War Department in 1859 as *The Prairie Traveler*. He was rewarded with promotion to major and assignment as a paymaster, and he served in the Northwest until May 1861.[2]

---

2. Heitman, *Historical Register*, 1: 689; *AMB*, 272; *DAB* 6: 273–74; Spaulding, *United States Army*, 237–38; Cecil Eby, *"That Disgraceful Affair, the Black Hawk War"* (New York: Norton, 1973), 217; Ezra J. Warner, *Generals in Blue: Lives of the Union Commanders* (Baton Rouge: Louisiana State University Press, 1964), 311.

Marcy was a large, handsome man who affected the cheek whiskers and mustache that became popular during the Civil War. He looked like a soldier and acted the part. He was energetic and—as his career demonstrated— bravely adventurous, a big-game hunter until his death. The new inspector general was also an affable man, a fund of anecdotes and generally popular among those who knew him. All those qualities might have fitted him for the role of inspector general, but in addition, according to Washington's long-time observer Ben: Perley Poore, Marcy was known as an experienced military counselor.[3] It was as a counselor that Marcy spent his first year and more as inspector general. The commander he served was his former partner in adventure, George B. McClellan, now a major

BRIG. GEN. RANDOLPH B. MARCY. *Inspector General and Inspector General of the Army, 9 August 1861– 2 January 1881.*

general. Marcy owed his appointment not to his character or qualifications, but to simple nepotism. McClellan had married Marcy's daughter Mary Ellen in 1860, and in June 1861 decided to ensure that his father-in-law would not spend the Civil War ignominiously as he had passed the Mexican War. McClellan invited Marcy to join him at Cincinnati that month to serve as his chief of staff during the campaign in western Virginia. This campaign's success propelled McClellan's rise to Commanding General of the Army.[4]

Making Marcy an inspector general in August 1861 was not in any way a restaffing of the Army's inspectorate. It was instead an exercise in expediency—taking a current vacancy merely to promote McClellan's chief of staff to colonel, followed by Marcy's appointment as brigadier general of volunteers on 23

3. Ben: Perley Poore, *Perley's Reminiscences of Sixty Years in the National Metropolis*, 2 vols. (Philadelphia: Hubbard, 1886), 2: 90–91. "Ben: Perley Poore" was the special affectation of one of Washington's most famous journalists and raconteurs, publisher of many essential catalogues of government documents. A more recent account of the Washington scene during the war is Margaret Leech, *Reveille in Washington, 1860–1865* (New York: Harper, 1941).

4. Warner, *Generals in Blue*, 311; Marcy to George W. Cullum, 12 Nov 65, Cullum Files, United States Military Academy Archives, West Point, New York (hereafter cited as USMA Archives). Marcy, understandably, did not credit his family connection with his appointments, but he was widely known in Washington as McClellan's father-in-law. Poore, *Perley's Reminiscences*, 2: 90–91. Until Grant became Commanding General in 1864, the highest officer was usually in command of the Army of the Potomac, and only nominally head of all military forces. McClellan relinquished command of the whole army on 11 March 1862, and was followed by Henry W. Halleck in the position of Commanding General. Heitman, *Historical Register*, 1: 17.

September. The latter promotion, however, not being confirmed by the Senate, expired the following July. The Senate, it appears, was not as inclined to indulge McClellan's family as was the President. Marcy's next appointment as brigadier general, 13 September 1862, also expired under senatorial inaction, on 4 March 1863. McClellan was by that time thoroughly discredited, and his disrepute affected those around him.[5] So Marcy was thus inspector general in title only while he actually served as chief of staff for the Army of the Potomac until 7 November 1862, shortly after McClellan had been removed from command. During that time, one of his principal activities was to relay McClellan's excuses for failure or inaction and other bad news to the War Department and the President. The emissary's duties were not happy ones, and Marcy regularly endured Secretary of War Edwin M. Stanton's furious outbursts about McClellan's failures.[6] Although Marcy went into limbo after McClellan's dismissal, he was too capable and well liked to remain hidden for long. After a while, he took up duties more appropriate to an inspector general. Eventually, he was to become the first senior inspector general to enjoy a higher rank than his colleagues.

Second to Marcy among the new inspectors general was Delos B. Sacket, a cavalryman who became a colonel and an inspector general 1 October 1861. A New Yorker, Sacket graduated from West Point in 1845 and entered the dragoons. As a brevet second lieutenant, he took part in the occupation and battles in Texas in 1846, earning his brevet for "gallant and meritorious conduct," then participated in the battle of Monterrey. He spent the rest of the war and its aftermath on frontier duty, mostly in New Mexico. Beginning in December 1850, Sacket spent five years as an assistant instructor of cavalry tactics at the Military Academy, then served successively as a recruiter, in garrison at Fort Leavenworth, on a board to revise the army regulations, as an inspector of horses and mules, and again on the frontier, fighting Indians. He was promoted to captain in 1855, and in 1861, after a year of leave in Europe, to major in January and to lieutenant colonel in May.

In fairly swift order, Sacket spent 1861 as an acting inspector general for the Department of Washington, then as a mustering and disbursing officer at New York City. While in New York, he was appointed a colonel, and an inspector general on 1 October. Two months later, on 13 December, he was appointed as the inspector general for the Army of the Potomac. Sacket, unlike Marcy, was able to survive McClellan's dismissal, but not that of his successor, Ambrose E. Burnside. He returned to Washington on 10 January 1863 and established the Inspector General's Office.[7] Sacket was a melancholy-looking

---

5. Heitman, *Historical Register*, 1: 689; Warner, *Generals in Blue*, 311.

6. Bruce Catton, *Terrible Swift Sword* (Garden City, New York: Doubleday, 1963), 195, 304, describes some typical encounters between Marcy and the Lincoln Administration.

7. Heitman, *Historical Register*, 1: 856; George W. Cullum, *Biographical Register of the Officers and Graduates of the U.S. Military Academy at West Point, N.Y.*, 3d edition (Boston: Houghton Mifflin, 1891), 2: 234–36. Sacket's actions during the battle of Antietam draw notice in several places in Stephen W. Sears, *Landscape Turned Red: The Battle of Antietam* (New York: Tichnor and Fields, 1983).

COL. HENRY VAN RENSSELAER.
*Inspector General, 12 November
1861–23 March 1864.*

man whose energy belied his appearance. He served with credit as an inspector general throughout the war. Alone among those appointed in 1861, he secured his position by merit, and lived up to his title. He succeeded Marcy as senior inspector general in 1881.

The third and last inspector general of 1861, Henry Van Rensselaer, was another matter. A member of a prominent New York family, he had graduated from West Point in 1831, but had resigned his commission within six months. He was among the numbers of politically connected former officers who presented themselves to the cause in 1861, and received an appointment as colonel and "additional aide-de-camp" on 5 August. Honorably discharged on 1 November, Van Rensselaer became a colonel and an inspector general eleven days later. He was an uncertain quantity, who thought himself bound for glory at the head of troops. His influence gained him appointment as a brigadier general of volunteers early in 1862, but the commission expired later in the year when the Senate refused to ratify it. Van Rensselaer was in his fifties and apparently not in good health. He drifted until his death on 23 March 1864, leaving behind an undistinguished record.[8]

Class of 1861: Assistant Inspectors

The President began to appoint assistant inspectors general on 11 November 1861. They were a mixed lot, although mostly creditable individuals. Their records during the war were also mixed, but reflected the many ways in which inspectors were employed in the conflict. Some, including Absalom Baird, John Buford, and James Totten, had little or no service as inspectors. They secured volunteer commissions as generals, and served as line commanders. Baird became a gallant leader and a winner of the Medal of Honor. Buford was a prominent cavalry commander, contributor to the Confederate entanglement at Gettysburg, who died of exposure and exhaustion in 1863, at the age of thirty-seven. Totten won distinction as a general, then reverted to the post of assistant inspector general after the war. Other assistant inspectors general spent most of the war at their jobs, inspecting troops. James Hardie became one

---

8. Heitman, *Historical Register,* 1: 983; GO No. 181, AGO, 1 Nov 62, in GORI&IG.

of the earliest bureaucrats of the inspectorate, Nelson Davis spent most of the war inspecting troops in the Army of the Potomac, while Roger Jones went wherever the Secretary of War sent him.[9] Three wartime assistant inspectors general later became senior inspectors general. Nelson Davis, appointed an assistant inspector general on 12 November 1861, graduated from West Point in 1846. He served as an infantry officer in the invasion of Mexico at Vera Cruz and the campaigns against Mexico City, during which he earned a brevet for "gallant and meritorious conduct" in battle. He spent the 1850s on the frontier in California and the Great Plains, rising to captain in 1855. His native state of Massachusetts appointed him a colonel of the 7th Massachusetts Infantry in 1861, but he resigned that post to become an assistant inspector general in November.

Davis spent the winter of 1861 to 1862 inspecting troops in the Army of the Potomac, and then in March became inspector of an army corps. After being attached to headquarters of the Army of the Potomac during the peninsula campaign, Davis was shifted from place to place—wherever an inspector or officer was needed—in the Army of the Potomac, carrying on the tradition of the inspector as available manpower. His "gallant and meritorious services" at the battle of Gettysburg in 1863 earned him a brevet lieutenant colonelcy. Davis next was assigned as an inspector general for the Department of New Mexico in November 1863. He spent the next two years, in his own words, "making Special investigations by Orders dpt. Comd'r. and Sec. War, exploring country, locating Mily Posts, directing movement of troops, scouting after Indians—in three attacks on Indians killing 51 and taking prisoners [sic] 16—arms, ammunition, property of various kinds captured, including $660.00 in gold." Once again, Davis' "gallant and meritorious services in action with the Apache Indians, Arizona," earned him a third brevet commission.[10] The quietly able Davis was not untypical of the crop of assistant inspectors general appointed in November 1861. He was in his forties, and had behind him a solid career as an infantry officer. He was intelligent and flexible, fit not only to be an inspector, but also for whatever assignments might come upon him. Service in the Southwest was an odd, frequently grueling ordeal during the Civil War, and Davis came through it well. By the time he became senior inspector general in the 1880s, his appearance was that of a large, calm, comfortable man.

Absalom Baird, who became an assistant inspector general the same day as Davis, 12 November, followed a somewhat different course during the Civil War. Of all the officers putatively in the Army's inspectorate, he compiled the

---

9. Sanger, "Inspector-General's Department," 244, offers a thumbnail sketch, not wholly accurate, of the wartime activities of inspectors general and assistant inspectors general. See Appendix B.

10. Cullum, *Biographical Register*, 2: 298–300; Heitman, *Historical Register*, 1: 359; Nelson H. Davis, "Summary of Services," 26 Mar 65, Cullum Files, USMA Archives. The variety of Davis' service in New Mexico is suggested by his role as the government's emissary in peace negotiations with the Apaches, who were in serious rebellion during the 1860s. The episode is recounted in Jacob Piatt Dunn, *Massacres of the Mountains: A History of the Indian Wars of the Far West* (New York: Harper and Brothers, 1886), 390–91.

most distinguished record—not as an inspector, but as a combat commander. He was a Pennsylvanian, who came from a prominent family with a strong military heritage. His grandfather was a surgeon in the Continental Army, and his great grandfather had fought in the French and Indian War. Baird initially intended to become a lawyer, but when trouble threatened between the United States and Mexico, he applied to the United States Military Academy; he graduated in 1849. The war then was over, and Barid went into the artillery, spending three years in campaigns against the Seminoles, then several more years on the Texas frontier. Promotions were slow for officers without war records in the 1850s, and he was still a first lieutenant when the Civil War broke out. Soon thereafter, Baird was appointed an assistant adjutant general with the brevet rank of captain in May 1861, and became a divisional adjutant in time for the battle of Bull Run. He was a permanent captain and an assistant adjutant general as of 3 August, before becoming a major and assistant inspector general on 12 November.

Baird's career in the inspectorate began inauspiciously. Until March 1862, he was assigned to the War Department staff as a functionary who managed to develop a sound understanding of the volunteers who were making up the majority of the wartime Army. He was then assigned as an inspector general and chief of staff of IV Corps, Army of the Potomac, taking an active part in operations on the Virginia Peninsula. He performed so ably that he was made a brigadier general of volunteers in April 1862 and sent to Kentucky, where immediately he led his brigade during the capture of Cumberland Gap in June. That earned him command of a division in the Army of Kentucky, and he organized his new force and had it ready within a month. Baird participated in various actions in Kentucky and Tennessee until August 1863 when, at the request of Maj. Gen. George H. Thomas, he and his division were transferred to Thomas' XIV Corps.

Then Baird came into his own. He was thirty-nine years old, energetic, and ambitious; popular with his men because he was a just, albeit hard, disciplinarian; and an aggressive commander. Baird led his division in the battle of Chickamauga in September, the first to enter and the last to leave the battle, repelling stout enemy attacks and sustaining heavy casualties. The erstwhile inspector led by personal example, and earned the first of many brevets at Chickamauga. His gallantry in the November assault on Missionary Ridge, near Chattanooga, earned him another. In the Atlanta campaign the next spring, Baird and his division were under fire every day for four months. At the battle of Jonesboro, he took personal command of one of his brigades and successfully stormed the enemy entrenchments. That earned him another brevet (he received five, in all, during the war) and a recommendation from General William T. Sherman that he be promoted to major general. It also brought him, thirty years later, the Medal of Honor.

Baird remained with Sherman until the end of the war, then spent a period as an assistant commissioner of the Freedmen's Bureau before reverting in 1866 to his old rank—almost forgotten—of major and assistant inspector general.

He followed Davis as a senior inspector general in the 1880s, but he was more fittingly Marcy's successor. By this time, this tall, dignified old soldier, like Marcy, was inclined to look to the past. Unlike Marcy, he was too reserved to be a great storyteller.[11] Baird's career was singular, but not unusual for a wartime inspector; several others spent more time commanding than inspecting.

Roger Jones, however, started out uniquely: He was made an assistant inspector general as a reward for heroism. Like Baird, he spent comparatively little time inspecting. But his wartime career was nevertheless ordinary, and not detached from the inspectorate. Jones was born in 1831, the son of Adjutant General Roger Jones. The younger Jones was destined for a military career, entering West Point at the minimum age of sixteen. Following graduation in 1851, his next decade was undistinguished. He was still a lieutenant of cavalry when the war started, his only special experience four years as regimental adjutant. Except for two years as an instructor at West Point and two assignments to Carlisle Barracks, Pennsylvania, Jones spent the 1850s in the Southwest.

Jones led about fifty recruits from Carlisle Barracks to Harpers Ferry, West Virginia, in January 1861, with orders to guard the place and its stores from Rebels, destroying the weapons and ammunition there if necessary to prevent their capture. He learned of the approach of the enemy on 18 April, sent out a call for aid, and announced his determination to destroy what he could not defend. That night, with more than a thousand Virginia troops at his doorstep, he destroyed the arsenal and its contents (including 15,000 muskets), and withdrew in the darkness with only four casualties. His steadiness in the face of overwhelming odds earned him the official thanks of the government. Jones became a captain and an assistant quartermaster general on 23 April. He spent the next several months in the Quartermaster General's Office, except for a few weeks as chief quartermaster of the Army of the Potomac. On 11 November 1861, he became a major and an assistant inspector general. He served as a War Department functionary until 17 July 1862, when he became an assistant inspector general for the Army of Virginia. He was relieved from that post on 1 September, and until June 1863 was in New York helping to organize and forward volunteer troops to the field. New York's draft riots interrupted recruiting work in the city, and Jones returned to service with the Secretary of War. As far as Jones was concerned, from September 1862 to the end of the war, he generally was on unimportant duty, away from the armies in the field. Like several other inspectors, Jones spent most of the war as a minor functionary in a department-full.

Jones had an unremarkable career partly because of lack of opportunity, but mostly because he lacked the ambition and will to advance his own interests.

---

11. *DAB*, 1: 507–08; Mark M. Boatner III, *Civil War Dictionary* (New York: McKay, 1974), 507–08; Heitman, *Historical Register*, 1: 182–83; Joseph P. Sanger, "Absolom Baird," *Annual Reunion of the Association of Graduates, 1905* (West Point: Association of Graduates, 1905), 114–24; John A. Baird, Jr., *Profile of a Hero: The Story of Absolom Baird, His Family, and the American Military Tradition* (Philadelphia: Dorrance, 1977); Baird, undated statement (early 1866), in Cullum Files, USMA Archives.

He was a quiet, reserved, calm, and exceedingly polite man whose face bespoke peaceful dignity. He was well liked, if not widely known. One of his West Point contemporaries remarked, "His whole life in the army, like that in the family circle, revealed only the charm of the lovely character with which nature and early family training endowed him." He was a "quiet, firm, conscientious soldier, ever alert in the performance of his duties, and always performing them with gentleness and distinguished courtesy." He lived "an admirable life full of grace and dignity." Although these values made close friendships, they were not the stuff of which glorious military careers were forged. He became senior inspector general solely as a result of promotion by seniority, and served less than a week in 1888 before taking leave for what proved to be terminal illness.[12]

Inspectors Without an Inspectorate

The appointment of inspectors general and assistant inspectors general during the fall of 1861 provided the officers who would preside over the Army's inspectorate during the quarter-century following the war. But it did not, as the varied careers of the appointees demonstrated, establish a formal inspection department for the wartime Army. The officers served in various capacities during the war, according to their talents or as the Secretary of War desired. And despite the presence of one or several of them in the War Department offices, there was not even a permanent office of the Inspector General in the department until January 1863. This lack of structure may be seen by the fact that the inspector general appointments appear to have been made, in the main, because the positions were vacant, and the candidates seemed worthy enough. But the inspector's job remained to be defined as the war advanced. Nevertheless, largely aside from the institution of inspectors general, inspection went forth. The regulations vested that responsibility in commanders, without clearly stating the place of inspectors general in the establishment. Armies, corps, divisions, brigades, and geographical divisions and departments almost all had inspectors general, assistant inspectors general, or acting assistant inspectors general, during the war, in the early period usually selected by the commanders. The formally designated inspectors were attached partly to armies or corps here and there, but mostly they did the bidding of the Secretary of War. Therefore, the army was inspected frequently by other officers from the line.[13]

The loose band of inspectors had no organization at the end of 1861, merely undefined purposes and varied assignments. But as the war advanced, a succession of small developments forced the evolution of an organization for the inspectorate, and a clearer definition of the inspectors' place and purpose.

---

12. Heitman, *Historical Register*, 1: 582; "A Classmate, Roger Jones," *Annual Reunion of the Association of Graduates, 1889* (West Point: Association of Graduates, 1889), 74–77; Roger Jones to George W. Cullum, 10 May 66, Cullum Files, USMA Archives.

13. It may be observed that Sanger is unaware of the gradual evolution of the inspectorate during the war, and even of the fact that it lacked the rudiments of an organization until 1863. Sanger, "Inspector-General's Department," 244.

Much went on without them. For instance, after receiving evidence of corrupt or negligent inspecting at an arsenal, the Secretary of War in February 1862 directed the Quartermaster General to overhaul his own inspection system, making it incumbent on all Quartermaster Department officers to report evidence of fraud on the part of contractors, or "where Inspectors have neglected their duty." In April 1862, legislation establishing the Medical Department assigned a Medical Inspector General, with the rank of colonel of cavalry, to the support of the Surgeon General.[14] Also during the second year of the war, Congress established programs without references to the inspectors general, but which eventually would require their official attention. The President was authorized on 17 July 1862 to buy grounds for national cemeteries "and cause them to be securely enclosed." That same year, the shortage of officers impelled Congress to include military instruction in the curriculum of colleges founded under the Land Grant Act. That farsighted provision for future volunteer officers was for some time ignored by the War Department, with each college remaining autonomous. But eventually, the department would want to know what the military college programs were doing, and turned to its inspectorate to provide this service.[15] More directly, Congress and the War Department added incidentally to the duties of inspectors general, focusing on problems as they developed but lacking any apparent general plan. In January 1862, for instance, the department grew concerned that some men were shirking combat by masquerading as musicians. Many regimental bands were of a low order in any case. "Inspectors General, while on their tours," ordered the Secretary, "will inspect the bands of all regiments, and discharge all men mustered therewith who are not musicians." That raised the question—never addressed in that context—of whether those officers had the authority to discharge soldiers, or even to transfer them within regiments.[16]

On 19 March 1862, Congress constituted the Inspectors General of the Army as a board of officers who were to prepare a schedule of articles that sutlers were to carry for the volunteer service. An extensive list of suggested items was provided in the regulation and the sale of all intoxicants was prohibited. Perhaps it was the presumed detachment and objectivity of the inspectors, but other than that why they received that particular assignment was not clear, unless it was believed that they had nothing better to do. Dispersed as the three inspectors general were, the War Department dutifully ordered them to prepare the list of 21 March, and instructed brigade staff officers, with divisional approval, to fix sutlers' prices. The inspectors general were also told to inspect sutlers' operations every fifteen days, or cause them to be inspected by "some

14. Russell F. Weigley, *Quartermaster General of the Union Army: A Biography of M. C. Meigs* (New York: Columbia University Press, 1959), 213; Ganoe, *History of the United States Army*, 178.

15. Act of 17 July 1862, 12 Stat. 596, quoted in Steere, "Genesis of Graves Registration," 151; Lyons and Masland, "The Origins of the ROTC," *Military Affair*, 23 (spring 1959), 2–3.

16. GO No. 4, AGO, 18 Jan 62, in GORI&IG.

competent officer,'' who was to report his findings to the appropriate inspector general.[17]

Whenever a problem arose, the War Department seemed inclined to assign an inspector to it. Cavalry was a growing subject of concern in 1862, because it did not always measure up to the Confederates' and, most important, because horses and equipment were expensive. The Secretary of War directed on 14 August that no one would be mustered into the cavalry service without being given a test of horsemanship and knowledge of horse care.[18] That, of course, was a duty of mustering officers rather than inspectors. But some of the inspectors (Roger Jones being one of them) served as mustering officers, as directed by the Secretary of War. The attention of inspectors general was directed more specifically to cavalry on 20 November, when all corps, division, and brigade commanders were instructed to order a special inspection of their cavalry by the end of the month. They were to report to the War Department the names of all officers whose horses appeared neglected or unfit, so that the officers could be dismissed from the service. Any commanders who had not already designated their inspecting officers presumably did so then, at least for that singular purpose.[19]

By that time, most of the people who carried the title of inspector general in some form were line officers detailed to inspection duty. The body of formally designated inspectors was too small to reach every brigade, or even every full field army, and many of them were busy mustering or conducting investigations ordered by the Secretary of War. Nearly 1,400 other officers were on orders at one time or another to perform various types of inspection duties. The only common ties these men had with the formally appointed inspectors were the regulations and orders which invoked similar inspection procedures. The inspectorate, in other words, still lacked an organization. Not even the organization of the larger fighting forces was uniformly established in the various regular and volunteer formations.

By 1862, the major fighting and command unit of the Army was usually the army corps, a grouping of divisions. But corps had not under the law been provided with staffs adequate to their emerging role on the battlefield. In fact, staff services were generally inadequate in the larger fighting units, and it was not only the inspectors general who fell into an undefined status. Adjutant General Lorenzo Thomas complained to Congress that adjutants general held too low a rank, for by law he could not recruit them from grades above lieutenant. The generally low rank of adjutants general made them ineffective and subject to the caprice of nearly every other functionary. ''As a consequence, then, of the very inferior rank held by these officers,'' said Thomas, ''they are thrust aside from their rightful positions. Inspectors general, additional aides-de-

---

17. The full text of the legislation appears in U.S. War Department, *Revised United States Army Regulations of 1861* (Washington: Government Printing Office, 1863), 529–31. See also GO No. 27, AGO, 21 Mar 62, which also reproduced the legislation, in GORI&IG.
18. GO No. 105, AGO, 14 Aug 62, in GORI&IG.
19. GO No. 192, AGO, 20 Nov 62, in GORI&IG.

camp, and officers of the line, are not only put over their heads, but actually put into their places."[20] Inspectors, in other words, often functioned as adjutants, merely because the latter lacked the status to be completely effective. That was another fruit of the absence of definition for the inspectorate, and of the generally inadequate provision of staffs for the combat organizations.

Congress moved to re-form the corps organization on 17 July 1862, when it determined that each army corps would have a staff comprised of an assistant adjutant general, a quartermaster, a commissary of subsistence, and an assistant inspector general—all to rank as lieutenant colonel and all assigned by the President from the Army or volunteer forces. Nine assistant inspectors general had been appointed and assigned to the staffs of major generals by 1 November 1862. Interestingly, they did not come from the number of the majors previously appointed as assistant inspectors general. Those who had not already moved into the volunteer organizations (as had Baird) remained in the Regular Army at their lower, but permanent, rank.[21] The War Department simplified and improved the appointment of army corps staffs on 23 December. The staff officers authorized in July were thereafter to be attached permanently to their units, not to their particular commanders. In addition, heads of the War Department bureaus were permitted to designate an adjutant general, quartermaster, commissary of subsistence and inspector general for each army corps. When it looked to the implementation of that order, the War Department probably noticed for the first time that it had no Inspector General's Bureau.[22]

There were assistant inspectors general available at the War Department, but the Secretary of War was in the habit of dispatching them to wherever he needed information. Nelson Davis, for instance, spent January 1863 making a special examination of a mutinous unit of the Army of the Cumberland, the Anderson Cavalry, at the Secretary's orders. He found merit in the men's complaints that they had been misled about their assignment, but believed that examples should be made of the more rebellious ringleaders.[23] The available assistant inspectors general were therefore too useful to restrict to performing desk work at the War Department. In any case, they were junior to the three

---

20. *Reorganization of the Adjutant General's Department*, H. Misc. Doc. 73., 37th Cong., 2d sess. (1862).

21. *An Act to amend the act calling forth the militia to execute the laws of the Union, suppress insurrection, and repel invasion, approved February twenty-eighth, seventeen hundred and ninety-five, and the act ammendatory thereof, and for other purposes*, Statutes at Large 12, sec. 10, 597 (1862); Thian, *Legislative History*, 112; GO No. 91, AGO, 29 Jul 62, and GO No. 181, AGO, 1 Nov 62, in GORI&IG. General Order No. 181, also announced the death of Joseph K. F. Mansfield at Antietam, 18 September 1862, and the fact that appointments as brigadier generals of volunteers for Henry Van Rensselaer and Stewart Van Vliet (a Quartermaster major) had expired 17 July.

22. GO No. 212, AGO, 23 Dec 62, in GORI&IG. When the regulations were reissued in 1863, that was the only noticeable change affecting the organization of inspectors general since 1861. *1863 Regulations*, 513.

23. Davis to AG, 4 Feb 63, in U.S. War Department, *The War of the Rebellion: A Compilation of the Official Records of the Union and Confederate Armies*, 70 vols. in 128 books (Washington: Government Printing Office, 1881-1900), 1st ser., vol. 20, pt. 2:345–75 (hereafter cited as *OR*).

inspectors general. Of the latter, Marcy was the senior and the logical candidate to hold forth in Washington. But he was for the moment serving as a brigadier general of volunteers. Moreover, his reputation was tarnished by his son-in-law's failures and he was decidedly out of favor with the Washington establishment, including Secretary of War Edwin M. Stanton.

Marcy would not have been a good addition to the War Department staff in that climate, so he was allowed to drift for a few months. Because he was an active man, one who enjoyed roaming the country, the War Department could not ignore him. Thus, from July 1863 until September 1865, he was constantly engaged in inspecting posts in the departments of the Northwest, Missouri, Arkansas, Mississippi, and the Gulf. His reports were in the fashion established by Croghan and Mansfield, although without the elaborate details and recommendations. They were addressed to the Adjutant General, not to a chief inspector at the War Department.[24]

A Presence in Washington

Before Marcy was dispatched to the western theater, Delos B. Sacket was reassigned from the Army of the Potomac to the War Department, on 10 January 1863. He was given no formal title, merely being placed in charge of the paper work of inspectors general at the War Department level. For convenience, he was commonly identified as the inspector general on duty at the War Department or at the U.S. Army headquarters. Because he was junior by date of commission to Marcy, he could not be regarded as the senior or supervisory inspector general, let alone as the Inspector General of the Army, counterpart to the Adjutant General. Nevertheless, even Marcy eventually regarded Sacket's position as "the office of the supervising inspector general at the headquarters of the army."[25]

Sacket's assignment to Washington cannot be regarded as the birth of the Inspector General's Department. It was, however, at least its starting point. Like a well-planted seed, the little organization took root and grew, and was thereafter a permanent fixture of the War Department establishment. In the course of events, when the staff had acquired the trappings of other staffs, it was generally assumed that it had always been there, a department or bureau equivalent to the establishments of the Adjutant General, Quartermaster General, and others. Sacket probably had no visions of founding a permanent bureau when he started work at the War Department. Rather, he found himself buried

24. Warner, *Generals in Blue*, 311; Marcy to George W. Cullum, 12 Nov 65, Cullum Files, USMA Archives. Marcy's first report was of inspections of posts in the Department of the Northwest. He worked from New York, and in 1863 toured the department from July to October, at which point he asked for further orders. Marcy to AG, 2 Nov 63, and Report (166 pages) dated 15 Oct 63, in Letters Received 1863-1894, Records of the Inspector General (ROIG), RG 159, National Archives.

25. Cullum, *Biographical Register*, 2: 235; *Annual Report of the Inspector General* (hereafter cited as *ARIG*) 1869, H. Ex. Doc. 1, 41st Cong., 2d sess., vol. 1, pt. 2:176.

in paper work. The Inspector General, at the request of the Adjutant General, made all final decisions correcting regimental muster rolls, showing in particular the effective dates of officers' commissions—the basis for their pay in volunteer regiments. It was tedious and demanding work, and not at all pleasing to Sacket.[26] In addition Sacket had other onerous burdens, while his fellows enjoyed great adventure and pursued promotions in the war. He provided the Adjutant General with exceedingly detailed reviews of the money and property accounts of Quartermaster Department officers, never finding more than very minor discrepancies. Another duty was review of pension applications. A typical case involved "Private Phillip [sic] Cole," who had lost an arm at Antietam. Sacket reviewed the man's record, and sent it on to the Adjutant General for further information and forwarding to the Pension Bureau with a favorable recommendation. The paper work multiplied endlessly.[27]

Sacket needed help. On 9 April 1863, he asked that Private Harris H. Stewart of the Rhode Island Light Artillery be detailed to duty in his office as a clerk. He asked on 7 June that an assistant inspector general, preferably Nelson Davis, also be assigned to his office. If that could not be done permanently, he wanted at least a temporary assistant while he served on the Invalid Board, to which he had recently been appointed. The Adjutant General's Office told him two days later that Davis could not be spared from the Army of the Potomac, and that there was no other officer available. Sacket obtained no professional assistance that year.[28]

Scattering the Inspectors' Attention

Sacket's difficulties were complicated by the fact that Secretary Stanton persisted in treating inspectors as if they were always available to satisfy his concerns. In May 1863, Stanton assigned Sacket and a surgeon to a special inspection of the sanitary condition of Washington and its suburbs, and to offer recommendations to prevent disease. They began with an interview with the mayor, who published clean-up notices to citizens. The city was replete with nuisances, and short on provisions for dealing with sewage. Dead animals were seldom buried properly, and all the corrals were adjoined by mountains of manure. Slaughterhouses adorned the environs of military hospitals and the Navy Yard, and streets went unrepaired. All Sacket could do was to urge that the city enforce the laws already on the books, and press others to clean up the

---

26. For typical examples, correcting muster roll entries for officers of the 103d New York Volunteers, see Sacket to Maj. R. Ringgold, 19 Feb 63, and Sacket to AG, 19 Mar 63, in Letters Sent 1863–1889, ROIG, RG 159.

27. A typical Quartermaster account examination is Sacket to Adjutant General, 20 May 1863, and the Cole case is covered in Sacket to Assistant Adjutant General Samuel Breck, 10 June 1863, both in Letters Sent 1863–1889, RG 159.

28. Sacket to AG, 9 Apr and 7 Jun 63, in Letters Sent, 1863–1889, RG 159, and Asst. AG E.D. Townsend to Sacket, 9 Jun 63, in Letters Received, 1863–1894, RG 159. He did obtain Private Stewart, however.

noisome capital city.[29] Sacket had no sooner finished combing Washington's filth than the Secretary, on 26 May, appointed him to the newly established Board to Organize the Invalid Corps. That was not his last assignment to such a body, as he also served on the Board to Retire Disabled Officers while trying to hold down his chair as an inspector general.[30]

The duties of inspectors general and their counterparts continued to increase during 1863. On 22 May, in connection with the raising of "colored" troops— federal and state volunteer regiments of black men—the War Department determined that three or more field officers would be detailed as inspectors to supervise the organization of colored units at places to be designated in the northern and western states. The department ordered on 25 June that any officer presenting property for condemnation certify that it had not previously been condemned. The inspector was to brand, chisel, cut, or punch "I.C." ("Inspected-Condemned," the initials required to mark condemned property as late as the 1940s) onto the property. If the inspector's findings were later disapproved, the marks were to be canceled and a certificate was to be presented to the accountable officer. And on 7 August, an order establishing transportation allowances and marching rations required that within one week of the order inspectors of armies and army corps were to report directly to the Adjutant General "every violation of this order, certifying in their reports that they have thoroughly inspected the several commands, and have reported therein every deviation from this order in regard to allowance of transportation."[31] . . .

The inspectors' attention was scattered further upon the establishment of the Cavalry Bureau on 28 July 1863. That organization was an attempt by the War Department to approach the needs of the mounted force more systematically. The new bureau was to supervise the organizing and equipping of cavalry regiments, and virtually all other requirements unique to the mounted service.

But the Cavalry Bureau also required information on the current state of the Army's cavalry forces. The order establishing the bureau directed that copies of all inspection reports covering cavalry troops be sent to the Cavalry Bureau. Thereafter, all cavalry units were to receive detailed inspection at the end of every month, and the report was to describe each unit's service during the month. Special attention was to be paid to the horses, classifying them into four groups: totally unfit for any use; unfit for cavalry, but useful for draft or herding (these to be turned over to the Quartermaster Department); unfit or nearly unfit, but could be rehabilitated (these to be sent to remount depots); and serviceable animals. Reports of cavalry inspections were to be sent to the Cavalry Bureau

---

29. Sacket and Medical Inspector Richard H. Collidge, to Surgeon General, 10 May 63, in Letters Sent 1863–1889, RG 159.

30. Sacket to AG, 7 Jun 63, in Letters Sent 1863–1889, RG 159; Cullum, *Biographical Register*, 2: 236. The Invalid Corps harked back to a predecessor during the Revolution. It was an attempt to preserve manpower by forming units of wounded soldiers who could undertake undemanding duties and free able men for the front.

31. GO No. 143, AGO, 22 May 63; GO No. 113, AGO, 25 Jun 63; and GO No. 274, AGO, 7 Aug 63, in GORI&IG.

through field army or department commanders.[32] The establishment of the Cavalry Bureau probably owed something to British practices, which had an Inspector General of Cavalry superintending the special needs of mounted units. But the American bureau chief mostly supervised a supply agency, and had very little in the way of an inspection service of his own. The business of providing him with current information rested with the inspectors general and assistant inspectors general, who found themselves going over part of the same ground twice when they examined cavalry—providing some information for their commanders, and some for the Cavalry Bureau.

Bringing the Inspectors Into Line

By the summer of 1863, the War Department was evidently determined to have the Army's inspectorate more systematically arranged and directed. The staffs of all corps included inspectors, and beneath them acting inspectors reviewing most divisions and brigades. The assistant inspectors general assigned to corps and field armies (a field army had only one inspector general on duty) were permanent War Department representatives on corps and army staffs. The order of December 1862 had in fact charged War Department staff bureaus with the selection of corps staffs. Assistant inspectors general and inspectors general alike were required, after Sacket's move to Washington, to submit routinely two kinds of reports: One was a summary of the condition of the forces within their purview; the other was a monthly account of what each of them was doing, and where. The inspectorate had become so scattered by special assignments and movements among stations that the War Department had lost track of its officers. Because of this dispersal, substantive reports of the military forces only occasionally reached the Washington office before mid-1863; they usually remained with field commanders. But one of the reasons Sacket was assigned to the War Department was to consolidate the results of inspections and prepare regular reports on the condition of the entire army. By the spring of 1863, he had distributed report forms to all inspectors, and responses began to arrive with middling regularity. But Sacket was soon distracted by the Invalid Board and other special assignments, and the consolidation task floundered. The Inspector General confessed to the Adjutant General in October that his other duties made it very difficult to monitor the incoming reports. He offered either to consolidate or to extract them for use by the rest of the staff.[33]

There were, however, difficulties, caused especially by assistant inspectors general who could not follow instructions. The return submitted in October by Lt. Col. James H. Strong of the Department of Virginia and North Carolina was worse than most. "The Grand Totals of the several columns should always agree according to the directions given on the margins of the report," Sacket

---

32. GO No. 237, AGO, 28 Jul 63, in GORI&IG.
33. Sacket to Assistant Adjutant General Col. J.C. Kelton, 21 Oct 63, in Letters Sent 1863–1889, RG 159.

told Strong, continuing, "the number and caliber of guns should always be given, and the names of all Officers absent especially those absent without leave, with the authority date &c. written in full."[34] Sacket had another means of monitoring the inspectors in the field. Besides requiring inspectors to report the results of their inspections, the regulations also required that they account for their own activities by means of monthly reports to the War Department. Very few of them did that, until the Adjutant General demanded that Sacket enforce the requirement. He then sent identical letters to nearly all his inspectors, exhorting them to get their reports in promptly as required and to assure that they were accurate.[35]

COL. EDMUND SCHRIVER. *Inspector General, 13 March 1863–4 January 1881.*

All the War Department wanted to know from its inspectors each month was their location, their activities during the month, and any changes of place or assignment; in other words, what they were doing and where. The requirement, however, was not heeded by many of the inspectors in the field, largely because they were too inexperienced to know to keep current with new regulations. Consequently, Sacket had to issue several explanatory letters specifying what he expected to receive from them.[36] The assistant inspectors general were not alone in their ignorance. Colonel Edmund Schriver, inspector general of the Army of the Potomac, the only inspector general working with a field army (while Marcy toured western posts in prewar fashion, and Sacket was desk bound in Washington) also did not appreciate what Sacket was trying to do, and asked for an explanation.

At Mansfield's death at Antietam in September 1862, his permanent position of inspector general became vacant. And when Sacket left the Army of the Potomac in January 1863, it became necessary to appoint an inspector general to replace him. Schriver occupied Mansfield's slot as of 13 March 1863, and remained inspector general of the Army of the Potomac to the end of the war. He earned two brevets (to major general) for "faithful and meritorious service" during the conflict.[37] He was a West Point graduate, class of 1833, who had

34. Sacket to Strong, 14 Nov 63, in Letters Sent 1863–1889, RG 159.

35. Sacket to Marcy, 6 Nov 63, in Letters Sent 1863–1889, RG 159.

36. Sacket to Strong, 18 Nov 63, in Letters Sent 1863–1889, RG 159. The file contains a very large number of identical letters to other assistant inspectors general.

37. Heitman, *Historical Register*, 1: 866.

enjoyed a successful career in the artillery before resigning in 1846 to become a railroad executive. He returned to the army in May 1861, serving as an infantry officer and corps chief of staff until he was appointed an inspector general in 1863. Schriver was a strong-willed man, who did not take lightly instructions from an unknown authority in the War Department. But Sacket let him know clearly that he must send his monthly reports of personal activities, just as other inspectors were required to do, saying he was no different from any other inspector and must comply with the regulations.[38]

Although not purposely, the enforcement of the monthly reporting requirement was another small step toward putting together an Inspector General's Department as a formal organization. Sacket's duty station represented a presence for the inspectorate at the top of the Army's pyramid. The reporting requirements connected all inspecting officers—formerly just a group of staff officers serving in discrete field units—to War Department headquarters. That was a long way from assembling them into a formal, let alone hierarchical, structure, but at least a new linking was developing. Inspectors general and assistant inspectors general mostly still obeyed their commanders, but they now had a slight attachment unique to them as inspectors. This distinctiveness of the Inspector General's Department was exceedingly tenuous, within the department and within itself. As late as January 1864, Sacket had to ask the Adjutant General to inform him of any orders assigning assistant inspectors general to different commands—supposedly his own responsibility to determine. His anomalous status is shown by his having to make a special request for a list of the geographical departments and districts to keep current with changing structures.[39]

Sacket's control over the inspectors was not much greater. In January 1864, he again demanded monthly returns from dozens of assistant inspectors general, and in fact many of them continued negligent to the end of the war. Nevertheless, early in February Sacket was able to tell the Adjutant General's Office, "I have the honor to enclose Reports of the Inspector General Dept USA for the months of 1863. Major Gen Buford is accounted for from memory his Report having never been received. The Reports of the Volunteer Inspectors have not all been received. If meeting with your approbation I can send them as they now stand trusting hereafter to forward them regularly."[40]

Although officers like Buford and Baird were serving as line commanders, they remained on the books as assistant inspectors general and were required to report their activities anyway. The delinquency of such officers was understandable, but a number of persons actually employed as inspectors were equally

---

38. Sacket to Schriver, 20 Nov 63, in Letters Sent 1863–1889, RG 159.
39. Sacket to AG, 5 Jan 64 (misdated 1863), and Sacket to Asst. AG Maj. Samuel Breck, 12 Jan 64, in Letters Sent 1863–1889, RG 159.
40. Sacket to Asst. IG, U.S. Volunteers (USV), 5th, 8th, 22d, and 23d Army Corps, 15 Jan 64; to Lt. Col. G.A. Kensel, AIG, 15 Jan 64; to Capt. Walter Cutting, 20 Jan 64; to Lt. Col. G.A. Kensel, 22 Jan 64; and many others of like import throughout the year; and Sacket to Asst. AG Maj. Samuel Breck, 7 Feb 64, all in Letters Sent 1863–1889, RG 159.

GOING INTO BATTERY BEFORE PETERSBURG, 1865. *Ordnance production was a traditional special item of inspection throughout the 19th century.*

negligent. Those who took their assignments seriously were certainly busy. "My position made it my duty to understand the condition of discipline, administration, and command in the forces gathered about Chattanooga," recalled James H. Wilson, inspector general for the gigantic army under Ulysses S. Grant in Tennessee. He was sufficiently conscientious that the monthly report of activities was but a minor extra burden for him. Wilson never received a demanding letter from Sacket.[41]

The general uncommunicativeness of the assistant inspectors general left Sacket in the dark when it came to knowing just who was inspecting the army. On 12 April 1864, the "Inspector General's Bureau" asked all assistant inspectors general in all departments and field armies for a list of all inspectors. "This list should contain the names of all Officers performing Inspection duty," the recipients were told, "whether members of the Inspector General's Department, or acting temporarily in that capacity, together with the . . . command to which they are attached."[42]

That was probably an impossible order, because inspections in the combat and occupation zones took many forms, under many names. Orders issued in

---

41. Wilson quoted in Baird, *Profile of a Hero,* 140. Wilson went on to become a brigadier general of volunteers in 1863, and major general two years later, earning several brevets as a gallant commander. He left the Army in 1870, but returned in 1898, became a very efficient general in Cuba, and retired a brigadier general of the Regular Army in 1901. Heitman, *Historical Register,* 1: 1046.

42. IG to AG, 12 Apr 64, in Letters Sent 1863–1889, RG 159.

the District of Tennessee in 1864 mentioned assistant inspectors of blockhouses, under the district's inspector of fortifications, along with inspectors and assistant inspectors for railroad defenses, Department of the Cumberland. Their relation to the regular inspectorate was doubtful.[43] Independent groups of War Department inspectors also began to develop. For example, there was a growing inspectorate in the Quartermaster Department, entirely unrelated to the inspectorate over which Sacket tried to preside. Quartermaster General Montgomery C. Meigs had six inspectors by 1864, all colonels, reporting directly to himself. They visited armies, depots, and military posts inspecting quartermaster officers and their duties, to detect abuses. Their reports were an important part of the information Meigs used to make decisions. When legislation reorganized the Quartermaster Department into nine divisions on 4 July 1864, the eighth division was "Inspection," its purpose to monitor honesty and quality assurance in the department's procurement and supply activities.[44]

The Washington Office

With a growing body of paper work to process, along with other responsibilities, Sacket found himself overwhelmed and in need of more clerical assistance. He asked the assistant adjutant general in early February 1864 for a fourth class clerk for his office, in case Congress let the War Department hire more clerks. Later in the month, he wrote directly to Senator William Sprague, saying that he had asked for a clerk for his office, and asking the senator to use his influence to get Private Harris H. Stewart the job. Stewart, the disabled soldier assigned at Sacket's request, had been working since April 1863, so productively that Sacket wanted to retain him. "He came to me a total Stranger highly recommended by good and gallant Soldiers," Sacket said, "and has proved himself worthy in every respect of their recommendations."[45] Sacket's duties involved the particular as well as the general. In January 1864 he had to inform the commander of Fort Randall, Dakota Territory, that the regulations requiring property inspections and condemnation applied to volunteer as well as regular officers. He advised the post commander to appoint an officer to inspect some unserviceable property, and to forward the report to the department commander for a final decision.[46]

In March, Sacket initiated a recommendation to the Secretary of War that an assistant commissary general of subsistence, Amos B. Eaton of New York, be assigned to conduct a special investigation of staff departments in the Department of the South. When the Secretary concurred, Sacket produced exceed-

---

43. See copies of orders appointing Arthur L. Conger, 115th Ohio, to both types of assistant inspector positions, 11 Jun, 24 Jul, and 7 Oct 64, in Arthur L. Conger Papers, United States Army Military History Institute (hereafter MHI), Carlisle Barracks, Pennsylvania.
44. Weigley, *Quartermaster General*, 223, 234;GO No. 231, AGO, 18 Jul 64 (reorganizing the Quartermaster Department), in GORI&IG.
45. Sacket to Asst AG, 11 Feb 64, and Sacket to Hon. William Sprague, 20 Feb 64, in Letters Sent 1863–1889, RG 159.
46. Sacket to Maj. Thomas N. Shephard, 16 Jan 64, in Inspection Reports 1863–1889, RG 159.

COL. JAMES A. HARDIE. *Inspector General, 24 March 1864–14 December 1876.*

ingly detailed instructions and a flurry of authorizing letters. Regular inspection reports he had received raised considerable concern about the conduct of financial disbursements and transportation in the South.[47] The growing number of special investigations for the Secretary of War finally liberated Sacket from the Washington office. In April an onslaught of orders dispatched several officers to examine various reported shortcomings in disbursements and supply operations. Lt. Col. J.F. Marsh, of the Veterans Reserve Corps was dispatched to all posts where prisoners of war were held. Capt. Elisha H. Ludington was to examine the accounts of Quartermaster and Subsistence Department officers in Washington, D.C. By 20 April that had earned Ludington a berth in the inspectorate as major and assistant inspector general. Sacket, meanwhile, went off to inspect the Commissary Department's operations in the departments of the Tennessee, the Cumberland, and the Arkansas.[48]

Of all the assignments, Marsh's activities proved to be the most interesting. His reports on prison camps began to arrive in late April, each one endorsed in the Inspector General's Office for the information of the Commissary General of Prisoners, the endorsements noting what orders had been given to correct shortcomings. And they were numerous, affecting almost every aspect of prison administration. Security, discipline, and conditions often were woeful. Marsh's inspection led the Inspector General's Office to recommend dismissal of a departmental provost marshal general, based in Saint Louis, for "neglect of duty" resulting in several poorly managed prisons.[49] Unlike Marsh, Sacket was apparently so happy to be free of Washington that he was not inclined to find fault as he made his rounds. He gave high praise to the military prison at Memphis, Tennessee, in June 1864, applauding the commander and reporting

---

47. Sacket to Secy of War, 31 Mar 64, to Eaton, 1 Apr 64, to CG, Dept of the South, and to others, 2 Apr 64, and to Eaton, 2 Apr 64, in Letters Sent 1863–1889, RG 159.

48. There is a variety of letters during April 1864 on these subjects in Letters Sent 1863–1889, RG 159. Ludington had joined the Army as an infantry captain in August 1861. He had been brevetted for "gallant and meritorious service" and twice more for "faithful and meritorious service." He remained an assistant inspector general and a major until he retired on 27 March 1879. Heitman, *Historical Register*, 1: 646. Heitman has no record of J. F. Marsh or anyone of similar name.

49. See the several endorsements, and IG to Secy of War, 19 Apr 64, in Letters Sent 1863–1889, RG 159.

that conditions were excellent there. But Marsh and a special commission that followed him had criticized the place thoroughly. Sacket was formally asked to explain the vast discrepancies between his report and all others.[50]

The man who asked Sacket to explain himself was James A. Hardie, an inspector whose presence had made it possible for Sacket to leave the office on the first of April. Hardie was the last inspector general (colonel) appointed during the Civil War. His commission dated from 24 March 1864, the day after Van Rensselaer died.

A New Yorker, Hardie had graduated from West Point in 1843. He was an artillerist, although he spent the Mexican War as a major of volunteers in the 1st New York Infantry, and became a captain in 1857. On 28 September 1861, he was elevated to the provisional status of lieutenant colonel and additional aide-de-camp. He held the grade until his appointment as Inspector General, but not without interruptions. Hardie was appointed a brigadier general of volunteers on 29 November 1862, but the assignment was revoked on 22 January 1863. On 19 February 1863 he became an assistant adjutant general with the rank of major. When Van Rensselaer died, therefore, and with the Secretary of War inclined to let Sacket go out of town, Hardie was available in the War Department. He became a new inspector general, bringing the complement to the maximum authorized four. More than available, he was competent, earning two brevets for "distinguished and faithful service" during the war and "faithful, meritorious and distinguished service in the Inspector General's Department," the Washington chair of which he held down until 1866. Hardie remained an inspector general until his death in 1876.[51]

Hardie, like Sacket before him, found himself fully occupied as the duties of inspectors multiplied. On 24 March 1864, the War Department decried once again the "existing evils in the waste and destruction of Cavalry horses." It ordered a board of three officers, to be appointed by the Secretary, to inspect all mounted troops in all armies. The board was to report to the Adjutant General—apparently the department did not think to put the Inspector General's Office at the center of a special inspection—all units that neglected or wasted horses and therefore should be dismounted or broken up. A month later, the department ordered all government horses to be turned in to the Quartermaster Department. Thereafter, no one was permitted to use a government horse or vehicle without written authorization from the Adjutant General's Office. The Offices of the Quartermaster General and Inspector General were both required to enforce the order through their department mechanisms.[52] Hardie sent copies of the second order to twenty-one officers of the inspectorate on 27 April, telling them that the Secretary of War directed a special effort at the next monthly inspection to find whether any officer was using a horse or vehicle for an unauthorized purpose. Such cases were to be reported to the Inspector General's Office

---

50. IG to Sacket, 25 Jun 64, in Letters Sent 1863–1889, RG 159.
51. Heitman, *Historical Register*, 1: 499–500.
52. GO No. 119, AGO, 24 Mar 64, and GO No. 177, AGO, 23 Apr 64, in GORI&IG.

without delay. "Any infractions of the order coming within the observation of inspecting officers at any time," he said, "will be promptly reported."[53]

An Undefined Inspectorate

The paper blizzard was unsettling to Hardie, who had had the Washington office duty descend upon him unexpectedly. This newest inspector general and Edmund Schriver corresponded concerning the uncertainties about the role of an Inspector General—but agreed that the Inspector General's Department should be an important part of the Army. Nevertheless, as Hardie pointed out, "In our military legislation, no provision has been made for such a department, there being only so many independent Inspectors." Hardie believed that the inspectorate's lack of achievement was due to deficiencies of organization. Failure to develop some system of inspection, he said, was a major lapse on the part of the inspectors. Hardie believed Schriver at the Army of the Potomac had gone further than anyone else in trying to systematize his inspectorate. He had given his inspectors rules and independence, and had overcome the natural reluctance of line officers to be inspected. Hardie doubted that a really independent inspectorate was possible at corps and division levels, and that inspectors at those levels would remain alter egos of the commanders they served. He thought a thoroughly independent Inspector General's Department might be a good idea, but one not likely to become reality; commanders would always want to control their inspectors, not have them agents of some higher or independent authority. In the meantime, Hardie asserted that the flurry of orders governing inspections merely multiplied paper work and diverted the inspectors' attention from the main issues of military efficiency.[54]

But the War Department was apparently more interested in economy than in military efficiency, and Hardie had to comply with its priorities as he struggled manfully to define his place in the department's establishment. In April, when he learned that a special War Department commission was investigating the ethics of New York City disbursing officers, he asked to see "notes or memorandum however rough or laconic, provided they be complete, of such frauds or improper transaction as may have come to [the commission's] notice affecting the fidelity, and honesty of any disbursing Officer of the Government within the sphere of [the commission's] observation." Such matters were, after all, the special interest of the inspectors general.[55] Even more than Sacket, Hardie found himself distracted from his duties in the inspectorate to answer to the authority of the Secretary of War. It appears that he spent much of the summer of 1864 acting as a special agent of the Secretary, conveying Stanton's messages and instructions to field army commanders. By using Hardie that way, Stanton was able to bypass the normal channel of communications—and the

---

53. IG to Totten et al., 27 Apr 64, in Letters Sent 1863–1889, RG 159.
54. Hardie to Schriver, 9 Apr 64, in Letters Sent 1863–1889, RG 159.
55. IG to Col. H.S. Olcott, 19 Apr 64, in Letters Sent 1863–1889, RG 159.

nominal chain of command. Much of his traffic was aimed at General William T. Sherman, then involved in a campaign of devastation against Atlanta, Georgia.[56]

However the Secretary might burden him with trifles, Hardie did his best to create some order in the Army's scattered inspectorate. He poured over every report that came into his office, and used his findings to try to impose some standards on work in the field. In July, for instance, various inspection reports of regiments at New Orleans described the same units as trained and untrained, ignorant of the regulations and well drilled in them, neat and sloppy, and so on. Hardie asked the assistant inspector general for the Department of the Gulf to "ascertain the exact condition of the Regts. referred to, and report the facts to this office, and be pleased to call upon the officers concerned, for an explanation of the discrepancy in their reports."[57] In another case, he rebuked an assistant inspector general in August for falling down on the job by not submitting reports explicit enough to allow positive action on the irregularities noted.[58] Hardie also had to become an arbiter of the inspectorate's frequently vague procedures. For instance, Hardie explained to a departmental assistant inspector general that he must inspect quartermaster and commissary depots if they were part of his department. If they had been established by orders from the War Department, and reported directly to the Quartermaster General or Commissary General of Subsistence, instead of to departmental quartermasters or commissaries, then the departmental inspector could not inspect the depots unless specially assigned by the War Department.[59]

The Inspectorate at War's End

So the affairs of the Washington office went until the end of the war. Preparing for peace, in early April 1865 the War Department recast the Army from a collection of field forces into the customary peacetime departments and districts—geographical compartments being the traditional means of administration. The staff of a department or district commander was limited to an assistant adjutant general, an assistant inspector general, a chief quartermaster, a chief commissary of subsistence, a medical director, a judge advocate, and two aides-de-camp. Thereafter, armies and departments were to hold inspection the last day of each month, the reports to be forwarded to the Adjutant General's Office in Washington.[60]

Hardie by that time enjoyed the assistance of Elisha H. Ludington, who had never strayed far from the Washington office anyway. Hardie was formally in charge of the office, Ludington signing letters by "direction" or "order" of

---

56. See *OR*, 1st ser., vol. 20, pt. 5: 247, 278-289, 300, for examples of these communications, which had nothing at all to do with the normal concerns of an inspector general.
57. IG to Lt. Col. W.S. Abert, 14 Jul 64, in Letters Sent 1863–1889, RG 159.
58. IG to Asst IG Lt. Col. A. Von Schroder, 8 Aug 64, in Letters Sent 1863–1889, RG 159.
59. IG to Maj. T.J. McKenny, 10 Aug 64, in Letters Sent 1863–1889, RG 159.
60. GO No. 54, AGO, 6 Apr 65, in GORI&IG.

Hardie. In that manner, Ludington picked up a large share of the work throughout 1865, beginning with a repetition of the request that all divisional and
departmental assistant inspectors general forward a complete list of inspectors
within their purviews. He did that simply by sending them a copy of Hardie's
earlier request of 12 April 1864.[61] This office was further augmented when
Hardie and Ludington were joined late in 1865 by acting assistant inspector
general Kilburn Knox, an infantry captain brevetted for "gallant and efficient
service in the attack on Atlanta." The office had by that time settled into a
routine and was almost indistinguishable from Washington's ink-splashing
norm.[62]

   In November, the office once again asked the assistant inspector general for
the Department of Texas to provide a complete list of inspectors, while a flurry
of letters asked division and department assistant inspectors general for copies
of all department and division orders, to complete the Inspector General's files.
Meanwhile, when inspectors discovered twelve cases of fraud and collusion
involving quartermaster officers and supply contractors in Philadelphia, Hardie
asked for authority to send Ludington to pursue the investigation and to interview the presumed culprits. The Secretary of War approved.[63] Lastly, permanent officers of the inspectorate not still in service to certain generals were
dispatched to new stations. There were two of them in 1865, and typically their
assignments reflected the War Department's divided feelings on whether Inspectors General were more valuable as inspectors or as something else. Absalom
Baird was appointed Assistant Commissioner of Refugees, Freedmen, and
Abandoned Lands for the state of Louisiana on 1 November. On 2 December,
Roger Jones became Inspector General of the Military Division of the
Mississippi.[64] There was nothing permanent about their arrangement, because
there was nothing permanent about the Army. Peace was at hand once again,
and the military force was bound to shrink to the minimum possible size. As
had happened before, it appeared likely that the lessons of the war and of
mobilization would be forgotten, as Congress and the public sought to embrace
the pleasures of peacetime. The Army was soon involved in an occupation of
the defeated South and in a demonstration on the Mexican border, but mostly
(as it had been after the last two wars) the Army was banished to the wilderness,
where it confronted increasingly violent Indian resistance.

   The legacy of the Civil War was mixed for the inspectors general. On the
positive side, their number had increased and their positions were filled by

---

   61. Ludington to Sir, 20 Jul 65, in Letters Sent 1863–1889, RG 159.
   62. IG to Asst. QM Capt. J. M. Moore, 16 Oct 65; Knox to Asst. QM Capt. J. H. Crowell, 19 Oct
and 21 Oct 65; IG to John Potts, chief clerk of the War Department, 7 Nov 65; to Capt. James M.
Moore, 7 Nov 65; to Capt. J. H. Crowell, 10 Nov 65; and to John Potts, 10 Nov 65; and Knox to
Capt. James M. Moore, 16 Nov 65; all in Letters Sent 1863–1889, RG 159.
   63. Knox to Actg. Asst. IG Dept of Texas, 9 Nov 65; letters to divisional and departmental
assistant inspectors general, Nov and Dec 65; and Hardie to Secy of War, 12 Dec 65, and
endorsements; all in Letters Sent 1863–1889, RG 159.
   64. Baird, undated statement (early 1866), and Jones to George H. Cullum, 10 May 66, in
Cullum Files, USMA Archives.

good officers with long careers ahead of them. Equally promising, if not so obvious, they now had a full-time presence in the War Department. They were increasingly regarded as an Inspector General's Department, although Hardie for one realized that there was no such thing. Their presence in Washington had given them direct communication with the Secretary of War, who had found inspectors general to be very useful in a variety of roles. They had been his chief insight into the military establishment, and—like Hardie in 1864—convenient personal agents when he wanted his own interests served. Service to the Secretary naturally promised permanence for the inspectorate. That came at a certain price, however. Stanton's use of the inspectors increased the gravitation of the inspectorate toward the Secretary and away

OHIO INFANTRY AT THE BLOODY ANGLE, 12 MAY 1864. *The quality of leaders routinely was evaluated by inspectors throughout the 19th century.*

from the Commanding General. When Commanding General Grant moved to Washington to take his place after the war, it remained to be seen whether the power of the inspectors general would be aligned with him, or with the Secretary of War.

On the more negative side, the record of the inspectorate during the war had not been altogether good. There were inspectors for all major command organizations, but they had been a varied lot, ranging from the diligent and effective to the barely competent. They all inspected, but not all of them did it well. Hardie perceived correctly in 1864 that part of the blame could be laid to an absence of organization, with a concomitant lack of central guidance and definite procedures. Even without a formal organization, the inspectorate could have performed better and more uniformly if it had been sufficiently regulated. The assignment of an inspector general to the War Department partly alleviated the shortcomings in the field, but could not eliminate them. This absence of any formal organization was the reason that, when the war started, the inspectorate dissolved, rather as it had in 1846. This time, however, it managed to recover part of its strength, especially after the Secretary demanded reports to his office, and put Sacket in place to reinforce his demands. But that came only after the Secretary had nearly disrupted inspection by letting inspectors become commanders without filling in behind them, and by sending one or another inspector off on secretarial errands. The whole operation bore an appearance of impermanence or expediency. The real inspectorate was established piecemeal, by field commanders. Even with one of the permanent officers in Washington, there was little real strength to tie it all together. This absence of structure meant that the experience of the war was mostly improvisation for the inspectors general. There was little about it that promised to be useful in the return to peacetime policing of the frontier. As the Army shrank and again took up its peacetime routine, necessity compelled the development of an inspectorate appropriate to its circumstances. As things worked out, it did so by organizational means. The Inspector General's Department finally became an organization as well as a name.

CHAPTER 14

Securing a Permanent Place

(1865–1866)

After the Civil War, the U.S. Army experienced the most precipitous strength reduction it had ever known. Most of the force was temporary, consisting of volunteers and draftees brought into service for the duration of the war. These men left with dramatic speed. Over seven hundred thousand were mustered out by August 1865 while another three hundred thousand were gone by November 1866. A small remainder augmented the Regular Army until December 1867 when it, too, was gone. The Regular Army had been a small part of these vast forces with 40,000 men authorized and an actual strength of around 34,000 men at war's end in April 1865. In brief defiance of tradition, it actually grew for a period after the war. The West was aflame with Indian troubles; Mexico was in the hands of the French; and Congress directed the military occupation of the defeated southern states. As a result, in July 1866 the authorized size of the Regular Army was raised to 54,641, a figure nearly matched by its actual strength within a year.[1]

As might be expected, the swiftly changing Army was in turmoil. The government believed that the great force available in April 1865 was a useful means of enforcing the Monroe Doctrine to persuade the French to withdraw from Mexico. Maj. Gen. Philip Sheridan was dispatched to Louisiana and Texas to make a demonstration of strength on the border. Other large forces were shipped to the West to quell a number of Indian uprisings. However, the volunteers who made up the largest share of the Army expected to go home. They had enlisted to subdue Rebels, not Frenchmen or Indians, and they voiced their complaints in the centers of political power. The troop movements of 1865 thus fell into confusion, in no small part because they occurred simultaneously with the mustering out of volunteer regiments. Any campaigns planned for that year were undone by chaos and shortages of manpower.[2]

A few major construction projects were begun during the next few years, but the army too often proved to be its own worse enemy. Posts started in Texas

---

1. *ARSecWar 1865*, H. Ex. Doc. 1, 39th Cong., 1st sess., pt. 1: 1, 19, 21; *ARSecWar 1866*, H. Ex. Doc. 1, 39th Cong., 2d sess., 3–6; *ARSecWar 1867*, H. Ex. Doc. 1, 40th Cong, 2d sess., 416; Weigley, *History of the United States Army*, 262; Heitman, *Historical Register*, 1: 598–605, 626.
2. Richard N. Ellis, "Volunteer Soldiers in the West, 1865," *Military Affairs*, 34 (April 1970): 53–56.

in 1867, for instance, were rather nicely designed, in comparison with earlier examples. But they were built under inept supervision because the Quartermaster Department was not allowed to send officers to direct the work; some of them were sited on inhospitable ground, and some buildings began to come apart even before they were finished. Worse, the money ran out before the projects were completed, and not all the buildings planned were started. Only two of six projected barracks at Fort Davis, Texas, were reasonably finished by the spring of 1868, and the unprotected adobe walls of a third were left to weather away for several years. And other similar mishaps occurred elsewhere, worsened by inconsistent and generally inadequate appropriations for construction and repairs. The result was that there were too few barracks for too many men. As authorized by regulations, the minimum-space requirements for enlisted men were totally inadequate.[3]

Sherman, commanding the Division of the West, made the Army's housing his special cause. In 1866, he sent Inspector General Sacket on a special tour of posts on the upper Missouri, to examine the barbarous living conditions of the soldiers, and to provide ammunition for his own bombardment of the Quartermaster Department. Sherman himself, eyeing the sod barracks at Fort Sedgwick, Colorado, said, "Surely, had the southern planters put their negroes in such hovels, a sample would, ere this, have been carried to Boston and exhibited as illustrative of the cruelty and inhumanity of the man-masters." The Quartermaster Department's own James F. Rusling agreed. "Dirt, dampness, disease, vermin," he told Meigs, "all infest such structures, and the United States Government, I take it, means better than that by the faithful troops that serve it." The poor sanitary condition of the Army's housing was reflected in serious cholera epidemics in 1866 and 1867. The surgeons attributed those calamities to overcrowding, poor diet, dirty water, and inadequate waste disposal.[4] In some cases, better accommodations might have been provided in rented buildings. But on 10 March 1866, the War Department made that impossible when it ordered all rented quarters to be vacated and the troops collected in regular posts. Housing allowances permitted by regulations were to be strictly observed, "Inspectors General," said the department, "will give their special attention of all commanding officers to the absolute necessity for economy, and will embrace it in their official reports to their respective headquarters."[5] As the years passed, housing, its quality as well as its quantity, became a subject of increasing concern to inspectors.

In 1866, the Regular Army, abandoned by the volunteers, was growing and disorganized, scattered across the wilderness in small bands. The troops hud-

---

3. Risch, *Quartermaster Support*, 488.
4. Robert G. Athearn, *William Tecumseh Sherman and the Settlement of the West* (Norman: University of Oklahoma Press, 1956), 51–52; Sherman and Rusling quoted in Risch, *Quartermaster Support*, 484; Ramon S. Powers and Gene Younger, "Cholera and the Army in the West: Treatment and Control in 1866 and 1867," *Military Affairs*, 39 (April 1975): 49–54. Sacket's report was published in H. Ex. Doc. 23, 39th Cong., 2d sess. (1866).
5. GO No. 14, AGO, 10 Mar 66, in GORI&IG.

dled in cramped, unsanitary, bug-infested shacks, and spent much of their time and energy in trying to hold their quarters together. They were poorly trained, indifferently fed, and not a happy group of men. They were also a varied lot, in keeping with tradition mostly societal misfits. George A. Forsyth said of a detachment he commanded that it included "a bookkeeper, a farm boy, a dentist, and a blacksmith, a young man of position trying to gain a commission and a salesman ruined by drink, an ivory carver and a Bowery tough."[6] Furthermore the well-being of the soldiers received only indifferent attention from Congress, which refused to appropriate enough money to house them decently. Extraduty pay was reauthorized in 1866 for work beyond ten days for the Quartermaster or another department—such work took most of the soldier's time at most posts. Mechanics (skilled craftsmen) received 35 cents a day, while laborers earned 20 cents. The scale was not raised until 1884, but that made little difference, because the soldiers were routinely deprived of the chance for the extra pay by successive nine-day assignments.[7] Also in 1866, Congress made a gesture at improving the intellect of the soldiers, when it authorized construction of schools and libraries at military posts. If no space was available, the Quartermaster Department could erect a building with the approval of the Secretary of War. The department interpreted the law as not applying to temporary posts—the Army had few of any other kind, and none in the West. With that, aggravated by low appropriations, little attention was given to instruction in "the common English branches of education" until 1877. Meanwhile, Congress authorized the detail of army officers to provide military instruction at land-grant colleges and military schools. But the Army showed little interest in that for some time. Finally, by 1866 the national cemeteries had become such a major class of property that the Quartermaster General saw fit to recommend some more permanent attention to their administration than had been devoted theretofore.[8]

New Orders for the Inspectors

Post schools, military colleges, and cemeteries eventually would become important subjects for inspectors general. But the inspectorate was more concerned in 1866 with establishing itself and defining its role in the Army. New orders on 22 January set forth detailed regulations and instructions for inspections of troops and military commands, infantry, artillery, cavalry, posts and garrisons, transports, administrative and disbursing departments, ordnance and stores, the Medical Department, and property presented for condemnation as well as for the stated monthly inspections and reports. The very detailed order

6. George A. Forsyth, *The Story of the Soldier* (New York: Brampton Society, 1908), 91.

7. Foner, *Soldier Between Wars*, 16–17. Extraduty pay had first been authorized in the 1820s (see above).

8. Risch, *Quartermaster Support*, 489; Robert D. Miewald, "The Army Post Schools: A Report from the Bureaucratic Wars," *Military Affairs*, 39 (February 1975): 8–11; Lyons and Masland, "Origins of ROTC," 3–4; Steere, "Genesis of Graves Registration," 160.

Charge of the 5th Regulars at Gaines Mills, Va., 27 June 1862. *The care of horses during the Civil War became a special item of interest requiring a distinct inspection program.*

stressed the close relationships of the inspectors to the Secretary or their commanders and specified that their sphere should be all-encompassing, limited only by specific orders. This was the strongest statement of authority for the inspectorate since the days of Macomb, although he might not have approved of the Secretary's evident ascendance over the Commanding General. Nevertheless, inspectors were clearly agents of the highest authority in the Army—except when they were "assigned to specific commands as Inspectors." That was an important exception, because in the coming years most of the inspectorate would be so assigned.

The order outlined in general terms what inspectors were to look for, providing the most convenient handbook to date for officers newly detailed to inspection duties. Except for the stated monthly inspections, inspection reports were to be held confidential, for the eyes of the commander only on whose staff an inspector served, with the stipulations that reports "may be withdrawn if desired." Inspecting officers had to know the regulations and pertinent laws: "Great care must be taken by Inspecting Officers," said the order, "that no injustice be done to organizations or individuals by reports not fully sustained by personal and thorough examination." It also said that "Inspectors will give orders only when specifically authorized to do so, and will then give them in the name of the officer authorizing it." When inspecting troops and commands, the inspector was specifically to present himself to the local commander, give him a copy of his order authorizing the inspection, and interview him. His examination was to cover the appearance and bearing of troops, officers, arms and equipment, supplies, health, diet—all the subjects that had occupied inspectors for generations, with special matters unique to infantry, artillery, and cavalry. At a post or garrison, inspectors were not only to determine how well the place was run and how well the troops were managed and military exercises conducted, but also to examine the handling of funds, the condition of buildings and hospitals, and the burden of labor imposed on the troops. Enlisted men were to be given notice that they could bring complaints to the inspector without officers present. The order also outlined the inspection of transports (physical condition and administrative matters like contracts), the administrative and disbursing departments (including habits of the officers as well as their accounts), ordnance and stores, the general operations of the Medical Department ("strictly medical inspections [were to] be made by the medical officers under the direction of the Surgeon General"), and property offered for condemnation (according to the orders issued in 1863). The order did not mention the Corps of Engineers, which by implication was not within an inspector general's purview. In addition, monthly inspections were required, on the last day of the month, for all commands less than brigade-size—something that had to be accomplished by others, since there were not enough inspectors general to go around.[9]

The order of January 1866 was a clearer statement of procedure than inspectors had enjoyed before. But it was not a charter for the "Inspection Department," which had yet to become a reality. Authorizations for inspections remained poorly defined somewhere between the Commanding General and the Secretary of War, although the implication of most of the order was that it would serve military more than civilian purposes. The order also included long-overdue encouragements to professionalism (inspectors must know the regulations, for instance) and it safeguarded the authority of inspectors to do their jobs once they had been ordered to embark upon them. But there was no clearly defined, separate inspectorate overseeing the Army. Rather, inspection occurred in discrete units surrounding commanders who could order them. Department and division commanders, by implication, established their own inspectorates, and nothing compelled them to relay their findings to higher authority. Nor did anything in the order require inspectors in lesser commands to communicate to the Inspector General's Office in Washington although the army regulations still carried this requirement. Inspectors general and assistant inspectors general were required to make monthly reports of their activities if they were detached from their duties in the inspectorate. Assistant inspectors general Nelson Davis and James Totten were taken to task by the Washington office in July 1866, because they had neglected that requirement.[10]

---

9. GO No. 5, AGO, 22 Jan 66, in GORI&IG.
10. Ludington to Davis, 12 Jul 66, and to Totten, 12 Jul 66, in Letters Sent 1863–1889, RG 159.

The inspectorate was scattered about the country. Sacket was at New York City in the early part of 1866, while Baird moved from the Freedman's Bureau to command of the Department of Louisiana on 23 May. He was on the scene when riots erupted in New Orleans on 30 June, and had to acknowledge responsibility for the events that led to the uproar. That cost him his post when his department was dissolved on 17 August. Baird became inspector general on General Sheridan's staff, continuing there after being mustered out of volunteer service on 1 September. The inspectorate reclaimed him on 17 September, assigning him as assistant inspector general on duty in the Department of the Lakes. He arrived at Detroit, the department headquarters, on 1 December—the last of the wartime inspectors to return to the fold of the inspectorate.[11] Hardie remained in charge of the Inspector General's Office in Washington during the early part of the year, still assisted by Ludington. Edmund Schriver joined them on 10 April 1866, and by virtue of seniority took charge. Hardie had signed his correspondence, and allowed Ludington to refer to him, as "Inspector General, USA." Schriver henceforth signed himself "the Inspector General of the Army."[12]

That change in nomenclature reflected Schriver's own ambition. He set out immediately to win status for his "department" equal to all others in the army hierarchy. On 22 May, Schriver, Hardie, and Ludington jointly proposed a regulation allowing to inspectors general and assistant inspectors general the same number of rooms for offices as that provided to other staff officers. Their own establishment in Washington had good space in a rented building, they said, but the subject was not addressed in the regulations. "Before the War, the Inspection Service was not what it is now," they said. "Offices were not perhaps so much of a necessity as they must be henceforth." Schriver clearly wanted to establish permanence and official respect for the inspectorate, although the joint request for office space related mostly to inspectors stationed at the department and division headquarters.[13] In future years the objection would be frequent that inspectors did not need bureaucratic overhead, because if they were on the job, they were in the field. Certainly they were, throughout 1866. But most of them were not permanent inspection officers, more commonly others were assigned to this duty. William B. Hazen, acting inspector general for the Department of the Platte, was a typical example. He enjoyed the duty so much that he continued in it after being appointed colonel of the 38th Infantry. In August he inspected posts on the Bozeman Road and upper Missouri River. His report was exceedingly critical, and provided the foundation for his reputation as being, in the words of a contemporary, prone to offer "unwanted criticism of his superiors." But when Hazen visited Fort Phil Kearny in late

---

11. Ludington to Sacket, 22 Jan 66, in Letters Sent 1863–1889, RG 159; Baird to George W. Cullum, 14 Oct 66, in Cullum Files, USMA Archives; Baird, *Profile of a Hero*, 181–86, 198.

12. Ludington to Capt. John T. Ritter, 10 Apr 66, and all subsequent correspondence document the change, in Letters Sent 1863–1889, RG 159.

13. Schriver, Hardie, and Ludington to Asst. AG E. D. Townsend, 22 May 66, in Letters Sent 1863–1889, RG 159.

August, the post commander said that "his visit was greatly enjoyed by us all."[14]

Service as acting inspector general could be pleasant or unpleasant, or a mixture of the two. Most officers welcomed the opportunity to undertake the work, because it was a break from the routine, and educational as well. Over the coming years, officers detailed to the duty would constitute a major part of the official inspectorate. If inspection broke the routine for officers, it did so equally for enlisted men. They led monotonous lives, especially at the western posts, and rarely saw an officer higher than captain. Inspectors could be visiting celebrities: When Hazen passed through Fort Laramie, Wyoming, in May 1866, at least one private was delighted enough to write his sister about it in an excited letter giving all the details.[15]

Reduction of the Regular Establishment

In 1866 it appeared that the functions of acting inspectors general might be abolished, as Congress debated an increase in the Army. But if Schriver hoped to see a force of inspectors large enough to serve the entire military establishment, organized into a formal department, his ambitions were dashed on 28 July. Although legislation raised the authorized strength of the Army to 54,641 officers and men, in an exercise in Reconstruction politics, the law also declared that the existing regulations would remain in force until Congress acted on a new code, to be prepared by the Secretary of War. The law omitted the inspectors general and the Signal Corps from the calculation of staff departments. Departments were headed by brigadier generals. The Signal Corps had one colonel. There were also to be five assistant inspectors general: three colonels and two majors. That merely kept the incumbents in place, and prevented their organizing into a formal department.[16]

Schriver reported in October 1866 that all assistant inspectors general authorized by the act of 17 July 1862 had been mustered out, the only officers remaining being "those of the regular establishment." None of the five majors had yet been promoted to lieutenant colonel. Schriver was assigned to inspection of the Military Academy, Hardie to "special duty" at the War Department, Sacket to the Department of the Cumberland, and Marcy to Sherman's Division of the Missouri. Assistant inspectors general were at the District of New Mexico, the Department of the East, the Division of the Pacific, the Department of the

---

14. William Reed, "William Babcock Hazen: Curmudgeon or Crusader," in Ray Brandes, ed., *Troopers West: Military & Indian Affairs on the American Frontier* (San Diego: Frontier Heritage Press, 1970), 137–38; Henry B. Carrington, *Ab-sa-ra-ka, Land of Massacre: Being the Experience of an Officer's Wife on the Plains*, 3d ed. (Philadelphia: Lippincott, 1878), 134.

15. Hervey Johnson to Sister Abie, 20 May 66, in William E. Unrau, ed., *Tending the Talking Wire: A Buck Soldier's View of Indian Country 1863–1866* (Salt Lake City: University of Utah Press, 1979), 337.

16. *An Act to increase and fix the military peace establishment of the United States, Statutes at Large* 14, sec. 11, 332 (1866); Thian, *Legislative History*, 112; Ganoe, *History of the United States Army*, 307–08; *Revised Army Regulations*, H. Rpt. 85, 42d Cong., 3d sess. (1873).

Lakes, and one (Ludington) in charge of the Inspector General's Office in Washington.[17] "The Inspection Service of the army has not been changed in the character by the return to a condition of peace," Schriver said in October 1866. "The system developed during the war, meeting as nearly as practicable all demands, is continued." However, orders issued in 1865 authorized the detail of officers as acting assistant inspectors general for all departments and divisions not having a permanent inspector assigned to them. That continued in 1866, unaffected by the legislation of 28 July, and "the operations of the Inspector General's department are extended to every military command."[18]

Serving the Secretary of War

From Schriver's standpoint, not much really had changed. Edwin M. Stanton remained Secretary of War, and he continued to use the inspectors general as it suited him. The big project for 1866 was a raft of investigations of alleged peculations and contract irregularities in the Quartermaster Department late in the war. The Inspector General's Office generated scores of letters, mainly asking Quartermaster Department officers and contractors for information and clarification. A major investigation involved the sales of surplus property since May 1865, totaling millions of dollars. Hardie and Ludington pored through the records, but could find only minor delinquencies in the accounts. Nevertheless, they told the Secretary that there was insufficient accountability in the Quartermaster Department's procedures.[19]

Schriver himself went off on a special inspection of family barracks maintained by the Freedman's Bureau in Washington for former slaves. He urged that better records be kept of families housed there, both as a means of ensuring War Department control of the former slaves before they were sent on to permanent homes, and as a way to limit overcrowding.[20] Most of the special inspections ordered during 1866 covered subjects like "posts and troops," "fort and troops." Some were directed at various "irregularities," occasionally "alleged frauds connected with the subsistence and quartermaster's departments." One special investigation examined the "alleged malfeasance of Sutler Seitz" at Fort Washington, Maryland, while another in South Carolina reviewed the "Condition of society as existing between the white population and freedmen, etc." Regular officers of the inspectorate made most of the special inquiries, although a few were conducted by officers detailed from the

17. *ARIG 1866*, H. Ex. Doc. 1, 39th Cong., 2d Sess., 33. Schriver did not mention names in his annual report; they are deduced from other information. Davis was in New Mexico, Baird at the Lakes, Jones in the Pacific Division, and Totten in the East. Schriver's assignment to the Military Academy reflected the removal of that institution from the Corps of Engineers and placement under the direct supervision of the Secretary of War, who appointed a Board of Visitors to help improve and guide its education programs.

18. Ibid., 32.

19. Hardie and Ludington to Secy of War, 26 May 1866, and reams of other correspondence on Quartermaster issues, in Letters Sent 1863–1889, RG–159.

20. Schriver to Commissioner of the Freedmen's Bureau, 30 November 1866, in Letters Sent 1863–1889, RG–159.

line or from staff departments. Their reports were, Schriver said, "confidential in character, [and] are not, as a rule, of record in this office."[21]

The Subsistence Sales List

Although Schriver was assigned to be the Secretary of War's inspector of the United States Military Academy, he actually spent most of his time in Washington where Ludington was nominally in charge of the office. In that location, Schriver acted as if he were head of the Inspector General's Department, and in doing so took charge of a new responsibility of the four inspectors general (colonels), imposed by the legislation of 28 July 1866. They were required "to designate, from time to time, what articles shall be kept by the Subsistence Department for sale to enlisted men"; the department's chief responsibility was to procure, distribute, and issue rations for enlisted men.[22] But in addition, it carried extra items for sale to officers at military posts, especially where household goods and foodstuffs could not be purchased locally. The law now extended the same services to enlisted men, mostly as a means of breaking the monopoly of sutlers.

Schriver told his colleagues on 20 November 1866 that the Commissary General of Subsistence had asked him to prepare regulations implementing the law. Schriver therefore asked all inspectors general to send proposed lists of items and their general views to his office. In his opinion, the list should vary from post to post according to location and "absolute wants." Posts near cities where men could buy everything should stock fewer goods than isolated stations. Schriver also believed that much of what sutlers carried was superfluous or harmful to the men. His own list carried articles categorized as "for toilet," cleaning of arms, "stationery etc.," clothing, and miscellaneous items.[23] Schriver received contradictory lists from Marcy and Sacket; while Hardie was agreeable to his desires. Suggesting that the inspectors general should be unanimous in their recommendations, Schriver sent a draft compromise list to Marcy and Sacket for approval: It included lists of toilet articles, arms cleaning supplies, clothing, stationery, "sporting articles," and miscellaneous articles. Items usually carried by sutlers were excluded. Schriver also recommended that the Subsistence Department be required to sell to enlisted men the same kinds of supplies it made available to officers. At very remote posts, the department should also be required to stock dry goods, house-furnishing articles, and kitchen utensils. Marcy and Sacket agreed to every particular, so Sacket's report with its lists and recommendations went forward the last day of 1866.[24]

---

21. Ibid., 32–33, 34–36.

22. *An Act to increase and fix the military peace establishment of the U.S., Statutes at Large* 14, sec. 11, 332 (1866). This provision was repealed a few years later. Thian, *Legislative History*, 112. The inspiration for this new activity probably was the wartime designation of items to be carried by sutlers of volunteer regiments.

23. Schriver, Circular, Office of the Inspector General (OIG), 20 November 1866, in Letters Sent 1863–1889, RG–159.

24. Schriver to Marcy and Sacket, 18 December, and Schriver to AG, 31 Dec 66, with enclosures, in Letters Sent 1863–1889, RG–159.

A Symbol of Permanence

The rather odd duty of preparing the subsistence sales list was a formal recognition of the presumed expertise of the inspectors general. But giving them that responsibility did not treat them as a department or bureau, because it did not require a department head to speak for his organization. The inspectors general, in that instance, were merely a committee of equals. Nevertheless, Schriver managed to give the inspectorate one more trapping of a bureau in 1866, when he published the first *Annual Report of the Inspector General's Department*. All other departments had prepared annual reports since 1822, which were published with the annual report of the Secretary of War. Publication of the Inspector General's report in 1866 was a welcome affirmation that the inspectors general were a permanent part of the establishment, and not just a collection of officers. It did not constitute them as a department, but it was another and very symbolic step in that direction.[25] Schriver's brief first annual report presented a general overview of the inspectorate and the stations of its officers; it included as well an excellent presentation on the mechanism of the regular "stated monthly" inspections of the Army.

Schriver also initiated in his report for 1866 what would become a routine, annual lament. "The clerical labor in this office has very materially decreased," he said, "and a corresponding reduction of employees has been made. There are now but two clerks and one messenger retained." He did not, of course, believe that constituted a sufficient staff. The Inspector General's Department may not yet have become a formal bureaucracy, but it was beginning to sound like one. In any case, by the end of 1866 that incipient department was securely in place, blessed by the Secretary of War. "The Officers of the Inspector-General's Department," Stanton told the President, "are now those of the regular establishment, and they are all engaged in their legitimate duties of stated and special inspections. No [special] appropriation is required for this service." The inspectors general had survived the war, and were an integral and permanent part of the Army.[26]

25. *ARIG 1866*. The report originated in a memorandum from Schriver to the Adjutant General presenting a "synopsis of the operations" of the Inspector General's Department during the year ending 20 October 1866. Schriver to AG, 20 Oct 66, and ind, in Letters Sent 1863–1889, RG–159. Inspectors General had made annual reports since before the 1820s, but the reports had been the privileged information of the Commanding General.

26. Ibid., 33; Stanton to the President, 14 Nov 66, in *OR* 3d ser., vol. 5, p. 1038.

CHAPTER 15

Foundations of a Bureaucracy

(1867–1869)

If there was any doubt that Schriver had begun, since early 1866, to regard himself as the head of a formal department, it was dispelled by his second annual report in 1867. He sounded like a full-fledged bureau chief intent on expanding his domain, devoting most of his brief text to a complaint that the Inspector General's Department was too small. That was a defect not to be remedied by the detail of a few line officers to inspection. Schriver felt that full satisfactory results could be gotten only by assignment of adequate numbers of permanent officers. The record of the war, he claimed, demonstrated the ill effects of inexperience in inspection; a thoroughly professional inspection service could have saved millions of dollars. More serious than any monetary waste, said Schriver, was the inefficiency of troops caused by an absence of inspection.[1]

Founding a Bureau

Edmund Schriver was a soldier by training but an adminstrator by inclination. He very much wanted to see his organization established on some permanent basis, equal to the other departments of the Army. Not altogether incidentally, he may have perceived the personal benefits of prestige, security, and protection from interference that bureaucratic formality would have provided. He probably believed more positively that a formal embodiment would make it possible for the inspectorate to become a permanent and more productive part of the War Department organization. After he arrived in Washington, the history of the Inspector General often became less a military story and more a managerial chronicle. There had been relatively little qualitative change in the inspectors' essential military function; that is, inspection, since the time of Steuben. Nor were the procedures of inspection likely to evolve significantly in the future. The dominating impulse in the inspectorate after the Civil War, accordingly, was to establish a permanent department structure and then to preserve and expand its domain. The arguments advanced by Schriver and his successors were familiar, echoing those justifying counterparts as diverse as the

---

1. *ARIG 1867*, H. Ex. Doc. 1, 40th Cong., 2d sess., 489–90.

Quartermaster General and the Chief of Engineers. Inspection was essential to the Army and to the War Department, and therefore demanded sufficient people and resources to serve the essential ends. Inspection was a demanding professional occupation that required full-time specialists; officers detailed to the duty were amateurs, who could not perform it as well as those who drew on a life's career of study and practice. Inspection was a technical specialty that must be protected from interference and the self-promoting demands of others; in other words, the inspectorate must be independent.

If the claims made for inspection were true, then the argument for a separate inspection department was valid. A separate department could organize and direct inspection on a professionally correct basis. Inspectors could become increasingly skilled and productive, and the client Army would benefit from their improved services. Inspectors could be freed from special-interest demands and threats, and their products would be the pure fruits of technical ability, untainted by politicial or selfish interests, free of unseemly compromise. Given the claims were true, this argument did have a negative aspect. Decrying the absence of organization (or enough manpower and budget) could be a convenient way of blaming others for the inspectorate's failures or unproductiveness. An organization, once established, can take on a life of its own, and ultimately find much of its energies diverted to its own sustenance. That may be expressed in attempts to increase the staff and budget and to expand the purview of the organization merely to raise its prestige and that of its leader. In extreme circumstances, the organization's entire energy can be devoted to self-justification or self-protection.

The postwar momentum toward a separate Inspector General's Department had a ramification that was accorded little consideration at the time, by the inspectors or by anyone else. Washington and Steuben had made inspection an integral function of command. Wayne had reinforced that principle, and Macomb had revived it. Even as late as the Civil War and its aftermath, inspectors served commanders, although after 1863 they increasingly catered also to higher inspectors. The Commanding General had no real authority over the staff departments, not even over that of the Adjutant General. But he did have nominal control—shared with the Secretary of War—over the higher inspectors general. If the inspectorate were to be separated into its own department, the senior inspector general could distance himself from the Commanding General, and look to the Secretary of War as his source of power, as was already happening in Schriver's time. A separate department could in an extreme case divide all inspectors from commanders, so that inspectors would serve the interests of inspectors. How these conflicting tendencies and competing interests would sort themselves out, Schriver did not consider. He merely started the campaign for a separate department. It remained for others to bring it into being in later years, and to leave to their successors the duty of preserving the organization once it was established.

Making the Organization Useful

Schriver devoted only a part of his energies to a crusade for a separate department. He continued as inspector general assigned to the United States Military Academy in 1867. His report on the academy that year comprised mostly an endorsement of recommendations offered by its Board of Visitors. The most important demanded an increase in the corps of cadets, because not enough officers were being produced to meet the Army's needs. Schriver and the board also believed that the academy's superintendent should receive the compensation of a brigadier general. Because the "public records and archives of the academy are in constant peril from fire," Schriver recommended construction of a fireproof building. Repairs to a wharf and the erection of a stable, he said, were also "absolutely necessary."[2]

Schriver reported no changes of station for the inspectors in 1867, although Nelson Davis, assigned to New Mexico, had "just gone on leave of absence." Two of the assistant inspectors general had been promoted to lieutenant colonel during the year. They were Roger Jones and Nelson Davis, both promoted from major on 13 June.[3] Schriver, Hardie, and Ludington remained in Washington at the Secretary's beck and call. The others continued as departmental or divisional inspectors, at the behest of the commanders. But Marcy, inspector general of Sherman's gigantic Division of the Missouri—everything between the Mississippi and the states of the Pacific Coast, and scene of most conflicts with the Indians—was less an inspector than a roaming observer and "experienced military counselor" for Sherman, as he had been for McClellan. Among his adventures in 1867, Marcy attended a conference of army and Navajo leaders to determine the future of the "experiment" that had uprooted them from their homes and planted them at Bosque Redondo, in eastern New Mexico. There, they were supposed to have become "civilized" agriculturists. The Indians were finally permitted to make a "long walk," as they recall it, home.[4]

Marcy's vast experience on the frontier, unmatched by that of anyone else in the inspectorate, induced him to prepare a paper of guidance on how to report on Indian tribes. He sent it to Schriver at the end of 1866. Schriver was then working on "Rules for the Inspection Service," to be included in the next revision of the regulations, and early in January wrote Marcy that he wanted to add the discourse on Indians to the new rules. Schriver then gave Marcy an essay of his own, concerning whether inspectors should be empowered to administer oaths. He said that he had administered oaths during investigations without the legal power to do so, and declared himself loath to request such authority. He ended his discourse with a statement that revealed who Schriver thought was in charge of the Inspector General's Department—and which Marcy, his senior, might have received as an insult, had he not been enjoying

---

2. Ibid., 490–91.

3. Ibid., 489; Heitman, *Historical Register*, 1: 359, 582.

4. Marcy's activities at Bosque Redondo are covered briefly in Gerald Thompson, *The Army and the Navajo* (Tucson: University of Arizona Press, 1976), 142.

his western adventures so thoroughly: "I shall always be happy to receive suggestions about Department matters from you."[5]

That letter showed both the strengths and the weaknesses of Schriver's views. On the one hand, he had a clear idea of the proper place of inspectors, and did not want their energies dissipated or their identities clouded by an extension of their authority. On the other hand, he lacked at least part of the ambitious bureaucrat's penchant for increasing his authority and expanding his purview. (His successors would take a different view of the power to administer oaths.) But he ended his letter with a clever piece of phrasing that underscored his own ascendancy in the embryonic Inspector General's Department. Meanwhile, he made his organization increasingly useful to the Secretary of War, whatever the Secretary's interests might be. When the Secretary of the Interior asked the War Department to provide housing for a large delegation of Sioux Indians scheduled to visit the nation's capital, Stanton handed the job to Schriver. He and Ludington were to confer with a number of officials, find an unoccupied barracks, and inspect it along with Interior Department representatives. When that was completed, Schriver made a full report for the Secretary's information.[6]

Also at the Secretary's request, Schriver sent Hardie off in January to investigate the qualifications of several bidders on construction contracts at Schuylkill Arsenal. Hardie returned with a report ranking them in order, based on background and reputation for such things as good work, surety, and business experience. In early February, when a fire alarm was raised in the War Department building, Stanton ordered Schriver to learn the cause. Schriver blamed mismanagement by the building's fireman, who had blown a steam valve by forgetting to open a return pipe after lighting the boiler. Schriver recommended corrective procedures. Later that month the Inspector General was charged with conveying captured Confederate property to the Secretary of the Treasury. When Schriver first attempted to do so, the Treasury's secretary was too busy, and he had to postpone an examination of the property inventory.[7]

Another special service to Secretary Stanton involved claims for damages and debts arising out of the war, which took most of Hardie's time. The trails of some cases had grown very cold by 1867. Hardie was handed a maddeningly frustrating example in early April, and was reduced to probing the memory of a cavalry officer then stationed in Baltimore in the hopes of getting something to go on.[8]

Schriver showed himself to be an increasingly able administrator. Proving his organization's usefulness to the Secretary of War was a means of ensuring its permanence, and its eventual growth. The Inspector General's Department became a repository for duties not clearly falling within the purview of another

---

5. Schriver to Marcy, 11 Jan 67, in Letters Sent 1863–1889, RG 159.
6. Schriver to Ludington, 16 Jan 67, in Letters Sent 1863–1889, RG 159.
7. Hardie to Secy of War, 4 Feb 67; Schriver to AG, 7 Feb 67; and Schriver to Secy of War, 27 Feb 67, in Letters Sent 1863–1889, RG 159.
8. Hardie to Capt. George T. Robinson, 3 Apr 67, in Letters Sent 1863–1889, RG 159.

bureau. When Congress formalized the system of national cemeteries on 22 February 1867, it required the Secretary to have them inspected annually by "some officer of the army, not under the rank of major," who would report their condition. That duty eventually ended up in the inspectorate (although the Quartermaster Department managed the cemeteries) because the inspectorate was an increasingly important adjunct to the War Department. Additional duties, of course, were ready-made justifications for additional inspectors.[9]

Taking Charge of the Inspectorate

Schriver also worked to increase his control over the inspectorate. When the Department of the East developed a system of property inspections that he considered especially sound, he sent a copy of the implementing order to every departmental inspector in the country, urging its adoption as a uniform approach to the problem. One acting assistant inspector general took that as an excuse to abandon inspections of troops, so Schriver had Ludington affirm that "the stated monthly Inspections of troops by subordinate Inspectors will not be discontinued. The department inspector will personally inspect each command once in three months, and oftener if practicable. It is desired that he will intrust to subordinate officers only such Inspections as he is unable to make himself."[10] Then Schriver issued a circular in April containing considerable administrative fine tuning. Acting assistant inspectors general were cautioned not to use the heading "Inspector General's Department" or "Inspector General's Office" on their communications. Instead, they should put "Acting Assistant Inspector General's Office" beneath the military department on their letterheads. Lastly, saying that he was gearing up for his department's inspection mission, the Inspector General asked all other staff departments for a complete set of their publications.[11]

Schriver thus established the Washington office's position as the final arbiter of rules and procedures. For example he had Ludington return a letter from Absalom Baird in May, correcting his erroneous actions affecting the disposal of Ordnance property. The Washington office was accepted as the reviewer and interpreter of all rules as they pertained to inspectors.[12] In all, Schriver was determined to defend his domain. He told Hardie to review a new set of infantry tactics proposed by Emory Upton, and authorized him to go directly to General Grant with objections to one paragraph. The offending passage said that if a

---

9. GO No. 8, AGO, 27 Feb 67, in GORI&IG.

10. Ludington to Sir, and Incls, 13 Feb 67; to Maj. James D. Roy, Actg Asst IG, Dept of the South, 23 Mar 67; to Chief of Engineers, 20 Mar 67; to Quartermaster General, 20 Mar 67; to Chief of Ordnance, 20 Mar 67, all in Letters Sent 1863–1889, RG 159.

11. Cir, IGO, 1 Apr 67, in GORI&IG. The Department of the East's property inspection procedure involved quarterly examinations by the departmental inspector or an assistant, inventory reports for unserviceable property, and special instructions to others detailed to such inspections. It eventually became the standard for property inspections throughout the Army.

12. Ludington, Ind on Ltr of Absolom Baird, of 27 Apr 67, returning it to Baird, 7 May 67, in Letters Sent 1863–1889, RG 159.

battalion was to be reviewed by an inspector junior in rank to the commander, the latter should "receive" the review. Hardie thought that reflected ignorance of the place of the inspector, whose rank was irrelevant because he had no power of command. The inspector should be understood instead as the eyes of the superior officer who ordered the inspection. As far as Hardie was concerned, Upton's proposal "trammelled" the authority of the inspector. It would allow him to see only what the commander wanted him to see, instead of what the higher authority most wanted to know, which was how well that commander could lead and maneuver his troops. Hardie said that the current regulations omitted only the personal salute from the commander leading the troops to an inspector junior in rank, but left the latter free to inspect without restriction. He saw no reason to change that procedure.[13]

Schriver demonstrated his organization's usefulness to the Army by assuming the mantle of arbiter of protocol. One typical question came from a quartermaster who wanted to know the proper uniform for staff officers in artillery regiments. Schriver began his response with, "My individual opinion—I am unauthorized to give any other." Since the officers belonged neither to batteries nor to the General Staff, he said, they should not wear the uniform of either. The only thing left was "the ordinary uniform prescribed for the Artillery Officer."[14] But Schriver's first concern was with the integrity of the Inspector General's procedures. He took important steps in two areas in late 1867. One was to protect the confidentiality of inspectors' reports, including those made by officers not permanently part of his department. Bvt. Col. Andrew J. Alexander had inspected troops in New Mexico while Nelson Davis was on leave, and apparently offered some disparaging remarks about Davis. The criticisms were leaked by the Adjutant General's Office, and Davis asked for a copy of the report so he could defend himself. Schriver turned him down, telling him that General Grant thought his own "inadvertance" had wronged Alexander by betraying the confidentiality of the report. Grant therefore told Schriver to soothe the ruffled feathers of both inspectors.[15]

The other important area in which Schriver sought improvement was ensuring that inspections produced results in the form of corrected deficiencies— what is now called follow-up. Inspection reports that did not say what happened to correct shortcomings detected during inspection were returned to their authors. A typical example went back to an acting assistant inspector general because it lacked "any letter of advice or any notification of the action, if known, taken by the Dept. Comdr. for the correction of the irregularities reported." Follow-up, Schriver believed, was essential not only to the effectiveness of inspection, but to the survival of the inspectorate. In December 1867, he told the inspectors to give him information that would support his case for a formal Inspector General's

---

13. Hardie to Grant, 2 Jul 67, in Letters Sent 1863–1889, RG 159.
14. Schriver to Lt. James L. Sherman, 28 Sep 67, in Letters Sent 1863–1889, RG 159.
15. Asst AG E. D. Townsend to Davis, true copy to IGO, 22 Oct 67, and Schriver to Davis and to Asst QMG H. M. Enas through the QMG, true copy to Alexander, 5 Nov 67, in Letters Sent 1867–1889, RG 159.

Department. He particularly wanted to know about improvements and econo-mies derived from inspecting.[16]

By the end of 1867, Schriver had gone far toward establishing the Inspector General's Department as a reality, if not as a legal formality. In doing so, he set a pattern for his successors, and created the arguments that they would use in pursuing the goal of a separate department. Congress had also been at work earlier that year. Reacting to complaints arising out of the war, it abolished the army's sutlers. That increased the importance of the Subsistence Department sales list maintained by the inspectors general, and eventually would give the inspectorate much to think about when it considered the amenities to which enlisted men were entitled. Also in 1867, Congress introduced black regiments into the Regular Army. Schriver would in due course have something to say about that as well.[17]

Inspection continued relatively unchanged into 1868, with inspectors mak-ing their rounds and writing their reports according to formulas that reached back to the days of Arthur P. Hayne. Marcy remained in the Division of the Missouri, serving more as Sherman's general factotum than as an inspector. He continued to devote his attention to finding a new home for the Navajo Indians, and his official writings became increasingly laden with reminiscences and references to his explorations before the Civil War.[18] Roger Jones, at the Division of the Pacific, included the new American possession of Alaska in his rounds in 1868, while Sacket continued his routine at the Department of the Cumberland. Hardie spent more than a year at the Washington office working full-time on investigations of claims arising out of the war. Schriver announced in October the War Department's intention to relieve Hardie "as soon as his services can be dispensed with, and to assign him to the charge of the inspec-tion service on the Pacific Coast." The only other change in the permanent complement of the inspectorate was the transfer of Baird to the Department of the Dakota, and Ludington to the Department of the South. Otherwise, depart-ments lacking a permanent inspector general received acting assistant inspec-tors general—officers detailed from the line for inspection duty. At least thir-teen were so assigned that year. "Their services have proved valuable and have been attended with good results," Schriver said blandly.[19]

---

16. Schriver, Ind on report of inspection of Camps Watson, Logan, and Harney, 22 Sep 67, submitted by Bvt. Col. Marcus A. Reno, 16 Nov 67, and Schriver, Cir, IGO, 11 Dec 67, in Letters Sent 1863–1889, RG 159. Reno was later to become famous as a survivor of the battle of the Little Bighorn, and then to become notorious for misbehavior that ended in his court-martial.

17. Tapson, "Sutler and Soldier," 181.

18. ARIG 1868, H. Ex. Doc. 1, 40th Cong., 3d sess., 776. Early in 1868, Marcy reported that former Choctaw and Cherokee lands in the Washita Mountains (Oklahoma) would be suitable for resettlement of the Navajos, whom he recommended be moved there. His report, laced with references to his prewar explorations, was picked up with interest by Army and Navy Journal, 5 (25 Apr 68): 571.

19. ARIG 1868, 776–77.

A Formal Bureau Is Acknowledged

Schriver said in his annual report for 1868 that the entire U.S. Army had been inspected, and that "the result has been an evident improvement in the discipline and carefulness in the disposition of the public moneys and property." Such self-generated praise was another tradition established by Schriver; it would be characteristic of the annual reports thereafter. Schriver promoted his program further, proclaiming that inspection was essential to the successful management of all armies. Inspection duties required experience, he claimed once again, and he announced that details to inspection duties would be limited to officers with a decade or more experience. "It is hoped," he concluded, "that this mode of detail will bring to the inspection service a sufficiency of officers properly suited therefor, and will obviate the necessity, at least for the present, of an increase of the regular organization."[20] What he referred to was a general order issued on 19 October 1868. It was a masterpiece of compromise, and on the whole a personal and official triumph for Schriver. At least for the moment he had to forego temporarily his campaign for a larger permanent force for the inspectorate. But Schriver himself gained from a formal affirmation (one had been lacking theretofore) that he be assigned to the War Department and in charge of the "Inspection Bureau," as well as to inspection of the Military Academy. The positions of all other permanent officers were likewise ratified by the order, but no one else received such an endorsement of his personal ambition as did Schriver. He was clearly and officially the supervisor of the inspectorate.

Schriver gained not only for himself but also for his interest in bringing about a formal Inspector General's Department. Divisions and departments lacking permanent inspectors were each to be inspected by a field officer with ten years of experience. It was in how such officers were to be selected, and in the way the Washington office could deal with them, that Schriver gained the most. The inspection process began with each division or department commander, who nominated three candidates to serve as acting assistant inspector general. The War Department—obviously meaning Schriver's office—would then select the acting inspector for each department or division. The officers so selected could not be relieved except by orders of the War Department or the Commanding General. And to extend Schriver's control over the inspectorate, the order concluded that the permanent officers, especially at division level, could direct the detailed officers, especially at the department level. Schriver presided over all in the Washington office.[21] Thus he had, with that order, achieved everything essential to a separate inspection department except for its formal recognition. Like quartermasters, inspectors were regarded as members of a distinct staff, with their own chain of communications apart from the Regular Army chain of command. Schriver's purpose quite obviously was to continue toward assem-

---

20. Ibid., 777. Note the qualification "at least for the present."
21. GO No. 87, AGO, 19 Oct 68, in GORI&IG.

bling a formal department. But the order was also another step in removing inspection from command, because commanders no longer enjoyed the unqualified services of inspectors as extensions of their own wills. Inspectors now served other masters, in a chain of communications that extended to the Secretary of War, the powerless Commanding General being of little account. George Washington, remembering the Conway affair, might have focused on the new arrangement as a symptom of the Commanding General's powerlessness.

Schriver had preceded the 19 October order with some minor moves that benefited the inspectors. On 25 August 1868, inspectors in the divisions of the Missouri and the Pacific became entitled to spring wagons, reserved for their exclusive use where the only mode of transportation available was animals or vehicles of the Quartermaster Department. But the free use of a vehicle was regarded as payment in full for transportation costs (figured by mileage). Also in August, Schriver added a number of fancy foodstuffs to the subsistence sales list, gaining the favor of officers and men—except, probably of those in the Subsistence Department. And on 21 September, he sent a circular to all his officers to point out the special position of inspectors in the evaluation of incompetent officers. Inspectors had special familiarity with army personnel, Schriver pointed out. They accordingly had a special duty "to aid the War Department in every proper way in its efforts to relieve the Army of Officers who unfit themselves for the service by indulgence in vicious habits."[22] More important was Schriver's other major accomplishment during the year—the promulgation of the rules for inspection he had been working on since early 1867. They appeared on 2 November 1868, offering instructions for inspectors similar to, but more concise than, the general order issued in 1866. The rules presented a basic outline of inspection duties and schedules, and required the use of prescribed forms (which could be expanded with additional information) for all reports. Economy in the management of public funds and property, said the rules, was of paramount importance to inspectors. Only they could condemn property, so they were advised to be cautious.

Troops were to be inspected before going into the field, and inspectors were required to learn the regulations governing all branches of the Army. In addition, in the first report after the issue of the rules, inspectors were to report carefully on the Indian situation in their respective purviews, following guidelines drawn on those Marcy had sent to Schriver. Inspectors were also to gather geographical information as they traveled, and forward it to Washington. To increase Schriver's control over the inspectorate, inspecting officers were required to keep good records, to submit their annual reports by 1 October, and to report to

---

22. GO No. 75, AGO, 25 Aug 68, in GORI&IG; Schriver to Marcy, Sacket, and Hardie, 29 Aug 68, and Schriver, Cir, IGO, 26 Sep 68, in Letters Sent 1868–1889, RG 159. In a minor development, GO No. 20, AGO, 21 May 68, in GORI&IG, said "Inspection reports of medical property will hereafter be referred to the Medical Director [of each department] before being acted upon by Department Commanders." That was a sign not so much of a loss of control of property condemnation by inspectors, as of the increasing tendency of the Medical Department to win control of its own affairs in every particular.

the Inspector General's Office in Washington their arrival at every assigned station.[23] However, Sacket noticed that Schriver's rules did not emerge from the War Department as a general order. Schriver had originally wanted his rules included in the next issue of the regulations, but those were hopelessly entangled in the bureaucracy. A general order would have had the same effect, and would have anticipated wholesale new regulations. Schriver apparently was not able to win the unqualified backing of the War Department for his rules, and he tried to impose them on the inspectorate in a brazen assertion of his own will—after carefully gaining the Secretary's approval. It was the first test of his power to direct subordinate inspectors under the 19 October general order. When Sacket called Schriver's bluff, the latter lamely responded that his circular should be treated as guidance to inspectors and commanding generals.[24] Making necessity a virtue, Schriver maintained that the rules, with the approval of the Secretary, were merely internal guidance for the inspection "department," similar to the internal governance of other staff departments, and need not take the form of a general order. The implication, however, was that inspectors should treat them as if they were orders. But the episode revealed that Schriver was not in as strong a position as he would like when it came to commanding the inspectorate. Sacket had had the temerity to question his action; until there was a clear organizational pyramid peaking with a senior in Washington, there could be no true inspection department.

It did not take Schriver long to butt heads with Sacket, in a circumstance where he could clearly affirm his own authority: On 2 December, he wired Sacket, who had transferred to the Division of the Atlantic on 29 October, to investigate and report on an accidental fire at Fort La Fayette, in New York Harbor.[25] Schriver had addressed Sacket at his last reported location. Paragraph X of his rules required inspectors to report their station and employment to the Inspector General's Office of the War Department every month. They were also to send copies of all orders given them for tours of inspection, including dates of departure and return. Despite that requirement, Schriver received a response from a third party that Sacket was out of the office. He immediately tracked down the wandering inspector general and fired off a stern rebuke to remind him to comply with reporting requirements.[26] Sacket finally replied two weeks later on 19 December, saying that a copy of his inspection orders had gone routinely to the Adjutant General's Office, and he believed that was sufficient notice of his whereabouts. Schriver retorted immediately that the purpose of paragraph X was to keep the Secretary of War advised of the status of every inspector, so that he might know whether the officer was immediately available—as had been the case with Fort La Fayette. Routine copies of orders

23. Schriver, Cir, IGO, 2 Nov 68, in Letters Sent 1863–1889, RG 159. This is also reproduced in GORI&IG.

24. Schriver to Sacket, 23 Nov 68, in Letters Sent 1863–1889, RG 159.

25. Schriver to Sacket, 2 Dec 68, in Letters Sent 1863–1889, RG 159.

26. Schriver to Sacket, 5 Dec 68, in Letters Sent 1863–1889, RG 159.

in the Adjutant General's Office, Schriver said, did not suffice to keep the Secretary of War informed, because routine paper work did not come to his daily attention, "nor are the means of administering the details of the Inspection service obtained through the Adjutant General's Office."[27]

Sacket's feelings may have been bruised, but Schriver was triumphant. With the backing of the Secretary of War, he had established the dominance of the Washington office over the entire inspectorate. Whoever held the chair there was effectively the head of the inspectorate—and in fact, if not in name, head of an inspector general's department. But Schriver was not the senior inspector general; Marcy was. In the rank-conscious Army, it was only a matter of time before it became necessary for the senior officer to put on his mantle. Marcy was having a thoroughly good time, roaming the West alone and with Sherman. But with the election of Grant to the presidency in 1868, Sherman was going to have to return from the wilderness to take up the amorphous post of Commanding General. Marcy's idyll could not long outlast Sherman's, so Schriver's days as head of the inspectorate were numbered.

The Inspectorate and Army Reorganization

Schriver remained in office long enough to see his organization through the trauma of another Army-wide reorganization. By early 1869, Congress was bent on a drastic reduction in the military force. But the legislature now numbered among its members quite a few who had been officers during the Civil War, and who took upon themselves the manner of military experts. One of them was James A. Garfield who, as chairman of the House Committee on Military Affairs, offered an ambitious plan for a thorough overhaul of the Army in January 1869. Taking testimony from the War Department hierarchy, most of which it ignored, Garfield's committee followed its own muse and concluded that the staff departments were "too numerous and too large in proportion to the line of the army." The legislators also believed that there were too many officers in higher grades.

Some of the proposed reforms would come later, such as merger of the Pay, Commissary, and Subsistence Departments. Equally farseeing was the committee's desire to make staff officers subordinate to the Commanding General. Other proposals, however, stood no chance of success; for example, merger of the Signal Corps into the Corps of Engineers and transfer to the latter of the Department of the Treasury's coast survey, and consolidation of the Ordnance Department and the artillery. The committee also proposed (against vehement War Department opposition) consolidation of the Adjutant General's and the Inspector General's Departments. But its proposal came to naught. The committee's only immediate contribution to the Army was the elimination of brevet promotions, although its desire to revoke brevets previously awarded went begging.[28] The committee's justification for merging the Adjutant General's

---

27. Schriver to Sacket, 22 Dec 68, in Inspection Reports 1863–1889, RG 159.
28. *Army Organization*, H. Rpt. 33, 40th Cong., 3d sess. (1869).

and the Inspector General's Departments was that both dealt with aspects of personnel. Their merger would also bring about some economies in manpower.[29] That throwback to the early nineteenth century would be heard again into the early twentieth century. The proposed merger obviated testimony regarding the substantial differences between the two assignments; Hardie for one had pointed out that at departmental headquarters "the adjutant general must be habitually present [while] the inspector general must be habitually absent." But the committee seemed more concerned in its questioning with the fact that the paper work of inspectors went forward wholly outside the channel of communications managed by the Adjutant General.

Schriver and Hardie both testified at length before the committee on 25 January. They had done much homework. Probably at Schriver's instructions, Hardie prepared histories of the Adjutant General and the Inspector General, with which he prefaced his testimony. His own department, understandably, received the longer treatment. Its chronology was up-to-date, but the bulk of the history focused on the Revolutionary period. Thanks to Hardie and Schriver, by 1869 the inspectorate had placed its roots very firmly in the soil tilled by Steuben.[30] Hardie's testimony offered a fine assessment of the work of the inspectorate, and of the Inspector General's Department's view of itself. In offering a general account of what the inspectorate did, Hardie especially underscored inspection's importance. Schriver, who probably approved Hardie's testimony in advance, must have been pleased. Hardie stressed the universal aspects of inspection and the value to the public and to commanders in knowing the condition of units. He testified that he saw no value in merging the two departments because, contrary to the committee's view, the two functions represented were not interchangeable. The missions of each required specific expertise and demanded flexibility on the part of the inspector so that he might go immediately to where he was needed. He could not be chained to a headquarters. The committee was particularly concerned that inspectors did not route their reports through the Adjutant General. To this, Hardie replied that the reports were intended only for commanders and were often confidential, never rising above the headquarters where appropriate action could be taken. He further pointed out that the Inspector General's Department was far from overstaffed given the volume of work that it accomplished.[31] Hardie was a conservative man who, like most of his uniformed contemporaries, favored no changes in the military establishment. He advised against proposed mergers of the Quartermaster, Subsistence, and Pay departments; the Ordnance organiza-

---

29. Ibid.
30. Ibid. Hardie's history of the Inspector General's Department apparently was the beginning of a historical consciousness in the organization, and the first revival of Steuben's memory in order to serve the department's current purposes. The rather terse institutional histories were updated periodically, and became an annual exercise early in the 20th century. The best example is Sanger, "Inspector-General's Department," which fails to mention Hardie's work, although it is clearly based on the earlier history.
31. *Army Organization* (1869).

tions of the Army and the Navy; the coast survey and the Corps of Engineers; and other suggested consolidations. He based his objections on the understanding that each activity was distinct and governed by regulations that only specialists could understand. American technical services, he maintained, were more efficient than some of the combined services in European armed forces.

Schriver followed Hardie to the witness chair. He lost no time in defending the department, even asking for its enlargement. After that opening, the committee asked Schriver whether the inspectors based in Washington in fact performed duties "that belong usually to the Adjutant General's department." He countered quickly by saying that there was "only one inspector here, and he performs appropriate duties, having charge of the inspection office and serving as inspector of the Military Academy, some of whose duties are similar to those of an adjutant general. I am that officer, but when not so engaged I am usefully employed in assisting the Secretary of War in certain branches of business which would require the special detail of an officer were I not serving as above. I am available for, and do make, special investigations and inspections under the Secretary's orders." Hardie's presence, he said, was accidental, because the Secretary had to detail someone to investigate claims against the War Department. Hardie had been assigned to the Pacific Coast, and would leave when his present duties were finished. When asked to whom as Inspector General he was responsible, Schriver said, "To the Secretary of the War and the General of the army." When asked if he reported to the Adjutant General, he merely said, "No." He also explained that all inspection reports were forwarded to him and that he called the attention of the Secretary, the Commanding General, and other officials to the parts of reports that concerned them "from time to time." Schriver then revealed the rather dubious status of his informal department, when it came to the Army's customary promotion procedures. He pointed out that assistant inspectors could not be promoted into vacancies created by departing inspectors because the Inspector General's Department had not been formally authorized by law. Schriver, like Hardie, objected to proposed consolidations of various staff departments, on the grounds that their missions were distinct and that it would be impossible for one person to adequately supervise them all, especially in wartime. Those objections would, by the early twentieth century, become hackneyed, but no less strongly voiced. In the meantime, Schriver, hoping to become head of a bureau, was not about to antagonize the influential heads of other bureaus by proposing the loss of any of their jobs, whatever the administrative efficiencies involved.

The committee was also concerned with the way the Army paid its troops, which was every two months (suggested as a cause of their disaffection for nearly half a century). So the members naturally looked to the Inspector General to provide an informed opinion. Schriver revealed himself to be a hard-nosed character of the old school, and generally unreceptive to any changes. He urged fewer pay periods on the premise that blocked pay would keep soldiers from deserting. The committee, unmoved, continued to favor some kind of reform. Then, ranging over other subjects at the committee's request, Schriver testified that he believed organizations of veteran reserves or invalids to be useful only during a big war, when much rear-echelon light duty was required and manpower was short. Such units should be abolished in peacetime, for they served no useful purpose, he averred. However, any influence Schriver may have had with the committee, several of whose members were Radical Republicans devoted to the elevation of the masses of former slaves, was eroded when he answered questions about the new black regiments. Like many of his white contemporaries, Schriver believed that black men were not ready for military service. He said he would rather not have any black units on the rolls because enough whites could be enlisted for all military needs. He said "antagonisms" between races would be better avoided if there were no black units in the army. He also was of the opinion that blacks would not make good NCO's, nor were they as physically fit as whites. Whatever his personal feelings about the qualities of black troops, his remarks reflected a central dilemma in the argument for an Inspector General's Department. He offered only one fact that could be represented as deriving from systematic inspection—that among poorly educated former slaves few men were prepared to be noncommissioned officers. Everything else was an opinion or an unsupported assertion. When Garfield asked Schriver for evidence of "antagonism which must always exist between white and black troops," he could offer no examples.[32]

Schriver and his successors who argued for a separate and independent inspection bureau placed great stock in the need for specialization, experience, and professional freedom for the inspector. That was as if inspection were a scientific profession—like engineering or forestry, for which similar claims were often advanced in the late nineteenth century. In fact, inspection was and is subjective, and its subjective nature surfaced most vividly whenever an inspector was asked for advice on policy. That the recommendations of an inspector, in other words, rested as much on the outlook of the inspector as on any objective facts is demonstrated by Schriver's belief that men should be paid infrequently; others before and after him believed just the opposite—both sides claiming the same evidence in support of their positions. The argument for an independent inspectorate was never persuasive so long as it was based on an assertion that inspectors were scientific specialists working on professional principles unaffected by the political or philosophical perspectives of the world at large. The facts, simply, countered the argument, and supported those opposed to an independent inspector general. Schriver might more successfully have advanced his case by acknowledging the subjective nature of inspection. Then he could have emphasized the beneficial effects of experience, prestige, and protection from interference on reducing subjectivity, personal or imposed, which accordingly would make the results of inspection more objective. When such arguments were advanced in the future, they proved to be more persuasive.

In any event, Schriver lost most of his skirmishes with the House Military Affairs Committee. But he won the war. Congress reduced the United States

---

32. Ibid.

Army on 3 March 1869, but it left the inspectors general and the adjutants general in their respective spheres. The legislation in fact accomplished little more than a drastic reduction in the authorized force—including the reduction, by consolidation, of the six "colored" regiments to just four—to a total of 37,313 officers and men. The staff departments emerged fairly unscathed, retaining virtually all their complements of officers, but their size remained large enough that regiments continued to be gutted by the detail of officers to other duties. The Inspector General's Department, now so-called (but still not established by law), retained its four colonels, three lieutenant colonels, and two majors. But thereafter, no promotions were permitted in the Adjutant General's, Inspector General's, Quartermaster, Subsistence, Medical, Pay, and Ordnance departments, or in the Corps of Engineers.[33]

Continuing the Routine

While Congress deliberated, Schriver's organization continued its varied routine. In February the Secretary of War decided that the Quartermaster Department had too many employees and too much rented property in the Washington area, so he sent Hardie to find out why. Hardie was also told that he should look for means to save money on such expenditures. That turned into a complete investigation of all expenditures and disbursements of the quartermaster depot at Washington. The Secretary called a few days later for a special investigation of reported timber thefts on the Fort Gratiot military reservation in Michigan, and Schriver dispatched the departmental acting assistant inspector general.[34] Schriver also continued to defend his operations with his customary vigor. When quartermaster and commissary depot heads objected to the use of the Inspector General's new inventory and inspection forms for condemned property instead of the forms of their own departments, Schriver reminded them firmly that general orders had required use of the "form furnished from Inspector General's Office, Washington." He also called for a republication of the regulations governing property condemnation in order to end such confusions and conflicts.[35]

Property condemnations received increasing attention, and the inspectors general emerged on top of the whole question. Property managing officers, especially in the Quartermaster Department, had a variety of forms serving overlapping purposes of their own department, the inspectors general, the Department of the Treasury, and other authorities. The appearance of a new

33. *An Act making appropriations for the support of the Army for the year ending June thirtieth, eighteen hundred and seventy, and for other purposes, Statutes at Large* 15, sec. 6, 315 (1869): Thian, *Legislative History*, 112; Heitman, *Historical Register*, 1: 606–09. The four regiments of the Veterans Reserve Corps, a largely meaningless organization anyway, were abolished, while the total number of infantry regiments fell from 41 to 25, including 2 of blacks where there had been 4. The 10 cavalry regiments (2 black) remained. Companies increased in size.

34. Schriver to Hardie, 1 Feb and 2 Feb 69, and Schriver to Jno. D. Hardin, 6 Feb 69, in Letters Sent 1863 1889, RG 159.

35. Schriver to Ludington, 4 Feb 69, in Letters Sent 1863–1889, RG 159.

Inspector General's inventory and inspection report form confused many quartermasters, particularly on the issue of accountability to the Treasury when property was disposed of. The Quartermaster General complained to Schriver, but while the latter acknowledged that the "desirability of simplifying the system . . . in any safe and practicable manner will surely not be disputed," he remained firm in his intention to add his form to the surfeit of paper. Schriver obtained the issue of a general order in early March, reminding inspecting officers "that there is hardly any species of material however worn, which cannot be put to some use." Thereafter, no property with any salable value was to be disposed of without special reason. The Army's shrinking budget was making it a pioneer in the recycling of used goods.[36]

Schriver enjoyed his final triumph as head of the inspectorate on 17 February 1869, when a general order permitted to inspectors general, assistant inspectors general, judge advocates, and chief commissaries of military departments the same allowances of office rooms and heating fuel as the regulations afforded to assistant adjutants general at the departments.[37] In trappings, if not in fact, the inspectorate resembled a formal department more closely than ever. By this time its de facto existence was acknowledged without question by legislators and army officers alike. Much of this can be attributed to Schriver's efforts at organization. However, equally instrumental in this phenomenon was the War Department's need for a sound inspection service.

The Senior Inspector Takes Over

Ulysses S. Grant became President 4 March 1869, and relinquished the office of Commanding General, which Sherman assumed four days later. Not much later, the senior inspector general came east—Marcy was ordered to Washington to take charge of the Inspector General's War Department office on 15 March, and began to sign its correspondence on the 20th. New orders on 12 April assigned all the inspectors general and assistant inspectors general, with Marcy formally coming to the "Headquarters of the Army," which he had already done. Schriver remained located there, assigned to the Secretary of War and to inspection of the Military Academy.[38]

Marcy devoted himself dutifully to the Washington office's paper work, although his heart continued to look west to the scenes of his adventures. One of his earliest duties was to notify his inspectors that, on 10 April 1869, Congress had given officers of the Inspector General's Department authority to administer oaths to affidavits taken during investigations of frauds or misconduct.

---

36. Schriver to Quartermaster General, 25 Feb 69, in Letters Sent 1863–1889, RG 159; GO No. 8, AGO, 3 Mar 69, in GORI&IG.

37. GO No. 5, AGO, 17 Feb 69, in GORI&IG.

38. Weigley, *History of the United States Army*, 559; *ARIG 1869*, H. Ex. Doc. 1, 41st Cong., 2d sess., pt. 2, 1: 175; GO No. 34, AGO, 12 Apr 69, in GORI&IG. The first mail signed by Marcy in Letters Sent 1863–1889, RG 159, is dated 20 March preceded by letters signed by Schriver on 25 February.

He reminded all officers on 27 May that orders since 1851 had required captains to write onto company musters and payrolls the paymaster's calculation of pay. Paymasters were not to be allowed to do that themselves. Marcy soon became bogged down in the minutiae that Schriver had found so enjoyable although, as he had told Marcy many months before, he had not wanted the inspectors to be required to issue oaths.[39] But in other respects, Schriver's influence lived on in the Washington office. A general order issued on 21 June reflected his attitudes more than Marcy's, as the latter appeared less inclined than his predecessor to take absolute control of the inspectorate. Inspectors, thereafter, while making their rounds in the field and at posts, were to send off their reports immediately, from each station inspected. And reflecting Schriver's interest in follow-up, inspectors were to endorse on their reports what remedies commanding officers had applied to correct deficiences. All commanders up the chain of communication also were to endorse their comments and corrective measures on nonconfidential reports. Finally, the paper work of inspectors was made uniform by the order. Schriver had not been able to finalize procedures for reporting condemned property, causing property departments to complain about the new form he had issued earlier in the year, but things were almost as he had wanted them to be.[40]

General Sherman told Marcy to look into the question of who was to issue inventory and inspection forms. The Inspector General said that the regulations had not changed since 1863, and did not say which office was responsible. However, he told the Adjutant General, General Order No. 5 of 1866 said that the Inspector General's Office was to prescribe forms. He defended the form devised there as "so simple and contains such ample directions" that even inexperienced officers had no trouble with it. The Subsistence Department had its own form, which Marcy thought no better than his own. He accordingly recommended the general adoption of the Inspector General's form to end the duplication and confusion.[41] Marcy was nothing if not diplomatic, so he set out to mend relations with the supply departments. He ordered a revision in the inventory and inspection report form, and in August sent it out for comment, offering it as the single property form for the whole Army. Schriver, resting on his prerogatives, would not have thought of such a civility. The Inspector General's Office was the only source of inventory and inspection forms for all species of property by the end of 1869, those of the other bureaus no longer being current. Marcy estimated that the supply of forms to the Army would increase his annual postage by $406.08, to cover the shipment of blank forms to all recipients.[42]

---

39. Marcy, Cir, IGO, 27 May 69, and Cir, IGO, 27 May 69, in Letters Sent 1863–1889, RG 159.

40. GO No. 55, AGO, 21 Jun 69, in GORI&IG.

41. Marcy to AG, 10 Jul 69, in Letters Sent 1863–1889, RG 159.

42. Marcy to Chief of Ordnance, Quartermaster General, Commissary General of Subsistence, Chief of Engineers, and Surgeon General, 24 Aug 69, and Marcy to Adjutant General, 13 Dec 69, in Letters Sent 1863–1889, RG 159. Why the forms could not be mailed postage-free is not clear.

Marcy issued his first annual report in October 1869. He proved rather more prolix than Schriver. Sacket, he said, had transferred to the Division of the Atlantic in October 1868, while Schriver had continued to inspect the Military Academy since his relief from the Washington office in March. "He has also acted as staff officer under the direction of the Secretary of War." Hardie had been in the Division of the Missouri since 26 April, supervising its inspectorate and serving both the division commander and the Commanding General of the Army. Davis had left New Mexico for the Department of the Missouri on 23 December 1868 and had spent most of that year inspecting its posts "and collecting information in regard to Indian raids upon the borders of Kansas, the destitution of the settlers, and their necessities for government aid resulting therefrom."[43]

Marcy had absorbed enough of Schriver's outlook that he lost no time in selling the importance of inspection and calling for an increase in his department. He said in his report that division and department commanders' duties prevented them from personally visiting every post and unit in their far-flung commands. Consequently, a sufficient number of proficient inspectors was essential as a reliable source of information for the commanders.[44] All inspecting officers, said Marcy, were under the direction of the commanders to whose staffs they were attached. They received only technical instruction from their superiors in the inspection service. They made inspection according to the judgments of their commanders, and copies of all their reports "except such as are of a strictly confidential character" were transmitted by way of the commanders to the Inspector General's Office, with the action the commander had taken "for the rectification of such evils or irregularities as have been brought to their attention indorsed [sic] thereon." Marcy then examined the reports and extracted from them information that should be brought to the notice of War Department authorities. Thus, he said, the Secretary of War and the Commanding General were kept informed of the state of the Army at every post and station.[45]

In support of his implicit argument that more inspectors were required, Marcy said, "Under existing regulations and orders inspectors are the only officers authorized to inspect public property with a view to its condemnation, which duty alone involves a great amount of labor and time." Despite that burden, he said that inspection was working, because the reports showed "continued improvement in the discipline and efficiency of the troops, as well as the promotion of a more discriminating and careful regard for the economical

---

43. *ARIG 1869*, 175. Of the assistant inspectors general, Totten had transferred from the Department of the East to the Division of the South. Roger Jones continued in the Division of the Pacific, earning high praise for his thorough reports. Baird had moved from the Department of the Lakes to the Department of the Dakota 1 October 1868, while Ludington went from the Department of the South to the Division of the Pacific on 1 April 1869. Eight departments and three districts were served by acting inspectors—1 colonel, 5 lieutenant colonels, 7 majors, 15 captains, and 4 lieutenants.
44. Ibid., 176.
45. Ibid., 176–77.

application of public money and property.'' He quoted in demonstration the statement of a department commander that the labors of Roger Jones ''have resulted in great saving to the government.''[46] Marcy was devoted to platitudinous praise of the ever improving condition of the Army, but he could admit that the state of training was not all that it should be. He blamed that on circumstances, but pointed out improvements made by his inspectors. These successes launched Marcy on a sermon about the importance of inspection, which led him to the conclusion that Schriver had voiced before: that the number of regular inspectors was too small, especially given the many duties thrust upon them. It was nearly impossible to inspect every post once a year, whereas the posts should be visited twice a year as was done in European armies. The use of acting inspectors was of limited value, Marcy opined, because inspectors needed time to study the regulations, and to gain the educational benefit of long experience on the job. The judgment of detailed officers was also suspect. Because most of the Army's officers were young, detail of field officers was detrimental to the regiments, while junior officers were ineffective inspectors because ''neither they nor their opinions would, as a general rule, command much respect from the troops.'' Marcy's solution, predictably enough, was to enlarge the permanent inspectorate. In a call so bold that even Schriver might have gasped, Marcy asked for enough assistant inspectors general to cover every division and department—six additional appointments in all. Since Congress had recently cut the army by nearly a third, and seriously considered eliminating a separate inspectorate, Marcy's optimism was clearly unfounded.[47]

By late 1869 Marcy was as firmly in charge of the inspectorate as he was capable. He was clearly influenced by the legacy of Schriver, but he was not the same sort of born bureaucrat as his predecessor. Nevertheless, he carried on in Schriver's spirit, proving his organization's usefulness to others and seeing to its well-being. In November, he assumed the role of arbiter of questions of ''relative rank'' among officers when decisions of the Adjutant General were appealed to the Secretary of War, reviewing the facts and presenting his opinion to the Commanding General. In December, he reaffirmed the right of inspectors in the West to the exclusive use of spring wagons for their travel.[48] The differences between Schriver and Marcy were reflected in their separate ways of compiling the Subsistence Department sales list. Schriver had simply prepared the list, sent it to his colleagues for comment and ratification, and got the minor business over with easily. Marcy, however, found agreement hard to come by. When the Subsistence Department proposed a number of changes— mainly deletion—in December, Marcy and Schriver agreed readily enough, but Hardie dissented vigorously. Marcy asked Sacket to comment, telling him that

---

46. Ibid., 177.
47. Ibid., 177–78.
48. Marcy to Sherman, 22 Nov and 21 Dec 69, in Letters Sent 1863–1889, RG 159; GO No. 81, AGO, 20 Dec 69, in GORI&IG.

if he agreed with Hardie the inspectors general would be split (they were a committee, not a board with a chairman, in this responsibility). It required a number of flow charts and memoranda before a final sales list was worked out. The Commissary General of Subsistence had proposed 30 deletions and 6 additions, reducing the list from 84 items to 63. The inspectors general finally settled on a total of 77 items to be offered for sale to officers and men.[49] So Marcy's leadership of the inspectorate was marked by a style quite different from that of Schriver for, although he shared his predecessor's interest in a larger and more formal department, he was not as bureaucratically oriented and accordingly was not inclined to make the issue the center of his existence. Schriver focused on the administration of his organization; Marcy was inclined to look more toward the condition of the Army as reflected in the reports coming across his desk. But the nostalgic old soldier had been in uniform for nearly four decades, and he was not inclined to find fault, whatever the facts told him.

The Army was scattered among 255 military posts in 1869. Its living conditions were atrocious, and that coupled with overwork and the lure of economic opportunity in the West raised desertion to phenomenal rates. The scale of the desertion problem had been demonstrated in 1868 when a first sergeant led thirty men in a midnight mass escape from the 7th Cavalry. Yet Marcy, in his first annual report, observed only continuing improvement.[50] In fact, just before Marcy moved to Washington, the New York *Tribune* of 19 February 1869 discussed the Army's desertion problem. The paper printed a letter from a deserter who complained that his company commander had put him in the guardhouse when he refused to serve as a menial, leaving him without food until he had to yield. "At times," said the deserter, "I felt like dying—the situation was so humbling to me who went into the army for love of my country, only to have to black a brute's boots and look after him when a return blow was death. It was hard . . . . Self respect was destroyed, it was misery. So, Mr. Greeley, I deserted, and glad I did it, and only sorry I did not do it sooner and defy the consequences."[51] That Marcy was somehow different from Schriver was reflected in his response to reports like that. Reflecting on practices early in his career, Marcy could see no validity to the soldier's complaint. In fact, repeal of the law forbidding officers to use enlisted men as their personal servants became his great crusade. Nothing seemed as important to him as that—not even the signal development of his time in Washington, the final emergence of an Inspector General's Department.

---

49. Marcy to Hardie, 15 Dec and 16 Dec 69; and Marcy to Sacket, 28 Dec 69, with accompanying attachments and memorandums, in Letters Sent 1863–1889, RG 159.

50. Weigley, *History of the United States Army*, 267; Don Rickey, *Forty Miles a Day on Beans and Hay: The Enlisted Soldier Fighting the Indian Wars* (Norman: University of Oklahoma Press, 1963), 150. Rickey records the mass desertion and a number of other interesting anecdotes illustrating the problem.

51. Quoted in Foner, *Soldier Between Wars*, 62–63.

Part Three

A Tradition of an Inspection Department, 1881–1898

Marcy and the Advent of the Department (1870–1881)

When William Tecumseh Sherman accepted the post of Commanding General in 1869, he did so with the understanding that he would serve in fact as well as in name; that is, that the Commanding General supervise the entire United States Army, staff and line. His old friend and new Commander in Chief, President Ulysses S. Grant, directed Acting Secretary of War John M. Schofield (himself a general in the Regular Army) to issue an order to that effect. But Schofield left the job at about the time Sherman arrived in Washington, in March 1869. Schofield was replaced by Grant's old chief of staff, John A. Rawlins, who told the President that the law required the Secretary's direct supervision over the staff bureaus. So Grant rescinded Schofield's order, and the volatile Sherman's temper was assuaged only by the fact that Rawlins was too ill to be very active. All secretarial orders went through the Commanding General's Office.

The Commanding General's Ordeal

Rawlins was followed in September 1869 by William W. Belknap, an ambitious man determined to wield every power at his command. Sherman found himself ignored as the Secretary directed the bureaus, and was increasingly upset as Belknap began to interfere in the command of the uniformed army by granting leaves of absence, transfers, and discharges. Belknap soon began to badger Sherman openly, and allied himself with powers in Congress not all favorably inclined toward the Commanding General. A crisis was reached when Belknap removed a post trader and replaced him with one of his own supporters, a man unacceptable to the garrison. When Sherman reinstated the former trader, Belknap persuaded Congress to remove control of post traders from the Commanding General's hands, and reimposed his favorite. Sherman then removed himself to Saint Louis, much as Scott earlier had decamped for New York. He finally left on a tour of Europe, while Belknap remained completely in control of the War Department and of the Army. Later, to Sherman's gratification, evidence surfaced in 1876 that Secretary Belknap had been profiteering, specifically by selling post traderships for his own profit. The public and Congress were outraged, and Belknap resigned to avoid impeachment.

He was followed by a series of unassertive secretaries, the first of whom, Alphonso Taft, begged Sherman to return to Washington. The triumphant Commanding General did so, the orders announcing his return reserving to him complete authority (under the President) for the military control and discipline of the Army. Over the next few years, until his retirement in 1882, Sherman made the office of Commanding General an important one, although its relationship with the Secretary was not yet clarified.[1]

Marcy Tries To Assert His Authority

It was in that distressing context that Randolph B. Marcy served as senior inspector general, and tried to establish a place for his emerging Inspector General's Department. That place had to be found in the shifting balance of power between the Secretary of War and the Commanding General. Even after Sherman was restored to his position, the power of the Secretary of War remained formidable. Marcy's first opportunity to clarify his position appeared on 15 July 1870, when Congress (while cutting the Army's authorized force slightly, to 35,353 officers and men) told the War Department to develop a new set of general regulations and to submit them for congressional approval. The Secretary eventually appointed a board of officers to draw up a revised code, which went to Congress 17 February 1873 although it received no action.[2]

Before the board was assembled, the Secretary asked bureau heads on 26 August 1870 to recommend regulations to govern their operations. Marcy sent up proposed regulations for the Inspector General's Department five days later. The regulations fell under three main heads: The "Inspection Service," under the laws and the orders of the Secretary of War and the Commanding General, "provides for the inspection of the Army, and of all matters relating to its operations." That was a sweeping grant of purview. Under "Assignment of Inspectors," the regulations would place the senior inspector general "near the person of the General in Chief" and under his immediate orders. Inspectors general and assistant inspectors general were to be assigned to the commanders of armies, divisions, and departments, and to other duties as the Secretary and Commanding General desired. When there were not enough permanent inspectors available, the regulations would permit the detail of officers from the line, the larger departments being entitled to two inspectors. The regulations also provided for acting inspectors when corps, divisions, and brigades were formed in field armies. As for reporting, the text mostly repeated the circular of rules distributed during Schriver's reign. The "Duties of Inspectors" called for a complete inspection of every aspect of the Army and the way it functioned. The "Special Duties of Inspectors" extended to "every branch of military affairs,"

---

1. Lloyd Lewis, *Sherman, Fighting Prophet* (New York: Harcourt and Brace, 1958), 601–25; William T. Sherman, *Personal Memoirs of W. T. Sherman*, 2 vols. (New York; Webster, 1892; reprinted Bloomington: Indiana University Press, 1957), 2: 441–63; Basil H. Liddell Hart, *Sherman: Soldier, Realist, American* (New York: Praeger, 1958), 412–19.

2. *Revised Army Regulations*, H. Rpt. 85, 42d Cong., 3d sess. (1873).

the sphere of inquiry being limited only by specific orders. Finally, the bulk of the regulations were long instructions on the inspection of troops, administrative and disbursing departments, the Ordnance Department, the Medical Department, property presented for condemnation, and such.[3]

Marcy had, it appears, become influenced by Schriver's administrative legacy. But its effects on him were not altogether positive. From the standpoint of what an inspectorate should be—the eyes of the commander—his proposed regulations were a disavowal of a tradition reaching back to Steuben, which had been eroded in recent decades. Marcy's regulations would have denied to Sherman something that Macomb had enjoyed: an inspectorate loyal only to himself, a tool with which he could assert his authority as Commanding General. Marcy wanted to be close to the Secretary also. It was not the good of the Army nor the integrity of its command that came first in Marcy's proposal; his regulations were an assertion of organizational integrity and independence which, with control theoretically divided between the Secretary and the Commanding General, gave the inspectorate considerable self-identity, and influence. Everything would be within the inspectorate's reach, and virtually no one but the Secretary could restrain its actions.

Despite high hopes, Marcy's proposal came to nothing, so he turned his attention to exerting greater control over his organization. That was not easy. Schriver contined as a free agent serving the Secretary of War independently, while also inspecting West Point. Sacket spent the last part of 1869 on "special duty in the State Department," although otherwise he inspected posts and department headquarters in the Division of the Atlantic. Hardie left Marcy's control for an extended period in September 1870, when the Secretary dispatched him to examine claims arising out of Indian wars in Montana. The assistant inspectors general continued in their customary routines, supplemented by eighteen line officers detailed to inspection. But it was among the assistants that the inspectorate suffered its first casualty due to the law reducing the force by attrition remaining in effect.[4] James Totten, inspector in the Division of the South, resigned 22 July 1870.[5] Because the law did not allow this position to be filled, Marcy could do nothing about Totten's departure so he turned his attention to bringing the other inspectors into line.

When it came to asserting his own primacy in the inspectorate, Marcy began to sound increasingly like Schriver. He wanted inspectors to know that he was in charge, and was not beyond sarcasm to make his point. When he learned that James H. Carleton, acting assistant inspector general for the Department of Texas, was writing "Notes for Inspecting Officers" to guide subordinate inspectors, Marcy told him, "The greater part of the information embraced

---

3. "Regulations for the Government of the Inspector General's Department. Submitted to the Secretary of War [by Marcy] 31 Aug 70," in Letters Sent 1863–1889, RG 159.

4. *ARIG 1870*, H. Ex. Doc. 1, 41st Cong., 3d sess., vol. 1, pt 2: 91–92. Ludington transferred from the Division of the Pacific to the Department of the Columbia late in 1869.

5. Marcy to Fry, 26 Jan 70, Marcy to Totten, 18 Feb 70, in Letters Sent 1863–1889, RG 159; *ARIG 1870*, 92; Heitman, *Historical Register*, 1: 966. See Appendix B.

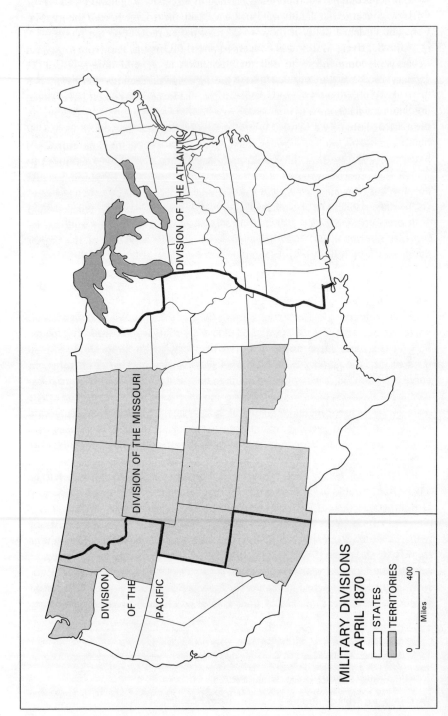

MILITARY DIVISIONS
APRIL 1870

DIVISION OF THE ATLANTIC

DIVISION OF THE MISSOURI

DIVISION OF THE PACIFIC

STATES

TERRITORIES

0   400
    Miles

MAP 2

in your notes outside the report is contained in the Army Regulations, and if the Officers concerned in the inspections do not take the trouble to read the Regulations and Orders I doubt if they would read the extracts upon the report."[6]

Like Schriver, Marcy was concerned about follow-up. He wrote to several department commanders to call their attention to general orders issued 21 January 1869 "and to say that unless the previous corrections that have been applied by Subordinates through whose offices the Inspection reports have passed are endorsed thereon, it is impossible to determine what action is necessary on the part of authorities here." When inspection reports showed an excessive number of horses, mules, vehicles, and civilian employees in the Quartermaster's Department at two posts in the Department of the Platte, Marcy refused to accept the reports from the departmental acting assistant inspector general because this inspector had not considered whether the numbers were necessary. "This matter should have been investigated and reported upon by you provided your orders contemplated a general inspection of those Posts," he said, knowing that the orders did just that, "in order that the attention of the proper authorities here might be called to the facts."[7]

The Inspectorate Declines

Even as Marcy tried to extend the influence of his inspectorate, and his own control over it, the War Department's tight budget interrupted him. The Secretary placed some curbs on the inspection service on 28 September 1870 by limiting the funds available for inspection tours and the number of officers who could travel.[8] That order appeared while Marcy was out of town, Marcy having persuaded the Secretary on 31 August to dispatch him on an inspection of the posts in the Department of the Lakes. The bulk of his inspection report on this particular trip was an ordinary account of each post in turn. His report was laced also with allusions to his past, especially when he visited posts such as Forts Mackinac and Gratiot where he had once lived.[9]

Very few important events punctuated the history of the inspectorate during 1871. Rather, a gradual fading of the influence of the Inspector General's Department continued, thanks to Marcy's preoccupation with other matters. Schriver remained the Secretary's assistant, while Hardie (nominally assigned to the Division of the Missouri) continued working on war claims arising out of the Montana Indian War of 1867, and as a "commissioner of Congress," investigating various wartime claims in Kansas and assessing the value of the Army's property at Fort Leavenworth. Assistant inspector general Davis was absent on leave the first half of the year, after which he was occupied with

6. Marcy to Carleton, 12 Jul 70, in Letters Sent 1863–1889, RG 159.

7. Marcy to Bvt. Maj. Gen. J. J. Reynolds and to Maj. Gen. John M. Schofield, both 20 Jun 70, and to Maj. N. B. Sweitzer, 31 Aug 70, in Letters Sent 1863–1889, RG 159.

8. GO No. 113, AGO, 28 Sep 70, in GORI&IG.

9. Marcy's report is Marcy to Adjutant General E. D. Townsend, 8 Oct 70, in Letters Sent 1863–1889, RG 159.

"special duty in New Mexico, and on other important duties under the orders of the department commander." Absalom Baird filled in behind Totten in the Division of the South, while Ludington's failure to see his posts in the Department of the Columbia more than once a year was attributed to transportation difficulties and the distances involved.[10]

The Army's inspectorate, under Marcy's inattentive leadership, was not in high repute. It could be, and was, represented as a disconnected lot of place-fillers headed by a wandering storyteller. "Cui Bono" ("for whose benefit?" or "to what purpose?") wrote to the editor of the *Army and Navy Journal* in September 1871 to castigate "that parasite of the Army called the Inspector General's Department." As far as that correspondent was concerned, the Inspector General's Department merely generated tons of useless, excessively detailed and analyzed reports.[11] Such sentiments were ominous at a time when Congress remained dissatisfied with the size and organization of the Army. A bill to reorganize the army staff appeared in the Senate and was referred to the Committee on Military Affairs on 11 December. The legislation proposed to the Senate actually would have permitted an increase in the number of inspectors general over the minimum they were to attain by attrition. But support for the inspectorate was on the wane, symbolized significantly early in 1872 when the *Army and Navy Journal* announced itself in favor of a consolidation of the offices of Adjutant General and Inspector General.[12]

Marcy apparently began to appreciate the vulnerability of his organization, and attempted a recovery. At the end of January he wrote the Secretary of War an impassioned argument for an independent inspectorate. Independence, said Marcy, was essential to the reliability of inspection. Inspectors should not be so placed that they were overly influenced by their commanders. Instead, they should be enabled to report freely, even if their findings were unfavorable to a department or its commanding officer. He claimed in support of his case that department and division commanders were suppressing confidential reports that the Secretary should see.[13] Marcy asked Belknap to revise the regulations to place the four inspectors general directly under the Secretary and the Commanding General, assigning the four assistant inspectors general to divisions and major departments. That was a bold grab for independent authority, and a clear attempt to establish a true department by connecting it to the Secretary of War. As Marcy pushed for an independent inspectorate, his campaign was interrupted by an outbreak of selfishness within his own organization. Nelson Davis had been one of the assistant inspectors general, ranking as major, appointed in November 1861; he became a lieutenant colonel in 1867. He developed an ingenious argument that he had been unfairly deprived of promotion to full

---

10. *ARIG 1871*, H. Ex. Doc. 1, 42d Cong., 2d sess., vol. 1, pt.2: 109–10.
11. *Army and Navy Journal*, 9 (2 September 1871): 39; *Congressional Globe*, 42d Cong., 2d sess. (11 December 1871): 56.
12. *Army and Navy Journal*, 9 (10 February 1872): 418.
13. Marcy to Secy of War, 30 Jan 72, in Letters Sent 1863–1889, RG 159.

colonel and an inspector general in 1864. He took his case to Congress in March 1872.[14]

Congress was, by 1872, in the middle of the Reconstruction period, accustomed to dealing directly in matters of army management. The lawmakers decided on 8 June that Davis had been entitled to promotion under legislation enacted in 1851 (which required promotion by seniority within corps) and by the Army's own regulations. Congress authorized the President to promote him to colonel and inspector general so as to precede Hardie, whom the legislation protected from loss of rank or pay. That raised the number of inspectors general to five, so the law also forbade any further promotions to that grade until the number reverted to four.[15] This was tantamount to a legislative finding that the Inspector General's Department was a duly constituted corps or bureau of the Army—at least, that promotion of its officers should be governed as if it were. That was a novel interpretation, one that not even the inspectors general had hitherto believed valid.

An Independent Inspectorate

Marcy, meanwhile, resumed his campaign for independence, and on 5 October 1872, he got it. To ensure that the War Department was kept informed of the personnel and materiel condition of the Army, said a general order, the inspectors general were to be assigned with one in Washington, in charge of the Inspection Office in the War Department, and the others assigned to stations after some brief training at the Headquarters of the Army. These officers were to receive instructions directly from, and report directly to, the Secretary of War and the General of the Army.[16] The senior inspectorate was now the personal agency of the Secretary of War, the current source of power. The mention of the Commanding General was a meaningless gesture, especially when Sherman then was based in Saint Louis. As surely as Conway would have been an agent for the Board of War, Marcy had become much the same for Belknap. It appeared that it was just a matter of time before there was an Inspector General's Department as permanent, prestigious, and independent as that of the Quartermaster General. Inspection seemed destined to part irrevocably from command.

The order attaching the inspectors general to the War Department clarified Marcy's position as senior inspector general. He soon began to assert himself. Early in November, he assigned Schriver, Sacket, and Hardie to thorough tours of certain geographical departments. He had asked the War Department bureaus what they would like to have inspected, and they generally emphasized finan-

---

14. The testimony was covered with great relish by *Army and Navy Journal*, 9 (30 March 1872): 524.

15. *An Act to authorize an appointment in the Inspector-General's Department, Statutes at Large* 17, sec. 1, 338 (1872): Thian, *Legislative History*, 113; Heitman, *Historical Register*, 1: 359.

16. GO No. 87, AGO, 5 Oct 72, in GORI&IG.

cial accounts. The inspectors general were advised to present themselves to the department commanders, to make any inspections those officers might request, and to report their findings to the commanders, with a copy to the Inspector General at Washington. The inspectors general, in other words, were to assist the department commanders, while serving the Washington office.[17]

Marcy had been involved also in the preparation of the regulations for uniforms that took effect in 1872, and it was perhaps through his influence that staff officers, including the Inspectors General, acquired a new distinction: "Whenever the full dress coat is worn by officers on duty the prescribed epaullettes or shoulder knots will be attached. Letters to be embroidered on shoulder knots in old English: *A.D.* Adjutant General's Department, *I.D.* Inspector General's Department."[18] This new insignia symbolized the growing independence of the inspectorate, while Marcy also began to restore his influence in the War Department. Beginning late in 1872 and on into the next year, the number of letters he addressed directly to the Secretary of War, instead of to the Adjutant General, increased, most of them offering formal opinions, advice, or information as requested.[19] Marcy was by then thoroughly independent of the command structure. He all but ignored the division commanders, merely informing them when his officers would enter their territories. Only after he had reported inspection findings to the Secretary of War and dispatched the inspectors general to their next assignments did Marcy send the Commanding General an extract of their reports. It was rarely substantive, merely stating how successful his inspectors were.[20] At the peak of his independence from the Commander and his connection to the Secretary early in 1873, Marcy received only one minor reversal: On 17 January the Secretary of War affirmed that the battalion, post, and depot at Willetts Point, New York, was under the orders of the Chief of Engineers, and not under those of any department or division commanders. Inspectors acting under the orders of department or division commanders were not to inspect any engineer establishments. Once again the engineers were protected from independent review.[21]

Marcy fared better with the House Committee on Military Affairs, which in 1869 had proposed a consolidation of the Adjutant General's and Inspector General's Offices. Just four years later, in February 1873, the panel reversed itself. The committee found no need for substantial changes in staff organization, despite generally favorable opinion in the army line for the establishment of a single supply department combining the Quartermaster's, Pay, and Subsistence

---

17. Marcy, identical letters to Schriver, Sacket, and Hardie, 5 Nov 72, in Letters Sent 1863–1889, RG 159.

18. Uniform and Dress of the Army of the United States, 1872, in *Uniform of the Army of the United States.*

19. See for instance Marcy to the several inspectors general, assigning them to stations, 20 Feb 73, Marcy to Secy of War, and attachments, 13 Mar 73, and Marcy to Schriver, Sacket, and Hardie, 18 Mar 73, in Letters Sent 1863–1889, RG 159.

20. Marcy to Generals Schofield and Pope, 18 Mar 73, and Marcy to Sherman, n.d. 1873, in Letters Sent 1863–1889, RG 159.

21. GO No. 9, AGO, 17 Jan 73, in GORI&IG.

Departments. The members did, however, propose a system of rotating details between line and staff that would appear again early in the twentieth century, and the establishment of bureaus for infantry, artillery, and cavalry. In respect to the Adjutant General and the Inspector General, the committee acknowledged the differences between the duties of the Adjutant General that tied him to a post and those of the Inspector General that required he be free to travel anywhere. The broader scope of the inspector's duties and the need for a more extensive knowledge of Army functions was noted also. "An excellent adjutant might be a poor inspector, while an excellent inspector could not fail to be a good adjutant." The committee further concluded that inspectors had to remain free from association with any other department and in an agency of their own to provide the best service.[22] In other words, a separate and independent inspectorate was judged essential to assuring worthwhile inspection. The opinions of officers responding to a questionnaire circulated by the House committee late in 1872 generally opposed merging the duties of the Adjutant General with those of the Inspector General. Most of the officers pointed out that the duties of the two positions were "dissimilar," and that adjutants had to remain in headquarters while inspectors must be absent most of the time. Although most of the officers opposed merging the duties of the Inspector General with those of the Adjutant General, the Inspector General's Department did not win a round of applause from the Army's leaders.[23] Most of them could probably have gotten along happily without an Inspector General, but they were loath to see one part of the organization nullified because it could just as easily be their own.

Reducing the Army and the Inspectorate

Things did not remain peaceful for the Army on Capitol Hill. On 16 January 1874, Senator John Logan, a bitter personal enemy of General Sherman, introduced Senate Bill 321 affecting aspects of the strength and organization of the Army.[24] The bill had much to say about the Army's staff organization. For the Inspector General's Department it provided one colonel, two lieutenant colonels, and two majors. It allowed the Secretary of War to detail no more than four line officers as assistant inspectors general, "and no new appointment shall be made in the Inspector-General's Department until the number of inspectors-general is reduced to five." Logan explained that the bill merely fixed the future size of the departments, would not cause the discharge of any incumbent, and would increase no department except for an additional position in the Commissary Department. The departments would all be reduced by not filling vacancies as they occurred. The Senate agreed, passing "A Bill Reorganizing the Staff Corps of the Army on 13 June."[25] The House of Representatives

---

22. *Army Staff Organization*, H. Rpt. 74, 42d Cong., 3d sess. (1873). The questionnaire responses discussed immediately below are presented in the same document.
23. Ibid.
24. *Congressional Record*, 43d Cong., 1st sess. (16 January 1874): 695; (28 April 1874): 3423; and (13 June 1874): 4941.
25. Ibid. (13 June 1874): 4941–42.

approved the bill ten days later.[26] Approved by the President the same day, the legislation reduced the inspectorate to five officers as Logan had wanted, with the reduction achieved by attrition. As far as the inspectorate was concerned, the law seemed finally to have settled on a ceiling of five officers, implying but not stating specifically that they were all to be entitled inspector general. The inspectorate's temporary force also was reduced, the law saying that a maximum of four line officers could be detailed "to act as inspectors-general."[27]

The officers of the Inspector General's Department took the reduction as a cruel, ungentlemanly blow. Five years later, the normally serene Roger Jones gave the Clerk of the House of Representatives a bitter account of how, in his opinion, the bill was promoted by members of other departments for their own purposes while most inspectors were away from Washington and could not defend their interests.[28] The severe reduction in Marcy's department indicated that his independence and increasing ties to the Secretary had earned him no friends in the Army and little influence in Congress.

Marcy Loses Control

Despite the reduction in strength, 1874 was not a completely bad year for the Inspector General's Department. Congress that year adopted the Revised Statutes, a recompilation of all the nation's laws. In specifying the Army, the revised legislation treated the Inspector General's Department as if it were a reality. The War Department's official historian deduced that the department's establishment dated from that event. Actually, however, Congress never deliberately created such an organization; rather it came into being through custom and practice. But by the time the second edition of the Revised Statutes appeared in 1878, the Inspector General's Department was legislatively entrenched.[29] Whatever the implication of the Revised Statutes, the Inspector General's Department was little more than a name. It lacked a clearly assigned principal charged with its management and its policy. When Marcy functioned as a bureau chief, it was largely as a conduit for the Secretary's orders. The number of individual assignments of inspectors general, mostly for special investigations, increased and this increase continued into 1875. Sacket went off to audit books at two arsenals, while Davis made miscellaneous investigations in Texas, Hardie did the same in New Mexico and Arizona, and Schriver in the Department of the

---

26. Ibid. (23 June 1874): 5442–43.
27. *An Act reorganizing the several staff corps in the Army, Statutes at Large* 183, sec. 1, 6, 244 (1874); Thian, *Legislative History*, 113–14. The permanent complement under the law was 1 colonel, 2 lieutenant colonels, and 2 majors.
28. Jones to Robert J. Stevens, 21 Jan 79, in Letters Sent 1863–1889, RG 159.
29. Ingersoll, *History of the War Department*, 145–46; Rev. Stat. 2d ed., sec. 1094; Thian, *Legislative History*, 114. The revised legislation mostly treated inspectors general as individuals or as a group, but did include the Inspector General's Department as among the things that composed the Army.

Missouri. The coordinated visits across departments that Marcy had previously organized had come to an end.[30]

In his wish to establish a formal Inspector General's Department with himself as its head, Marcy shared Schriver's inclinations. But he had lacked the latter's bureaucratic skills. Marcy's continual distraction by official and personal interests repeatedly interrupted his control of the organization, and made him ineffective when the organization was threatened by others. Even his attempt to gain status by attaining independence for inspectors general backfired. Belknap soon began to regard them more as a group of individual agents rather than as a consolidated unit, and wrested control of them from Marcy. Worse, the attainment of "independence" under the Secretary soon erased the credit of Marcy's organization in the Army. Belknap had departed in disgrace by early 1876, and Sherman returned in triumph.

Sherman agreed to reestablish himself in Washington only on his own terms. He could not take control of the supply departments, but he did manage to get the line Army into his uncontested hands. On 6 April 1876, orders announcing that the headquarters of the Army was reestablished at Washington said that all orders from the President through the Secretary of War would be promulgated to the Army by the Commanding General. The departments of the Adjutant General and the Inspector General would thereafter "report to [the Commanding General] and be under his control in all matters relating thereto." Beginning with that order, the Adjutant General no longer signed the Army's instruction "By order of the Secretary of War." Now it was "By command of General Sherman."[31] Sherman also imposed his views by reassigning the inspectors general on 29 May 1876, calling the attention of division and department commanders to the general orders governing inspections issued in 1869. Reports of inspections thereafter were to be forwarded via the Adjutant General to the Inspector General's office at Army headquarters. Inspectors were told to note in their reports the remedies that commanders had instituted for deficiencies they identified, while other high-ranking inspectors were to endorse their own actions on each report. Things were as they had been before Marcy had won his short-lived independence. The order left Marcy in charge of the Washington office: Hardie was retrieved from special investigations and claims work to serve as his assistant; Schriver terminated special investigations of disbursements and recruiting depots, and went to the Department of the Pacific; Davis also ceased the Secretary's work and went to the Division of the Atlantic; and Sacket similarly went to the Division of the Missouri. Of the assistant inspectors general, Jones had already left the Division of the Pacific for the Division

---

30. For examples, see Inspector General USA (no signature) to Sacket, 26 Feb; to Davis, 4 Mar; to Hardie, 4 Mar; and to Schriver, n.d. Apr and 12 Apr, all in 1875, in Letters Sent 1863–1889, RG 159.

31. GO No. 28, AGO, 6 Apr 76, in GORI&IG; *ARIG 1876*, H. Ex. Doc. 1, 44th Cong., 2d sess., vol. 1, pt. 2 : 74; Thomas H. S. Hamersly, *Complete Army Register for 100 Years (1779–1879)* (Washington: Hamersly, 1881), pt. 2, 271. Beginning in 1876 Marcy's annual reports were no longer addressed to the Secretary of War.

of the Atlantic in February, and was unaffected. The same was true of Baird in the Division of the Missouri, while the order moved Ludington from the Department of the Platte to the Division of the Pacific. Released by the Secretary, the inspectors general once again worked for the Commanding General and his subordinate division and department commanders.[32]

The Army and its inspectorate suffered further blows in 1876. Congress, which had been whittling away at the military force throughout the 1870s, reduced the authorized force to 27,472 officers and men on 26 June, with a ceiling on enlisted men of 25,000. Reconstruction was drawing to an end, and Congress desired to keep the U.S. Army at its minimum size. Budgets dropped accordingly. Congress set new rules for reimbursement of travel expenses in July, substituting actual costs for mileage. For the hard-traveling inspectors, that was particularly distressing.[33] Marcy was annoyed about what had happened to his inspectorate in the recent past. Complaining that the 1874 legislation reduced his department to five officers by attrition, leaving only one of them a colonel, he observed that no inspectors general since the War of 1812 had been ranked less than colonel. He also asserted that the work could not be done properly by officers of inferior rank. "Indeed," he said, "it cannot be expected that officers of experience and high rank will cheerfully submit to the criticisms of inspectors who are much junior to themselves." The present complement, he said, was barely sufficient and should be raised to pre-1874 levels. If Congress would not go along with that, Marcy asked at least that all five inspectors be graded colonels, while line officers detailed as departmental inspectors be selected from among the Army's majors.[34]

Denied the outward signs of a large staff and spacious offices that connoted bureaucratic status, Marcy was forced to watch his inspectorate erode: When Hardie died on 14 December 1876, the 1874 legislation prevented his being replaced.[35] Marcy even had to prepare a special testimonial to help Mrs. Hardie gain her widow's pension. In early January, the Senate discussed clarifying a conflict in legislation governing the number of inspectors general and, after a long, rather pointless discussion, it voted to amend the law to permit no promotions until the Inspector General's Department consisted of only four officers.[36] In such a climate the Army, and its inspectorate, drifted. Marcy made some efforts to restore his former independence, but that required a direct connection to the Secretary of War. After Belknap's resignation in March 1876, there was no Secretary of comparable energy and influence. In fact, when George W. McCrary took office in March 1877, he was Belknap's third successor in a year.[37]

---

32. GO No. 45, AGO, 29 May 76, in GORI&IG; *ARIG 1876*, 73–74.
33. Weigley, *History of the United States Army*, 267; Heitman, *Historical Register*, 612–13; GO No. 97, AGO, 8 Sep 76, in GORI&IG.
34. *ARIG 1876*, 77–78.
35. Ibid., 78; Marcy to Secy of War, 4 Jun 77, in Letters Sent 1863–1889, RG 159.
36. Heitman, *Historical Register*, 1: 500; Marcy to Mrs. J. A. Hardie, 1 Jan 77, in Letters Sent 1863–1889, RG 159; *Congressional Record*, 44th Cong., 2d sess. (10 January 1877): 530–31.
37. Weigley, *History of the United States Army*, 287, 557.

Shortly after McCrary arrived at the War Department, Marcy delivered to him a short statement on the size, role, and function of the Inspector General's Department, along with the current assignments of its officers. He uttered a strong plea for his lost independence. Bureau heads, he told McCrary, should be able to communicate with the Secretary or with post commanders in their areas of official interest without going through the Adjutant General's Office, unless some action by the Commanding General was required. That, Marcy said, would avoid "necessary circumlocution."[38] To achieve efficient staff departments, Marcy believed that ultimate independence, including the authority to give orders to their own officers, was required. Sherman's ascendance over the uniformed Army prevailed despite Marcy's desires. In fact, it stabilized the Inspector General's Department. No changes of station and few extraordinary assignments were made during 1877. Marcy's greatest break from the routine was to serve as a pallbearer for the funeral and reburial of George A. Custer, loser of the battle of the Little Bighorn in June 1876.[39]

The Inspector General's Department Emerges

One of the principal bureaucratic and political weaknesses of the Inspector General's Department was that its chief was not specifically designated by law. Marcy was the senior inspector general by date of his commission, and its presumed leader by virtue of assignment to the Washington office. But he was not formally the head of a department, and his position could not be equated with that of the Quartermaster General or the Adjutant General, who outranked their subordinates and represented their departments by virtue of something more than date of commission. The War Department and the Commanding General alike were accustomed to thinking of the inspectors general as many independently functioning colonels.

Marcy, frustrated in trying to establish his organization as a semiautonomous department under the Secretary of War, in 1877 decided to try a different approach. After once again complaining about the relatively few and low-ranking inspectors, he concluded his annual report with the heartfelt lament that his duties were equal to that of the other department chiefs, all of whom were brigadier generals. He felt that the senior inspector should also be in that grade to symbolize his department's importance.[40] Marcy's motives in raising the

---

38. Marcy, "Memorandum submitted by Inspector General Marcy for the Information of the Honorable The Secretary of War," 17 Mar 77, and Marcy to Secy of War, 17 Apr 77, in Letters Sent 1863–1889, RG 159.

39. *ARIG 1877*, H. Ex. Doc. 1, 45th Cong., 2d sess., vol. 1, pt. 2: 51–52; Telg, Marcy to Mrs. E. B. Custer, 1 Oct 77, and Marcy, draft of remarks upon proposed rules and regulations for Ordnance Department submitted to the Secy of War by Inspector General Marcy, 11 Aug 77, in Letters Sent 1863-1889, RG 159.

40. *ARIG 1877*, 54. Actually, Marcy was not the only bureau chief not a brigadier general. The Chief Signal Officer was regarded as the head of the Signal Service—a quasibureau at that point, but formally established, as the Inspector General's Department was not—but he was only a colonel. Heitman, *Historical Register*, 1: 44, and 2: 612.

issue of his rank probably were twofold. On the one hand, he had his own interests at stake; on the other, he knew that the Inspector General's Department would never be fully recognized until its leader could deal with the other bureau chiefs on equal terms. Colonels simply did not prevail over generals as interbureau rivalries grew increasingly serious. Marcy's promotion became the most important business of the Inspector General's Department for over a year; otherwise no important changes occurred in the organization.[41] On 13 March, asking for a "simple act of justice," he sent the Secretary a resume of his career, testimonials from his former superiors, and a letter of support from Sherman, who portrayed the Inspector General as the alter ego of the Commanding General. Secretary McCrary sent the whole package to Congress the same day, along with his own statement of support for Marcy's position.[42]

The Senate Committee on Military Affairs, after hearing Marcy's personal appeal, observed on 2 April that the Inspector General's Department was the only department in the Army with a chief ranked lower than brigadier general. The committee members saw no reason for such a discrimination to exist, and recommended that Marcy get his promotion.[43] Congressional solicitude for Marcy's status was remarkable. It came from a body that recently had almost subsumed Marcy's operations into those of the Adjutant General, and had threatened to reduce the inspectorate to a four-man force headed by a solitary colonel. When the Senate considered Marcy's promotion on 25 April, a member of the Military Affairs Committee avowed that, while Marcy's record should be acknowledged, the real purpose of the measure was to put the head of the Inspector General's Department on a par with other staff chiefs. He observed in response to questions that the promotion would entail no increase of duties; it would just raise Marcy's pay. The committee had already amended a bill authorizing such a promotion in the inspectorate to prevent an increase of rank of any subordinate officer in the act of 23 June 1874, he said, and the panel passed the measure unanimously. Satisfied with that, the whole Senate agreed to the amendment and passed the bill.[44]

On 12 December 1878 Congress declared that the rank of the senior inspector general of the United States Army would be brigadier general. The Adjutant General announced the news to the Army on 27 December, by publishing the act in general orders.[45] If it could be said that there was a year in which the Inspector General's Department really came into being as a formal organization,

---

41. There were again no changes of assignment of the permanent officers during 1878, and most inspection was performed by the usual rotation of officers detailed from the line—seven that year, for the first time all of field grade ARIG 1878 H. Ex. Doc. 1, 45th Cong., 3d sess., vol. 1, pt. 2: 30–31.

42. Marcy to Secy of War, 13 Mar 78, Sherman, "opinion," 13 Mar 78, and McCrary to George E Spencer, chairman, Senate Committee on Military Affairs, 13 Mar 78, all in Letters Sent 1863–1889, RG 159.

43. *Report* (to accompany bill S. 824), S. Rpt. 221, 45th Cong., 2d sess. (1878).

44. *Congressional Record*, 45th Cong., 2d sess. (25 April 1878): 2842.

45. An Act Establishing the Rank of the Senior Inspector-General, approved 12 December 1878, 20 Stat. 257; Thian, *Legislative History*, 114; GO No. 92, AGO, 27 Dec 78, in GORI&IG.

that year was most likely 1878. The discussion in the Senate of Marcy's promotion showed that the whole justification rested on Marcy's position as the head of a department. The legislation raising him treated him only as the senior among inspectors general. However, it also limited the rank of other officers of the Inspector General's Department.

While it debated Marcy's betterment, Congress also issued the second edition of the Revised Statutes of the United States. Section 1094 declared as it had in 1874 that "An Inspector-General's Department" was a component of the Army. But the rest of the nation's body of law addressed inspectors general only as so many individuals, not as part of an organization. Congress had never formally created it, but the Inspector General's Department nevertheless existed, with all the trappings of the War Department's other staff bureaucracies, including a bureau chief who shared a brigadier's stars with people like the Commissary General of Subsistence.[46] Even before his promotion, Marcy behaved as a bureau chief should. When he saw the draft of the War Department appropriations request for fiscal year 1879, he protested that the measure would reduce the pay of his messenger by $120.00 per year. The man was a nineteen-year army veteran, he said, who had worked in the office since 1863, and was chiefly responsible for the burden of packing and mailing the large volume of blank inspection forms and other important products of the organization. Marcy also tried, and failed, to get a third office, but instead he had to move out of the two he already had.[47]

Another Reorganization Scare

Marcy's elevation went forward during a period when Congress once again grappled with the further reduction and possible reorganization of the Army. Congressman Henry B. Banning, a Civil War hero, introduced a bill late in 1877 to reduce the Army to 20,000 enlisted men by July 1878, cutting the number of cavalry regiments to six, artillery to four, and infantry to fifteen. The size of mounted regiments would be increased at the expense of the infantry and the artillery. Among the bill's provisions, the Inspector General's Department would be reduced to one Inspector General with the rank of colonel and two assistant inspectors general ranked lieutenant colonel. Inspection of the Army would generally be performed by line officers on detail, not to exceed one to a department. The House Committee on Military Affairs once again surveyed opinion among army officers to find answers to its questions. Regarding the inspectorate, Maj. Gen. Winfield Scott Hancock responded by sending a copy of a letter he had written to an earlier request in 1876, which among other things called for a substantial inspectorate of experienced and high-ranking officers. Marcy also presented his views. He said that it was a mistake to believe that only cavalry could chase Indians, and that having mounted men

---

46. Revised Statutes, 2d ed., secs. 1094, 1131, 1194, 1348; Thian, *Legislative History*, 114.
47. Marcy to Secy of War, 17 Apr and 5 Dec 78, in Letters Sent 1868–1889, RG 159.

compose over half the Army would be a serious mistake. Marcy wanted to preserve as well the regimental organization of the artillery, mostly because it served as infantry on the frontier. Urging the importance of strong staff organizations as preparation for war, he advised against any changes in the present staff organization, especially consolidations.

Marcy continued with a renewed plea for his own independence. Control of staff departments, he said, should rest with the Secretary of War administratively, and with the Commanding General militarily, but commanders of field armies and geographical divisions and departments should have absolute control over their own staffs. The only changes Marcy recommended in the staff departments were, predictably, more inspectors general for his own, all of them ranked at least as colonels. Finally, he said that getting rid of laundresses in the Army and reducing the retired list would save $100,000 per year.[48] Whatever Marcy thought, Congress was determined to overhaul the Army, or at least the former Civil War generals among its members were so determined. A joint committee of members of the House and Senate assembled in June 1878 to hold hearings and consider the many issues. The committee members were ready with a legislative bill by November. The measure began by proposing to reduce the number of generals in the Army from eleven to six, including the elimination of the offices of general and lieutenant general when the incumbents (Sherman and Sheridan) retired.

The proposed legislation would consolidate the Inspector General's Department and the Adjutant General's Department into a new "general staff" organization, reducing the total number of officers there by six. All other staff departments, except for the Corps of Engineers, also would be drastically reduced. The measure would eliminate two regiments of cavalry and seven of infantry, and would give each regiment four battalions, of which only three would be organized (in the infantry and artillery, only two manned) in peacetime. The enlisted force would remain limited to 25,000 men, while the retired list would be permitted an unrestricted increase. There were many other provisions in the awesomely comprehensive bill—the Ordnance Department, for instance, would be prohibited from manufacturing its own supplies, post traders would be abolished, generals would be required to retire at age sixty-five, others at age sixty-two, and so on. All members of the joint committee were Civil War veterans, who felt assured that they knew what was best.[49]

Inspector General Marcy, newly commissioned as a brigadier general, saw his organization threatened on every side in 1879. The joint committee was not the only part of the Congress that tried to reduce the military force. The House of Representatives devised its own bill, which among other things would retain an Inspector General's Department, but would reduce it to one colonel, one

---

48. *Reorganization of the Army*, H. Misc. Doc. 56, 45th Cong., 2d sess. (1878); Marcy to the Hon. Levi Maish, Edward S. Bragg, Henry White, Subcommittee on Military Affairs, House of Representatives, 1 Jan 78, delivered to clerk of Military Committee, 8 Jan 78, by messenger, in Letters Sent 1863–1889, RG 159.

49. *Reorganization of the Army*, H. Rpt. 3, 45th Cong., 3d sess. (1878).

lieutenant colonel, and two majors. The Committee on Appropriations asked Roger Jones to comment on the measure's possible effects on military efficiency. He responded with Marcy's by-now customary long discourse on the Inspector General's Department, its history, its size, and its importance, emphasizing that all inspectors be awarded colonelcies. The department had already been cut too far in 1874, he said, attributing the deed to the "machinations of other Staff offices."[50] The move for reorganization declined as quickly as it arose. By 1879, the army was arrayed in eight departments, eleven districts, and three divisions, and it remained that way. The Secretary of War vouched for the importance of inspection in August by requiring that every post, station, and command be inspected at least once a year by division and department inspectors. In addition, post, station, and other permanent commanders were to make similar inspections annually in early September, and to forward their reports to the Inspector General's Office in Washington. The order included a blank form to be used in commanders' inspection reports. That year division and department inspectors were also told to report occasionally on the number and duties of the army's civilian employees, especially when the number appeared excessive. The complement of the Inspector General's Department, meanwhile, declined further when Ludington retired on 27 March.[51]

Marcy's Last Year

Marcy's last year as Inspector General was 1880. Evidently satisfied with his promotion, he ceased trying to reassert his independence from Sherman and settled into a comfortable routine. His department continued as it had been for some time. Marcy remained in Washington, although he made several inspections of disbursing accounts at the Secretary's behest. Schriver was at the Division of the Pacific; Davis was at the Division of the Atlantic. Of the assistant inspectors general, Jones, Marcy's assistant in Washington, performed important services under the orders of the Secretary of War. Baird was in the Division of the Missouri. Two lieutenant colonels, four majors, and one captain performed most inspections to which officers had to be detailed. With "very few exceptions," said Marcy, all garrisoned posts were inspected that year. He continued to maintain that the force of permanent inspectors was too small and issued one more call for more inspectors at higher ranks. He also requested authority to assign clerks for inspectors at department or division headquarters.[52]

Of all the inspectors general, Sacket had the most interesting year in 1880. He was relieved from his duty in the Division of the Missouri on 1 July and assigned as a member of a board of officers in Washington to examine and

---

50. Jones to Robert J. Stevens, clerk, House Committee on Appropriations, 21 Jan 79, in Letters Sent 1863–1889, RG 159.

51. Weigley, *History of the United States Army*, 267; Sanger, "Inspector-General's Department," 246; GO No. 106, AGO, 9 Dec 79, in GORI&IG; Heitman, *Historical Register*, 1: 646.

52. *ARIG 1880*, H. Ex. Doc. 1, 43d Cong., 3d sess., pt. 2, 1: 48–51.

BRIG. GEN. DELOS B. SACKET. *Inspector General, of the Army, 2 January 1881–8 March 1885.*

report on the codification of the Regulations of the Army.[53] The War Department had, at last, decided to force the issue of the Army's dormant regulations. Marcy spent his last year in office in a futile attempt to straighten out the status of the Inspector General's Department. Several laws had put conflicting ceilings on the number and ranks of the department's officers. As attrition continued, the correct figure needed to be determined. Secretary McCrary agreed, and in fact wanted to raise the legislated ceiling from four to seven. Marcy, of course, was delighted, and together they proposed new legislation to the Senate in 1879 and early 1880. But McCrary left office at the end of 1879, and Marcy had to explain the whole thing to the new Secretary of War, Alexander Ramsay. When he did so, in May, he took the opportunity to set the proposed new ceiling at eight officers, suggesting that McCrary had favored that as well. Ramsay, however, was unenthusiastic. In a last effort, Marcy said that with his approaching retirement the law would not permit the Secretary to appoint any new inspectors. If Schriver retired also, however, the Secretary could appoint one, but the new inspector could be only an assistant in the grade of major. Again Marcy urged an increase in the inspectorate, but he had to leave office frustrated on that point, as he had been for years.[54] Despite claims of understrength, the inspectorate gained another minor responsibility when a general order declared on 9 April 1880 that the periodicals, newspapers, and school books provided by the Quartermaster's Department were for the use of enlisted men. They were not to be taken from post libraries or school rooms, and officers were entitled to use the materials only when duty forbade use by enlisted men. All officers, however, were encouraged to promote study and learning among their men. Inspecting officers were to inquire into observance of the order and to report any violations.[55]

53. *ARIG 1880*, 48.

54. Marcy to Hon. T. F. Randolph, chairman, Committee on Military Affairs, United States Senate, 30 Apr 80, enclosing copy of McCrary to Randolph, 11 Dec 79; and Marcy to Secy of War, 10 May, 14 Jul, and 8 Nov 80, all in Letters Sent 1863–1889, RG 159.

55. GO No. 23, AGO, 9 Apr 80, in GORI&IG. The distribution of reading matter was ordered in 1878 and began in 1879. Risch, *Quartermaster Support*, 489–90; *ARSecWar 1881*, H. Ex. Doc. 1, 47th Cong., 1st sess., pt. 2: 23.

Special Investigations and Services

One of the most important duties of inspectors general, especially while Belknap was in office, was to undertake special investigations and other services for the Secretary of War. Marcy, for instance, provided official opinions. In 1871, he evaluated the claim of an officer for commutation of fuel and quarters and gave his views on issues like authorizing the transportation of horses and on questions of relative rank. He also provided official criticisms of new cavalry tactics and recommended explorations of some mountains in Texas.[56] Marcy recommended to the Secretary in 1873 that the volume and excessive number of returns and other paper work be reduced, especially in the Quartermaster's Department. Two years later, he advised the Secretary on review of court-martial judgments regarding officers convicted of misconduct, and looked into cases where accusations of intemperance had been made. In 1877, in the case of a lieutenant convicted of negligent loss of some government-owned property, Marcy recommended leniency because the court record did not show the value of the property lost or destroyed. His advice was to uphold part of the man's conviction but to offer leniency in punishment. And in 1878, he made a special project of constructing the regulations to cover transfer of officers from one corps or regiment to another. He also drafted a general order to resolve questions of relative rank in such circumstances.[57] In a unique case, under orders of the Commanding General, Marcy published the annual *Outline Description of Military Posts* in 1872, usually a function of the Quartermaster General. The reason he did so is not apparent, for Marcy's compilation was less complete in its descriptive content than the Quartermaster General's *Outline Description* prepared that year.[58]

The special investigations done for the Secretary were time-consuming, and even Congress felt free to request them too. In 1874, the lawmakers requested an investigation of the expenses incurred by the territory of Dakota in raising volunteer forces during the Indian uprising of 1862 and also a list of private claims against the government. Inspector General Hardie undertook the work and discovered that the utter chaos of events was reflected in the equally chaotic records. In the end, he was able to find only about half the claims valid.[59] Matters of conduct were also the objects of inspectors' interest. A

---

56. Marcy to Adjutant General E. D. Townsend, 4 Feb 71; to Secy of War, 8 Feb and 14 Feb 71; and to Sherman, 4 Mar and 15 Mar 71, all in Letters Sent 1863–1889, RG 159.

57. Marcy, endorsement on communications of Secy of War and QMG, 25 Sep 73; IG to Secy of War, 15 May 75; IG to Sacket, 21, 22, and 28 Jun 75; IG to Maj. Gen. W. S. Hancock, 22 Jun 75; IG to Col. J. B. Fry, 28 Jun 75; Marcy to Secy of War, 6 Mar 77 and 22 Apr 78, all in Letters Sent 1863–1889, RG 159.

58. U.S. War Department, *Outline Description of the Posts and Stations of Troops in the Geographical Divisions and Departments of the United States*, compiled by Inspector General R. B. Marcy by Order of the General in Chief of the Army (Washington: Government Printing Office, 1872); U.S. War Department, Quartermaster General's Office, *Outline Description of U.S. Military Posts and Stations in the Year 1871* (Washington: Government Printing Office, 1872).

59. Hardie's report, accompanied by 130 pages of documents, appeared as *Dakota Indian War Claims of 1862*, H. Ex. Doc. 286, 43d Cong., 1st sess. (1874).

general order in 1874 made misbehaving officers the subjects of special investigations, although every attempt was made to ensure that no man be slandered. When an inspector had to investigate an officer, he was to inform the subject of the accusations and give him an opportunity to present his own case in writing so that it might accompany the inspector's report.[60] Consequently, "Rumors injurious to the reputation of an officer or liable to produce mischief if incorrect" were not reported by Inspectors without careful investigation and definite ascertainment of facts.

Some special investigations were impossible. In 1875 the Inspector General's Office tried to defend the Army in a six-year-old case, arising from the supposed delivery by a contractor of stolen cattle at Camp Supply in Indian territory. Working under the Secretary's orders, the inspectors general were reduced to asking the current post commander whether anybody in the neighborhood remembered the incident. They learned nothing, and the aggrieved owner of the cattle put through his claim.[61] A rare foray into engineer matters occurred at the surprising request of the Chief of Engineers when, in 1876, Marcy ordered Hardie to make a special investigation into citizens' complaints about the personal habits and conduct of a Corps of Engineers officer in Wisconsin. The next year, at the Secretary's orders, Marcy himself went to Salt Lake City, Utah, to look into requests of two churches for army land at Fort Douglas, to be used as a public cemetery. In this case, Marcy advised granting the request and approving the churches' plan of operation. His officers also looked into rumors of Indian depredations in Arizona in 1877, and discovered them to be unfounded.[62]

Reflecting his divided supervision, in 1878 Marcy was ordered by the Secretary of War and directed by the Commanding General to investigate a petition for conveyance of part of the reservation at Fort McHenry, Maryland, and to examine the possibility of reclaiming land there by filling in the harbor. He also made a long and detailed study for the Secretary on the issue of transferring the Indian Bureau from the Department of the Interior back to the War Department, its original location. He favored the move, citing the Army's previous good performance, its honesty, and the location of its posts in Indian country. In other investigations that year, Marcy examined the availability of quarters at Washington Arsenal, and the feasibility of moving interred bodies from the post cemetery at Fort McHenry to a national cemetery (he favored the move). Acting under the Secretary's orders, Col. Roger Jones made a special investigation into charges that the civilian superintendent of the national cemetery at Winchester, Virginia, was a drunkard and a gambler. Jones declared the charges unfounded and the superintendent a model citizen[63]

---

60. GO No. 5, AGO, 23 Jan 74, in GORI&IG.
61. IG to CO, Camp Supply, 12 Oct 75, and IG, Ind on Inspector General Hardie's Report, n.d. Dec 75, in Letters Sent 1863–1889, RG 159.
62. Marcy, Ind on Ltr of Chief of Engineers, n.d. Feb 76, and Marcy to Secy of War, 28 Sep 76, both in Letters Sent 1863-1889, RG 159; *ARIG 1877*, 54.
63. Marcy to Adjutant General E.D. Townsend, 4 Mar and 25 Jul 78; Marcy endorsement on communication from Capt. J.C. Breckinridge, 25 Oct 78; Marcy to Sherman, 16 Nov 78; Jones to AG, 9 Dec 78, all in Letters Sent 1863–1889, RG 159.

The department stayed busy in the area of special investigations, usually at the Secretary's behest. When citizens in New Mexico accused Bvt. Maj. Gen. Edward Hatch of dereliction of duty and various sorts of negligence in association with the uprising of Apaches under Victorio, Marcy dispatched Maj. John J. Coppinger, an acting assistant inspector general, to investigate. Coppinger declared the charges baseless and Hatch's record commendable. Marcy himself went to investigate conflicts of authority reported to the Secretary at Washington Arsenal. He found that petty feuding occurred there between artillery and ordnance officers because of a divided command. That, he said, was an invitation for trouble. The two commanding officers were irreconcilable, and unless one was moved out or a field officer put over them, there was no possibility of any harmony developing.[64] The artillery commander at Washington Arsenal was Capt. Joseph C. Breckinridge. Marcy did not know it, but Breckinridge would eventually become an inspector general and succeed him as the head of the inspectorate. In the interim, when Marcy examined ungarrisoned Fort McHenry's fitness to house troops in May 1880, he suggested moving Breckinridge's unit there to end the divided command at Washington Arsenal. That would also free space at the latter location for a national repository of the nation's official records.[65]

Special investigations continued a varied responsibility throughout Marcy's term. During June of 1880, at the Secretary's orders, Jones examined complaints about the quality of the men's food at Fort Whipple, Virginia. The Secretary had received an anonymous letter, but Jones found few complaints among the soldiers. Marcy undertook his last special investigation in December 1880, when the Secretary sent him to Fort Wingate, New Mexico, to see what additional buildings were needed there. As with most other special investigations, that was something that could more economically have been determined by the local inspector, but it showed how thoroughly the inspectors general remained the personal agents of the Secretary of War.[66]

Property Inspections

The inspectors' secretarial assignments were varied and unpredictable. More enduring, and in their view more important, was their responsibility for the Army's property and its management—especially its condemnation when unserviceable. That responsibility grew steadily and came into its own during Marcy's tenure. In 1870, Marcy reviewed and clarified the procedures for boards of survey determining the condition of property, especially as they

---

64. Special Report of Major J. J. Coppinger, Actg Asst IG, in *ARComGen*, H. Ex. Doc. 1, 46th Cong., 3d sess., vol. 1, pt. 2: 104–05; Marcy to Secy of War, 11 Feb 80, in Letters Sent 1863–1889, RG 159.

65. Marcy to General of the Army, 10 May 80, in Letters Sent 1863–1889, RG 159.

66. Jones to Marcy, 18 Jun 80, and Marcy to Secy of War, 28 Dec 80, in Letters Sent 1863–1889, RG 159. Jones' letter was a rare instance of an inspector on special assignment reporting to Marcy instead of to the Secretary directly.

affected an officer's accountability. The regulations, he admitted, were vague. That same year, at the Secretary's request, Marcy gave the Adjutant General's Office a clarification of the relative roles of inspectors and boards of survey. One was not a substitute for the other, he pointed out. While inspectors condemned property, boards fixed responsibility for any damage or loss.[67]

By 1875, the property condemnation activities of inspectors had produced enough information to support a general order declaring that the troops were not taking care of the Army's goods. The order enjoined greater care and supervision, especially over weapons. Property was to be brought before an inspector only if it was unserviceable, not merely because it was ugly. Objects going to depots were to be packed carefully to avoid further injury. Inspectors general, when inspecting unserviceable property, also were to report whether the responsible officers had exercised "due care." Finally, only obsolete arms and ammunition could be sold, not any .45-caliber weapons or ammunition. Another order that year forbade condemnation of canteens merely because the covers, straps, or corks were worn out or missing. Troops were to repair such damages, while officers were to make timely requisitions for replacement parts.[68]

An 1876 order stated that the copies of property inventory and inspection reports, required since 1869 to be kept in inspectors' offices at division and department headquarters, were no longer required. In 1877, the Secretary ordered that all public property found by inspectors to be worthless and without monetary value was to be destroyed in the concerned inspector's presence. "The action of an Inspector, on property of this character," said the order, "will be final, and his inspection report on the same will be a valid voucher for the officer responsible for the property. In the discharge of the duty devolved upon Inspectors in this regulation, they are reminded they will continue to be regarded as answerable that their action is proper and judicious according to the circumstances of the case."[69] That measure was undoubtedly a relief to hundreds of property-managing officers, but it increased the burden of accountability resting on inspectors general. Later in 1877, another order instructed medical officers to ensure that hospital bedding and other property was not used for other than hospital purposes, or outside hospital buildings. All borrowed property was to be returned to hospitals, and an accounting made to the Surgeon General. "Inspectors will carefully note and report every instance in which these orders are violated or neglected," warned the Secretary of War.[70]

Orders governing property continued to multiply. In 1878 orders declared that property condemned by an inspector, or by a board of survey, could not be purchased by the officer accountable for it or by any officer involved in the condemnation. Another order said that articles of clothing found incomplete but in good condition could not be presented to an inspector for condemnation, but

---

67. Marcy, Ind, 15 Jan 70, and Marcy, Ind on Communication of General Schofield, 24 Jan 70, in Letters Sent 1863–1889, RG 159.
68. GO No. 55, AGO, 29 Apr 75, and GO No. 58, AGO, 11 May 75, in GORI&IG.
69. GO No. 40, AGO, 11 May 76, and GO No. 85, AGO, 8 Sep 77, in GORI&IG.
70. GO No. 99, AGO, 22 Oct 77, in GORI&IG.

should be returned to a depot for completion, or fixed locally. The next year, the advertisement and sale of condemned horses was limited to a ten-day period; if the condemned animals were not sold, they were to be shot on the eleventh day. The Quartermaster General was to be informed of either event. Inspectors were to exercise greater care in branding the animals "I.C.," which meant Inspected-Condemned. Meanwhile, Roger Jones discovered that many officers avoided the condemnation process by transferring worn-out goods to depots; he thought such objects should go before an inspector before transfer. Finally, in 1880 two new orders required boards of survey to examine damaged property at depots before presenting it to an inspector.[71]

Disbursing Accounts

Long before Marcy left office, the inspectors general had become the War Department's chief agency for safeguarding its public property. They had also become the chief examiners of the thousands of separate financial accounts kept by disbursing officers. In early 1872, the department distributed the Department of the Treasury's "Instruction Relative to Public Moneys and Official Checks of United States Disbursing Officers." Further orders the next year required that reports of inspections of the accounts of disbursing officers were to be filed where they could be reviewed by the commander ordering the inspections. Any discrepancies between officers' statements and inspectors' verifications were to be reported to the Adjutant General via the Inspector General in Washington. Under those orders, inspectors scrutinized the accounts of all disbursing officers, verifying them against statements from the Treasury and from authorized money depositories. Marcy complained that some of the depositories, mostly regional banks, did not furnish statements. Nevertheless, he thought the system would prevent losses to the government, "and it is gratifying to state that no embezzlement and but three cases of misapplication of funds have been reported during the year, the latter being small sums which probably will not result in any loss to the Government."[72]

In April 1874, Congress directed the Secretary of War to audit the books of all officers handling appropriated money. The audits were to be done by inspectors general or others detailed for that purpose, provided the latter were not connected with the department or corps making the disbursements. The requirement greatly expanded the duties of the Inspector General's Department. At first the law was interpreted as requiring monthly inspections, but that was soon changed to inspections once every two months. A flurry of orders finally settled on requiring six examinations of every account in a year. Besides the monstrous work load, inspectors found themselves liable for any frauds or losses which

<hr>

71. GO No. 45, AGO, 2 Jul 78; GO No. 89, AGO, 9 Dec 78; GO No. 35, AGO, 26 Mar 79; GO No. 29, AGO, 29 Apr 80; and GO No. 79, AGO, 2 Dec 80, all in GORI&IG; and Jones to AG, 15 Sep 79, in Letters Sent 1863–1889, RG 159.

72. GO No. 1, AGO, 9 Jan 72, and Cir, AGO, 25 Jun 73, conveying and elaborating on GO No. 87, in GORI&IG; *ARIG 1873*, 86-87.

"an active vigilance on their part might have detected"—a novel and distressing transfer of culpability from an embezzler to his examiner. This ignored the fact that inspectors were not public accountants or auditors, but merely observers of whether officers complied with the law in keeping books and making deposits.[73]

Examinations of accounts were the prime occupation of inspectors general by 1875, and most of their correspondence related to that activity. The exceedingly dull routine revealed only a few minor discrepancies, and was interrupted when disbursing officers occasionally were not present when they should have been and had to be summoned for their audits. Uncooperative depositories and unhelpful Treasury Department operatives were reported to the Secretary of War. The following year, Marcy could only say that the procedure had revealed that accounts were kept well and that money was handled properly. Recent changes in travel cost compensation procedures, however, had complicated matters unnecessarily. In reality, reports of account inspections were not always being made, so Marcy persuaded the Secretary to specifically order department commanders to require regular inspections. And to his relief, in July the Secretary changed the inspection schedule from a bimonthly one to a quarterly one.[74] "These inspections," Marcy said in 1877, "have promoted care in the system of keeping accounts, as well as having inculcated a more faithful compliance with the laws and the Treasury regulations affecting disbursements and deposits." To that end, the Secretary told division commanders to order inspections of the accounts of officers not under their commands but within their territory; that is, at facilities of staff departments. The burden on the inspectors increased steadily, but only occasionally did they find anything wrong, other than clerical errors (all "promptly rectified," reported Marcy). In 1880, Inspector Nelson Davis alone examined disbursements exceeding $4 million, and felt compelled to call for a uniform system of keeping cash and checkbooks.[75]

No matter how the inspectors general justified their existence as the alter ego of the Army's commander, the growing burden of account inspections increasingly compelled them to move from purely military concerns to those of the Secretary in regard to financial economy and propriety. The Army's disbursements were large enough, and scattered among so many recipients, that some sort of regular supervision was essential. But the institution of account inspections after 1874 was undoubtedly excessive; it is questionable whether the total saved in corrected errors and the rare detections of fraud equaled the

---

73. *An Act to provide for the inspection of the disbursements of appropriations made by officers of the Army, Statutes at Large* 18.3, sec. 1, 33 (1874); GO No. 33, AGO, 28 Apr 74, GO No. 45, AGO, 22 May 74, and GO No. 64, AGO, 23 Jun 74, all in GORI&IG; *ARIG 1874*, H. Ex. Doc. 1, 43d Cong., 2d sess., pt. 2, 1:93.

74. IG USA to Secy of War, 24 Nov 74, and reams of letters and endorsements in the months following, and AG, identical letters to all department and division commanders, 13 Jul 76, in Letters Sent 1863–1889, RG 159; *ARIG 1876*, 76; GO No. 67, AGO, 25 Jul 76, in GORI&IG.

75. *ARIG 1877*, 54; Adjutant General E. D. Townsend, identical letters to department and division commanders, 20 Dec 77, in Letters Sent 1863-1899, RG 159; *ARIG 1878*, 31; *ARIG 1880*, 49.

cost of the inspections. Not only did the system turn the inspectorate into an auditing service, it was insulting to the Army as a whole. There were some dishonest men in uniform, as there were in any group, but the vast majority of officers were honest and conscientious. Many of them were young and prone to make errors, for no person could ever grasp all of the Army's complicated accounting procedures, but they were not as a group likely to plunder the public treasury. Nevertheless, as the years passed, the inspectors general began to emphasize increasingly the importance of their accounting work. That was to a great extent a means of building a reputation as necessary by catering to the economical sentiments of politicians. In due course, account inspection would be presented as a principal justification for the inspectorate, with the unfortunate implication that, but for the inspectors general, the Army's officers would send the country into bankruptcy. Given that attitude, it is not surprising that inspectors general also complained increasingly that officers resisted inspection.

Other Occupations of the Inspectors

Account examinations were not the only paramilitary occupation of the inspectors general. Throughout the 1870s they remained the authors of the Subsistence Department's sales list. In 1872, Marcy reviewed the history of the abolition of sutlers in 1866–1867 and of the sales list, considering whether post traders might be done away with. He thought it might be useful for the Subsistence Department to carry all items then stocked by traders, but they lacked the storage space. Nevertheless, he advised expanding the list beyond its present seventy-two items.[76]

The inspectors general's control over the list gained the inspectors attention from the growing processed food industry. In a typical encounter, early in 1880 Marcy received political pressure urging upon him the merits of Tobin's Chili Sauce and "Florida Orange Marmalade." He politely turned the proffers aside with a promise to investigate the goods. Somewhat later, the inspectors general acceded to the Commissary General's request that canned crabs and shrimp be substituted for lobster when desired. In Marcy's last connection with the list, the Inspectors General unanimously turned down a request for additions that they believed similar to items already carried. The Secretary of War concurred.[77] That the entire body of inspectors general could spend weeks debating whether to add a bottle of chili sauce to the list might now seem remarkable, but it was a matter of law. The list was certainly a wasteful use of their time, but it reflected the rather vague ideas Congress and the War Department continued to hold about what inspectors general were for. Simply put, they were handed whatever did not neatly fit someone else's pigeonhole, or were told to act when an

---

76. Marcy, "Memorandum upon the subject of supply Officers and enlisted men of the Army with Articles not pertaining to the Army ration," n.d. Jul 72, in Letters Sent 1863–1889, RG 159.

77. Marcy to Hon. C. Upson, House of Representatives, 5 Jan 80, Marcy to Mr. L. Warrock, 15 Jan 80, and increasing correspondence from industry in succeeding months, all in Letters Sent 1863–1889, RG 159.

independent voice in someone else's activity (in the present case, that of Subsistence) was thought to be desirable. Nor was the devotion of high talent to something like the sales list unremarkable at the time. This was the same U.S. Army in which a broken teacup had to be accounted for separately, taken before an inspector, condemned, and disposed of—with a form for every move—before it could leave some unfortunate officer's accountability. Although the inspectors general might deliberate over the matter, the Secretary of War himself had to give the sales list his personal attention and final approval.

Much more estimable than subsistance minutiae was the growing system of national cemeteries. The Secretary of War directed in 1876 that division commanders order the inspectors general assigned to their commands to inspect all seventy-three national cemeteries, and send their reports to the Inspector General in Washington. The "whole subject" was consolidated in the Quartermaster's Department, but inspectors general were to make annual inspections "in the course of their tours of inspection." The Secretary sent Marcy himself out the next year to visit some cemeteries, and he returned with simple, detailed physical descriptions but few recommendations. He was by that time saying repeatedly in his annual report that the cemeteries were "in excellent order" and that the superintendents were doing their jobs well. It was obvious by 1879 that the cemetery visits were a waste of the inspectors' time, so the Secretary ordered the annual examinations dispensed with, unless specifically ordered. Soon thereafter, inspectors were told to examine post cemeteries when they inspected military posts.[78]

Another miscellaneous duty of the inspectors general was the United States Military Prison, established at Fort Leavenworth, Kansas, under legislation passed in 1873. The law establishing the prison required that "one of the inspectors of the Army shall, at least once in three months, visit the prison" to make a complete inspection. Most of the quarterly inspections during the 1870s were made by Marcy himself, as the Secretary of War directed. The growing institution employed the latest in penology, the men well housed and increasingly productive in making things like shoes, chairs, and kitchenware for the Army. Marcy was enthusiastic about the place, and never found anything to complain about. If he ever had any influence on its operations, it is not evident in his reports, which over a seven-year period read very much alike.[79] The inspectors general examined the Military Prison because the law told them to. Unlike the commissary sales list, the prison was something that both Congress and the Secretary of War believed to be very important. Therefore they wanted the best information about it, from a reliable source.

---

78. AG, identical letters to division commanders, 3 Aug 76; AG to Marcy, 16 May 77, and Marcy to Secy of War, 6 Jun 77, all in Letters Sent 1863–1889, RG 159; *ARIG 1876*, 74–75; *ARIG 1878*, 32; *ARIG 1879*, 32; GO No. 68, AGO, 25 Jul 76, GO No. 84, AGO, 14 Aug 79, Cir, AGO, 29 Sep 79, and GO No. 61, AGO, 18 Jun 79, all in GORI&IG.

79. *An Act to provide for the establishment of a military prison and for its government, Statutes at Large* 17, sec. 5, 582 (1873); Thian, *Legislative History*, 113; GO No. 12, AGO, 19 Feb 77, in GORI&IG; *ARIG 1878*, 32; *ARIG 1879*, 32; Letters Sent 1863–1889, RG 159.

Something not held in as high regard during the 1870s was the potential wartime army represented in the National Guard and the expanding range of colleges or universities offering military instruction. To most regular officers, the growing National Guard was nothing more than the discredited militia with a new label. It was, in fact, something else, because it was completely voluntary. Military formations began to appear in one state after another in the 1870s, manned by young men from society's middle and upper reaches and fueled with a remarkable military spirit that sometimes appalled their war-weary elders. They did their best to train and equip themselves, and endeavored to attain proficiency. In 1879 they formed the National Guard Association to serve as their political lobby, and increasingly the Guard asked for attention from the Regular Army. However, it received no such notice for most of the 1870s, except for occasional expressions of disdain. But the great national railway strikes of 1877 brought the Regular Army into an unaccustomed role, that of keeping civil order. Few regular officers thought that the Army was well adapted for that role. Over the next few years, their professional journals filled with talk about civil disorders, but the regulars were happy enough to leave the job to the National Guard. The guardsmen prospered from public fears of radicals and anarchists, who were blamed often for labor unrest, and spent about a third of their time after 1877 on strike duty. Marcy's son-in-law McClellan perceived as early as 1878 that the Guard might have a greater value than he presumed and he urged federal assistance and support for the developing new units.[80]

The Regular Army's official involvement with the National Guard began only at the end of Marcy's time. During the summer of 1880, the Secretary sent Roger Jones to attend the encampment of the Connecticut National Guard. Jones' long report was favorable to what he had seen, although not by any means uncritical. His most important recommendation was that the officers spend more time studying tactics.[81] The National Guard became a subject of increasing importance for the Inspectors General after Marcy's time. Another such matter was military education in the colleges. Marcy himself initiated the Army's first attention to that subject early in 1880, when the Secretary dispatched him to four colleges in Pennsylvania where army officers served on the faculties. Colleges and officers, he said, both were doing their part. Because Pennsylvania's quota of officers had been exceeded, Marcy recommended removing one from a certain college because it had two West Point graduates on its civilian faculty.[82]

---

80. McClellan quoted in Frederick P. Todd, "Our National Guard: An Introduction to Its History," *Military Affairs*, 5 (1941): 159. Besides Todd's article, the foregoing summary is based on Graham A. Cosmas, "From Order to Chaos: The War Department, the National Guard, and Military Policy, 1898," *Military Affairs*, 29 (fall 1965): 105-21.

81. Jones to AG, 6 Sep 80, in Letters Sent 1863–1889, RG 159.

82. Marcy to Secy of War, 9 Feb 80, in Letters Sent 1863–1889, RG 159. After 1880, college inspections grew in response to the need to keep track of the federal property at the institutions.

Things like the property procedures and the national cemeteries were important objects of the inspectors' attention during the 1870s, but Marcy and his associates were military men first. It was the men of the Army who claimed first place in their attention. The inspectorate continued on its rounds among the posts and garrisons throughout Marcy's tenure, looking into every aspect of soldier life and military affairs. But they did so from a perspective formed in the "old army" before the Civil War. Winds of change were blowing in the 1870s, especially in the management of the enlisted men. Marcy, for one, did not approve of all that was beginning to happen in the Army.[83]

The Old Soldier Retires

Marcy's views on reform were, characteristically, a rearguard action, with his trying vainly to preserve the memory of the rugged past from the advance of changing times. He was too much a soldier of the old army to adapt happily to the conditions of the new army. He must have found one cause for satisfaction as he faced retirement, beyond his stabilization of the Inspector General's Department and the elevation of its chief to brigadier general. The permanent officers behind him on the scale of seniority were, in order, Delos B. Sacket, Nelson H. Davis, and Absalom Baird. They also were veterans of the old army. Marcy could be confident that they would keep the faith, defending the old virtues from the frivolities of the new generation.

Marcy retired from the Army 2 January 1881. He left behind him an Inspector General's Department, or at least the makings of one, something the Army had never formally had before. It was up to his successors to preserve the department and to define its mission more fully. For whatever he accomplished, Marcy had not really forged a systematic organization. Although he had systematized many things, especially property procedures, and had ensured his organization's permanence, inspection itself had not been improved. In his own service as an inspector, he was inclined to act on his personal sentiments, rather than on an objective examination of what was before him. He remained too much the man of action to measure up to Joseph P. Sanger's description of the ideal inspector: "The best characteristic of an inspector next to thoroughness is impartiality and absolute reticence," wrote future inspector Sanger in 1880. "He should remember that it is his duty simply to examine and report facts, and that if he forms opinions they are to be expressed *first* to his general, or the officer who ordered the inspection."[84] As it happened, Inspector General Marcy too often had proven unable to so contain himself, although he remained an estimable man. A general order on 3 January 1881 announcing his retirement

---

83. On army reform generally in the 1870s see Donna Marie Thomas, *Army Reform in America: The Crucial Years, 1876-1881* (Ph.D. Dissertation, University of Florida, 1981), and Donna Thomas, "Ambrose E. Burnside and Army Reform, 1850–1881," *Rhode Island History*, 37 (1978): 3–13.

84. J. P. Sanger, "The Duties of Staff Officers," *United Service*, 2 (June 1880): 754–73. Edmund Schriver retired immediately after Marcy, and therefore is not listed above among Marcy's successors.

said that "throughout his long period of constant duty, the career of Brigadier-General Marcy has been marked by distinguished military service." The best-known inspector general after Steuben, "military counsellor" and storyteller, popular author and noted big-game hunter, old soldier from the old army, Randolph B. Marcy retired to West Orange, New Jersey, where he died 2 November 1887.[85]

---

85. GO No. 1, 3 Jan 81, in GORI&IG; *ARIG 1881*, 75; *DAB*, 6: 274.

CHAPTER 17

Passing of the Old Guard
(1881–1889)

When Marcy left the Army in 1881, the military force was scattered among 190 posts, 16 arsenals, 3 recruiting depots, and an engineer depot. Eighty-four of those installations were on the Great Lakes or the Atlantic or Gulf Coasts; 11 were on the Pacific coast; and the remaining 115 were scattered inland. The Army was still very much in a posture to fight the Indian Wars of the 1860s and 1870s.[1] The needs of its scattered condition were diminishing rapidly. Yet, pressures against redeployment prevented any immediate readjustment to the new circumstances. Concurrent with the fading of the frontier came the first pressures for institutional reform and reorganization necessary to meet the perceived demands of the new era.

Portents of Reform

Nothing else in its administrative history was so reflective of the Army's difficulty in breaking with the past than its lack of a modern code of regulations. Two full decades had elapsed since the last revision of the general regulations. The previous edition, based on earlier rules of the 1840s, had appeared in 1861, followed by only a simple reissue with minor amendments two years later. That volume remained in force until 1881, but was increasingly inapt. At least three times since the Civil War, efforts had been made to develop a new code of regulations, but they were frustrated repeatedly by bureaucratic and political turmoil during the period of Reconstruction. The difficulties grew out of the ceaseless debates over the size of the permanent military establishment. The stalemate was finally broken by the appropriations act of 23 June 1879, authorizing and directing the Secretary of War to codify and establish all regulations and orders in force. The U.S. Army therefore marked the advent of its modernization with the publication, in 1881, of a new edition of its general regulations.[2]

For the inspectorate, the new regulations offered little that was new. They were in fact much the same as those of 1863, adding changes made by general

---

1. *ARComGen 1881*, H. Ex. Doc. 1, 47th Cong., lst sess., vol. 1, pt.2: 36.
2. U.S. War Department, *Regulations of the Army of the United States and General Orders in Force on the 17th of February 1881* (Washington: Government Printing Office, 1881) (hereafter cited as *1881 Regulations*).

order during the 1870s. Substantially they described the schedules of inspections by inspectors general and various commanding officers. Inspectors still were not to give orders unless expressly authorized, nor were they to indulge in "informal conversation" regarding their inspections. As they had been for some time by orders, inspectors were enjoined from using hearsay against individuals or organizations. In investigating charges, they were to offer the accused an opportunity to present his own case. Otherwise, the new regulations concisely listed the subjects of inspections of posts and troops. Marcy's former emphasis on reporting the Indian situation was dropped, except for a general reference to the number and disposition of Indian tribes. The detailed text's guidance for quarterly inspections of disbursements, transports, and condemned property, however, had increased in a reflection of that growing part of an inspector's sphere.[3]

Breckinridge Joins the Department

General Marcy's departure marked a period of change for the Inspector General's Department. Edmund Schriver also retired in January, being over sixty-two years old and therefore eligible for the retired list. For the first time in many years, that created a vacancy in the Inspector General's Department.[4] Delos B. Sacket, next after Schriver in the order of seniority, was Marcy's proper successor. There was, however, some unexplained delay in his confirmation. Not until 20 April did the War Department announce his assignment as senior inspector general, effective 2 January (the date Marcy left); he had, however, been in the Washington office since January. The same order announced that Capt. Joseph C. Breckinridge of the 2d Artillery had been appointed assistant inspector general with the rank of major, to date from 19 January, replacing Schriver. Breckinridge was assigned to the Military Division of the Pacific, after an orientation in Washington.[5]

Breckinridge was the artillery officer who had been unable to get along with his Ordnance counterpart at Washington Arsenal during the 1870s. As that incident suggested, he was a man of strong will, sensitive about his prerogatives and determined to have his own way. Born in Maryland and raised in Kentucky, he was a member of Kentucky's most prominent family. His relatives figured on both sides of the Civil War in military and political capacities, and others were represented in state and national politics and journalism. Breckinridge joined the Army as lieutenant and aide-de-camp of volunteers in 1861, then accepted a regular commission as a second lieutenant of the 2d Artillery in 1862. He was captured before Atlanta fell and spent the last months of the war as a prisoner. A lieutenant by the end of the war, he did not become a captain

---

3. *1881 Regulations*, passim.
4. *ARIG 1881*, H. Ex. Doc. 1, 47th Cong., 1st sess., vol. 1, pt. 2: 75. *ARIG 1881* says that Schriver was retired 19 January; Heitman, *Historical Register*, 1: 866, dates it 4 January, two days after Marcy's departure.
5. GO No. 37, AGO, 20 Apr 81; *ARIG 1881*, 74, 75.

until 1874, and moved from that position to his majority in the Inspector General's Department seven years later. He earned two brevets for "gallant and meritorious service" during the Civil War.[6]

Breckinridge's personality would become more apparent later. For the moment, he was a harbinger of change in the Inspector General's Department, whose other officers had been secure in their positions since the Civil War. All were growing older, and none had personally commanded troops since the war. Breckinridge, however, like the acting inspectors, was a troop commander, sensitive to the realities of life in troop units and isolated garrisons. Moreover, he was an artillerist, whose men suffered the Army's worst conditions, men dismayed by an absence of clear identity as artillerists, indifferently trained, and most likely required to inhabit those man-made caves, the casemates, at the major fortifications. Breckinridge was very much in touch with the Army, and he was inclined to use his position to do something about what he believed was wrong.

Breckinridge's arrival was accompanied by a general reorganization of the inspectorate. Baird had spent so long in the West that he fairly begged to be assigned to the Washington office. Sacket agreed, although Baird's presence in the head office would leave few permanent officers out among the Army. In April 1881 Sacket told the Secretary of War that he would prefer to have all his officers at headquarters, where they would be available for special assignments. The Inspector General's Department was too small, had been "for many decades," he said, and in the circumstances, central assignment would be most advisable.[7] The Secretary concurred, but only in part. Baird was established as assistant in the Inspector General's Office as of 1 July 1881. Thereafter, he was in charge of the office whenever the senior inspector was out of town. The Secretary would not allow concentration of the entire department there, however. Breckinridge went to the Division of the Pacific on the same day, and Jones, who had been in Washington for a long time, to the Division of the Atlantic. Davis moved from the Atlantic to the Division of the Missouri, which had been established since the late 1860s as the proper place for the second-most senior inspector general.[8]

Sacket was the nominal head of his department, but his authority to dispose of its staff as he thought fit was limited. The Secretary believed that the greater number of the permanent inspectors should be assigned to the divisions to pursue regular duties. In order to meet this requirement, the inspectorate relied upon the four acting inspectors general who had been authorized since 1874. These men were used to fill the additional spaces which required an inspector in excess of authorized IG strength. One of these officers detailed as an acting inspector got into a situation which led Sacket early in his tenure to make a case for independence for all inspectors. In January 1881, this officer, assigned as a

6. Heitman, *Historical Register*, 1: 242.
7. Sacket, Ind on application of Lt. Col. Baird, 16 Apr 81, in Letters Sent 1863–1889, RG 159.
8. *ARIG 1881*, 74–75.

departmental inspector in the Military Division of the Missouri, had to comment unfavorably on an action of the colonel commanding the regiment to which he would return after his detail. This obviously posed an uncomfortable and embarrassing conflict of interest to both officers. The Inspector General's Office, acting after a strong comment from Baird, went to the Commanding General to request an end to details of line officers as inspectors in departments where their regiments and permanent commanders were located.[9]

Most of Sacket's first year on the job was taken up with ordinary matters. He wrote to the four acting assistant inspectors general in March to advise them, while inspecting troops, to identify officers especially qualified for special details such as staff assignments, surveys, and the like. In May, responding to a request, Sacket submitted a thorough plan for simplification of the Army's profuse returns, rolls, books, and other paper work. His suggestions, however, were limited only to format; they would have eliminated or consolidated nothing.[10] Because he was not willing to commence his job with major challenges to the existing order, the new senior inspector looked first to his surroundings. The appropriations act of 3 March 1881 allowed him one clerk of class four, and one assistant messenger, for a total payroll of $2,520. He asked for more, to put his office on the "same status" as other staff offices, because he found the repeated need to borrow clerks from other departments humiliating. "The officers of this department are gentlemen of rank and of many years' service, and their status should not be that of beggars," he said.[11]

Sacket also asked, not surprisingly, for a larger complement of officers for the Inspector General's Department, requesting nine additional majors. In contrast to the Marcy years, when the department was in repeated danger of vanishing from sight, Sacket's first year brought him welcome help. Secretary of War Robert Todd Lincoln supported his views, urging that the nine officers be allowed. Then, each division and department would have one inspector.[12] General Sherman concurred most heartily with Sacket's request, asking further that the President be allowed to select any additions to the Inspector General's Department from the majors as well as the captains of the line.[13] Thus did Sacket's campaign to increase his department receive some hope of success late in 1882. The House Committee on Military Affairs took issue on 27 December with the Adjutant General's interpretation of the 1870 law promoting Marcy. The Adjutant General contended that the measure would abolish the rank of colonel behind the senior inspector general, leaving the department with 1 brigadier general, 2 lieutenant colonels, and 2 majors. The committee reviewed the history of the Inspector General's Department and the repeated assertions of

9. Roger Jones to General of the Army, 29 Jan 81, in Letters Sent 1863–1881, RG 159.

10. Sacket to Sir, 10 Mar 81, and Sacket to AG, 24 May 81, in Letters Sent 1863–1889, RG 159.

11. GO No. 28, AGO, 12 Mar 81, in GORI&IG; *ARIG 1881*, 80. Sacket asked for $4,800 per year to hire three clerks at the division headquarters.

12. *ARSecWar 1881*, 7.

13. *ARComGen 1881*, 34–35.

the War Department that more officers were needed. The committee foresaw consolidation of the Army's posts, and suggested that a total of 9 officers would suffice. In substitution for an alternative bill, which the committee thought had too many colonels and lieutenant colonels, it proposed a complement of 1 colonel, 2 lieutenant colonels, and 5 majors under the senior inspector general.[14]

Sacket did some inspecting, of a sort, on his own in 1882, and played a small part in a significant development in the history of conservation in the United States. He accompanied General Sheridan on a tour of the most scenic parts of Sheridan's Division of the Missouri during August and September and was particularly taken by Yellowstone National Park, which he called "Wonder Land" in his annual report. The reservation was then a decade old, and indifferently administered. When Sacket returned from his long journey (3,307 miles, mostly by train) he found himself regarded as an authority on the first national park. At the end of the year Senator Benjamin Harrison asked him his opinion on a number of issues affecting Yellowstone, including proposed leases of land there and its transportation and management requirements. The Inspector General recommended in the strongest terms the stationing of troops in the park to fight forest fires and to protect the thermal wonders. A troop of cavalry would suffice, he said. Based on this, on 17 August 1886, one troop of cavalry arrived in the park, and three days later its captain became acting superintendent. That was the start of national park management by the Army that would continue until the establishment of the National Park Service in 1916. The military not only protected the growing number of parks from fire and trespass, and regulated visitors, but it also undertook the construction of roads and other improvements and supervised private development by permittees. That history all started with Sacket's junket to "Wonder Land" in 1882.[15]

Success for the Inspector General's Department seemed assured in 1883, when Sacket was listed casually among those bureau chiefs entitled to receive copies of orders and circulars issued by division and geographic department headquarters. However, little else was new because the bills to expand the department failed in a short session of Congress, causing Sacket to issue another plea for more officers. His permanent complement remained where they had been sent in 1881, and all posts were inspected. Sacket revealed how he was able to circumvent the law limiting the number of officers detailed to inspection to four. Department commanders assigned four others to serve as acting assistant inspectors general.[16] . . . Near the end of the year, Breckinridge made a

14. *Inspector General's Department of the Army*, H. Rpt. 1839, 47th Cong., 2d sess. (1882). *The Army and Navy Journal* gave extended treatment to the committee's finding that the Inspector General's Department should be increased by additional majors. *Army and Navy Journal*, 20 (30 December 1882): 486–87.

15. *ARIG 1882*, 76–77; Sacket to G. G. Vest, U. S. Senate, 3 Jan 83, in Letters Sent 1863–1889, RG 159. The principal study of the Army's administration of the National Parks is H. Duane Hampton, *How the U.S. Cavalry Saved Our National Parks* (Bloomington: Indiana University Press, 1971).

16. GO No. 76, AGO, 24 Oct 83, in GORI&IG; *ARIG 1883*, H. Ex. Doc. 1, 48th Cong., 1st sess., vol. 1, pt.2: 98–103. On the last day of the year, the annual inspection of posts by commanders was clarified further. Cir, AGO, 31 Dec 83, referring to letter, 19 Dec 83, 4915 AGO, 1883, in GORI&IG.

suggestion that revealed viewpoints in the Inspector General's Department indicative of the growing difference between officers of the old army and those of the new army. The weekly inspection of companies had been scheduled for Sunday since 1841, after a brief period in the 1830s when Macomb had given the men a day off. Breckinridge believed that an unnecessary and onerous imposition upon the soldiers, and proposed that it be moved to Thursday. Sacket opposed any such change, and compared the Sunday ritual to the sprucing up of children on that day in civilian family life. Breckinridge let the matter rest there, but he did not forget it.[17]

Sacket's hopes for expansion of his department revived early in 1884, when the House Committee on Military Affairs expressed its belief that the present force was grossly inadequate for its assignment. More generous than before, the committee recommended increasing the permanent force to 11 officers—1 brigadier general, 2 colonels, 2 lieutenant colonels, and 6 majors—and wanted to lift the ceiling on details from the line. The department's majors, said the committee, should be promoted from among the captains of the line, and "all other promotions [including those to brigadier general] shall be by seniority in the corps." Almost echoing Marcy, the committee expressed the opinion that inspectors should be permanent and of sufficiently high rank. "In one word," said the panel's report, "the inspection of officers of high rank by those far below them is liable to be accompanied by circumstances which may prejudice good order and military discipline."[18] However, nothing came of the congressional activity. The only change in the Inspector General's Department in 1884 was the dispatch of Breckinridge to his home on sick leave in May. A lieutenant colonel of infantry was detailed to substitute for him. Sacket again said nearly every post was inspected, and that things as usual were greatly improving. Target practice, he said, had received increasing emphasis, with good results. Sacket had managed an increase in his clerical force that year: 1 class-four clerk, 1 class-one clerk, and 1 assistant messenger, for a payroll of $3,725— but he said it was not enough, and again "request[ed] that some prompt action be taken to afford the relief so urgently demanded."[19]

The Department Enlarged and Ratified

Sacket's request that additions be made to his department was finally answered, although not without a last-minute hesitation. On 20 January 1885, the Senate passed H. R. 1017, a bill previously passed by the House to add two officers to the Inspector General's Department. The Senate Committee on Miltary Affairs strongly endorsed the increase on the floor; and expressed its agreement with its counterpart in the House. The legislation passed without

---

17. Sacket to Breckinridge, 21 Dec 83, in Letters Sent 1863–1889, RG 159.

18. *Reorganization of the Inspector-General's Department*, H. Rpt. 330, 48th Cong., 1st sess. (1884).

19. *ARIG 1884*, H. Ex. Doc. 1, 48th Cong., 2d sess., vol. 1, pt. 2: 81–84, 97; GO No. 69, AGO, 14 Jul 84, in GORI&IG.

substantive comment except for the committee's report, and went to President Chester A. Arthur. Approved on 5 February, the law increased the complement of the department while also specifying grades and promotion procedures.[20] That legislation finally removed the conflicts and ambiguities in the law governing the Inspector General's Department. It did not formally establish such an organization—no law ever did—but it ratified the department's existence and affirmed that it should be governed by the the rules applicable to all other staff departments. It also clarified the complement of the department: The number of officers now stood at seven, and any conflicting earlier legislation was repealed. That was not as much as Sacket would have preferred, but it was more than his department had enjoyed for some time. The requirement that promotions occur within the bureau ratified one of the inspectorate's long-standing watchwords, that inspection is a specialty requiring permanence and experience.

An interesting part of the law, one not explained either in its text or in the legislative history behind it, was the quiet dropping of the grade of assistant inspector general. All permanent inspectors, from major to brigadier general, were thereafter to be entitled inspectors general. For the majors, this did not quite constitute a promotion to colonel, something Marcy and Sacket believed to be the minimum proper rank for an inspector general, but it was the next best thing in terms of prestige. This legislation expanding the Inspector General's Department was followed by a reallocation of personnel. The assistant inspectors general moved up on 5 February. Roger Jones became a colonel, and Joseph Breckinridge, a lieutenant colonel. Two line officers became majors and inspectors general in the department's permanent complement on 19 February. One was Robert P. Hughes of the 3d Infantry, who had already proved himself energetic and effective as an acting inspector. The other was Edward M. Heyl of the 4th Cavalry. On 2 March 1885, Hughes was assigned to the Department of the Dakota, Heyl to the Department of Texas. Only majors, each was called inspector general, just as their superiors were.[21]

Davis Has a Brief Reign

The expansion of the Inspector General's Department was a triumph for Sacket, but it was his last. The senior Inspector General died on 8 March 1885. In the words of Absalom Baird, Sacket's loss was "deeply felt and sincerely mourned. . . . As a man, his exemplary character and charming social qualities made him respected and loved by all who knew him." His death, however, was beneficial to his colleagues. On 11 March, Nelson Davis became brigadier

---

20. *Congressional Record*, 48th Cong., 2d sess. (20 January 1885), 849; *Message From the President of the United States, Returning a Bill H. R. 1017 Relating to the Inspector-General's Department of the Army*, H. Ex. Doc. 155, 48th Cong., 2d sess. (1885); An Act Relative to the Inspector-General's Department of the Army, approved 5 February 1885, 23 Stat. 297; Thian, *Legislative History*, 115; GO No. 17, AGO, 18 Feb 85, in GORI&IG. See also *ARIG 1885*, H. Ex. Doc. 1, 49th Cong., lst sess., vol. 1, pt. 2: 102.

21. *ARIG 1885*, 102–03. See Appendix B.

general and senior inspector general; Baird became a colonel behind Davis; Hughes, so recently a major, became lieutenant colonel behind Baird. Capt. George H. Burton, 21st Infantry, was appointed inspector general with the rank of major, filling Hughes' former position on 27 March 1885. Burton was as promising an acquisition as Hughes. He remained in the Inspector General's Department thereafter, and was the first Inspector General of the Army in the new staff organization instituted in 1903.[22]

Burton became Davis' assistant in the Washington office on 2 April 1885. After the reorganization of late winter, the inspectors general were assigned on 16 April as follows: Jones to the Division of the Atlantic and Department of the East; Baird to the

BRIG. GEN. NELSON H. DAVIS. *Inspector General of the Army, 11 March 1885–20 September 1885.*

Division of the Missouri; and Hughes to the Division of the Pacific and Department of California. Heyl was assigned to the Department of Texas, while Burton left Washington for the Department of the Missouri. Acting inspectors general, four in all, took up duties in the Departments of the Dakota, the Platte, Arizona, and the Columbia. The detailed officers were two majors and two lieutenant colonels. The order assigning the officers contained two provisions that would have pleased Sacket immensely. One was the entitlement of each division or department inspector to one general-service clerk with the rank of corporal and one private to serve as messenger. The other was an order allowing direct communication between the senior inspector and inspectors in the field.[23] That verified the inspectorate's status as a regular staff department, and suggested the independence that Marcy and Sacket had so greatly desired. Nelson Davis never had a chance to take hold of the Inspector General's Department, with its larger complement and partial autonomy. His sixty-fourth birthday was 20 September 1885. He had to retire, and who should replace him became the question. The seniority system, it turned out, offered no clear answer, because the system had been muddled by Davis' and Baird's special promotions years before. Davis evidently assumed that Jones would be his successor, because in August he asked the Secretary of War to detail Jones to the Washington office to write the annual report.[24]

22. *ARIG 1885*, 103. See Appendix B.

23. GO No. 47, 16 Apr 85, in GORI&IG; *ARIG 1885*, 104. The closed channel of communication was a privilege held by all other staff departments, but rarely before granted to the inspectorate, which recurrently had to route all correspondence through the Adjutant General's organization.

24. Davis to Secy of War, 13 Aug 85, in Letters Sent 1863–1889, RG 159.

Baird Succeeds Davis

When Davis actually retired, the President promoted Absalom Baird to his place, as of 20 September. That ended what the *Army and Navy Journal* described as "one of the most spirited, and yet friendly, contests ever known between two officers." Jones was senior to Baird on the department's list, but he was junior in the line. In a friendly exchange of letters, Baird made known his intention to seek the promotion, while Jones responded with his sympathy and support for Baird's feelings, and with a declaration that he could not in principle favor promotion of someone else arguably not his senior. The *Journal* suggested that the deciding issue between the two was age. Baird was scheduled for retirement during the current administration of President Grover Cleveland, while Jones had seven years yet to serve. He was therefore practically guaranteed the position of senior inspector general when Baird retired, while the converse appointment would have prevented Baird from ever getting his general's star.[25]

Davis' departure and Baird's elevation set off another round of reassignments and promotions in the Inspector General's Department. The fast-rising Breckinridge became a colonel on 22 September, and Heyl, a lieutenant colonel. Capt. Henry J. Farnsworth, 8th Cavalry, became a major and inspector general behind Heyl. Breckinridge moved to the Division of the Missouri on 10 October, and on 15 November Farnsworth was assigned to the Washington office. Over the next year, four departments continued to be served by acting inspectors general.[26]

Baird was not the instinctive bureaucrat that Schriver had been, nor was he as forceful as Marcy or Sacket. In fact, the gallant combat leader of the Civil War had aged into something much more mellow. His erect bearing, sweeping white mustaches, and tall beaver hat made him a noticeable figure at the War Department, and a popular one. But he was not the sort of person to make great innovations. Baird reveled in technical assignments. He was delighted early in 1886 when he and the Quartermaster General were assigned jointly to produce an official publication describing the army uniform. He felt that was a proper use of his time, because inspectors were always answering questions about the uniform regulations and ceremonies. It also gave him another opportunity to discourse on scores of minor questions, often with no conclusion.[27] Neither did Baird conduct himself as the leader of a staff department. He complained to the Adjutant General early in 1886 of the discontent in the Army about the inspectors general, and the moves afoot to limit their authority. The chief threat, he believed, was Emory Upton's infantry tactics, which limited the inspector's actions at reviews. Baird felt called upon to expand the role of inspectors under the regulations that, unlike Upton's text, were to govern the

25. *ARSecWar 1885*, 12; *Army and Navy Journal*, 23 (26 September 1885): 167. No one had shown such solicitude toward Schriver.

26. *ARIG 1886*, H. Ex. Doc. 1, 49th Cong., 2d sess. vol. 1, pt. 2: 106. See Appendix B.

27. See Baird to AG, 12 Feb 86, and to QMG, 19 Feb 86, in Letters Sent 1863–1889, RG 159.

BRIG. GEN. ABSALOM BAIRD. *Inspector General of the Army, 20 September 1885–20 August 1888.*

army. He then produced a long discourse on the role of an inspector general as an alter ego of the commander and so on. Most problems in inspection, he averred, were caused by misbehaving department and division commanders. They detailed officers to inspect their own colonels, for instance, or allowed confidential inspection reports to circulate in department or division headquarters for staff review. Commanders, Baird implied, were the enemies of inspectors. That was a novel position, and one not likely to win support for the Inspector General's Department.[28]

Baird's second annual report reflected this outlook. The four officers detailed to inspection, he said, were fine men; he would like to retain them permanently. To that end, he recommended adding 6 captains to the Inspector General's Department, 4 to replace those on detail and 2 as assistants in the Washington office. Baird noted briefly that all posts had been inspected during the year, as had all financial books, and then got down to the most important business. His officers traveled constantly, he said, and had to pay 15 to 20 percent of their expenses because the compensation allowed them by law was too little. Moreover, the Inspector General's Department was treated unfairly by its not having its own clerks: "No other branch of the staff is hampered in this way. A young captain in the Subsistence or Quartermaster's Department has all the assistance he demands, limited only by the amount of work he has to perform. The Inspector-General's Department alone is left with undefined and doubtful rights in this regard."[29] And Baird occasionally got himself into bureaucratic difficulties. He received a reproof from the Commanding General in February 1887 after having direct correspondence with the Quartermaster General on a purely fiscal matter. Communications involving two departments were to go through the Adjutant General's Office. Baird protested to the Secretary of War, referring to a circular issued by Secretary George W. McCrary on 2 April 1877, and underscoring the Inspector General's dual relationship to the Secretary of War and the Commanding General. Although his position in that regard was like that of the Adjutant General, Baird

28. Baird to AG, 10 Feb 86, in Letters Sent 1863–1889, RG 159.
29. He also said, "There is no more urgent and crying need in the Army than a new revision of the Army Regulation . . ." *ARIG 1886*, 112.

said that the Inspector General necessarily had greater difficulty in balancing the two relationships.[30]

Baird attempted to extend his department's purview in July 1887, when he reminded the Secretary that all posts and stations were to be inspected annually by divisional or departmental inspectors and the reports forwarded to the Inspector General in Washington. There was, he said, one post not under a division or department that had never been inspected. He therefore recommended that the post and battalion of the Corps of Engineers at Willetts Point, New York, be inspected and the findings reported to the Secretary of War. He got nowhere with that suggestion.[31] But, the Inspector General's Department did receive a new, if ordinary, responsibility during the summer, following the creation of the Hospital Corps. The corpsmen were excused from attendance at review, parades, or any other military duty. They were to be inspected and mustered at the hospitals they were attached to. The implementing order specified that officers of the Inspector General's Department, among others, would examine the members of the Hospital Corps and the company bearers to determine their efficiency during regular inspections.[32]

Baird's biggest interest in 1887 was not the American army, but rather the French. The French authorities invited foreign officers to observe their maneuvers in September, and the War Department sent Inspector General Baird. Along with the Commandant of Cadets at West Point, Baird spent about two months overseas. Six months after his return he submitted a nineteen-page report of his observations. His chief conclusion was that the three-battalion infantry regiment, something the Army's leaders had been begging for since the Civil War, was a bad idea. The French also, in a diplomatic nicety, wanted to confer honors on the leaders of visiting delegations. American law, however, forbade acceptance of foreign offices without action in Congress. Baird worked earnestly, and on 19 October 1888 a joint resolution of Congress authorized him to accept from the President of France a diploma honoring him as Commander of the National Order of the Legion of Honor. For Baird and his family, it was the high point of his entire career.[33]

Baird was scheduled for retirement in August 1888. He spent the time remaining to him more actively than he had the period before, often in opposition to proposed changes. The Secretary of War had at last persuaded Congress to consider legislation reorganizing the Army, based on a 3-battalion infantry regiment. When it came his turn to comment, Baird cited his forty-three years of experience in the Army—like Marcy, Baird was inclined to remind everyone within earshot that he had been around in the old days—and reaffirming his opposition to any changes in the organization. The 1-battalion infantry regi-

30. Baird to AG, 28 Feb 87, in Letters Sent 1863–1889, RG 159.
31. Baird to Secy of War, 11 Jul 87, in Letters Sent 1863–1889, RG 159.
32. GO No. 56, AGO, 11 Aug 87, in GORI&IG.
33. Baird to AG, 15 Mar 88, in Letters Sent 1863–1889, RG 159; GO No. 88, AGO, 29 Oct 88 (printing the resolution), in GORI&IG. Baird, *Profile of a Hero*, reflects great pride over Baird's French honor.

ment had always worked well, he said, and the 3-battalion organization was a mistake. He preferred large companies (100 men) in strong battalions, with the main maneuver force a 5-battalion brigade. The French troops he had observed were arrayed in 3-battalion regiments, but Baird said those had worked only because their battalions were large; that is, 2 regiments formed a brigade. But in Baird's opinion, command difficulties made the 3-battalion regiment the weakest part of the French system. As for artillery, Baird did favor a change, abandoning regiments in favor of one large corps, with a two-gun section the basic unit. But in general, Baird opposed all reorganization proposals, maintaining that the Army as organized in 1865 had been the best institution possible.[34]

In a more positive vein, Baird recommended that the status of the Army's veterinary surgeons be established by law, and he drafted a bill to that end. He also was successful in persuading the Secretary and Maj. Gen. Philip H. Sheridan, who had replaced Sherman in 1883, to urge Congress to expand the Inspector General's Department once again. The lawmakers considered such legislation, but did not act immediately. And because divisional or departmental inspectors might be reluctant to undertake the work critically, Baird recommended that divisional or departmental headquarters be inspected occasionally by a high-ranking officer answering to the Secretary of War. His purpose was partly selfish. He wanted to make a farewell journey around the army, and the Secretary of War allowed the senior inspector general to go on an eleven-stop tour of the country.[35]

Breckinridge Takes Charge

Baird retired because of age on 20 August 1888, his tenure marking a period of quiet stability in his department. He was replaced by his old "friendly" rival, Roger Jones, a reserved, introspective individual suffering ill health, who did not promise to infuse the organization with much energy either. On 1 September 1888, he went home—the ailing man never returned; he died at Fort Monroe, Virginia, on 26 January 1889.[36] The Army also lost its Commanding General in August 1888, when Sheridan died on the 5th. John M. Schofield was detailed to the command of the Army on 14 August. It remained for a new Commanding General and a new Inspector General to work out their

34. Baird, endorsement on communication of the Secretary of War referring for remark as to merits or demerits, H. R. Bills No. 1177 and 1347, 10 Feb 88, in Letters Sent 1863–1889, RG 159.

35. Baird to CG, 20 Feb 88, and to AG, 25 Apr 88, in Letters Sent 1863–1889, RG 159; Secy of War William C. Endicott to William C. P. Breckinridge, 17 Mar 88, Endicott to R. W. Townshed, 17 Mar 88, and General Sheridan to Secy of War 17 Feb 88, in *Inspector-General's Department,* H. Rpt. 4091, 50th Cong., 2d sess. (1889). In March 1888, orders directed every post commander to inventory all books received from the Adjutant General's Office, and to do so annually. Inspecting officers were supposed to verify books on hand as compared with the inventory, condemn and destroy unserviceable books, and report their actions in their inspection reports. GO No. 12, 5 Mar 88, in GORI&IG.

36. *ARIG 1889,* H. Ex. Doc. 1, 51st Cong., 1st sess. vol. 1, pt. 2: 118; *Annual Reunion of the Association of Graduates 1889,* 77. Jones' ailment is described in the sources only as a "serious illness."

relationship not only between themselves but also to the Secretary of War. All such questions had drifted in recent years, because of weak direction from all three parties. Schofield observed in his memoirs that by the time of Sheridan's death, the Commanding General had long since ceased to command.

Not even the Secretary of War was exercising much control of military affairs in 1888. Each department chief was in effect his own Secretary of War and, with the concurrence of the titular Secretary, could issue orders in his own name with the full weight of the War Department behind him. Only the Adjutant General bothered to use the name of the Secretary of War or the Commanding General. As far as Schofield was concerned, the only course was to transform his own office into that of a chief of staff to the Secretary. To that end he cracked down on the Adjutant General, forbidding the latter from continuing to issue orders in Schofield's or the Secretary's name without either's knowledge. But with Jones incapacitated by illness, there was little that Schofield could do about the Inspector General's Department for the moment.[37]

Baird's retirement and Jones' elevation caused another series of shifts in the Inspector General's Department. Robert P. Hughes became a colonel on 31 August, and George H. Burton a lieutenant colonel. Capt. Henry W. Lawton, 4th Cavalry, hero of the campaign against Geronimo, was appointed major and inspector general on 2 October. Hughes was for a time temporarily in charge of the office while Jones was out, and authored the 1888 annual report. Heyl moved to the Division of the Pacific, while Lawton was temporarily assigned to Washington. Burton had gone to the Department of Arizona before Baird's retirement.[38] This rapid shuffling of the Inspector General's Department had accelerated the rise of Joseph C. Breckinridge. On 27 October, as the senior officer under Jones, he was moved to the Washington office to assume responsibility for the department in the latter's extended absence. He was by the end of the month, as he signed his correspondence, "in charge." He wasted no time in writing a very forceful appeal for an increase in the Inspector General's Department, urging the Secretary in the strongest terms to support legislation to that end. After the drifting of recent years, it was apparent that when Breckinridge became senior inspector general, the department was destined to receive strong leadership.[39]

Special Investigations in the 1880s

During the time of Breckinridge's rise, the decade of the 1880s, the inspectors general continued to perform a number of services that had become traditional for them in recent years. A few new duties were added as well. One

---

37. *ARSecWar 1888*, H. Ex. Doc. 1, 50th Cong., 2d sess., vol. 1, pt. 2: 4; John M. Schofield, *Forty-Six Years in the Army* (New York: Century, 1897), 468–70; Russell F. Weigley, "The Military Thought of John M. Schofield," *Military Affairs*, 23 (summer 1959): 82–83.

38. *ARIG 1888*, H. Ex. Doc. 1, 50th Cong., 2d sess. vol. 1, pt. 2: 98–99. See Appendix B.

39. *ARIG 1889*, 118; Breckinridge to Secy of War, 1 Dec 88, in Letters Sent 1863–1889, RG 159. Breckinridge's signature begins appearing on correspondence 30 October, preceded by Hughes'.

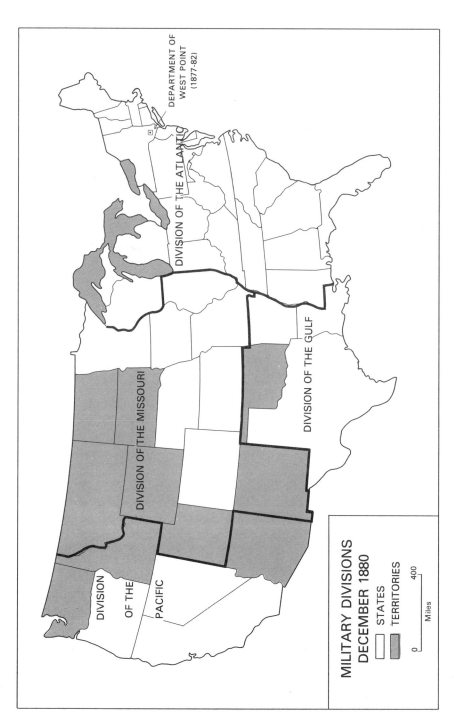

MILITARY DIVISIONS
DECEMBER 1880

☐ STATES
▨ TERRITORIES

0   400
Miles

DIVISION OF THE ATLANTIC

DEPARTMENT OF
WEST POINT
(1877-82)

DIVISION OF THE GULF

DIVISION OF THE MISSOURI

DIVISION
OF THE
PACIFIC

MAP 3

responsibility customary since the Civil War, that is, special investigations for the Secretary, continued to be imposed, but it declined in proportion to the other departmental activities. The secretaries of the 1880s were not as interested as their predecessors in maintaining their own personal corps of investigators. The inspectors general were more closely associated with the Commanding General and the uniformed Army during the decade, and, besides, they were mostly assigned to divisions and departments.

There were some special assignments, however, especially during the early part of the decade. In 1881, when the Surgeon General complained about the conditions in which his clerical staff worked, the Secretary of War sent Roger Jones to make a "sanitary inspection" of the room occupied by the Medical Department's clerks. He found 136 people and 17,000 volumes of records crammed into insufficient space, the place's oxygen further consumed by the gaslights with which it was illuminated. Conditions, in other words, were beastly, the air almost poisonous. Jones pronounced them unhealthy, and urged immediate relief.[40] However, The Army's Signal Service became the object of the greatest number of special investigations on the Secretary's behalf. That was because it was new, and engaged in the mysterious arts of telegraphy, meteorology, and other arcana. Its staffing was also erratic, which caused personnel problems, while its telegraphic operations involved a lot of money generated in thousands of small message charges. Moreover, the Signal Service, like the Corps of Engineers, was a self-contained technical establishment that paralleled, but was uncontrolled by, the rest of the Army. It therefore needed watching, and unlike the Corps of Engineers was not well enough established or powerful enough to resist inspections.

Absalom Baird's first special assignment in the Washington office in 1881 was to investigate the Signal Service, beginning with its fiscal operations. His first recommendation was that a certain captain be assigned as the service's auditor of accounts, and that an incompetent lieutenant detailed to the work be sent back to his regiment. Meanwhile, the Chief Signal Officer objected to inspections of his organization by the inspectors general. His justification, echoing those of Ordnance and the Engineers over many years, was that his agency was specialized, accessible only to specialists. Sacket responded smartly that he had no objection to signal officers inspecting purely technical matters, but he insisted that inspectors general be allowed to inspect Signal Service operations as they made the rounds of military posts.[41]

Most of the Signal Service's facilities were small telegraph and weather stations at military posts. They were the responsibility of the Signal Service, not the post commanders, who were in that context unwilling landlords. The Signal Service establishment depended on a scattering of young officers, each of whom supervised a number of stations under the immediate management of

---

40. Jones to Secy of War, 18 Feb 81, in Letters Sent 1863–1889, RG 159.
41. Baird to AG, 24 Oct 81, and to IG, 10 Nov 81; Sacket, Ind on Ltr from Chief Signal Officer, 24 Oct 81; all in Letters Sent 1863–1889, RG 159.

enlisted men. By 1883, the Inspector General's Department was involved in one squabble after another over the subject of inspections of Signal Service operations. At the same time, it appears that telegraph operators routinely pocketed "line receipts," and there was no way Signal Service officers over them could be held accountable for the widespread embezzlement. That did little to encourage tighter supervision in an organization that was very loose.[42] So, responding to the reports of inspectors and complaints from line commanders, the Secretary of War exerted his jurisdiction on the Signal Service at the end of 1883. Department commanders were told to extend their authority to include Signal Service men in their territories. The control was not to interfere with signal duties, but was to ensure proper military behavior on the part of signalmen. For that purpose, an immediate general inspection of all departmental Signal Service operations was ordered, except that inspectors were not permitted to examine telegrams, books, or matters related to weather and money accounts.[43]

It proved impossible to bring the Signal Service completely in line with the ordinary standards of the Army. Its enlisted men were technically proficient, and by training and situation, independent. The service's officers were also capable technicians, but not necessarily good managers of men who sometimes bordered on the rebellious. In 1885 Baird was sent to make a special investigation at Fort Myer, Virginia, the service's home base. A garrison court-martial there had tried a very large number of men for insubordinate behavior. Baird believed that the men had been tried wrongfully, and that they had legitimate grievances. But, except for the chief signal officer, the entire commissioned complement of the Signal Service was a gathering of second lieutenants too green to handle wisely the odd collection of individualists that comprised the enlisted force. Baird concluded that if the men at Fort Myer had been permitted to take their complaints to the Chief Signal Officer, the whole contretemps would have been avoided.[44]

Soldiers' Home, Military Prison, Cemeteries

Another special investigation eventually led to a permanent assignment for the Inspector General. The United States Soldiers' Home was established by Congress in the 1850s to provide a refuge for retired enlisted men otherwise unable to take care of themselves. Located in Washington, D.C., the establishment was supported by deductions from the pay of active soldiers, and was modeled on similar institutions in Europe. It first came to the attention of the inspectors general in 1882, when Baird was sent to look into alleged conflicts of interest involving contracts to supply meat. He found some unseemly overlaps in the contractor's selling of meat to officers running the home and his contract with the home itself.[45] Subsequently, Congress imposed a code of

---

42. See, for instance, Baird, Ind on papers, responsibility of certain officers for public funds, 4 May 83, in Letters Sent 1863–1889, RG 159.
43. GO No. 105, AGO, 29 Dec 83, in GORI&IG.
44. Baird to AG, 31 Dec 85, in Letters Sent 1863–1889, RG 159.
45. Baird to AG, 12 Dec 82, in Letters Sent 1863–1889, RG 159.

regulations on the home in March 1883. This code directed "that the Inspector-General of the Army shall, in person, once in each year thoroughly inspect the Home, its records, accounts, management, discipline, and sanitary condition, and shall report thereon in writing, together with such suggestions as he desires to make." By "Inspector-General of the Army" Congress clearly meant the senior inspector general, who had occasionally been referred to in that way, but never before in the law. That the senior inspector himself was to examine the home may have underscored the care Congress wanted the place to be shown, but it was an assignment that could have been filled as well by any inspector. Nevertheless, Sacket and his successors dutifully made their annual visits each fall, beginning in 1883. Interest in Soldiers' Home activities remained at a high level. For instance, in 1885, General Sheridan sent Baird to investigate anonymous complaints about the food at the Soldiers' Home. Baird made several surprise mealtime visits, and found no grounds for complaint. Otherwise, the Soldiers' Home became an ordinary part of the senior Inspector General's routine, although its inspection was reported with unusual meticulousness and an eye to administrative improvement. More worth noting is the fact that the inspection of the home was a duty that the Inspector General owed directly to the Secretary of War. The reports were not brought to the attention of the Commanding General; they were addressed to the Secretary. The legislated authority for the annual inspection was a further wedge into the divided subordination of the Inspector General's Department to two masters.[46]

The inspection of the Military Prison was already routine by the 1880s. In a typical comment, Sacket said in 1881 "the government of the convicts is humane and kind, but withal firm and uniform." The place was clean and in good order and well supplied, while the convicts were busy making boots, shoes, harnesses and barracks chairs for the Army. The place needed either expansion or limits on its population. Sometimes the inspection caused the visiting officers to ponder more fundamental questions, as when Jones said in 1881 that the absence of uniformity of sentences throughout the Army was brought home to him on a visit to the prison. Penal reform was needed, he said. Otherwise, the inspections were ordinary, but far from perfunctory.[47] Because of growing interest in army reform, the Secretary made the Military Prison his personal concern. In 1883, new regulations for the prison, replacing a code adopted in 1877, called for the place to be inspected every three months by one of the inspectors of the Army, who was to report to the Secretary. The inspectors (Davis most often) dutifully related what they found, observing the expanding work program and physical plant. But when Baird became senior inspector

---

46. An Act Prescribing Regulations for the Soldier's Home Located at Washington, in the District of Columbia, and for Other Purposes, approved 3 March 1883, 22 Stat. 564; GO No. 24, AGO, 11 Apr 83, in GORI&IG; Baird to Sheridan, 22 Jan 85, in Letters Sent 1863–1889, RG 159. The annual inspection reports were often published in *ARSecWar*. The National Home for Disabled Volunteer Soldiers, a separate establishment, was created later, and is discussed later.

47. *ARIG 81*, 78; Jones to AG, 18 Mar 81, and Sacket to AG, 20 Jul 81, in Letters Sent 1863–1889, RG 159; *ARIG 1882*, 72–73.

general, his resistance to modern leniencies came through. The Military Prison, he said, had proved a failure in its purpose, and should be discontinued and the inmates returned to the ball-and-chain routine of post guardhouses. He felt the recent experiments absorbed too much manpower which could be used better elsewhere. Nevertheless, the prison continued past Baird's time, and in 1888 the quarterly secretarial inspections were continued in new regulations.[48]

The inspection of national cemeteries became in the 1880s another duty the Inspector General's Department accrued from the Secretary of War, not the Commanding General. In 1882 Sacket declared these cemeteries a marked contrast to the disgraceful condition of most post cemeteries, and asked that the latter be upgraded. But he found the special inspection of the national properties an onerous duty, and asked that the governing regulation be revoked. The Secretary agreed, and in February 1882 required that national cemeteries, and other army installations, be inspected annually by division or department inspectors under the direction of their commanders. By 1883 the Quartermaster Department was spending over $8,000 per year at post cemeteries, and vastly more at the national cemeteries, transferring remains, repairing headboards, and building fences. With such heavy Quartermaster involvement in cemetery management, in 1883 the Secretary permitted department commanders to designate Quartermaster Department officers in charge of national cemeteries to be their special inspectors. For several years, then, national cemeteries became the least of the concerns touching the Inspector General's Department.[49] Sacket was not the type of administrator to perceive the utility of national cemetery inspections as another direct connection to the Secretary of War and a justification for greater bureaucratic independence under the Secretary. He merely saw the duty as a waste of his department's time because no more than a perfunctory inspection was required. His successors were only slightly quicker to realize that the growing system of military colleges might provide the occasion for an expansion of authority, and manpower, in the Inspector General's Department.

Military Colleges

The Army as a whole gave civilian military instruction little notice for several years. A few incidental inspections of Regular Army officers detailed to colleges had been made during Marcy's last year, but no systematic attempt was made to inspect them until the mid-1880s. Baird visited several colleges in Ohio in 1884, but was not enthusiastic at first. In July 1884, when Congress permitted the detail of as many as forty officers as presidents, superintendents, or professors at colleges or universities, followed by the assignment of thirty-

48. GO No. 100, AGO, 21 Dec 83, and GO No. 5, AGO, 4 Feb 88, in GORI&IG; *ARSecWar 1884*, H. Ex. Doc. 1, 48th Cong., 2d sess., vol. 1, pt 2: 10; *ARIG 1884*, 84; *ARIG 1886*, 111.

49. *ARIG 1882*, 70; Sacket to AG, 30 Jan 82, in Letters Sent 1863–1889, RG 159; GO No. 17, AGO, 9 Feb 82, and GO No. 73, AGO, 20 Oct 83, in GORI&IG; *ARQMG 1883*, H. Ex. Doc. 1, 48th Cong., 1st sess., vol. 1, pt. 2: 561.

nine officers and the transfer of ordnance and stores to thirty-seven colleges, Baird recommended an inspection program to protect the federal interest. The Inspector General's Department was directed to inspect the college programs in 1885. Although no inspections had yet been made, Baird expected them to be worthwhile.[50] Division and department inspectors general began to examine colleges with military programs annually in February 1886. Before long, the great number of such programs put most inspections in the hands of officers, mostly young, detailed especially to the purpose.

A number of thoughtful officers believed that collegiate military instruction would not only provide potential officers in future wars, but would inculcate military virtues and sympathy for the Army among society's leaders. Even Baird had become an advocate of military colleges by 1887. That year, he said, his officers had inspected nearly all the colleges before the travel budget ran out. He believed that colleges receiving federal personnel and assistance should be subject to a code of regulations that defined the duties of detailed officers and specified what was expected of the colleges in return for the loan of an officer and equipment. Baird also urged a maximum four-year detail for instructors, and the issue of a federal diploma to the students. But there were limits to Baird's enthusiasm, as there were to any new venture. He feared that officers might come to enjoy campus life rather too much, when they should be with their regiments. "The fact is," he said, "every officer should be in the place to which his commission assigns him, and when it becomes distasteful to him he ought to retire."[51]

Baird's temporary successors (Jones being sick at home) were somewhat more favorably inclined. Inspection reports showed that a number of colleges had introduced target practice, but not enough ammunition was provided. The colleges would become the source of officers for any great emergency, said the annual report of the Inspector General's Department, and ensuring the proficiency of the new officers would be wise because "fire tactics" had replaced "shock tactics" on the battlefield. The report accordingly recommended giving the colleges all the ammunition they wanted, in the hope that rifle competitions would become a popular college sport. As with the National Guard, college military instruction increasingly would become an object of the Inspector General's attention in the following years.[52]

Disbursing Accounts

Inspection of the accounts of disbursing officers was an old subject for the inspectors general, but it also grew steadily, and virtually all books were gone over in tedious detail every year. In 1881 the Adjutant General asked that

---

50. *ARIG 1886*, 113; Baird to AG 31 Mar 84, in Letters Sent 1863–1889; *ARIG 1885*, 117. Sanger, "Inspector-General's Department," 246, mistakenly says that inspections of the colleges were assigned to the department in June 1886.

51. *ARIG 1887*, 112–13.

52. *ARIG 1888*, 118.

divisional and departmental inspectors be directed to make quarterly inspections of the contingent expense accounts of Adjutant General's Department officers at the geographic headquarters. During that year (fiscal year 1882), under the 1874 legislation, the Inspector General's Department audited all accounts, covering disbursements totaling $53,854,922.86, 92 percent of which was verified by the department's permanent or acting inspectors and the rest by special inspectors. "This large aggregate," Sacket explained, "is caused by the fact that much of the funds was transferred from one officer to another, and thus became several times the subject of examination."[53] In 1883 Sacket reported that the inspections revealed public funds "have generally been disbursed properly. One exception is noted, where official action has been taken and the offender convicted and sentenced to the penitentiary." The Paymaster General that year reported the dismissal of a paymaster "for misappropriation of the public funds." The man "was a defaulter in the sum of $5,452. The amount was made good to the United States during the progress of his trial." That was a triumph for the inspectors. In 1884, Sacket recommended some protection for officers, especially in the Corp of Engineers, who carried large amounts of cash as payment for civilians and were thus vulnerable to robbery or accidents. As for the Army generally, the inspectors had detected several cases of fraud, ending with the dismissal of misbehaving officers, but the Army suffered scandal for their work. The most prevalent offense was duplication of pay accounts by drawing pay from more than one paymaster. Sacket believed that could be ended by giving each paymaster an exclusive list of the officers he must pay, revising the lists whenever officers transferred.[54]

The account inspections were a monstrous burden, and a growing one. The load was in fact excessive for inspectors and audited officers alike, so in August 1885 the War Department reduced the inspection schedule from six times a year to "once every four months, allowing a reasonable interval between any two examinations," beginning in fiscal year 1886 (which had begun the month before). The inspection system was amended once again the following March, although the thrice-yearly schedule remained, "at irregular intervals." Division and department commanders were to order inspections of the books of officers under their command, by their regular inspectors or others detailed to the duty. But disbursing officers not under the geographic commanders, that is, staff department officers answering to the War Department, were inspected in a national system. The Inspector General in Washington would inform division and department inspectors of those staff officers. The lesser inspectors were to submit to Washington a plan for inspecting those officers, and to request orders. They would be ordered to such inspections by the War Department, and would send their reports directly to the Inspector General's Office in Washington.[55]

53. AG to IG, 28 Oct 81, in Letters Sent 1863–1889, RG 159; *ARIG 1882*, 67.

54. *ARIG 1883*, 99; *AR Paymaster General* 1883, H. Ex. Doc. 1, 48th Cong., 1st sess., vol. 1, pt. 2: 633; *ARIG 1884*, 94–95, 96–97.

55. GO No. 87, AGO, 7 Aug 85, and GO No. 14, AGO, 29 Mar 86, in GORI&IG.

The inspection of accounts had been part of the department's divided accountability to the Secretary of War and the Commanding General. Previously it had gone forward in one system, relying mainly on the department inspectors. But staff department officers at depots and other War Department installations had resisted inspection by officers under the order of geographic department or division commanders. The commanders had no direct authority over those staff officers, who answered to their chiefs in Washington. The new order introduced in 1886 resolved that dilemma, and also gave the Secretary an independent look into the operations of the staff departments, which spent most of the Army's money. It also gave the Inspector General's Department a closer connection to the Secretary of War, and another range of activity wholly separate from the concerns of the Commanding General. Now even departmental inspectors served two masters, which was bound to have its influence in later years as the Inspector General's Department continued to seek recognition as an independent staff department comparable to all others. More immediately, the arrangement was politically useful to the Secretary. When the Washington *Post*, in July 1887, quoted a Second Comptroller of the Treasury as claiming that books of some army and navy paymasters had not been examined in five years, Baird was able to send the news clipping and a detailed refutation to the Secretary of War—along with a list of all paymasters and the date each was last audited.[56]

Property Inspections

Inspections of condemned property were another old responsibility of the inspectors general. They gave little scope for the expansion of departmental influence, however, so they were considered merely routine. They were mostly the subject of endless meddling at the hands of the money-conscious War Department. Orders announced in 1881 that subsistence stores not fit to eat but having value in manufacturing or as animal food were not to be destroyed after condemnation, but were to be advertised and sold instead. If the items were dangerous to purchasers or consumers, their unfitness as human food must be part of the sale notice. Inspectors were required to certify that any subsistence stores condemned had no monetary value at or near the military post where they were located.[57] Other orders in 1882 announced technical changes in the marking of condemned property and the methods of canceling the inspectors "I.C." Trivial alterations in property condemnation procedures continued to appear the principle governing subsistence stores was extended to all property that year, inspectors being allowed to order the destruction of unserviceable property only if they certified it was worthless. In addition, the inspection of unserviceable ordnance property was restricted to Ordnance Department officers. Two years later, unserviceable telescopes and signaling gear issued to compa-

---

56. Baird to Secy of War, 23 Jul 87, in Letters Sent 1863–1889, RG 159.
57. GO No. 56, AGO, 21 Jun 81, in GORI&IG.

nies was similarly removed from the purview of inspectors. It was to be reported to the Chief Signal Officer, who would order its disposition.[58]

The War Department never lost an opportunity to save a dollar. It declared in 1886, "Inspecting officers will not order the destruction of any saddles until the action of the Secretary of War is had upon the inspection reports, as there is a good market with constant demand for the unserviceable Army saddle even when only the tree remains." When inspectors were less than diligent the War Department was aware of it. In 1888 a decision of the Secretary of War reminded inspectors that they must state in their certificate of inspection, if such was the case, that the property was worthless, had no monetary value near the depot where it was housed, and had been destroyed in the inspector's presence.[59]

The Sales List

Another old responsibility, that of preparing the Subsistence Department sales list, gradually fell away during the 1880s. It was still the responsibility of the inspectors general under the law, but they were more interested in other things. It was through Marcy's efforts that, in January 1881, the Secretary of War ordered the Subsistence Department at all posts to stock clothes and hair brushes, combs, towels, needles, and thread. At recruit depots, the sales inventory was also to include tin plates and cups, knives and forks, and button sticks (hooks) and brushes. Once the supplies were on hand, stoppages against the men's pay in favor of post traders was to cease "absolutely." But a month later, the Secretary directed the Ordnance Department to furnish to soldiers as regular equipment tin silverware and a meat can, plate, cup, and button sticks and brushes. Those objects therefore fell off the subsistence list. The inspectors general continued to tamper with the list during the decade, but it received progressively less attention.[60]

Signs of Change

Hughes' 1889 report and the advent of Joseph C. Breckinridge, who expected his brigadier general's stars at any moment, were both indications of new things to come. Breckinridge soon demonstrated that Hughes' insights were not really exceptional, but rather the epitome of the new class of inspectors who had so recently taken over the Inspector General's Department. That a different style would now characterize the Inspector General's Department was suggested with respect to a specific item, that is, horses, something dear to the heart of the bluegrass Kentuckian, Breckinridge. When he learned that authority had

---

58. GO No. 4, AGO, 16 Jan 82; GO No. 5, AGO, 17 Jan 82; GO No. 22, AGO, 8 Mar 82; and GO No. 125, AGO, 20 Nov 84, all in GORI&IG.

59. Decision of Secy of War, 2 Mar 86, in Cir No. 3, AGO, 14 Apr 86, and *Decision of Secy of War*, 7 May 88, in GO No. 5, AGO, 9 Jun 88, both in GORI&IG.

60. GO No. 2, AGO, 4 Jan 81, and GO No. 14, AGO, 7 Feb 81, in GORI&IG; Davis to Secy of War, through AG, 30 Apr 85, in Letters Sent 1863–1889, RG 159.

BRIG. GEN. ROGER JONES. *Inspector General of the Army, 20 August 1888–26 January 1889.*

been granted for the Army to buy horses, Breckinridge stepped in uninvited to urge that none over seven years of age be bought, at least for the artillery.[61] Neither Sacket nor Baird would have done any such thing; they would have permitted the purchase by the proper authorities. They would have observed the results of the purchase, and if the animals were especially defective might even have said so in guarded terms. The old-timers would never have taken it upon themselves to step in and advise preventive measures before a problem arose. But the class of 1861 was gone now. Breckinridge's department had for over two decades been a center of conservatism in the Army. He wanted to make it a wellspring of progressivism. He also set out to make it a truly independent bureau of the War Department. How far he would get with either depended, in the final analysis, upon his own strengths and limitations.

The declining interest of the Inspectors General in items like the sales list reflected their growing interest in greater things. No longer a purely military eye on the Army, the Inspector General's Department was becoming the War Department's chief auditor of accounts. Its attention also was expanding beyond the War Department, encompassing military colleges and the National Guard. It was a far different organization from the one that Marcy and the others had composed in 1861 and led since the Civil War. Its differences were reflected in changes in its personnel: Roger Jones had been the last of the inspectorate's class of 1861, the inspectors general and assistant inspectors general appointed during the Civil War's first year. These men had been veterans of the old army before the war, so that great conflict, although an instructive experience for them, was not a formative one. They all recognized intellectually that times must change, in the Army as elsewhere, but they all instinctively preferred things as they once had been. Sometimes, as when Marcy resisted modern barracks lighting or Baird the three-battalion regiment, the inspectors general bordered on the reactionary. Despite their conservatism, however, the Army did begin to reform in the decades after the Civil War. The inspectors general, sometimes grumbling, sometimes optimistic, went along, but they were never leaders of reform.

---

61. Breckinridge to AG, 28 Dec 88, in Letters Sent 1863–1889, RG 159.

Jones was replaced on 30 January 1889 by Breckinridge. Like Jones, Breckinridge was a veteran of the Civil War, but the resemblance goes no further. The war had been the start of Breckinridge's military career, which had begun in volunteer service, not at West Point. Furthermore, Breckinridge had spent most of the postwar period as a troop commander, not as an inspector. Behind Breckinridge was a completely new generation of inspectors general. None had much of an emotional investment in the way things once had been. None had been in the Army before the war, and all had joined the Inspector General's Department since the early 1880s. Not all of them had even been veterans of the war, nor had all of them begun their careers at West Point, or even as officers. They were, in fact, creatures of the new army, and bound to share its emerging outlook. And last, Breckinridge and the others were far younger than Marcy's company of old warriors. They were certain to make their energy felt, and wanted only an equally energetic leader to make them effective. Breckinridge promised to be that man, but it remained to be seen just what kind of a leader he really was.

When Breckinridge took over the Inspector General's Department, the Army was at the midpoint of a slow, painful transition. A small frontier constabulary, long accustomed to life in the wilderness, earnestly wanted to become a modern military force and neighbor to the civilized parts of the nation. The inspectors general had watched the changes creeping up for the past decade, altering the conditions that had been accepted before the Civil War. If Breckinridge was the character he appeared to be, the inspectors general would not merely watch changes come in the future, but would labor to bring them about. The old inspectorate was gone. A new Inspector General's Department had arrived.

CHAPTER 18

Breckinridge's Widening Scope

(1889–1898)

Roger Jones' death on 26 January 1889 had been preceded by that of Henry J. Farnsworth on 19 November 1888. The two events initiated another rearrangement of personnel within the department, and two appointments to keep its complement at full strength. Breckinridge became senior inspector general on 30 January 1889. Edward Heyl was promoted to colonel and Henry W. Lawton to lieutenant colonel on 12 February. To fill Farnsworth's vacancy, Capt. Peter D. Vroom, 3d Cavalry, had already become a major and an inspector general, on 10 December 1888. On 12 February 1889, Capt. Joseph P. Sanger, 1st Artillery, joined the department, also as a major and an inspector general.[1] Experienced troop leaders who had entered the army during or after the Civil War were beginning to fill the inspectorate's ranks.

New Department Under New Leadership

Vroom had entered the Army as first lieutenant and adjutant of the 1st New Jersey Infantry in 1862. He resigned that position to become a major in the 2d New Jersey Cavalry, where he remained until mustered out in October 1865. He earned a brevet in the interim for "gallant and meritorious service during the war." He joined the Regular Army in February 1866 as a second lieutenant and was promoted to first lieutenant within five months, in the 3d Cavalry. His experience included half a year as regimental commissary and two and a half years as regimental adjutant before his promotion to captain in May 1876. Vroom was a solid officer with an unremarkable career, who may never have become a major had it not been for the opportunity in the Inspector General's Department. He pursued an equally steady course there, rising through the seniority system until a graveyard promotion to senior inspector general, with the rank of brigadier general just one day before he retired on 12 April 1903.[2]

Sanger had entered the service in much the same fashion as Vroom, as a second lieutenant of the 1st Michigan Infantry in May 1861. There the similarity ended, for Sanger was anything but an ordinary man. The Michigan native was

---

1. *ARIG 1889*, H. Ex. Doc. 1, 51st Cong., 1st sess., vol. 1, pt. 2: 118.
2. Heitman, *Historical Register*, 1: 990.

inducted into the Regular Army on 5 August 1861 as a second lieutenant of the 1st Artillery, and was promoted to first lieutenant in October. He earned two brevets for gallantry during the Civil War while serving with the Army of the Potomac. Sanger spent two years as regimental adjutant of the 1st Artillery before his promotion to captain in 1875, retaining that rank for three weeks after his promotion to the Inspector General's Department in 1889. By the time he arrived in the inspectorate, he was already well known as a thoughtful contributor to the professional literature of the military, with articles on many subjects to his credit. He was also a great favorite of the Commanding General, John M. Schofield, serving him as aide in the Division of the Atlantic in 1886 and after. Schofield recalled that his work on improving the instruction of artillery with new weapons was "ably and zealously assisted" by the labors of Sanger, whom he invited to write a summary of the work for the general's memoirs. Schofield approved Sanger's promotion to inspector general and declared it "well-merited." In 1895, Sanger was again attached to Schofield as an aide-de-camp (with the rank of lieutenant colonel) during the general's farewell tour of the Army before retirement. He authored the commander's tour report.[3] Sanger, thanks to his literary inclinations, became the department's first official historian, something that earned him Breckinridge's gratitude because, as chief, he justified his department's very existence with arguments from history. Sanger followed the course of the seniority system in the department only so far, however, becoming a lieutenant colonel in July 1898. Meanwhile he had already served as a lieutenant colonel and inspector general of volunteers for one month; then he became a brigadier general of volunteers during the Spanish American War. Mustered out of volunteer service in June 1899, Sanger returned to the inspectorate, where he became a colonel in February 1901. He had proved his military merits during the war, and was promoted to brigadier general of the line in July 1902, having a distinguished career thereafter.[4]

When the Army received a new senior inspector general in 1889, a revision of its general regulations had occurred as well. The Army's stated inspections, including company inspections on Sundays, were defined as they had been before, except that company commanders were now enjoined additionally to make daily inspections of barracks and kitchens, while surgeons did the same in hospitals. Post commanders were to inspect their facilities in July, reporting to the Inspector General in Washington on forms furnished for the purpose. "Methods of Inspection" had been revised somewhat, but the content of reports remained traditional, with added attention to subjects like post gardens. The regulations emphasized that inspection reports should discuss the remedies instituted for any deficiencies reported. The reports were to go to the Inspector General in Washington "through the regular channels," but only commanding

3. Ibid., 1: 859; Schofield, *Forty-Six Years*, 458–60. Many of the important documents in the John M. Schofield papers, Manuscript Division, Library of Congress, dating from the 1880s and 1890s were produced by Sanger, including the report of Schofield's farewell inspection.

4. Ibid.

officers could forward confidential reports. The extended attention to subjects like disbursing accounts and condemned property reflected the War Department's endless tampering with minor details, for property alone took up two full pages in the new regulations.[5]

Having disposed his people and examined the new regulations, Breckinridge began to assert himself. He was the only officer to attain a general's stars before 1898 who had ranked less than captain in the reorganization of 1866. Of course, a series of deaths and retirements in the inspectorate had enabled his rise, which otherwise would have been impossible under the hard rule of seniority. But it is not beyond reason to suspect that Breckinridge calculated the odds, or at least counted the scheduled retirements ahead of him, before seeking a position in the Inspector General's Department. If anyone in the Army had the personal ambition and energy to make the system work in his own behalf, that man was Breckinridge.[6] He used this energy in a long campaign to establish the independence of the Inspector General's Department, and to raise its strength and prestige. Much of that effort involved careful maneuvers within the split leadership of the War Department. The Inspector General answered jointly to the Secretary of War and the Commanding General of the Army. Breckinridge adjusted to the contradictions in that divided authority by moving away from the weaker power (the Commanding General) and closer to the stronger (the Secretary of War). Redfield Proctor became Secretary of War 5 March 1889. He was a man of known reformist inclinations, and, in fact, proved himself able to carry through the sorts of real reforms that secretaries like Lincoln had only talked about. Breckinridge had reformist tendencies of his own, compatible with Proctor's views.

Ending Sunday Inspections

On 8 March 1889, three days after Proctor took office, Breckinridge personally handed the Secretary a "Draft of a proposed General Order amending the Regulations," together with "Memoranda in connection with draft of General Order submitted to Secty of War March 8, 1889." Breckinridge proposed to end the weekly inspection of companies on Sundays, moving the procedure to Saturday morning and giving the soldiers a day and a half off every weekend. He told Proctor that Sunday had been a day of rest in the Army previously, by orders of two Presidents. "If President Washington and Lincoln do not represent the best sentiment of the American people when they addressed the Army on this subject, then to whose instructions ought the Army to conform?" he

---

5. U.S. War Department, *Regulations for the Army* (Washington: Government Printing Office, 1889).

6. The recognition that Breckinridge was the only person to become general before 1898 who had not started at least as a captain in 1866 is in Arthur P. Wade, "Roads to the Top—An Analysis of General-Officer Selection in the United States Army, 1789–1898," *Military Affairs*, 40 (December 1976): 162–63.

asked with his distinctive flourish.[7] He had, in fact, proposed the same thing several years before, and had been squelched by Sacket. But aside from its accord with his own sentiments as a former battery commander, it was definitely an idea whose time had come. Proctor was taken with it immediately, and very quickly word spread that the Secretary was preparing an order to abolish Sunday inspections and exercises. However, many high-ranking officers protested, saying that a day of leisure for the soldiers would cause nothing but trouble. Schofield, however, favored the change, so Proctor decided to pursue the idea, but cautiously.[8]

Breckinridge personally handed Proctor a draft of the proposed general order on 7 June. His text cited President Lincoln's establishment in 1862 of Sunday as a day of rest. Proctor took the order to the White House the same day. President Benjamin Harrison imposed it in his capacity as Commander in Chief of the Army and the Navy. Weekly inspections were moved to Saturday morning, and Saturday afternoon became a holiday for sports and recreation. Soldiers were to have no work on Sunday except guard and police duty. Any change in general orders in the future would have to be presidential.[9]

Proctor's caution was justified, because the order met with widespread resistance. Breckinridge told him on 6 August of the various ways in which officers defied or subverted the order, and suggested one way of enforcing that inspections be held on Saturday was to order company commanders to submit weekly reports of their inspections. He provided a draft of a general order to that effect. In October he recommended that the Secretary approve the request of the superintendent of the Military Academy that the cadets' Sunday dress parade (which with preparation took three hours) be dispensed with, thus reinforcing the spirit of the general order across the Army. Breckinridge went so far as to propose ending the cadets' Saturday evening parade. Finally, in February 1890 Schofield interdicted the widespread defiance of the order, which had permitted routine inspections without arms on Sundays. Some captains had turned that into a full-blown inspection, so Schofield ordered them to do all such things only on Saturday.[10] By his efforts to abolish Sunday inspections, Breckinridge had accomplished a significant change. For the Army the new order represented a fundamental change in the management of the enlisted men. The conditions of enlisted life were unpleasant enough, given the Army's

---

7. "Draft of a proposed General Order amending the Regulations handed to the Secretary of War in person by General J.C. Breckinridge Inspector General March 8/89," and "Memoranda in connection with draft of General order submitted to Secty of War March 8, 1889," in Letters Sent 1863–1889, RG 159.

8. Foner, in *Soldier Between Wars*, 91, summarizes the situation, but is evidently unaware of Breckinridge's role.

9. "Draft of an order relative to Sunday Inspections handed by General J.C. Breckinridge Inspector General, in person to the Secretary of War June 7, 1889," in Letters Sent 1863–1889, RG 159; GO 50, AGO, 12 Jun 89, announcing the President's order of 7 Jun 89, in GORI&IG; Foner, *Soldier Between Wars*, 91.

10. Breckinridge to Secy of War, and Incls, 6 Aug 89, and Memo handed to Secy of War by Inspector General Breckinridge, 16 Oct 89, in Letters Sent 1863–1889, RG 159; Cir No. 2, AGO, 12 Mar 90, conveying: Decision of the Commanding General, 15 February 1890, in GORI&IG.

INFANTRY TACTICAL DRILL, SUMMER 1892. *Observation of exercises became a part of each general inspection.*

circumstances, but it was a major grievance to the soldiers that the Army never gave them any rest. That complaint was answered at a stroke. More fundamentally, for the first time the Army had officially told the men that it trusted them to act as soldiers without constant supervision. Some of the officers may have grumbled, but the enlisted men felt that at last they were treated with some respect. The end of Sunday inspections was a major step in the current transformation of the Army.

Building a Definite Sphere

In June 1889 Breckinridge persuaded the Secretary to add West Point to the list of posts to be examined by the Inspector General's Department. He ordered the first inspection in July. He then asserted strongly that his office, not that of the Adjutant General, was the proper repository for inspection reports on military colleges, and, by extension for all inspection reports. As the activities of the inspectorate increased, he resumed in the strongest terms, his customary appeals for more clerks for the inspectors general at the various geographical headquarters.[11] So Breckinridge had unfettered control of all inspection during his first year in office. His was the designated office to receive reports of

---

11. Breckinridge Ind or Ltr of Col. J.G. Parke, 19 Jun 89, and chief clerk of the War Department, Ind on same, 24 Jun 89; Breckinridge to IG USA, Governors.Island, 5 Jul 89; Breckinridge, Ind on Ltr of AG requesting originals or full copies of inspection reports of colleges, 15 Jul 89; and Breckinridge to Secy of War, 16 Aug 89, all in Letters Sent 1863–1889, RG 159.

National Guard inspections, inspections of the recruiting service, and even the construction projects of the Corps of Engineers. As he frequently apprised the Adjutant General, he was very close to the Secretary of War. He told Proctor early in November that he hoped that year to have the first complete inspection of all branches of the Army. On 22 November he handed the Secretary a draft of an order directing the Inspector General's Department to inspect all army facilities not under divisional or departmental commanders, or not otherwise provided for in the regulations. That especially included the facilities of the Corps of Engineers and the Ordnance Department.[12] Thanks to Breckinridge and Proctor, paragraph 955 of the general regulations was revised to say that the entire military establishment was to be inspected annually. That included public works under the Corps of Engineers as well as the arsenals, armories, depots, and other facilities of the several staff departments, in addition to the entire uniformed Army in all its posts and stations.

There were other additions to the department's responsibilities during Breckinridge's first year. The duty of inspecting the accounts of the War Department's Supply Division was transferred from the Quartermaster to the Inspector General on 19 January 1889, apparently because the establishment was, in the main, operated by the Quartermaster. Breckinridge's purview over the Signal Service was extended in February, when orders appeared to train officers and men in signaling. Every post was to be visited annually by an inspector so that the signaling efficiency of all officers and enlisted men who had had instruction and practice could be rated. Divisional and departmental commanders were told in August to inscribe on inspection reports the instructions intended to remedy defects. Finally, in September the Secretary expressed his displeasure that the ban on hard liquor had not been enforced. Moreover, post traders thenceforth could sell light wine and beer only in unbroken packages, and then only to officers or post canteens. Inspectors' reports were to set forth any violations of the order, and remedies were to be instituted.[13]

Breckinridge appreciated the value of symbolism, and no detail was too insignificant to escape his notice. The Army's uniform regulations were reissued on 5 May 1889, accommodating changes made since the last general revision in 1881. Officers of the Adjutant General's and Inspector General's Departments and aides-de-camp to general officers wore the same shoulder knots—gold cord on a blue cloth ground, and aiguillette. Officers of other staff corps wore the same shoulder knot, but without the aiguillette. Most staff departments identified themselves with initials, as they had since 1872, but the Signal Corps now displayed two crossed signal flags and a burning torch, the

---

12. Breckinridge to AG 14 Nov and 16 Nov 89 (two letters); Breckingridge, Ind forwarding to Secy of War copies of letters and endorsements relative to the inspection of West Point and Willetts Point, N.Y., 11 Nov 89; copy (of order) received by Secy of War from IG, 22 Nov 89, all in Letters Sent 1863–1889, RG 159. See also Sanger, "Inspector-General's Department," 247.

13. Orders, Secy of War, 19 Jan 89; GO No. 19, AGO, 20 Feb 89; Cir No. 7, AGO, 3 Aug 89, conveying: Decision of the Secretary of War, 5 July 1889; and GO No. 75, 27 Sep 89, all in GORI&IG.

Corps of Engineers a turreted castle, and the Ordnance Department a shell and flame. Officers of arms wore crossed muskets, sabers, or cannons. The age of insignia had dawned, and Breckinridge wanted to be a part of it. He complained to the Adjutant General on 22 July 1889, "If something is deemed necessary on our shoulder knots and epaulettes, it should not be anything like a lettered brand that is placed upon public animals and property. . . . I will be glad to submit an approved design to have an acceptable insignia made from." Receiving approval, he solicited designs for insignia from several jewelers and uniform manufacturers. First Lieutenant William P. Van Ness suggested a fasces as a fitting symbol for the Inspector General's Department. An axe enclosed in a bundle of rods, it was a sign of public office in ancient Rome. (Until made disreputable by the Fascists of Benito Mussolini during the twentieth century, the fasces long stood as an emblem of civil authority, and of unity forged from diversity.) Breckinridge concurred with Van Ness and collaborated with Mr. C. H. Ourand of the Adjutant General's Office, an authority on such symbolism, to develop the final design. Breckinridge gave his department a motto, *Droit et Avant*, emblazoned on the insignia, which reportedly came from the family coat of arms of Joseph P. Sanger, the newest inspector. Breckinridge said he wanted something that would express the sentiment, "Be sure you are right, then go ahead," which strongly exemplified his attitude toward life. The French phrase (literally "Right and Forward") expressed this adequately.

Breckinridge was ready to present his proposed insignia to the Secretary of War on 14 February 1890. It comprised a crossed sword and fasces surmounted by a wreath bearing the motto. The sword, of course, symbolized military power, but it was subordinated to the fasces, the emblem of civil authority— symbolic of the image Breckinridge wished to promote for his department. The wreath, combining ancient symbols of peace and honor, was composed of two branches, an olive branch on the left and a laurel on the right, which were tied at the base by a ribbon. The Secretary approved the new insignia a few days later and it was authorized to be worn beginning on 23 May.[14] The adoption of unique insignia was only one way in which Breckinridge stressed his department's distinctiveness. Another symbol of the inspectorate's changing role in 1890 was Breckinridge's issuing of two annual reports—one to the Commanding General and a longer one to the Secretary of War. Although the two overlapped somewhat, Breckinridge constructed them so that they reflected the separate and significant spheres of inspection that related to one, not both, of his masters. He continued this practice until just before he retired.[15]

Breckinridge had carved out a considerable position for himself, enjoying close association with the Secretary. But he remained subject to the orders of

14. The history of the insignia is presented in "A Brief History of Insignia, Branch of Service, Officers, Inspector General," (duplicated, files in OIG at the Pentagon), which includes Breckinridge to Secy of War, 14 Feb 90, Ind by Asst AG, 20 Feb 90, endorsement by Secy of War, 26 Feb 90, and the original design, with specifications, issued 15 Jun 64 and 20 Jun 66.

15. For purposes of convenience, both will be cited as *ARIG*. Only twice, in 1900 and 1901, did they have overlapping page numbers, although sometimes they were in different volumes of the War Department annual reports. For those two years the exact report will be reflected in citations.

the Commanding General, whereas most of his officers were answerable to the divisional commanders. The officers of the Inspector General's Department, supplemented by a shifting group of acting inspectors general, remained stable during most of 1890. Vroom moved from the Department of the Platte to the Department of the Missouri on 9 September to replace Sanger, who had spent most of the year in the Washington office and was officially transferred there from the Division of the Missouri. The part of Breckinridge's scope visible in Washington (in bureau circles, the most important part) had thereby increased.[16] Despite this, the number of officers in the Inspector General's Department, Breckinridge told a sympathetic Secretary, was "utterly inadequate" for all the duties imposed upon them. The few details of officers from the line were not enough help he said; besides, some inspections could not be done by transients, it required experienced personnel. A bill then before Congress would add six officers, two of them field-grade, to the department, and Breckinridge yearned for its passage. The volume of the department's work, he said, had grown phenomenally, and if the inspecting officers decided to obey the law limiting their workdays to eight hours, it would not get done. He was equally strong on his proclaimed need for clerical assistance to replace the "uncertain detail of general-service men." Good, permanent civilian clerks under full control of the Inspector General's Department, he claimed, were essential, and he offered a full page of examples on how the lack of clerical assistance hampered the department's labors.[17]

Breckinridge continued to increase his department's authority and its work load. Every inspector was told in January 1891 to give each commander, at the end of an inspection, a written statement of deficiencies detected, which was to be kept on file for future information. The commanding officer was told to report to the officer who ordered the inspection not only the remedies he had applied but also the recommendations for actions beyond his ability to effect them. That statement was to be forwarded to the headquarters of the Army. Every officer required to take action on inspection findings was to note on the report his actions, and to make a supplementary report to army headquarters for the information of the Commanding General. After the Commanding General was satisfied, all reports were to be filed with the Inspector General's Office. Like his predecessors, Breckinridge was obsessed with follow-up: the positive effects of inspection, in terms of administrative action. But he was also establishing his authority over inspection by keeping the paper work safe in his own hands.[18]

Breckinridge maintained later in the year that he had solved the problem of follow-up:

Remedial action usually follows inspections swiftly and surely. The inspector, without unnecessary delay, furnishes commanding officers of posts a memorandum of the defects

16. *ARIG 1890*, 119–21, 122–23.

17. Ibid., 123–25. The department's payroll for fiscal year 1891 was $29,500. GO No. 69, AGO, 27 Jun 90, in GORI&IG.

18. GO No. 11, AGO, 30 Jan 91, in GORI&IG.

and irregularities which came under his notice during inspection, and commanding officers report what remedial action they have applied in each instance; and if no such action has been applied, then they explain why it has not. The benefits arising from such speedy, intelligent, and concerted action are great, and must necessarily grow greater and more far-reaching in their effects as the system becomes familiar and perfected.[19]

The senior inspector general was proud of the work his men accomplished, because it was considerable. The work of the inspectors general in 1891, Breckinridge explained to Schofield, was divided into two classes: those for the Secretary of War and those for the department commanders in the Army line. Only permanent officers of the department, he said, were entrusted with the matters of interest to the Secretary. These included such things as inspections of cemeteries, rivers and harbors, depots, and the recruiting service. In all, during fiscal year 1891, permanent and detailed department members had inspected 740 money accounts representing a value of $63 million. They had also looked at 87 line posts, 41 bureau posts and depots, 5 prisons, 53 military units at colleges and universities, 63 public works, 61 national cemeteries, 36 recruiting rendezvous and 21 special investigations had been made. During this same period, inspectors had filed about 1,600 inventory and inspection reports involving over $1,800,000 worth of property.[20]

The Army's big event during fiscal year 1891 was the winter campaign against the Sioux Indians at Wounded Knee in South Dakota. Breckinridge never mentioned the battle there, or the loss of life that had stunned the nation. Rather, to him the whole campaign showed a need for exercise in cold-weather mobilization. Staff and line both, he said, had performed well, while the Medical Corps deserved special mention. "These larger concentrations are as readily made habitual as the mere company affairs," maintained the Inspector General "and familiarity with them is essential before an organization can be called an army, or be considered either instructed or equipped to meet modern requirements; and the concentration of the past winter was so well considered and conducted as to deserve special study."[21]

A Setback and Renewed Advance

Redfield Proctor resigned from the War Department in November 1891 to take a seat in the Senate. He had been a popular man in the Army, its most productive reformer in recent times. During his relatively brief period in office, the post consolidation program had made progress, work had started on modern coastal defenses, and the lives of the enlisted men had been improved. Proctor's departure deprived Breckinridge of a patron. The Inspector General had greatly expanded his power and influence during the previous two years, an impossible

19. *ARIG 1891*, 10.
20. Ibid., 23–24.
21. Ibid., 19.

feat without making enemies or at least incurring the resentment of others. Breckinridge, in a memorandum to the files, wisely predicted trouble.[22]

Proctor was replaced on 17 December by Stephen B. Elkins, who remained until March 1893. Breckinridge enjoyed Elkins' warm support during his secretaryship, but the close personal relationship and patronage he had received from Proctor was lacking. Adroit as he was, the Inspector General managed to survive Proctor's departure with only one important loss to his power. Congress had directed in March 1891 that the Inspector General's Department provide detailed supervision of the receipts and disbursements of the new National Home for Disabled Volunteer Soldiers. This modest increase was offset when Secretary Elkins removed an important aspect of inspection activities. Officers and staff departments chafing under the Inspector General's increased oversight had become decidedly restive since Secretary Proctor had departed. No department was more fiercely protective of its own independence than the Corps of Engineers, one of the more effective combatants in the War Department's bureaucratic dogfighting. The Chief of Engineers curtailed Breckinridge's increasing scope on 5 July 1892, when that part of paragraph 955 of the regulations authorizing the Inspector General's Department to inspect engineering works was revoked. The responsibility for inspections reverted to the Chief of Engineers and his commanders of engineer divisions. All Breckinridge salvaged was continued authority to inspect Engineer disbursements and financial accounts.[23]

Much of the increase in the department's work load could be attributed to duties imposed by Congress. But in fact Breckinridge himself was generating additional work, especially by having secretaries of war assign it. One of his motives was an honest belief, shared by others, that inspection was beneficial to the Army and the War Department. Equally strong in Breckinridge's thinking was that additional work represented both an expansion of influence for his department and a justification for its increase in size and budget. By 1893, he had added to his store of justifications for increase of his department a growing series of arguments from history. His staff, that year, had prepared a brief history of the Inspector General's Department since 1778, which allowed him to refer to the glories of his predecessors, reaching back to "Baron Steuben, practically the first Inspector-General of the Army." The history was the work of clerk A. C. Quisenberry, who compiled a documentary record and a list of all inspecting officers. Breckinridge used this example to show inspection as one of the training grounds for the great military leaders of all wars; 2 major generals, 7 brigadier generals, 18 colonels, 118 lieutenant colonels, and 149 majors of the Regular Army, he pointed out, had performed inspection duty during the Civil War.[24]

---

22. Breckinridge, Memo, 6 Nov 91, in Letters Sent 1891–1894, *Records of the Inspector General's Office* (hereafter cited as RIGO), RG 159; Cir No. 3, AGO, 5 Dec 91, conveying: Decision of the Commanding General, 21 Nov 91, in GORI&IG.

23. GO No. 45, AGO, 5 Jul 92, in GORI&IG.

24. ARIG 1893, 6. In June 1893, Breckinridge told the Secretary that Quisenberry was working on the project, had gone through all War Department records, and needed authority to examine

(Continued)

INSPECTION AT PROVING GROUND, 12-INCH HOWITZER ON CANET CARRIAGE, 1892. *The activities of the Coast Artillery Corps increased in inspection importance at the end of the 19th century.*

Quisenberry's history soon fell into the hands of Joseph P. Sanger, the inspectorate's most prolific writer. In 1895, Sanger expanded the text into a narrative history of the Inspector General's Department, which was published the next year in a project of the Military Service Institution of the United States, *The Army of the United States: Historical Sketches of Staff and Line with Portraits of Generals-in-Chief*, and which Breckinridge reproduced in 1900 as an appendix to his annual report. Thus Breckinridge, as Inspector General, once again demonstrated that he was a highly imaginative bureau chief by using history to justify his current policies. What was interesting about the published versions of Sanger's history was that they were abridged, because Sanger told the editors to cut it if it was too long. What was not printed was a biased closing that argued at length for a bigger, higher ranked, and above all thoroughly independent Inspector General's Department. Independence, Sanger claimed (probably reflecting Breckinridge's influence) was necessary because of the fragmented War Department organization, little of which answered to the Commanding General. If each War Department bureau had its own inspection

(Continued)
the records of the State Department (the government's chief record keeper for much of the 19th century). Breckinridge to Secy of War, 7 Jun 93, in Letters Sent 1891–1894, RG 159. The main fruit of Quisenberry's labors is: General Orders Relating to Inspection and the Inspector General's Department (GORI&IG). Some of his notes covering the late 1860s are now in RG 159, entry 26, box 6, file 323 miscellaneous, RIGO, Secret Correspondence 1917–1934, National Archives, Washington National Records Center, Suitland, Maryland.

system, the result would be further fragmentation which would reduce the possibility of the Secretary or Commanding General receiving unbiased information. Sanger argued that it was thus particularly important for the Secretary to have his own separate Inspector General's Department to maintain control of War Department affairs through the information provided by its impartial observers.[25]

The interests of the eclectic Breckinridge knew no bounds. Unlike his predecessors, he felt no compunction about offering broad recommendations for the improvement of the military force, even if they involved the terrifying prospect of a reorganization. Breckinridge was one of the first of the Army's top leaders to call for the establishment of a modern general staff, although the idea had been current in American military circles for some time. The Inspector General's version of a "higher general staff" was so couched that it posed no bureaucratic threat to the "lower general staff," for his own organizational mandate included the following specification: "The simple thing we need is that one branch of the staff shall be wholly devoted to strategy, simply the mental part of war, and be constantly accustomed to field service, with each individual fully and permanently under the well-graded authority of those whose province it is to command troops. In short, we need a higher general staff."[26]

More peculiar was Breckinridge's first call, in 1893, for the establishment of a homing pigeon service. After elaborating on the value of pigeons, which he said every modern army used, the Inspector General pointed out there were clubs of pigeon fanciers in all cities. He assured the Secretary that they would be willing to lend their help in the establishment of a national pigeon service. The War Department, Breckinridge suggested, should work to obtain favorable transportation rates for pigeon racers, or subsidize transportation with a small appropriation, out of which also would come prizes for the "best results obtained during the year as is now done in Europe." Every pigeon club should in return make annual reports to the War Department.[27]

An Uncertain New Patron

In March 1893, Secretary Elkins was succeeded by Daniel S. Lamont, whose progressive inclinations were as strong as those of Proctor. Lamont was cautious during his first year or two on the job, however, contenting himself only with a call for an increase of the enlisted force, echoing arguments that had been advanced many times in the past. Rather than condone Breckinridge's ambitions, Lamont made some effort to discourage him. The new Secretary did stop the excessive printing costs associated with the Inspector General's

25. Sanger, "Inspector-General's Department"; Theo. F. Rodenbaugh and William L. Haskins, eds., *The Army of the United States: Historical Sketches of Staff and Line with Portraits of Generals-in-Chief* (New York: Maynard, Merrill, 1896). The complete text of Sanger's history survives in the manuscript, located in file 372, RIGO, Index to General Correspondence 1894–1916, RG 159.

26. *ARIG 1893*, 31–32.

27. Ibid., 33–34.

extremely long annual reports and, beginning in 1894, the Inspector General's report no longer was published in a separate volume. In his annual report of that year, Breckinridge told the Secretary and the Commanding General that, for the first time in several years, a complete inspection had been made of all garrisons and posts within a single fiscal year, for which he said the inspectors should be credited. Inspections that year included 928 disbursement accounts involving over $68 million and inspections of 90 posts; 50 staff facilities, prisons, and ungarrisoned posts; 82 military colleges; 51 national cemeteries; 27 recruiting stations; and 28 special investigations: a total of 1,256 inspections. Regretfully Breckinridge had to report that the annual inspection reports of post commanders, which had been required for about fifteen years, came to an end in 1894. He credited the post commanders' reports with much good, and obviously regretted the loss of that source of information and influence for his department.[28]

By 1894 it was clear that Breckinridge's ambitions continued to earn him enemies. But that resourceful inspector general was ready for any emergency. Asking the Secretary, "Is the Army inspected to death?" "This department," he said, "has not contended for frequent so much as for thorough and complete inspections, equally and fairly applied, or excluded alike from all." Retrenchments in mileage appropriations had curtailed inspections that year, but Breckinridge said that all in the Army realized that inspections were in the interest of discipline. He claimed, "Only a few officers" had objected to inspection, but the implication of his own words was that there had been many complaints about the Inspector General's Department.[29]

Breckinridge began 1895 with a rearrangement of personnel. Edward M. Heyl died on 2 January, making way for George H. Burton's rise to colonel and Peter D. Vroom's to lieutenant colonel. The vacancy for one major was filled by promotion of Capt. Ernest A. Garlington of the 7th Cavalry. Garlington was a certified hero, winner of the Medal of Honor for "distinguished gallantry in action against hostile Sioux Indians on Wounded Knee Creek, South Dakota, 29 December 1890, where he was severely wounded while serving as first lieutenant, 7th Cavalry." Garlington proved to be an effective and energetic addition to the Inspector General's Department.[30]

Independence Gained

Secretary Lamont, his earlier hesitancy put aside, proved a strong supporter of the Inspector General after all. Breckinridge gained one of the greatest triumphs of his career: The Secretary granted nearly complete independence for the Inspector General's Department. Breckinridge had managed to persuade Lamont not only that inspection was in the Secretary's interests, but also that the many complaints from the Army were attempts by commanders to interfere

28. *ARIG 1894*, H. Ex. Doc. 1, 53d Cong., 3d sess., vol. 1, pt. 2: 90–91, 101, 214.
29. Ibid., 214–15.
30. *ARIG 1895*, H. Doc. 2, 54th Cong., 1st sess., vol. 1, pp. 107–08; See Appendix B.

with inspection, and therefore to hide something from the War Department. Schofield apparently voiced no strong objections to Breckinridge's scheme, and was in fact looking forward to retirement in the fall. The Commanding General had been thoroughly dismayed by the War Department's bureaucratic dogfighting since taking office, and chose not to spend his last months involved in another controversy. As a result, On 30 March 1895 the Secretary ordered that, effective 30 April, the United States be divided into six inspection districts "whose limits," reported Breckinridge, "were determined by the questions of economy of travel and equalization of work. The number of acting inspectors-general was reduced from six to one." The new system put the entire inspectorate directly under the Secretary of War and (nominally) the Commanding General. What was really important about the new arrangement was that department commanders no longer controlled officers of the Inspector General's Department, who now covered territories that took in, with equal interest, military posts and secretarial concerns such as staff facilities and cemeteries.[31] Breckinridge had evoked George Washington's inspectorate to justify this new structure. This was imaginative, but also inaccurate and self-serving, to say the least. If anything had characterized Washington's attitude toward inspection, it was its utter absorption into the military command. The army commander, not its Inspector General, answered to the civil authority for the Army's performance. In Breckinridge's scheme, the Inspector General served the civil authority represented by the Secretary of War, and only nominally served the Commanding General. That was a logical product both of the division of authority in the War Department and of Breckinridge's ambitions for bureaucratic independence, but it effectively separated inspection from command.

Despite the predictable complaints from department commanders, the *Army and Navy Journal* observed the new inspection system with interest and a great deal of favor. The dual system of department commanders and inspectors general, each making annual inspections and reporting to the Secretary of War, said the editors, was very promising. The *Journal* emphasized Lamont's involvement in the new district inspection system on 20 April, and printed a list of the districts and the facilities they contained, along with inspection schedules. Finally, on 22 June, the editors reported, "The first inspections under the new method . . . were made during the past few weeks by the Inspection Corps, and the result has been all that its advocates have claimed for it." Inspections, said the periodical, had been complete, thorough, in accord with the Secretary of War's desires, and reduced travel costs.[32] The system had begun so quickly because Breckinridge had arranged his officers as soon as possible once the district system took effect. Hughes held the North Atlantic District, with an office in New York City. Burton reported on the Pacific District from San

---

31. GO No. 18, AGO, 30 Mar 95, in GORI&IG; *ARIG 1895*, 106.

32. *Army and Navy Journal*, 32 (2 March 1895): 434 (6 April 1895): 518 (13 April 1895): 541 (20 April 1895): 555, and (22 June 1895): 702; U.S. War Department, *Regulations for the Army of the United States 1895* (Washington: Government Printing Office, 1895), passim.

Francisco, Lawton the Southern District from Santa Fe, and Vroom the Middle District from Chicago. On 30 April, Sanger was detached as Military Secretary to Schofield, who embarked on his farewell tour of the Army. Garlington, based in Washington, D.C., served as Inspector General of the South Atlantic District, and was also assistant to "the Inspector General of the Army" (Breckinridge). Major Francis Moore, 5th Cavalry, the only line officer detailed to inspection, covered the Northern District from Denver.[33]

General Schofield was replaced by the new Commanding General, Nelson A. Miles, who took office on 5 October 1895. Miles was the most critical occupant the office had known since Winfield Scott. Schofield had acknowledged the powerlessness of the top office by trying to make himself a Chief of Staff to the Secretary of War. Miles, in contrast, was selfish of his prerogatives and wanted the Commanding General to command in fact as well as name. It was, therefore, only a matter of time before he came into conflict with Breckinridge, whose bureaucratic independence was neither as complete nor as traditional as that of other staff heads. But as Miles said in his memoirs, the Army as a whole suffered in 1895 because of its rigid size and hidebound ways.[34] Trusting in support from Secretary Lamont, Breckinridge managed to get through Mile's first year without serious incident. His inspection system peaked in 1896 with its personnel unchanged and its work load continuing to increase. To assure Miles that he had the best interest of the Army at heart, Breckinridge reported that his inspectors had visited 82 garrisoned posts that year, thus demonstrating the thoroughness of his program.[35] He also told Miles that inspection under the new system was both more comprehensive and economical than that under previous systems. Fewer officers were doing more work. He may have believed that this positive assessment would calm Miles, for the department commanders were complaining frequently about the independent inspectors roaming their domains. Breckinridge's independence was derived from Secretary Lamont, whom he had convinced of the merits of the district inspection system.[36]

Independence Lost

Secretary of War Lamont left office in March 1897 and was replaced immediately by Russell A. Alger, a genial, well-meaning man of average ability. He was interested in his position, but was unfortunately naive and no match for the unprincipled bureaucrats who were his nominal subordinates. When the war with Spain erupted, Alger proved a welcome scapegoat for everyone's complaints about the Army's problems. Before that, he had fallen into the most vicious feud between a Secretary of War and a Commanding

    33. *ARIG 1895*, 106–07.
    34. Nelson A. Miles, *Serving the Republic: Memoirs of the Civil and Military Life of Nelson A. Miles* (New York: Harper and Brothers, 1911), 260–61.
    35. *ARIG 1896*, H. Doc. 2, 54th Cong., 2d sess., 1: 100–103.
    36. Ibid., 125, 209.

General since Sherman had departed for Saint Louis. At the start, however, Alger wanted only to please Miles, and his first annual report urged that the Commanding General be promoted to lieutenant general, as Schofield had been earlier.[37] Alger's approach to Miles had little effect at first on Breckinridge's department. There were only minor changes in the inspectorate the year Alger took office. Lawton moved his headquarters from Santa Fe to Los Angeles, while Sanger and Garlington divided their time between the South Atlantic District and the Washington office. The total of inspections continued to climb, and Breckinridge was pleased to report that the work was all done by his regular complement, except for twenty-one military college inspections made by officers under detail. In troop inspections, he felt that practical exercises posed by inspectors were increasingly part of the routine, while follow-up, the correction of deficiencies reported by inspectors, had improved, except for unsolvable problems related to army buildings.[38] Breckinridge complained as usual that his officers were overworked, and that more were needed. Nevertheless, he thought that the dual system of inspections, as performed by Inspectors General and department commanders, was working well enough.[39]

However, by the end of 1897 Breckinridge must have known that his organization had serious problems. The department commanders were not satisfied with the district system and neither was Miles, who rightly perceived that he had no control over the inspectorate. Breckinridge requested a legislatively established department with mandated duties, but he failed to win the active support of Secretary Alger, who at the time respected and feared Miles. The Commanding General, meanwhile, was trying to assert his own authority, and his conflicts with Alger increased. The Secretary tried to placate Miles even as he battled to restrain him. Thus, the Inspector General's Department became a casualty of the growing controversy between the power-hungry Miles and the ineffective Alger. Alger had not the ambitions for the close relationship with the inspectorate that his predecessors had cherished. He would not grant Miles any control over the regular staff departments, but he decided that he could not refuse him the kind of connection to the Adjutant General and Inspector General that his predecessors had held. The first sign of Breckinridge's changing fortunes was his loss, on 12 March 1898, of authority to inspect the War Department Supply Division, a minor task filled by an inspector general since 1889. That was a small event, but it marked only the second time since Breckinridge's advent that his department's service to the Secretary had decreased.[40]

---

37. *ARSecWar 1897*, H. Doc. 2, 55th Cong., 2d sess., 1: 9–10. Alger's background is addressed in Margaret Leech, *In the Days of McKinley* (New York: Harper, 1959). Alger was brevetted twice, to major general of volunteers, during the Civil War, but resigned under accusations of cowardice in 1864. He was politically well-connected as a governor of Michigan and a power in the Grand Army of the Republic.

38. *ARIG 1897*, H. Doc. 2, 55th Cong., 2d sess., 1: 117–18, 120, 146.

39. Ibid., 265–66.

40. War Department Cir, 12 Mar 98, cited in "History of the Inspector General's Department," 31 Dec 04, in file 372, Index to General Correspondence 1894–1916, RG 159. The first loss was purview over the Corps of Engineers, in 1892.

The great blow fell on 23 March 1898, when the Secretary abolished the inspection districts and assigned the inspectors general, and as many acting inspectors general as were necessary to be detailed, to the eight geographical departments. They were to serve under the orders of the department commanders. Only inspectors general not assigned to departments now served the Secretary of War or the Commanding General. Correspondence in the Inspector General's Department could be direct for purposes of instruction or information for inspectors but could not extend to matters of administration pertaining to military commanders.[41] Breckinridge' s cherished independence, unprotected by the legislative charter he had asked for and undefended by a disinterested Secretary, was crushed, as was Breckinridge. The change, Alger said later, was to put the inspectorate on a footing for a war that seemed imminent. The enraged Breckinridge, instead of staying in Washington while the army was engaged in war, left his department leaderless while he took to the field in pursuit of glory on the battlefield. His departure at such a critical time almost cost the Inspector General's Department its very existence.

---

41. GO No. 11, 23 Mar 98, in GORI&IG. The officers were assigned to the departments by orders of 16 April 1898.

CHAPTER 19

The Department in Service to the Secretary (1889–1898)

During Breckinridge's leadership of the Inspector General's Department, the range of its ancillary inspection duties increased and the number of special investigations at the Secretary's behest decreased. That was mostly because Breckinridge was able to develop a comprehensive inspection system for activities that had formerly received only sporadic attention through special investigations. In the 1890s, rarely did the Secretary of War call one of the inspectors general off his regular tour to make a special review. An isolated instance occurred in April 1897, when Sanger, at the Secretary's request, was sent to Memphis, Tennessee, to inspect flood damage on the Mississippi and to report directly to the Secretary on what the War Department could do to relieve distress in the area.[1]

Paragraph 955

Breckinridge justified his department's independence and direct connection to the Secretary on inspections required by paragraph 955 of the regulation. That paragraph, in accordance with the law, directed the inspectors general to examine facilities not under the authority of department commanders and to report their findings to the Secretary of War. That introduced recurrent conflicts with department commanders, who resented the inspectors' freedom. The commanders triumphed momentarily in August 1890, when Breckinridge was ordered to keep departmental and divisional inspectors informed, through the commanders, of the paragraph 955 inspections desired by the Secretary. Each inspector was to submit his plan of inspection to his commander, who must approve it and give orders for the necessary travel.[2] At the other extreme was Breckinridge's triumph in freeing his officers of any control by departmental commanders through the institution in 1895 of inspection districts. The great number of paragraph 955 inspections, combined with the need to control travel time, justified the district system. . . . In 1891 Breckinridge explained that the attention of inspectors under paragraph 955 went only to business and adminis-

---

1. Correspondence on this assignment is located in file 2544, Index to General Correspondence (hereafter cited as Gen Corresp) 1894–1916, RG 159.
2. GO No. 95, AGO, 26 Aug 90, in GORI&IG.

trative matters, not to technical or scientific concerns. He pointed out, for example, that his inspectors looked into business practices as well as into financial accounts to determine how the public's money was spent. Otherwise, he feared, "There is great danger which can not be too carefully guarded against that our officers will degenerate into mere auditors, which evidently is not the intention of the law."[3]

Breckinridge ceased lamenting the 1892 loss of engineering inspections and concentrated on his otherwise expanding purview. His judgments on staff department facilities continued mostly favorable, although he did not hestitate to recommend improvements, from repair of dilapidated buildings to the institution of uniform pay scales for civilian employees. The Quartermaster Department's depots, he declared in 1896, were especially commendable for their adoption of a uniform business method. The Army and Navy General Hospital was usually described as in "excellent condition," while in 1897 he declared the Subsistence Department depots "well administered, as usual," although the Medical Department supply depots tended to be cluttered with too many objects. And although he steered clear of the Corps of Engineers' technical operations, the Inspector General still examined their books, and in 1897 advised that staff officers needed some accounting assistance so they could devote full time to supervising their employees.[4] Although willing to render advice to another bureau, Breckinridge was quick to defend his department's prerogatives when he saw his own province threatened. A case in point was property condemnation and disposal procedures. With variations in practice, since 1825 the law had required that each useless item, from riverboat to teacup, be taken before an inspector general for condemnation before it could be disposed of. That procedure was excessively cumbersome, with the kind of inventories the Army was accumulating by the late nineteenth century. But when some of the staff departments proposed to simplify matters, the Inspector General was quick to give them a reprint of the 1825 legislation and a dose of his own sentiments favoring no change.[5]

One of the Inspector General's paragraph 955 responsibilities continued to be the system of national cemeteries. By the mid-1890s the need for annual inspections was excessive, in terms both of burden upon the inspectors and of the real value derived. The places were usually found to be well run, and the occasional dilapidated building or missing fence was seldom news that an inspector brought to the superintendent or the Quartermaster General. Inspections ultimately were made biennial by 1895, and only ten were made the following year. The Inspector General successfully urged that Confederate dead in Federal cemeteries be treated and memorialized in the same manner as Federals. He also suggested that, because deceased honorably discharged soldiers were entitled to burial in national cemeteries, most of which were in the

3. *ARIG 1892*, 20–26.
4. *ARIG 1894*, 213–14; *ARIG 1895*, 221–25; *ARIG 1896*, 218–21; *ARIG 1897*, 242–43, 253–55.
5. *ARIG 1896*, 211–20.

South, new cemeteries should be established near the regional homes for disabled volunteers and near selected northern cities.[6]

West Point

The Military Academy at West Point returned to the Inspector General's purview in the early 1890s, an annual duty owed to the Secretary of War. Typically, as in 1894, the inspection report spoke in "high terms of the excellent management of this institution." The inspector also listed the deficiencies corrected on the recommendations of previous inspections. Breckinridge proposed that year the coordination of all officer instruction in the Army, involving West Point and the officers' schools for application in infantry, artillery, and cavalry, as well as the lyceums beginning to appear at posts. In that, Breckinridge presaged the systematic educational program that would appear early in the twentieth century. He extended his attention to the West Point Special Contingent Fund in 1895, which was supported by rentals of the hotel on the academy grounds and other incidental sources, and used for minor expenses. It was, he said, "appropriately handled."[7]

The Military Prison

Inspection of the United States Military Prison at Fort Leavenworth, Kansas, continued as a responsibility conveyed upon the Inspectors General by Congress in the 1870s. It was another duty they owed to the Secretary, not the Commanding General. Since 1881, the inspections had usually been made by divisional or departmental inspectors, and on 2 March 1889 the Secretary directed the inspector general of the Military Division of the Missouri to make quarterly inspections of the prison. In August Breckinridge complained that inspections by divisional or departmental inspectors had always caused friction, because the prison superintendent owed no allegiance to any geographical area commander. He asked Proctor to return the duty to the Inspector General's Department in Washington. The agreeable Secretary concurred early the next month, while Breckinridge was on tour in the West.[8] Advised by the Secretary of War, who learned what he knew from Breckinridge, that the quarterly inspection schedule was excessive, on 19 January 1891 Congress revised the law governing inspections of the prison, requiring a single annual inspection.[9]

On 1 November 1890, the United States Military Prison became an independent military post under the immediate authority of the Commanding General of

---

6. *ARIG 1893*, 21–22; *ARIG 1894*, 214; *ARIG 1896*, 221–22; *ARIG 1897*, 255–56. The figure of ten cemeteries for 1896, a remarkable drop from recent years, is correct.

7. *ARIG 1894*, 203–04; *ARIG 1895*, 214–15.

8. Breckinridge to IG, Division of the Missouri, 8 Mar 89; Breckinridge to AG, 16 Aug 89; and Telg, Lawton to Breckinridge, 5 Sep 89, all in Letters Sent 1863–1889, RG 159.

9. *An Act to amend sections thirteen hundred and forty-six and thirteen hundred and forty-eight of the Revised Statutes of the United States, in reference to the visitation and inspection of the Military Prison and examination of its accounts and government, Statutes at Large* 26, sec. 1348, 722 (1891). Thian, *Legislative History*, 115; GO No. 8, AGO, 27 Jan 91, in GORI&IG.

the Army, for the convicts and their keepers were the only troops he really commanded. The board of commissioners reformed the applicable governing rules in May 1891, permitting the prisoners holiday and letter-writing privileges. Those reforms did not entirely erase confusion at the prison. Both the commandant and the inspector were required by law to hear and investigate all prisoner complaints. Breckinridge maintained that that merely invited complaining, and claimed that at least a third of the time which boards and inspectors spent in looking at the place was devoted to reviews of nonsense generated by chronic malcontents. His answer to that problem was to change the procedure, to require that a complaining prisoner show how the prison rules had been violated.[10] The handling of complaints was not the only matter of concern: In the two decades of the prison's existence, there had been much grumbling in the higher officer corps about the coddling of criminals and the encouragement of crime by less than rigorous treatment; before Breckinridge's time, some of that complaining had come from the Inspector General's Office. The government finally decided to end this experiment in modern penology, and in August 1895 it terminated the United States Military Prison. Within the next few months, the prisoners were dispersed to guardhouses at the larger permanent posts, while the officers and men of the staff returned to their line positions. The inspectors general, of course, lost one of their special attachments to the Secretary of War when the prison shut down.[11]

The Soldiers' Home

The inspection of the Soldiers' Home was another secretarial attachment, begun in 1883, which Breckinridge took seriously. Besides meticulous reviews of the financial accounts, the Inspector General kept the place in the public eye. His inspection in 1892 reported some improvement, but suggested that the home's managers needed to do much more to provide comfort for the old soldiers. Better meal service, elevators, bathing facilities, warmer floors, and more fresh produce were all, in Breckinridge's opinion, wanted. He suggested forming a board of officers to work on improving the home's food.[12] The next year he said that the exterior had always looked good, but recently there had been improvements to the internal condition of the buildings, bedding, and cleanliness, "and this at least extends to the facilities provided the inmates to enjoy the same virtue." Additional bathing facilities were still required, however, but the Inspector General was pleased to announce an increase in the water supply. He complained that there were still too few elevators for the feeble, and that some men slept in substandard conditions. The mess had improved, but the practice of buying from selected suppliers was expensive and unsatisfactory.

10. *ARIG 1891*, 14–15.

11. *ARSecWar 1896*, H. Doc. 2, 54th Cong., 2d sess., 1: 15; Foner, *Soldier Between Wars*, 120.

12. *ARIG 1892*, 43. For a general history of the Soldiers' Home, see Paul R. Goode, *The United States Soldier's Home* (Richmond, Virginia: William Byrd Press, 1957).

Breckinridge also asked that "means [be] provided for the innocent diversion and recreation of these old and disabled veterans," including a post exchange ("dry if preferred") and amusement rooms like those at the military posts. He was not pleased to report the destruction of the home's dairy herd and the reduction of its garden. Finally, he suggested that the "funding basis" of the home "seems somewhat questionable," although he did not say precisely what that meant.[13] Breckinridge's interest in the home's operations continued at a high level, and he agitated for further improvements continually. Although there was now a recreation room, it was dingy and inappropriately located in a basement. In 1896 he reported a need for more improvements, and he listed them, including the construction of more walkways on the grounds. The home's books were "neatly and properly kept, but the habit of keeping cash balances on hand seems dangerous and undesirable, and where the depository is so easy of access it is also unnecessary. It is understood that two separate sets of accounts are kept, one as is usual with public accounts which are submitted for inspection, the other in some special manner not recognized elsewhere in the authorized system of accounting for public moneys."[14] Inasmuch as double bookkeeping arouses suspicion in any auditor; the Soldier's Home had apparently ended the practice, whatever its original purpose, by 1897 and the Inspector General commended the staff and recommended that an additional officer be assigned to accounting.[15]

Home for Disabled Volunteer Soldiers

Breckinridge was interested in the extension of his department's influence over the Army, but he was also a sincere humanitarian, a quality reflected in his concern for the nation's "old soldiers," and for the young soldiers he helped to relieve of Sunday inspections and exercises. Both facets of his personality were satisfied when Congress extended his purview over the National Home for Disabled Volunteer Soldiers, established to care for the growing numbers of indigent Civil War veterans. In 1893 Breckinridge reported that the appropriation acts and certain orders required his department to audit the accounts of the National Home quarterly. Transactions in the accounts that year amounted to about a million and a quarter dollars per quarter, and one appropriation for transportation had been overdrawn by $54.11. Breckinridge suggested that audits be made monthly to ensure better control. The Inspector General also stressed the need for routine close acountability of both property and money at all times. In the meantime, Breckinridge and the Treasury Department had developed an accounting system for the National Home.[16]

---

13. *ARIG 1893*, 26–27.

14. *ARIG 1895*, 220–21; *ARIG 1896*, 217–18.

15. *ARIG 1897*, 243–44.

16. *ARIG 1893*, 27–30. The National Home was a predecessor of the Veterans Administration, established by Executive Order 5398, 21 July 1930, in accordance with the act of 3 July 1930 (46 Stat. 1016), authorizing the President to consolidate and coordinate the United States Veterans

(Continued)

The National Home for Disabled Volunteer Soldiers was actually a collection of branch homes scattered across the country. Their administration was inevitably less professional than that of the Soldier's Home, which was a War Department operation housed in one place. In August 1894 Congress agreed that the National Home should receive closer supervision, but instead of monthly audits, it required regional annual inspections conducted by the Inspector General's Department.[17] The National Home, because of the political influence of Civil War veterans, was a politically sensitive subject that attracted close congressional attention. It was also a perennial headache for the inspectors. Breckinridge reported all branches generally in good condition in 1894, except for repairs needed to some buildings. Staff overhead duplicated excessive effort, he complained, and technical changes were needed in business procedures, along with some clarifications of the law. Most recommendations made by the inspectors general were adopted by the Board of Managers and the appropriations committee in Congress, and the adoption of new accounting forms and methods improved the records systems.[18]

Breckinridge himself inspected the branches of the National Home in 1896. He reported their newer barracks better than their antecedents, offering more air and light and improved comfort for the inmates. But the National Home's population was growing while its appropriations were decreasing. However, because of the administrative improvements he had encouraged, care of inmates continued adequate, economies had been instituted, and surpluses had been turned back to the Treasury. In Breckinridge's opinion, more savings were possible. The National Home's operators still did not conduct all of their affairs according to law, but defects in their vouchers were on the decline. As for the residents, the Inspector General had tried to visit every healthy inmate. "They seem to be generally contented," he said.[19] His personal interest meant that the scale of the inspectorate's involvement would be high. The size of the inspection responsibility may be seen in the fact that it took the Inspector General's Department fifteen man-weeks in 1897 to inspect the "whole plant, valued approximately at $7,500,000, and of the methods, more or less intricate, of its fiscal department and its great mass of accounts and vouchers, which aggregated more than $5,000,000." The National Home for Disabled Volunteer Soldiers by then housed 18,000 men in hundreds of buildings and the number of eligible users was increasing. Breckinridge declared the branch homes generally in good condition, and although appropriations had been reduced again, increased efficiency had cut maintenance costs.[20]

(Continued)

Bureau, Bureau of Pensions, and National Home for Disabled Volunteer Soldiers. The Veterans Administration also eventually took over national cemeteries, except for those operated as historic sites.

17. *An Act making appropriations for sundry civil expenses of the Government for the fiscal year ending June thirtieth, eighteen hundred and ninety-five, and for other purposes,* Statutes at Large 28, sec. 1, 372 (1894); Thian, *Legislative History,* 116.

18. *ARIG* 208–11.

19. *ARIG 1896,* 213–17.

20. *ARIG 1897,* 244–50. The National Home by this time had its own supply service, with a central depot at Columbus, Ohio.

Disbursing Accounts

Breckinridge was obsessed with the National Home's bookkeeping because inspections of disbursing accounts had become his department's greatest area of concern. During his first year in Washington, inspectors general submitted 1,204 reports of inspections of accounts covering transactions amounting to over $52 million. Only twenty-three, about 2 percent, had had to be returned for correction. Nevertheless, in the spring of 1889 the Secretary expressed his displeasure over two cases of gross carelessness in records of the Pay Department. He reminded disbursing officers to follow the rules on record-keeping. The Secretary also told the Inspector General's Department to give "special attention to these matters, and promptly report, for the action of the Secretary of War, all infractions of those rules and regulations."[21]

Auditing the Army's financial transactions was the department's most seriously taken service to the Secretary of War. The activity provided a strong justification for the department's existence. No one approves the waste of public funds, and Breckinridge was quick to proclaim his department's role in monitoring disbursements. By 1892 Breckinridge's office was responsible for producing forms for inspection of money and property accounts, new versions of which appeared that year. The Secretary ordered earlier that any officer relieved from disbursing duty was to send "Form 3, Inspector General's Department," to the inspector who looked after his accounts. The inspector would make an examination if practical, and in any case was to forward the form to the Inspector General's Office in Washington.[22] This, too, was a huge task: The volume of accounts inspected increased to over $71 million in 1892. Officers of the Inspector General's Department made about a hundred account inspections per week, while other officers did the remaining quarter of the audits. Breckinridge concluded that it was absolutely vital that uniform methods of accounting and disbursing be adopted and enforced. Various staff departments made very broad interpretations of the law, accounting for 60 percent of the "exceptions" in inspectors' reports of audits. Inspectors had uncovered voucher frauds that had led to prosecutions. He suggested that the Treasury Department ought to compare every check and voucher it acted upon.[23]

Breckinridge also advised managing public works by contract, rather than having officers hire, subsist, and oversee gangs of construction laborers. Outstanding checks were a burden to disbursing officers, who must report them monthly until cashed. There was a slight decline in total disbursements in 1893, for which Breckinridge claimed credit for the inspectors general. He further claimed that since he had first started working on the problem in 1891, the percentage of final balances as part of the average of total monthly disburse-

21. *ARIG 1889*, 122; Cir, AGO, 20 Apr 89, in GORI&IG.
22. *ARIG 1890*, 281–84; Cir No. 15, AGO, 11 Dec 90, and Cir, AGO, n.d. 1891, both in GORI&IG.
23. *ARIG 1892*, 17–18.

ments had fallen from 186 percent to 99 percent in 1892 and to 94 percent in 1893.[24] Breckinridge also suggested that the congressional policy returning any savings to the Department of the Treasury was misguided, because it removed any incentives toward economy for officers in charge of projects. There were also other reasons that savings might be transferred from one account to another to support needed work, such as in barracks construction. In his view, all army appropriations should be transferrable among the many accounts, which would not affect the total appropriation.[25]

Property Inspections

In its service to the Secretary of War's interest in economy, the department's attention to disbursing accounts was closely related to its inspection of property. The War Department meddled with property procedures endlessly. Inspection of ordnance property was transferred from the inspectors general to the Ordnance Department in 1890. Later that year, the regulations were revised to permit department and division commanders to give orders to dispose of condemned property, except in two instances. Only the Secretary of War could order the disposal of ordnance property, while the Surgeon General had first to give his opinion on the disposal of medical property. The Secretary was the arbiter of all disputes.[26]

Nothing revealed the administrative complexities of the War Department more than the subject of property management. Officers presenting property for inspection were told in January 1892 to inventory it in quadruplicate, on prescribed forms. Inspection reports on condemned property also were to be prepared in quadruplicate, on other specified forms. If valueless property was destroyed, one copy of the report went to Breckinridge's office; otherwise, all copies were to be held at department headquarters. Orders for the disposition of property were to be endorsed on inspection reports. One copy went to Breckinridge, one to the head of the staff department holding the property, and the other two to the accountable officer. In November, the War Department changed the inventory and inspection reports from quadruplicate to triplicate, with a copy to Breckinridge's office and two to the accountable officer. The staff department heads had to consult the Inspector General or their field officers if they wanted to know the fate of some discarded object.[27]

The reasons for those orders Breckinridge made clear later in 1892. Hitherto, there had been no record kept of property inspected and condemned. Breckinridge avowed that the level of information was improved, but the reports involved considerable speculation about the value of condemned property. The problem, he maintained, was that there was no uniform system in the War

24. *ARIG 1893*, 12–13.
25. Ibid., 16.
26. GO No. 90, AGO, 15 Aug 90, and GO No. 118, AGO, 7 Oct 90, in GORI&IG.
27. GO No. 8, AGO, 29 Jan 92, and GO No. 76, AGO, 9 Nov 92, in GORI&IG.

Department, so that "on the one side an officer disposes of steamboats or vehicles without any outside inspection, and on another side extra officers are ordered to inspect property like pots and pans and bed linen before they can be disposed of." Only the Quartermaster and Subsistence Departments then had to present property for review by an inspector general before it could be disposed of, and Breckinridge thought the procedure should be extended to the whole Army.[28] Orders regarding property continued to multiply. In January 1893, the head of the Recruiting Service received the same authority as department commanders to appoint inspectors to examine property offered for condemnation by his officers. In August, the War Department made minor amendments to the regulations, emphasizing that inspections for condemnation must be wholly separate from boards of survey examining property from other perspectives.[29]

Finally, in 1894 the Secretary of War directed that inspections of unserviceable property be made by the Inspector General's Department. All inspections were to be made by inspectors general, acting inspectors general, or specially designated officers not connected with the organization possessing the property. Breckinridge applauded the development, and reported that he had received 2,392 inspection and inventory (I. and I.) reports that year—84 percent of them made by officers of his department, who prepared 8 to 10 per working day. He said also that his officers still had some difficulty in fixing the costs of the property they inspected, and that they had met some resistance in performing their work.[30] Although it was very heavy, the enormous burden of property inspections was a principal means in which the inspectorate's influence was felt throughout the Army. But it was also a self-inflicted wound, bogging inspectors down in tedious paper work and diverting them from larger issues. Breckinridge placed much importance on property inspections as the sort of economically oriented activity that justified his proposed increases in the Inspector General's Department. But, when the increases did not develop, the department was left with an almost unmanageable burden.

Military Colleges

Another activity of the Inspector General's Department that increased dramatically during the 1890s was the inspection of officers detailed to colleges and universities as professors of military arts and tactics. There were fifty such officers when Breckinridge became senior inspector general in 1889, only three of whom he said received inadequate support from their colleges. The collegiate programs were highly varied, but were generally improving. Breckinridge expressed high hopes that, with increased uniformity and support from the War Department, the nation would receive its future supply of wartime officers from

---

28. *ARIG 1892*, 40–41. By the whole Army he meant especially the Corps of Engineers.

29. Cir No. 1, AGO, 10 Jan 93, conveying: Decision of the Secretary of War, 10 Dec 92, and GO No. 66, AGO, 7 Aug 93, in GORI&IG. The Recruiting Service was an arm of the Adjutant General's Office.

30. *ARIG 1894*, 100–01.

the civilian colleges.[31] His opinions show that Breckinridge was a strong supporter of collegiate military education, and as such was years ahead of most
officers of the Regular Army. He found cause to complain during the summer
of 1889 that there was strong opposition in the Army to the program, and some
resistance from the colleges against more effective supervision by the War
Department. He pointed out that there were discrepancies between the laws
which authorized military studies at land grant colleges and those which allowed
the detail of military faculty to the colleges. He urged strongly to the Secretary
that regulations be developed clarifying the relationship and responsibilities of
the army and colleges to each other. The regulations would also establish
standards and performance criteria for the professors of military science. When
a board of officers was formed to draft rules and regulations for college programs,
and its report circulated, Breckinridge offered as comment seven legal-size
pages of remarks, including his own proposed version of the regulations.[32]

Breckinridge ensured from the outset that his inspectorate would play a
significant role in guiding the development of collegiate military education.
The President imposed rules on 12 February 1890 for the detail of army officers
to colleges and universities. The military department of any college accepting
such a detail was then subject to an annual inspection near the end of the school
year, and the college president, like a militia commander, would receive from
the War Department a copy of the inspection report. Inspectors were told to
report first to the college head, then to remain on campus long enough to
understand the place of the military department within the entire institution.[33]
The college program and its accompanying inspections consumed a great deal
of time and manpower. In fact, the detail of officers to college programs,
Breckinridge said in 1893, was large enough to staff a regiment, but in his
opinion fully worth the investment. Officers were present at every type and size
of college, Breckinridge said, and "these schools deserve the most favorable
attention and zealous support of the national government." But given Congress'
failure to pass the law providing uniforms and equipment, the Inspector General
said that the government was denying the colleges that support. In demonstration of the program's worth, he pointed to the "commendable character" of
civilians commissioned in the Regular Army after graduation from civilian
military programs.[34] His views persuaded the War Department to support the
growth of the program. The number of institutions with active or retired army
officers assigned to them rose to 106 in 1896, by which time Breckinridge had
begun to add to his detailed surveys of the programs accounts of some difficul-

---

31. *ARIG 1889*, 122–23. He also reported that equipment furnished to the colleges was well
cared for.

32. Breckinridge to AG, 13 Jun 89, and scores of endorsements related to this subject, in
Letters Sent 1863–1889, RG 159. His comments on the board's recommendations in the same file
are Breckinridge, Endorsement on report of Board . . . , 16 August 1889.

33. GO No. 15, AGO, 12 Feb 90, and Cir B, AGO, 13 Feb 90, both in GORI&IG.

34. *ARIG 1893*, 8–9.

EIGHTEENTH PENNSYLVANIA INFANTRY REGIMENT AT THE ALLEGHENY CO. CENTENNIAL, 1888. *The Inspector General's Department was one of the first War Department agencies to stress the importance of the revived National Guard.*

ties in inspecting them. Most colleges wanted their inspections near the end of the academic year, understandably enough, but that was a sore trial for inspectors. His officers, the Inspector General said, nevertheless performed commendably and got the job done. He urged more exchanges of information, by means of inspection reports, among colleges.

The National Guard

Breckinridge disagreed with those people, such as Emory Upton, who believed that the country must create a large military establishment founded on universal military training. Having himself entered the Army as a volunteer, he believed firmly that the nation could rely for its future defense upon the voluntary resources of citizens who would agree to a part-time commitment to military service. He counted upon them to come forward, in an emergency, better prepared than their predecessors in 1812 or 1861, provided they received proper encouragement and guidance from military professionals. He was for that reason quite at odds with those regular officers who wanted to ignore the college military programs. For the same reason, he disagreed with those who viewed the growing National Guard movement with disdain. Breckinridge perceived that both programs could satisfy his objectives: They accorded with his personal military philosophy and they provided opportunities for expansion of his department's purview. Even as the Inspector General's Department extended its reach over the college community, it became the War Department's ambassador to the reviving state militias.

The growing numbers and political influence of the state militias (now most calling themselves the "National Guard" in etymological distinction from the discredited militia of the old days) caused the Army in the 1880s to revive a duty it had never really performed fully. That was the annual inspection of the militia, which in November 1889 Breckinridge managed to have consolidated into his own hands. He was almost, but not quite, the only regular officer who wanted anything to do with it. At least one other, 1st Lt. John P. Wisser, also believed that the militia should be inspected annually by regular officers. Inspections, he said, could be used to improve the National Guard and to demonstrate that drill was not an end in itself but a means to military efficiency. Inspection, Wisser maintained, was the only way of making professional expertise available to the part-time soldiers of the Guard. Breckinridge could not have said it better himself.[35] Despite his strong interest, Breckinridge entered the National Guard program cautiously. In 1890 he said that officers had been detailed from the Army to inspect and advise the militia, and from his vantage point over them all, he detected variations in all respects from state to state. Some states were very lax, or had no militia at all. In general, he thought the organizations had improved in recent years, but only a few states had decent camp and garrison equipment. Their officers were "zealous," and Breckinridge thought that army officers should be assigned to advise governors full time, rather than just at summer camps, which he also believed could stand improvement.[36]

In 1891, fifty-seven officers had been detailed to forty-nine National Guard encampments in twenty-seven states and territories, while twenty-one states and territories either had no militia or held no encampments. That was the most complete inspection ever, because nearly every state that did hold an encampment had been visited by an army officer, who in many cases served as an instructor as well as an inspector. Federal-state relations were good, and the work continued to improve. Breckinridge had two major recommendations that year. One was that no officer ranked less than captain should be detailed to militia inspection, as the "worthiest men of wide experience" would have the most beneficial influence. The other was a grand, national encampment involving the militia of all states and territories, to be held in association with the planned Columbian Exposition in Chicago.[37]

The inspectorate temporarily lost its hold on the National Guard in 1892, when the Bureau of Information was established and inspection of militia went to the Adjutant General's Office. Breckinridge was outraged, and in June

---

35. Sanger, "Inspector General's Department," 247; John P. Wisser, "The Annual Inspection of the National Guard by Army Officers," *United Service*, n.s., 2 (December 1889): 607–14.
36. *ARIG 1890*, 271–78.
37. *ARIG 1891*, 7–8, 95, 97.

INSPECTION OF ENGINEER TROOPS, Washington Barracks (now Ft. McNair) 1892.

complained that when officers were detailed to militia inspections the word "inspect" was deleted from their orders by the Adjutant General, and "no officer has been ordered to report to me, according to existing instructions and former practice." "In 1892," he wrote later, "this Department was for a time debarred from any participation in the work of instructing and inspecting the militia, and this work which had grown up and developed so considerably under its fostering care was somewhat retarded." But the function was returned by September 1892.[38] At the same time, The National Guard Association was asked to help with systematic scheduling of state encampments. If the camps in each military department met consecutively and progressively, it would be possible to provide more complete instruction from basics to army-corps maneuvers. And although the Guard was organized by state, such coordination would encourage the "most reliable national feeling and effective comradery between the States"—the very purposes of the National Guard Association.[39]

Breckinridge had nothing but praise for the National Guard, saying that their encampments had overcome historical difficulties in militia training. He said that although criticisms of their inexperienced efforts were to be expected, the inspecting officers were always friendly and constructive. "With the en-

---

38. Breckinridge to Secy of War, 11 Jun 92, and Breckinridge to A.R. Kieffer, House of Representatives, 21 Dec 93, in Letters Sent 1891–1894, RG 159; *ARIG 1892*, 6; Sanger, "Inspector General's Department," 247.

39. Ibid., 6–7.

thusiasm, superior intelligence, willingness and promptness displayed by the militia forces the task was not difficult, and the troops received many warm commendations." Support for this assertion came from carefully selected quotations from inspection reports. Relations between the Guard and its inspectors were obviously not always smooth. Reports of unhappiness over inspectors' criticisms caused the War Department to consider ending the inspection duties of officers assigned to the militia. That issue was resolved, but later the Inspector General asked the Secretary to require officers detailed to the National Guard to be "authorized to make a report to this office."[40] Criticisms were important, he said, and most Guard officers wanted them for use in improving their own organization. Breckinridge cited in his support a letter he had received in 1890 from the president of the National Guard Association, and quoted another letter from a colonel of the Illinois National Guard, who said, "To have the inspections and publications of your department cease would be a damage to the National Guard for which nothing else could possibly compensate."[41] This warm appreciation indicates that the reach of the Inspector General's Department extended during Breckinridge's years to cover every sphere of military activity. Breckinridge was perhaps first among the Army's hierarchy to recognize that the National Guard and the military programs of civilian colleges were worthy of serious official attention. But ultimately, there was only so much an inspector could do in the face of state-level independence, War Department indifference, congressional restraints, and the concomitant general disorganization of every part of the national defense except the Regular Army. When war erupted in 1898, most of the Regular Army distrusted the National Guard, and therefore denied it the kind of guidance that Breckinridge had long suggested. The result was a succession of disasters attributable in equal measure to the ineptitude of the guardsmen and the indifference of the regulars.

Balancing Two Interests

The inspection of the National Guard continued during Breckinridge's regime thanks to his own persistence in the face of opposition from within the Army and without. Because the Guard was politically a force to reckon with, the inspection system also provided a valuable service to the politicians who served as secretaries of war, providing them with a dependable source of information. It was in that sense part of a larger package of inspection activities catering to the interests of the Secretary, and only occasionally touching those of the Commanding General. Breckinridge quite obviously organized and increased his department's attention to paragraph 955 properties, staff departments, disbursements, and other such concerns with two purposes in mind. One was to strengthen his department's influence and growing independence by basing its

---

40. Breckinridge to Secy of War, 4 Sep 93, in Letters Sent 1891–1894, RG 159.
41. *ARIG 1893*, 7–8, 34–35.

authority on an unfettered connection to the Secretary of War. But he lacked a formal charter for his organization, and in that context could be successful only so far as the changing secretaries permitted, as witnessed by the vacillating status of the district system of inspections. Breckinridge's other motive reflected the broader part of his interests. He simply wanted to get the job done better, more systematically, and with some demonstrable product. Before Breckinridge's tenure, except for purely military inspections, secretaries of war had been wont to scatter inspectors indiscriminantly on this or that errand, usually in response to some report of trouble. Breckinridge ended that waste of his manpower and thereby attained greater administrative control over his people. He did that by organizing all subjects of inspection into a set of systematic routines. It was no longer necessary to make so many special investigations as before, because a prearranged annual routine usually disclosed any trouble before the Secretary would sense a problem. That systematization was most apparent in the miscellany of ancillary, nonmilitary objects of inspection.

Despite his difficulties and his frustration at not attaining complete departmental independence, Breckinridge came closer than any of his predecessors to serving equally his two masters. Inspectors general had looked mostly at purely military subjects for many years, serving the Commanding General. When they answered to the Secretary, as had Wool before and others since the Civil War, their dispersal while satisfying secretarial requests had interrupted their attention to things military. Breckinridge had found a way to balance the two interests, although his solution made his inspectors' work load almost unbearable. Except for the period of the district inspections, most of his officers remained under department commanders, and therefore primarily conducted military inspections. Breckinridge had ensured that they looked after the Secretary's interests as they did so. Equally, his district system, which was constructed with secretarial interests in mind, also permitted systematic military inspections, its audience being the Commanding General directly rather than the department commanders. The achievement of this balance marks the department's entering maturity. The Inspector General's Department had been a linguistic convenience since the Revolution and the War of 1812. As a quasi-legal entity, it may have existed since the year Marcy became a brigadier general. But it was only due to Breckinridge's influences that it became a real "department," a carefully managed, smoothly working organization. If any person could hold the title of "father" of the Inspector General's Department, that man was Joseph C. Breckinridge.

CHAPTER 20

Reform During the Breckinridge Era
(1889–1898)

When Breckinridge assumed the mantle of senior inspector general in 1889, the Army's greatest single problem remained its staggering desertion rate. That had declined somewhat, but desertion continued to curtail seriously the available military force. The winds of reform were blowing strongly, however, and much of the Army's leadership had begun to recognize that conditions in the Army itself were partly to blame for the problem. Many senior officers began to see that changes would be necessary to solve the Army's problem. The last decades of the century saw a wave of reform movements developing throughout American society. In many ways the Army was in the vanguard of this movement, led by dynamic young officers intent on making it a modern force.

Soldier Life and Discipline

Most of the inspectors perceived that there were flaws in the system that required renovation. Their reports reflected a keen interest in sensible change and experimentation. As a result, the inspectorate kept a firm watch on developments within the Army that were intended to improve morale and discipline. Issues involving pay and the operations of soldier canteens and post exchanges were evaluated and suggestions were made for further improvements. Breckinridge was for the most part enthusiastic over this positivism, adding his own recommendations for further advances. He pressed for reforms in military justice and promotion systems that would enhance the lot of the private soldier. Inspectors also noted an improvement in the quality of the individuals enlisting, and attributed this progress to the reforms and changes in recruiting and medical standards. The inspectors' observations were a valuable sounding board to the Commanding General and the Secretary as to the value and effect of the attempted changes.

Breckinridge continued to speak glowingly about the Army's discipline in the year preceding the Spanish-American War. Training of recruits, he believed, continued successfully at the company level. He did pass on a suggestion from Inspector General Sanger that training detachments might be established at every post for efficiency's sake, although Breckinridge concurred only so far as the recruit's connection to his company continued unbroken. Discipline remained strong, and, not for the first time, Breckinridge proposed good-conduct badges as a reward for good behavior, and as a boost to morale.[1] That common soldiers might be entitled to privileges and consideration would have been unheard of a generation earlier. Some of the older officers, those few who remembered the old army before the Civil War, might not approve of the modern state of affairs, but the enlisted men did. The changes in enlisted life were justified by the lowest rate of desertion and the highest state of discipline, by 1898, the U.S. Army had ever known. If old-timers objected, the Inspector General had proof in the form of facts and figures, and strong personal opinions, on matters of justice.

Educating the Enlisted Men

One of the modern measures that Breckinridge wanted imposed on the Army was a respectable system of education for enlisted men. He came into office determined to do something about the much-neglected post schools, just as he was determined to attack Sunday inspections. Shortly after his accession, on 31 January 1889, a general order raised education to the status of a military duty. All soldiers were required to receive some instruction during duty hours, and no discretion was allowed to line commanders on the subject. The Inspector General's Department was required to inspect the post schools, examine instruction, and advise commanders of defects. The inspectors were also to work with adjutants to improve the schools and induce uniformity. Their reports were to be forwarded through channels for the information of the Commanding General.[2] Not wholly the work of Breckinridge, the precept also reflected the views of Schofield and Proctor, both of whom believed strongly that education could elevate the character of enlisted men, make them more efficient, and prepare them for civil life after discharge. Also, both felt that something had to be done about the many illiterates in the ranks, and they were not alone in those sentiments. But some company officers believed that the general order was a denial of their responsibility as line commanders, unnecessarily increasing their work load. As a result, the schools were often perfunctory efforts to please the War Department bureaucrats, and a "disappointing and melancholy spectacle," according to one officer.[3] Breckinridge had to acknowledge by 1897 that the post school system was a failure, useful only to children. But he was never short of solutions, telling the Secretary, "The enlistment of the ignorant is now prohibited by law, so post schools should be made military schools intended more for the professional advancement of the enlisted men than for their education in merely the common English branches." Moreover, the Army needed "a single system of schools" for noncommissioned officers, to make them as

---

1. *ARIG 1897*, 122, 137–38, 143–44, 240.

2. GO No. 9, AGO, 31 Jan 89, in GORI&IG.

3. *ARComGen 1889*, 62; William P. Burnham, "Military Training of the Regular Army of the United States," *Journal of the Military Service Institution of the United States*, 10 (1889): 613–39; Miewald, "Army Post Schools," *Military Affairs* 39 (February 1975) 10–11.

efficient and professional as possible. As for officers, their service schools were excellent but were underfunded.[4]

The development of a system of education in the Army was one of Breckinridge's greatest frustrations during the 1890s. He correctly stressed the importance of instruction, and offered a number of workable proposals. But neither he nor the other proponents of education had any success with an Army that was generally indifferent to official self-improvement. Part of the problem was bureaucratic. Breckinridge very correctly predicted an unsuccessful program unless someone was clearly responsible for it and charged with making it work. But the system also suffered from a lack of focus. Its original justification had been to cure the prevalent illiteracy in the ranks. But that purpose became dubious as illiteracy disappeared because of the changing character of recruits. Breckinridge had always wanted a system of enlisted education to parallel that accorded officers, but in an army whose officer corps partly believed that men were not entitled to even Sundays off, too few people shared his egalitarian views. And last, the overworked soldiery themselves had never shown enough interest in schooling to assure success.

Military Training

Greater success attended physical training and practical military instruction. That went hand in hand with the upgrading of general discipline, the two being the pillars of military efficiency. Breckinridge declared in 1889 that generations of contending with "savages" had done nothing to sharpen the Army's professional skills in modern warfare. Nor had its other circumstances: "The first duty of our Army to the country is perfected military instruction; but probably all professional soldiers recognize that perfect instruction is impossible with depleted skeletons." The reduction in manpower of the Army in pursuit of economy, he maintained, had come at the price of military efficiency. Units were often barely of cadre strength. Furthermore, the heavy burden of manual labor interfered with the training of the enlisted men, while their officers were a widely varied lot as leaders.[5] Inspector General Breckinridge offered a laundry-list description of the Army's military readiness in 1890. The officers, he said, were improving, but their level of instruction varied. The cavalry needed to work on its horsemanship, while practice marches were to be encouraged for all troops. Although camps of instruction and field maneuvers, when held, had been a great success, drill was nothing but parade practice and did not prepare troops to meet an enemy. As for target practice, too much of it was on fixed ranges. When Inspector Robert P. Hughes took soldiers to rough and timbered ground, the best shots did poorly; only those who were hunters did well. Unless the men were trained to shoot at moving targets on uneven terrain, and rewarded with

---

4. Breckinridge to Secy of War, 26 Oct 97, in *ARSecWar 1897*, 21; *ARIG 1897*, 133, 135–37, 240.

5. *ARIG 1889*, 123–26.

MAJ. GEN. JOSEPH C. BRECKIN-
RIDGE. *Inspector General of the
Army, 30 January 1889–11 April
1903.*

marksmanship badges, Breckinridge said that target practice would accomplish nothing. As for field artillery, none of the batteries had a practice range, while the heavy artillery's guns were so obsolete that Breckinridge declared practice a waste of time.[6]

Modern tactics placed a great deal of independent responsibility on private soldiers who worked the battlefield in squads, unlike their predecessors who had been tightly organized in larger formations. That was one of the motivations behind the reform of discipline and enlisted life generally. If the soldier must be trusted to act individually or as a member of a small group often indirectly supervised by an officer, he must be accorded respect and given responsibility for his own conduct in peace as well as on the battlefield. The days of volley fire and the massed bayonet charge had long since passed, and people like Breckinridge maintained that the hard discipline that had once supported those tactics should also be dispensed with. Something fundamental as weapons training had many flaws: Infantry and cavalry target practice, said Breckinridge, usually went forward systematically, although not often appropriately, while only part of the artillery had practice at all. Only at some of the posts were troops trained to estimate distances, and practice firing had not yet been added to practice marches or encampments on unfamiliar ground, nor was firing practiced with moving targets. And only part of the army engaged in field exercises: "Nothing can be more necessary to an army in time of peace than the experience of marches and encampments," Breckinridge said, "and it is to be regretted that they do not form an unflexible part of the annual training of every soldier. It is especially desirable just now, when new equipments and drill regulations are under consideration."[7] The Regular Army's unwillingness to embrace the need for a high level of practical training sorely frustrated the senior inspector general, which may have been one reason why he looked with such favor on the National Guard whose volunteer citizen-soldiers took to their summer encampments with such great enthusiasm. In any event, by 1893

---

6. *ARIG 1890*, 106–10.
7. *ARIG 1893*, 718–19. Breckinridge also reported difficulties in giving infantry the extended-order drill required by the new tactics.

Breckinridge had adopted a very comprehensive view of the national defense establishment, embracing the Regular Army, the National Guard, and college cadet corps.[8]

Even ordinary drill was beset with obstacles. The organization was defective, some reservations were too small, and there were no large assemblies of troops. Nevertheless, Breckinridge maintained that post commanders could do better than they had and should be required to report in advance what exercises they would have during the year. In the absence of scheduled exercises, at least one acting inspector general had started to teach minor unit tactics at every post he visited. He was really doing the job of a unit officer. But, as for the training of officers at posts, Breckinridge said the lyceums recently established provided good theoretical instruction when well conducted, but the topics presented for essays were usually too complex and arcane. Troops generally lacked training in estimating distances and tracking moving targets, while too few men were adequately trained in signaling. As for target practice, too little emphasis was placed on moving targets and unknown distances.[9]

A former gunner himself, Breckinridge felt the artillery especially needed tutelage, while the cavalry was showing slow improvement. Infantry drill in extended formations, he believed, did not appear adaptable to the battlefield. Practical problems had been tested during all inspections, and except for the coastal artillery, those exercises came off well. The men of the Medical Department earned special praise for their handling of "wounded" during exercises, but Sanger suggested that the troops generally needed more training as stretcher bearers. Despite training efforts, target practice had declined by 1897 with skirmish training remaining the weakest part of that program. The artillery was generally unprepared and its practice ammunition was in short supply, but moving targets were beginning to come into use, much to Breckinridge's satisfaction. Nevertheless he complained that no one had given much thought to having artillery posts coordinated to repel attack; hence the nation's coastal defense was piecemeal. Breckinridge listed the fundamental rules of infantry training, one of which was "The spade is raised almost to the rank of a weapon." The new weaponry and new conditions of warfare, he maintained, meant, "For the infantry the proficiency required was never so great, and the time, if not the means, for instruction and preparation may seem severely limited; so the efforts of the officers have to be redoubled." To prepare for a major war, he once again urged that, it being impossible to assemble the scattered Regular Army into a full corps, regulars and guardsmen of several states should assemble for maneuvers.[10]

When the American army first acquired its Inspector General, during the Revolution, his first job was to train the troops. Thereafter, the primary respon-

8. Ibid., 6.

9. *ARIG 1894*, 92–94, 96.

10. *ARAG 1897*, H. Doc. 2, 55th Cong., 2d sess., 1: 101; *ARIG 1897*, 119, 122–23, 124–27, 133–34, 1. 1–40, 151–53, 241; Breckinridge to Secy of War, 26 Oct 97, in *ARSecWar 1897*, 21.

sibility of inspectors general remained the monitoring of the training and military proficiency of the soldiers. Breckinridge took that responsibility very seriously, and there is little doubt that the inspectors general played a significant part in revitalization of that army as a fighting force in the 1890s. They encountered resistance, from circumstances as much as from the officers and men, but by the mid 1890s their ceaseless criticism had caused line commanders to reenliven the training program, neglected for many years. By the time war erupted in 1898, the Army was probably as well trained as it had been since 1865, and the line and mass of troops had made significant progress in overcoming the deadening effects of a long peace.

INSPECTOR GENERAL INSIGNIA, 1895–1961.

That the emphasis on training revived rather late was not as damaging as it might seem. The average soldier was far more intelligent than his predecessors, and his improved lot in life had made him more receptive to instruction. Reforms in his living conditions had helped diminish the amount of time taken from training by manual labor, while his shortened enlistment period meant that training had to be intensified. There was simply no time for the leisurely approach that had characterized professional armies a century earlier, something that Steuben had perceived at the American army's inception. The state of training was not all that Breckinridge would have preferred, but even he had to concede a high degree of improvement in a short span of years. However, no matter how thorough, training remained somewhat academic. Its real results were to be demonstrated on the battlefield, when the next war started. The enlisted men at least were as ready as possible. It remained to be seen whether their officers, especially those in high command, were equally prepared to do their part.

Supply Services

Officers as a class called forth only selected proposals from the inspectors general, but in fact the inspectors spent most of their time observing officers—in their roles as troop leaders, staff administrators, disbursing officers, and so on. The Army's supplies and equipment were managed by officers, and as had always been true the inspectors general had much to say about such matters in the 1890s. Characteristically, Breckinridge was wont to offer recommendations on things other bureau chiefs might have said should not concern him. In 1890 he averred that the rigid advertised contract system for procurement often forced the government to pay the highest price fixed by trusts, as anyone offering a lower price "will be discovered and made to suffer." Testifying to the trustworthiness of the Army's supply officers, he urged that they be allowed to depart from advertisement if they could find cheaper ways of procurement. The Quartermaster Department probably enjoyed that, but not the Inspector General's occasional barbs about horses, the baggage allowance, the "inferior quality of campaign shoes," fading dye on dress coats, and other details. Breckinridge did say in 1896, however, that the inspectors generally believed quartermasters to be overworked.[11]

One of the Quartermaster Department's major responsibilities was transportation. Thanks to the fact that the U.S. Army had spent decades scattered throughout a continental wilderness, by the end of the Indian wars it had perhaps the finest field transportation system and equipment in the world. But in a shortsighted economy measure, and as part of post closings and consolidations, in 1890 Congress ordered the department to sell off most of its equipment and draft animals. Breckinridge was quick to join the Quartermaster General in pointing out the error of that command, stressing that discarding the system would make it impossible to develop officers and men with experience in organizing transport, and that was one thing, he said, that necessitated experience.[12] He could not have been more prophetic, because the mobilization of 1898 turned into a transportation disaster; in fact, nearly all other shortfalls in supply and operations could be attributed to a combination of equipment shortages and general inexperience in organizing transport. It was apparent to Breckinridge by 1896 that some such disaster was in the winds, if an emergency arose, because the transportation inventory was by then insufficient even for peacetime needs.[13]

Besides the quartermasters, the Army's other principal supply service was the Subsistence Department. Breckinridge regarded that much as he had the Quartermaster Department, although it was excellently managed and its supplies were usually of good quality, there were a few complaints. Sometimes supplies were delayed, there was not enough soap issued, rations for field service hampered mobility, and an "emergency ration" was needed. Breckinridge was also opposed to the Subsistence Department's often repeated request that it be allowed to stop selling sundry items to the soldiers. This service was a convenience for the troops, the predecessor of an exchange system. Breckinridge rightly felt that the effect of ending such a program would be disastrous to morale.[14]

---

11. *ARIG 1890*, 98, 102; *ARIG 1894*, 96; *ARIG 1895*, 117–18; *ARIG 1896*, 119–20; *ARIG 1897*, 138–39. One or another item of clothing was the most common subject of complaint. See *ARIG 1890*, 103; *ARIG 1891*, 18; *ARIG 1892*, 35; and *ARIG 1893*, 724–25. For persistent complaints about shortages of tentage, see *ARIG 1892*, 38, and *ARIG 1895*, 118. The issue of waterproof overcoats, incidentally, recommended by inspectors before Breckinridge's time, began in 1890. *ARQMG 1890*, 774–75.

12. *ARIG 1891*, 17.

13. *ARIG 1896*, 120.

14. *ARIG 1893*, 723–24; *ARIG 1894*, 97; *ARIG 1895*, 119; *ARIG 1896*, 120; *ARIG 1897*, 139–40.

Important to the Army's health as was its food, also was its medical service. Like inspectors general since the 1820s, those of the 1890s had nothing but praise for the Medical Department, which continued to modernize during the period. The enlisted Hospital Corps and detailed stretcher bearers also performed commendably during the period, and when the Army Medical School was established in 1893 to give four months of instruction to new surgeons, Breckinridge found that an estimable development. He was also pleased with the Medical Department's educational and training programs for enlisted men. "The Medical Department seems to be generally in excellent condition," he said in 1897. "The Hospital Corps has frequently been specially mentioned for excellence in appearance and efficiency."[15]

Breckinridge addressed the Ordnance Department, as he did the other supply departments, in two terms—according to its operations, and according to its products. The department's operations he usually commended, but occasionally he complained: The blanket bag was unpopular, he said; both heavy and light artillery equipment was a neglected subject; and a magazine explosion in 1894 demonstrated occasional carelessness in handling stores. As for weaponry, Breckinridge complained for every year beginning in 1893 that the Army with its .30-caliber rifle and the Navy with its rifle bore of .236-caliber should find some common cartridge, as "a difference of 20 percent between the two services as to the theoretically perfect calibre seems excessive, and might be reconciled prior to the issue of a single weapon." He was a strong proponent of "a small-caliber bullet and a large-caliber field cannon, and there is some gratification in seeing the tendency now generally established in this direction." When a new .30-caliber cavalry carbine was adopted in 1896, Breckinridge was delighted, except for the absence of a windage gauge on the rear sight. But the difference between Army and Navy calibers aside, in 1897 the Inspector General proclaimed the Army well-equipped, and even coastal armanent was improving at a slow pace.[16]

The Army, the Inspectors—Ready for War?

Since the time of Steuben, the main purpose of the Inspector General was to determine and report upon the Army's preparation for war. Under Breckinridge's guidance, the Inspector General's Department did that throughout the 1890s. Breckinridge had concluded by 1897 that the Regular Army was essentially ready, and when the test came the next year, at least as far as the fighting quality of the officers and men was concerned, he proved correct. But he and his inspectors had also continued to detect flaws in the system, and those flaws worked their own effects during the war with Spain. Breckinridge's complaints about the loss of transportation and the cumbersome procurement procedures

---

15. *ARIG 1893*, 721; *ARSecWar 1893*, 9–10; *ARIG 1894*, 94; *ARIG 1896*, 113; *ARIG 1897*, 140.

16. *ARIG 1890*, 104–05; *ARIG 1893*, 30–31, 721–22; *ARIG 1894*, 95; *ARIG 1896*, 113; *ARIG 1897*, 140–42, 241.

proved especially well founded. Furthermore, the establishment had other short-comings that were not so apparent to the inspectors. In finding the reactionary ways of the supply services, and their rigid defense of the fragmented staff system of the War Department, generally commendable the inspectors general did not ask whether the Army was prepared for the logistical demands of a real emergency. They had paid much attention to the National Guard, but they never really addressed the relationship between the Guard and the Regular Army in any possible war. Especially, in focusing on the need for defense, they did not consider how the Army might go on the offensive and carry a war overseas.

Another thing that Breckinridge and his men failed to plan for was the proper role of the Inspector General's Department in the next major war. The inspectorate had fallen apart in the last two conflicts, although it had emerged from the Civil War with some semblance of order. Most of the Army's leaders, Breckinridge included, were veterans of Grant's Grand Army of 1865, and very conscious of that fact. Breckinridge was more forward-looking than most, and perhaps partly for that reason failed to consider how an inspectorate might be organized in the next grand army. But when the emergency erupted, it was not lack of foresight that hampered Breckinridge's customary adaptability. Rather, it was his outrage over the disruption of the district system of the Inspector General's Department that made him look for a change of scene away from Washington and Nelson Miles.

In one subject, however, Breckinridge proved more farsighted than any of his contemporaries: that was thinking about the next, unpredictable war. Beginning in 1892, he mounted a strong campaign to establish a fund for widows and orphans of military men, supported by interest-earning deducations from soldiers' pay and by fines levied by courts-martial. Compulsory life insurance, he maintained, was essential for soldiers, because the military was a hazardous occupation. The best soldiers were those most likely to put themselves in danger in the heat of battle, and also the least likely to plan for the future. When the war broke out in 1898, many new widows and orphans found cause to wish that the government had heeded the words of Inspector General Breckinridge.[17]

17. *ARIG 1892*, 121–22; *ARIG 1897*, 144–45; Breckinridge to Secy of War, 26 Oct 97, in *ARSecWar 1897*, 21.

Part Four

The Inspector General's Department
of the New Army

(1898–1903)

CHAPTER 21

Inspection During the War with Spain (1898)

In his postwar memoirs, Secretary of War Russell A. Alger commented on his department's preparedness for events that propelled it into war in April 1898: "[The department] had, during thirty years, been called upon only to plan for and meet the requirements of the regular army in time of peace, and naturally enough had become quite fixed in the narrow grooves of peace."[1] The Secretary's observation accurately summarizes the United States Army's situation at the time of the declaration of war with Spain in April 1898. Numbering a little more than 23,000 men, it was scattered in small garrisons throughout the country. The bureau structure at the War Department, adequate for peace, could not meet the demands of mobilization and deployment. Its mission had never been to plan and prepare for such contingencies and thus the predominantly older bureau chiefs had to improvise based on vague memories of the Civil War. The weakness inherent in the duality between the Secretary of War and the Commanding General became immediately apparent as policies and plans were hastily developed.[2]

The Situation in 1898

The tremendous surge of enthusiastic but largely untrained and unequipped manpower accepted by the President proved to be the source of most of the War Department's problems during, and after, the war. Although conditioned by years of congressional parsimony, tight accountability procedures, and severe limits on any kind of stockpiling, the bureau chiefs unstintingly executed their responsibilities. Despite many critical problems, some of which should have been avoided, these leaders succeeded remarkably well under the circumstances. One minor and two major expeditions were equipped and transported to three completely different locations and successfully discharged. By the end of the war in August 1898, the Army numbered 274,714 men, far more than were

---

1. Russell A. Alger, *The Spanish American War* (New York: Harper, 1901), 7.
2. Weigley, *History of the United States Army*, 289, 305; Ellen Maury Slayden, *Washington Wife: Journal of Ellen Maury Slayden from 1897-1919* (New York: Harper & Row, 1962), 17; Edward Ranson, "Nelson A. Miles as Commanding General, 1895–1903," *Military Affairs*, 29 (winter 1965–1966): 179–200.

needed. Most were concentrated in large training camps, the foremost of which was Camp Thomas in Georgia, on the old Chickamauga battlefield. The deficiencies exacerbated by the hasty mobilization of these untrained masses were most evident at such camps, as were the newspapermen eager for a story but ignorant of the overall problems experienced by the War Department.[3]

Most difficulties during the war came from shortfalls in transportation, just as Inspector General Breckinridge had feared. No one, apparently, consulted the Quartermaster on the selection of camp locations. Most had poor transportation facilities, and Tampa, the best embarkation point for Cuba, was a terminus served by fewer than adequate railroad tracks and inadequate roads. Volunteer quartermasters proved unable to execute the marshaling and unloading of railroad cars, and a system for the transshipment and loading of water transports was generally lacking. When the Army had sold off its wagon and pack train equipment during the years preceding the war, wagons flooded the market, leaving the wagon industry unable to supply new wagons on short order. Ocean transportation at times nearly brought disaster.

Even more serious was the defective medical service during the war, also attributable in part to the transportation shortfall. Not enough medical supplies reached the front, and transportation for the wounded was extremely primitive. But the greatest disasters occurred in the camps, stateside, where the Medical Department thought that circulating a pamphlet on hygiene satisfied the supervision of inexperienced volunteers. Epidemics, especially of typhoid fevers, swept the camps, taking more lives during the war than both the enemy and tropical diseases took in Cuba. To be sure, the volunteers had too few physicians, but the death toll in their camps could have been reduced had elementary precautions in siting, sanitation, and troop management been applied. The result of the Medical Department's failings paralleled that of the purchase of unpalatable canned beef by the Subsistence Department, which led to a major scandal and the overhaul of the department.[4]

The war itself was brief and surprisingly successful. General William "Pecos Bill" Shafter led a force of 14,412 regulars and 2,465 volunteers to Cuba, followed eventually by about 5,000 additional volunteers. They landed on 20 June 1898, established themselves ashore, and began ten days later to march from Siboney toward Santiago. The Americans cleared the heights around Santiago on 1 July, forcing the Spanish fleet to flee the safety of the city's harbor, whereupon the American fleet destroyed it. The campaign had involved three engagements; just two of them, El Caney and San Juan, had any real significance. Meanwhile, Miles led an expedition into Puerto Rico in late July, landing his forces at five separate places and quickly subduing the dispirited enemy on the island. An armistice concluded both campaigns on 12 August.

---

3. General accounts of the war include David F. Trask, *The War With Spain in 1898* (New York: Macmillan, 1981); Graham Cosmas, *An Army for Empire: The United States Army in the Spanish-American War* (Columbia: University of Missouri Press, 1971).

4. Leech, *Days of McKinley*, 300–04; Weigley, *History of the United States Army*, 304–05.

Much of the U.S. Army's Cuban force, meanwhile, had been evacuated because of sickness. President McKinley directed the mustering out of all volunteers after the armistice, except for the regiments sent to the Philippines to capitalize on the Navy's victory there. The Spanish at Manila had given up swiftly, but the American volunteers continued mired in jungle warfare for another year fighting Emilio Aguinaldo's revolutionaries who cared no more for American rule than they had for that of the Spanish. Things were more peaceful in the Caribbean, where the Army embarked upon the unfamiliar duties of military government without much strong guidance from the War Department.[5]

The Spanish-American War, in short, demonstrated that the War Department was seriously flawed. As a result of its organization it could not perform the fundamental duties of planning and supervising a mobilization or deployment. The supply and medical departments had done well in serving the Regular Army, but they were unable to extend their operations sufficiently to ensure that like service be given the larger force of volunteers. Volunteer supply and medical officers did their best in the circumstances, but were mostly unguided by their more experienced counterparts in the permanent establishments. The situation inevitably led to the creation of conditions that reflected adversely on the War Department's management of the war.

Where Were the Inspectors?

The War Department's failures were demonstrated to the public by the transportation calamities, the epidemics in the southern camps, and the tales of food that was either inedible or undelivered. These problems all reflected command and management inefficiencies that should have been detected early by the Inspector General's Department and righted, following its advice; but they were not. Breckinridge and his department could perhaps be excused for not predicting the wartime disasters. But as the war faded, Breckinridge soon learned that he would not be excused for failing to report trouble when it developed. The other departments may have been less than perfect, but they at least tried to fulfill their obligations. The Inspector General's Department at War Department level, however, did little inspecting during the war. Its preoccupation with its structure and members' careers caused it to give little guidance to the many inspectors scattered throughout the Army, who had, they thought, nowhere to refer their findings. This drift began with Breckinridge making a fight for his department. He still chafed at the termination of his district system by Miles, who as the Commanding General was endeavoring to assert his authority over the Adjutant General and the Inspector General alike, clashing with both in the process. Breckinridge's response was an attempt to reassert the status of his own organization as a bureau of the War Department.

---

5. Besides the general accounts of the war identified above, on Cuba see Joseph Wheeler, *The Santiago Campaign* (1898; reprinted Port Washington, New York: Kennikat, 1971), and Charles Johnson Post, *The Little War of Private Post* (Boston: Little, Brown, 1960).

Congressman John Handy of Kentucky, Breckinridge's nephew, introduced legislation on 1 April 1898 to "define and prescribe the duties of the officers of the Inspector-General's Department of the Army." The bill began by asserting that the department was a bureau of the War Department. It also would have established its complement at thirteen inspectors general and one accountant, with provisions for inspectors for brigades, divisions, and army corps in the event of mobilization. Furthermore, each inspector general would have been entitled to a clerk and messenger. Although Breckinridge generated a mountain of justifying paper work, the bill got nowhere against the strong opposition of the Adjutant General, whom the Inspector General believed in league with General Miles in an effort to suppress the Inspector General's Department.[6] Breckinridge said later that the Handy bill would have been sufficient for the circumstances of the war, but that the legislation that actually did pass was insufficient, because it did not allow for enough officers. He was trying to shift to others the blame for any wartime failure, while nevertheless asserting that his department had performed as well as it could during the war. In any case, the first legislation, on 22 April, increasing the Army and mobilizing volunteers, permitted the assignment of inspectors general to the staffs of army corps and divisions.[7]

Meanwhile, on 16 April, the War Department reassigned the six junior inspectors general and one acting inspector general from the inspection districts to duty as inspectors of the eight military departments, which had been reorganized on 11 March 1898. This realignment required the detail of additional officers to act as inspectors. But before the change could be effected, the country was at war, and the Inspector General's Department began to disintegrate.[8] Even as its officers were leaving Washington for field duty, a development occurred on 3 May in response to a request from Breckinridge, which seemed to improve the department's status. The Judge Advocate General rendered an official opinion on the question "whether the Inspector-General's Department is now legally a bureau of the War Department, similar to the Quartermaster's, Subsistence, and other bureaus therein, in its character and in the status and authority of its chief." The chief legal officer's finding was that, despite the absence of a specific law, precedent made the Inspector General's Department a department or corps of the Army, while the Office of the Inspector General was a bureau of the War Department. To Breckinridge's delight, he thus possessed status equal to the other bureau chiefs. "So, on the whole," said the Judge Advocate General, "it would seem that the offices usually called bureaus in the War Department are all bureaus in their character, and that all the

---

6. *ARIG 1898*, H. Doc. 2, 55th Cong., 3d sess., 1: 580, including a copy of the bill. Breckinridge's enormous file on the Handy bill, including his personal opinions about Miles, is in file 3314 A–I, K–P, Index to General Correspondence, RG 159.

7. *ARIG 1898*, 580–81; *An Act to provide for temporarily increasing the military establishment of the United States in time of war, and for other purposes*, Statutes at Large 30, sec. 10, 361 (1898); Thian, *Legislative History*, 116.

8. *ARIG 1898*, 563, 564.

chiefs of these bureaus are practically alike in the status and authority as chiefs of bureaus and heads of corps in the Army."[9]

The Judge Advocate General's opinion was so qualified that it accorded Breckinridge the status of bureau chief only by custom, not by law. But that did not disconcert the Inspector General, who asserted his equality with other bureau heads and used his organization's departmental status as justification to revive the issue of district inspectorates. He said again that the supervision of a bureau of the War Department should not be interrupted by departmental commanders. He implied later that these interruptions were the reason that his office had received few inspection reports during 1898.[10] The day after receiving his declaration of departmental independence, Breckinridge responded to a request from the Secretary for an estimate of the extra manpower his department would need for the war. He assumed that four corps and twelve divisions would require permanent inspectors general, each with a clerk and a messenger. On 7 June, Sanger, acting for the absent Breckinridge, told the War Department's chief clerk that his office required eight more clerks and three more messengers, as well as additional office space. If the war lasted past December, Sanger said, eight additional clerks would be needed. Also that month, Warren H. Orcutt, Breckinridge's senior clerk, was temporarily promoted to chief clerk, whose duties he had been performing for years, and in August his promotion was made permanent.[11]

Trying to assert his independence and enlarge his organization, which was suspended between the district inspection system and a return to departmental inspections, Breckinridge had not yet clarified how he intended to employ his department in the war effort. When Maj. Gen. Joseph Wheeler asked for Ernest A. Garlington to serve as inspector general of his volunteer division, Breckinridge said, "And to suggest now taking his inspector from the regular establishment and from this bureau must now be regarded as exceptional." Breckinridge revealed that with his "inadequate force" he wanted junior officers to run the Washington office, while more senior officers were to join the field force. The best way "to provide for such exceptional requests as General Wheeler's and yet obviate the weakening or disintegration of this Department and bureau is by a proper increase of the permanent corps," he said. Complaining that Handy's bill had been killed by the Adjutant General's opposition in April, Breckinridge asked Adjutant General Corbin to prepare a new bill supporting his proposals for increases. That request, apparently, was answered when Corbin's comments and Alger's endorsement went to Congress.[12] Because no permanent increase was allowed, the work of inspecting the masses of troops for the most part fell to the inspectors general of volunteers, of whom at least thirty-six were

9. Ibid., 589–90; another copy of the opinon is JAG to Asst Secy of War, 3 May 98, in file 3314, Gen Corresp 1894–1914, RIGO, RG 159.

10. *ARIG 1898*, 360–63.

11. Correspondence on this is in file 2912, Index to Gen Corresp 1894–1916, RG 159.

12. Breckinridge, memorandum for Henry C. Corbin, 13 May 98, in E.A. Garlington personal records, 5574–ACP–1877, box 493, personnel records, RAGO, RG 94.

assigned during the war. About two-thirds of them were assigned from the Regular Army; the others, from volunteers, with the approval of the War Department. It is clear from Breckinridge's record of their assignments that not all spent the entire war as inspectors; they had various other staff or command duties. Moreover, Breckinridge did not assert control over the volunteer inspectorate, and as a consequence he heard very little from the volunteer inspectors. That was in striking contrast to his formerly incessant demands to have all inspection paper work flowing quickly to his office.

Breckinridge's failure to direct the inspectorate and make it work was a primary factor in his department's ineffectiveness during the war with Spain. It was also a principal reason why the authorities in the War Department remained, until too late, uninformed about conditions in the southern camps. By the time the war was over, the Inspector General's Department was under considerable journalistic criticism for not doing its job. Breckinridge, predictably, would not concede that. The high rate of sickness in the volunteer camps, he said, was attributable to the absence of experienced officers and noncommissioned officers to teach camp discipline and sanitation. Clearly on the defensive, he claimed that the volunteer inspectors had done their job well. He said the inspectors were well selected and had done good work but sometimes had problems with "intercommunication."[13] Breckinridge implied that, because of Miles' obtrusion, his communications with inspectors were interrupted by commanders; therefore his department was not culpable for any lack of information in the War Department on conditions in the camps. In fact, he made no attempt to assert his own control over information produced by the inspectorate.

Besides being displeased over the abolishment of his district system, as senior inspector general, he had ambitions of his own. He wanted to go to the field, preferably as a line commander. He and other senior officers such as Miles still remembered the precedent of the Civil War. Overlooking the benefits of Hardie's and Schriver's work in consolidating the department, these senior officers seemed only to remember Marcy's role as McClellan's chief of staff. Every one of their memories seemed to call for the senior inspectors to betake themselves to the field, with the further emotional impulse of old warriors to advance toward the sound of the guns for one last time. Breckinridge went so far as to tell his nephew he felt it more honorable to be near danger with no particular job than to be safe at home on the staff.[14] As a "loyal Southerner" he was selected by President McKinley to be commissioned a major general of volunteers, junior only to Nelson Miles and John R. Brooke. Miles originally intended for Breckinridge to serve as his inspector general and chief of staff, assuming that he would accompany the main army into the field.[15] When other

13. *ARIG 1898*, 564–65. A list of volunteer inspectors and their assignments is in *ARIG 1898*, 586–89.

14. Joseph C. Breckinridge, Ltr to Desha Breckinridge, 11 Jul 98, in file 3409, Index to Gen Corresp 1894–1916, RG 159, entry 24.

15. Orders dated 30 May 98 in ACP file B203 CB 1866, microfilm 1064, reel 240, National Archives.

circumstances prevented this from happening, Breckinridge was somewhat disconcerted, although before that happened he had spent much of May and June inspecting volunteers at the largest gathering, Camp Thomas, at Chickamauga National Military Park in Georgia. Rather than any case study of an inspection by a volunteer inspector (he apparently had none in his office), Breckinridge selected that journey as the subject of his "summary outline of a single inspection" for his annual report. Miles had sent him out on 17 May to inspect camps at Chickamauga, Atlanta, New Orleans, Mobile, Tampa, Miami, and Key West. He took with him Garlington, Inspector General of Volunteers John J. Astor, and two lieutenants. The senior inspector general had to develop his procedures as he went along: "As the inspection of an improvised army preparing for the field was almost unprecedented and absolutely new to us, our progress in the earlier stages of the inspection was necessarily slow." It should take three days for four inspectors to cover a division, he said, but he was soon behind schedule.[16]

To his credit, Breckinridge's telegrams revealed that serious problems existed in the organization, training, equipment, transportation, supplies, and medical services at Chickamauga. He was inclined to state things positively, however, and did not hint at any serious defects in sanitation there, although there was only a meager water supply. That he perceived problems was suggested by his request that Colonels Vroom and Burton be assigned to join him on the tour. It is also apparent that the troops he examined were far from prepared for action, and would require a long period of training. He was nevertheless able to drill them in some battle maneuvers. Breckinridge's last telegram from Chickamauga, on 4 June, asked the Secretary to give him a command commensurate with his new grade of major general of volunteers. Although Breckinridge should have been more informative and critical about what was going on in the camps before the worst epidemics erupted, the confusion over his status as a member of Miles' field staff is partial mitigation. His own tour covered only Chickamauga, one of several camps he was to observe, while his going to Cuba meant he received few reports from inspectors in the departments or in the camps and field.

Despite Breckinridge's absence, his proposed expansion of the Inspector General's Department was progressing. Because he was not around to advance his own case, Congress followed the course laid out by the Adjutant General. A bill to add three officers to the department passed the House of Representatives on 28 June 1898. The approved bill became law on 7 July 1898, increasing the

---

16. The "J. J. Astor" who accompanied Breckinridge to Chickamauga was John Jacob Astor of the New York family. Breckinridge was not impressed, as he wrote his nephew Desha from Santiago: "I recommend that the volunteer officers appointed for this war in the IGD should be subjected to a suitable examination, then volunteers would have been protected from the suffering which was shown along the sick-line at Chickamauga and Tampa . . . . And the country might have been spared the discredit of having to have such asses as Jack Astor . . . . pretend to direct & instruct soldiers for the absolute and fateful requirements of war." Breckinridge to Desha Breckinridge, 11 Jul 98, in file 3409, Index to Gen Corresp 1894–1916, RG 159.

Inspector General's Department by a colonel, a lieutenant colonel, and a major. The law provided that these new slots were to be filled first by promotion within the department according to seniority, and that after the volunteers were mustered out and the Regular Army reduced, the department would decline by attrition to its former level of seven officers.[17] As a result of that legislation, Lawton became a colonel and Sanger and Garlington became lieutenant colonels. Major Charles H. Heyl became an inspector general on 8 July, joined on 25 July by Capt. Stephen C. Mills, promoted to major. "Following the honored precedent established early in its history," Breckinridge said, "the policy of this department was to secure service for as many of its officers as possible with the fighting line."[18]

This view meant that although the Inspector General's Department was significantly expanded, its members were dispersed almost immediately. Robert P. Hughes, assigned in late May to accompany troops bound for the Philippines, became a brigadier general of volunteers on 3 June; he ended the year as provost marshal in Manila. George H. Burton was ordered to the Washington office on 6 June, but he fell ill with typhoid later in the month and spent the rest of the year on sick leave. Henry W. Lawton, assigned as inspector general on Shafter's staff for the invasion of Cuba late in April, became a brigadier general of volunteers on 4 May, and then a major general of volunteers two months later; he never returned to inspection. Joseph P. Sanger, who began the war in the Washington office, was a brigadier general of volunteers by 27 May; he ended the war as division commander. Thus, besides Breckinridge, four Inspector General's Department senior officers were otherwise occupied during the war. Of those remaining on the permanent staff, Peter D. Vroom eventually became inspector on General Miles' staff during the invasion of Puerto Rico. Garlington started the war attached to Breckinridge, whom he accompanied to Chickamauga, but he was soon assigned as the inspector to Wheeler's cavalry division, which he accompanied to Cuba. He returned to duty in Washington at the end of August. Of the newcomers, Heyl found himself administering the Washington office after 14 July. He was joined there two weeks later by Mills, who left on 4 August to become the recorder for a commission investigating the conduct of the war. Another new inspector, Maj. Thomas T. Knox, was with his regiment in Cuba at the time of his 25 July appointment. There he was severely wounded. On 18 August he was ordered to report for duty, after convalescence, in the Washington office.[19]

The Inspector General's Department, as it had during the Civil War, existed mostly on paper. Two very junior officers in Washington could not begin to establish a systematic and responsible inspectorate over the whole Army, and in fact such an organization never evolved. The volunteer inspectors did their

---

17. *An Act to Provide for a Temporary Increase in the Inspector-General's Department of the Army, approved 7 Jul 98*, 30 Stat. 720; Thian, *Legislative History*, 116.

18. *ARIG 1898*, 564, 587. See Appendix B. Incidentally, Congress also provided in July for temporary increases in rank for four inspectors reporting to the Quartermaster General. Risch, *Quartermaster Support*, 518.

19. *ARIG 1898*, 585–86.

best, interpreting the regulations as well as they were able. Inspection went forward, sometimes well, and sometimes not, in most divisions and corps, but it lacked the direction or overview of the Inspector General's Department. Meanwhile, at least seven officers served as acting inspectors general on the staffs of the geographical departments. As Breckinridge admitted, they sent him no reports. The only positive note, from his point of view, was an order on 30 July that told the senior inspector general to report to the departmental inspectors, via their commanders, those inspections required of them by the Secretary of War. Inspections of staff facilities, cemeteries, and the like were explicitly excluded from supervision by the department commanders.[20]

The Whereabouts of General Breckinridge

The Secretary's order should have pleased Breckinridge, who in earlier times would have used it as an initiative to reinstate his independence. But this time he was not present to notice. On 3 June, while Breckinridge was at Chickamauga, Miles ordered him to Tampa, where he arrived on 5 June. The Secretary of War later said that the Commanding General, Miles, had sent Breckinridge to observe operations in Cuba and to report on them. Actually, on 6 June the Adjutant General telegraphed him, allowing him to accompany Shafter if he desired, which, of course, he did.[21] His purpose in going to Cuba has never been explained fully, but Breckinridge did perform as an inspector on occasion. When he arrived in Tampa he decided that the expedition's transports had not been examined by an inspector general as "suggested" in the regulations, and he observed that some of the ships were unsuitable. So he sent telegrams to Miles, Alger, and the "Acting Inspector General of the Army" (probably Burton, who had not yet arrived) after he had talked with Shafter and the chief surgeon. But all he suggested was that someone be assigned to perform the inspection; he did not do it himself.[22] Breckinridge sent at least three telegrams to the War Department pointing out that the transports had not been properly inspected. He also reported that the troops at Tampa were in considerable "discomfort," aggravated by "the unsystematic and unsupervised methods, or lack of inspections of volunteers by capable inspectors hitherto prevailing." The best he could do was to ask the War Department to provide instructions on the duties of corps and division inspectors. Why, from his position on Shafter's staff, he did not work to straighten things out in the command by his own devices, he never explained satisfactorily.[23]

In his annual report for that year, Breckinridge tried to justify himself and avoid criticism: The volunteer inspectors were incompetent or undirected, or the

---

20. Ibid., 586; "History of the Inspector General's Department," 31 Dec 04, in file 372, Index to Gen Corresp 1894–1916, RG 159. The order was: GO No. 109, AGO, 30 Jul 98, which is not included in GORI&IG.

21. *ARIG 1898*, 570–71, 575; *ARSecWar 1898*, H. Doc. 2, 55th Cong., 3d sess., p.3.

22. *ARIG 1898*, 575.

23. Ibid., 575–76.

BLOODY FORD, CUBA. *Private Post met General Breckinridge at this site during the fighting for San Juan Hill, 1898.*

inspectorate had tried to do its job but was obstructed. Nowhere did he provide any evidence that he had tried to organize an effective inspectorate for Shafter's expedition; he seemed to have expected someone else to do that. Rather than immerse himself in the mechanics of inspection, Breckinridge regaled Miles and Alger with optimistic telegrams. Only rarely did the Inspector General find problems to report; these few were mainly related to supplies and were usually reported without details, as on 4 July when he complained of insufficiency of medical supplies. If anything positive came of Breckinridge's presence, it was his summary, "Report of a Tour of Duty with the Army of Invasion of Cuba," which offered a number of recommendations for changes in uniforms, equipment, supplies, maps, mail service, facilities for foreign observers, and so on. But mostly, his report, like his telegrams, was devoted to lavish praise of officers and men.[24]

Breckinridge had no clearly defined place in Shafter's army, and he evidently made no attempt to establish one. Lt. Col. John D. Miley served as Shafter's inspector general and was effectively his chief of staff, issuing orders to the generals. He also did investigative work, such as when he went out to learn why firing suddenly broke out during the night among troops investing Santiago. Breckinridge seemed content to accompany the investing force as an

---

24. Ibid., 576–79, 590–601.

observer, providing an occasional source of speculation to others with authentic jobs to do, including Pvt. Charles Johnson Post, who met him one night:

> Bloody Ford was our nearest watering place. I was in the ford filling our squad's canteens when a general and his staff rode through. A Mauser bullet from a sharpshooter smacked into the stream not six inches from my dipping hand. It had just missed the general. "Didn't miss by much, did he?" said the general mildly.
> "Do you mind filling my canteen for me, my man?" He reached over his canteen. I filled it. I had never known a general, and I was curious.
> "General," I asked, "do you mind telling me what general you are?"
> "I am General Breckinridge," he answered.
> And to this day, I do not know who General Breckinridge is, or was, or what he was doing at that Cuban ford.[25]

On 31 July 1898, acceding at last to his appeals for a command in the line, the department assigned Breckinridge to command of "all the troops at Camp Thomas, Ga." He assumed charge at the camp in Chickamauga National Military Park on 2 August.[26] To some extent, Breckinridge redeemed his neglect of the inspectorate in his performance at Camp Thomas. The place, housing the largest gathering of green volunteers, was in a deplorable state, with diseases taking a ghastly toll, and a promise of worse to come. The new commander began his work with attention to the hospitals, which he told the War Department on 4 August were "inadequate and unsuitable." A War Department board (one of its members, Maj. Walter Reed, was the future conqueror of yellow fever) was examining the conditions of sanitation at Chickamauga. According to Breckinridge, "All testimony and every appearance indicated that we were on the verge of an experience with a diseased camp that required prompt, decisive, and united effort to fully meet." The inspector-turned-commander went right to work rectifying camp discipline and moving camps out of unhealthy locations.[27]

Camp Thomas housed 40,000; these men were supervised by a commander unable to meet the special challenges of a large gathering of undisciplined volunteers and unable to enlist the support services that his situation required. The Army was then preparing for an advance on Havana, and Breckinridge was to lead his 40,000-man force in that campaign. In any case, too many of the men were ill or dying from patently preventable causes, and the place had become a national disgrace. Within a week, however, it was apparent that there would be no advance on Havana. The Spanish in Cuba had yielded to American pressure. This fact did not slow down Breckinridge. He took considerable satisfaction from his accomplishments in two months as a line commander. After correcting the sanitary defects at Chickamauga, he put into practice what he had long preached as an inspector general: He thoroughly formed and

25. William Henry Bisbee, *Through Four American Wars: The Impressions and Expressions of Brigadier General William Henry Bisbee* (Boston: Meador, 1931); Post, *The Little War of Private Post*, 219, 226–27 (quotation), 229.

26. *ARIG 1898*, 582.

27. Ibid., 582–83.

organized the army, and trained it from top to bottom, to the point where it was proficient en masse in reviews and battle exercises. But as hard as he worked he said he was plagued by "constantly changing circumstances," his army was dissolving around him. He was compelled to begin mustering troops out in late August, finding himself the target of bad news reports which he attributed to complaints from men discontented because some regiments were mustered out ahead of their own. The last of the first-draft volunteers were gone on 14 September. On the same day, Breckinridge began to march what was left of his command, now an army corps, to Knoxville, Tennessee, then to Lexington, Kentucky, drilling and training the troops all the way. Secretary Alger paid him the honor of reviewing the troops at Lexington on 20 September. Breckinridge turned over his corps to his replacement on 20 October and returned to Washington. He resumed his duties as senior inspector general on 24 October, and on 30 November his honorable discharge from the volunteer service took effect.[28]

The Aftermath

The Inspector General's Department was at the time disorganized. In theory, Hughes was supposed to be at the Department of the East, Burton at the Department of the Lakes, Lawton at the Department of California, Vroom at the Department of the Gulf, and Sanger and Garlington on duty in Washington. The newest inspectors general had not received departmental assignments and few of the others were in their assigned places. Actually, Hughes was in the Philippines and Lawton was on his way there, both officers with line duties. Burton was home with typhoid fever, while Vroom was in the Caribbean, Sanger was commanding a division at Lexington, and Mills was on special assignment with the presidential commission. Only Garlington, Heyl, and Knox were accessible; all were in Washington.[29] When he returned to Washington, Breckinridge found himself and his department under heavy criticism in the press and among politicians. A few might acknowledge that he had worked manfully to ameliorate the miserable sanitation at Camp Thomas, but the general thinking was that the Inspector General's Department should have informed the authorities that such disasters were in the making. With his customary aplomb, Breckinridge tried to turn the situation to his own advantage, saying again that his department's ineffectiveness was attributable to the end of its independence in the spring and to its being too small.

A renewed drive for an expanded Inspector General's Department depended upon a decision on the size of the permanent military establishment. Late in 1898 Secretary Alger told Congress that the new island possessions made an increase in the army advisable. President William McKinley agreed, and in his annual message on 5 December 1898 gave "unqualified approval" to Alger's

---

28. Ibid., 584, 585, 601–11.
29. Ibid., 563–64, 585–86.

request for a 100,000-man Regular Army. Congressman John A.T. Hull, retired General Schofield, and even the National Guard Association supported such an expansion. But central to the issue was a reform of the staff department system, increasingly regarded as the cause of all the problems that had characterized the mobilization of 1898. Line officers seized the opportunity to argue strongly for an end to permanent staff departments, to be replaced by temporary rotations of line officers, along with other administrative changes. The staff departments, led by Adjutant General Henry C. Corbin, offered their own arguments in return, and the old issue of the relation between the Commanding General and the rest of the War Department arose once again.[30]

Congressman George B. McClellan, the late Inspector General Marcy's grandson, introduced a bill on 12 December 1898 to reorganize the Army. His measure proposed merger of the Inspector General's and Adjutant General's Departments into a "general staff" headed by the most formidable of the staff chiefs, Adjutant General Corbin. General-staff officers would have permanent tenure, but would be required to have two years of service in the line every ten years. McClellan's bill would also have consolidated some other staff departments and put all of them under the direct control of the Commanding General, who would be graded lieutenant general, this an attempt to win Miles' support. Over the next two days, Miles, Schofield, Corbin, and others testified on various army expansion bills, with Schofield and Miles debating the proper status of the Commanding General.[31]

Breckinridge also testified, saying again that the Handy bill, introduced in the spring, would have provided all the organization necessary for his department. It would have extended his purview over all inspecting officers, "or others, under the control of the Secretary of War," excepting only the purely technical work of the Corps of Engineers and Ordnance Department. In a sense Breckinridge's ambitions paralleled Miles'. The *Army and Navy Journal*, a spokesman for much current military thinking, perceived what he was intriguing to do, and suspected that his emphasis on independence went too far. The periodical did not oppose reorganization of the Inspector General's Department, but avowed that the Handy bill circumscribed the authority of the President as Commander in Chief. Breckinridge wanted too much independence, and in reaching too far, as did Miles, he very nearly lost his department's identity altogether.[32] Breckinridge spent November and December 1898 building a great file of paper work justifying his designs for a large and thoroughly independent Inspector General's Department. He assailed congressmen and army officers with correspondence. When he had his opportunity to testify on Capitol Hill in December, however, he found himself faced with considerable skepticism among congressional committee members. They were not immediately interested in an expansion of the Inspector General's Department, they

30. Graham A. Cosmas, "Military Reform After the Spanish-American War: The Army Reorganization Fight of 1898-1899," *Military Affairs*, 35 (February 1971): 13.

31. Ibid., 14–15.

32. *Army and Navy Journal*, 35 (9 April 1898): 609, and (16 April 1898): 626.

questioned whether the organization had accomplished anything of value during the war, and they were definitely unsympathetic to Breckinridge's ambitions.[33]

The issue of expanding the Inspector General's Department was not resolved in 1898, partly because the larger issues arising from the War Department's conduct of the war, and the department's efficiency generally, had not all been thoroughly aired. But Breckinridge had by the end of the year acquired an important political ally in the person of the Secretary of War. The two now perceived that they had a common enemy in Miles. Alger was beginning to incline toward support of Breckinridge, as a way of curbing the troublesome Commanding General. In his report for 1898, Alger quoted Breckinridge's recommendations at length, strongly endorsing his proposal that the Inspector General's Department be extended in wartime to even the brigade level. But whether Alger's growing support of Breckinridge would prove beneficial would depend ultimately on the strength of Alger's own position. As scandal heaped upon scandal in the press at the end of 1898, Alger appeared less and less secure as Secretary of War.[34]

Breckinridge had to admit at the end of the year that the Inspector General's Department had not provided its usual services. Many of the regular inspections, he said, were deferred or omitted because of the war's pressing demands. Even the "customary third inspection of the accounts of most of the staff officers was not had." About a quarter of the garrisoned posts and camps had been inspected (by acting inspectors), but none of the military colleges had. There had not been an inspection of the National Home for Disabled Volunteer Soldiers in more than a year. As for property, Breckinridge detected a movement to end the cumbersome condemnation procedures that had been in effect since 1825, and he resisted vigorously any attempt to curtail the purview of his department.[35] In other concerns, Breckinridge advised the establishment of an indemnity fund to compensate farmers for damages incurred during troop maneuvers; he also proposed a permanent maritime military transport service. Breckinridge renewed an earlier suggestion that a corps of "trained civilian teamsters and packers" be organized to prevent taking soldiers from the line for land transportation service; he recommended a renewed stockpile of transportation equipment, and an increase in the enlisted Hospital Corps. The ration, he said, should be "changed or made more elastic to meet the new conditions of service in the tropics; and articles required by convalescing patients, suffering from fever and disturbances of the alimentary tract, should be added to some branch of supply." Breckinridge further suggested that the appointment of graduates from college cadet corps to volunteer commissions be made a matter of policy.[36]

33. Breckinridge's file on this issue at the time is in file 3314 Q–U, W, Gen Corresp 1894–1914, RG 159.

34. *ARSecWar 1898*, 154.

35. *ARIG 1898*, 347–49, 352–53, 356–58, 363–64, 611; GO No. 56, AGO, 27 May 98, in "History of the Inspector General's Department," 31 Dec 04, in file 372, Index to Gen Corresp 1894–1916, RG 159.

36. *ARIG 1898*, 154–55.

With ideas like that, Breckinridge had for several years shown himself ahead of the mass of the Regular Army in predicting the future shape of the military establishment, which in the next generation would be based on the permanent Regular Army, the National Guard, a system of reserves, and volunteer armies for large wars. Simultaneously, he was reactionary in his devotion to the idea that the staff departments should continue as independent satraps in a War Department organized as they had always known it. Breckinridge was not blind to the forces of change; he merely wanted his organization to be as little affected by their consequences as possible.

CHAPTER 22

Inspecting the New Army

(1898–1903)

Commenting on a bill in the Senate that would have demolished the Inspector General's Department, on 22 February 1902 the editors of the *Army and Navy Journal* stated: "The most striking comment on the importance of a separate department of inspectors general is the action of the officers who abandoned the department during the Spanish war to seek more distinguished, or more congenial, services in command of troops, thus seriously crippling it at a critical time."[1] With this as their image among many of their colleagues, the inspectors seemed to be facing an insurmountable task to redeem themselves and their department's reputation.

Breckinridge and the Dodge Commission

Notwithstanding, on the question of whether the senior inspector general should have ordered more wartime inspections, Breckinridge, like the rest of the War Department, was somewhat hampered by circumstances in the highly charged political climate of 1898. The mobilization for the Spanish-American War had indeed had its unfortunate aspects, for it appeared to some people that much of the War Department had not done its job, or at least had not done it well. Moreover, this was the great age of "yellow" journalism, with newspapers competing viciously in circulation wars. Their weapons were sensational stories, preferably of scandals in high places. With reports of unpalatable food and sickness in the southern camps emerging even before the war was over, the papers initiated their accusations against the War Department. To quiet the controversy, President William McKinley appointed an investigating commission, chaired by Grenville M. Dodge, to investigate the War Department's conduct of the conflict with Spain. The members of the commission were upright and distinguished, none more so than the chairman, a Civil War hero, politician, and builder of the Union Pacific Railroad. Inspector Stephen Mills was its secretary. People looking for scandal recognized early that Dodge was a friend of Secretary Alger, and was so impeccably honest that he would not allow his panel to be a billboard for unsupported allegations. Nevertheless,

---

1. *Army and Navy Journal*, 39 (22 February 1902): 624, and (1 March 1902): 650.

Dodge gave everyone who so desired an opportunity to testify; nearly 500 people did so, and not all were friendly to the War Department.[2]

The commission held its hearings during the fall and into the winter of 1898, meanwhile conducting a large investigative correspondence with the War Department and others. Breckinridge testified before the panel in the middle of November. What he had to say was lost in a controversy that began a few weeks later between Miles and Charles P. Eagan, the Commissary General, and was remembered only after the testimony of Miles had become old news. The exchanges between Miles and Eagan dominated the public's attention for several months before becoming passe. Almost unnoticed in the uproar was the Dodge Commission's report, which cleared all War Department officials of any charges. The report, issued in February 1899, attributed the war's shortcomings to the understandable results of unpreparedness for hasty mobilization. The panel found the War Department's organization less than adequate for war, but it said that despite all obstacles the soldiers had all been sheltered, clothed, fed, and transported. All bureaus, save one, had done the best possible under the circumstances. That one exception was the Inspector General's Department.[3]

The members of the commission were especially interested that almost no reports ever reached the Inspector General's Office; those that Breckinridge had sent in comprised the bulk of the available information. Alger was sensitive to the charge that his department had not used its inspectorate to apprise itself adequately, and he repeatedly emphasized that all correspondence for the attention of the Inspector General went swiftly to that office. None, he said, had been held in the office of either the Adjutant General or the Secretary of War. As for the rule of the Inspector General's Department during the war, the Secretary acknowledged that four of its officers had been commissioned as volunteer generals for service as commanders.[4] When it issued its report, the Dodge Commission expressed concern that inspectors were required to inspect only when ordered to do so, and that orders to that effect were not always forthcoming. Furthermore, although some officers of the department had been assigned to field commands, others had remained in Washington, where they could have exercised a general oversight if directed to do so. The inspectorate's field organization was "ample," but reports often were not acted on or for-

2. The background to the appointment of the Dodge Commission is presented in Stanley P. Hirschson, *Grenville M. Dodge: Soldier, Politician, Railroad Pioneer* (Bloomington: Indiana University Press, 1967), 234–35, and Weigley, *History of the United States Army*, 310–11. A more recent study of army reforms during the period is Barrie E. Zais, "The Struggle for a 20th Century Army: Investigation and Reform of the United States Army after the Spanish American War, 1898–1903" (Ph.D. dissertation, Duke University, 1981).

3. Hirschson, *Grenville M. Dodge*, 236; Risch, *Quartermaster Support*, 555–56. The Dodge Commission's report was published as *Report of the Commission Appointed by the President to Investigate the Conduct of the War Department in the War with Spain*, S. Doc. 1, 56th Cong., 1st sess. (8 vols., 1900). The findings, but not the testimony, were released on 13 February 1899.

4. Alger to Dodge, 29 Nov 98, and GO No. 81, AGO, 27 Jun 98, in *Report of the Commission*, 1: 427–32.

warded to Washington. The commission recommended a three part "better system" for the Inspector General's Department. First, inspectors general should be required to submit to the Secretary of War at stated intervals their plans for inspecting camps and troops. Second, the corps of inspectors general should be large enough to do the job. Third, inspection reports should be forwarded promptly by the Inspector General's Department to the Secretary of War.[5]

More important, however, was the fact that the commission dismissed Breckinridge's contention that his work was made impossible by the demise of the district system and by delays in reporting attributable to the necessity for routing correspondence through the Adjutant General. Most stinging was the implication in the commission's report that the inspectors general did not do their jobs during the war. Eventually, the commissioners were not too upset about the transfer of some inspectors to line commands, but they did point out that other inspectors remained in the department and implied that those officers by indirection, including Breckinridge, should not have awaited specific orders to do their work. The commissioners believed that Breckinridge and his people could have had the Army inspected adequately had they wished to, for no good reason existed why they could not have submitted plans and requested orders without higher authority speaking first. Characteristically, Breckinridge reacted sharply to the commission's remarks. His first action, when he heard of the criticisms, was to tell Maj. Thomas T. Knox to obtain a report from all inspectors general in the field, recounting their wartime activities. He also requested testimonials from commanders on the value of inspectors general's services to the Army. The senior inspector general anticipated a fight to save his department, and began collecting information in its defense.[6]

Increasing the Army Temporarily

The fate of the Inspector General's Department quickly became entwined with the larger questions of the size and shape of the entire Army. With peace concluded, the military force was intended to decline to its prewar level, which was grossly insufficient for serving a colonial empire especially when rebellion raged in the Philippines. So the War Department submitted a plan to retain the necessary force. The measure called for an increase of the Regular Army, made the three-battalion infantry formation permanent, authorized the President to raise a force of volunteers for the Philippines, and had a number of reform provisions, including the authorization of company clerks. In basic form, this act of 2 March 1899 raised the Army to 65,000 enlisted men until 1 July 1901 and allocated 35,000 volunteers. Both forces were nearly all recruited by the fall of 1899, and the infantry was permanently arrayed in the three-battalion formation.[7] The act of 2 March 1899 also affected the inspectorate. It

---

5. Ibid., 1: 124.
6. The file he built is file 4122/7, Index to Gen Corresp 1894–1916, RG 159. It also has some miscellaneous material on his tour of Cuba in 1899.
7. Ibid., 2371; Cosmas, "Military Reform, 1898–99," 14–17; ARSecWar 1899, 3–4, 45.

made permanent the slots of the three new inspectors general which were added during the war. It permitted the appointment of volunteers to be additional inspectors general, raising their number to eight lieutenant colonels and nineteen majors. The law also required that any captains who had "evinced marked aptitude in the command of troops" be reported by their colonels to the War Department, thereby becoming eligible to fill any vacancies in the Adjutant General's and Inspector General's Departments.[8] Despite the increase in his permanent force, Breckinridge pointed out that in addition to the five officers who were on other duty, many of the volunteers were doing something else besides inspecting.

Serving the Secretary's Interest in Economy

The Inspector General's Department ended the Spanish-American War with its complement dispersed because of continued line service by some of its officers and a shifting corps of officers detailed to inspection. However, the organization soon functioned smoothly again. The department's mandate once more was diffused over a bewildering variety of secretarial duties, and across a uniformed army now spread around the world. As it had been for a quarter century, inspection of disbursement accounts remained a significant burden. The Inspector General's Department inspected accounts involving $325 million in fiscal year 1899, the largest amount inspected in any one such year. That figure included accounts missed the previous year, which was the organization's auditing backlog, so the total declined to $280 million in 1900 while the number of inspections increased to 1,406. Breckinridge estimated that he needed thirty full-time inspectors to do the job properly, and also that he would require more clerical help. In 1901 inspectors made 2,197 reports, while in 1902 (Breckinridge's last year on the job) the 3,040 inspection reports received in the Washington office represented $301 million worth of disbursements.[9]

Property inspections and condemnations were also a growing burden, albeit essential, while proposals for legislation to simplify the cumbersome procedures were resisted. Only 6 percent of property inspections were made by permanent inspectors in 1899; those remaining were made by special inspectors and officers detailed to inspection. This work load increased steadily through 1902, with Breckinridge defending its necessity. The growing assignment of special inspectors, he said, justified an increase in the permanent complement

---

8. *An Act for increasing the efficiency of the Army of the United States, and for other purposes*, Statutes at Large 30, sec. 1, 6, 14, 977 (1899): Thian, *Legislative History*, 116–17; *ARIG 1899*, 80.

9. *ARIG 1899*, H. Doc. 2, 56th Cong., 1st sess., 1: 90; *ARIG 1899* (to Secy War), H. Doc. 2, 56th Cong., 1st sess., pt. 2, 1: 122; *ARIG 1901* (to Secy War), H. Doc. 2, 57th Cong., 1st sess., pt. 2, 1: 134–38; *ARIG 1902*, H. Doc. 2, 57th Cong., 2d sess., 1: 454–55. Breckinridge's separate reports to the Secretary and to the Commanding General fell into two separate parts of the War Department annual reports in 1900 and 1901. (The report to the Secretary both years was in part 2, that to the Commanding General in part 3. Hereafter, the former will be cited as *ARIG 1890*, Secy, p. no.; the latter as *ARIG 1890*, CG, p. no. The practice of separate reports ended in 1902.)

of the department. Nevertheless, he continued to gain better control of substantive and item-pricing information in the work. He also recommended regulation of auctioneers of discarded property and reforms in the management of subsistence stores in the tropics, an important loss of inventory. He was receiving over 7,500 condemnation reports a year by 1902, and said in justification of the program that it was comprehensive, including funds as well as property.[10]

The Inspector General's Department also returned its attention to staff facilities such as the depots of the supply departments. As before the war, these were usually pronounced well managed, although there was comment on occasional overcrowding or defective buildings. The worst problems occurred in the tropical Philippines, where many stores of all types suffered from the climate and vermin. As for the national cemeteries, the Soldiers' Home, and the Army and Navy General Hospital, Breckinridge seldom found anything to criticize. By 1899, he had made himself a strong proponent of electric lighting in War Department facilities.[11]

Inspections of the National Home for Disabled Volunteer Soldiers resumed in late 1898, helped by a change permitted by orders on 27 May. Any officer of the Inspector General's Department, not just the senior inspector, now could perform this function. The home's greatest problems were serious overcrowding and an absence of outdoor recreational amenities. Furthermore, when its long-time manager retired in 1900, it came under a series of short-term managers who did not give it their full attention. Therefore, Breckinridge attributed any progress made to the inspections and noted a recently expanded population of 19,000 inmates in 1900. The next year, the Sundry Civil Appropriations Act of 3 March 1901 removed inspections of the National Home's accounts from the purview of the Inspector General's Department, transferring it to the Department of the Treasury's auditors. Inspectors, however, were still permitted to inspect the National Home's physical properties. This led to the discovery of a discrepancy in the accounts of deceased inmates, for which a treasurer was fired. The National Home had eight branches by 1902, with another about to open, and a sanitorium in South Dakota, with all facilities in "excellent condition generally" but badly overcrowded.[12]

Military Colleges and the National Guard

The Inspector General's Department also returned its attention to the military programs at colleges in 1899, finding that only some had continued to operate during the war. By 1900 the inspection program was fully operational again, including reviews of 101 of the colleges, only some of which were

---

10. *ARIG 1899*, 97–102; *ARIG 1900*, Secy War, 140–46; *ARIG 1901*, Secy War, 138–42; *ARIG 1902*, 459–66.

11. *ARIG 1899*, 109–12; *ARIG 1901*, Secy War, 163–90.

12. GO No. 56, AGO, 27 May 98, in "History of the Inspector General's Department," 31 Dec 04, in file 372, Index to Gen Corresp 1894–1916, RG 159; *ARIG 1899*, 92–94; *ARIG 1900*, Secy War, 127–32; *ARIG 1901*, Secy War, 132, 147–51; *ARIG 1902*, 469–70.

SECOND KANSAS NATIONAL GUARD, FIELD INSPECTION. FORT RILEY, KANSAS, 1898.

staffed with regular officers. The number of officers assigned as instructors increased to fifty-eight in 1901 and to seventy-four in 1902. The programs continued to grow, and although they became so numerous that not all could be inspected each year, inspectors continued to examine as many as possible, whether or not Regular Army officers were present. Inspection support for the program was as great as ever by 1902: Recommendations included that another 100 officers be assigned to colleges and the number of direct commissions of college graduates be increased in the Army.[13]

A more important long-term subject than the military colleges was the National Guard, whose record during the Spanish-American War had not earned it the favor of the regulars. When Elihu Root became Secretary of War in 1899, at first he shared the general disdain of professional soldiers for the National Guard. He did not want the Guard set up for wartime service, believing instead that volunteers should continue to be the basis of expansion of the national army, as had been the case when the force was increased in 1899 for service in the Philippines.[14] Both Root's attitude and the National Guard legislation had evolved considerably by 1902. The National Guard wanted not only federal money but also its independence from federal control. Root originally preferred the volunteer system as the basis for mobilization, since it would be federally

13. *ARIG 1899*, 94–95; *ARIG 1900*, Secy War, 135–40; *ARIG 1901*, Secy War, 159–63; *ARIG 1902*, 384–89.

14. Colby, "Root and the National Guard," *Military Affairs*, 23 (spring 1959): 30.

controlled, but he recognized the inevitability of the Guard's existence. Accordingly, he decided to seek its conversion into an effective national reserve. The legislation that eventually emerged, the Dick Act of 21 January 1903, repealed the Militia Act of 1792 and made the Guard the nation's first source of wartime manpower.[15] The Dick Act imposed certain performance standards on the National Guard, specifying the number and frequency of drills and encampments. It also directed the Secretary of War to inspect the Guard annually, to monitor its efficiency. Root started the job immediately in 1903 and claimed many benefits, including some major reorganizations. But the inspection program, which really had evolved under Breckinridge's hands in the 1890s and had become one of his department's most cherished responsibilities, no longer was the exclusive province of the Inspector General's Department. Now the Adjutant General kept the Secretary informed on the state of the militia.[16]

Special Assignments for the Secretary

The Inspector General's Department, even as it lost the Secretary's attention on matters affecting the National Guard, received from him a somewhat growing number of special assignments after the war with Spain. The first notable call was for Breckinridge himself, who conducted a detailed inspection of the U.S. forces in Cuba and Puerto Rico at the Secretary's personal request.[17] Breckinridge said "Nothing was left undone," and, indeed, he was thorough. He returned with a large number of recommendations on the quality of housing in Cuba and Puerto Rico, on the disposal of garbage and sewage, and on civil affairs, which he said were well managed. He proposed a public works program to relieve native unemployment and also suitable summer clothing and rain gear for the soldiers. The "extraordinary infusion of new recruits," he also said, had disrupted the discipline of many units.[18] This was the first of many special reports from the new colonies. A year later, one of the volunteer inspectors general went to observe the transition from military to civilian rule in Puerto Rico, which he said went well. The indifference of the natives to the change in rule he attributed to their appreciation of the high quality of the military government. Breckinridge also reported improvements in public health on the island, which he credited to the Army's surgeons. He further praised his department's accountant, William T. Kent, who had made a number of special investigations in the West Indies. Finally, in 1902, at Breckinridge's suggestion,

---

15. *ARSecWar 1902*, 38–40; Louis Cantor, "Elihu Root and the National Guard: Friend or Foe?" *Military Affairs*, 33 (December 1969): 361–73; *ARSecWar 1903*, H. Doc. 2, 58th Cong., 2d sess., 1:13; Colby, "Root and the National Guard," 28. The law was named for its sponsor, Congressman Charles Dick, a major general in the Ohio National Guard.

16. *ARSecWar 1903*, 16–18, *ARAG 1903*, H. Doc. 2, 58th Cong., 2d sess., 1:180–89. The subject of the National Guard is not mentioned in *ARIG 1903*, H. Doc. 2, 58th Cong., 2d sess., vol. 1.

17. *ARIG 1899*, 437–38.

18. Ibid., 466–96. Breckinridge's reports are in file 4122, Index to Gen Corresp 1894–1916, RG 159. They were also published in the *Army-Navy Register* during June and July 1899.

the Secretary recommended the disbandment of the Puerto Rico Regiment, with Puerto Ricans permitted to enlist in the Regular Army, and the withdrawal of all forces of occupation.[19]

The Secretary of War required sources of information as he tried to develop policies for the War Department's new colonial responsibilities. The Inspector General's Department, he quickly perceived, was a convenient source of such advice. By 1900, Breckinridge could report his department's "unusual activity," caused by a considerable expansion of inspection duties. These not only included more inspections of property, finances, and new units leaving the country, but also meant a return to inspection of West Point, and resumption of the prewar routine at its fullest. The most "notable development" that year was the work of Inspector General Burton, who exposed certain "Cuban postal frauds," the only malefaction detected that year not made good to the Treasury.[20] Burton's skill in detecting these so-called Neely frauds demonstrated further the value of having qualified inspectors in the new territories. Experience, Breckinridge said in 1900, had proved the necessity of a high-ranking inspector general in each of the overseas military divisions. Burton, he cited as an example, had thoroughly overhauled and organized the inspectorate in Cuba, and his disclosure of frauds had led to several trials and convictions. Garlington had provided such oversight in the Philippines before his return to America, and in Breckinridge's opinion, replacing him was essential. Meanwhile, Breckinridge himself resumed the inspection of the Military Academy, the first since 1897. "If general inspections are to continue in the Army," he said, "the cadet should be familiar with it [sic] as in times past." The academy curriculum was not subject to the inspectors' purview.[21]

The special investigations performed by the members of the Inspector General's Department had increased by 1902 to 133, of which 31 related to the conduct of officers, 16 to insular and municipal government affairs, 10 to transport services, and 5 each to conduct of enlisted men, to accommodations for troops and garrisons, to sanitary conditions, and to financial claims. The growing volume of special inspections reflected a continued erosion of the independent control that Breckinridge had achieved of his department's affairs in the early 1890s. Once again, as they had been in the 1870s, the inspectors general seemed less a department than a group of individuals serving at the Secretary's behest.[22]

Old Business and New

Some old responsibilities of the inspectors general returned early in the twentieth century. A system of military prisons was revived at the start of the

---

19. *ARIG 1900*, Secy War 105, 150–52; *ARSecWar 1902*, 4. One proposal was for the time-being unsuccessful. The Puerto Rico Regiment continued until March 1915. Ganoe, *History of the United States Army*, 451.

20. *ARIG 1900*, Secy War, 106.

21. Ibid., 112–13, 134–35.

22. *ARIG 1902*, 389–90.

century, and inspectors were required to examine the United States Penitentiary at Fort Leavenworth, the prisons at Alcatraz Island, and two prisons in the Philippines in 1901; and a total of seven institutions in 1902. Breckinridge also reasserted his control over the subsistence sales list in 1901, and was pleased to be able to talk the Secretary into an extensive revision. In addition, he recommended special lists for the Philippines and for Alaska.[23] His concern for the individual welfare of the soldiers was reflected in his interest and in the many reforms or improvements he recommended in each of these areas.

Breckinridge proved himself exceedingly far-sighted in 1899 when he presumed to question the wisdom of separate governmental departments for the Army and the Navy. "Perhaps it was a wise provision of our institutions," and worked well enough, he said, but some consolidation in the defense establishment might be advisable. As examples of difficulties caused by the separation of the armed services, he pointed out the Army's ineptitude in equipping itself with boats, the Navy's failure to cooperate in selecting troop-landing sites, and the difference in the bore of the small arms used by the two services. His solution to the confusion was to create a joint board whose decisions on interservice matters would be binding on both services.[24] Whether through Breckinridge's influence or not, the Joint Army and Navy Board, composed of four officers from each service, was established on 17 July 1903, just after he left the service. Only much later would there be a combined Department of Defense, this was nevertheless a tentative step in that direction.[25]

The State of the New Army

As earnestly as the inspectors general applied themselves to things like disbursements, property, and other concerns of the Secretary, the first object of their attention remained the Army, which was considerably different from its previous form. No longer a desertion-prone, continental constabulary, it was becoming a disciplined, modern military force, now distributed around the world. The Army had not only global concerns, but it was also brought into contact with other nations' forces, increasing its awareness of the need to remain current in ideas and equipment. Inspector General Breckinridge urged greater thought be given to mobilization and the requirements implicit in defending new overseas possessions.[26] Predictably, he maintained that if the Army was to come through changing times successfully, it must rely on its inspectors. He told the Secretary that "It is an aphorism that a good army responds like a willing charger to inspections."[27]

---

23. *ARIG 1901*, 180–82; *ARIG 1902*, 451–54; *ARIG 1901*, 182–86.

24. *ARIG 1899*, 102–03.

25. *ARSecWar 1903*, 8–10. The Joint Army and Navy Board was another of Root's reforms of the defense establishment. Breckinridge's influence on it is not clear, but he seems to have been the first War Department official to publicly propose such an idea.

26. *ARIG 1899*, 81–86.

27. *ARIG 1901*, CG, 174.

Inspecting a Worldwide Army

The greatest hindrance to training in the "old" Army was the dispersion of its force across a continent. After 1898, its troops were scattered around the world, occupying the Caribbean Islands or trying to suppress the growing rebellion in the Philippines. As for the former, in 1899 Beckinridge declared Puerto Rico a healthy enough locale, but in Cuba the troops were facing typhoid fever, smallpox, and the constant threat of epidemics of yellow fever and malaria, all aggravated by crowded, substandard quarters. The story of the Cuban occupation, he believed, was mainly medical, and he devoted most of his attention to the admirable clinical and research work being performed by the Medical Department in that strange tropical land.[28] The inspectors general reported conditions generally fair in the Philippines, although they varied greatly from place to place. The troops there were mostly recruits, which impaired the efficiency and discipline of some of the regular and all of the volunteer units, and all their arms and equipment were becoming well-worn. The Army's heavy wool clothing, Breckinridge said, was unsuited to the climate, and American horses and mules appeared to founder under strange local rations. The mess's food was standard, but in that climate sometimes more was condemned than issued. In general, Breckinridge attributed most shortcomings to hasty preparation for the expedition to the Philippines.[29]

By 1900, the Inspector General's Department could inspect all regiments before they left for the Philippines, thus correcting some of the effects of the former hastiness in preparation, and had instituted a systematic inspectorate in the islands. One of the acting inspectors general there was William Carey Brown, who received the assignment as light duty after a sickness. But inspecting the scattered forces of the Army in the Philippines was anything but light duty, and Brown's faithful diary records a schedule that would tax a healthy man in a temperate climate. As always, troop inspections were only part of a program that included military and civil disbursements. "In inspecting public civil funds, investigate the necessity, economy, and whether in strict conformity with the authority appropriating money," Brown recorded his instructions in his diary.[30]

Inspections were more routine in the Caribbean in 1900, where the Army was not fighting the natives, but was merely running their government for them. Not so routine was the United States' first joint interallied military campaign, the relief of the legations at Peking, China, during the Boxer Rebellion. No one from the Inspector General's Department was directly involved in that operation. Maj. John M. Lee, 15th Infantry, and Capt. Grote Hutcheson, 6th Cavalry, were assigned as acting inspectors. Breckinridge said that reports

---

28. *ARIG 1899*, 90–92.

29. *ARIG 1899*, 438–46.

30. *ARIG 1900*, CG, 146–47, 154–57; Brown's diaries and other papers are in William Carey Brown Papers, United States Military History Institute (MHI), Carlisle Barracks, Pa.

he had seen showed that American soldiers compared favorably with their allies. A Japanese officer, to Breckinridge's positive delight, had said, "The American soldier is the best soldier in a fight and the poorest soldier out of a fight that I have seen in North China."[31]

Inspector General Sanger made a special inspection of the Signal Corps' operations in the Orient in 1901 and concluded, "Very little need be said of the Signal Corps except by way of commendation." The difficult transportation and poor mail service of the Philippines had literally made the Signal Corps the Army's lifeline, and the corps was profiting handsomely from its service charges for nonmilitary telegrams. In fact, the organization had given the Philippines their first communications system, which Breckinridge in 1902 declared marvelous and a testimony to the "admirable work and gallantry" of the signalmen. However, it should, in his opinion, be doubled, and a connection between the Philippines and Hawaii secured by undersea cable. The telegraphy of the Philippines led the Inspector General to predict that "wireless telegraphy" would be the norm in the future.[32]

Communications in the Philippines in the year of the Army's first radio set made Breckinridge ponder the marvels of the future, but the distressing conditions of service in that territory also made him look to the old-fashioned issue of follow-up to inspection reports. Thanks to some creative but unnamed member of the inspectorate, in 1901 a means was developed to overcome the problems caused by the inadequate mail service, which had made this issue nearly unsolvable later. Before leaving a post, the inspector now would hand the commander a written statement of "irregularities," and would receive in return the commander's statement of remedial actions taken for forwarding with the inspection report. The procedure, said Breckinridge, was developed "with the hearty cooperation of commanders and inspectors . . . . so expedition and efficiency are secured amidst unusually adverse surroundings."[33]

Supply Services

Breckinridge's praise of the Quartermaster Department was positively lavish during the years after the war. He was almost equally positive about the Subsistence, Medical, Ordnance, and Pay Departments, all of which adapted well to greatly increased work loads, the peculiar demands of the Philippines service, and the heady winds of changing times and technologies. Some complaints remained to be sure, the most persistent being the loss of foodstuffs and drugs due to the climate and vermin of the Philippines. Breckinridge also reported in 1902 that staff departments frequently violated regulations by giving orders to their subordinates without the controlling line commanders' knowing anything about them.

31. *ARIG 1900*, CG, 149, 157–63.
32. *ARIG 1901*, Secy War, 158; *ARIG 1902*, 448–51.
33. *ARIG 1902*, 376.

One logistical service of growing importance after the war was transportation, particularly over water. Breckinridge offered general praise of the Army's transport fleet in 1899, but he complained that the inspectorate was not allowed to inspect any of the transports. He warned that "perhaps the exclusion of disinterested general inspectors even from examining the disbursements as required by law may disarm all criticism of this Department." On 16 September 1899, by telegram and followed by instructions from the Adjutant General's Office, the Secretary told the appropriate department commanders to order their inspectors to begin looking at the transport fleet.[34] Inspections began immediately, and the results were often dismaying. The transport service was usually satisfactory, but many transports were old and defective, overcrowding and poor ventilation being common problems. Furthermore, the hiring of transports was unregulated, and the relative duties of contractors and army transportation officers were unclear: "As the law now stands, the Government is at the mercy of owners of ships, brokers, and others." But, thanks in large measure to ceaseless inspections of both government and chartered vessels, the general condition of the Army's transports improved rapidly. Breckinridge was still calling for improvements in 1902, but by then reforms were comparatively minor, covering such things as the cost of meals on board and the transportation of unattached civilians, "especially women and children without male escort."[35]

Inspector General Breckinridge was in his sixties by the time the new century dawned, but he remained as ever a forward-looking man, delighted with each new development in the soldier's life and art. In 1900 he declared "road locomotives" obviously the transportation system of the future, because they were more efficient than animals. The next year he expanded on the virtues of "mechanical transportation" of men, supplies, and armaments. France and Germany, he said, were prepared to commandeer automobiles during mobilization, while the German Army had begun to mechanize: All staff officers were now supplied with autos, motorcycles, or bicycles. The English, meanwhile, had offered a prize for the best design of a "self-propelled lorrie or wagon for military purposes." The same year he urged that the U.S. Army take a serious interest in development of the new devices for its purposes.[36]

The Inspector General's Wide View

Breckinridge sometimes could look both ways on the time line. In 1899 he complained that the Army "has neither trained dogs nor a pigeon service. . . .

---

34. *ARIG 1899*, 454–55; Telg, AGO, 16 Sep 99, AG to CG, Department of the East, 13 Oct 99, and AG to CG, Department of California, 3 Mar 1900, cited in "History of the Inspector General's Department," 31 Dec 04, in file 372, Index to Gen Corresp 1894–1916, RG 159.

35. *ARIG 1900*, Secy War, 117–21; *ARIG 1901*, Secy War, 151–57; *ARIG 1902*, 419–25. After his trip to the Orient in 1901, Breckinridge also recommended placing good libraries, especially for professional development, on board transports. See file 6355, Index to Gen Corresp 1894–1916, RG 159.

36. *ARIG 1900*, Secy War, 121–22; *ARIG 1901*, Secy War, 157–58; *ARIG 1901*, CG, 172–73.

The Spanish war has taught us that we should be prepared beforehand at all times.'' The next year he offered a far-sighted proposal that a special body of rangers or guards be employed for the national parks. Troops were too expensive for park administration because of the associated costs of feeding and maintaining their animals. That was sixteen years before the establishment of the National Park Service. Finally, in 1902 Beckinridge urged the Army to adopt modern methods of copying and bookkeeping, and to expand its use of typewritten multiple copies to replace the old-fashioned letter-press books and pigeon-hole filing systems. The Army, he said, had buried itself in paper:

> When General [Adna R.] Chaffee was detailed on duty in the Inspector General's Department as a major the reduction of paper work in the Army was specially invited to his attention, but despite his forcefulness of character this incubus seems to have grown instead of diminished, and we find great tomes filled with longhand at almost every military center, while line officers in the fighting force feel hardly fairly treated when their clerks are taken to headquarters, and reports and returns are still demanded ad nauseam.[37]

Despite the paper work, Breckinridge had rescued his department from its disfavored status of 1898. He had revitalized it and shown it to be effective and necessary to the Army's operations. What is most remarkable about his success after the war was that it came during conditions that usually demoralize organizations and make them ineffective or merely self-serving. The Inspector General's Department continued to function even when the Secretary refused to clarify its authorities, compromising its independence. It kept its reports flowing even when events happened that would thoroughly undo most bureaucracies. First, the tenure of its officers was cancelled, albeit by attrition. Then, a seemingly irresistable movement took shape that would not only end the last traces of independence, but could altogether eradicate the Inspector General's Department. Breckinridge managed to bring his organization through that crisis, and at the last moment to preserve it intact. But it is to his great credit that, amid all that turmoil, he kept his people on the job and producing useful work for commanders at every level.

---

37. *ARIG 1899*, 455–56; *ARIG 1900*, Secy War, 148–50; *ARIG 1902*, 474–75.

CHAPTER 23

Inspection and Reorganization of the War Department

(1898–1903)

The reaction to the findings of the Dodge Commission combined with the evident failings of the War Department made it apparent that some kind of reorganization was required. Thus, the passing of Secretary Alger marked only a brief hiatus in the continuing examination of the Inspector General's Department, along with the entire bureau system that had been going on since 1898. The changes in the National Guard, previously cited, were only the first of many that were even more far-reaching. The appointment of a new Secretary of War with an interest in reform presaged a fundamental restructuring of the War Department, a result which would affect many of the basics of inspection.

Secretary Root Takes Charge

"Really, you know, I do not need to know everything about armies and their organization, for the five reports of Elihu Root, made as Secretary of War in the United States, are the very last word concerning the organization and place of an army in a democracy."[1] Thus spoke no less an authority than Britain's great reformist Secretary of State for War, Lord Haldane, upon taking office in 1905. Unlike his predecessors, Root did not owe his job to political favoritism, regardless of his long-standing association with Vice President Theodore Roosevelt. Instead, he was an accomplished lawyer, and President McKinley believed that a lawyer's skills were needed to oversee the Army's new and greatest task of governing the territories acquired from Spain. But Root soon realized that the Army had to become an effective fighting force, especially with a rebellion raging in the Philippines, and this led him to a larger perception that both the Army and the War Department required an overhaul. "[T]he American soldier today," he said in October 1899, "is part of a great machine which we call military organization. . . . The machine today is defective; it needs improvement; it ought to be improved."[2] Root, like most efficiency-

---

1. Root's tenure as Secretary of War is covered well in Philip C. Jessup, *Elihu Root* (New York: Dodd, Mead, 1938), 1: 215–410. See also Weigley, *History of the United States Army*, 313 (Haldane quotation), and 313–26; and Millis, *Arms and Men*, 157 (Root quotation).
2. Ibid.

minded Progressives of his generation, placed great faith in planning as the cure for all public evils. He appreciated especially that effective mobilization in war required planning in peacetime, but good planning was impossible under the present organization of the War Department and the Army. The Commanding General lacked any clear-cut authority in peacetime, and none at all over most of the staff bureaus. The division of responsibility between the Secretary of War and the Commanding General led to conflicts. The bureaus were responsible to the Secretary, if they were responsible to anyone, and most bureau heads had well-developed connections in Congress. In that context, Root did not want to fragment the War Department further until he had developed a sound understanding of what was wrong with it and how the defects might be repaired.

Root began to educate himself on the workings of a proper national military establishment. He had not developed a coherent philosophy by the time of his first annual report, but he did see the need for specific changes. Proposing an increase and reorganization of the fighting force, he also offered a number of other innovations: First among them was the Army War College. He perceived that as the sort of central planning agency which his Progressive outlook thought proper; the War College became the seed of a general staff. "The real object of having an army is to provide for war," he said. But the college was also to be the pinnacle of a comprehensive system of officer education, which Root thought woefully deficient in the Army. To correct other glaring problems, the Secretary proposed that all staff appointments, except those in the Medical Department, be filled by rotations from the line on fixed terms; in other words, permanent tenure in the staff departments would be abolished. Root also proposed to modify the seniority system to allow promotions according to fitness as determined by boards of officers, a separate artillery corps, and improvements in the militia system.[3]

Before Root could make his organizational ideas more precise, Congress threatened to do some interfering of its own. Early in 1900 the lawmakers considered a bill to authorize transfers to the Adjutant General's and Inspector General's Departments of officers of the line then serving in those departments in the volunteer army. The measure had other restrictive provisions that would be inconsistent with previous legislation governing appointments and promotions in the two departments. Adjutant General Corbin objected on the grounds of fairness to the regular complement of the departments. Breckinridge joined him, and the Senate Committee on Military Affairs recommended against the bill.[4] The measure thus died in Congress, and Root turned his attention to a more fundamental review of the Army's organization. He convened a board of officers in the spring of 1900 to consider whether or not an army war college should be established. But its long report went far beyond its original charter and addressed the need for a general staff. The first idea proposed that the

---

3. *ARSecWar 1899*, 44.
4. *Transfer of Certain Line Officers*, S. Rpt. 605, 56th Cong., 1st sess. (1900).

general staff could be created by a simple consolidation of the Adjutant General's and Inspector General's Departments (an old suggestion) but it soon became apparent that this would not produce the desired result. "I was opposed to forming a General Staff by a consolidation of the Adjutant General's and Inspector General's Departments," Root said later, "because that would carry over to the General Staff a great mass of such [administrative] duties."[5]

While Root was trying to reorganize the Regular Army, Breckinridge continued to press for an increase in his own department and its clerical staff. He was still sensitive to his organization's bad wartime reputation. He pointed broadly to cases where inspection had been "hampered" or "trammeled," presumably by department commanders, and rightly complained that no orders had been issued to clarify the change in procedures with the shift from inspection districts to geographical departments, "So the work of the Department is occasionally questioned." But more fundamentally, he said that the Inspector General's Department needed "judicial independence and subordination to higher authority" in order to do its work properly. Furthermore, Breckinridge remained sensitive to complaints about delays in the transmission of inspection reports. The problem, he said in 1900, had been solved after hard work on his part. Describing the chain of communication from the inspector through various headquarters to the Adjutant General before it reached his office, he said that it took an average of 17.5 days for reports to reach him from posts in the United States. Reports on depots (under his juridiction, not the department commander's) took only 12.5 days; on property, 22.4; and on disbursements, 24.1. "Prompt remedial action is the soul of effective inspections," he said, so prompt reporting was essential. In other words, he still objected to the remaining delays imposed by the requirement that his paper work go through the normal channel of the Adjutant General's Office.[6]

Secretary Root achieved his first legislative victories on 2 February 1901, when Congress fixed the size of the Regular Army between 59,131 and 100,000 officers and men, according to the President's discretion. Because the war in the Philippines had abated, on 8 May the strength was fixed at 77,187 enlisted men. The actual strength, including native units, stood at 84,513 in the fall, with about two-thirds stationed overseas. The legislation increased the number of infantry and cavalry regiments and established the Corps of Artillery. The new organization was flexible, permitting fluctuations in enlisted manpower once the base number of officers or organizations had been decided. To reach the base desired, the law allowed the appointment of 298 staff officers and 873 line lieutenants that year—mostly from the volunteer army, which was brought home and mustered out by 30 June.[7]

_____

5. Vaulx 8, "The Evolution of a General Staff," *Journal of the Military Service Institution of the United States*, 33 (1903); *Elihu Root*, 1: 262 "Vaulx 8," it is apparent from his writing, was William H. Carter.

6. *ARIG 1900*, 106–08, 111–12, 126–27, 152–53; *ARIG 1900*, 111–12, 136

7. *ARSecWar 1901*, 7–9.

One of Root's principal objectives was to expunge the isolation of the staff bureaus within the War Department. His first act in that direction was to end the old system of permanent tenure and promotion by seniority within the bureaus. The bureau chiefs, naturally, fought that idea as they always had, but despite their political connections, their credibility after the war was weak, while that of Root was on the rise. The Secretary triumphed. The end of permanence in staff assignments was the most important and enduring feature of the legislation of 2 February 1901. Under the new law, permanent appointments to any staff department were prohibited, except for technical professions as represented by the Medical, Engineer, and Ordnance Departments and the Signal Corps. Vacancies were to be filled by detail, without promotion, from the line, for a period of no more than four years. Furthermore, no officer below the grade of lieutenant colonel could return to a staff assignment until he had served at least two years in the line. The law also corrected an old problem when it specified that the army could fill by promotion any line position vacated by an officer detailed to a staff. The comfortable isolation of the staff bureaus was at long last ending. The process would be gradual, however, and no incumbent with a permanent appointment would be terminated. Vacancies in any permanent position, including that of bureau chief, were to be filled first by promotion from among the remaining permanent officers, according to seniority. When no permanent officer was available to fill a vacancy, it would be filled by four-year detail. When all permanent staff officers had retired, their positions would cease to exist.

Another gesture to please the bureau chiefs was an increase in the size of their departments. The new positions would be filled first by promotions of permanent officers present, then by detail. That was the only gratifying part of the measure for Breckinridge. The law now gave the Inspector General's Department 1 brigadier general, 4 colonels, 4 lieutenant colonels, and 8 majors—a total of 17 officers. But exactly one month later, the annual appropriations act altered the department. After the present lieutenant colonels had been promoted or retired, no vacancy in the grade of colonel could be filled. Thereafter, the complement of the department would be 1 brigadier general, 3 colonels, 4 lieutenant colonels, and 9 majors—still 17 officers, but on the average graded lower than before.[8] Of the 31 officers detailed to staff departments by November 1901, 12 went to the Adjutant General and 8 to the Inspector General, along with 5 to the Quartermaster, 2 to the Subsistence, and 4 to the Pay Department. Breckinridge still maintained that his department was understaffed. In 1900 he had complained that the assignment of inspectors to geographical departments had been inefficient, because the work loads varied widely. He repeated that

8. *An Act for increasing the efficiency of the Army of the United States, and for other purposes,* Statutes at Large 31, sec. 17–37, 748 (1901); *An Act to increase the efficiency of the permanent military establishment of the United States,* Statutes at Large 31, sec. 14, 26, 895 (1901); Thian, *Legislative History,* 117–18.

claim in 1901, saying that with fourteen departments and headquarters he had too few inspectors to permit assigning 2 to one place even if they were needed.[9]

Despite the increase in the complement of his department, and the concomitant growth of its work load, Breckinridge had received no expansion of his clerical staff, which he complained was unfairly graded lower than that of other departments. Moreover, inspectors at the departments had no civilian clerical help, and the department's "contingent fund," first authorized in 1900 to cover office expenses, had disappeared from appropriations in 1901. So, along with the inevitable request for more officers, the Inspector General asked for more and higher ranked clerks. He did not get them, and in October the Secretary authorized him to require that those he did have work overtime, until they caught up with their work. More positively, Capt. John L. Chamberlain, 1st Artillery, had joined the department as a major on 10 November 1900, the last permanent officer assigned to the inspectorate. But Hughes was promoted to brigadier general on 5 February 1901, leaving a vacancy that could be filled only be detail. Despite these strength problems, Breckinridge boasted that during the year there were 10,333 inspections of different kinds made, or over 28 per day for every day of the year, including Sundays.[10]

The General-Staff Idea and Inspection

While Breckinridge was citing the inadequate size of his department and the great amount of work it still managed to accomplish, events that would threaten its very existence began to appear. The person responsible was an assistant adjutant general named William H. Carter, a formidable soldier and an even more formidable intellect. Carter became a major and assistant adjutant general in January 1897, six years after earning the Medal of Honor at Cibicu Creek, Arizona. Carter shared many of the views of his intellectual predecessor, Emory Upton, who had favored a strong defense establishment founded upon a general-staff system comparable to similar systems used in Europe. But Carter was more realistic than Upton, perceiving that the latter's more extreme proposals for an exceedingly large Army and universal military training were politically unacceptcle in the United States. Carter was to have considerable influence over the development of the new Secretary's views. Root encountered Carter, and through him Upton, early in his self-education on military subjects. Shortly after entering office, the Secretary began to read with great avidity everything he could get his hands on, beginning with the Dodge Commission report, then progressing to critical and academic studies of foreign armies and their staff systems. Carter brought him Upton's published study of the armies of Asia and

---

9. *ARSecWar 1901*, 14; *ARIG 1901*, Secy of War, 131. The Inspector General's Department had used detailed officers for so many years that in practical terms the new arrangement did not affect operations immediately.

10. *ARIG 1901*, Secy of War, 131–34, 186–87; receipt of letter from the Secretary ordering an extension of working hours of clerks in the Inspector General's Office "until the public business is caught up," 19 Oct 01, card 3236, in Index to Gen Corresp 1894–1916, RG 159. See Appendix B.

Europe, then Peter Smith Michie's biography of Upton, which included an analysis of the dead author's critique of American military policies, and finally Upton's unpublished manuscript on American policies. It was characteristic of Root's practical mind that he paid less attention to Upton's grand general themes than to his detailed proposals for reform. The latter included the three-battalion infantry regiment, a termination of the seniority system for promotion, and the establishment of a general staff for the United States Army.[11]

When the receptive Secretary asked him for more information, Carter began to send him a series of memorandums that eventually led to a formal proposal for an American general staff. It was clear from the outset that there was no place in Carter's scheme for Breckinridge's notion of an independent inspection department. Carter had no specific complaint against the Inspector General's Department. Rather, he maintained that inspection was an essential process of information-gathering and self-education for a properly conceived general staff, and that a separate inspectorate would merely duplicate the procedures and confuse the command structure. In the fall of 1901, in a more elaborate and much longer memorandum on the general staff, he once again reviewed his idea of its proper organization, and explained that the Adjutant General's Office should continue to exist as an administrative organization separate from the general staff. He reported, therefore, that the Inspector General's Department should be dissolved because it would merely duplicate the functions of the general staff.[12] In Carter's all-encompassing vision, his general staff, headed by a chief, would eradicate the divided authorities and administrative confusion that had hampered the military establishment for nearly a century. In place of a titular Commanding General, this chief would be the principal adviser to the Secretary of War, whose supervision of all War Department operations and the line of the Army would be combined in one channel of authority through the general staff. As for inspection, Carter had grasped instinctively what Washington, Wayne, and Macomb had known: that inspection was essential to command and, if it was a separate power, it could threaten command. Consequently Carter's comprehensive vision of the military organization did not include space for a separate inspection bureau. So, Carter had almost, but not quite, won Root to his cause by September 1901. The Secretary still placed his Progressive's faith in planning as the guarantee of successful public administration, and to that end he remained oriented toward a war college and its academically based war college board. The latter became the nucleus of Root's early general-staff ideas. But in one form or another, he had decided to seek legislation establishing a general staff and, on 27 September, summoned the bureau chiefs to his office to give them the news they dreaded to hear.[13]

---

11. Heitman, *Historical Register*, 1: 288; Weigley, *History of the United States Army*, 315; William Harding Carter, *Creation of the American General Staff: Personal Narrative of the General Staff System of the United States Army*, S. Misc. Doc. 119, 68th Cong., 1st sess. (1924).

12. Carter, *Creation of the American General Staff*, 20.

13. Memo from the Secretary of War, 27 Sep 01, card 6652, in Index to Gen Corresp 1894–1916, RG 159; *ARSecWar 1901*, 25. Breckinridge was not present at the September meeting because he was in the Orient.

Since 1872, possibly evoking the precedent of the old Adjutant and Inspector General, proposals had been advanced for consolidating the Adjutant General's and Inspector General's Departments. Upton, among others, had suggested forming a general staff in that way. But such a simple notion did not suit Carter and Root, who believed that the administrative responsibilities of the Adjutant General were best left separate, sparing the general staff the overwhelming paper work that could divert its attention from study and planning. But inspection was integral, they believed, to the proper functioning of a general staff, and it could not be divorced from the staff's mission. Breckinridge apparently misinterpreted Root's intentions, and in his annual report for 1901 once again reproduced all the testimony and committee reports from 1872 that argued against a consolidation of the functions of Adjutant General and Inspector General. He also complained about the end of permanence for his department's officers under the legislation enacted in February, pointing to the need for experience in the details of inspection work. In this regard Breckinridge offered an interesting point related to the planning and reform that the general staff was to provide. He did not compare his organization explicitly with the proposed general staff, but he said that the many changes in the Army since 1890 were attributable to his department's "agitation" for better men and horses and to such reforms as improved recruiting, better rations, and the end of Sunday duties. That was something more than a desperate bureaucrat's defense of his threatened empire; it was rather Breckinridge's imaginative way of trying, once again, to attain his goals of independence and clear authority under the Secretary of War.[14]

But Root was already moving ahead as far as his powers, and the support of the President, would permit. The establishment of a general staff required legislation, but the Army War College did not, so the college was established by executive order in November 1901. Explaining that the demands of field service since 1898 had nearly ended officer education, Root pointed out that two-thirds of new lieutenants in recent years had come into the Army from civilian life. Given that the lore of military science was changing swiftly, the Secretary averred that it was crucial for officers to remain professionally current. Accordingly, he directed the establishment of officers' schools of instruction at every post; the revitalization of the five special service schools; the establishment of a general service and staff college at Fort Leavenworth; and the formation of the Army War College, "for the most advanced instruction," at Washington, D.C. Moreover, officers of the National Guard, the volunteer army, and graduates of military colleges would be admitted to army schools. "This order, if loyally and persistently followed," said the Secretary, "will result in the building up of what is practically a university system of military education." He said in the fall of 1902, a year later, that the development of the

14. *ARIG 1901*, 161–672.

"general scheme of systematic instruction" adopted in November 1901 had made "satisfactory progress."[15]

The establishment of the Army War College, supervised by the war college board, was Root's essential first step on the way to achieving a general staff. His next endeavor was more cosmetically initiated, but it was perhaps equally significant in terms of symbolism, for Root understood that such was often very important: In 1902, he did as much as he could to create a single channel of authority within the War Department. The independent bureau chiefs historically had reported directly to the Secretary, but for many years the Adjutant General and Inspector General, the two officials nominally controlled by both the Secretary and the Commanding General, had issued separate annual reports to both of their putative masters. Now, in 1902, each official submitted only one report, to the Secretary. Root's actions thus foreshadowed the demise of the office of the Commanding General. Root hoped, before long, to have a chief of the general staff between him and all of the bureau chiefs.

By the fall of 1902, Beckinridge was in the final throes of the fight to save his department. His permanent force continued to erode, as Sanger became a brigadier general of the line on 23 July. Heyl was promoted to colonel behind him, leaving one more vacancy to be filled for details. Vroom and Chamberlain departed for the Philippines to "take over the duties there recently vacated."[16] The Inspector General's Department, large though it was with temporary inspectors on detail, was approaching the semblance of a relic. . . . So Breckinridge, knowing that direct action would be required to save the Inspector General's Department, began cultivating his connections on Capitol Hill. From the time that Root had revealed his notion of a general staff exclusive of a formal inspectorate, Breckinridge had become one of his strongest opponents. But Root, knowing how to avoid open confrontation sent Breckinridge on tour to Hawaii, China, and the Philippines from 10 August 1901 until 6 March 1902. The Inspector General returned to Washington only to find Root's reorganization well under way.[17]

The General Staff Bill

Root decided to move ahead with the general staff measure in February 1902, and William H. Carter drafted the legislation. The bill consolidated the Quartermaster, Subsistence, and Pay Departments but protected the careers of officers in the Inspector General's Department. Inspectors with permanent tenure were assigned to the general staff, while those on detail were returned to the line. Carter said later that he had been greatly influenced in his conception

---

15. *ARSecWar 1901*, 20–25; *ARSecWar 1902*, 30.

16. *An Act making appropriation for the support of the Army for the fiscal year ending June thirtieth, nineteen hundred and three*, Statutes at Large 32, 509 (1902); *ARIG 1902*, 375–76; 477–79.

17. *ARIG 1902*, 375.

of a general staff by the findings of the Dodge Commission, particularly by its criticisms and recommendations regarding the Inspector General's Department.[18] The bill was introduced in both the House and the Senate on 14 February 1902. Carter and Root then went to work to ensure its success. The chairman of the Senate Committee on Military Affairs asked Root about the elimination of the Inspector General's Department, the only part of the Army organization to disappear in the proposed new system. Root explained once again that the proposed general staff was expected to assume inspection functions, obviating the need for an Inspector General's Department, whose finance functions would be transferred to the Treasury Department.[19]

It was apparent by 20 March that Breckinridge was beginning to mount a campaign of resistance against the general staff proposal, at least so far as it affected his department. Carter sent Root a memorandum suggesting that the best solution for any threatened impasse would be "to gradually consolidate" the Inspector General's Department with the General Staff Corps. Carter still wanted to eliminate disbursement and property inspections immediately, but he would at least retain the identity of the Inspector General's Department for the length of Breckinridge's and the other permanent officers' tenures. On that same day, General Miles appeared on Capitol Hill to declare his absolute opposition to the entire proposal.[20]

On 7 April 1902, Root directed Breckinridge to see him at one o'clock on the first of Monday of each month.[21] Perhaps the Secretary wanted to keep up with the machinations of his most persistent opponent, who in any case now had a regular opportunity to spar verbally with his nemesis. Breckinridge's objection to the general staff proposal was understandable because, as presented, it called for the elimination of everything he had labored for over these many years. Breckinridge always made certain that his organization did its job, but he was equally interested in its continued well-being. He did not become Inspector General merely to preside over the destruction of his department, and in July 1902 he prepared "Some Remarks on the Proposed Destruction of the Inspector General's Department." Using the Filipino water buffalo incident that had so interested him in a report a few years earlier, he asserted that the Treasury Department was incapable of adequately auditing the Army's accounts. Witness the fact that even War Department auditors were loath to pay for the hire of a "carabao and cart" in the Philippines when only the hire of a "bull cart" had been authorized. Inasmuch as it had taken months, apparently, to establish the equivalency of these terms Beckinridge used this case to illustrate the general inability of auditors to see the real purpose of inspection in the Army. "The

18. Carter, *Creation of an American General Staff*, 22–25, 30–35. This also includes the text of the bill.

19. Root to Chairman, Senate Committee on Military Affairs, 3 March 1902, in Elihu Root *The Military and Colonial Policy of the United States: Addresses and Reports by Elihu Root*, eds., Robert Bacon and James Brown Scott (Cambridge: Harvard University Press, 1916), 405–06.

20. Carter to Secy of War, 20 Mar 02, in Carter, *Creation of an American General Staff*, 34.

21. Card 3236, in Index to Gen Corresp 1894–1916, RG 159.

necessity, propriety, and economy of the expenditure in the first place was the real matter for inspection," he said, "and no one but an officer familar with the work of troops is competent to make that inspection."[22] Breckinridge said that transferring his account inspection responsibilities to the Treasury would be equivalent to transferring the Army's water transportation to the Navy (he momentarily forgot that he had once proposed that very thing), the Judge Advocate General's duties to the Justice Department, and so on. The War Department, he alleged, could not rely on other departments to service its needs. As for property inspections, he delivered a long essay on the importance of preventing waste, which he said was the Inspector General's very purpose. His people, he claimed, saved the government a half-million dollars a year in property condemnation, by returning to service goods that should not have been presented for condemnation. Trained officers in a separate Inspector General's corps, he asserted, were as necessary to the Army as were specialists in the Medical Department, the Corps of Engineers, and the other technical services. The Inspector General must be a soldier first, not an accountant, because he was most essential during wartime.[23]

By the summer of 1902, Carter was in the midst of an equally vigorous propaganda campaign, designed to persuade the Army to accept the approaching order. Root's adviser was the single most prolific contributor to the professional military literature in the early twentieth century, producing article after article. By early 1903, the publication of "Training of Army Officers" had swelled the Army War College and promoted the idea of a general staff, while in the publication "Recent Army Reorganization" Carter said, "A number of minor changes which require legislative authority have been asked for, but the final step in the general movement and one which is far-reaching in its effects is the organization of a general staff corps, and incidentally, the abolition of the office of commanding general of the army and of the Inspector General's Department as a separate and distinct corps." Carter told his colleagues that change was overdue: "The present administration and supply system is the result of a gradual growth." Carter continued, "Through a century of effort at meeting emergencies . . . it is now, and has always been, almost impossible to obtain legislation of a general character for the Army." Legislative challenges aside, Carter acknowledged that reorganization would be hard on the staff bureaus. But he reminded them that they were also soldiers, who had taken an oath of obedience to the government they served and to its appointed officials.[24]

Whatever Carter had to say, "soldierly loyalty to the Secretary of War" was a scarce commodity among the War Department's highest officers in 1902,

22. Breckinridge, "Some Remarks on the Proposed Destruction of the Inspector General's Department," July 1902, in file 5066/A/I, Index to Gen Corresp 1894–1916, RG 159.

23. Ibid.

24. William H. Carter, "The Training of Army Officers," *United Service*, 3d ser., 2 (October 1902): 337–42; Carter, "Recent Army Reorganization," *United Service*, 3d ser., 2 (August 1902): 113–20; and Carter, "A General Staff Corps," *United Service*, 3d ser., 3 (January 1903): 677–81, quotations on 677–78.

at least when it came to the subject of a general staff that would subsume their customary independence. The bureau chiefs mobilized their connections in Congress and did what they could to sabotage the Secretary's plans. General Miles proved especially obdurate. Miles had also participated in ruining Root's proposed consolidation of military posts early in the year, thus winning gratitude from congressmen who might have lost posts in their districts. When the Commanding General appeared before the Senate Military Affairs Committee, he made much of his record during the Civil War, saying that a general staff was something characteristic of Old World despotisms, not the American Republic and its grand army that had performed so gloriously in 1865.[25]

Catering to the nostalgia of the Civil War veterans who dominated the military committees in Congress was used to advantage. As Carter observed in 1903, "The Senate and House of Representatives soon [after the Civil War] became filled with ex-volunteers, and from that time to the present day, it has always been more or less difficult to convince committees composed of gentlemen who have seen service in the Civil War that the methods in vogue during that war can be improved upon." Indeed, as the military policy of the United States in 1812 was dominated by relics of the Revolution who wanted the Army to be as they vaguely remembered Washington's to have been, in 1902 the aging congressional Civil War Veterans wanted to cast the Army forever in the imagined mold of Grant's victors of 1865.[26]

Root, however, had broken the opposition to the general-staff proposal by the fall of 1902, except for that of one man, Inspector General Breckinridge, who continued to fight against the eradication of his department, building a monumental file of correspondence with influential persons, keeping track of press notices, and finally taking his case directly to Congress. Far less disagreeable than Miles, Breckinridge nevertheless proved exasperating to Root.[27] Breckinridge never directly challenged the general-staff idea; rather, he was concerned only that his own department would continue to exist. If the general staff transpired, he did not want any of his organization's activities curtailed or restricted. The proof of his argument, he claimed, lay in the visible positive effects of inspection as seen in increased efficiency and economy throughout the Army.[28]

Breckinridge benefited from the fact that the criticisms of his department's wartime record had begun to abate under the press of current events. By December, Root and Carter feared that the Inspector General's relentless lobbying, together with that of Miles and the heads of the three main supply

25. Carter, *Creation of the American General Staff*, 31–36; Jessup, *Elihu Root*, 1: 251–53; Weigley, *History of the United States Army*, 319–20; William H. Carter, "The Evolution of Army Reforms," *United Service*, 3d ser., 3 (May 1903): 1192.

26. Carter, "Evolution of Army Reforms," 1192.

27. Jessup, *Elihu Root*, 1: 261; Breckinridge's files on the last fight for his department, including documentation on the measures he personally had taken to improve the Army, are in file 5066, Index to Gen Corresp 1894–1916, RG 159.

28. *ARIG 1902*, 375, 485–88.

departments, might destroy the whole scheme. So the Secretary decided to drop the side issues, such as the consolidation of the supply departments, and concentrate on the single issue of creating a general staff—still at the expense of the Inspector General's Department. Carter drafted a bill "of the simplest character" to authorize a General Staff Corps and "combine with it the military duties of the Inspector General's Department."[29] Root also elicited an opinion from Maj. Gen. Samuel B. M. Young. As the president of the Army War College, Young was destined to be the first Chief of Staff if the new organization came about, and he heartily approved of Carter and Root's notion that inspection should be integrated into the general staff's program. Young felt that remedial action on inspection findings would be more certain under the proposed system.[30] Preparing for his last assault on the general-staff issue, Secretary Root decided to lay down the law to the bureau chiefs.

Breckinridge had by that time earned the favor of Congressman James Slayden of Texas, a member of the Military Affairs Committee, who was sympathetic to his pleas to retain the Inspector General's Department in any new army organization. Slayden and his wife were on far more intimate terms with Brig. Gen. Fred Ainsworth, head of the Record and Pensions Office, who kept them informed of developments within the War Department, where Breckinridge's frantic efforts to save his own organization had become a source of some amusement. Ellen Slayden recorded in her diary what happened when Root tried to bring his bureaucrats to heel:

December 14. The chiefs of bureaus were summoned by Secretary Root to hear the government's side of the new hoped for General Staff bill before the Military Affairs Committee, and General Ainsworth said it was Root's way of letting them know what his opinion was and serving notice on them to keep their mouths shut, so he just decided not to go so he could remain comfortably ignorant of the Secretary's opinion. General Breckinridge was there and talked all the time that was allowed him. General A. says it is true of Breckinridge as was said of Joe Blackburn in the House that he "would borrow time to talk from a man on the gallows."[31]

Breckinridge Saves His Department

Unwilling to restrain himself, Breckinridge had his moment before the House Military Affairs Committee three days later, and all Washington listened in. He limited his testimony to those parts of the general-staff bill that would abolish the Inspector General's Department. According to a press report, he began by quoting "at length" generals from Washington to some still living, praising the work of his department, which he asserted was essential to the service.[32] Certain members of the committee were sympathetic to his cause, providing him with leading questions. One was to describe the discovery of the

---

29. Carter, *Creation of an American General Staff*, 42–43.
30. S.B.M. Young to Secy of War, 12 Dec 02, in ibid., 42.
31. Slayden, *Washington Wife*, 44–45.
32. Breckinridge's testimony appears in *Army and Navy Journal*, 40 (20 December 1902): 377.

Cuban postal frauds by an inspector general (Burton). He answered, and added an account of commissary frauds in the Philippines. "Our method is not to have scandals," he said, "but to prevent them. Abolish the inspection and there will be no end of frauds."[33] As always, Breckinridge lavished praise on the Inspector General's Department, never exhausting his source of favorable examples to recount. The only general officer killed in the recent conflicts, he pointed out, was a member of the Inspector General's Department (Lawton). More pertinently, he asserted, "The military critics of the world have declared that our Army in the last war was the best the country ever raised, and its efficiency was the work of the Inspector General's Department. Whatever fault there may have been was in those who were above inspection. Those who were subject to inspection were found to be all right."[34] Whether his extravagant self-promotion impressed anyone or not, 17 December was one of Breckinridge's finest hours, because he saved his beloved Inspector General's Department. "During its progress through the committee of the House the Inspector General was given every opportunity to present his objections," William H. Carter recalled blandly, "and he succeeded in eliminating the proposed reorganization of the department of which he was the head."[35] Indeed, by the next day, the committee had cut into pieces the original bill, eliminating the two sections that would have changed the system of inspections in the Army.

How had Breckinridge done it? It is not likely that his ceaseless praise of his department persuaded many members of the committee. It is more probable that Breckinridge benefited from the organizational conservatism that characterized the old "Civil Warriors" who dominated the committee. As he reminded them, Washington had had an inspector general, and the victorious Scott and Grant had had inspectors general. Even Schofield, who favored the general staff, had in the past commended the inspectors general; Breckinridge had the quotations to prove it. In the minds of the committee, therefore, the Army had always had an inspector general, as it always should. Besides, even when the Congress wanted to reduce the War Department, it had shown a great deal of solicitude for incumbents whose jobs would be eliminated: they usually were allowed to remain until retirement. Beyond being able to take advantage of these factors, there is reason to believe that Breckinridge was able to capitalize on his personal connections. He had never been as assiduous a cultivator of political influence as some other bureau chiefs, but the general-staff crisis had

33. Ibid.

34. Ibid.

35. Carter, *Creation of an American General Staff*, 43, 45–47. Philip L. Semsch, "Elihu Root and The General Staff," *Military Affairs*, 27 (spring 1964): 26–7, offers a somewhat erroneous interpretation of what happened. As for Breckinridge's promotion, Semsch is evidently unaware that it immediately preceded his retirement, and was by no means the only graveyard promotion in 1903, as Root tried to clear away as much of the War Department's dead wood as he could. Another interpretation is: Otto L. Nelson, *National Security and the General Staff* (Washington: Infantry Journal Press, 1946), 58–59, which attributes that event to Breckinridge's "political adeptness," and says that Root believed that the general staff needed eyes and ears for its studies and planning, while Congress thought an inspection service not necessary to a general staff.

mobilized him into action. He was familiar to members of the Military Affairs Committees by virtue of his position, and by December 1902 he was even more familiar with some of them.

Congressman James Slayden's wife reported three days after Breckinridge's testimony, "December 20. Met J. [James, her husband] down at Brentano's to buy Christmas cards and books. General _____'s wife was there, and I was surprised to find how well we knew each other. J's work to save her husband's place on the General Staff has advanced our acquaintance by ten years." "General _____" could be no one but Breckinridge, for of the entire War Department bureaucracy, only he would have lacked a place in the new organization.[36] When Root learned of Breckinridge's feat, he was not as pleased. The informative and supervisory potential of inspection had been essential to his vision of how the general staff would keep the Army ready for war. The angry Secretary went directly to his predecessor, Redfield Proctor, who was now the chairman of the Senate Committee on Military Affairs. "The House committee has also stricken out sections 5 and 6 of the bill relating to the Inspector General's Department," he told Proctor on 30 December. "I think that change is unfortunate and that those sections ought to be retained."[37] Congressman George B. McClellan, grandson of Inspector General Marcy, agreed. On 6 January 1903 he told his colleagues that restoring the Inspector General's Department might weaken aspects of the general staff's operations.[38]

That lukewarm concurrence was as much support as Root was able to receive over the issue of the inspectorate. The House indulged in a long and tumultuous debate over the general staff bill, paying the greatest attention to the protection of the War Department's incumbent bureaucrats. Whether the Inspector General's Department should continue to exist was not a subject of great moment, and the sentiment was not strong to change the committee's bill. Fred Ainsworth's name, however, was mentioned often, and his position defended frequently, loudly, and gratuitously. So long as the guardianship of the pension records would remain unaffected by the reorganization, the lawmakers acquiesced to the measure. The bill passed through the House, then went to the Senate where its passage was quieter. Proctor was either unable or unwilling to challenge his Military Affairs Committee counterparts in the House, and on February 1903 sat quietly as the clerk read a message from the President. An Act to Increase the Efficiency of the Army had just become law.[39]

A Charter for the Future

In the hands of Elihu Root, the War Department had just received the most thorough overhaul it had known since 1821. Although it would take time to

---

36. Slayden, *Washington Wife*, 45.

37. Root to Proctor, 30 Dec. 02, in Carter, *Creation of an American General Staff*, 47.

38. *Congressional Record*, 57th Cong., 2d sess. (6 January 1903): 533.

39. Ibid. (6 January 1903): 533–40; (14 February 1903): 2240. The legislation and orders implementing it are in *ARSecWar 1903*, 59–72.

demonstrate just how valuable the general staff could be, of immediate benefit was the unification of authority within the department, which was achieved by eliminating the Commanding General and channeling all power through the Secretary and the Chief of Staff. Otherwise, the general staff would have had only potential, not immediate, use. Because too many old-time bureau chiefs, accustomed to their independence, were in place, and other permanent officers were scheduled to replace them as they retired, the legislation of 1901 had first to work its effects to curb bureaucratic independence by eliminating these permanent tenured bureaucrats through attrition. Still other problems confronted the new organization. Proposing that the general staff would merely coordinate the staff bureaus and not involve itself in current operations was unrealistic. Inevitably the staff would participate in operations, setting the stage for conflicts with the bureau heads. Moreover, American officers had no experience in working with a general staff in 1903, and although many of the strongest proponents of the new system had made a great study of the Prussian Army, they had concentrated on campaigns and maneuvers instead of the activities of the staff system that had made those campaigns so admirable.[40]

The general staff system was scheduled to become effective immediately after the mandatory retirement of the quarrelsome Nelson A. Miles. On 15 August 1903, Samuel B. M. Young, president of the Army War College, became the first Chief of Staff of the United States Army. Root declared the establishment of the general staff "the important military event of the year," more than equal to the nearly simultaneous reform of the militia. As soon as the legislation passed, the Secretary appointed a board to work out the details of its implementation, and to select forty-two officers "for detail, upon their merits as exhibited by their military records," for service in the general staff.[41] The board also became an interim general staff to develop organizational and procedural guidelines. The Secretary, explaining that the new position of Chief of Staff would continue the civilian control of the American military, said that this arrangement would eliminate the problems caused by dual control. With the new organization in place, the National Guard beginning to come along, and the educational system showing early progress, the satisfied Secretary of War said, "Aside from such action as may be called for by a further study of coast defense problems, I do not think that any important legislation regarding the Army will be advisable for some time to come."[42]

The grounds for disagreement between the Secretary and the Inspector General lay in an honest difference of opinion. Root believed that the purposes served by inspection were essential to the operation of the general staff as he conceived it. In that view, things like property and disbursement account inspec-

---

40. Some of these issues are explored in James Hewes, "The United States Army General Staff, 1900–1917," *Military Affairs*, 38 (April 1974): 67–71; and Edward M. Coffman, "Sidelights on the War Department General Staff in Its Early Years," *Military Affairs*, 38 (April 1974): 71–72.

41. *ARSecWar 1903*, 3–6, 10–13, 36.

42. Ibid.

tions were minor administrative matters that could be handled by other means; they should not be allowed to divert the general staff from its fundamental supervision of the Army through inspection. Root's general staff would in that sense have presented the fullest integration of command and inspection since Anthony Wayne's Legion of the United States in the 1790s. All power of command would ultimately rest in the Secretary as the designated agent of the Commander in Chief. The general staff would be the agents of that power, and also its inspectors: The power to command and the power to inspect were one. That philosophy would have satisfied George Washington and Alexander Macomb, as well as Anthony Wayne, although all three had inhabited different political and bureaucratic climates. But it was not quite the philosophy that Breckinridge expressed, despite the frequency with which he raised old ghosts in his own support.

Breckinridge was interested in results, in a measurable and useful product. As in the case of post schools, he thought it impossible to achieve results unless some person or organization was put in charge of a program and told to make it work. So it was with inspection. Unless the inspectors held full-time appointments, he asserted, inspection would not be properly or efficiently conducted, and much important information would be lost. He did not consciously want to separate inspection from command, although that was the tendency of some of his actions. He believed that inspection should serve command, by providing it with a body of impartial information upon which decisions could be made. In Breckinridge's opinion, general staff officers would have too much on their minds to make them effective as inspectors, and he believed that a great many important matters should be inspected. His difference with Root over property and disbursement accounts, therefore, was more than a selfish attempt to shore up his organization by demonstrating that the work load required a separate organization; it also represented his conviction that if the responsibility for inspection was not discharged, many things could go wrong. Root was a politically adept administrator who believed fully in the Progressive era's notions of "scientific management" and the gospel of efficiency. He wanted those philosophies to govern the War Department. Breckinridge, on the other hand, was a production-oriented soldier, who saw his department's output as the measure of its intrinsic worth. Root had an unbounded faith in planning; Breckinridge's lay in doing. Both recognized that a competent and efficient Army served the public interest, but each had his own perspective on how that service might be provided.

Inspection could remain in a separate department, thanks to Breckinridge, but Root ensured that it was restored so far as possible to its central place in the operations of the general staff. The Secretary's board of officers labored mightily to define the duties of the general staff, and on 3 August 1903, the President imposed them on the Army in the form of twenty new regulations. Inspection received special attention, with the General Staff Corps "charged with the duty of investigating and reporting upon all questions affecting the efficiency of the Army and its state of preparations for military operations, and to this end, considers and reports upon all questions [and] exercises supervision over inspections,'' among a great many other things. The Chief of Staff ''is charged with the duty of supervising, under the direction of the Secretary of War, all troops of the line, the Adjutant General's, Inspector-General's [and all other] departments.'' His supervisory power encompassed duties pertaining to everything about the Army, including inspections of both regulars and the militia. He also had the sole power to keep the Secretary informed about all questions affecting the War Department, and ''in the performance of the duties . . . the Chief of Staff calls for information, makes investigations, issues instructions, and exercises all other functions necessary to proper harmony and efficiency of action upon the part of those placed under his supervision.''[43]

In 1903 it was not clear just how the general staff and the Inspector General's Department would interact. If the senior inspector general, despite his supervision by the Chief of Staff, proved uncooperative, the Army could well find itself under the eyes of two inspectorates: that of the Inspector General's Department, along its customary lines, and another in the general staff serving that organization's interests. On the other hand, a cooperative Inspector General might willingly bend his organization's programs to the interests of the supreme authority represented by the Chief of Staff. In that case, inspection would be completely integrated in command for the first time since the Revolution, when Washington supervised not only the Army but the staff services later embodied in the War Department. Root might regard the Inspector General's Department as unnecessary, but if it bent itself to the will of the General Staff, it could make his new organizational system work as he wanted it to. However, the actual definition of the general staff and its place in the Army and the War Department would depend upon the individuals involved. Those would not be the same people who had fought so earnestly over whether the general staff should exist at all. Root retired in January 1904, as did Chief of Staff Young. Carter became a major general in 1906. Quartermaster General Ludington left in 1903, and the days of a number of the other conservative bureaucrats were numbered by the mandatory retirement law. A few personalities involved in the struggles of 1902 remained for some time yet, among them Fred C. Ainsworth, who would follow Henry C. Corbin as Adjutant General in 1904. But Ainsworth would no longer have Inspector General Breckinridge to amuse him as he pursued his own ambitions. Before the new regulations for the general staff were even promulgated, the man who had saved the Inspector General's Department had left the scene. He was honored in a farewell *Army and Navy Journal* article as an exceptionally inspiring leader and the officer most responsible for the improvements in the life of the enlisted men since the Civil War.[44]

---

43. Regulations for the general staff were published in *ARSecWar 1903*, 63–68,
44. ''Army Promotions and Retirements,'' *Army and Navy Journal*, 18 (April 1903), 808–09.

The Veterans Depart

Breckinridge left the scene with his beloved department intact. Despite its survival and the apparent congressional indifference to consider its elimination, several members of the new general staff continued to be critical. Foremost amongst these was Carter. He considered the continued existence of the Inspector General's Department as one of only two defects in the War Department organization that still required correcting in 1903. Inspections of troops, he said, were the duty of commanders and the General Staff Corps. Worn-out property was not a big enough issue to require a separate bureaucracy, while money accounts could be "safely provided for." He then predicted that the Inspector General's Department would eventually vanish from lack of work and from the departure of its permanent members.[45] That prediction was as interesting as it was wrong. Did Carter mean to imply that the Secretary had struck a deal with one or another of Breckinridge's successors? That is not likely. More probably he believed that the workings of the law of 1901, ending permanent tenure in the staff departments, would soon eliminate those who had a lifelong emotional investment in the Inspector General's Department. Rational officers on four-year assignment, free of personal attachment to the Inspector General's Department, he seemed to say, would recognize that the organization was superfluous beside the General Staff Corps. What he failed to recognize was that it is the nature of bureaucracies often to have lives of their own, outlasting the people who serve them. The Inspector General's Department did not vanish from the scene in Carter's professional lifetime, let alone Breckinridge's. Nevertheless he had grounds for hope in 1903, because the Inspector General's old, permanent cadre diminished significantly that year. Joseph C. Breckinridge was promoted to the rank of major general of the line and then retired on 11 April. Peter D. Vroom became brigadier general and senior inspector general on the same day; he retired the next day. Also, on 11 April, Thomas T. Knox became a colonel; he retired on 13 April. The remaining officers were promoted behind them, leaving vacancies that could be filled only by successive four-year details.[46]

George H. Burton succeeded Breckinridge and Vroom as senior inspector general on 12 April 1903. He remained in the position until illness caused his retirement on 30 September 1906. By then, few officers remained who remembered the Inspector General's Department during the heady days of the 1890s, when under Breckinridge's strong leadership it aspired to bureaucratic independence. The department remained a part of the army, because it had accommodated itself to the new order of things. Breckinridge was not the only old soldier to receive a promotion as inducement to retire in 1903. Secretary

---

45. Vaulx 8, "Evolution of a General Staff," 203–04. Why "Vaulx 8," William Carter, chose a pseudonym is unclear.

46. *ARIG 1903*, 443. Vroom was senior inspector in the Division of the Philippines at the time of his promotion and retirement.

Root did his best to clear the War Department of those remaining from the old army. Among those who became one-day major generals was the redoubtable Marshall I. Ludington, Quartermaster General, who also left in April. The Congress might still have its share of aging Civil War veterans, but they were decidedly scarce in the Army by the end of 1903. It was time for them, Breckinridge included, to go. They were artifacts of the most recent old army, and another new army was at hand.

The new army of the early twentieth century was, like previous new armies, a product of a war and of new postwar realities. But something more had been at work, long before any purely high-level reorganization in 1903. This new army was more care-

BRIG. GEN. PETER D. VROOM. *Inspector General of the Army, 11 April 1903.*

fully crafted than any of its predecessors had been, being slowly molded in the reforms and consolidation that had taken place during the 1880s and, especially, the 1890s. Inspector General Breckinridge had played an important, sometimes decisive, role in every one of those changes. The new army was not his work alone, of course, but he must be acknowledged as one of its creators. However, like many founding fathers, Breckinridge discovered that his creation had no place for him, nor for the other old army reformers who had helped to bring it about. Only the future could tell whether, in preserving the Inspector General's Department, Breckinridge had done the Army a service or had burdened it with a relic of the old days. If he had done one thing for the Inspector General's Department, Breckinridge had made it adaptable. In that regard, the future boded well for both the new army and its inspectors general.

The War Department's dichotomy was theoretically resolved by the reorganization of 1903. The useless Commanding General was discarded, and soldiers, staff and line alike, had to acknowledge the real power over the military. It came from the President through the Secretary to all parts of the War Department. Instead of a rival for power, the Secretary had a loyal agent in the Chief of Staff, through whom he addressed the whole establishment. That unity of authority erased the division of power over the inspectorate. The people behind the reorganization understood as fully as Breckinridge that inspection was an essential function both of military command and of War Department administration. With command and administration unified in the general staff, they wanted inspection placed there also. Like General Washington, the Chief of

Staff was to be solely accountable for the performance of the Army according to the government's wishes. Like Washington, the reorganizers believed that the chief military officer must control his inspectorate absolutely. Breckinridge did not disagree with either the principle of inspection in service to the commander, or with the establishment of the general staff to unify authority within the War Department. But he had an emotional stake in the Inspector General's Department and labored successfully to preserve it, if not the permanence of its personnel.

Root and Carter may have regarded the continued existence of a separate inspection department as an affront, but in fact they overreacted. The Chief of Staff, acting under the orders of the Secretary of War, had supervisory authority over the Inspector General's Department, as over all other bureaus. The danger that the inspectors general could gravitate toward the Secretary at the expense of the Chief of Staff threatened no longer, because the inspectors had to go through the Chief of Staff to reach the Secretary. In 1903 there was every reason to expect, therefore, that the Inspector General's Department would integrate its programs into the new system and become the eyes and ears of the Chief of Staff and his superior, the Secretary.

Breckinridge made a career of claiming that he merely pursued the course that history had mapped out for the Inspector General, that he acted as Steuben would have in the same circumstances. Many of his historical allusions were overdrawn, but there was a fundamental correctness abut his basic position. He wanted inspection to serve "higher authority," and he tried to ensure that it did. But there was a similarity between Breckinridge and Steuben that the former did not detect. Steuben had struggled with Washington before he was able to work out his proper place in the Army. Breckinridge had his own struggle in 1902, and when he had finished this struggle, his position was firmly established in a workable system.

As the new century brought with it increasingly complex challenges, it became apparent that, in their own ways, Root and Breckinridge each had made significant contributions to the Army's capabilities. While the general staff successfully coped with steadily growing demands, the inspectorate became its handmaiden to judge, to evaluate, and to assist in the implementation of its plans and policies. Global conflict and commitment became the tragic norm, causing ever greater pressures on men, units, and resources. The Inspector General's Department in this context proved to be a vital extension of the War Department staff; without it, the many demands could not have been met. In the tradition of Steuben and his successors, the inspectorate continued to serve as the alter ego of the chain of command. Phoenix-like, it survived because of the consistent need for unbiased, concerned analyses and appraisals of every facet of the Army's activities. The old traditions continued into the twentieth century virtually intact. That Breckinridge was successful at the end was to be credited to his own ability and determination, but it also reflected an aggressive spirit that had infused the inspectors general since Steuben arrived at Valley Forge. That spirit was expressed by Breckinridge himself on the eve of his departure for Cuba in 1898, when he sent Sanger a telegram that said simply, ''Galatians Six Nine.'' The text he cited reads: ''And in doing good, let us not fail; for in due time we shall reap, if we do not become faint-hearted.''

Appendix A

Inspectors General of the United States Army[1]

(1777–1903)

Inspector-General of Cavalry

Col. Augustin Mottin de la Balme   08 July 1777–13 February 1778[2]

Inspector-General of Ordnance and Military Manufactories

Maj. Gen. P.C. Jean-Baptiste Tronson   11 August 1777–16 September 1777
du Coudray

Inspector-General of the Continental Army

Maj. Gen. Thomas Conway   13 December 1777–28 April 1778[3]
Vacant   13 December 1777–

Volunteer Inspector-General of the Main Army

Friedrich W. A. von Steuben   28 March 1778–05 May 1778

Inspector-General of the Main Army

Maj. Gen. Friedrich W. A. von Steuben 05 May 1778–18 February 1779

---

[1] From 1777 to 1903 the Inspectors General of the United States Army encompassed the following military personnel: predecessors and equivalents to the position, persons holding the position or fulfilling the duties comparable to those of the senior inspector general of the Army, and persons entitled inspector general or the equivalent.

[2] Mottin de la Balme sent Congress his resignation on 3 October 1777; it was noted by Congress on 11 October 1777 and accepted on 13 February 1778.

[3] Congress authorized two inspectors general on 13 December 1777, and immediately appointed Conway; the other position was never filled. Conway did not actually serve as an inspector general, making relinquishment of the title meaningless by the time he resigned on 28 April 1778.

Inspector-General to the Armies of the United States

Maj. Gen. Friedrich W. A. von Steuben 18 February 1779–15 April 1784

Inspector of Troops[4]

Maj. William North   15 April 1784–25 June 1788

Adjutant and Inspector-General[5]

Vacant   05 March 1792–

Persons Acting as Inspectors of the Legion or Army

Maj. Michael Rudulph	1792–
Lt. Henry DeButts	10 March 1792–23 February 1793
Maj. Michael Rudulph	23 February 1793–17 July 1793
Capt. Edward Butler	18 July 1793–13 May 1794
Maj. John Mills	13 May 1794–27 February 1796
Maj. John Haskell	27 February 1796–01 August 1796
Capt. Edward Butler	01 August 1796–27 February 1797
Maj. Thomas H. Cushing	27 February 1797–18 July 1798

Inspector-General[6]

Maj. Gen. Alexander Hamilton   26 July 1798–15 June 1800

---

[4] North served as acting adjutant and inspector general to 28 October 1787. Congress abolished the position of Inspector of Troops (originally called Inspector to the Troops Remaining in the Service of the United States) on 25 June 1788. When required thereafter, the function of inspector general was served by War Department clerks.

[5] Although unclear, the act of 5 March 1792, Section 7, stated that the "Adjutant General shall do the duty of Inspector General." Initially, it was offered to only one person, Winthrop Sargent, Adjutant General of the St. Clair expedition. Even though he was a prominent territorial politician, Sargent declined the position. Until Anthony Wayne assumed command, inspection was mostly mustering to verify payrolls, a function routinely served by adjutants and brigade majors. Wayne's acting inspector for most of 1792 was Maj. Michael Rudulph. Thereafter the duty rotated among Wayne's aides: Michael Rudulph, Henry DeButts, John Mills, and Edward Butler. Butler bore the title Deputy Adjutant and Inspector General *pro tem* from 28 September 1792. The list of acting inspectors that follows relies on Heitman's *Historical Register*. Wayne nominated Mills to be the Adjutant and Inspector General in 1794, but no action was taken on the nomination. In 1796, legislation gave the Inspector General the duties of an adjutant general, a provision not made in the law. The following year, the office was retitled *Brigade Inspector*.

[6] The Inspector General, as authorized 28 May 1798, was nominally the second highest office of the Army, and de facto commanding general. Hamilton devoted himself to general administration and planning for a provisional army that was never tested. The office was abolished 14 May 1800, and Hamilton was honorably discharged a month later.

Acting Adjutant and Inspector

Maj. Thomas H. Cushing   15 June 1800–26 March 1802

Adjutant and Inspector of the Army[7]

Col. Thomas H. Cushing   26 March 1802–09 May 1807
Maj. Abimael Y. Nicoll   02 April 1807–14 July 1812

Inspector-General[8]

Brig. Gen. Alexander Smyth   06 July 1812–03 March 1813

Adjutant and Inspector General[9]

Brig. Gen. Zebulon M. Pike   12 March 1813-27 April 1813
Vacant   27 April 1813–09 May 1814
Brig. Gen. William H. Winder   09 May 1814–02 July 1814
Vacant   02 July 1814– 22 November 1814
Brig. Gen. Daniel Parker   22 November 1814–01 June 1821

Inspector General of the Army[10]

Col. Arthur P. Hayne   03 May 1816–30 September 1820
Col. James Gadsden   01 October 1820–13 August 1821

---

[7] The Office of Adjutant and Inspector General was authorized by the act of 16 March 1802. The act of 26 June 1812 also authorized an adjutant and inspector of the Army. The Secretary of War merged it with the Adjutant General's Office 14 July 1812, making the incumbent an assistant to the adjutant general.

[8] The position of inspector general was authorized 11 January 1812. Regulations adopted 4 May 1812 prescribed duties similar to those of Steuben in the Continental Army. In practice, however, inspecting and mustering services were performed mostly by assistants. The Secretary of War attempted to manage the war without a commanding general of the whole Army giving the title of inspector general to the current favorite brigadier general. Smyth was dismissed when the Office of Inspector General was abolished by the act of 3 March 1813. He functioned in practice as commander in the most active theater while inspector general.

[9] The act of 3 March 1813 stated that the Inspector General's Department would include an adjutant and inspector general appointed from among the brigadier generals commanding armies, with lesser officers including inspectors general, adjutants general, and assistants. Pike, as had Smyth, functioned mostly as a troop commander; the actual administration of the office rested with various staff members. Interpretation of the law kept the office vacant for a year after Pike's death allowing the duties to fall on various members of the staff. Winder served briefly before becoming a district commander at Washington, D.C. When Parker was appointed, the Secretary of War announced that the position was ''not connected with the line of the Army.'' With the reduction of the Army in 1821, the office vanished and the functions were replaced by the Adjutant General and the Inspectors General. Persons bearing the title inspector general or assistant inspector general during this period are not listed.

[10] The act of 24 April 1816 established that the general staff should include one adjutant and
(Continued)

Col. Samuel B. Archer   10 November 1821–11 December 1825
Col. John E. Wool[11]   01 June 1821–25 June 1841
Col. George Croghan   21 December 1825–08 January 1849
Col. Sylvester Churchill   25 June 1841–25 September 1861
Col. George A. McCall   10 June 1850–29 April 1853
Col. Joseph K.F. Mansfield   28 May 1853–14 May 1861
Col. Henry L. Scott   14 May 1861–31 October 1861
Col. Randolph B. Marcy   09 August 1861–02 January 1881
Col. Delos B. Sacket   01 October 1861–08 March 1885
Col. Henry Van Rensselaer   12 November 1861–23 March 1864
Col. Edmund Schriver   13 March 1863–04 January 1881
Col. James A. Hardie   24 March 1864–14 December 1876

Inspector General Stationed at the War Department
(Supervising Inspector General at Army Headquarters)

Col. Delos B. Sacket   10 January 1863–01 April 1864
Col. James A. Hardie   01 April 1864–10 April 1866
Col. Edmund Schriver   10 April 1866–15 March 1869
Col. Randolph B. Marcy   15 March 1869–12 December 1878

Inspector General at Army Headquarters
(Senior Inspector General, Inspector General of the Army)[12]

Brig. Gen. Randolph B. Marcy   12 December 1878–02 January 1881
Brig. Gen. Delos B. Sacket   02 January 1881–08 March 1885
Brig. Gen. Nelson H. Davis   11 March 1885–20 September 1885
Brig. Gen. Absalom Baird   20 September 1885–20 August 1888
Brig. Gen. Roger Jones   20 August 1888–26 January 1889
Brig. Gen. Joseph C. Breckinridge[13]   30 January 1889–11 April 1903
Brig. Gen. Peter D. Vroom   11 April 1903–12 April 1903
Brig. Gen. George H. Burton   12 April 1903–30 September 1906

(Continued)
inspector general and one inspector general, with an assistant inspector general to every brigade. The act of 2 March 1812 authorized two inspectors general, the other positions ceasing to exist. The act of 6 August 1861 added two more inspectors general. Until an inspector general was stationed permanently at the War Department in 1863 inspectors general were functionally coequal, relative seniority in grade notwithstanding. Assistant inspectors general are not listed here.

[11] Because of division rivalries between north and south, the commander of the Northern Division, Jacob Brown, appointed Wool to be his inspector general on 29 April 1816. Wool held this position for five years before his status was authenticated.

[12] Officers junior to the senior inspector general and bearing the title of inspector general or assistant inspector general are not listed.

[13] Breckinridge was promoted to major general of the line and retired on 11 April 1903.

Appendix B

Biographical Notes

These biographical notes on men who served as inspectors contain information that may not bear directly on the story of the inspectorate but that fills out the records and provides further insight into the character of the personalities mentioned in the text. Often, other aspects of these men's careers have been of greater significance or interest, and any summary of their lives given in response to an inquiry about them would need their inclusion. These individuals appear alphabetically. Sufficient information on other inspectors whose names do not appear below is in the body of the text.

ARCHER, SAMUEL B. (c. 1790–1825) entered the Army in 1812 as a captain of artillery. The next year he was brevetted major for his gallantry in operations against the British garrisoned at Fort George, Ontario. He was again cited for distinguished conduct at the battle of Stony Creek. He remained in the artillery after the War of 1812 until his promotion to colonel and inspector general on 10 November 1821. His selection for the job over other candidates is most likely attributable to his reputation as an artilleryman, a skill given emphasis by Secretary of War John C. Calhoun. Archer's Virginia origins also balanced against those of the other inspector at the time, the New Yorker John E. Wool. [Heitman, *Historical Register*, 168; *Appleton's Cyclopaedia of American Biography*, 1: 87.]

BALME, MOTTIN DE LA (1736–1780), following the acceptance of his resignation as inspector of cavalry in February 1778, continued to serve as a colonel without pay. He became active in trying to stimulate rebellion in French Canada, serving first with Maj. Gen. Horatio Gates' command near Albany in 1778. Later he shifted his activities to Maine where he conducted raids using the local Indians, again hoping to lure French Canadians to the American cause. He spent three months in the summer of 1780 recruiting amongst Frenchmen living in the Illinois country. On 5 November 1780, he was killed near the site of modern Fort Wayne, Indiana, while leading an ill-advised expedition of his recruits against Detroit. Somewhat unconventional, his actions and tragic death are proof of the sincerity of his support for the American cause. [Boatner, *Encyclopedia of the Revolution*, 749; Bodinier, *Dictionnaire des Officiers*, 355.]

BURTON, GEORGE H. (1843–1917) was the first officer to become senior inspector general after the firing on Fort Sumter who was not a veteran of Civil War fighting. He was born in Millsboro, Delaware, on 12 January 1843, and graduated from the Military Academy in June of 1865, too late to see any action. He joined the 12th Infantry in Petersburg, Virginia, where he served on occuption duty. Later, he served with the 21st Infantry in Richmond (until 1869). He then moved with his regiment to the West, where he was to serve for nearly ten years, except for two years' recruiting duty in Columbus, Ohio. He was cited for bravery in the fighting at the Lava Beds in January 1873, during the Modoc War. He later participated in the campaign against the Nez Perce during 1877 and 1878, and was brevetted for gallantry at the battle of Clearwater, 11–12 July 1877, where he was cited "for coolness and gallantry . . . in close combat with a superior number of enemy."

Despite his apparent success as a combat leader and the esteem of his superiors, Burton does not appear to have been content as an infantry officer. As early as 1877, he submitted a standing request for assignment to the Quartermaster or Commissary Department whenever a vacancy should open. At another time, he had an approved request for transfer to the 1st Artillery, which he eventually refused. More and more influential individuals pressured the War Department to get Burton an appointment in the East during the late 1870s. In August 1879, Burton himself wrote the Secretary of War requesting appointment in either the Adjutant General's or Inspector General's Department. Despite the support of several of his former commanders and members of Congress, his request was denied. This agitation for a staff appointment was not uncommon. Officers who had served fifteen or twenty years with troops on hard service at the company level no doubt felt the physical burdens and could see no charms in continuing them. Furthermore, appointment to the staff must often have seemed to be the only way to achieve promotion to major, given the longevity of the regimental field-grade officers. Finally, coming from the Atlantic Coast states, as did Burton, and with the only prospect being more time in godforsaken western posts, a job on the staff may have been seen as the only way of returning to civilization.

In September 1880, Burton rejoined his regiment at Fort Klamath, Oregon. There he was given the major additional duty of building the Fort Klamath and Ashland Military Telegraph Line. He became in the course of this project the de facto signal officer for the region. Later he requested that he take the examination for transfer to the Signal Corps and was favorably supported in this by Brig. Gen. Adolphus W. Greeley, its chief. For a while, his status in the 21st Infantry was unclear, as he responded to tasks sent to him direct by the chief signal officer. It took a three-way correspondence among General Sherman at army headquarters, General Miles at the Pacific Division, and General Greeley to settle the fact that Burton's company duties should always take priority. The restless Burton continued in his regimental duties for another five years with one six-month tour as an inspector of horses at Oakland, California.

Finally, he returned on leave to Washington in early 1885 and personally submitted his application for an inspector's position that would be available. He cited his many previous good references and added more, including one from

Governor A. G. Thurman of Ohio whom he had impressed while on recruiting duty. This time he was accepted, going on temporary duty to the Washington office of the Inspector General at the end of March 1885, before being assigned to the Department of the Missouri. He served throughout the West, enjoying two promotions and attaining colonelcy in 1895. (In 1892, he had worked directly for General Breckinridge inspecting colleges at the outset of this program.)

When the war with Spain began, Burton tried to get an appointment as a brigadier general of volunteers. On 27 April 1898 he telegraphed the Adjutant General, asking that General Miles consider him for brigade command. He said he wanted to participate in the fighting. Miles forwarded the request to Secretary Alger with a strong favorable comment, but Alger turned down the request because all the vacancies of that grade had been filled. Burton was initially assigned as inspector of the 1st Corps at the request of its commander, John R. Brooke, but his orders were changed to report to the Office of the Inspector General for duty in Washington. There he was diagnosed as having typhoid fever and was placed on sick leave from October 1898 to August 1899. The surgeon's report shows that he was critically ill.

After recovering, he was assigned to the Cuban Division as Gov. Gen. Leonard Wood's senior inspector. This was perhaps his finest hour. His work was described by General Wood as a "most valuable service in connection with postal frauds, inspection of public works, Department of Finance and much special work . . . he was thorough and fearless." His duties in connection with the Neely postal frauds also brought him into close contact with Secretary Root.

The esteem of these major figures as well as that of others such as Adna R. Chaffee unquestionably confirmed Burton's place as the senior inspector when Breckinridge retired. Unfortunately, he was not to have much time after his 12 April 1903 appointment. For four months, from 12 November 1904 to 12 February 1905, he was detained as a witness on the Neely postal fraud case and then, in December 1905, he went on extended leave for health reasons, never to return to duty. He retired on 30 September 1906 and died at his home in Los Angeles on 20 October 1917. The *Army and Navy Journal* credited him with restoring to the department "much of the high regard it has held throughout so many years of its existence." [George W. Cullum, *Biographical Register of the Officers and Graduates of the Military Academy* (Boston and New York: Houghton Mifflin & Co.), vol. 3, nos. 1001 to 2000 and no. 2080) (hereafter cited as Cullum, *Register*); "Recent Deaths," *Army and Navy Journal*, 27 Oct 17, 311; Fred H.E. Ebstein, "Twenty-first Regiment of Infantry," *Journal of the Military Service Institute of the U.S.*, no. 12, (1892): 844–850 (hereafter cited as *JMSI*); National Archives, RG 159, ROIG, files 3 and 518.]

CHAMBERLAIN, JOHN L. (1858–1948), was the last living member of the Class of 1880, as well as the last permanent member of the Inspector General's Department. He was born in Livonia, New York, on 20 January 1858, the son of a Baptist minister and farmer. He left the New York State Normal School to enter the Military Academy, and was commissioned into the artillery. After three years' regimental duties in New York and California, he joined the Military Academy faculty in 1884 as an instructor in chemistry. One of his students was John J. Pershing with whom he was to form a lasting friendship. Following that, he returned for a short time to his regiment before being assigned in 1890, first to the Artillery School at Fort Monroe, and then to the Washington Navy Yard, to study heavy-gun construction. He took time off from his duties to rejoin his regiment, serving with it during the Wounded Knee campaign in January 1890. After completing his work at the Navy Yard, in which he was engaged in metals chemistry, he returned to the 1st Artillery with the praise of the Navy Yard's commodore.

In 1892, he considered applying for a position in the Subsistence Department but decided against it, and continued to spend a great deal of time on details away from his battery. He was finally directed by the War Department to rejoin (July 1893), after serving more than a year as Ordnance Officer in the Department of the Missouri. Previously, he had been aide to Brig. Gen. Nelson Miles at the 1892 Chicago Exposition. No sooner had he reported than he began to press for reassignment as professor of military science at the military academy in Peekskill, New York. The Adjutant General did not want to assign him because he had been away from his unit seven and a half years out of the previous fourteen. Pressure prevailed, however, and he joined the Peekskill faculty in January 1895. He continued to impress all those with whom he came into contact, and soon was teaching arithmetic and geology as well as military science. Inspector Capt. William P. Van Ness especially cited his energy and hard work, crediting him with improving the military program at the school considerably. He mentioned Chamberlain in his 1896 report for his complete dedication and "well known ability" as a disciplinarian.

Chamberlain remained at Peekskill until September 1896 when he became commander of Battery E of the 1st Artillery at Fort Sheridan, Illinois, which was located later at Washington Barracks, Washington, D.C. Once again, his superiors expressed their high esteem for his professional knowledge and dedication. Then, in July 1897, he was sent to Vienna, Austria, as attache to the Austro–Hungarian Empire. His task was difficult and delicate because of Austria's sympathy for Spain in the growing tensions between that country and the United States. When it became apparent that the two nations would go to war, Chamberlain again began to agitate for a more active assignment. In March 1898, he cabled the Adjutant General, asking for reassignment, and he left Europe on 21 May.

Upon his return to the United States, Chamberlain was on recruiting duty for a short time in New York City; then he was assigned as adjutant of the Siege Artillery Train located at Tampa, Florida. He was appointed a major of volunteers and ordnance officer of the 1st Division, 7th Army Corps, after the train was disbanded in August. He became the division acting adjutant general in September. In that capacity, he mustered out most of the unit before collapsing with typhoid fever on 31 October. He resumed light duties in February 1899.

Chamberlain returned to the 1st Artillery as regimental adjutant in April

1899, joining it at its headquarters at Sullivan's Island at Moultrieville, South Carolina. Despite the praise of his commander, Maj. Gen. Arthur Murray, who characterized him as "one of the ablest and best officers I ever met," Chamberlain's request for a volunteer commission and duty in the Philippines was turned down. He then wrote General Miles asking for a volunteer appointment, saying he missed combat in Cuba and he wanted to prove himself in the Philippines. He asked further that if that was not possible, he would like to be considered for a position in the Adjutant General's or Inspector General's Department.

Shortly thereafter he requested, formally, examination for entry into either of the two departments. He submitted eleven letters of recommendation with his request, signed by such officers as Generals Miles and Merritt, and former inspector Joseph P. Sanger, among others. He appeared before the examining board in New York City on 26 February 1900. The required examination took almost six hours and consisted of tactical, logistical, and administrative questions requiring fully developed, written answers. He was accepted and commissioned a major in the Inspector General's Department, the last man to undergo such an ordeal and the last to hold such a commission.

He was first assigned to the Washington office of the Inspector General, from which he made a circuit through organizations in Pennsylvania and Maryland inspecting financial accounts. This was a tutorial period before he received his first independent assignment as inspector for the Department of California with headquarters at the Presidio of San Francisco. While en route to California, he was promoted to lieutenant colonel. Once there, he soon became involved in a special investigation of the Army Transport Service on the West Coast, establishing for himself a reputation as an expert in the field.

Chamberlain left California on 1 October 1902 for the Philippines, eventually going to Zamboanga where he served as inspector for the Department of Mindanao. While there, he frequently accompanied units on tactical operations as an observer. In June of the next year he went to Manila to assume the duties of inspector general for the Philippines Division. He later described his duties there as routine: inspecting various posts and making special investigations, making vast numbers of money and disbursing accounts inspections, as well. His commander, Maj. Gen. George W. Davis, specifically praised him for his skillful handling of an atrocity case. Later, Chamberlain accompanied his friend and former student, John J. Pershing, on the successful Lake Lanao expedition against the Moros.

The detail law of 2 March 1901 precluded Chamberlain's automatic promotion to colonel to fill the vacancy created when Col. Thomas T. Knox retired in April 1903. A special bill was later passed by Congress to adjust his date of rank. But, before that, Chamberlain had received his promotion on a seniority basis to colonel in the Inspector General's Department on 30 November 1904. This was the last permanent commission granted in the department; thereafter, any vacancies were filled by detail in accordance with Secretary Root's reforms.

Still the Philippines Division inspector, Chamberlain spent most of August and September 1904 in China inspecting the U.S. legation in Peking and troops at Tientsin Barracks. Shortly after his return to Manila, he was stricken with malaria and ordered to return to the United States for medical reasons. He was authorized a circuitous boat trip by way of China and Japan as a form of convalescence. Chamberlain left Manila in January 1905 and finally arrived in Washington in April to assume the job of assistant to the Inspector General. For the next year and a half, he assisted in the management of the office and participated in several major inspections of depots, arsenals, the Leavenworth prison, and the National Home for Disabled Volunteer Soldiers. He also conducted an extended special investigation of conditions in Puerto Rico. General Burton called Chamberlain "one of the most efficient all-around officers in the service."

Chamberlain's rise was marked by assignment for a year to the Pacific Division under Frederick Funston and then by transfer to the prestigious Department of the East at Governors Island, New York. There, he first worked under Maj. Gen. Frederick Dent Grant who characterized him as "one of the best officers I have had with me, a valuable officer for the General Staff, excellent." Grant's successor, Maj. Gen. Leonard Wood, called Chamberlain painstaking and efficient. Throughout 1908 and early 1909, Chamberlain covered the vast department, inspecting posts and training activities as well as conducting numerous special investigations on topics ranging from race relations to officer conduct. He returned briefly to the Philippines and then to the West Coast before attending the Army School of the Line at Fort Leavenworth. Of special interest was his membership in the U.S. delegation to Hong Kong sent from Manila in June 1911 as part of King George V's coronation observances.

Chamberlain enjoyed the Leavenworth course (School of the Line), which he attended between his Philippine and Pacific Divisions assignments. He wrote General Garlington for permisssion to succeed it with attendance at the Army War College. He thought attendance would sharpen his inspecting skills. He also mentioned it was extremely likely that the Inspector General's Department, then under examination again, would be abolished. A War College diploma, would ensure his competitive skills if he was thrown back into the line. Garlington and General Murray, now of the Western Division, approved, and Chamberlain attended the War College from August 1912 to June 1913. The school commandant, Brig. Gen. William Crozier, cited Chamberlain as qualified for high command at the time of his graduation.

Chamberlain stayed in the West only until September 1914, when he returned to Governors Island to serve under General Wood again. Wood said he was "delighted to have him," calling him "a remarkably able and efficient officer. Far and away the best inspector I have ever had under my command and especially well fitted" to be the Inspector General of the Army. Wood continued to speak highly of Chamberlain until he was reassigned to replace Garlington in February 1914. His appointment was greeted with Army-wide approval. He served throughout World War I as the Inspector General of the Army, finally retiring in November 1921. He spent the remainder of his life in various business activities, dividing his time between Washington and Rhode Island. Chamberlain died in Washington on 14 December 1948. [National Archives, records of TAG, RG 94, 2566 ACP 1883; records of TIG, RG 159, entry 24, file 693–20; Obituaries, *Washington Post*, 15 Nov 48, *New York World Telegram*, 15 Nov 48, Assoc. of Grads., USMA, *Assembly* (Jul 50): 53–54; Cullum, *Register* (Boston and New York: Houghton Mifflin & Co., 1891–1950) no. 2831; USMA Archives, Cullum Files, Chamberlain.]

CONWAY, THOMAS (1735–1795), the fractious Irishman, returned to France in 1779 where he reentered that country's army as a staff officer in Flanders. He was named a brigadier general on 1 March 1780 and assigned to duty in the French possessions in India. Promoted to marshal in 1784, he eventually became governor of all French colonies in the Indian Ocean area. He returned to Europe in July 1790 during the first stages of the French Revolution and there he took up the loyalist cause, first in a scheme to raise a force in the Midi. When that failed, he commanded an Irish regiment in British service until his death in June 1795. [*DAB*, 4:366, Bodinier, *Dictionnaire des Officiers*, 105–06.

DEBUTTS, HENRY (birth and death dates unknown), born in Maryland, was a militia veteran of the Revolution who returned to military service in 1791 as a lieutenant during the activation of forces under Maj. Gen. Arthur St. Clair. He survived that officer's defeat to be commissioned in the 4th Sublegion, becoming a captain in December 1792. He served in various staff capacities until he returned to the infantry line in November 1796, where he resigned on 31 December 1797. [Heitman, *Historical Register*, 1:363–64; *National Cyclopaedia of American Biography*, 12:336.]

FARNSWORTH, HENRY J. (birth date unknown), entered the army from civilian life in New York in early 1864. He became a captain and assistant quartermaster of volunteers in July 1864, earning two brevets for his service during the war. He moved to the 34th Infantry as a first lieutenant in June 1867 and, when that unit was inactivated, joined the 8th Cavalry at the end of 1870. Having been promoted to captain in 1876, he transferred on 22 September 1885 as a major to the Inspector General's Department. He died at Fort Monroe, Virginia, while still on active duty, on 19 November 1888. [Heitman, *Historical Register*, 1:413.]

GARLINGTON, ERNEST A. (1853–1934), was the first young man from his Georgia congressional district to enter the U.S. Military Academy after the Civil War. Born in Newberry, South Carolina, on 20 February 1853, he was the son of a prominent lawyer and planter who became a Confederate general. He studied at the University of Georgia for three years before receiving an appointment to West Point from Congressman W.P. Price in 1872. He graduated from the academy in 1876 and was commissioned in the 7th Cavalry. His appointment in the cavalry was influenced by a request from former Confederate Vice President Alexander H. Stevens to President Grant. There was some further pressure to have the young man assigned as a military professor to a Georgia school but that ended with news of the battle of the Little Big Horn. As soon as he heard of Custer's disaster, Garlington wrote the Adjutant

General on 10 July 1876, requesting that he be allowed to turn in the remainder of his graduation leave and be given orders to join his depleted regiment. His request was granted and he went west to command G Troop of the 7th Cavalry in operations along the Powder River in Montana Territory. There were so many vacancies created by Custer's casualties that Garlington was promoted to first lieutenant in August 1876, almost as soon as he joined his unit. He spent the next several years in operations against the Indians and was cited for gallantry in action at Canyon Creek, 13 September 1877, during the Nez Perce campaign.

He remained with his regiment until 1883, when in April he was placed under the control of the chief signal officer, Brig. Gen. William B. Hazen. Garlington had volunteered to lead an expedition for the relief of the Adolphus W. Greeley party stranded in the Canadian Arctic at Lady Franklin Bay. Unfortunately, his ship, the *Proteus*, was wrecked in Smith Sound, and Garlington was lucky to be able to extract his own crew in a 600-mile trip in open boats to safety aboard a second rescue vessel.

After his Arctic adventure, Garlington resumed service with his regiment in Kansas and the Dakotas. In the spring of 1890, he assumed command of A Troop and served with it in the Wounded Knee battle at Pine Ridge Agency, South Dakota, in December 1890. He was severely wounded in the battle and later was awarded the Medal of Honor for "distinguished gallantry." He rallied his men at the critical moment and, despite pain and loss of blood, continued to direct them, thus determining the outcome of the fight. After a year's convalescence, Garlington returned to Fort Riley where he was an instructor in horsemanship and a member of the Cavalry Board. Within a year, he had published a small volume on cavalry tactics. His commander, Col. James W. Forsyth, considered him "one of the ablest young cavalry officers in the service with the ability to perform well in any position." He later called him "an unusually successful drillmaster."

Secretary of War Daniel Lamont noted Garlington's handiwork while on a visit to Fort Riley in 1894 and shortly thereafter appointed him a major in the Inspector General's Department. Also in 1894 Garlington wrote a history of his old regiment for the Military Service Institute. His selection as an inspector precluded his assignment to the military department at Clemson University, which the school had requested. He was assigned instead as the assistant to the inspector of the South Atlantic District, where he served until the war with Spain when he joined the Cavalry Division as its inspector. Garlington's assignment to the Cavalry Division in June 1898 was paralleled by an unsuccessful effort on the part of the South Carolina congressional delegation to have him appointed a brigadier general of volunteers. He remained instead with the Cavalry Division in Cuba where he participated in the operations against Santiago and was again cited for gallantry. He returned to the Washington office of the Inspector General in October 1898 and served for the next year as Breckinridge's senior assistant. Garlington was involved in many special investigations, including one looking into General Miles' allegations about the beef furnished the Army. He then served as the senior inspector in various departments including two tours in the Philippines, but both of his Philippine tours were curtailed because of illness. The last time this happened was in 1906 when he was hospitalized at the San Francisco Army Hospital in time to witness the earthquake and great fire in which he lost most of his personal property, just arrived from Manila.

Garlington's performance of duty between the war with Spain and his 1906 return from the Philippines was praised by his superiors. Major General Arthur MacArthur considered him "fit for any duty." Adjutant General Henry C. Corbin recommended him for duty on the new general staff, characterizing him as "exacting, yet generous and broad minded," fully capable of serving as a general officer. Later, Corbin recommended him to be superintendent of the Military Academy, saying that he was "an excellent soldier and a very fine gentleman."

In late May 1906, General Burton notified the Adjutant General that his health was not improving and that he intended to remain on sick leave over the summer of 1906 to try to recuperate. He was not optimistic and said the War Department should anticipate his retirement in September. He recommended that Garlington be designated his successor and be assigned as acting inspector general. Accordingly, Garlington was ordered off sick leave to go to the Secretary of War's summer home for consultation. He began running the Washington office on 8 June 1906. Burton's eyesight continued to deteriorate and Garlington was formally designated Inspector General on 1 October 1906. He was reappointed in 1910 and again in 1914, serving over ten years before retiring for reasons of age in February 1917.

Shortly after his retirement, Garlington was recalled to active duty to serve as a special assistant to the Chief of Staff, his West Point classmate Tasker H. Bliss. He began that job on 30 April 1917, but was reassigned at Secretary of War Newton B. Baker's request on 26 June to serve the remainder of the war as the Army representative on the Cantonment Adjustment Commission. This was a labor relations board agreed to by unions and management to assure fair conditions in the settlement of disputes while continuing to rush the building of barracks. At war's end, Garlington returned to retirement to live in San Diego, California. There he led a quiet, scholarly life until his death on 16 October 1934. [National Archives, records of TIG, RG 159, entry 24, files 693–720 and 12179; entry 35, misc. office files; records of TAG, RG 94, 5574 ACP 1877; USMA Archives, Cullum file, class of 1876; Assoc. of Grads., USMA, *Annual Report, June 11, 1935*, "Ernest Albert Garlington," 90–94; "Obituaries," *Army and Navy Journal*, 20 Oct 34, 173; Cullum, *Register*, no. 2622; Maj. E. A. Garlington, "The Seventh Regiment of Cavalry," *Journal of the Military Service Institute of the United States*, January 1895, 16:649–65.]

HASKELL, JONATHAN (birth date unknown) born in Massachusetts, enlisted in the Massachusetts Continental Line in December 1776 and served in various regiments throughout the Revolutionary War, about half the time as regimental adjutant. He was discharged on 20 June 1784 with the last infantry unit of the

Continental Army, Henry Jackson's Continentals. He was appointed an infantry captain in March 1794. He relieved John Mills as adjutant and inspector on 27 February 1796 but returned to his unit, the 4th Sublegion, on 1 August. When it was disbanded in November 1796, Haskell returned to Massachusetts, where he died on 13 December 1814. [Heitman, *Historical Register*, 1:509.]

HEYL, CHARLES H. (1849–1926), entered the Army from civilian life in New Jersey as a second lieutenant of infantry in October 1873, rising to first lieutenant in 1892. On 19 May 1898 he was appointed a major and an inspector general. He had been brevetted for gallantry during the Indian Wars and in 1897 was awarded the Medal of Honor for his gallantry in action in 1876. He remained in the Inspector General's Department, becoming a colonel in 1902, and retired in 1904. Recalled to active duty during the First World War, he became chief of the Inspections Division where he effectively streamlined operations and guided them into the postwar era. He retired again in 1919 and died in Washington, D.C., on 12 October 1926. [Heitman, *Historical Register*, 1:527.]

HEYL, EDWARD M. (1834–1895), entered military service in August 1861 as a quartermaster sergeant, later becoming a first sergeant in the 3d Pennsylvania Cavalry. Promoted to second lieutenant in September 1862 and captain in May 1864, he served until his regiment was mustered out in August 1864. Among other locales, he had seen action at Brandy Station and Gettysburg. He returned to the Army as a lieutenant of the 9th Cavalry, a black regiment, in 1866, and was promoted to captain within the next year. He transferred to the 4th Cavalry in 1870, from which he was promoted to major and inspector general. Heyl had seen hard service before becoming an inspector and in 1890 he was brevetted for gallantry in three actions against Indians in Texas in 1869—in the inspectorate, he became lieutenant colonel in September 1885, and colonel in February 1889. Heyl died on 2 January 1895 in Chicago, Illinois. [Heitman, *Historical Register*, 1:527.]

HUGHES, ROBERT P. (1839–1909), a graduate of Jefferson College, Pennsylvania, joined a three-month Pennsylvania infantry regiment as a private at President Lincoln's first call for volunteers in April 1861. When that unit was mustered out, he became a lieutenant in the 85th Pennsylvania Infantry Regiment. After that unit's service expired in 1864, he was promoted to lieutenant colonel in the 199th Pennsylvania Infantry. His extended service was rewarded with a brevet for gallantry and merit at the time he was mustered out in 1865. He rejoined the Army as a captain in 1866, remaining as such until his appointment in 1885 as a major and an inspector general. He rose to colonel in 1888 and was commissioned a brigadier general of volunteers during the war with Spain, after which he commanded troops during the insurrection in the Philippines. In 1901, he became a Regular Army brigadier, then a major general in 1902. He retired in the wholesale retirements of April 1903, and died in Philadelphia, Pennsylvania, on 21 October 1909. [Heitman, *Historical Register*, 1:267.]

KNOX, THOMAS T. (1849–1927), the son of Scottish immigrants living in

Tennessee, graduated from West Point in 1871. Commissioned in the cavalry, he soon saw action in the Modoc War in 1872–73. After three years' staff duty, he returned to a line troop in time to take part in most of the battles of the Nez Perce campaign of 1876. He continued to see action with his regiment in the northwest until he was assigned to Washington, D. C., in 1881 to work in the Adjutant General's Office as part of the group producing the official record of the Civil War. During this period, he earned two law degrees from George Washington University and was admitted to the District of Columbia bar. In 1891 he rejoined his regiment, the 1st Cavalry, and served with it on the frontier until it deployed to Cuba in June 1898 as part of Shafter's Corps. At the battle of Las Guasimas, he was critically wounded, but remained on the field directing his unit. His inspiring conduct led to the award of the Distinguished Service Cross for what Maj. Gen. S.B.M. Young called "conspicious gallantry, stoicism and devotion to duty." A month later his appointment to the Inspector General's Department was approved. There, he became an expert on the National Home for Disabled Volunteer Soldiers and, when offered a position on its board, retired from the Army on 13 April 1903, becoming a board member. In 1905, he became governor of the Hampton branch of the home, and remained there until 1915. Following that, he retired to Washington, D.C., where he died on 16 May 1927. [Assoc. of Grads., USMA, *Annual Report, June 9, 1932*, "Thomas Taylor Knox," 87–92; Heitman, *Historical Register*, 1:607.]

LAWTON, HENRY W. (1843–1899), was born in Ohio and was reared in Indiana. He entered the Army as a sergeant of the 9th Indiana Infantry Regiment in 1861 and was soon raised to first lieutenant in the 30th Indiana Infantry. He became a captain within a year, and was promoted to lieutenant colonel in November 1864. His gallant and meritorious service earned him a volunteer brevet during the war, and he was mustered out in November 1865. He returned in July 1866 as a second lieutenant of the 41st Infantry (a black regiment), spent two years as regimental quartermaster, and went to the 24th Infantry in the merger of the black regiments in 1869. The 6-foot, 3-inch, 210-lb. giant transferred to the 4th Cavalry in 1871, continuing to distinguish himself as a combat leader. He participated in the Sioux War of 1876 and in operations against the Utes in 1879. His most famous campaign occurred in 1886 when he led a gruelling 1,300-mile successful chase after the Apache, Geronimo, in the mountains of Mexico. By then one of the Army's foremost soldiers, he transferred to the Inspector General's Department on 17 September 1888, where he performed the usual duties until appointed a brigadier, and then major general of volunteers in 1898. In that year he was awarded a brevet for gallantry for his conduct at El Caney. Transferred to the Philippines in March 1899, he commanded a division in a series of spectacular successes against the *insurrectos* until he was killed at the battle of San Mateo on 19 December 1899. His death was cause for national mourning. His remains were returned to the United States, where he was buried at Arlington on 9 February 1900. [Heitman, *Historical Register*, 1:620; L. R. Hamersly, *Biographical Sketches of Distinguished Officers of the Army and Navy* (New York: Hamersly, 1905) 253;

Major General Henry W. Lawton of Ft. Wayne, Indiana, Ft. Wayne: Staff of Public Library of Ft. Wayne and Allen County, 1954; ARIG to the Com. Gen., 1900 (Washington: Government Printing Office, 1900), 85–91.]

MILLS, JOHN (birth date unknown), entered the Massachusetts militia in May 1775, early in the Revolution. In January 1776 he transferred to the Massachusetts Continental Line where he served in various units until his discharge as a captain in June 1784. He returned to the army in 1791 as a captain of infantry, and rose to major by February 1793, acting as adjutant and inspector from 13 May 1794 to 27 February 1796. He was the only one of Wayne's acting inspectors to receive the general's formal nomination to be Adjutant and Inspector General, but no action was taken. He died on 8 July 1796. [Heitman, *Historical Register*, 1:713; *National Cyclopaedia*, 12:336.]

MILLS, STEPHEN C. (1854–1914), a native of Illinois, graduated from West Point in 1877, immediately joining the 12th Infantry Regiment in California. He saw action in the Bannock War the next year, then served four arduous years commanding Apache scouts in Arizona. He was twice brevetted for gallantry during this period. Following that, he was on college duty, was a general's aide, and was attache at Copenhagen, Denmark, for two years. When war with Spain erupted, he was made a major and inspector general of volunteers and given the duty on 12 May 1898 of mustering in state volunteer units. In July 1898, he was given a regular appointment to the Inspector General's Department. Following further mustering and demobilization duties, he was appointed recorder of the Dodge Commission investigating wartime problems. He served as Philippine Division Inspector from 1899 to 1902, during which period he was promoted to lieutenant colonel. After promotion to colonel in 1903, he returned to the Philippines where he eventually served as division chief of staff from 1907 to 1909. Mills returned to the United States where he assumed the same duties first at the Department of the Lakes and then at the Department of the East. While at the latter, he was selected to serve as chief of staff of the temporary maneuver divisions formed annually as part of the army's tactical improvements. His ability and seniority marked him as General Garlington's successor, but for his death on 3 August 1914. He was one of the army's most admired officers, noted for his fair-mindedness and leadership. [Heitman, *Historical Register*, 1:714; Assoc. of Grads., USMA, *Annual Report, June 11th, 1915*, "Stephen Crosby Mills," 94–98.]

NORTH, WILLIAM (1755–1836), born in Maine, moved while young to Boston, where he was educated to become a merchant. He began his military career in 1776 as an artilleryman and then served in various Continental Massachusetts infantry regiments until assigned as Steuben's aide in May 1779. After the war, he served as the senior inspector in the army from 15 April 1784 to 25 June 1788. There is considerable controversy over his rank during this period, but most authorities give his rank as major. Through his marriage he had acquired an estate in the Hudson River Valley, to which he returned after army service, becoming active in state politics. He served several terms in the state legislature and then in 1798 was appointed by Governor John Jay to a vacant

United States Senate seat. On 19 July 1798 he was appointed adjutant general of the provisional force in which Alexander Hamilton was inspector general. After his discharge, North returned to New York where he again was elected to the legislature. His colleagues appointed him to the Erie Canal Commission in 1809, where he was active in assuring the adoption of that great commercial venture. Offered the adjutant general position again in 1812, he wisely turned it down in favor of his local activities. He died in New York City in 1836. Along with Benjamin Walker, North was named Steuben's son and heir in Steuben's will. [Doyle, *Steuben*, 356–60; Ryan, *Salute to Courage*, 302–20; Heitman, *Historical Register*, 1:751; *DAB*, 7:563–64.]

RUDULPH, MICHAEL (1758–1793), spelled "Rudulph" so consistently in Wayne's correspondence and in family papers that unquestionably this form was used by him instead of the suspect form "Rudolph," began his military service in 1778 as sergeant major of "Light Horse" Henry Lee's battalion of dragoons. He quickly rose through the ranks to captain in 1779. That year, he was cited by Congress for his bravery at the battle of Paulus Hook, New Jersey. Lee's unit, now designated a legion, was moved to the Southern Department in early 1781, where it remained for the rest of the war. Rudulph accepted his discharge there in May 1783 and settled in Sunbury, Georgia, where he became active in politics and led the local militia in skirmishes with the Indians. He reentered the army in June 1790 as a captain. Rudulph served in the northwest under Harmer and St. Clair and was commissioned major of dragoons in March 1792. Then, he spent a frustrating year trying to organize the cavalry of Wayne's Legion. Wayne appointed him acting adjutant and inspector general on 23 February 1793. At almost the same moment, he granted Rudulph's request for a furlough. Rudulph apparently never returned to duty and his resignation was approved on 17 July 1793. He disappeared after sailing on board ship from Elkton, Maryland, shortly after his resignation. It seems likely that this colorful and magnetic character drowned at sea. [Rudulph, Marilou A., "Michael Rudulph, Lion of the Legion," and "The Legend of Michael Rudulph," both in vol. 45 (1961), *Georgia Historical Quarterly*; Heitman, *Historical Register*, 1:850; *National Cyclopaedia*, 12:335.]

SANGER, JOSEPH P. (1840–1926), born in Detroit, Michigan, on 4 May 1840, was a student at the University of Michigan at the outbreak of the Civil War. In addition to service in Michigan infantry units, he served briefly as an aide-de-camp to President Lincoln. After the war he enjoyed a variety of assignments, to include duty against Fenians along the Canadian border, professorship of military science at Bowdoin College, Maine, and membership in General Emory Upton's 1875–76 worldwide military tour. Two years after coming to the inspectorate, he served as President Benjamin Harrison's secretary and aide in 1891. At the outbreak of the war with Spain, he held various commands in Cuba, then served as director of the census for Cuba and Puerto Rico. He returned to the inspectorate for duty in the Philippines, and there was promoted to brigadier general of the line and served as director of the Philippines census. He retired in the grade of major general in January 1904. During

1908–09 he served on the court of inquiry that investigated the Brownsville incident in which black soldiers had allegedly rampaged in a Texas town. Later, from 1916 until his death, he served on the War Department Medal of Honor Board. Fluent in French and German, he also continued to write scholarly articles on military and literary topics. He died in Washington, D.C., on 15 March 1926. [Heitman, *Historical Register*, 12:859; *National Cyclopaedia*, 27:311–12.]

TOTTEN, JAMES (1818–1871), a Pennsylvanian appointed to the Military Academy from Virginia, graduated in 1841. He was commissioned in the artillery and spent most of the next twenty years assigned to coastal defense activities. Totten saw action against the Seminoles in 1849–50 and frontier duty in Kansas in the late 1850s. Although among the first group of majors (assistant inspectors appointed in November 1861), he actually spent the next eighteen months in command of Missouri infantry and artillery units. This duty was followed by ten months' service as inspector general for the Department of Missouri in 1863–64. After that he commanded siege artillery units in operations in Arkansas and Alabama until the end of the war. He was brevetted four times for gallantry, rising to brevet brigadier general, U.S.A., in 1865. After the war, he served first as inspector for the Department of the East (until 1869), being promoted to lieutenant colonel, Inspector General's Department, in 1867. Transferred to the Department of the South as its inspector, he was relieved in April 1870 and dismissed in July after conviction on various charges of personal misconduct. He died on 2 October 1871 at Sedalia, Missouri. [Heitman, *Historical Register*, 1:966; Cullum, *Register*, 2:21–22, 3:145.]

VROOM, PETER D. (1842–1926), was born in Trenton, N.J., on 18 April 1842. His father's and mother's families had both been prominent in New Jersey affairs for generations. The elder Vroom had been governor of the state and was for many years a well-known jurist. Immediately after graduating from Rensselaer Polytechnic Institute in 1862, young Vroom entered the Army as an officer in the 1st New Jersey Cavalry. In 1863, he was appointed major in the 2d New Jersey Cavalry. He was severely wounded at the battle of South Mountain and later participated in the battles of Fredericksburg and Gettysburg. He ended the Civil War as the inspector of Maj. Gen. Benjamin Grierson's cavalry force on its devastating raid across Mississippi. Both Grierson and the famed cavalryman Joseph Karge praised Vroom as a brave and able officer. He was later awarded a brevet for gallant and meritorious service during the war.

Vroom was given a regular commission as a second lieutenant in the 3d Cavalry in April 1866, based on recommendations from General Grierson and Senator Stockton of New Jersey, among others. For the next ten years he performed regimental duties at various posts in the West. He then participated in the Big Horn and Yellowstone expeditions. At the battle of the Rosebud in June 1876, he again distinguished himself for what George A. Forsyth described as "great coolness and management of his force in a tight situation." He spent the next several years in campaigns against the Sioux and the Ute Indians.

By the early 1880s Vroom was beginning to feel the physical effects of his hard twenty years of service and asked his brother, George, a prominent New Jersey politician, to press discreetly to get him some kind of staff appointment in one of the bureaus or departments. As the decade proceeded, more and more prominent New Jersey politicians indicated their support for Vroom's appointment, citing his long service and professional reputation. Finally, in December 1888, he was appointed and promoted to major in the Inspector General's Department.

Vroom spent his first three years as an inspector assigned to the Department of the East, during which time he became somewhat an expert on financial accounts. When he was reassigned to the Department of Texas, Nelson Miles characterized him as "zealous" while Breckinridge praised him as a quiet, extremely able "gentleman of fine presence." He recommended that Vroom be considered for attache duty. When the war with Spain commenced, Vroom's political friends urged that he be promoted to brigadier general. Instead, however, he was assigned as inspector for various corps before accompanying General Miles to Puerto Rico as his inspector general. He was there less than two months when he contracted malaria and had to return to the United States.

After convalescing, he was again assigned to the Department of the East. During this tour, he was promoted to full colonel in January 1900. In July 1902, he was reassigned as inspector general for the Philippine Division, but was soon overtaken by the events surrounding General Breckinridge's retirement. A delicate situation developed, in that, although second in rank to George Burton in the department, Vroom was senior to him in the Army line. A graceful solution was proposed by Senator John Kean, no doubt at George Vroom's suggestion. Vroom accepted promotion to brigadier general and Inspector General, with the agreement that he would retire as soon as he was promoted. He thus became the senior inspector of the Army for one day only, 11 April 1903, but never served in that capacity as he was en route home from the Philippines at the time. He returned to New Jersey, where he was active in several veterans' organizations and also established a reputation as a scholar and collector of military literature. He died in Atlantic City on 19 March 1926. [*Who Was Who in America*, vol. 1 (1897–1942); "Retired U.S. Army Officer is Dead," The *State Gazette* (Trenton, N.J.), 20 Mar 26; National Archives, RG 94, records of AGO, 814 ACP 1883, 2762 ACP 1890; George A. Forsyth, *The Story of the Soldier* (New York: D. Appleton & Co., 1900). 319.]

WALKER, BENJAMIN (1753–1818), migrating when young from England, became a merchant in New York City. He joined a New York infantry regiment at the start of the Revolution and served with it until appointed to Steuben's staff. In 1781 he transferred to Washington's staff until returning to civilian life in 1782. There, he served first as a private secretary for the governor of New York, and later as naval officer for the Port of New York. Then he spent a term as a congressman. In 1803 Walker moved to Utica, New York, where he spent the rest of his life as agent and manager for a group of land speculators in the central part of the state. He also became prominent in the development of the Utica area until his death in January 1818. Walker and Steuben remained close until Steuben's death, with Walker attending to Steuben's burial. Steuben made Walker and William North his adopted sons and heirs in his will. [Doyle, *Steuben*, 360–61; *National Cyclopaedia*, 5:239.]

WILLIAMS, JONATHON (1750–1815), was a grandnephew of Benjamin Franklin, whom he served as secretary in Paris. Following this, he earned a master's degree from Harvard and then became secretary, and later counselor, of the American Philosophical Society. He developed such an interest in fortifications that in February 1801 he obtained appointment as a major in the 2d Regiment of Artillerists and Engineers with duty as inspector of fortifications in charge of the school at West Point. When the army was reduced in 1802, Williams became the first chief of the Corps of Engineers and the first superintendent of the Military Academy. He resigned in 1803 over issues of command, but was reinstated in 1805. Among other fortifications, he built castle Williams on Governors Island, New York. Williams resigned in 1812 and died in 1815. [Heitman, *Historical Register*, 1:1041; Arthur P. Wade, "A Military Offspring of the American Philosophical Society," *Military Affairs*, Sep 44, 38.]

Selected Bibliography

Archival Collections

The basis for a study of the Inspector General's Department in the eighteenth and nineteenth centuries must rest on the holdings of the National Archives in Washington, D.C., Record Group (RG) 159, Records of the Office of the Inspector General, naturally, should be the starting point. These are somewhat uneven before the Civil War. Most of the records that have survived between 1814 and 1842 are on three microfilm rolls available for sale from the National Archives. The records become increasingly voluminous after 1862, and they are listed in a preliminary checklist prepared by the Archives, which indicates those entries in the group containing indexes. The nature of the work of the Inspector General's Department has involved it with many other bureaus and staff departments. Often, replies to correspondence or duplicate copies of Inspector General material may have survived in the records of these while perishing in those of RG 159.

Particularly helpful in this study were the records of the Secretary of War (RG 107), the Adjutant General (RG 94), the Quartermaster General (RG 92), the Surgeon General (RG 112), and in those of various Continental Commands (RG 98). Each of these has a checklist and inventory available from the National Archives as well. The documentation in the Archives is for the most part highly impersonal and formal. The holdings of the Military History Institute, Carlisle Barracks, contain the personal papers of several officers who served as inspectors general in the late nineteenth century. Excellent biographical material on many inspectors may be found in the holdings of the U.S. Military Academy, West Point, particularly in its Cullum files. The Military History Institute and the Indiana University Library, Bloomington, Indiana, archives also contain large collections of published military documents.

Printed Documents

A large part of the research for this volume relied on printed official documents. One of the most important of these was the various *Annual Reports* of the Secretary of War, Commanding General (title varies), Adjutant General, Inspector General, Surgeon General, Quartermaster General, Commissary General of Subsistence, Judge Advocate General, Commissary General of Purchases, Ordnance Department (title varies), Corps of Engineers, and others, 1822–1920. All reports until 1920 were grouped together with the *Annual Report of the*

Secretary of War, and began publication in 1822 or when the issuing official was established. The first *Annual Report of the Inspector General* appeared in 1866. From 1822 to 1838, the *War Department Annual Reports* appear in *American State Papers*, Class V, Military Affairs; thereafter, they appear in the Congressional Documents Serial Set, usually as Document No. 1 for the year. From 1861 to 1920 the *War Department Annual Reports* were also published separately. The congressional publication, however, was used during the course of this research. Each report is given a complete citation the first time it appears in the footnotes.

Also helpful were several published collections of congressional documents. These include Paul H. Smith, ed., *Letters of Delegates to Congress, 1774–1789*, (8 vols., Washington, 1976–1981) and the *Index: Journals of the Continental Congress, 1774–1789* published by the National Archives in 1976. The *Journals* themselves had been published by the Government Printing Office between 1934 and 1937. William H. Carter's narrative of the creation of the general staff appears as Senate Misc. Doc. 119, 68th Cong., 1st sess., 1924. Reports by various inspectors have also appeared as public documents: Edward P. Gaines' report on western posts is in *American State Papers*, 19: 103–41. Marcy and McClellan's Red River exploration was published as House Executive Document (n.n.), 33d Cong., 1st sess. (1854). The Dodge Commission's report may be found in Senate Document 221, 56th Cong., 1st sess. (1900). The second session of this Congress produced Joseph Sanger's IG History (House Document 2) and Raphael Thian's history of the general staff (Senate Document 229).

Useful along this line were publications such as the *Annals of Congress*, the *Congressional Globe*, and the *Congressional Record*. All the issues of the *Army Regulations* need to be reviewed to see the various duties imposed on the inspectorate or expected of it. Many of these are cited in Virgil Ney's *Evolution of the United States Army Field Manual* prepared for the Army Combat Development Board in 1966. Especially valuable is the unique collection of General Orders compiled by A. C. Quisenberry for General Breckinridge. The original is in the National Archives and a copy is in the Office of the Inspector General. The *Official Record of the War of the Rebellion*, known to all Civil War students, can be useful if a particular name or incident is known.

Books and Reports

A great deal of information on inspectors and their activities during this era may be gotten from secondary sources through a careful gleaning. A few inspectors' reports have been published in full. Some men such as Steuben and Hamilton are the subjects of biographies. Numerous general or campaign histories mention inspectors' activities, often without realizing their significance. The titles listed below were helpful in providing background or in mentioning an inspector general in the performance of his duties.

Adams, Henry. *The War of 1812*. Edited by Harvey A. DeWeerd. Washington: Infantry Journal, 1944.

Alden, John R. *A History of the American Revolution*. New York: Knopf, 1969.

Alger, Russell A. *The Spanish-American War*. New York: Harper, 1901.

Ambrose, Stephen E. *Duty, Honor, Country: A History of West Point*. Baltimore: Johns Hopkins University Press, 1966.

———. *Halleck, Lincoln's Chief of Staff*. Baton Rouge: Louisiana State University Press, 1960.

Annual Reunion of the Association of Graduates, United States Military Academy, West Point, New York. West Point: Association of Graduates, 1889.

Annual Reunion of the Association of Graduates, United States Military Academy, West Point, New York. West Point: Association of Graduates, 1905.

Armstrong, John. *Notices of the War of 1812*. 2 vols. New York: Wiley & Putnam, 1840.

Ashburn, P. M. *A History of the Medical Department of the United States Army*. Boston: Houghton Mifflin, 1929.

Athearn, Robert G. *William Tecumseh Sherman and the Settlement of the West*. Norman: University of Oklahoma Press, 1959.

Babcock, Louis L. *The War of 1812 on the Niagara Frontier*. Buffalo: Buffalo Historical Society, 1927.

Baird, John A., Jr. *Profile of a Hero: The Story of Absalom Baird, His Family, and the American Military Tradition*. Philadelphia: Dorrance, 1977.

Baldwin, Leland. *The Whiskey Rebels*. Pittsburgh: University of Pittsburgh Press, 1939.

Bandel, Eugene. *Frontier Life in the Army, 1855–1861*. Edited by Ralph P. Bieber. Glendale, Calif.: Arthur H. Clark, 1932.

Bauer, K. Jack. *The Mexican War, 1846–1848*. New York: Macmillan, 1974.

Berton, Pierre. *Flames Across the Border: The Canadian-American Tragedy, 1813–1814*. Boston: Little, Brown, 1981.

———. *The Invasion of Canada, 1812–1813*. Boston: Little, Brown, 1980.

Billings, John D. *Hardtack and Coffee: The Unwritten Story of Army Life*. Edited by Richard Harwell, 1887. Reprint. Chicago: R. R. Donnelley, The Lakeside Classics, 1960.

Bisbee, William Henry. *Through Four American Wars: The Impressions and Experiences of Brigadier General William Henry Bisbee*. Boston: Meador, 1931.

Boatner, Mark M. III. *Civil War Dictionary*. New York: McKay, 1959.

———. *Encyclopedia of the American Revolution*. New York: McKay, 1974.

Bodinier, Gilbert. *Dictionnaire des Officiers de l'armee royale qui ont combattu aux Etats-Unis pendant la guerre d'Independance 1776–1783*. Vincennes: Bureau d'histoire, 1982.

Bolton, Charles Knowles. *The Private Soldier Under Washington*. New York: Scribner, 1902.

Bourke, John G. *On the Border with Crook*. 2d ed. New York: Scribner, 1892.

Bowman, Allen. *The Morale of the American Revolutionary Army*. Port Washington, N.Y.: Kennikat, 1964.

Boyd, Thomas. *Mad Anthony Wayne*. New York: Scribner, 1929.

Brackett, Albert G. *History of the United States Cavalry, From the Formation of the Federal Government to the 1st of June, 1863*. New York: Harper & Bros., 1865.

Brandes, Ray, ed. *Troopers West: Military and Indian Affairs on the American Frontier*. San Diego: Frontier Heritage, 1970.

Brant, Irving. *James Madison*. 6 vols. Indianapolis: Bobbs-Merrill, 1941–1961.

Brown, John Howard, ed. *Lamb's Biographical Dictionary of the United States*. Boston: James H. Lamb, 1900.

Butterfield, C. W. *Washington-Irvine Correspondence: The Official Letters Which Passed Between Washington and Brig.-Gen. William Irvine and Between Irvine and Others Concerning Military Affairs in the West from 1781 to 1787*. Madison, Wis.: David Atwood, 1882.

Carroll, John M., ed. *The Black Military Experience in the American West*. New York: Liveright, 1971.

Carter, George H. *Proceedings Upon the Unveiling of the Statue of Baron von Steuben, December 7, 1910*. Washington: Government Printing Office, 1911.

Carter, William Harding. *The Life of Lieutenant General Chaffee*. Chicago: University of Chicago Press, 1917.

Churchill, Franklin Hunter. *Sketch of the Life of Bvt. Brig. Gen. Sylvester Churchill, Inspector General U. S. Army, with Notes and Appendices*. New York: Willis McDonald, 1888.

Clarke, Dwight L. *Stephen Watts Kearney: Soldier of the West*. Norman: University of Oklahoma Press, 1961.

Clary, David A. *A Life Which Is Gregarious in the Extreme: A History of Furniture in Barracks, Hospitals, and Guardhouses of the United States Army 1880–1945*. Report DAC–9, prepared for the National Park Service. Bloomington, Ind.: David A. Clary & Associates, 1985.

———. *"The Place Where Hell Bubbled Up": A History of the First National Park*. Washington: Government Printing Office, 1972.

———. *These Relics of Barbarism: A History of Furniture in Barracks, Hospitals, and Guardhouses of the United States Army, 1800–1880*. Report DAC–7, prepared for the National Park Service. Bloomington, Ind.: David A. Clary & Associates, 1982.

Commager, Henry Steele, and Morris, Richard B., eds. *The Spirit of Seventy-Six: The Story of the American Revolution as Told by Participants*. 2 vols. Indianapolis: Bobbs-Merrill, 1958.

Concise Dictionary of American Biography. 2d ed. New York: Scribner, 1977.

Cooper, Jerry M. *The Army and Civil Disorder: Federal Military Intervention in Labor Disputes, 1877–1900.* Westport, Conn.: Greenwood, 1980.

Cosmas, Graham. *An Army for Empire: The United States Army in the Spanish-American War.* Columbia: University of Missouri Press, 1971.

Coues, Elliott, ed. *The Expeditions of Zebulon Montgomery Pike.* 3 vols. New York: Harper, 1895.

Cronau, Rudolf. *The Army of the American Revolution and Its Organizer.* New York: Cronau, 1923.

Crook, George. *General George Crook: His Autobiography.* Edited by Martin F. Schmitt. Rev. ed. Norman: University of Oklahoma Press, 1960.

Cross, Trueman. *Military Laws of the United States.* Washington: Edward DeKraft, 1825.

Cullum, George W. *Biographical Register of the Officers and Graduates of the U.S. Military Academy at West Point, N. Y..* 3d ed. Boston: Houghton Mifflin, 1891.

David, Jay, and Crane, Elaine, eds. *The Black Soldier from the American Revolution to Vietnam.* New York: Morrow, 1971.

Dictionary of American Biography. 20 vols. New York: Scribner, 1928–1936.

Dippel, Horst. *Germany and the American Revolution, 1770–1800: A Sociohistorical Investigation of Late Eighteenth-Century Political Thinking.* Translated by Bernhard A. Uhlendorf. Chapel Hill: University of North Carolina Press, 1977.

Doyle, Joseph B. *Frederick William von Steuben and the American Revolution.* Steubenville, Ohio: H. C. Cook, 1913.

Drake, Francis S. *Dictionary of American Biography Including Men of the Time.* Boston: James R. Osgood, 1872.

Dupuy, R. Ernest. *The Compact History of the United States Army.* Rev. ed. New York: Hawthorn Books, 1961.

Dupuy, R. Ernest, and Baumer, William H. *The Little Wars of the United States.* New York: Hawthorn Books, 1968.

Dupuy, R. Ernest, and Dupuy, Trevor N. *Brave Men and Great Captains.* New York: Harper & Bros., 1959.

Elliott, Charles Winslow. *Winfield Scott: The Soldier and the Man.* New York: Macmillan, 1937.

Fitzpatrick, John C., ed. *The Writings of George Washington, from the Original Manuscript Sources.* 39 vols. Washington: Government Printing Office, 1931–1944.

Fletcher, Marvin. *The Black Soldier and Officer in the United States Army, 1891–1917.* Columbia: University of Missouri Press, 1974.

Flexner, James Thomas. *George Washington and the New Nation (1783–1793).* Boston: Little, Brown, 1970.

———. *George Washington: Anguish and Farewell (1793–1799).* Boston: Little, Brown, 1972.

———. *George Washington in the American Revolution (1775–1783).* Boston: Little, Brown, 1968.

————. *George Washington: The Forge of Experience, 1732–1775*. Boston: Little, Brown, 1968.

Flipper, Henry O. *The Colored Cadet at West Point*. New York: Homer & Lee, 1878.

————. *Negro Frontiersman: The Western Memoirs of Henry O. Flipper, First Negro Graduate of West Point*. Edited by Theodore D. Harris. El Paso: Texas Western College Press, 1963.

Foner, Jack D. *Blacks and the Military in American History: A New Perspective*. New York: Praeger, 1974.

————. *The United States Soldier Between Two Wars: Army Life and Reforms, 1865–1898*. New York: Humanities Press, 1970.

Foreman, Grant. *Advancing the Frontier 1830–1860*. Norman: University of Oklahoma Press, 1933.

————. *Marcy and the Gold Seekers: The Journal of Captain R. B. Marcy, with an Account of the Gold Rush over the Southern Route*. Norman: University of Oklahoma Press, 1939.

Fowler, Arlen L. *The Black Infantry in the West, 1869–1891*. Westport, Conn.: Greenwood, 1971.

Frazer, Robert W., ed. *Mansfield on the Condition of the Western Forts, 1853–54*. Norman: University of Oklahoma Press, 1963.

————, ed. *New Mexico in 1850: A Military View by Colonel George Archibald McCall*. Norman: University of Oklahoma Press, 1968.

Frederick II ("the Great") of Prussia. *Frederick the Great on the Art of War*. Translated and edited by Jay Luvaas. New York: Free Press, 1966.

Freeman, Douglas Southall. *George Washington*. 7 vols. New York: Scribner, 1948–1957.

Freidel, Frank. *The Splendid Little War*. New York: Scribner, 1958.

Funston, Frederick. *Memories of Two Wars: Cuban and Philippine Experiences*. New York: Scribner, 1914.

Ganoe, William A. *History of the United States Army*. Rev. ed. New York: Appleton-Century, 1942.

Garrison, Fielding H. *John Shaw Billings: A Memoir*. New York: Putnam, 1915.

General Orders of George Washington, Commander in Chief of the Army of the Revolution, Issued at Newburgh on the Hudson, 1782–1783. Compiled and edited by Edward C. Boynton, 1909. Reprint, Harrison, N.Y.: Harbor Hill, 1973.

Goetzmann, William H. *Army Exploration in the American West, 1803–1863*. New Haven: Yale University Press, 1959.

Goff, John S. *Robert Todd Lincoln.: A Man in His Own Right*. Norman: University of Oklahoma Press, 1959.

Goode, Paul R. *The United States Soldiers' Home*. Richmond, Va.: William Byrd Press, 1957.

Greene, Francis Vinton. *General Greene*. 1893. Reprint. Port Washington, N. Y.: Kennikat, 1970.

Hamersly, L. R. *Biographical Sketches of Distinguished Officers of the Army and Navy.* New York: Hamersly, 1905.

Hamersly, Thomas H. S. *Complete Army Register for 100 Years (1779 to 1879).* Washington: Hamersly, 1881.

Hampton, H. Duane. *How the U.S. Cavalry Saved Our National Parks.* Bloomington: Indiana University Press, 1971.

Hart, Basil H. Liddell. *Sherman: Soldier, Realist, American.* New York: Praeger, 1958.

Hatch, Louis C. *The Administration of the American Revolutionary Army.* New York: Longmans Green, 1904.

Heitman, Francis B. *Historical Register of Officers of the Continental Army During the War of the Revolution, April, 1775, to December, 1783.* Rev. ed. Washington: Rare Book Shop, 1914.

———. *Historical Register of the United States Army, From Its Organization, September 29, 1789, to September 29, 1881.* Washington: National Tribune, 1890.

Heyman, Max L., Jr. *Prudent Soldier: A Biography of Major General E.R.S. Canby, 1817–1873.* Glendale, Calif.: Clark, 1959.

Higginbotham, Don. *The War of American Independence: Military Attitudes, Policies, and Practice, 1753–1789.* New York: Macmillan, 1971.

———, ed. *Reconsideration of the Revolutionary War: Selected Essays.* Westport, Conn.: Greenwood, 1978.

Hill, Jim Dan. *The Minute Man in Peace and War: A History of the National Guard.* Harrisburg, Pa.: Stackpole, 1963.

Hirschson, Stanley P. *Grenville M. Dodge: Soldier, Politician, Railroad Pioneer.* Bloomington: Indiana University Press, 1967.

Hitchcock, Ethan Allen. *Fifty Years in Camp and Field: Diary of Ethan Allen Hitchcock.* Edited by W. A. Croffut. New York: Putnam, 1909.

Hollon, W. Eugene. *Beyond the Cross Timbers: The Travels of Randolph B. Marcy, 1812–1887.* Norman: University of Oklahoma Press, 1955.

———. *The Lost Pathfinder: Zebulon Montgomery Pike.* Norman: University of Oklahoma Press, 1949.

Huston, James A. *The Sinews of War: Army Logistics 1775–1953.* Washington: Department of the Army, 1966.

Idzerda, Stanley J., ed. *Lafayette in the Age of the American Revolution: Selected Letters and Papers, 1776–1790.* 4 vols. Ithaca, N. Y.: Cornell University Press, 1977–1981.

Ingersoll, L. D. *A History of the War Department of the United States, with Biographical Sketches of the Secretaries.* Washington: Francis B. Mohun, 1879.

Jackson, Donald, ed. *The Journals of Zebulon Montgomery Pike, With Letters and Related Documents.* 2 vols. Norman: University of Oklahoma Press, 1966.

Jacobs, James Ripley. *The Beginning of the U.S. Army, 1783–1812.* Princeton: Princeton University Press, 1947.

————— Tarnished Warrior: Major-General James Wilkinson. New York: Macmillan, 1938.

Jessup, Philip C. Elihu Root. 2 vols, New York: Dodd, Mead, 1938.

Johnson, Virginia Weisel. The Unregimented General: A Biography of Nelson A. Miles. Boston: Houghton Mifflin, 1962.

Kapp, Friedrich. The Life of Frederick William von Steuben, Major General in the Revolutionary Army. 2d ed. New York: Mason Brothers, 1859.

Kemble, C. Robert. The Image of the Army Officer in America: Background for Current Views. Westport, Conn.: Greenwood, 1973.

Kieffer, Chester L. Maligned General: The Biography of Thomas Sidney Jesup. San Rafael, Calif.: Presidio Press, 1979.

Knopf, Richard C., ed. Anthony Wayne, a Name in Arms; Soldier, Diplomat, Defender of Expansion Westward of a Nation: The Wayne-Knox-Pickering Correspondence. Pittsburgh: University of Pittsburgh Press, 1960.

Koenig, William J. Americans at War, from Colonial Wars to Vietnam. New York: Putnam, 1980.

Kohn, Richard H. Eagle and Sword: The Federalists and the Creation of the Military Establishment in America, 1783–1802. New York: Free Press, 1975.

Kreidberg, Marvin A., and Henry, Merton G. History of Military Mobilization in the United States Army 1775–1945. Washington: Department of the Army, 1955.

Kurtz, Stephen G. The Presidency of John Adams: The Collapse of Federalism, 1795–1800. Philadelphia: University of Pennsylvania Press, 1957.

Leach, Douglas Edward. Arms for Empire: A Military History of the British Colonies in North America, 1607–1763. New York: Macmillan, 1973.

Leckie, Robert. The Wars of America. 2 vols. New York: Harper & Row, 1968.

Leckie, William H. The Buffalo Soldiers: A Narrative of the Negro Cavalry in the West. Norman: University of Oklahoma Press, 1967.

—————. The Military Conquest of the Southern Plains. Norman: University of Oklahoma Press, 1963.

Leech, Margaret. Reveille in Washington, 1860–1865. New York: Harper, 1941.

—————. In the Days of McKinley. New York: Harper, 1959.

LeRoy, James A. The Americans in the Philippines: A History of the Conquest and the First Years of Occupation. Boston: Houghton Mifflin, 1914.

Lewis, Lloyd. Sherman, Fighting Prophet. New York: Harcourt & Brace, 1958.

Lodge, Henry Cabot, ed. The Works of Alexander Hamilton. 9 vols. New York: Putnam, 1885–1886.

Lord, Walter. The Dawn's Early Light. New York: Norton, 1972.

Lossing, Benson J. The Pictorial Field Book of the Revolution. 2 vols. New York: Harper & Bros., 1860.

—————. The Pictorial Field-Book of the War of 1812. New York: Harper & Bros., 1896.

Malone, Dumas. *Jefferson and the Ordeal of Liberty*. New York: Little, Brown, 1962.

Maltby, Isaac. *The Elements of War*. Boston: Thomas B. Waite, 1811.

Marcy, Randolph B. *Border Reminiscences*. New York: Harper & Bros., 1872.

———. *The Prairie Traveler: A Hand-Book for Overland Expeditions*. New York: Harper & Bros., 1859.

———. *Thirty Years of Army Life on the Border*. New York: Harper & Bros., 1866.

Marcy, Randolph B. and McClellan, George B. *Adventure on Red River: Report on the Exploration of the Headwaters of the Red River*. Edited by Brant Foreman. Norman: University of Oklahoma Press, 1937.

Meneely, A. Howard. *The War Department, 1861: A Study in Mobilization and Administration*. New York: Columbia University Press, 1928.

Meriwether, Robert, and Hemphill, W. Edwin, eds. *The Papers of John C. Calhoun*. 13 vols. Columbia: University of South Carolina Press, 1959–1980.

Merrill, James M., ed. *Uncommon Valor: The Exciting Story of the Army*. Chicago: Rand McNally, 1964.

Michie, Peter S. *The Life and Letters of Emory Upton*. New York: Appleton, 1885.

Miles, Nelson A. *Personal Recollections and Observations of General Nelson A. Miles*. Chicago: Werner, 1896.

———. *Serving the Republic: Memoirs of the Civil and Military Life of Nelson A. Miles*. New York: Harper & Bros., 1911.

Miller, John C. *The Federalist Era, 1789–1801*. New York: Harper & Row, 1963.

Millis, Walter. *Arms and Men: A Study in American Military History*. New York: Putnam, 1956. Reprint. New York: New American Library, n.d.

———. *The Martial Spirit: A Study of Our War with Spain*. Boston: Houghton Mifflin, 1931.

Montross, Lynn. *Rag, Tag and Bobtail*. New York: Harper & Bros., 1952.

Mooney, Chase C. *William H. Crawford, 1772–1834*. Lexington: University Press of Kentucky, 1974.

Morgan, H. Wayne. *William McKinley and His America*. Syracuse: Syracuse University Press, 1963.

Morris, Richard B., ed. *Alexander Hamilton and the Founding of the Nation*. New York: Dial Press, 1957.

Morton, James Kirby, and Lender, Mark Edward. *A Respectable Army: The Military Origins of the Republic, 1763–1789*. Arlington Heights, Ill.: Harlan Davidson, 1982.

Myers, Minor, Jr. *Liberty Without Anarchy: A History of the Society of the Cincinnati*. Charlottesville: University of Virginia Press, 1982.

The National Cyclopaedia of American Biography. New York: James T. White, 1909.

Neff, Jacob K. *The Army and Navy of America*. Philadelphia: J. H. Pearsol, 1845.

Nelson, Otto L. *National Security and the General Staff*. Washington: Infantry Journal, 1946.

Palmer, John McAuly. *General Von Steuben*. New Haven: Yale University Press, 1937.

———. *Washington, Lincoln, Wilson: Three War Statesmen*. Garden City, N. Y.: Doubleday, Doran, 1930.

Patterson, Samuel White. *Horatio Gates: Defender of American Liberties*. New York: Columbia University Press, 1941.

Peters, Virginia Bergman. *The Florida Wars*. Hamden, Conn.: Archon Books, 1979.

Pickering, Timothy. *An Easy Plan of Discipline for a Militia*. Salem, New England: Samuel and Ebenezer Hall, 1775; 2d ed. Salem: S. Hall, 1776.

Poore, Ben: Perley. *Perley's Reminiscences of Sixty Years in the National Metropolis*. 2 vols. Philadelphia: Hubbard, 1886.

Post, Charles Johnson. *The Little War of Private Post*. Boston: Little, Brown, 1960.

Pratt, Fletcher. *Eleven Generals: Studies in American Command*. New York: Sloane, 1949.

Preston, John Hyde. *A Gentleman Rebel: The Exploits of Anthony Wayne*. Murray Hill, N. Y.: Farrar & Rinehart, 1930.

Prucha, Francis Paul. *Broadax and Bayonet: The Role of the United States Army in the Development of the Northwest, 1815–1860*. Madison: State Historical Society of Wisconsin, 1953. Reprint. Lincoln: University of Nebraska Press, 1967.

———. *A Guide to the Military Posts of the United States, 1789–1895*. Madison: State Historical Society of Wisconsin, 1964.

———. *The Sword of the Republic: The United States Army on the Frontier, 1783–1846*. Toronto: Macmillan, 1969.

———, ed. *Army Life on the Western Frontier: Selections from the Official Reports Made Between 1826 and 1845 by Colonel George Croghan*. Norman: University of Oklahoma Press, 1958.

Rankin, Hugh F. *The American Revolution*. New York: Putnam, 1964.

———. *The War of the Revolution in Virginia*. Williamsburg: Virginia Independence Bicentennial Commission, 1979.

Reade, Philip. *History of the Military Canteen*. Chicago: Burroughs, 1901.

Reinhardt, George C., and Kintner, William R. *The Haphazard Years: How America Has Gone to War*. Garden City, N. Y.: Doubleday, 1960.

Rickey, Don. *Forty Miles a Day on Beans and Hay: The Enlisted Soldier Fighting the Indian Wars*. Norman: University of Oklahoma Press, 1963.

Riling, Joseph R. *Baron Von Steuben and His Regulations*. Philadelphia: Ray Riling Arms Books, 1966.

Rippy, J. Fred. *Joel R. Poinsett Versatile American*. Durham: Duke University Press, 1935.

Risch, Erna. *Quartermaster Support of the Army: A History of the Corps, 1775–1939*. Washington: Department of the Army, 1962.

Robinson, Fayette. *An Account of the Organization of the Army of the United States.* 2 vols. Philadelphia: E. H. Butler, 1848.

Rodenbaugh, Theo. F. and Haskin, William L., eds. *The Army of The United States: Historical Sketches of Staff and Line with Portraits of Generals-in-Chief.* New York: Maynard, Merrill, 1896.

Root, Elihu. *The Military and Colonial Policy of the United States: Addresses and Reports by Elihu Root.* Edited by Robert Bacon and James Brown Scott. Cambridge: Harvard University Press, 1916.

Rossie, Jonathan Gregory. *The Politics of Command in the American Revolution.* Syracuse: Syracuse University Press, 1975.

Scheer, George F., and Rankin, Hugh F. *Rebels and Redcoats.* New York: World, 1957.

Schoenbrun, David. *Triumph in Paris: The Exploits of Benjamin Franklin.* New York: Harper & Row, 1976.

Schofield, John M. *Forty-Six Years in the Army.* New York: Century, 1897.

Scott, Winfield. *Memoirs of Lieut.-General Scott, LL.D.* 2 vols. New York; Sheldon, 1864.

Sherman, William T. *Personal Memoirs of W. T. Sherman.* 2 vols. New York: Webster, 1892. Reprint. Bloomington: Indiana University Press, 1957.

Slayden. Ellen Maury. *Washington Wife: Journal of Ellen Maury Slayden from 1897 to 1919.* New York: Harper & Row, 1962.

Smith, Page. *John Adams.* 2 vols. Garden City, N. Y.: Doubleday, 1962.

Spaulding, Oliver Lyman. *The United States Army in War and Peace.* New York: Putnam, 1937.

Steiner, Bernard C. *The Life and Correspondence of James McHenry, Secretary of War under Washington and Adams.* Cleveland: Burrows Bros., 1907.

Stern, Philip van Doren, ed. *Soldier Life in the Union and Confederate Armies.* New York: Bonanza, 1961.

Strode, Hudson. *Jefferson Davis, American Patriot, 1808–1861.* New York: Harcourt Brace, 1955.

Thane, Elswyth. *The Fighting Quaker: Nathanael Greene.* New York: Hawthorn, 1964.

Thayer, Theodore. *Nathanael Greene: Strategist of the American Revolution.* New York: Twayne, 1960.

Thomas, Benjamin P., and Harold M. Hyman. *Stanton: The Life and Times of Lincoln's Secretary of War.* New York: Knopf, 1962.

Trask, David F. *The War with Spain in 1898.* New York: Macmillan, 1981.

Trussell, John B., Jr. *Birthplace of an Army: A Study of the Valley Forge Encampments.* Harrisburg: Pennsylvania Historical and Museum Commission, 1976.

Tucker, Glen. *Poltroons and Patriots: A Popular Account of the War of 1812.* 2 vols. Indianapolis: Bobbs-Merrill, 1954.

Upton, Emory. *The Armies of Asia and Europe*. New York: Appleton, 1878.

———. *The Military Policy of the United States*. 3d impression. Washington: Government Printing Office, 1912.

Utley, Robert M. *Frontier Regulars: The United States Army and the Indian, 1866–1891*. New York: Macmillan, 1973.

———. *Frontiersmen in Blue: The United States Army and the Indian, 1848–1865*. New York: Macmillan, 1967.

Walker, Paul K. *Engineers of Independence: A Documentary History of Army Engineers in the American Revolution, 1775–1783*. Washington: Corps of Engineers, 1981.

Ward, Harry M. *The Department of War, 1781–1795*. Pittsburgh: University of Pittsburgh, 1962.

Warner, Ezra J. *Generals in Blue: Lives of the Union Commanders*. Baton Rouge: Louisiana State University Press, 1964.

Webster's American Military Biographies. Springfield, Mass.: G. & C. Merriam, 1978.

Weigley, Russell F. *The American Way of War: A History of United States Military Strategy and Policy*. New York: Macmillan, 1973.

———. *History of the United States Army*. New York: Macmillan, 1967.

———. *Quartermaster General of the Union Army: A Biography of M. C. Meigs*. New York: Columbia University Press, 1959.

———, ed. *The American Military: Readings in the History of the Military in American Society*. Reading, Mass.: Addison-Wesley, 1969.

Wheeler, Joseph. *The Santiago Campaign*. 1898. Reprint. Port Washington, N. Y.: Kennikat, 1971.

White, Leonard D. *The Federalists: A Study in Administrative History*. New York: Macmillan, 1956.

———. *The Jacksonians: A Study in Administrative History, 1829–1861*. New York: Macmillan, 1954.

———. *The Jeffersonians: A Study in Administrative History, 1801–1829*. New York: Macmillan, 1959.

———. *The Republican Era, 1869–1901: A Study in Administrative History*. New York: Macmillan, 1958.

Williams, T. Harry. *Americans at War: The Development of the American Military System*. Baton Rouge: Louisiana State University Press, 1960.

———. *The History of American Wars From Colonial Times to World War I*. New York: Knopf, 1981.

———. *Lincoln and His Generals*. New York: Knopf, 1952.

Wilson, James Grant, and Fiske, John, eds. *Appleton's Cyclopaedia of American Biography*. New York: Appleton, 1888.

Wilson, James Harrison. *The Life of John Rawlins*. New York: Neale, 1916.

Who Was Who in American History: The Military. Chicago: Marquis Who's Who, 1975.

Wiltse, Charles M. *John C. Calhoun, Nationalist, 1782–1828*. Indianapolis: Bobbs-Merrill, 1944.

Wisley, Edgar B. *Guarding the Frontier: A Study of Frontier Defense from 1815 to 1825*. Westport, Conn.: Greenwood, 1970.

Wolff, Leon. *Little Brown Brother: How the United States Purchased and Pacified the Philippine Islands at the Century's Turn*. Garden City, N. Y.: Doubleday, 1961.

Wright, Robert K., Jr. *The Continental Army* (Washington: Center of Military History, U.S. Army, 1983).

Unpublished Academic Dissertations

Andrews, Richard Allen. "Years of Frustration: William T. Sherman, the Army, and Reform, 1869–1883." Ph.D. dissertation, Northwestern University, 1968.

Bell, Rodney E. "A Life of Russell Alexander Alger, 1836–1907." Ph.D. dissertation, University of Michigan, 1975.

Carp E. Wayne. "Supplying the Revolution: Continental Army Administration and American Political Culture, 1775–1783." Ph.D. dissertation, University of California at Berkeley, 1981.

Chase, Philander D. "Baron Von Steuben in the War of Independence." Ph.D. dissertation, Duke University, 1973.

Childress, David Ted. "The Army in Transition: The United States Army, 1815–1846." Ph.D. dissertation, Mississippi State University, 1974.

Graham, Stanley S. "Life of the Enlisted Soldier on the Western Frontier, 1815–1845." Ph.D. dissertation, North Texas State University, 1972.

Hinton, Harwood P. "The Military Career of John Ellis Wool, 1812–1863." Ph.D. dissertation, University of Wisconsin, 1960.

Hughes, J. Patrick. "The Adjutant General's Office, 1821–1861: A Study in Administrative History." Ph.D. dissertation, Ohio State University, 1977.

Nesmith, Vandell E., Jr. "The Quiet Paradigm Change: The Evolution of the Field Artillery Doctrine of the United States Army, 1861–1905." Ph.D. dissertation, Duke University, 1977.

Skelton, William Barrett. "The United States Army, 1821–1837: An Institutional History." Ph.D. dissertation, Northwestern University, 1968.

Smith, Carlton Bruce. "The United States War Department 1815–1842 " Ph.D. dissertation, University of Virginia, 1967.

Thomas, Donna Marie. "Army Reform in America: The Crucial Years, 1876–1881." Ph.D. dissertation, University of Florida, 1981.

Wright, Robert K., Jr. "Organization and Doctrine in the Continental Army, 1774–1784." Ph.D. dissertation, College of William and Mary, 1980.

Zais, Barrie E. "The Struggle for a 20th-Century Army: Investigation and Reform of the United States Army after the Spanish American War, 1898–1903." Ph.D. dissertation, Duke University, 1981.

Articles in Journals and Collections

Ambrose, Stephen E. "Emory Upton and the Armies of Asia and Europe." *Military Affairs* 28 (spring 1964): 27–32.

———. "The Union Command System and the Donelson Campaign." *Military Affairs* 24 (1960–1961): 78–80.

Applegate, Howard L. "The Medical Administrators of the American Revolutionary Army." *Military Affairs* 25 (spring 1961): 1–10.

Benton, William A. "Pennsylvania Revolutionary Officers and the Federal Constitution." *Pennsylvania History* 31 (1964): 419–35.

Betz, I. H. "The Conway Cabal at York, Pennsylvania, 1777–1778." *Pennsylvanian German* 9 (1908): 248–54.

Bowen, Francis. "Life of Baron Steuben." In *Sparks' American Biography*, vol. 8, 117–202. New York: Harper & Bros., 1902.

Brenneman, Gloria E. "The Conway Cabal: Myth or Reality." *Pennsylvania History* 40 (April 1973): 169–77.

Brown, Richard C. "General Emory Upton—The Army's Mahan." *Military Affairs* 17 (fall 1953): 125–31.

Burnham, William P. "Military Training of the Regular Army of the United States." *Journal of the Military Service Institution of the United States* 10 (1889): 613–39.

Calkin, Homer L. "Changes in Providing for Army Enlisted Men (1846–1946)." *Military Affairs* 11 (winter 1947): 241–44.

Call, Luther P. "The History, Organization, and Function of the Inspector General's Department." *Reserve Officer* 16 (October 1939): 11–13.

Cantor, Louis. "Elihu Root and the National Guard: Friend or Foe?" *Military Affairs* 33 (December 1969): 361–73.

Carter, William H. "The Decadence of the Brevet." *United Service*, 3d ser., 3 (April 1903): 1009–14.

———. "The Evolution of Army Reforms." *United Service*, 3d ser., 3 (May 1903): 1190–98.

———. "A General Staff Corps." *United Service*, 3d ser., 3 (January 1903): 677–81.

———. "The Passing of a High Office." *United Service*, 3d ser., 3 (March 1903): 901–08.

———. "Recent Army Reorganization." *United Service*, 3d ser., 2 (August 1902): 113–20.

———. "The Training of Army Officers." *United Service*, 3d ser., 2 (October 1902): 337–42.

Clarke, C. J. T. "The Post Mess." *Journal of the Military Service Institution of the United States* 15 (1894): 545–52.

Clary, David A. Introduction to *Early Forest Service Research Administrators: Interviews with Verne Lester Harper, George M. Jemison, Clarence L. Forsling, Conducted by Elwood R. Maunder*. Edited by Linda Brandt and Linda Burman. Santa Cruz, Calif., Forest History Society, 1978.

———. "The Role of the Army Surgeon in the West: Daniel Weisel at Fort Davis, Texas, 1868–1872." *Western Historical Quarterly* 3 (January 1972): 53–66.

Coffman, Edward M. "Army Life on the Frontier, 1865–1898." *Military Affairs* 20 (winter 1956): 193–201.

———. "Sidelights on the War Department General Staff in Its Early Years." *Military Affairs* 38 (April 1974): 71–72.

Colby, Elbridge. "Elihu Root and the National Guard." *Military Affairs* 23 (spring 1959): 28–34.

Cooke, Jacob E. "The Whiskey Insurrection." *Pennsylvania History* 30 (1963): 316–46.

Cooper, Jerry M. "National Guard Reform, the Army, and the Spanish-American War: The View from Wisconsin." *Military Affairs* 42 (February 1978): 20–23.

Cosmas, Graham A. "From Order to Chaos: The War Department, the National Guard, and Military Policy, 1898." *Military Affairs*, 29 (fall 1965): 105–21.

———. "Military Reform After the Spanish-American War: The Army Reorganizaton Fight of 1898–1899." *Military Affairs* 35 (February 1971): 12–18.

———. "Securing the Fruits of Victory: The U.S. Army Occupies Cuba, 1898–1899." *Military Affairs* 38 (September 1974): 85–91.

"Coudray's Observations on Forts for Defense of the Delaware, July 1777." *Pennsylvania Magazine of History and Biography* 24 (1900): 343–47.

Crackel, Theodore J. "Jefferson, Politics, and the Army: An Examination of the Military Peace Establishment Act of 1802." *Journal of the Early Republic* 2 (spring 1982): 21–38.

Crimmins, Martin L., ed. "Colonel J. K. F. Mansfield's Report of the Inspection of the Department of Texas in 1856." *Southwestern Historical Quarterly* 42 (October 1938, April 1939): 122–48, 215–57, 351–87.

———. "W. G. Freeman's Report on the Eighth Military Department." *Southwestern Historical Quarterly* 51 (July 1947–April 1948): 54–58. 167–74, 252–58, 350–57; 52 (July 1948–April 1949): 100–08, 227–33, 349–53, 444–47, 53 (July 1949–April 1950): 71–77, 202–08, 308–19, 443–73, 54 (October 1950): 204–18.

DeWeerd, H. A. "The Federalizaton of Our Army." *Military Affairs* 6 (1942): 143–52.

Echeverria, Durand, and Murphy Orville T. "The American Revolutionary Army: A French Estimate in 1777." *Military Affairs* 27 (spring 1963): 1–7.

———. "The American Revolutionary Army: A French Estimate in 1777. Part II: Personnel." *Military Affairs* 27 (winter 1963–1964): 153–62.

Fisher, Vincent J. "Mr. Calhoun's Army." *Military Review* 37 (September 1957): 52–58.

Fletcher, Marvin. "The Black Volunteers in the Spanish-American War." *Military Affairs* 38 (April 1974): 48–53.

———. "The Negro Volunteer in Reconstruction, 1865–66." *Military Affairs* 32 (December 1968): 124–31.

Foote, Morris C. "The Post Mess." *Journal of the Military Service Institution of the United States* 14 (1893): 519–24.

Ford, Worthington C. "Defenses of Philadelphia." *Pennsylvania Magazine of History and Biography* 18 (1894): 334–37.

Forman, Sidney. "Thomas Jefferson on Universal Military Training." *Military Affairs* 11 (fall 1947): 177–78.

———. "Why the United States Military Academy Was Established in 1802." *Military Affairs* 29 (spring 1965): 16–28.

Freidel, Frank. "General Orders 100 and Military Government." *Mississippi Valley Historical Review* 32 (March 1946): 541–56.

Fritz, David L. "Before the 'Howling Wilderness': The Military Career of Jacob Hurd Smith, 1862–1902." *Military Affairs* 43 (December 1979): 186–90.

Fry, James B. "The Adjutant General's Department." *Journal of the Military Service Institution of the United States* 12 (1891): 686–96.

———. "Compulsory Education in the Army." *Journal of the Military Service Institution of the United States* 9 (1888): 429–44.

Futrell, Robert J. "Federal Military Government in the South, 1861–1865." *Military Affairs* 15 (winter 1951): 181–91.

Gaines, William H., Jr. "The Forgotten Army: Recruiting for a National Emergency (1799–1800)." *Virginia Magazine of History and Biography* 56 (July 1948): 267–79.

Godfrey, Carlos Emmor. "Organization of the Provisional Army of the United States in the Anticipated War with France, 1798–1800." *Pennsylvania Magazine of History and Biography* 38 (1914): 129–82.

Gow, June I. "Military Administration in the Confederate Army of Tennessee." *Journal of Southern History* 40 (May 1974): 183–98.

———. "Theory and Practice in Confederate Military Administration." *Military Affairs* 39 (October 1975): 119–23.

Hacker, Barton C. "The United States Army as a National Police Force: The Federal Policing of Labor Disputes, 1877–1898." *Military Affairs* 33 (April 1969): 255–64.

Hardin, E. E. "Army Messing." *Journal of the Military Service Institution of the United States* 6 (1885): 274–75.

Hewes, James. "The United States Army General Staff, 1900–1917." *Military Affairs* 38 (April 1974): 67–71.

Hickey, Donald R. "Federalist Defense Policy in the Age of Jefferson, 1801–1812." *Military Affairs* 45 (April 1981): 63–70.

Higginbotham, Don. "The American Militia: A Traditional Institution with Revolutionary Responsibilities." In Don Higginbotham, ed. *Reconsideration of the Revolutionary War: Selected Essays*, 83–103. Westport, Conn.: Greenwood, 1978.

Horsman, Reginald. "The British Indian Department and the Resistance to General Anthony Wayne, 1793–1795." *Mississippi Valley Historical Review* 49 (September 1962): 269–90.

Hughes, Robert P. "The Campaign Against the Sioux in 1876." *Journal of the Military Service Institution of the United States* 18 (January 1896): 1–44.

Jackson, Donald. "How Lost Was Zebulon Pike?" *American Heritage* 16 (February 1965): 10–15, 75–80.

Knollenberg, Bernhard. "John Adams, Knox, and Washington." *Proceedings of the American Antiquarian Society* 56, pt. 2 (October 1946): 207–38.

Kohn, Richard. "American Generals of the Revolution: Subordination and Restraint." In Don Higginbotham, ed., *Reconsiderations of the Revolutionary War: Selected Essays*, 104–23. Westport, Conn.: Greenwood, 1978.

Lane, Jack C. "American Military Past: The Need for New Approaches." *Military Affairs* 41 (October 1977): 109–13.

Linn, Levon P. "Army Inspector General System." *Army Information Digest* 19 (October 1964): 13–17.

Lyons, Gene M., and Masland, John W. "The Origins of the ROTC." *Military Affairs* 23 (spring 1959): 1–12.

Mahon, John K. "Anglo-American Methods of Indian Warfare, 1676–1794." *Mississippi Valley Historical Review* 45 (September 1958): 254–75.

———. "A Board of Officers Considers the Condition of the Militia in 1826." *Military Affairs* 15 (summer 1951): 85–94.

———. "Pennsylvania and the Beginnings of the Regular Army." *Pennsylvania History* 21 (1954): 33–44.

Maurer, Maurer. "Military Justice Under General Washington." *Military Affairs* 28 (spring 1964): 8–16.

McAnaney, William D. "Desertion in the United States Army." *Journal of the Military Service Institution of the United States* 10 (1889): 450–65.

Miewald, Robert D. "The Army Post Schools: A Report from the Bureaucratic Wars." *Military Affairs* 39 (February 1975): 8–11.

Molineaux, E. L. "Riots in Cities and Their Suppression." *Journal of the Military Service Institution of the United States* 4 (1883): 335–60.

Morris, Richard B. "Andrew Jackson, Strikebreaker." *American Historical Review* 55 (October 1949): 54–68.

Morrison, James L., Jr. "Educating the Civil War Generals: West Point, 1833–1861." *Military Affairs* 38 (September 1974): 108–11.

Morton, Louis. "The Origins of American Military Policy." *Military Affairs* 22 (summer 1958): 75–82.

Mullins, George G. "Education in the Army." *United Service* 2 (April 1880): 478–85.

Murphy, Orville T. "The French Professional Soldier's Opinion of the American Militia in the War of the Revolution." *Military Affairs* 32 (February 1969): 191–98.

Nelson, Paul David. "Citizen Soldiers or Regulars: The Views of American

General Officers on the Military Establishment, 1775–1781." *Military Affairs* 43 (October 1972): 126–32.

———. "Legacy of Controversy: Gates, Schuyler, and Arnold at Saratoga, 1777." *Military Affairs* 37 (April 1973): 41–47.

Nichols, Roger L. "Army Contributions to River Transportation, 1818–1825." *Military Affairs* 33 (April 1969): 242–49.

Owen, Arthur F. "Opportunities for Research: The Early Records of the Office of the Inspector General, 1814–48." *Military Affairs* 7 (1943): 195–96.

Pierson, William W., Jr. "The Committee on the Conduct of the War." *American Historical Review* 23 (1917–1918): 550–76.

Preston, John F. "Inspector General's Department of the Army." *Army and Navy Journal* 71 (7 October 1933): 103, 116.

Prucha, Francis Paul. "Distribution of Regular Army Troops Before the Civil War." *Military Affairs* 16 (winter 1952): 169–73.

———. "The United States Army as Viewed by British Travelers, 1825–1860." *Military Affairs* 17 (fall 1953): 113–24.

Quaife, Milo M., ed. "General James Wilkinson's Narrative of the Fallen Timbers Campaign." *Mississippi Valley Historical Review* 16 (June 1921): 81–90.

———, ed. "A Picture of the First United States Army: The Journal of Captain Samuel Newman." *Wisconsin Magazine of History* 2 (September 1918): 40–73.

Ranson, Edward. "The Endicott Board of 1885–86 and the Coast Defenses." *Military Affairs* 31 (summer 1967): 74–84.

———. Nelson A. Miles as Commanding General, 1895–1903." *Military Affairs* 29 (winter 1965–1966): 179–200.

Rickey, Don, Jr. "The Enlisted Men of the Indian Wars." *Military Affairs* 23 (summer 1959): 91–96.

Riepma, Siert F. "Portrait of an Adjutant General: The Career of Major General Fred C. Ainsworth." *Journal of the American Military History Foundation* 2 (spring 1938): 26–35.

Robertson, S. C. "The Remount Question in the United States Cavalry." *Journal of the Military Service Institution of the United States* 8 (June 1887): 111–29.

Sanger, J. P. "Absalom Baird." In *Annual Reunion of the Association of Graduates, 1905*. West Point: Association of Graduates of the United States Military Academy, 1905. 114–24.

———. "The Duties of Staff Officers." *United Service* 2 (June 1880): 754–73.

———. "Inspector General's Department." In Theo. F. Rodenbaugh and William L. Haskin, eds., *The Army of the United States: Historical Sketches of Staff and Line with Portraits of Generals-in-Chief*. New York: Maynard, Merrill, 1896. 12–32.

Sargent, Winthrop. "Winthrop Sargent's Diary While With General Arthur St. Clair's Expedition Against the Indians." *Ohio Archaeological and Historical Quarterly* 33 (July 1924): 237–73.

Semsch, Philip L. "Elihu Root and the General Staff." *Military Affairs* 27 (spring 1963): 16–27.

Shannon, Fred A. "The Federal Government and the Negro Solier." *Journal of Negro History* 11 (October 1926): 563–83.

Sharpe, A. C. "Military Training in Colleges." *Journal of the Military Service Institution of the United States* 8 (1887): 405–13.

Shippee, Lester B., ed. "Report of [Arthur P. Hayne's] Inspection of the Ninth Military Department, 1819." *Mississippi Valley Historical Review* 7 (December 1920): 261–74.

Shy, John. "American Society and Its War for Independence." In Don Higginbotham, ed., *Reconsideration of the Revolutionary War: Selected Essays*. Westport, Conn.: Greenwood, 1978. 72–82.

Silver, James W. "Edmund Pendleton Gaines and Frontier Problems." *Journal of the Southern Historical Association* 1 (1935): 320–44.

Skelton, William B. "The Commanding General and the Problem of Command in the United States Army, 1821–1841." *Military Affairs* 34 (December 1970): 117–22.

Smith, Carlton B. "Congressional Attitudes Toward Military Preparedness During the Monroe Administration." *Military Affairs* 40 (February 1976): 22–25.

Smith, Dwight L. "Wayne and the Treaty of Greene Ville." *Ohio Archaeological and Historical Quarterly* 63 (January 1954): 1–7.

Snow, Richard F. "Henry Ware Lawton." *American Heritage* 33 (April–May 1982): 40–41.

Spaulding, Oliver L., Jr. "The Military Studies of George Washington." *American Historical Review* 29 (July 1924): 675–80.

Steere, Edward. "Genesis of American Graves Registration, 1861–1870." *Military Affairs* 12 (fall 1948): 149–61.

Tapson, Alfred J. "The Sutler and the Soldier." *Military Affairs* 21 (winter 1957): 175–81.

Todd, Frederick P. "Our National Guard: An Introduction to Its History." *Military Affairs* 5 (1941): 73–86, 152–70.

True, Marshall M., ed, "Ethan Allen Hitchcock and the Texas Rebellion: A Letter Home." *Vermont History* 45 (spring 1977): 102–06.

Vaulx 8. "The Evolution of a General Staff." *Journal of the Military Service Institution of the United States* 33 (1903): 200–06.

Wade, Arthur P. "A Military Offspring of the American Philosophical Society." *Military Affairs* 38 (September 1974): 103–07.

———. "Roads to the Top—An Analysis of General-Officer Selection in the United States Army, 1789–1898." *Military Affairs* 40 (December 1976): 157–63.

Watson, Richard L., Jr. "Congressional Attitudes Toward Military Preparedness, 1829–1835." *Mississippi Valley Historical Review* 34 (March 1948): 611–36.

Weigley, Russell F. "The Military Thought of John M. Schofield." *Military Affairs* 23 (summer 1959): 77–84.

Wensyel, James W. "The Newburgh Conspiracy." *American Heritage* 32 (April–May 1981): 40–47.

Wesley, Edgar Bruce. "Life at a Frontier Post: Fort Atkinson, 1823–1826." *Journal of the American Military Institute* 3 (winter 1939): 203–09.

Williams, T. Harry. "The Committee on the Conduct of the War: An Experiment in Civilian Control." *Journal of the American Military History Institute* 3 (fall 1939): 139–56.

———. "Investigation, 1862." *American Heritage* 6 (December 1954): 16–21.

Wisser, John P. "The Annual Inspection of the National Guard by Army Officers." *United Service* 2 (December 1889): 607–14.

Wyche, Ira T. "Mission and History of the Inspector General's Department." *Armored Cavalry Journal* 56 (March–April 1947): 38–41.

List of Abbreviations

Actg Asst IG	Acting Assistant Inspector General
AG	Adjutant General
AGO	Adjutant General's Office
A&IG	Adjutant & Inspector General's Office
AMB	*Webster's American Military Biographies*
ARAG	*Annual Report of the Adjutant General*
ARComGen	*Annual Report of the Commanding General*
ARIG	*Annual Report of the Inspector General*
ARQMG	*Annual Report of the Quartermaster General*
ARSecWar	*Annual Report of the Secretary of War*
ASP	*American State Papers*
ASP–MA	*American State Papers–Military Affairs*
Asst QMG	Assistant Quartermaster General
CDAB	*Concise Dictionary of American Biography*
CG	Commanding General
DAB	*Dictionary of American Biography*
DAE	*A Dictionary of American English on Historical Principles*
DAHP	*A Dictionary of Americanisms on Historical Principle*
GenCorresp	General Correspondence
GO	General Order
GORI&IG	General Orders Relating to Inspection and the Inspector General's Department
H. Doc.	House Document
H. Rpt.	House Report
JAG	Judge Advocate General
JCC	*Journals of the Continental Congress*
JMSI	*Journal of the Military Service Institute of the U.S.*
LBD	*Lamb's Biographical Dictionary of the United States*
Ltr	letter
Ltr Bk	letter book
MHI	USA Military History Institute
Mil Aff	Military Affairs
NCAB	*The National Cyclopaedia of American Biography*
OED	*The Oxford English Dictionary*
OIG	Office of the Inspector General
OR	*The War of the Rebellion: A Compilation of the Official Records of the Union & Confederate Armies*
QMG	Quartermaster General

RAGO	Records of the Adjutant General's Office
RG	Record Group
RIGO	Records of the Inspector General's Office
ROIG	Records of the Inspector General
ROQMG	Records of the Office of the Quartermaster General
S. Doc.	Senate Document
SO	Special Orders
USMA	United States Military Academy
USV	United States Volunteers

Index

Adams, John: 75, 76, 77, 79, 81, 82
Adjutant General: 24, 65, 74, 82, 126, 127,
  132, 272–73. *See also* Inspector General;
  Secretary of War.
  as controller of Army's communications: 103,
    143, 158, 187–88, 217–18, 222, 287,
    377–78, 382
  as inspector: 65
Adjutant General's Office: 53, 226–27, 251–52,
  254, 256, 312–13, 390–91
Adjutant and Inspector General: 65, 67, 92, 125,
  126, 131, 132. *See also* Adjutant General.
  as assistant to Adjutant General: 93
  as chief administrative official: 107, 111,
    112–13, 115–16
  as chief of staff: 99–100, 103–04, 108
  as head of adjutants and inspectors: 108
  as Secretary of War's adjutant: 87–90
  as troop commander: 105
Aguinaldo, Emilio: 363
Ainsworth, Brig. Gen. Fred C.
  as Adjutant General: 405
  as head of Record and Pensions Office: 400,
    402
Alexander, Bvt. Col. Andrew J.: 247
Alexander, Brig. Gen. William. *See* Lord
  Stirling.
Alger, Russell A.: 332–34, 361, 365, 369,
  372–73, 374, 390
Alien and Sedition Acts: 77
American army. *See* Continental Army.
American Revolution: 8, 12–14, 42–43
  at Brandywine: 22
  at Germantown: 22
  at Morristown: 16
  at Philadelphia: 22, 31
  at Point of Fork, Virginia: 55
  at Saratoga, New York: 22
  at Schuylkill River: 42
  at Valley Forge: 28–29, 31, 35, 36
  at York: 22, 29, 31, 35, 36
  Battle of Monmouth: 46
  campaigns of 1777: 21–22
  final battles: 56
Anglo-American relations: 73–74
Appalachian Mountains: 62
Archer, Col. Samuel B.: 124*n*, 136–40, 142,
  143–45, 147, 151
Apothecary-General: 99*n*
Armstrong, John: 98, 99, 103, 105, 106, 107,
  109, 111, 115
Army. *See* United States Army.

Army and Navy Journal: 270, 298*n*, 302, 331,
  373, 377, 405
Army of the Potomac: 207*n*, 210, 217, 218
Army War College: 390–91, 395–96
Arthur, Chester A.: 300
Articles of War: 153
Artillery: 138, 280
Astor, John Jacob: 367
Atkinson, General Henry: 123
Auditing accounts: 287–89, 303, 403–04. *See
  also* Inspection reports; Inspections;
  Inspectors general; Inspectors general,
  special assignments.
  as strong justification for existence of
    inspectorate: 341–42, 348–49, 379, 397–98,
    404
  as Treasury Department function: 397–98
  of Corps of Engineers: 327, 336
  of division and department commanders: 313
  of National Home for Disabled Volunteer
    Soldiers: 327, 339–41
  of Pay Department: 313, 341
  of staff department officers: 313
  procedures: 287–88, 313

Bailey, Capt. William: 120
Baird, Brig. Gen. Absalom: 209, 210–12, 222,
  292, 300–301, 306, 310–12, 314, 316
  as a commander, Department of Louisiana:
    237
  as assistant commissioner, Freedmen's
    Bureau: 211–12, 229, 237
  as assistant inspector general, Department of
    the Lakes: 237, 239*n*
  as Commander of National Order of the
    Legion of Honor: 304
  as division commander, Army of Kentucky:
    211
  as inspector, Department of the Dakota: 248,
    259*n*
  as inspector, Division of the Missouri: 276
  as inspector, Division of the South: 270, 301
  as inspector, Washington office: 296–97,
    308–10
  as inspector and chief of staff, IV Corps,
    Army of the Potomac: 211
  as Inspector General: 302–305
Baird, Spencer F.: 200
Bankhead, Maj. James: 120
Banning, Henry B.: 279
Barbour, James: 147, 150, 152
Beall, Col. William: 90

Beaumarchais, Caron de: 34–35
Belknap, William W.: 265–66, 275, 276, 283
Bell, John: 171
Bell, Maj. John R.: 108
Benton, Thomas Hart: 157, 168–69
Biddle, Capt. John: 120n
Bissell, William A.: 197
Black regiments: 248, 255–56
Blue book: 49–50, 59–60, 64–65, 67, 196. See also Steuben, Maj. Gen. Friedrich W.A. von.
Board of War: 17, 25, 47
    relationship to Inspector General: 26–27
    role in Conway affair: 28–29
Board of War and Ordnance: 16, 17
Board to Organize the Invalid Corps: 219
Board to Retire Disabled Officers: 219
Boxer Rebellion: 385–86
Breckinridge, Brig. Gen. Joseph C.: 298–99, 300, 372–75, 391, 392–93, 395, 396, 397, 398, 399–402, 404–05
    as artillery commander, Washington Arsenal: 285
    as assistant inspector general, Division of the Pacific: 295–96
    as inspector, Division of the Missouri: 302
    as Inspector General and reformer: 318, 320–58, 362, 363–65, 376–80, 382–88
    as inspector running Washington office: 306
    as troop commander: 296
    roles in Spanish-American War: 365–72
British Army: 6–7
    at New York City: 56
    in campaigns of 1777: 21–22
British Articles of War: 12–13
Brock, General Isaac: 95
Brooke, Maj. George M.: 120
Brooke, John R.: 366
Brown, Lt. Ethan Allen: 77n
Brown, Maj. Gen. Jacob: 106, 109–10
    as commander, Northern Division: 117, 120n, 124–25
    as Commanding General: 128, 131–33, 136, 137, 139, 141–42, 151
Brown, William Carey: 385
Budget: 198
    Army: 123, 126–27, 131, 184–85, 193–94
    Inspection: 144, 269, 279
    War Department: 123, 143, 183–84
Buford, John: 209, 222–23
Bureau of Pensions: 339–40n
Burgoyne, Maj. Gen. John: 22
Burnside, Ambrose E.: 208
Burr, Aaron: 87
Burton, Brig. Gen. George H.: 330, 367, 368, 369, 372
    as Davis' assistant in Washington office: 301
    as inspector, Department of Arizona: 306
    as inspector, Department of the Missouri: 301
    as inspector, Pacific District: 331–32

as Inspector General: 406
as organizer of inspectorate in Cuba: 383, 400–401
Butler, Capt. Edward: 66, 67–68, 69
Butler, Col. Robert: 136

Cadwalader, Brig. Gen. John: 30
Calhoun, John C.: 121–23, 125, 126–28, 131–34, 135–37, 186
Cameron, Simon: 198–99
Camp Thomas, Chickamauga National Military Park, Georgia: 367, 371–72
Canadian border problems: 168
Canby, Bvt. Capt. Edward R. S.: 192–93
Caroline: 168
Carleton, James H.: 267
Carter, William H.: 393–95, 396–97, 398–400, 401, 405, 406, 408
Cass, Lewis: 159–60, 166
Cavalry, 81, 215, 226–27, 279–80. See also Inspection reports; Inspections; Inspectors general, special assignments.
Cavalry Bureau: 219–20
Chaffee, General Adna R.: 388
Chamberlain, Capt. John L.: 393, 396
Champlain Department: 106n
Chase, Salmon P.: 203
Chief of Engineers: 243. See also Corps of Engineers.
Chief of Staff: 403, 407–08. See also General staff.
Churchill, Brig. Gen. Sylvester: 106n, 148, 172–73, 175–77, 190, 203, 204
    as acting inspector general: 166
    as inspector, Department of the East: 194–95
    as inspector, Eastern Division: 187–88, 192
    as inspector general, Army of the South: 166–67
    as inspector general, Washington office: 186
    as inspector general and chief of staff: 177–78
    as second in command: 178
    revision of drill manual and army regulations: 195–200
Civil War: 200, 201–02, 207, 210
    assault on Missionary Ridge: 211
    Battle of Antietam: 203, 221
    Battle of Bull Run: 211
    Battle of Chickamauga: 211
    Battle of Gettysburg: 210
    Battle of Jonesboro: 211
    capture of Cumberland Gap: 211
    firing on Fort Sumter: 198
    inspectors' role in: 202–03
Clarke, Bvt. Brig. Gen. Newman S.: 195
Clay, Henry: 118–19, 126
Cleveland, Grover: 302
Clothier General: 57
Commander in Chief. See Commanding General.

Commanders: 191
  company: 57–58
  department: 134, 140–41
  division: 174–75
  field: 167
  post: 305*n*
  regimental: 25–26
Commanding General. *See also* General staff;
    Secretary of War; War Department; *by
    name.*
  as chief of staff of Secretary of War: 167,
    306, 332
  as field commander: 178–79, 185–86
  as nominal commander of line: 174–75, 243
  as supervisor of U.S. Army, staff and line:
    133–34, 252, 265–66, 332, 363
  loss of control over army and staff: 167–69,
    172, 179–80, 205, 243, 250, 390
  relationship to Corps of Engineers: 161–62,
    171
  relationship to Secretary of War: 66, 179,
    181–82, 314, 330–31
  toward abolition: 398
Commissary Department: 126, 252. *See also*
    Staff departments.
Commissary Generals
  of Ordnance: 99*n*
  of Purchases: 99*n*, 126, 142
  of Subsistence: 126, 240
Congress: 141, 150, 164, 166, 214. *See also*
    Continental Congress; House of
    Representatives; Senate.
  establishment of War Department: 56
  expansion of national defense: 73–74, 177,
    232, 238, 364, 372–73
  legislation affecting inspectorate and its
    duties: 91–93, 142–43, 144–45, 150–51,
    168, 175, 184, 204–05, 246, 248, 278–79
  postwar: 61–62, 356
  reduction of size of military force: 58–59,
    112–113, 131, 175, 183, 252, 255–56, 266,
    276, 279–80
  reorganization of Army and staff departments:
    122, 159–60, 216, 252–56, 270–71, 304–05,
    373–74, 391
  wartime: 91–93, 177
Conrad, Charles M.: 184
Construction: 145. *See also* Housing; Inspection
    reports; Inspections; Inspectors general,
    special assignments.
  of posts: 73, 232–33
  of schools and libraries: 234
Continental Army: 3, 7, 12*n*, 21, 61–62. *See
    also* Steuben, Maj. Gen. Friedrich W.A.
    von; Washington, General George.
  against British at Barren Hill: 42–43
  as mixed force of regulars and militia: 11–13,
    17
  at Charleston: 56
  at Hudson Highlands: 56

  at Middlebrook, New Jersey: 50–51
  at Morristown, New Jersey: 52
  becomes U.S. Army: 62
  campaigns of 1777: 21–22
  demobilization: 58–59
  first inspector: 8
  meeting British invasion of New York: 15–16
  mounted force: 18–19
  officers: 13–14
  problems: 12–15, 36–38
  successes: 16–17
  under authority of Continental Congress:
    12–13
Continental Congress: 29, 48, 53–54
  authority over American army: 12, 14, 16, 17
  commissions to Europeans: 17–21, 22–23,
    33–35
  concept of inspector general: 3, 5–6, 27–28, 31
  development and support of effective fighting
    force: 11, 12–13, 16–17
  establishment and use of Inspector General:
    24–28, 45–46, 47, 50, 53–54
  move to York: 22
  organization of line command: 12–13
  organization of staff departments: 12–13
Continental forces. *See* Continental Army;
    Militia; Volunteers.
1st Continental Regiment: 12*n*
Conway, Maj. Gen. Thomas: 22–25, 26–27,
    28–31, 39, 44, 250, 271
Cooper, Bvt. Maj. Samuel: 164, 188–90, 195,
    198
Coppinger, Maj. John J.: 285
Corbin, Henry C.: 365, 373, 390–91, 405
Cornell, Col. Ezekial: 57
Corps of Artillerists: 69
Corps of Engineers: 69, 87, 121, 127, 141,
    158–59, 161–62, 168, 174, 190–91, 192,
    202, 236, 239*n*, 256, 272, 284, 304,
    308, 323, 327, 373. *See also* Inspectors
    general, special assignments; United States
    Military Academy.
Corps of Topographical Engineers: 127, 168
Crawford, George W.: 195
Crawford, William H.: 113–14, 115
Croghan, Col. George: 145–48, 150–51, 152,
    153–54, 156, 157–58, 159, 160–62, 163–64,
    167, 168, 169, 171, 172, 173, 174,
    176–77, 178, 182, 191–92, 200
Cromwell: 12
Cushing, Col. Thomas H.
  as Acting Adjutant and Inspector: 67–70, 82
  as Adjutant General: 93
  as Adjutant and Inspector of the Army: 87–88
  as brigade inspector: 73
  as line commander: 88

D'Arendt, Baron: 29
Davis, Jefferson: 186, 191, 196–97

Davis, Maj. John M.: 119–20, 124, 125
Davis, Brig. Gen. Nelson Davis: 216–17, 236, 270–71, 274, 288, 292, 310–11
  as assistant inspector general, Army of the Potomac: 210, 218
  as inspector, Department of the Missouri: 259
  as inspector, Department of New Mexico: 210, 239n, 244, 247
  as inspector, Division of the Atlantic: 275, 281
  as inspector, Division of the Missouri: 296
  as Inspector General: 212, 300–302
  on special duty in New Mexico: 269–70
Deane, Silas: 17–18, 20–21, 22–23, 34–35
Dearborn, General Henry: 85–86, 87–88, 95, 96, 103–04, 105, 106, 109
DeButts, Lt. Henry: 65–66, 68
Departments. See also Districts; Divisions.
  Eastern: 128, 133, 142, 151–52
  9th Military: 190
  of California: 184n
  of New Mexico: 184n
  of Oregon: 184n
  of Texas: 184n, 229
  of the East: 238–39, 246
  of the Lakes: 238–39
  Southern: 55
  Western: 128, 133, 151–52
Desertion: 15, 96, 118, 123, 141, 145, 149–50, 157, 160, 182, 194, 254–55, 261, 351.
  See also Discipline; Enlisted men.
Dexter, Samuel: 82
Dick Act of 21 January 1903: 382
Disbursements and receipts. See Auditing accounts.
Discipline: 80–81, 82–83, 88, 92, 96, 108–09, 141, 149–50
  Continental Army problems of: 15, 37
  reform of: 156–57, 204, 350–51
District of Columbia: 133
Districts
  9th Military, in the North: 106
  of New Mexico: 238–39
  of Tennessee: 224
Divisions
  Eastern: 167, 188
  Northern: 116–17, 120n, 125
  of the Atlantic: 251
  of the Missouri: 244, 250, 298, 337
  of the Pacific: 238–39, 250
  Pacific: 188
  Southern: 116–17, 120, 122, 123–24
  Western: 167, 188
Dodge Commission report: 376–78, 389, 393, 397
Dodge, Grenville M.: 376
Dodge, Col. Henry: 164
Doughty, Capt. John: 61
Draft: 80, 232
Drillmaster. See Inspectors general.

Du Coudray, Maj. Gen. Philippe Charles Jean Baptiste Tronson. See Tronson du Coudray, Maj. Gen. Philippe Charles Jean Baptiste.
Duponceau, Pierre: 40–41, 48

Eaton, Amos B.: 224
Eaton, John H.: 157
Education. See Military education.
Elizabethtown, New Jersey: 167
Elkins, Stephen B.: 327, 329
Ellery, William: 28
Enlisted men
  education of: 351–52, 387n
  management of: 250–51, 358
Eustis, Col. Abram: 136
Eustis, William: 89, 91, 93–94, 96–97, 98

Fallen Timbers, Ohio: 68
Farnsworth, Maj. Henry J.: 302, 318
Federalists: 73–74, 75, 82, 84. See also Republicans.
Floyd, John B.: 198, 201
Forsyth, George A.: 234
Fort Davis, Texas: 233
Fort Jesup, Louisiana: 164
Fort Leavenworth: 164
Fort Pitt: 61
Fort Shelby: 119n
Fort Snelling, Minnesota: 164
Fort Towson: 164
Franklin, Benjamin: 17–19, 34–35
Franklin, Brig. Gen. William B.: 199
Frederick the Great of Prussia: 5
French and Indian War: 6, 11

Gadsden, Col. James
  as Adjutant General: 132, 136
  as inspector general, Southern Division: 124–25, 126n, 127
Gaines, Brig. Gen. Edmund P.: 108, 120, 124, 125, 132–33, 136, 137
  as commander, Western Division: 166, 167–68, 171–72, 173
  as department commander and own inspector: 140–42, 151–52, 156–57, 159
  Remarks Concerning the Militia of the United States: 156
Garfield, James A.: 252, 255
Garlington, Lt. Col. Ernest A.: 330, 332, 333, 365, 367, 368, 372, 383
Gates, Maj. Gen. Horatio: 14, 22, 24–25, 27, 29–30
General of the Armies of the United States. See Commanding General.
General staff: 329
  of early staff departments: 69, 74, 82, 87, 98–99, 113, 122
  as unity of authority: 394–406

Gibson, Capt. James: 90
Governors Island, New York: 133
Grant, General Ulysses S.
    as Commanding General: 205, 207n, 223,
        230, 246, 247, 401
    as President: 252, 257, 265
Greene, Maj. Gen. Nathanael: 20, 30, 36–37,
        41, 55–56

Hall, Nathaniel N.: 108–09
Halleck, Henry W.: 207n
Hamilton, Maj. Gen. Alexander: 25, 28, 40, 41,
        46, 61, 74. See also Adams, John.
    as Treasury Secretary: 64
    as Inspector General: 75–83, 88
Hammond, Lt. Richard P.: 177
Hancock, John: 18
Hancock, Maj. Gen. Winfield Scott: 279
Handy, John: 364, 365–66, 373–74
Hardie, Col. James: 209–10, 261, 267, 271,
        274–75, 276, 283–84, 366
    as inspector, Division of the Missouri: 259,
        269
    as inspector general at Washington office: 226–31
        237, 240, 253–54
    as inspector on special duty at War
        Department: 238, 244, 245, 246–47, 248,
        256
Harrison, Benjamin
    as Senator: 298
    as President: 321
Harrison, Lt. William Henry: 68
Harrison, General William Henry: 121, 145–46,
        147
Haskell, Maj. Jonathan: 68
Hatch, Bvt. Maj. Gen. Edward: 285
Hayne, Col. Arthur P.
    as adjutant general: 113
    as inspector general, Southern Division:
        116–17, 120, 123–24, 136, 248
Hazen, William B.: 237–38
Heyl, Col. Charles H.: 368, 372, 396
Heyl, Col. Edward M.: 330
    as assistant inspector general, Department of
        Texas: 300, 301, 302
    as assistant inspector general, Division of the
        Pacific: 306, 318
Hicks, Maj. John: 120
Hindman, Bvt. Lt. Col. Jacob: 139
Hitchcock, Bvt. Maj. Gen. Ethan Allen: 171–72,
        197
    as acting inspector general: 166
    as inspector general and chief of staff: 180
Holt, Joseph: 198
Hortalez and Company: 34
House of Representatives: 159–60, 176, 273–74,
        280–81. See also Congress; Senate.
    Committee on Military Affairs: 166, 176,
        255–56, 272–73, 279–80, 400–401
    H. R. 1017: 299

Housing: 145, 169, 193–94, 232–34, 285. See
        also Construction; Inspection reports;
        Inspections; Inspectors general, special
        assignments.
Howe, Maj. Gen. Sir William: 22
Hughes, Maj. Daniel: 109
Hughes, Brig. Gen. Robert P.: 393
    as brigadier general of volunteers, Philippines:
        368, 372
    as inspector, Department of California: 301
    as inspector, Department of the Dakota: 300
    as inspector, Division of the Pacific: 301
    as inspector, North Atlantic District: 331–32
    as inspector running Washington office: 306
Hull, John A.T.: 373
Hull, General William: 95
Hutcheson, Capt. Grote: 385–86

Indians: 123–24, 149, 188, 210, 229, 232, 244,
        248, 250–51, 259, 267, 269, 294, 295. See
        also Inspection reports; Inspectors general,
        special assignments.
    and British: 62–64, 67–69, 95–96
    relocation: 164–66, 168
Inspecting and Mustering Department: 53, 57
    as general staff: 54–55
    relationship to Commander in Chief: 54–55
Inspection reports: 27, 57–58, 108–09, 113–14,
        118–20, 137–40, 153, 155–56, 157–58,
        161–62, 166, 174, 181, 191–92, 193–94,
        201, 219–21, 253–54, 312, 321–23, 366.
        See also Auditing; Cemeteries;
        Construction; Property condemnation and
        inspection; Returns; United States Military
        Prisons.
    chain of communication for: 187–88, 217,
        275–76, 391
    confidential: 102, 108, 125, 133, 144n, 155,
        162, 235–36, 239–40, 247, 253
    guidelines for: 220–21, 222
    on administration: 47–48, 137–38
    on arms and equipment: 47–48, 151, 163–64,
        191–93
    on conduct of officers: 119–20, 124, 139,
        144, 162, 192, 200
    on discipline: 47–48, 119–20, 124, 137–38,
        191–92
    on Eastern Department: 156
    on follow-up: 247–48, 269, 275, 319–20, 386
    on Fort Stockton, Norfolk Harbor, Virginia:
        137
    on horses: 123–24
    on Indians: 123–24, 152, 186–87, 193
    on police: 137–38
    on post gardens: 192, 319–20
    on posts: 119–20, 123–24, 192, 193–94,
        144–45
    on property management: 139–40, 200–201,
        320

Inspection reports (cont.)
  on Quartermaster Department, Department of
    the Platte: 269
  on reform: 158–59
  on Southern Division: 123–24
  on supplies: 47–48
  on Western Department: 156
Inspections: 57–58, 154–56, 158n, 223–24,
    253–54, 258, 281, 302–03, 365–67. See
    also Inspectors general.
  as a form of specialization: 136–37, 143–44,
    299–300
  as a responsibility of commanders: 144, 213,
    228, 230–31, 236
  as a source of information: 150–51, 153, 404
  as a tool of command: 5–7, 42, 43–44, 46, 49,
    58, 60, 65, 100–102, 125, 134, 135, 141–42,
    156, 180, 202, 243, 394, 404–05
  as civil oversight of military: 5–6, 56–57, 58
  as management: 135, 249
  concept of: 3–4
  divisions of: 83, 332, 334, 335–36, 349, 358,
    363, 364–65
  encourage efficiency: 201
  essential to general staff operations: 403–05
  follow-up: 258, 325–26, 333
  frequency of: 144, 235
  guidelines for: 134–35, 235–36
  in absence of inspectorate: 61–62, 63, 70
  of accounts of War Department Supply
    Division: 323
  of Camp Montgomery: 119
  of care of the sick: 51
  of Corps fortification construction projects:
    161, 192
  of Cuban postal frauds: 383, 400–401
  of Department of California: 191, 192–93
  of Department of Oregon: 191
  of Department of Texas: 191
  of Department of the East: 194–95
  of Department of the Lakes: 159, 269
  of Department of the Northwest: 217
  of Division of the Pacific: 191
  of Fort Claiborne: 109
  of Fort Columbus, New York: 195
  of Fort Delaware: 161
  of Fort Monroe, Virginia: 154, 195
  of Fort Saint Charles: 109
  of Fort Scott, Georgia: 124
  of Fort Shelby: 119
  of Fort Stockton: 137
  of Fort Sullivan: 140, 157
  of forts in Louisiana: 137
  of forts on East and Gulf coasts: 137, 152,
    217
  of horses: 101–02
  of 2d Infantry: 109, 159
  of 3d Infantry at Fort Trumbull, Connecticut:
    195–96
  of 5th Infantry: 159
    of 7th Infantry: 151
    of 29th Infantry: 108
    of Jefferson Barracks, Missouri: 195
    of New Mexico Territory: 186–87, 191, 192
    of New Orleans: 109, 151
    of Niagara, New York: 137, 158
    of Ordnance Department facilities: 137,
      139–40, 151, 154–55, 158–59, 323
    of posts on Missouri and Mississippi rivers:
      144, 150, 151, 166, 217, 237–38
    of Red River posts: 144, 193
    of 1st Regiment of Light Dragoons: 108
    of 2d Regiment of Light Dragoons: 108
    of 13th Regiment of Light Dragoons: 108
    of 1st Rifle Regiment: 108–09
    of target practice: 299
    of the West: 159, 160, 194, 237–38
    of United States Military Academy: 139–40,
      152, 158, 160–61, 321–22, 337
    of paragraph 955: 323, 335–37, 348–49
    on military and civil subjects: 349
    separated from command: 31, 45–46, 249–50,
      330–31
    serving higher authority: 50, 134, 408
    serving military more than civil purposes: 5–6,
      236
  Steuben imprint on: 101
  systematized: 248–49
  systems of, as models: 4–8
  worldwide: 385–86
Inspector General: 50–51, 52–53, 57, 91–93,
    131–32, 228–29, 302, 328–29, 335, 336.
    See also by name.
  as chief of staff: 52–53, 60, 74, 99–100
  as commander: 79, 80, 83, 94
  as Commander in Chief's principal inspector:
    55
  as drillmaster-general: 24, 38–42, 44, 47, 55
  as muster master-general: 55
  as second in command: 75–76, 78–79
  as staff officer: 47
  as standardizer of Army procedures: 43–44,
    50–51, 53–55, 57–58, 228
  duties: 54, 93–94, 217–18, 224–26, 227,
    335–36
  Hamilton's imprint on: 92
  relationship to Adjutant General: 46, 52–53,
    79
  relationship to Board of War: 27–28, 50,
    54–55
  relationship to Commander in Chief: 30–31,
    43–44, 47–48, 50, 53–55
  relationship to Continental Congress: 53–55
  relationship to Secretary of War and
    Commanding General: 131, 132, 162,
    227–28, 229–30, 278, 303–04, 324
  status with other department chiefs: 93,
    277–79
  Steuben's imprint on: 74, 91–92
Inspector General's Department: 96, 102–03,

Inspector General's Department (cont.)
    256, 385, 390–91. *See also* Congress;
    Corps of Engineers; Adjutant General; Staff
    departments; United States Army.
  abolition of: 82, 96–97
  annual report of: 241, 249, 259, 302 306,
    315, 324, 329–30, 369–70, 395
  as arbiter of protocol: 247
  as arbiter of questions of relative rank: 260
  as duplication of general staff: 394–95, 396–98,
    400–401, 404–05
  as group of individual agents: 275, 277
  as staff of Commanding General: 65–66
  as War Department chief auditor of accounts:
    316
  authority and work load of: 325–26, 327,
    333–34, 348–49, 383
  centralized authority of, over inspectors:
    153–54, 178–80, 222, 236, 246–47, 250–52
  clerks as status of: 224, 297, 299, 301, 303,
    322, 325, 365, 391, 393
  deterioration of, after Legion dissolves: 68
  during Civil War: 229–31
  during Spanish-American War: 334, 357–58,
    363, 364, 365–69, 372, 374
  during War of 1812: 106
  formalization and status as separate
    department: 90, 201, 202, 229–31, 242–43,
    248, 249–50, 255, 257, 270–71, 273, 275,
    276, 277–79, 363, 364–65
  history of: 253–54, 327–29
  in low repute: 270
  independence of: 227, 242–43, 255, 270–71,
    272–73, 275, 277, 281, 289–90, 296–97,
    301, 320, 328–29, 330–31, 334, 335–36,
    348–49, 365–66, 373–74, 391
  lacking head of department: 274–75, 277–78
  legislation authorizing personnel and
    functions: 98–101, 115–16, 259–60,
    273–74, 297–98, 299–300, 319–20, 365–66,
    367–68, 390–93, 406
  permanence of: 217–18, 241, 242–43, 245–46,
    271, 292–93
  post-American Revolution: 61–62, 63
  post-Civil War: 243
  post-Spanish-American War: 372, 376–78
  post-War of 1812: 113–14
  relationship to Adjutant General's Office:
    252–53, 301*n*
  relationship to Secretary of War and
    Commanding General: 229–30, 254, 285,
    310, 311, 314, 320, 324–25, 330–31,
    335–36, 348–49, 391, 394
  rules of inspection: 227, 250, 292–93, 335–36
Inspectors
  brigade: 39, 46, 50, 73, 89, 92
  divisional: 46
  of Artillery: 82
  of contracts and supplies: 57
  of Fortifications: 82, 86
  regular: 17
  sub: 38, 39, 45, 53, 57, 74, 92
  volunteer: 366, 369–70
Inspectors general: 4, 21, 26–27, 52–53, 56–58,
    63, 65–66, 91–93, 99–101, 102–03, 142,
    162–63, 176, 213–15, 219–21, 226–27,
    235–36, 245–46, 259–60, 282, 299, 330–31,
    401–02
  acting assistant: 239, 248, 296, 301
  administering oaths: 244–45, 257–58
  as a group of independently functioning
    individuals: 277, 279, 383
  as adjutants: 50, 53, 69, 79, 88, 168, 215–16
  as agents of civil oversight of military: 26–28,
    92, 174–75
  as agents of commanders served: 43–44, 46,
    50, 60, 66, 102–03, 125, 132–33, 134, 167,
    180, 227, 235, 246–47, 302–03, 306–08,
    334
  as auditors: 25, 26, 92, 174, 175–76, 201,
    271–72, 287–89
  as chiefs of staff: 103–04, 163, 167–68,
    177–78, 181
  as commanders: 46–47, 179–80, 210–11,
    230–31, 376, 378
  as muster masters: 52–54, 57, 67–68, 92,
    100–101, 163, 166–67, 170, 179
  as second in command: 65–66, 177–78
  as specialists: 242–43, 249, 255
  as training officers: 24, 25–26, 31, 45–46, 58,
    64–65, 106
  assistant: 39*n*, 53, 58, 74, 92–93, 105–06,
    209–13, 222–23
  chain of communications: 187–88, 195–96
  charter: 50–51
  concept of: 4–5, 37*n*, 43–44
  establishment of: 24, 25
  granting discharges: 152–53, 160
  independence: 125, 249
  inspection of United States Military
    Academy: 162
  legislation authorizing personnel and
    functions: 91–92, 105–06, 127, 204–05, 269
  noting condition of buildings: 91–92, 162,
    232–34
  observing conduct of officers: 25, 118–19,
    152–53
  promotion of discipline: 25, 26–27, 91–92,
    101–02
  property management: 65–66, 91–92, 142–43,
    163, 246*n*, 250
  relationship to Commander in Chief: 31,
    56–58, 163
  relationship to Congress: 56–58
  relationship to Secretary of War and
    Commanding General: 56–58, 88–89, 133,
    142–43, 152, 167–69, 173–75, 187–88, 205,
    213, 229–30, 239, 249–50, 275–76, 285

Inspectors general (cont.)
	relationship to War Department: 101, 181
	review of troops: 25–26, 27, 50, 64–66,
		170–71, 179–80, 250–51, 292
	supervision of camp selection and security:
		45–46, 100–103, 163
Inspectors general, special assignments: 163–64,
		218–19, 225–26, 256, 274–75, 283–85,
		309–11, 326, 335, 382–83
	auditing: 224–25, 229, 239–40, 257–58
	cavalry: 215, 216
	cemeteries: 284, 311
	conduct of officers: 250, 283–84, 285, 309
	construction: 245
	Corps of Engineers: 174, 284
	housing: 239–40, 284, 285
	Indians: 194–95, 283, 284, 285
	ordnance: 194
	Signal Corps: 308–09, 386
Invalid Board: 218, 219n, 220. See also Board
	to Organize the Invalid Corps.
Izard, Capt. George: 77n, 106n

Jackson, Andrew: 112, 116–17, 120, 121,
		122, 125, 132–33, 134, 136
Jay Treaty of 1794: 73–74
Jefferson Barracks, Missouri: 167
Jefferson, Thomas: 84–86
Jesup, General Thomas S.
	as field commander: 166–67
	as Quartermaster General: 142, 147, 160,
		169, 193–94, 202
Johnston, Bvt. Col. Joseph E.: 198, 202
Joint Army and Navy Board: 384
Jones, Col. Roger (father)
	as Adjutant General: 150, 158
	as adjutant general, Northern Division: 124,
		136, 187–88, 195–96
Jones, Brig. Gen. Roger (son): 212–13, 244, 300
	as assistant inspector general, special
		assignments: 210
	as assistant inspector general, Army of
		Virginia: 212
	as assistant quartermaster general: 212
	as chief quartermaster, Army of the Potomac:
		212
	as inspector, Department of the East: 301
	as inspector, Division of the Atlantic: 275–76,
		296, 301
	as inspector, Division of the Mississippi: 229
	as inspector, Division of the Pacific: 239n,
		284, 285, 291, 302
	as inspector, Washington office: 305, 306,
		316–17, 318
	as Inspector general: 305, 306, 316–17, 318
Judge Advocate General: 364–65

Kent, William T.: 382
King, Capt. William: 93n

Kirby, 1st Lt. Edmund: 132
Knox, Brig. Gen. Henry: 37, 38
	as chief of artillery under Washington: 20
	as Secretary at War: 62, 64–68, 76
Knox, Kilburn: 229
Knox, Col. Thomas T.: 368, 372, 378, 406
Knoxville, Tennessee: 372

Lafayette: 29–30, 41, 42–43
Lamont, Daniel S.: 329–32
Land Grant Act: 214
Laurens, Henry: 29–30, 32, 34–35
Laurens, Col. John: 30, 32, 40–41
Lawton, Col. Henry W.: 306, 318, 332, 333,
		368, 372
Leadership: 95–96
	Continental Army: 13, 18
	reform of: 98–99, 106–07
Lee, Francis Lightfoot: 28
Lee, Maj. John M.: 385–86
Legion of the United States: 404
	at Legionville: 64–67
	basis for the U.S. Army: 69, 70–71
	expedition in the Northwest: 67–68
L'Enfant, Pierre Charles: 48
Lewis, Capt. T.: 68
Lexington, Kentucky: 372
Lincoln, Abraham: 198
Lincoln, Benjamin: 56–57
Lincoln, Robert Todd: 297
Logan, John: 273
Lord Cornwallis: 55, 56
Lord Haldane: 389
Lord Stirling: 25
Louis XIV: 4
Louisville, Kentucky: 133
Ludington, Capt. Elisha H.: 281
	as assistant inspector general: 225, 228–29,
		237
	as inspector, Department of the South: 248
	as inspector, Department of the Columbia:
		270
	as inspector, Division of the Pacific: 259n,
		276
	as inspector running Washington office: 239,
		240, 244, 245, 247
Ludington, Maj. Gen. Marshall I.: 405, 407

McCall, Col. George A.: 186–88, 190, 195–96
McClellan, Maj. Gen. George B. (father): 195,
		199, 206–08, 217, 291, 366
McClellan, George B. (son): 373–74, 402
McCrary, George W.: 276–77, 278, 282, 303–04
McDonald, Eleazer W.: 120
McDowell, Maj. Gen. Irvin: 199
McHenry, James: 74, 76, 78, 79–80, 81–82
McKinley, William: 363, 366, 372–73, 389
Macomb, Alexander: 106n
	as Chief of Engineers: 150, 152

Macomb, Alexander (cont.)
  as Commanding General: 152, 153–54, 157–59, 161, 162, 163–64, 166, 167–68, 169, 171–72, 174, 182, 187–88, 299, 404
Macon, Nathaniel: 157
McRae, William: 120
Madison, James: 89, 90–91, 110, 112–13, 115–16
Mahan, Denis: 197
Mansfield, Col. Joseph K.F.: 190–92, 193, 197, 203, 204, 221
Marcy, Brig. Gen. Randolph B.: 199, 206, 221, 240, 302, 316
  as brigadier general of volunteers: 207–08, 217
  as chief of staff, Army of the Potomac: 207, 366
  as inspector, Department of the Lakes: 269
  as inspector, Division of the Missouri: 238, 244–45, 248, 250, 252
  as Inspector General: 212, 257–61, 266–93, 294, 295, 311–12, 315
  Outline Description of Military Posts: 283
  The Prairie Traveler: 206
Marcy, William L.: 176
Marigault, G. H.: 120n
Marsh, George P.: 197
Marsh, Lt. Col. J. F.: 225
Medical Staff: 99n
Medical Department: 127, 256, 336, 386
  Army Medical School: 357
  Army and Navy General Hospital: 380
  Hospital Corps: 304, 357, 374
  as own inspector: 154, 214, 250n
Meigs, Montgomery C.: 224
Medal of Honor: 211
Mentges, Col. Francis:
  as acting inspector of Southern Army: 57
  as inspector of contracts: 62, 63
Mexican War: 183
  at Battle of Buena Vista: 178
  at San Antonio: 177–78
  inspectorate during: 177, 179–80
Mifflin, Thomas: 30
Miles, General Nelson A.: 332–33, 358, 362–63, 366–67, 368, 369, 373–74, 397, 399–400, 403
Miley, Lt. Col. John D.: 370
Military education. See also Army War College; Enlisted men.
  civilian, at colleges: 234, 291, 311–12, 333, 343–45, 380–81
  university system of: 395–96
Militia: 7–8, 11–13, 14–17, 62–64, 67–68, 88–89, 97, 150, 157, 164, 169, 198–99. See also Continental Army; National Guard; Volunteers.
Militia Act of 1792: 382. See also Dick Act of 21 January 1903.

Mills, Maj. John: 65–66, 67–68
Mills, Maj. Stephen C.: 368, 372
Mingo River, Ohio: 61
Monroe Doctrine: 232
Monroe, James
  as Secretary of State: 110, 111
  as President: 121, 127, 136
Moore, Maj. Francis: 332
Morris, Gouverneur: 77
Morris, Robert: 34, 56
Mottin de la Balme, Col. Augustin: 18–19, 20
Mustering: 11–12, 100–101, 215. See also Inspecting and Mustering Department; Inspectors general; Mustering Department.
  for pay: 52, 101, 102n, 107–08, 112, 163, 170
  of militia and volunteers: 102n, 163, 168, 170, 195
  with company muster rolls: 143, 177–78
Mustering Department: 52–53
Muster master: 8
Muster master-general: 8

National conscription. See Draft.
National Guard: 291, 345–46, 375
  Connecticut: 291
  encampments of: 346, 347–48
  inspection of: 346–48
  military training of: 353–54, 381–82
National Guard Association: 291, 347, 348, 373
National Home for Disabled Volunteer Soldiers: 339–41, 374, 380
National military cemeteries: 184n, 214, 234, 246, 284, 290, 311, 336–37, 339–40n, 380. See also Inspection reports; Inspections; Inspectors general.
National Park Service: 298, 388
Nicoll, Maj. Abimael Y.: 88–89, 93, 106
North, Maj. William
  as Adjutant General: 79, 93n
  as inspector: 59, 61, 62
  as Steuben's aide: 48, 49, 51
North American Review: 149

Office of the Inspector General. See Inspector General's Department.
Orcutt, Warren H.: 365
Orderly books: 48
Ordnance: 138, 142–43, 151, 154–56, 158–59. See also Inspection reports; Inspections; Inspectors general.
Ordnance Department: 99, 142–43, 151, 154–56, 158–59, 168, 202, 256, 357, 373–74, 386
Orne, Maj. Azor: 106–07
Ourand, C. H.: 324

Parker, Brig. Gen. Daniel
  as Adjutant and Inspector General: 111–14, 116–17, 124, 125, 133

Parker, Brig. Gen. Daniel (cont.)
    as Paymaster General: 127–28, 132
Pay: 138, 149–50, 160, 254–55. *See also*
    Desertion.
Pay Department: 127, 252–53, 256, 386
Paymaster General: 69–70, 74, 101–02, 126,
    127–28, 313
Philadelphia: 47, 48
Physician and Surgeon-General: 99*n*. *See also*
    Surgeon General.
Physician General: 74
Pickering, Col. Timothy: 15
Pierce, Franklin: 186
Pike, Brig. Gen. Zebulon Montgomery: 103–06,
    110
Pinckney, Charles Cotesworth: 75, 76–77
Poinsett, Joel R.: 167–69, 186
Polk, James K.: 176–77
Poore, Ben: Perley: 207
Porter, Maj. Gen. Fitz-John: 199
Porter, James M.: 175–76
Porter, Peter B.: 152
Portsmouth, New Hampshire: 35
Post, Pvt. Charles Johnson: 371
Post school system. *See* Enlisted men.
Pratt, Capt. James: 118–19
Prisons. *See* United States Military Prisons.
Proctor, Redfield
    as chairman, Senate Committee on Military
        Affairs: 402
    as Secretary of War: 320–23, 337, 351–52
    as senator: 326–27
Property condemnation and inspection: 139,
    142–43, 144, 200–201, 219, 249, 250,
    256–57, 258, 259–60, 336, 342–43, 374,
    379–80, 397, 398, 403–04. *See also*
    Inspection reports; Inspections; Inspectors
    general.
    boards of survey for: 285–87
    of horses: 215, 219–20, 226–27, 287, 314–15
    of medical supplies: 286, 342
    of ordnance: 154–55, 170–71
    of signaling gear: 314–15
    of subsistence stores: 314, 342–43
    procedures: 285–86, 342–43
Provisional army: 74, 75–76, 77, 78–79, 82. *See
    also* Hamilton, Maj. Gen. Alexander.
Pulaski, Casimir: 19
Punishment. *See* Discipline.
Purchasing Department: 122, 126

Quartermaster Department: 63, 91, 99, 101–02,
    123, 127, 156, 174, 183–84, 233–34,
    239–40, 255–56, 303–04, 336. *See also*
    Inspectors general, special assignments;
    Staff departments.
    as own inspector: 153–54, 213–14, 223–24

    involvement in construction and repairs: 145,
        233–34
    management of cemeteries: 245–46, 290, 311
    management of transportation: 355–56, 362,
        374, 386–87
    supply problems: 14
Quartermaster General: 57–58, 69, 74, 91, 99*n*,
    113, 122, 242–43, 283, 286–87, 290,
    302–03, 336–37
Quisenberry, A. C.: 327–28

Ramsay, Alexander: 282
Rawlins, John A.: 265
Reconstruction: 271, 276, 294
Recruitment: 16, 103, 106
Reed, Maj. Walter: 371
Regular Army: 157, 169, 362–63, 365–66,
    372–73, 375. *See also* United States Army.
    during peacetime: 90–91, 121–22, 233–34
    expansion: 73–74, 89
    problems: 80–81
    relationship with National Guard: 291, 347–48
Regulations: 102–03, 133, 238, 274–75, 282.
    See also Inspector General's Department.
    defining authority of Commanding General:
        134, 179, 201
    defining duties of general staff: 405
    defining inspectorate: 133, 201
    making inspection duty of company
        commanders: 42, 319–20
    establishing relationship of inspectors to
        Secretary of War: 201, 234–35, 367
    outlining inspectors' duties: 134–35, 144, 162,
        179, 200–201, 202*n*, 234–36, 266–67,
        294–95, 319–20
    outlining inspection report format: 63, 200
    outlining inspection procedures: 163, 236,
        267, 294–95, 319–20
Republicans: 75, 77, 82, 84–85
Returns: 25–26, 56, 101–02. *See also* Inspection
    reports.
Reserves: 375. *See also* National Guard.
Revolutionary France: 73
Revolutionary War. *See* American Revolution.
Robinson, Fayette: 181
Roosevelt, Theodore: 389
Root, Elihu: 381–82, 384*n*, 389–92, 393–400,
    401*n*, 402–05, 407–09
Rudulph, Maj. Michael: 65–66
Rusling, James F.: 233

Sacket, Brig. Gen. Delos B.: 240, 260–61,
    271–72, 281–82, 292, 302, 305, 310–11,
    313, 316, 321
    as establisher of Inspector General's
        Department: 208–09
    as head of Inspector General's Department:
        217–19, 220–26, 227, 233, 237

Sacket, Brig. Gen. Delos B. (cont.)
　as inspector, Department of the Cumberland:
　　238, 248
　as inspector, Division of the Atlantic: 250–52,
　　259, 267
　as inspector, Division of the Missouri: 275
　as inspector, Washington office: 295, 296–301
St. Clair, Maj. Gen. Arthur: 63–64
St. Germain, Comte de: 34
Sanger, Brig. Gen. Joseph P.: 292, 324, 332,
　　335, 350–51, 354, 386, 396
　as brigadier general of volunteers: 318–19,
　　368
　as division commander: 368
　as inspector, Division of the Missouri: 325
　as inspector, South Atlantic District: 333
　as inspector at Washington office: 325, 333,
　　365, 368, 372
　*The Army of the United States: Historical
　　Sketches of Staff and Line with Portraits of
　　Generals-in-Chief*: 328–29
Sargent, Lt. Col. Winthrop: 63–64, 65
Scammell, Col. Alexander: 40
Schofield, General John M.: 373–74, 401–02
　as Acting Secretary of War: 265
　as Commanding General: 305–06, 319,
　　321–22, 332, 351
Schriver, Col. Edmund: 271, 282, 292n, 295,
　　302, 366
　as agent of Secretary of War: 257–61, 266–69
　as head of Inspector General's Department:
　　237, 238–57
　as inspector, Army of the Potomac: 221–22,
　　227
　as inspector, Department of the Missouri:
　　274–75
　as inspector, Department of the Pacific: 275
　as inspector, Division of the Pacific: 275
　as inspector of the U.S. Military Academy:
　　281
Schuylkill Arsenal: 245
Scott, General Winfield: 49n, 94, 96, 108, 150
　as Adjutant General: 109–10, 113–14
　as commander and adjutant: 106–07
　as Commanding General: 172, 174, 176,
　　179–80, 185–86, 187–88, 198, 203, 205,
　　401
　as department commander and own inspector:
　　132–33, 134–35, 137, 139, 151–52, 167,
　　171, 185–86, 191, 192–94
　Scott's Exercise: 113
Second Seminole War: 166–68, 174, 175–76
Secretary at War: 56. *See also* Secretary of War.
Secretary of War: 151–52, 157–58, 167, 239n,
　　241, 257, 287–88, 289–90, 304–05, 314,
　　315, 322–23, 334, 377–78, 383, 394
　as all staff departments: 85
　as commander: 85, 92, 96–97, 98–99, 101
　as voice of government Army served: 173–75

　relationship with Commanding General:
　　87–88, 174–75, 201, 249–50, 265–66,
　　389–90, 402–03
　responsibilities: 63n
Seminole Wars: 164–65
　Dade massacre: 166
　role of inspection in: 166–67, 168
Senate. *See also* Congress; House of
　　Representatives.
　Bill 321: 273–74
　Committee on Military Affairs: 149–50,
　　151–52, 176, 198, 278, 299–300, 390–91,
　　398–99
Sevier, Ambrose H.: 159
Shafter, General William "Pecos Bill": 362–63,
　　369–71
Sheridan, Maj. Gen. Philip H.: 232, 298, 305
Sherman, General William T.: 211–12, 227–28
　as commander, Division of the West: 233, 252
　as Commanding General: 257, 258, 265–66,
　　271, 273–74, 275–76, 281
Signal Corps: 238, 308–09, 323, 386
Slayden, James: 400, 402
Smith, Col. Persifor F.: 166–67
Smyth, Brig. Gen. Alexander: 93–97, 103–04,
　　150, 152
Society of the Cincinnati: 59, 82n
Soldier's Book: 169–70
Spanish-American War: 361–63, 366–67
　at El Caney: 362
　at Havana: 371–72
　at Manila: 363
　at San Juan: 362
　at Santiago: 362
　at Siboney: 362
　Cuban landing during: 362
　mobilization for: 376–78
　on the Philippines: 363
　on Puerto Rico: 362
Spencer, John C.: 175–76
Sprague, William: 224
Staff departments: 301n, 380. *See also by name.*
　in peacetime: 85, 228, 280
　in wartime: 215–16
　independence of: 173–74
　of the Continental Army: 12–13, 14, 52, 56–57
　personnel appointments: 390, 392–94, 406
　relationship to Secretary of War and
　　Commanding General: 158, 280, 306,
　　389–90
Stagg, John: 62
Stanton, Edwin M.: 208, 217, 218–19, 227–28,
　　239, 245
Steuben, Maj. Gen. Friedrich W.A. von: 33–36,
　　42–43, 62, 64–65. *See also* Blue book;
　　Continental Army; Continental Congress;
　　Washington, General George.
　as drillmaster-general: 37–40, 44
　as Inspector-General: 39–44, 52–60

Steuben, Maj. Gen. (cont.)
    as line commander: 46–47, 55
    as muster master-general: 53–55
    as Washington's adviser: 36–37
    as de facto chief of staff: 52–53
    concept of an inspectorate: 43–44, 45–46
    development of American drill regulations:
        40–42
    establishment of inspection system: 47–48
    reformation of the Continental Army: 36–38,
        40–42
    *Regulations for the Order and Discipline of
        the Troops of the United States*: 48–50
Stewart, Pvt. Harris H.: 218, 224
Strong, Lt. Col. James H.: 220–21
Subalterns: 58, 92–93. *See also* Inspectors.
Subsistence Department: 122, 240, 252–53, 256,
    356, 362. *See also* Staff departments.
Subsistence sales list: 240, 248, 250, 260–61,
    289–90, 315, 384, 386
Sullivan, Maj. Gen. John: 20, 24
Sunday inspections: 160, 171, 299, 320–22. *See
    also* Enlisted men.
Sundry Civil Appropriations Act: 380
Supply: 91, 95
    Continental Army problems of: 31–32, 36–37,
        56–57
    reforms: 98–99, 169, 355–56

Taft, Alphonso: 266
Taylor, General Zachary: 166–67, 177
    as commander, Western Division: 185–86
    as President: 185–86
Temporary armies. *See* Legion of the United
    States.
Thayer, Sylvanus: 158
Thomas, Maj. Gen. George H.: 211
Thomas, Brig. Gen. Lorenzo: 198–99, 215–16
Thompson, Maj. John L.: 96
Three-battalion infantry regiments: 203, 304–05,
    378–79, 394
Totten, James: 209–10, 236, 239n, 259n, 267,
    270
Training: 15, 16–17, 68, 95–96, 102–03, 326,
    352–55
Transportation: 183–85. *See also* Quartermaster
    Department.
Treasury Department: 64, 179, 339, 380, 397
Treaty of Ghent: 112
Tronson du Coudray, Maj. Gen. Philippe
    Charles Jean Baptiste: 20–21, 23, 39, 44
Twiggs, Brig. Gen. David: 203

Uniforms: 115n, 195, 272, 323–24
United States Army: 361, 385–86
    and the inspectorate: 87–88, 153–54, 181, 228,
        230–31, 257–58, 366–67
    as modern military force: 384, 390–91

as peacetime continental constabulary: 70, 71,
    85, 118, 149–50, 153, 182, 183, 185–86,
    191, 229, 230–31, 294, 317
comparison with the Legion and Continental
    Army: 70–71
expansion: 62–63, 73–74, 91, 98–99, 160
legalization by Congress: 62
permanence: 69
reduction: 82, 84, 86–87, 111–13, 123, 183,
    232
reformation: 159–60, 294–95, 316, 321–22
reorganization: 64, 69, 390–91
United States Military Academy: 61, 81, 82–83,
    84–85, 86–87, 157, 171, 179, 238–39, 244,
    321–22, 337, 383
United States Military Prisons. *See also*
    Inspectors general, special assignments.
    at Alcatraz Island: 384
    at Fort Leavenworth, Kansas: 290, 337, 384
    at Memphis, Tennessee: 225–26
    in the Philippines: 384
    inspection of: 225–26, 290, 310–11, 337–38,
        383–84
United States Soldiers' Home: 309–10, 338–39,
    380
United States Veterans Bureau: 339–40n
Upton, Emory
    general staff concept: 393–95
    infantry tactics: 246–47, 302–03
    universal military training: 345–46

Van Ness, 1st Lt. William P.: 324
Van Rensselaer, Col. Henry: 95
Van Rensselaer, Maj. Gen. Stephen: 209, 226
Varnum, Brig. Gen. James Mitchell: 36
Veterans Administration: 339–40n
Volunteers: 63, 67–68, 177–78, 195, 202–03,
    211, 212, 215, 232, 361–63, 365, 375,
    378–79
Vroom, Brig. Gen. Peter D.: 318, 330, 367, 396
    as inspector, Department of the Gulf: 372
    as inspector, Department of the Missouri: 325
    as inspector, Middle District: 332
    as inspector during invasion of Puerto Rico:
        368
    as Inspector General: 406
    as inspector in Caribbean: 372

Walker, Capt. Benjamin: 40, 41, 48, 51
War of 1812: 94–95, 121–122
    at Albany: 95
    at Chippewa: 106–07, 109–10
    at Detroit: 95
    at Fort George: 95
    at Lake Champlain: 95
    at Lake Erie: 95
    at Lake Ontario: 104–05
    at Lundy's Lane: 106–07

War of 1812 (cont.)
    at Montreal: 95
    at Niagara River: 95–96
    at Queenston Heights: 95–96
    at Sackets Harbor: 104–05, 106–07, 109–10
    at York, upper Canada: 104–05
    in Canada: 95
War Department: 56, 61, 63–64, 88, 103–04,
        121, 122–23, 128, 142–43, 151, 154,
        164–67, 170–71, 176, 196–97, 200, 213–17,
        228, 243, 245, 277, 344–46, 390, 396
    and the inspectorate: 131–32, 143–44, 178–80,
        205, 213–14, 215, 220, 236
    as a collection of independent bureaucracies:
        157–58
    establishment: 62
    interest in economy: 227–28
    problems during the Spanish-American War:
        361–65, 366–67
    property management of: 142–43, 144,
        200–201, 314–15
    regulations: 164, 266–67
Wars. See by name.
Washington, General George: 65, 66, 81, 404,
        405, 407–08
    and Conway affair: 22–31
    and Steuben: 36–40, 42–48, 50–57, 59–60
    as Commander in Chief of Continental Army:
        11–17
    as Commander in Chief of provisional army:
        75–77
    as own staff: 14, 23–24
    as President: 63
    attitude toward commissioned Europeans: 18,
        20–21
    concept of an inspector general: 3, 24, 26–27,
        30–31, 36, 43–44, 47
    selection of inspectors general: 43–44, 50

Washington Post: 314
Wayne, Maj. Gen. Anthony: 64–68, 71, 85,
        109–10, 141–42, 404
Webb, Capt. Nathaniel: 41
West Point. See United States Military
        Academy.
Wheeler, Maj. Gen. Joseph: 365–66
Whipple, General William: 28
Whiskey Rebellion: 77
Whiting, Col. John: 89–90
Wilkinson, Brig. Gen. James: 86, 87–88, 106n
    as Army's brigadier general: 70–72, 73,
        78–79
    as Gates' aide: 25
    as own inspector: 70–72, 87
    running the War Department: 82, 83, 85
Willetts Point, New York: 272
Williams, John: 122
Williams, Maj. Jonathan: 86
Wilson, James H.: 223
Winder, Brig. Gen. William H.: 107–08, 109–10
Wool, Maj. Gen. John E.: 126n, 128, 131–32,
        147, 148, 158–59, 166, 171–72, 173,
        177–78, 199–200
    as division commander's chief of staff: 167
    as inspector, Northern Division: 117, 120n
    as inspector of infantry: 136–37, 140, 142,
        143–44
    as inspector of seaboard posts and ordnance:
        151, 152, 153–56, 160–61, 163–64, 169–70
    working with Indians: 164–65, 168
Wright, Clinton: 120

XYZ Affair: 74

Yellow journalism: 376
Yellowstone National Park: 298
Young, Maj. Gen. Samuel B. M.: 400, 403, 405